ELEMENTARY SCHOOL CURRICULUM

Edited by **J. MICHAEL PALARDY**

University of Georgia

The Macmillan Company, New York

Collier-Macmillan Limited, London

ELEMENTARY SCHOOL CURRICULUM

An Anthology of Trends and Challenges

DEDICATED TO MARY ELLEN, TERRI, MIKE

The Macmillan Company
866 Third Avenue, New York, New York 10022
Collier-Macmillan Canada, Ltd., Toronto, Ontario

Library of Congress catalog card number: 79–123146
First Printing

Preface

Teachers who have never had a course in curriculum often have different perceptions of what it is. Some believe it has to do with subject matter; others are convinced it deals with methodology. Many think it is more than this, but they are not quite certain how much more. It was with teachers such as these in mind that the idea for this book was conceived.

Curriculum is usually defined as all the experiences of the learner for which the school accepts responsibility. As such, it is often conceived of as a series of tasks that must be performed before, as, and after the learner has the experiences. This task-oriented approach to curriculum serves as the unifying theme of this book. The tasks it lays out are these: establishing goals and objectives, fostering students' cognitive development, promoting students' psychosocial health, organizing students for learning, using instructional resources, understanding and teaching the "different" student, evaluating pupils and programs, and keeping abreast of current trends. Stated very simply, the better teachers perform these eight tasks, the better students' learning experiences will be. This, after all, is the purpose for studying curriculum, as well as its justification.

Any editor of a book of readings is confronted with the difficult assignment of selecting manuscripts. For this book, three criteria were employed in the selection process. First, manuscripts were chosen that were judged by the editor to be *most* appropriate for in-service teachers taking their first course in

v

curriculum. Second, manuscripts were selected that seemed to have the ingredients needed to evoke and facilitate individual thought and collective discussion. And third, an effort was made to include in the book only recent selections. To the writers and publishers who kindly granted the editor permission to reprint their materials, sincere thanks are extended.

The last word in the subtitle of the book is *challenges*. The eight tasks constitute what the challenges are. It is the editor's hope that through a careful study of the book you, its readers, will be better prepared to meet these challenges.

J. M. P.

Contents

vii

PART 1

Establishing Goals and Objectives

No need in education deserves more attention than the one addressed in this part. Indeed, the kinds of educational objectives that are set in hundreds of thousands of classrooms across the country will determine in large measure the kinds of products those classrooms ultimately will produce. And yet this need is the one that is probably most often shunted aside by teachers as they go about meeting the daily exigencies of classroom life.

There are two reasons primary in accounting for this. First, it is often believed that educational objectives are established in places other than the classroom, perhaps in the board of education building, in the state department of education, or in a textbook publisher's office. To an extent, this is true; to an extent, it is even desirable. But it is the contention here that classroom teachers must assume greater responsibility than they have in the past in establishing their own *objectives* for their own *groups* of students. This can and must be done if the real educational needs of all America's youth are to be met.

The second reason is that establishing educational objectives is no easy academic task. It requires, at the very least, an understanding of children and of the way they learn and an understanding of our changing society. In addition, it demands choosing, from all that could be learned, the small percentage of knowledge that children need most to learn. And finally it demands a philosophy of life, a philosophy enabling one to say,

"This is the kind of human being I want to help mold. This is the kind of world I see him helping to build. Yes, this is what I think the schools are for."

What are the schools for? What is their purpose? In the first article, Tyler gives his opinion about the answer to these questions. His thesis is that, for the most part, the major purposes or functions of America's schools have not changed over the past ten years or, in most cases, over the past thirty or forty years. These functions he identifies as educating for individual self-realization, developing literate citizens, providing the vehicle for social mobility, educating for vocational ends, developing understandings and appreciations of goods and services, and developing the capacity to learn how to learn. Tyler points out, however, that even though these basic functions may not have changed they are in need of continual reinterpretation.

The three authors following Tyler are also concerned with the question of the purposes of education. One very important item needs to be kept in mind as their articles are read and contrasted. That is that each of the authors has a different interpretation of what the major purposes are and of what means are needed to achieve them. These selections are included to help the reader see the complexity of the task and to give him some guidelines for determining the purposes that to him seem most legitimate.

In the selection by Havighurst, major attention is devoted to four forces of present-day social change. These are listed as: contraction of space and time, technological development, urbanization and metropolitan development, and world interdependence and cooperation. Havighurst explores in considerable depth the implications of these forces for education. The reader is asked to note particularly his discussion of the role of the educator in teaching the structure of a subject. Is it a different role from the one Ammons proposes in the selection that follows?

In reading the Ammons paper, perhaps it would be most beneficial to read the last paragraph first. Her assignment, to construct and justify a curriculum for elementary school children that is "way out," was no easy charge. Whether she has succeeded must be determined by each reader using as criteria his own ideas about the tasks of the elementary school. At least in this writer's opinion, however, she has succeeded in raising some questions about elementary education that deserve the most thoughtful consideration.

If Ammons' proposals are perceived by the reader to be "way out," Goodman's discussion in the fourth article may not even be taken seriously. But Goodman, one of the so-called new breed *of critics in education, is not to be lightly regarded. In this opinion, his dissatisfactions with all phases of education, from preschool to postgraduate, are for the most part valid. Although the alternatives Goodman proposes may not now be realistic, his comments should serve as a reminder to educators that all is not well in the establishment.*

In the fifth and sixth selections, Krathwohl and Atkin discuss, respectively, some of the potential advantages and disadvantages inherent in the current emphasis upon establishing educational objectives in behavioral terms. Krathwohl contends that objectives that are stated behaviorally and at several levels of specificity provide the educator with the means of improving significantly the process of curriculum building and instructional development. Three of the available frameworks designed to facilitate construction of these objectives are described in the article in considerable detail. As will become apparent upon a reading of the article, few people are as qualified as Krathwohl to discuss these frameworks.

Atkin sees some potential dangers in the use of behavioral objectives that he believes are often overlooked. One such danger is that important learning outcomes that can be stated behaviorally only with great difficulty may tend to be bypassed in favor of less important outcomes that can be translated easily into behavioral terms. Another danger lies in the number of behavioral goals toward which the teacher directs his attention. If too few, his range may be limited and some important goals disregarded. If too many, his teaching style may become mechanical and spontaneous interaction with the class lost. Atkin's final plea for a rational debate among educators on the positive and negative potential of behavioral objectives is, in this writer's opinion, very legitimate and very necessary.

Goldman, in the last article in the section, presents his views of the goals of education during what he calls the three American revolutions. He believes that America has just entered into the third of these revolutions, one far more complex in its educational implications than either of the previous two. Goldman's challenge will require education's greatest effort ever if it is to be met. That challenge is to help build a truly democratic society, a society dedicated to the principle of improving for all the quality of living and among all the quality of human relationships.

Purposes for Our Schools

RALPH W. TYLER

From their beginning the schools of our country have been sensitive to the needs and opportunities of our changing society. In the debates that took place in the early days of our nation over the establishment of free public education, two primary purposes were emphasized. For the individual child, education was to provide the opportunity to realize his potential and to become a constructive and happy person in the station of life which he would occupy because of his birth and ability. For the nation, the education of each child was essential to provide a literate citizenry. Since the new nation was ruled by its people, ignorance among the people would threaten the survival of the country.

INDIVIDUAL SELF-REALIZATION

Today, these remain two of the educational functions of our schools, recognized by the public generally and firmly imbedded in our thinking in the light of changed social conditions, new knowledge, and prevailing attitudes of the times. The goal of individual self-realization is even more necessary for the schools to stress in our mass society where economic, political, and social demands are frequently heard more distinctly than demands of the individual for education that will enable him to use the rich resources of an industrial society for his own fuller life. Kenneth Boulding, speaking in June, 1966, at the Eight-State Conference on "Prospective Changes in Society by 1980," eloquently expressed the contemporary problem in achieving this purpose.

> The final problem is subtle and hard to put one's finger on; nevertheless, it may be the most important problem of all. This is the problem of the role of the educational system in creating what might be called a moral identity. The

Reprinted from *The Bulletin of the National Association of Secondary School Principals,* 52 (332): 1–12 (December 1968), by permission of author and publisher.

obsolescence of older moral identities in the face of enormous technological changes is a problem which underlies almost all others in the social system. In its solution, the educational system would play an absolutely crucial role. It would be precisely indeed in the things which our conservatives despise as "frills" that the development of satisfying human identities may have to be found. It must never be forgotten that the ultimate thing which any society is producing is people. . . . If this principle is stamped firmly in the minds of those who guide and operate our educational system, we can afford to make a great many mistakes, we can afford to be surprised by the future, we can afford to make some bad educational investments, because we will be protected against the ultimate mistake, which would be to make the educational system a means, not an end, serving purposes other than man himself.

One test of our success in educating the individual for self-realization is whether at the end of each year of education he has a wider range of realistic choices in life available to him. If he is being narrowly specialized to fit into a niche in life with a real possibility of very limited choices, he has been miseducated. Each year should open new doors for him and develop new abilities to enable him to go through these doors as he chooses.

LITERATE CITIZENS

The reinterpretation of the development of literate citizens is profoundly important today when both the political problems and the functioning of the political system have increased enormously in scope and complexity. When the activities of government were largely restricted to maintaining law and order, providing schools, roads, and postal services, and protecting property from fire, the issues were easily grasped, and the agents and officers of government were generally known to a majority of the community. Now, the preservation of the nation, the health of the economy, the welfare of those in need, as well as education, have become mammoth operations with national and international implications. The agents and officers of government are known personally to only a small fraction of the people. Moreover, effective citizenship requires participation in a much more complex social system. A few years of schooling are not sufficient to prepare an intelligent and effective citizen, nor are the simple myths, which pass for American history in many places, adequate background for reasoned understanding. Educating a literate citizenry is in itself a major educational task.

SOCIAL MOBILITY

A third purpose of our schools has been recognized ever since the immigrating tide from Europe reached massive proportions in the latter part of the last century. As the children of recent immigrants became a considerable proportion of the school population in several of the states, many of the new citizens began to perceive the American schools as a means by which their children could have a chance through education to get better jobs and to enjoy the benefits of American life which they had been unable to do. Hence, in addition to providing opportunities for individual self-realization and educating for intelligent citizenship, the American schools have become a major avenue for social mobility—the means by which the American dream has been made a reality by many thousands of families and by which new streams of vigorous leadership have been injected into our maturing society.

But educating for social mobility has also required new interpretations with each generation. In the '90's, the prevailing notion among educators was that there were a few children among the many immigrant families whose moral character and native intelligence were equal to those of pupils from the middle class, old-American stock. They could make superior records in school if certain handicaps were eliminated. The handicaps recognized then were: limited knowledge of English, little time for study because of the need for their wages or help at home, and lack of supporting encouragement. Equality of educational opportunity meant, in that day, to furnish special help in acquiring the English language, raising money to reduce the time the child had to work, and for teacher and principal to give him friendly encouragement.

Now, we have learned that most children have capabilities in one or more areas and that, in place of estimating educational potential by a single scale of scholastic aptitude, we need to use various means of finding the strengths of each child on which further educational development can be based. Not only do we now expect to find many more children with potential social mobility than did our predecessors, but we have also learned about a broader range of handicaps that we need to eliminate in order that children and youth may move ahead. These include limited experience with standard English, limited access to the influence of educated people, nutritional and other health problems, lack of experience in successful learning, lack of disciplined work experience, and lack of confidence in ability to learn. The particular learning objectives and the kinds of educational programs that can enhance social mobility, we now know, must be designed in terms of the particular strengths and limitations of the pupils concerned.

Preparation for the World of Work

The expectation that the public elementary and secondary schools would prepare the workers needed in our expanding economy was not commonly held until the close of World War I. Farm laborers, construction workers for railroads and highways, domestic servants, and unskilled "helpers" comprised the majority of the labor force. Skilled tradesmen came from Europe or were trained through apprenticeship in this country. But the rapid rate of industrialization and business development after 1910 required many workers with higher levels of skills and understanding such as mechanics, stenographers, clerks, and salespeople. The level of education required came to be expressed increasingly in terms of a high school diploma. Furthermore, specific vocational education was introduced in many high schools with grants-in-aid provided by the federal government. By 1925, the public generally, and the schools as well, were including as one of the purposes of American education the preparation of young people for the world of work.

Since 1925, and particularly since World War II, the rapid rate of technological development in agriculture, industry, commerce, defense, and the health services has so changed the occupational distribution of the total labor force that the chance for a youth or young adult without high school education to obtain employment is less and less. Farmers and farm laborers, who made up 38 percent of the labor force at the turn of the century, now comprise only 7 percent. Similarly, opportunities for employment in unskilled occupations have almost disappeared. Last year, only 5 percent of the labor force was unskilled. The proportion employed in skilled trades is not likely to increase. But there are large increases in the percentage of people employed in engineering, science, the recreational fields, accounting, and administration. Now, not only is high school education essential for most employment, but the percentage of jobs requiring college education is increasing at a rapid rate. Education as preparation for employment is more important than ever before.

But this function also requires continuing reinterpretation. Recent reports, such as the one by President Kennedy's Commission on Vocational Education, chaired by Benjamin Willis, and that of the National Association of Secondary School Principals, have documented the failures of our schools to maintain continuing contact with the needs, problems, and opportunities in educating youth for the world of work.

Mention was made earlier of the sharp shifts taking place in the composition of the labor force. In 1960, only 45 percent of the U.S. labor force was engaged in the production and distribution of material goods, while 55 percent was employed in providing non-material services in areas like the health services, education, recreation, social services, science and engineering, accounting, and administration. In 1967, it was estimated that only 40 percent of our labor force was required to produce and distribute material goods, and this is predicted to shrink to 25 percent by 1980. In spite of these great changes, high school vocational programs are still predominantly focused on production jobs, including farming, although only 7 percent of the labor force is engaged in agriculture.

The shift in demand to persons who provide non-material services poses a particular problem for males. A majority of boys from working-class homes have a self-image of being strong and manually dexterous. This is their notion of a "real man." But the opportunities for employment where physical strength and manual dexterity are important are becoming more and more limited. Instead, the new jobs that are increasingly available require primarily intellectual competence and social skills. Education that helps boys to prepare for employment really begins in the early grades, aiding them to develop a more realistic picture of the world of work and to perceive more clearly what characteristics are required for employment. In these early years, children can develop habits of responsibility, of thoroughness in work, of punctuality, as well as intellectual and social skills. In the junior high school period, career exploration and planning are important phases of the program. One of the most significant changes in occupational education is based on the recognition that every child needs to learn things that will prepare him for the world of work, that what is to be learned is much more than certain specific vocational skills, and that appropriate educational experiences will need to extend throughout the school years. Furthermore, the continuing transformation taking place in the nature and distribution of jobs requires not only the use of current projections of employment demands but also emphasis upon the development of generally useful abilities and skills, rather than confining the training to skills limited to specific jobs. This shift of emphasis will insure that re-education and training, when needed, will be more easily accomplished.

WISE CHOICES OF NON-MATERIAL SERVICES

To maintain and to increase the productivity of the American economy requires not only an ample supply of workers at higher levels of competence but also consumers who want and are willing to pay for the wide range of consumer goods and services which the economy can produce. If the American people wanted only food, clothing, and shelter, a major fraction would be unemployed because these goods can be produced by a small part of our labor force. The desire and the willingness to pay for health, education, recreation, including art, music, literature, sports, and the like create the demand which enables the economy to shift its patterns of production to take advantage of the greater efficiency of technology, without stagnation. This sets a fifth major function of American education, namely, to develop in students understanding and appreciation of the wide range of experiences, services, and goods which can contribute much to their health and satisfaction. Only through education can people learn to make wise economic choices as well as wise choices in the personal, social, and political fields.

The consumer education courses which were constructed in the '20's and '30's emphasized the development of the abilities required to make choices among material products, using information about the serviceable qualities and relative costs of these goods. The chief consumer problem of that period was believed to be to obtain useful products at lowest prices commensurate with necessary quality. Few of these courses dealt with the problems involved in making wise choices of goods and services that furnish non-material values, like the aesthetic values in music, art, and drama; the recreational values of sports; the personal and social values in various educational opportunities; the health values in different forms of health and medical programs. Frequently, English courses sought to develop an appreciation for literature that could afford continuing meaning and satisfaction to the reader, and a small number of courses were devoted to motion picture appreciation aimed to help students make wise choices of the movies they viewed.

Now that a majority of the labor force is engaged in the production of non-material services, the range of possible choices for the consumer is increasing greatly. Hence, the reinterpretation of this purpose in our age opens up a whole new area of consumer education and requires the development of relevant objectives and learning experiences. The wise choice of these services is profoundly important, in the development both of individuals and of our culture. Choices of literature, art, music, recreation, leisure time, educational opportunities, health services, and contributing social services have more to do with the quality of life than most of our material choices.

However, the relatively simple calculations involved in comparing the value of steak at one price with that of chicken at another is not the kind of decision process involved in choosing among non-material alternatives. The educational program will need to extend the opportunities for students seriously to explore experiences and services in ways that help them to perceive values, to find meaning in them, to discover how far they afford satisfaction. Furthermore, to help in making rational decisions, students will need opportunities to review their experiences, to reflect on their impact, to assess the probable future consequences, and to develop the habit of appraising the values of non-material experiences. This is a new area for many schools.

LEARNING TO LEARN

Teaching students how to learn has, in the last ten years, been accepted as another function of our schools. With the rapid acquisition of new knowledge, it is no longer possible to give the student in school an adequate command of the facts in each major subject which will serve him throughout the balance of his life. The school can only start him on a life-long career of continued learning. Hence, an important educational aim today is to teach students to learn and to develop in them a strong interest in continued study together with the skills required to keep on with their learning after graduation.

At educational gatherings, the comment can be heard that this has always been a major purpose of our schools. It has certainly been stated as a desirable aim by educational leaders for centuries; but not only have the particular sources of learning and procedures for study changed with the times but for generations the pattern of school performance has been in sharp contrast to what is involved in learning outside of the formal school situation. In life outside the school, one encounters problems that are not clearly formulated, and he must analyze the situation sufficiently to identify particular problems or to see what questions are involved. He needs to know where he can get relevant information; he needs to be able to attack the particular problems appropriately in terms of the fields in which they can be placed—that is, science, literature, economics, politics, and the like. He needs to be able to verify or validate the procedures he follows and/or the answers or solutions he proposes.

These abilities can be acquired through experience which requires their use. But most schools do not provide much opportunity for this. Typically, the teacher poses the problems or questions rather than the student finding them as he works. The textbook or the teacher is most likely to furnish the answers rather than to require the student to work them out or to find dependable sources. If this new purpose is to be attained, the contrast between traditional study in school and the procedures of life-long learning must be eliminated through making the school experiences examples of continued learning. This requires teachers and students to take on new roles.

The increase in the number of functions which the American schools are expected to serve is the natural result of the changes in our whole society. In the nearly 200 years since this country was founded, society has increased enormously in complexity. Yet, today, the human individual at birth does not differ appreciably from the babies born at the time of the American Revolution. All of the knowledge, skills, and attitudes required to live in modern society must be acquired by each individual after birth. Since society is continuing to increase in complexity and scope, the development of youth for effective modern life increases in difficulty and in magnitude with each generation.

CRITICAL NEW TASKS

The aforementioned six still remain the major functions of American schools, but from time to time special tasks take on immediate urgency. Two of them are stressed today.

We have seen that with the increasing use of technology the demand for unskilled labor has diminished to about 5 percent of the labor force. Yet, in the United States and in other advanced nations, between 15 percent and 20 percent of the population have not acquired sufficient skill and general literacy to qualify for skilled or higher levels of employment. The fact that more than 80 percent of our children have achieved an educational level above the minimum requirements for modern literacy and employment is a tribute to the determination of our people and the efforts of our schools. But this is not enough. Today, 19 out of every 20 of our children can and must be effectively reached by education. We know how to stimulate and guide the learning of children who come from homes where education is valued and where the basis for it has been laid in the home experiences. However, we do not have widely accepted means for reaching children whose backgrounds have given them little or no basis for school work. To reach all or nearly all of these children is a critical task of the present period.

A second urgent task of today is also partly a result of modern technology. As automation has sharply reduced the demand for unskilled labor, the occupations in which there are increasing demands, as noted earlier, are those requiring a fairly high level of education. However, to provide employment opportunities for all our people and to keep our economy fully productive requires a much larger proportion of our youth to complete high school—many more than in the past—to gain professional, semi-professional, or technical competence. To provide these educational opportunities and to insure effective learning for youth from varied backgrounds of training, experience, and outlook is another new and important educational task which we now face. Neither the U.S. nor any other country has previously attempted it.

Mention is made of these two new tasks that the schools are being urgently asked to undertake, not because they involve additions to the basic functions or purposes of the schools but because they should be viewed as important tasks with purposes of their own.

Both of them—reaching the disadvantaged and making the high school effective for a large proportion of the population—must be undertaken with the six basic purposes in mind: to help each individual achieve his highest potential, to develop a broader base of intelligent and active citizens, to make possible social mobility, to prepare each person for the world of work, to help him choose non-material services that will furnish the greatest meaning and satisfaction, and to become a life-long learner.

In making education effective for a larger number of students, consideration must be given to the criticism made by students themselves of the high school program.

The most common complaint they make is its "irrelevance." In many cases, what is being taught could be highly relevant to the activities, interests, and problems of the students, and they fail to perceive the connection. Much of this is due to the separation of the school from the rest of life. For example, the separation of the school from the world of work and the world of community service results in several unfortunate consequences. Many students see the school as something apart from the adult world into which they will be going. This is one of the factors in dropping out of school; and for many students who do not drop out, the apparent lack of connection between the school work and their future lives results in low interest and effort in their studies. From the standpoint of the society, the separation of the school makes more difficult the transition from school to work and from school to constructive community membership. What is needed is the development of bridges to the rest of the community and greater openness in the school to outside persons and activities. We need to be providing cooperative education (work-study programs), community service programs, and other means by which school youth can be actively involved in work experiences, in community services, in joint civic participation with adults, and the like. Students are not likely to use what they learn unless they have practice in identifying problems and difficulties. Dealing with these requires learning—and practice in using what is learned —in situations outside of school.

RESPONSE OF THE SCHOOLS TO CHANGE

Although the American schools, when compared to those of Western Europe, have not rigidly adhered to obsolete programs but have been responsive to the changing needs and opportunities of the times, these educational changes have lagged some years behind the initiating forces, and the adaptation or transformations required in the schools have not always been largely effective. The lag appears to have been due both to the lack of continuing attention within the school to developments in the society and to the common failure of school leaders to translate needed changes into educational purposes and operations that guide the actual conduct of school work.

It has become modern business practice for the corporation to make continuing projections of environmental factors, such as population shifts, new technologies becoming available, and changing patterns of consumer preferences, that importantly affect its work. From these assessments and reassessments of changing conditions, the corporation commonly plans its production and distribution programs, adjusting the future plans each year in the light of facts of the past year. In this way, the company is able to respond quickly to changing conditions and frequently anticipates the changes before they actually take place. Educational systems and organizations could benefit from similar practices. A rationale for such planning procedures exists, and modifications to fit a particular system can be worked out. With such studies and with the attitude that change is the natural characteristic of our society and its institutions, our schools in the future can anticipate new educational needs as well as respond to present conditions more promptly.

Our failure to translate changing needs into guiding purposes and operational plans seems to be largely due to our following the pattern of leadership characteristic of a slowly changing society. Under conditions of very gradual shift, the operational modifications in the system are commonly made by the operators before they are recognized by the leaders. Then, the role of leadership is to explain these changes in terms of accepted principles so that the new practices now in operation are legitimized. Many statements of educational policy have been justifications of changes already under way rather than pointing the direction for new efforts.

Because our society is changing more rapidly with each decade, we must develop educational procedures that can reduce the lag between changing needs and educational programs that meet the needs. The American schools have shown their flexibility in responding to needs in the past. By developing procedures to scan the social horizon, we can anticipate impending changes and understand their probable impact. By employing task forces of scholars, scientists, curriculum makers, and teachers to translate needs into educational objectives and operational plans, we can expect to respond more promptly and more effectively in the future than we have in the past. Over the years, the purposes for our schools have been expanding, and in each generation older purposes require reinterpretation. This is necessary for schools to serve adequately the individual and the society of the times.

The Challenge of Social Change to Education

ROBERT J. HAVIGHURST

Education operates in a social situation which conditions its aims and its methods. At the same time, education is based on what we know about the intellectual and social development of children and upon the state of the art of teaching.

SOCIAL FORCES AND TRENDS

Just now our society is going through a period of extremely rapid social change which compels us to modify and adapt our education. The major

From *Educational Imperatives in a Changing Culture* (Philadelphia, Pa.: University of Pennsylvania Press, 1966), pp. 9–20. William B. Brickman, editor. Reprinted with permission of publisher.

social forces and social trends have been described by many writers and are known to anybody with open eyes and an open mind. In order to see them at a single glance and to note their bearing on the schools, we may consider them under four headings.

Contraction of Space and Time

Owing to the speeding up of travel, we have extended our reach. When the wind and the muscles of a horse provided the energy for locomotion, a man could travel thirty to one hundred miles a day. Soon we will travel with the speed of sound. Thus, we cover more space and compress more action into a unit of time than was conceivable a few decades ago.

The world has grown so small that people can begin the day in Chicago, eat a leisurely breakfast on the way to New York, do a day's work in New York, and have a comfortable dinner on the way back, arriving in Chicago in time to attend the evening performance of the Chicago Symphony. Time has become so crowded with action that a man can go around the world in eighty hours, instead of the eighty days that Jules Verne's hero required.

These changes are comparable in their effect on education to the disclosure by Columbus that the earth is a sphere. School courses in geography could never be the same after Columbus. Modern courses in geography must be modified to give children the feel of rapid and extensive movement in space and time. Modern man crowds a tremendous amount of action into a unit of time. How do we convey this knowledge effectively to children? Not only geography, but also history and government and the social sciences must be taught so as to help students get the feel of this kind of a world.

Technological Development and Change in the Labor Force

In the nineteenth century, the muscles of a man were important to the productivity of an economy. At that time, it was calculated that an average man can do about forty-eight kilowatt-hours of useful work in a year. Then the various kinds of engines were created to supply energy, and now the electric energy alone generated in the United States is the equivalent of eighty-five men for every man, woman, and child in the country.

Not only was energy supplied, but machines were created to do work more rapidly and with as much efficiency as men could do it. The man-hour productivity in 1960 was three times that of 1900 in the United States. The American people elected to produce more goods and many new products with this increasing productivity. At the same time, they elected to shorten the work week from about 60 to about 40 hours.

Increased productivity showed its effects on the labor force first in agriculture, where the proportion of workers shrank rapidly to the present level of about 8 per cent of the labor force. This started the migration from farm to city that has provided most of the new industrial workers since World War I. The manufacturing industry at first expanded to produce many new goods, but productivity increased even more rapidly. From 1950 to 1960, the quantity of manufactured goods increased nearly 50 per cent, while the number of workers employed in manufacturing stayed constant. From now on, the number of production workers will decline. The General Electric Company increased its output by 8 per cent from 1956 to 1959 and at the same time reduced its production workers by 25 per cent. It has been predicted that factory workers will be as scarce in the year two thousand as farm workers are today.

The emphasis in the affluent society has shifted from the production of goods to the distribution and consumption of goods. These are the problems today—how to distribute the goods that we produce in such volume, and how to consume this volume of goods.

We now employ 60 per cent of the labor force in the United States to do work that is concerned with distribution and consumption of goods, whereas, in 1900, this proportion was 30 per cent of the labor force. By increasing the proportions of jobs not directly involved in producing consumable goods, we have provided nearly full employment and have given people the purchasing power to consume an increasing volume of production.

Urbanization and Metropolitan Development

Not long ago an editor of a newspaper in the South presented his readers with the following little thought:

Changing Times

We live in a time
　When cotton has gone west,
Cattle have gone east,
　Yankees have gone south,
Negroes have gone north,
　And we've all gone to town.

Now, 70 per cent of our population live in places defined as urban by the census, and 65 per cent of the population are clustered together in 228 Standard Metropolitan Statistical Areas. The Big City is in a crisis—financial, political, social, and moral. With growing slums and a lowering of the average occupational level of city residents, it is losing the middle classes to the suburbs. Vast sums of money are going into physical urban renewal, in an effort to make the city once more a place in which all kinds of people will live and raise their children.

The earlier term—urbanization—no longer describes the process that we are concerned with. It is not the growth of a city, but the development of a metropolitan area, on which our attention will be fixed during the remainder of the century.

The standard metropolitan statistical area, as defined by the Census Bureau, is a city of 50,000 or more with its surrounding county and any contiguous counties that are functionally bound to the major city.

Between 1950 and 1960, the central cities of the country showed relatively small growth, and many of the larger cities actually lost population. Meanwhile the suburbs grew very rapidly, until by 1960 the population of suburban areas was practically equal to that of the central cities.

It is the metropolitan area—the central city and its suburbs—with which the new Federal Department of Housing and Urban Development will be concerned.

From 1925 to 1960, the metropolitan areas of the eastern and northern sections of the country became polarized, with people of high income and high educational level moving to the suburbs, while their places in the central city were taken by poorly educated and low-income families. Thus, the educational and the economic level of the central city fell, while suburban levels rose. In the larger metropolitan areas a gulf separated the two parts, and neither showed an interest or a sense of unity with the other.

World Interdependence and Cooperation

The day of political and economic isolation for any nation is past. Vast areas of the world that in 1900 were known only as places for missionary effort, are now independent countries and co-members of the United Nations with the rich and powerful nations whose power and riches depend in part on their trade and their political cooperation with the have-not nations. Africa is no longer the Dark Continent; now it is the mother of new nations, which are slowly forming themselves into a United States of Central Africa and will soon rival Europe in economic and political power. South America has awakened from a century of stagnation into a period of economic growth and social revolution that will make it an economic rival of North America in a few decades, if it does not become an economic partner with North America.

The modern era of history is often said to have started in 1453, when the Turks conquered Constantinople and Western Europe took to the ocean and the building of overseas empires. It seems probable that historians of the future will declare that this era closed about 1950, when the hegemony of white men came to an end. During these five centuries, the West Europeans and the North Americans dominated the world through their superior technology applied to material production and to warfare. On these terms, the Caucasian race was clearly superior to the other races.

Only at the beginning of the twentieth century did a non-white nation (Japan) defeat a white nation (Russia) in war and become a world power. The Chinese gradually awakened and in the second half of the century have become the great question mark around which the speculations and the strategies of the white nations turn. During the twentieth century, India established herself as a moral force in the parliament of nations. Africa developed after World War II a set of independent nations which slowly learned to live and work together toward the goal of bringing enormous economic and political influence to bear on the rest of the world. Only the indigenous peoples of South, Central, and North America, among the colored peoples of the world, did not rise to power during the twentieth century. They were too much integrated into a white-dominated society, or too much subordinated, or too much isolated, to be able to assert themselves politically as a nation or nations of colored people.

Thus, the twentieth century marks the close of the white man's dominion. In the twenty-first century, *if color means anything at all,* the white man will have to come to terms with his inferiority in numbers and in political and economic power.

The growing interdependence of nations has been matched by a growing movement toward cooperation and understanding among the religions of the world. The Roman Catholic Church has moved toward closer cooperation with other Christian churches since 1962, when Pope John XXIII convened the Vatican Ecumenical Council and set up the Vatican Secretariat for Christian Unity.

The World Council of Churches has gained strength rapidly since World War II. Extension of the ecumenical movement to encompass all world religions is only a matter of time. The leaders of the Christian churches plan to encourage a worldwide dialogue among religions that will strengthen them as religious systems and at the same time contribute to greater understanding. Others, following the lead of Arnold Toynbee, boldly predict the coming of a single world religion with branches that fit the religious traditions of various parts of the world.

In any case, we see the nations and the churches—earlier the exponents of war and dissension in the world—seeking now to promote peace and good will.

WHAT THESE SOCIAL CHANGES REQUIRE OF EDUCATION

These social changes require two things of the school. First, textbooks must be completely rewritten, which we all take for granted. What we call the Explosion of Knowledge requires books and films which record the vast increase of knowledge and also an approach to knowledge that stresses the ability of the pupil to find and acquire the knowledge that he needs. This second requirement is the one that affects most deeply the ways we teach. It forces us to treat the mind of a child in a different way from that of the past.

The traditional view of the human mind that has dominated our methods of teaching sees the mind as a storehouse of knowledge. The aim of teaching, therefore, is to put a stock of facts into the mind. The mind is a kind of filing cabinet. Sometimes we help the student set up a good filing system by giving him a curriculum that organizes his facts into fields so that he can consult his files quickly and economically. A good mind, according to this view, has a good filing system.

But, as the amount of knowledge has grown so rapidly during the present century, we have been forced to give up the hope that any human mind, however well organized, could contain all useful knowledge or could keep up with the growth of knowledge. Therefore, we have been forced to change our view of the human mind.

The human mind is now seen as an instrument for learning. We train the mind so that it can learn quickly and economically the knowledge that is important about a particular subject. Therefore, we train the child to use the library to look up knowledge that he needs, and thus train him in the method of inquiry. We train for problem-solving, for the making and testing of hypotheses. Our aim is to help the pupil develop a flexible and continually learning mind.

The basic elements of the curriculum, then, are as follows:

1. The fundamental concepts on which the subject is based. This is what is meant by the current phrase—the *structure* of a subject. In teaching geography, for example, we determine a few fundamental concepts of geography and we teach around them. The specific topics or units in geography are selected for the purpose of illuminating the structure of the subject. The teacher may select from a wide variety of topics, and may ask the pupils to help in choosing topics. There may be an element of chance in the topics studied by a particular class. But there should not be any element of chance in the underlying concepts that are taught. This is the teacher's responsibility—to cover the structure of the subject.
2. A set of learning experiences that emphasizes inquiry, induction, organizing data, testing hypotheses, drawing conclusions. This is why the current interest in teaching the method of inquiry is so important, and why the experimental work in creativity is so useful.
3. A variety of instructional materials, with textbooks, library collections, workbooks, laboratory exercises, tape recordings, films, and programmed study material. This variety is needed to provide for a variety of ways of learning, and to provide for individual differences among pupils.

INDIVIDUALIZED INSTRUCTION

The call today is for individualized instruction, but there is some ambiguity in this term. It does not mean instruction of children individually, by a tutorial method, but rather relating the instruction to the individual child's level of mental skill, intellectual development, and social development. Generally, it means instructing the child in a group that is like him in mental skill, such as in reading or arithmetic, as well as keeping him in a group of his peers in social and emotional development so that he can master the tasks of social and emotional development in an orderly fashion under guidance. Individualized instruction certainly involves self-directed study, after about the age of 8 or 9, because self-directed, self-initiated study is an important outcome of education at that age.

Perhaps the best way to think usefully about individualized instruction is to conceive of education as consisting of five phases extending over a period from about 3 years of age to about 18. For each phase there are developmental tasks in the areas of mental skill, intellectual development, physical development, and social development. Then the function of the school is to provide a learning situation in which each child makes appropriate progress on the tasks of his stage of development.

The five phases and their principal developmental tasks are:

PHASE I. Early Childhood—Age 3 to 5 or 6.
    Command of oral language.
    Development of concepts of the physical world.
    Learning to play in groups of children under adult direction.
    Developing an internalized conscience.
    Developing motor coordination.
PHASE II. Lower Elementary Phase—Age 5 or 6 to 8 or 9.
    Skill in reading.
    Skill in simple arithmetic.
    Development of concepts of the immediate social world.
    Learning to play in the peer group without adult direction.
PHASE III. Upper Elementary Phase—Age 8 or 9 to 11 or 12.
    Learning independently.
    Learning to inquire.
    Expanding concepts in space and time.
    Becoming physically independent of parents.
    Becoming an active member of the democracy of peers.
    Learning the physical skills necessary for ordinary play with the same sex.
PHASE IV. Junior High School—Age 11 or 12 to 14 or 15.
    Learning the complex mental skills of logic and mathematics.
    Developing mental and moral perspective. Gaining some rational control over one's conscience, through evaluating the moral consequences of behavior.
    Acquiring self-esteem based on objective evaluation of one's abilities.
    Becoming loyal to the values of one's society and religious group.
PHASE V. Senior High School—Age 14 or 15 to 17 or 18.
    Learning the structures of the basic disciplines of knowledge.
    Developing basic vocational attitudes and skills appropriate to vocational goals.

Becoming emotionally independent of parents and other adults.
Learning to get along with the opposite sex.
Developing a scale of values.
Developing an identity based on career plans and personal values.

When one thinks in terms of these phases and of the developmental tasks appropriate to them, one can see how individualized instruction and cooperative or team teaching should operate.

It is assumed that the teaching team includes a counselor who has information and skills on the basis of which he can diagnose the strengths and weaknesses of each pupil. To this team are assigned one hundred or two hundred pupils who are spread over the age range of their phase of development. The school building has a library and rooms of various sizes with a variety of equipment. The teachers and teacher aides work with pupils in large or small groups, the groups having been formed on the basis of diagnoses of the pupils' standing on the various developmental tasks. Pupils are also free for self-initiated and self-directed work in the library and laboratory and in the community as they grow older.

THE SCHOOL AND THE COMMUNITY

Up to this point, the argument of this essay has been that social change places a responsibility on the schools to educate the individual so that he can understand social change and can learn independently to keep up with the flow of new knowledge in areas of importance to him. Very little has been said about the content of his education, and it may appear that the specific content is unimportant as long as it is chosen by the pupil or the teacher to aid the development of mental skills and to help along the processes of inquiry and creativity. This would certainly not be an appropriate conclusion, for there is much specific knowledge which is important for every pupil in an American school to learn, and also much to know in the area of his general vocational goal.

The knowledge which takes on the most importance through social change is largely knowledge of the social world in which we live. We have noted the development of the metropolitan area as the natural unit for planning and conducting the human enterprise on a local scale, and we have noted the development of an interdependent world. These are two centers around which much of the instruction should be organized.

The Metropolitan Community

We have seen how the metropolitan areas became polarized before 1960. The central city developed serious civic problems, and commenced to work on them by means of urban renewal. But the problems grew worse. At first, the suburbs were complacent, and suburban residents quietly rejoiced in their good judgment or good luck at getting out of the city.

A new balance between suburb and central city is now taking place. The economic and racial polarization between them has probably reached its maximum and is already receding. From now on, it is likely that the suburbs and central cities will become more like one another, rather than more different from one another.

From now on, suburbs and central cities will increasingly recognize their similarity and their common interest in cooperation. This will come soon in the more technological aspects and processes of the human enterprise, such as in water supply, sewage disposal, streets, and fire protection. It has already come in the area of communication, with newspapers, radio, and television serving the entire area.

Cooperation between suburbs and central city will come slowly and with more difficulty in the areas of government and education. These complex social systems are so entrenched in law and custom that they will be hard to change. For instance, the six counties around and including Detroit have more than four million inhabitants and will reach five million before 1970. In this metropolitan "community," there are 214 local governmental units, with seventeen special districts and 159 school districts. The Detroit area will soon become one continuous community in the physical urban sense. It is already a community to the newspapers and television stations. How rapidly will it become one community in the governmental sense and the educational sense?

The first steps toward true metropolitan area cooperation are likely to be taken by volunteer and non-official groups which meet to study the problems of a metropolitan area and to plan for possible cooperation. A Metropolitan Area Council on Higher Education is an example. The new Federal Aid to Higher Education Law will give a substantial push to cooperation in library and extension work by colleges in metropolitan areas. Some form of metropolitan education authority will come into existence as a means of correlating the work of the many school districts, of equalizing educational opportunity, and carrying on certain functions that should be conducted on an area-wide basis.

The time has come for the school to treat the metropolitan area as the pupil's local community. From as early as the fifth grade, pupils should learn the boundaries of the metropolitan area as the boundaries of *their* community. They should be taught to see the social and political and economic problems of the entire metropolitan area as *their* problems.

The World Community

The fact of world interdependence needs no further demonstration. But we need a great deal of experimentation and innovation in teaching world history and world affairs. Our young people are going to be citizens of the world. They are going to help decide major questions concerning the relations of the United States to South America, to Africa, to China, and to

Russia. They are going to help decide how we should use our armed forces in relation to the rest of the world. They are going to help decide on momentous changes in the character and functions of the United Nations Organization. We have to use all of our imagination and understanding in the choice of what and how we should teach about the world community.

CONCLUSION

Social change is producing a new material and social setting for Americans with such speed that the schools cannot keep abreast of them by sheer teaching of knowledge. Therefore, we must help boys and girls become independent and self-directing learners, equipped with the basic skills and the interest in learning that will enable them to become life-long learners. Our educational research workers have given us valuable assistance during the past decade with this task. At the same time, we should give priority in our teaching of social studies to the kind of content that provides a base of knowledge for citizenship in the metropolitan community and citizenship in the world community.

Communication: A Curriculum Focus

MARGARET AMMONS

Given the charge of preparing an example of a new way to organize a curriculum for children, I have found my paper falling into what seems to me to be four natural sections. Three of these are in essence a foundation for the fourth, the proposal of a new curriculum design focused on communication. The paper opens with some remarks that provide general background, after which I define key terms and then proceed to spell out the basic assumptions on which the design proposal itself rests.

In any one of the sections you must recognize that much of what is set down is sheer assertion or assumption, although I may sometimes neglect to identify for the reader just where this is so. I defend myself in this regard on the grounds that where curriculum, as defined here, is concerned, we have little other than organized assumptions to go on. Therefore, I will try to present as tight a case for what I propose as I am able to do, be-

From *A Curriculum for Children* (Washington, D.C.: Association for Supervision and Curriculum Development, 1969), pp. 105–122. Alexander Frazier, editor. Reprinted with permission of the Association for Supervision and Curriculum Development and Margaret Ammons. Copyright © 1969 by the Association for Supervision and Curriculum Development.

lieving firmly that in our present stage of professional development, there is no viable alternative to our doing so. Hopefully, this reasoning will be exonerated by the end of the paper.

GENERAL BACKGROUND

My first assertion is that "The elementary school as we know it is largely the product of historical accidents." That is to say, the graded school for children roughly five or six to eleven or twelve years of age was not a result of national studies or assessment, nor careful experiments regarding child growth and development, nor an adoption or revision of what knowledge is of most worth, nor surveys to determine the most pressing needs of children in the given age bracket. I need not here catalogue the critical dates of the history of the elementary school in its entirety. Most assuredly, some few changes have occurred. The changes, however, were again not the result of the kind of thoughtful inquiry and introspection to which we would be pleased to admit. Rather, decisions regarding the elementary school have been made in response to such questions as "What will we do with rapidly increasing numbers of children?" And thus grades. Then, "What will be studied in each of these grades?" Thus graded textbooks and graded teachers. Not one of such decisions or answers was responsive to searching questions which, to me at least, appear relevant to children.

Given such decisions, we have then attempted to justify them after the fact, as in the following statement: "The best basic unit of organization yet devised is the self-contained classroom in which a group of children of similar social maturity are grouped together under the extended and continuous guidance of a single teacher." This statement was published originally in 1950 and quoted in 1960.[1] At the time of either publication, there were no other basic units of organization in sufficient numbers to have made a thorough-going comparative study which would have allowed such an assertion to be made.

Furthermore, programs established on such bases as described above have been maintained *in essence* in spite of data which point to something other than the present elementary school program and organization. Perhaps most critical, however, is that while we have tinkered with such elements as flexible buildings, team teaching, computers, nongrading, and so on, the curriculum has remained in essence the same.

To repeat: the curriculum, or in general those things which have been proffered to children to learn, has not changed in essence. By essence, I mean simply that, when the trimmings have been peeled away, what re-

---

[1] Association for Supervision and Curriculum Development. *The Self-Contained Classroom.* Washington, D.C.: the Association, 1960.

mains as the core around which the curriculum is built has remained un-altered for decades. One piece of evidence for this is a number of studies conducted in response to charges that schools of the 'fifties were not doing as well as schools of the earlier part of this century. In spite of the fact that we claimed to be doing something different, in which case we should simply have said, "You're right, we're not trying to do the same thing," we hastened to haul out tests which would, for example, measure in 1953 what the tests were initially designed to measure in 1933. If there is no difference between 1933 results and 1953 results on tests designed to measure 1933 performances, it would appear on the surface that whatever happened to children in 1953 was at least similar to what happened in 1933; that is, what happened to them in terms of learning opportunities.[2]

Let me put it in another way. Once upon a time we were faced with the task of making members of our society literate. Initially, this meant teaching the three R's. Slowly literacy came to be defined to include in addition the possession of certain information, social science information, for example. That is, subject matter "mastery" somehow came to be equated with success and literacy. Obviously, the school was the place where such mastery should occur.

Supposedly, however, our expressed purpose now is somewhat different from mere literacy. We speak of producing persons who possess such attributes as critical thinking, or analytical abilities, or abilities to sort out fact from fiction, or appreciation of the humanities. Yet the studies we have available reveal at least two unsettling generalizations about what transpires in elementary classrooms. First, teacher classroom behavior is determined more by textbooks than by any other single factor.[3] Second, approximately 90 percent of teachers' questions require no more of the learner than that he recall some specific piece of information or that he be able to put someone else's idea into his own words.[4]

The point is this: Despite aspirations and claims to the contrary, what actually happens in elementary classrooms, at least in large numbers of them, puts a ceiling on what children are expected to do. And ceilings are placed in the traditional subject areas. When children are given grades, they are typically evaluated in terms of performance in subject areas. Some attention is given to such other factors as the quality of their citizenship and their effort; but these are often judged as children function in subject areas. Furthermore, a rapid survey of statutory requirements regarding the

[2] V. V. Miller and W. C. Lanton. "Reading Achievement of School Children—Then and Now." *Elementary English* 33: 91–97; February 1956.

[3] D. Gilmore. "A Critical Examination of Selected Instructional Practices." Unpublished doctoral dissertation. East Lansing: Michigan State University, 1963.

[4] F. J. Guszak. "A Study of Teacher Solicitation and Student Response Interaction About Reading Content in Selected Second, Fourth, and Sixth Grades." Unpublished doctoral dissertation. Madison: University of Wisconsin, 1966.

elementary school program reveals that these are typically set down in terms of subject matter to be taught and amount of time to be spent per week on certain areas.

Thus, mastery of subject matter or literacy is still the operational goal in elementary education. Earlier, the expressed goal and the operational goal were the same and a program appropriate for their attainment was developed. Now there is a basic discrepancy between expressed and operational goals; the program is reflective of the operational, not the expressed goal. The reasons for this situation constitute an interesting problem for exploration, but such explorations are beyond the limits of this paper.

Thus while we want to change, while we alter school organization, we still divide the child's school world into the same subject areas which have been the basis for schooling for decades. Furthermore, with such notable exceptions as the work of Suchman, new projects have been developed within the framework of disciplines or academic specialties. The apparent objective in some such projects has been to make better mathematicians of elementary school children, or better scientists, or better historians, or better users of the mother tongue.

The question which cries for thoughtful consideration is whether the goal of the elementary school is to prepare young children for more adequate performance in the academic disciplines at later educational stages by earlier and earlier concentration on the disciplines—or whether the purpose of the elementary school is something quite different. While this question will be dealt with in some detail at a later point, let me assert now my own position—the purpose of the elementary school is *not* to create academicians at earlier and earlier ages.

DEFINITIONS

Let us turn now to the definition of some terms which will recur and upon the definition of which much of what is to follow hangs. There are five such terms: curriculum, instruction, communication, objectives, and evaluation.

By *curriculum* I mean an educational plan which includes a statement of objectives, a description of exemplary learning situations, and a description of exemplary evaluation techniques, the latter two designed in relation to objectives. This plan is drawn for a group of learners for whom the planners have responsibility, as, for example, all the children in a school district.

Instruction in this context is defined as the interaction between teacher and pupil or pupils which is intended to assist the learner toward the achievement of specified objectives.

Communication here is a rather simple concept. It is not burdened with the theoretical constructs of communications specialists, though such specialists have much to contribute. Here communication is defined as a two-way process in which one individual intends that a particular meaning be grasped by another or others, and in which others grasp the intended meaning. I acknowledge that the word "meaning" is fraught with ambiguity and various philosophical and psychological over- and undertones. But if I were to use the word "message," I would be in similar difficulty. When I use the word communication, I hope the reader will decode it with the same interpretation that I place upon it.

Objectives are statements of purpose which describe the desired student behavior and the content in relation to which the student is to behave. Objectives have as their function guiding, not dictating to, teachers in selecting appropriate learning situations and evaluation techniques. Parenthetically, both behavior and content are conceived of here in very broad terms.

Evaluation is intended to mean a description of an individual's progress toward one or more objectives. So much for terms.

BASIC ASSUMPTIONS

There is a set of assumptions which I make about the nature of man, the knowable, the good society, and man's relation to it. From these, hopefully, grow some assumptions which relate directly to elementary education.

First, man is rational. By this I mean that man can see alternatives and choose among them. Further, in my frame of reference, rationality in man means that man does not act capriciously, whimsically, or without some justification which to him makes sense; that is, man behaves with reason. Even further, man can learn to increase his ability to act with reason, to improve through his own power his grounds for choosing. Man desires to improve, has the courage to improve, is curious and enthusiastic about things which have meaning for him. And finally, man is a social animal, requiring direct and vicarious human contact and response for survival. If I did not hold this belief, I would have little purpose in teaching.

Second, I assume that much is knowable which cannot be accounted for through the perception of the senses. I can know what it is like to be lonely or happy, but I know this in a way that is probably different from the way I know that something is blue, or hard, or sweet, or true, or harmonious. If this is so, then what I offer to a learner to know must include knowing in many ways. Knowledge cannot be limited to what is measured by responses to a paper and pencil test. What I accept as knowledge, and therefore knowable, must allow for empathic knowing, for sensitivity to another's perceptions of occurrences. It means that much of worth is known without my intervention or awareness. Learners do come to know without me. I assume that knowledge and knowing are a means, not an end. Finally, knowing, and thus learning, is deeply personal for each individual.

The good society is one in which man is free to choose, to make of himself what he will, to participate in the business of living according to his own lights. Such a society encourages independence of mind and spirit and does not bend humankind to its own ends, however magnanimous these may be. It is a society which provides the context for freedom of choice of the individual. The individual, in turn, has the obligation to behave as a human being, with the capacity for reasoning and choosing, with the ability to add to his store of knowledge whatever will allow him to become what he potentially is and to contribute to the good of all. It is a society which exists for the individual as he lives with others, not one for which the individual exists. It accords to the individual the ability to make his own rational and informed decisions.

The foregoing statements represent only a brief summary of where I stand on the questions which each of us must answer for himself as he contemplates the task of educating the young. If I am able to be consistent, these assumptions, or this value position, if you prefer, would seem to give rise to some further assumptions regarding elementary education:

1. The purpose of elementary schools is not to prepare a child for "a" or "the" next step in the sense of "getting him ready" for first grade or sixth grade, or high school, or college.
2. The best preparation for "next steps" is success at tasks which are valuable and relevant to a learner wherever he is.
3. Instruction and the plans for it derive or should derive from the curriculum of a particular school system or district.
4. Schools must define their curricula in terms of something which hopefully is relevant to the elementary child as he is.
5. Performing is different from learning. Performing is a short-lived change in behavior displayed in order to meet some external standard; learning is a persistent change in behavior displayed because the individual has "internalized" a new way of behaving or because he values it sufficiently to make it characteristic of his behavior patterns.[5]
6. Currently in elementary education, as elsewhere, we emphasize performance rather than learning.
7. Possession of information does not guarantee a permanent change in behavior.
8. The study of academic subject matter for its own sake does not guarantee an "educated" individual or one who has learned.
9. Mastery of academic subject matter is currently the end of elementary education. Some evidence in support of this assumption

[5] Margaret P. Ammons. "Do We Really Want Students to Learn?" *Oregon Foreign Language Newsletter,* October 1967.

is the fact that success or failure is determined in part by this criterion.

10. Conditions are changing so radically and rapidly that educational needs of elementary children as defined in the past are no longer relevant.

11. Academic subject matter can in fact become the means not the end of education.

12. Academic subject matter can be justified in the curriculum as it contributes to the individual's ability to communicate.

13. To change the essence of the elementary curriculum, we must alter our pattern of thinking and talking about the elementary curriculum.

14. As long as we segment the elementary program without some unifying theme, we deny what many assert to be true in the lives of human beings, namely the need to see the world as a whole piece.

15. Given such conditions, I am willing to put my money on communication as relevant at any point in a human's life.

A COMMUNICATIONS CURRICULUM

Given the foregoing rationale, what follows is a justification for a curriculum or the skeleton of a curriculum that I would propose as being more responsive to the child and his real world. The questions whose answers suggest or at least allow this curriculum are perhaps more important than the program itself. The curriculum proposal to follow is an illustration of a process in application more than it is a full-blown description of a program. Many of the questions it tries to answer have already been identified or implied.

Justification

Earlier I have denied either implicitly or explicitly that simple literacy is an acceptable purpose if it is the main or only purpose. I have also rejected the purpose of elementary education as that of preparing an individual for any next stage of education. Let me again disavow the notion of some that the purpose of elementary education is to teach children to think as does a scientist, a mathematician, or any other scholar in any other discipline.

The reasons for such rejections are probably obvious from what has been said to date. Let me here state some of these reasons briefly. I reject literacy as the end of education because it restricts the view held by the child of himself and his world. I reject preparation for next stages because in the main any stage of education has been artificially and arbitrarily determined; thus such preparation is also artificial and arbitrary. I reject the purpose of having children think as does a scholar because at the level of the elementary child, it is presumptuous to pretend that he is, in any real sense, capable of such activity. To assume that one child can think in the pattern of scholars in some seven to nine different fields is unrealistic and perhaps undesirable.

To try to force a child to choose a discipline of special interest at the elementary level, which might be an alternative, is to violate several of my basic assumptions. It would deny him the opportunity to become sufficiently acquainted with his world so that his choice would be informed and suitable. Inherent is the danger that the choice will be made for him in relation to something other than his individual welfare. Furthermore, to place such emphasis upon the disciplines is to make them become ends in themselves rather than means to be used by individuals for their own ends.

From these assertions an acceptable purpose of elementary education seems to me to emerge. In its broadest terms, the purpose of elementary education is to assist the individual child to cope with the world as he finds it. Such coping involves understanding, a major part of which is to be able to interpret accurately the stimuli he receives from his world. Here I include stimuli to the emotional or affective "senses."

More specifically, the purpose of elementary education is to help the child acquire the attitudes and skills he needs to interpret his world and to clarify for himself what the implications for him and for his own choices might be. As a child, it is more important for him to understand his world in his own terms than to behave in the mode of a scholar in any one or all of the disciplines. The term I have chosen for this kind of interpretation is communication.

My focus on the child's ability to communicate rests upon these facts: (a) communication is essential to both communal and individual living; (b) communication may be one of the activities in which we engage with the least skill; [6] and (c) maintenance of the fabric of our own society may be dependent upon communication. On this last point, for example, Richard Sanger suggests that one factor which may affect what happens in the expression of political feeling, whether it becomes violent or not, is the gap in communications between the ruling group and the discontented. [7]

Further, given individual differences, it seems likely that each of us may communicate effectively in only a small number of media, meaning by media language, body movement, painting, and the like. For example, when some 110 children were asked how many different ways they could think of to help someone understand what they meant, almost without exception they relied upon words as the medium. My own belief is that we fail to exploit many media as means of communication, thus reducing the

[6] Ladislas Farago. *The Broken Seal.* New York: Random House, Inc., 1967.
[7] "Is Insurrection Brewing in U.S.?" Interview with Richard H. Sanger. *U.S. News and World Report* 63: 32–37; December 25, 1967.

possibilities for any one individual to choose the medium most appropriate for him and the particular message he is intent upon sending or receiving.

In any case, I view communication as a legitimate core around which to plan the program of the elementary school so that areas of study may contribute to the child's ability to cope with his world on his own terms. These areas of study—reading, mathematics, social sciences, the arts—can thus become functional as means rather than as ends. If we speak of the needs of children as a factor in organizing the elementary school, we may concede that one need to which the school can turn its attention in a unique fashion is communication; for it would appear that the elementary school is *the* agency which can utilize the "disciplines" in helping children to sharpen their communication. Since communication appears to be a need which will exist as far into the future as I care to predict, and a need which exists at any level of development, I am willing to posit this area as the basis for organizing the elementary program.

With such an overall purpose, I would hope each child would be given the opportunity to:

1. Experience real communication with peers and with representatives of the appropriate academic disciplines
2. Participate in activities in which communication is essential to the individual in acquiring what he wants
3. Explore a variety of ways and means for getting messages across to others, particularly ways which he has not explored heretofore
4. Examine what ideas may most appropriately be communicated through the language of the different disciplines
5. Conversely, examine the role of mathematics, drama, and music in communication
6. Interpret the "messages" from the various disciplines and use such messages in making decisions about himself, his world, and his relation to it
7. Examine feelings, his own and those of others, to explore how these are communicated among humans and to comprehend the effects of feelings among humans
8. In general, increase sensitivity to his own communication as well as to the communication of others.

If these are at least some of the parameters of a curriculum with a communications focus, what comprises the substance? Time does not permit a detailed specification; however, I will list the objectives which I see as essential for elementary education, some description of organizing elements which bind the curriculum together, some illustrative activities, and several evaluation techniques which allow us to make some judgment regarding the progress of individual children.

Objectives

As I see it, there are four major objectives for the elementary school child: (a) that he be able to make reasoned and wise choices regarding his own behavior in a radically changing social context; (b) that he acquire the tools which allow such wise choices; (c) that he become increasingly independent in his learning; and (d) that he value learning as a means of coping with his world. Given what I believe regarding learning and the necessity for it to be a personal and individually internal affair, and given the definition I offered of communication, then communication is the key to the contribution which the elementary school can make to the individual child.

Elements

The organizing elements which run throughout the curriculum could be more clearly set forth with a diagram; however, let me try to construct a verbal diagram for you. Imagine a two by three table; that is, three columns and two rows, six cells. Across the top are three types of behavior; down the side are two types of activities.

Although there are many ways to categorize human behavior, *e.g.*, Guilford or Gallagher-Aschner, I find the work of the committee of University Examiners and the home economics group at the University of Illinois the most useful and presently the most comprehensive. These groups have described human behavior as having three dimensions: cognitive, affective, and psychomotor. No claim is made that these are absolutely discrete, but rather that any given behavior is more of one type than of the other two. No claim is made either that these descriptions are final. In any case, they are helpful in talking about what is possible in terms of human behavior. So across the top of the diagram place these three terms.

One way to talk about the manner in which these behaviors are put into operation is modes of behavior. I am not fond of the term, but it is intended to distinguish between *types* of behavior and the way in which one *uses* each behavior. The modes which seem most appropriate in the present context are verbal and nonverbal. Down the side of the diagram, then, place those two words.

Given this arrangement, it is possible to talk about engaging in behavior in either a verbal or nonverbal way. Thus we may speak of verbal-cognitive behavior, verbal-affective behavior, verbal-psychomotor behavior, and nonverbal-affective behavior, nonverbal-cognitive behavior, and nonverbal-psychomotor behavior.

Thus we have the elements around which the program is to be built. The next major task is to determine what broad categories of schoolroom activities can be developed to allow the child to participate in the various types of communication and how they might be arranged both horizontally and vertically, a rather difficult consideration.

Organization

Recalling one of the major problems I now see with the program of the elementary school, it is incumbent upon me to suggest an alternative. The problem is fragmentation or splitting of the child's academic world into unrelated parts. Perhaps what I am about to suggest is simply another type of fragmentation, and I suspect that it is. Yet I believe the proposed approach exhibits more unity than do other plans and may serve at least to reduce the problem of fragmentation.

Over the years there have been various attempts to relate horizontally all the aspects of the elementary program. These attempts have included, among others, the integrated curriculum, the fused curriculum, and the core curriculum. The present proposed solution sounds similar to some aspects of each of these, but the intent is different. The intent is to relegate the disciplines to the level of tools rather than to consider these as something to be dealt with for their own sake. Some may interpret this as anti-intellectualism. Not so. I contend that the most intellectually respectable activity in which a child can engage is that of relating to his world in such a way that he can fulfill the objectives I set forth earlier. If independence in and love of learning are anti-intellectual, so be it.

Now what kind of horizontal organization makes sense for the elementary school child who is exposed to a curriculum built around communication? It is *not* relating or attempting to relate to communication the instructional areas as they are presently structured; that is, there is no concern with maintaining the present boundaries of the subject areas. If it should occur in the process that language arts, as this area is currently construed, is most useful in the form now taught, then it should be retained in that form. However, the major concern is that the program be organized so that children have opportunities to engage in verbal-cognitive behavior so that some aspects of language instruction would be essential. Such instruction, however, would be in relation to a type of communication rather than in relation to mastery of an area of study.

Another example of horizontal organization may be taken from mathematics. This field, of course, has significant impact upon the world of children. The contention here is that for the elementary school child, understanding the contribution of the various areas of scholarship to his own personal world is more appropriate than becoming a master of the field itself. Thus, learning what the mathematician has to say to the individual, learning how these ideas are expressed, and grasping the implications of mathematical ideas is to be emphasized.

Further, since nonverbal-cognitive behavior is one of the elements to be stressed throughout the curriculum, opportunities to wrestle with the area of nonverbal symbolism become relevant and crucial. To illustrate, and parenthetically I am not a numerologist, mathematical operations are not the only contribution made by the field. In Wisconsin I wager if one says the number 15 something exciting is communicated. Or if one is a Cub fan, then the number 14 is significant. One kind of communication is non-verbal-cognitive, and it seems that restricting children's exposure to the symbols typically associated with mathematics to the study of mathematics *qua* mathematics is limiting the opportunity of children to develop their sensitivity to the ideas communicated most appropriately through nonverbal symbols.

Another form of communication is nonverbal-affective. According to those who have tilled the field of affective behavior, this is the most neglected area in the schools. Yet many assert that unless and until the affect is involved, little learning of a permanent nature will occur.[8] If, then, we are concerned with the affective behavior of elementary school children, we must design the curriculum to account for such behavior. Since by definition communication of any kind necessarily involves the affect, nonverbal-affective behavior is legitimate and necessary. What this implies for the classroom is a study of the "silent language" described by Hall.[9] It involves work with ballet, pantomime, and other vehicles for communicating feelings to others. It involves offering children the chance to explore their own feelings, how they communicate these to others, and how they can be increasingly certain that they are accurately interpreting the feelings and messages of others.

When verbal-affective behavior is under consideration, we can turn to the general semanticists. A study done with sixth-grade children showed among other things that children of that age can deal with ideas in general semantics and that they find such involvement exciting. There is some reason to think that the materials used in that study could be adapted for younger children if this were desirable.

Looking, then, at horizontal organization, imagine a circle containing smaller, overlapping circles formed with broken lines. These six circles represent the six types of communication. You will recall the six: verbal-cognitive, verbal-affective, verbal-psychomotor, nonverbal-cognitive, nonverbal-affective, and nonverbal-psychomotor. The large circle represents a slice from the total curriculum, which may be thought of in this context as a cylinder. The area surrounding the six smaller circles contains the ideas from academic areas I have mentioned, along with whatever additional ideas are needed to complete the curriculum. It should be noted that the smaller circles are composed of broken lines and are overlapping, suggesting that at least theoretically fragmentation is reduced and that appropriate aspects of areas of study feed directly into one or more types of communication, with the types of communication forming a whole.

---

[8] See: *Learning and Mental Health in the School.* Walter B. Waetjen and Robert R. Leeper, editors. Washington, D.C.: Association for Supervision and Curriculum Development, 1964; see particularly the chapter by: Donald Snygg. "A Cognitive Field Theory of Learning." pp. 77–96.

[9] E. T. Hall. *The Silent Language.* New York: Doubleday & Company, Inc., 1959.

Vertical, or overtime, organization of the curriculum requires a different approach. Whereas horizontal organization accounts for what we now call scope, vertical organization is concerned with sequence. Two major sets of ideas must be brought into relation in determining sequence. These are ideas from child development and ideas from areas of study. Please notice I have shifted terminology from discipline to areas of study. The reason is that we may be caught in the present trap of a disciplines curriculum if we persist in adopting a discipline *in toto*. Rather we need to look to areas of study to determine what ideas from each area are relevant to the various types of communication.

At this point, I must remind myself that the six types of communication run throughout the entire program, and that each will always receive either major or minor emphasis, depending upon the developmental level of the child. If we look at the two modes of behavior, we have verbal and non-verbal. Included in the verbal mode are the usual oral, written, read, and heard. Early in the child's school career, I would place almost all emphasis upon the oral, spoken, and heard, moving to read and written only when the child has almost done it himself. This would apply across the board to all three types of behavior. Urgent attention, however, would be given to the nonverbal mode in all types of behavior at all points along the curriculum. The purpose of this progression is to allow the child to become increasingly proficient in the types of communication with which he is already familiar, assuming that more attention can be paid to the quality of his communication and his ability to interpret his world than if we force upon him a type of communication with which he has to struggle.

The foregoing illustrations give the general idea of the direction in which I would move in building a curriculum. To make the intent hopefully more clear, let me cite some specific classroom examples. Were I actually writing a curriculum for the use of teachers, I would describe such activities solely for the purpose of making clear the intent of the curriculum, not to prescribe what teachers must do with their own children.

Activities

First, classrooms would be characterized by talk, not silence, and the preponderance of such talk would be by children—among children and between children and the teacher. Where we now have reading groups, we would find discussion groups, painting groups, dance groups, drama groups, listening groups.

While there would be a professional teacher present, other adults would play a major role in the elementary school. Who better can discuss the language of the dance than someone who is in dance as a professional? Who better can help children to see what scientists are trying to say to the world than a scientist? Who better can explain the contribution of mathematics than the mathematician? Who better can help children understand the language of the fields than the scholars in the field? The role of the teacher becomes that of mediating for individual children and helping each child make personal use of what he has gleaned from the specialist.

Such activities require teachers who are skilled at ferreting out with each child the meaning of all such activities, teachers who honestly ask children questions which allow children to see for themselves what something means to them and for them. These are simple questions, which go something like this: What do you mean? Why does it mean that to you? How do you know? How do you feel about it? What difference does it make to you that you feel that way rather than another? What seems important to you? How do you think you come to know something? Why? Does this add to anything you already have found out? Does it make something clearer than it was before? Does it make you feel better about yourself? Do you now feel more comfortable about things than you did before you had the talk with the gentleman about matter and energy? Conversely, children will be asking similar questions of each other and of teachers.

As children acquire facility in communicating with spoken and heard language, they may work toward such facility with the written word— their own and that of others. The necessity for dialogue with other children, with the teacher, with other adults, and with materials does not decrease, however. For now children need to be asking of what they read the same questions teachers have been asking of children. The time at which this becomes appropriate will differ for each child. The determination is made on the basis of what is known about the child, not upon such an extraneous measure as how long he has been in school, nor upon some such astrological grounds as the number of years he has been alive or in what month he was born.

Other kinds of activities are relevant to other kinds of communication. As I have already mentioned, the performing arts offer children the opportunity to see themselves and what they have to say to the world in a light different from that shed upon them when they are limited to communicating with words. Creative dramatics gives a chance for "talking with" others in a unique way. And this talking lets others see an individual in a way he may not be able to demonstrate with verbal language alone. Sports of many types can be drawn upon in the same way and for the same reasons.

Evaluation

Evaluation techniques become more critical in the curriculum I have only hinted at than they have been in more traditional types of approaches. You will recall that I am using the term evaluation to mean a description of progress of an individual child toward specified objectives. The techniques are little different from the kinds of activities described earlier. Through questions and discussions, teachers will be collecting evidence to let them know whether children are becoming increasingly abler to cope with their world on and in their own terms.

Teachers will be able to tell whether and in what ways a child needs something in particular—stimulation, sympathy, a sensitive ear, a group opportunity, or solitude in which he may struggle with an idea with which he is involved. The core of the techniques to be employed is sensitive observation by teachers of individual children and thorough, comprehensive record keeping. It should be noted here that there is an important distinction to be made between and among evaluation, grading, and reporting. The latter two are based upon the first and therefore related to it. Yet grading and reporting are not synonymous with evaluation. In passing, if I were to have my way, regardless of the curriculum, I would abolish grading and improve techniques of evaluating and reporting.

The reason for stressing evaluation is that, in my judgment, we ought to be concerned with a child's progress, not with developing categories for him to fit or labels for him to wear. True evaluation is a learning experience for the child and is not judgmental. Nor is it used to threaten or cajole, or to elevate, or to make odious comparisons. It has as its purpose assisting each child to grow in whatever direction has been set by him or with him. It is to gather information with and about each child so that he may see himself in relation to goals of which he is at least aware.

Let me give just one simple illustration. Suppose that a physician were brought to a classroom to discuss his field with children. The teacher knows each child well. During the discussion she observes each child but in all likelihood with a different purpose for each child. She makes a careful record of the amount and nature of the interaction and communication. This information will be used in subsequent discussions with an individual child to chart his next moves. This, in my estimation, is evaluation.

In conclusion, certainly all the foregoing has implications for teaching and instruction, for school organization, for buildings, for nonprofessional personnel, for materials, for deployment of teachers and pupils. These, however, go much beyond the scope of this paper's purpose. It is important to note that these latter considerations follow, not precede, the establishment of a purpose of education and the curriculum.

It is also vital to keep constantly in mind that a curriculum as I have used the term is nothing more than a plan. It is also nothing less. For years in education we have traveled on the assumption that there is some relation between curriculum and instruction. Richard Hawthorne has developed a model which allows us to examine the extent and nature of this assumed relation; his study reveals that this relation is at best tenuous. Therefore, it is essential that we do not rely upon plans, no matter how well done, to make the changes so vitally needed in elementary education.

Many questions can be raised about the proposal I have made for the restructuring of the elementary curriculum. One of the most common reservations expressed about such new ventures is that children will not be prepared for any one of a number of things: junior high school, high school, college, or a vocation. My response has to be that that is not our problem. It is the problem of the junior high school, the high school, the college, the vocations. We might even influence education at these levels. Let us counter with the charge that these institutions have the shoe on the wrong foot; they are not prepared for individuals who are learning to live in the world.

My assignment for this paper was to construct a curriculum that is "way out" and to justify it. Whether or not I have succeeded is at best doubtful. Perhaps the task could have been carried out in four sentences: (a) The job of the elementary school is to start each child on the road to accepting himself and to coping successfully with the world in his own way and on his own terms. (b) The present program of the elementary school cannot do this job. (c) To construct a program that holds promise of allowing the elementary school to do the job, we must change the essence of the way we think and talk about the elementary school program, not simply try to make the same old things over into a new image. Communication offers *one* possibility. (d) To build a new elementary curriculum which is relevant and real to the child requires untold intellectual and moral courage, as does any change in the face of opposition. However, given my position on the nature of man, I must make one last assertion: educators, being a part of humankind, are by nature courageous.

Freedom and Learning: The Need for Choice

PAUL GOODMAN

The belief that a highly industrialized society requires twelve to twenty years of prior processing of the young is an illusion or a hoax. The evidence is strong that there is no correlation between school performance and life achievement in any of the professions, whether medicine, law, engineering, journalism, or business. Moreover, recent research shows that for more modest clerical, technological, or semi-skilled factory jobs there is no advantage in years of schooling or the possession of diplomas. We were not exactly savages in 1900 when only 6 per cent of adolescents graduated from high school.

Reprinted from *Saturday Review*, 51 (20): 73–75 (May 18, 1968), by permission of author and publisher. Copyright © 1968 by Saturday Review, Inc.

Whatever the deliberate intention, schooling today serves mainly for policing and for taking up the slack in youth unemployment. It is not surprising that the young are finally rebelling against it, especially since they cannot identify with the goals of so much social engineering—for instance, that 86 per cent of the federal budget for research and development is for military purposes.

We can, I believe, educate the young entirely in terms of their free choice, with no processing whatever. Nothing can be efficiently learned, or, indeed, learned at all—other than through parroting or brute training, when acquired knowledge is promptly forgotten after the examination—unless it meets need, desire, curiosity, or fantasy. Unless there is a reaching from within, the learning cannot become "second nature," as Aristotle called true learning. It seems stupid to decide a priori what the young ought to know and then to try to motivate them, instead of letting the initiative come from them and putting information and relevant equipment at their service. It is false to assert that this kind of freedom will not serve society's needs —at least those needs that should humanly be served; freedom is the only way toward authentic citizenship and real, rather than verbal, philosophy. Free choice is not random but responsive to real situations; both youth and adults live in a nature of things, a polity, an ongoing society, and it is these, in fact, that attract interest and channel need. If the young, as they mature, can follow their bent and choose their topics, times, and teachers, and if teachers teach what they themselves consider important— which is all they can skillfully teach anyway—the needs of society will be adequately met; there will be more lively, independent, and inventive people; and in the fairly short run there will be a more sensible and efficient society.

It is not necessary to argue for free choice as a metaphysical proposition; it is what is indicated by present conditions. Increasingly, the best young people resolutely resist authority, and we will let them have a say or lose them. And more important, since the conditions of modern social and technological organization are so pervasively and rigidly conforming, it is necessary, in order to maintain human initiative, to put our emphasis on protecting the young from top-down direction. The monkish and academic methods which were civilizing for wild shepherds create robots in a period of high technology. The public schools which did a good job of socializing immigrants in an open society now regiment individuals and rigidify class stratification.

Up to age twelve, there is no point to formal subjects or a prearranged curriculum. With guidance, whatever a child experiences is educational. Dewey's idea is a good one: It makes no difference *what* is learned at this age, so long as the child goes on wanting to learn something further. Teachers for this age are those who like children, pay attention to them, answer their questions, enjoy taking them around the city and helping them explore, imitate, try out, and who sing songs with them and teach them games. Any benevolent grownup—literate or illiterate—has plenty to teach an eight-year-old; the only profitable training for teachers is a group therapy and, perhaps, a course in child development.

We see that infants learn to speak in their own way in an environment where there is speaking and where they are addressed and take part. If we tried to teach children to speak according to our own theories and methods and schedules, as we try to teach reading, there would be as many stammerers as there are bad readers. Besides, it has been shown that whatever is useful in the present eight-year elementary curriculum can be learned in four months by a normal child of twelve. If let alone, in fact, he will have learned most of it by himself.

Since we have communities where people do not attend to the children as a matter of course, and since children must be rescued from their homes, for most of these children there should be some kind of school. In a proposal for mini-schools in New York City, I suggested an elementary group of twenty-eight children with four grownups: a licensed teacher, a housewife who can cook, a college senior, and a teen-age school dropout. Such a group can meet in any store front, church basement, settlement house, or housing project; more important, it can often go about the city, as is possible when the student-teacher ratio is 7 to 1. Experience at the First Street School in New York has shown that the cost for such a little school is less than for the public school with a student-teacher ratio of 30 to 1. (In the public system, most of the money goes for administration and for specialists to remedy the lack of contact in the classroom.) As A. S. Neill has shown, attendance need not be compulsory. The school should be located near home so the children can escape from it to home, and from home to it. The school should be supported by public money but administered entirely by its own children, teachers, and parents.

In the adolescent and college years, the present mania is to keep students at their lessons for another four to ten years as the only way of their growing up in the world. The correct policy would be to open as many diverse paths as possible, with plenty of opportunity to backtrack and change. It is said by James Conant that about 15 per cent learn well by books and study in an academic setting, and these can opt for high school. Most, including most of the bright students, do better either on their own or as apprentices in activities that are for keeps, rather than through lessons. If their previous eight years had been spent in exploring their own bents and interests, rather than being continually interrupted to do others' assignments on others' schedules, most adolescents would have a clearer notion of what they are after, and many would have found their vocations.

For the 15 per cent of adolescents who learn well in schools and are interested in subjects that are essentially academic, the present catch-all high schools are wasteful. We would do better to return to the small preparatory academy, with perhaps sixty students and three teachers—one in physical sciences, one in social sciences, one in humanities—to prepare for college board examinations. An academy could be located in, and administered by, a university and staffed by graduate students who like to teach and in this way might earn stipends while they write their theses. In such a setting, without dilution by nonacademic subjects and a mass of uninterested fellow students, an academic adolescent can, by spending three hours a day in the classroom, easily be prepared in three or four years for college.

Forcing the nonacademic to attend school breaks the spirit of most and foments alienation in the best. Kept in tutelage, young people, who are necessarily economically dependent, cannot pursue the sexual, adventurous, and political activities congenial to them. Since lively youngsters insist on these anyway, the effect of what we do is to create a gap between them and the oppressive adult world, with a youth subculture and an arrested development.

School methods are simply not competent to teach all the arts, sciences, professions, and skills the school establishment pretends to teach. For some professions—e.g., social work, architecture, pedagogy—trying to earn academic credits is probably harmful because it is an irrelevant and discouraging obstacle course. Most technological know-how has to be learned in actual practice in offices and factories, and this often involves unlearning what has been laboriously crammed for exams. The technical competence required by skilled and semiskilled workmen and average technicians can be acquired in three weeks to a year on the job, with no previous schooling. The importance of even "functional literacy" is much exaggerated; it is the attitude, and not the reading ability, that counts. Those who are creative in the arts and sciences almost invariably go their own course and are usually hampered by schools. Modern languages are best learned by travel. It is pointless to teach social sciences, literary criticism, and philosophy to youngsters who have had no responsible experience in life and society.

Most of the money now spent for high schools and colleges should be devoted to the support of apprenticeships; travel; subsidized browsing in libraries and self-directed study and research; programs such as VISTA, the Peace Corps, Students for a Democratic Society, or the Student Nonviolent Coordinating Committee; rural reconstruction; and work camps for projects in conservation and urban renewal. It is a vast sum of money—but it costs almost $1,500 a year to keep a youth in a blackboard jungle in New York; the schools have become one of our major industries. Consider one kind of opportunity. Since it is important for the very existence of the republic to countervail the now overwhelming national corporate style of information, entertainment, and research, we need scores of thousands of small independent television stations, community radio stations, local newspapers that are more than gossip notes and ads, community theaters, high-brow or dissenting magazines, small design offices for neighborhood renewal that is not bureaucratized, small laboratories for science and invention that are not centrally directed. Such enterprises could present admirable opportunities for bright but unacademic young people to serve as apprentices.

Ideally, the polis itself is the educational environment; a good community consists of worthwhile, attractive, and fulfilling callings and things to do, to grow up into. The policy I am proposing tends in this direction rather than away from it. By multiplying options, it should be possible to find an interesting course for each individual youth, as we now do for only some of the emotionally disturbed and the troublemakers. Voluntary adolescent choices are often random and foolish and usually transitory; but they are the likeliest ways of growing up reasonably. What is most essential is for the youth to see that he is taken seriously as a person, rather than fitted into an institutional system. I don't know if this tailor-made approach would be harder or easier to administer than standardization that in fact fits nobody and results in an increasing number of recalcitrants. On the other hand, as the Civilian Conservation Corps showed in the Thirties, the products of willing youth labor can be valuable even economically, whereas accumulating Regents blue-books is worth nothing except to the school itself.

(By and large, it is not in the adolescent years but in later years that, in all walks of life, there is need for academic withdrawal, periods of study and reflection, synoptic review of the texts. The Greeks understood this and regarded most of our present college curricula as appropriate for only those over the age of thirty or thirty-five. To some extent, the churches used to provide a studious environment. We do these things miserably in hurried conferences.)

We have similar problems in the universities. We cram the young with what they do not want at the time and what most of them will never use; but by requiring graded diplomas we make it hard for older people to get what they want and can use. Now, paradoxically, when so many are going to school, the training of authentic learned professionals is proving to be a failure, with dire effects on our ecology, urbanism, polity, communications, and even the direction of science. Doing others' lessons under compulsion for twenty years does not tend to produce professionals who are autonomous, principled, and ethically responsible to client and community. Broken by processing, professionals degenerate to mere professional-personnel. Professional peer groups have become economic lobbies. The licensing and maintenance of standards have been increasingly relinquished to the state, which has no competence.

In licensing professionals, we have to look more realistically at functions, drop mandarin requirements of academic diplomas that are irrelevant, and rid ourselves of the ridiculous fad of awarding diplomas for every skill and trade whatever. In most professions and arts there are important abstract parts that can best be learned academically. The natural procedure is for those actually engaged in a professional activity to go to school to learn what they now know they need; re-entry into the academic track, therefore, should be made easy for those with a strong motive.

Universities are primarily schools of learned professions, and the faculty should be composed primarily not of academics but of working professionals who feel duty-bound and attracted to pass on their tradition to apprentices of a new generation. Being combined in a community of scholars, such professionals teach a noble apprenticeship, humane and with vision toward a more ideal future. It is humane because the disciplines communicate with one another; it is ideal because the young are free and questioning. A good professional school can be tiny. In *The Community of Scholars* I suggest that 150 students and ten professionals—the size of the usual medieval university—are enough. At current faculty salaries, the cost per student would be a fourth of that of our huge administrative machines. And, of course, on such a small scale contact between faculty and students is sought for and easy.

Today, because of the proved incompetence of our adult institutions and the hypocrisy of most professionals, university students have a right to a large say in what goes on. (But this, too, is medieval.) Professors will, of course, teach what they please. My advice to students is that given by Prince Kropotkin, in "A Letter to the Young": "Ask what kind of world do you want to live in? What are you good at and want to work at to build that world? What do you need to know? Demand that your teachers teach you that." Serious teachers would be delighted by this approach.

The idea of the liberal arts college is a beautiful one: to teach the common culture and refine character and citizenship. But it does not happen; the evidence is that the college curriculum has little effect on underlying attitudes, and most cultivated folk do not become so by this route. School friendships and the community of youth do have lasting effects, but these do not require ivied clubhouses. Young men learn more about the theory and practice of government by resisting the draft than they ever learned in Political Science 412.

Much of the present university expansion, needless to say, consists in federal- and corporation-contracted research and other research and has nothing to do with teaching. Surely such expansion can be better carried on in the Government's and corporations' own institutes, which would be unencumbered by the young, except those who are hired or attach themselves as apprentices.

Every part of education can be open to need, desire, choice, and trying out. Nothing needs to be compelled or extrinsically motivated by prizes and threats. I do not know if the procedure here outlined would cost more than our present system—though it is hard to conceive of a need for more money than the school establishment now spends. What would be saved is the pitiful waste of youthful years—caged, daydreaming, sabotaging, and cheating—and the degrading and insulting misuse of teachers.

It has been estimated by James Coleman that the average youth in high school is really "there" about ten minutes a day. Since the growing-up of the young into society to be useful to themselves and others, and to do God's work, is one of the three or four most important functions of any society, no doubt we ought to spend even more on the education of the young than we do; but I would not give a penny to the present administrators, and I would largely dismantle the present school machinery.

Stating Objectives Appropriately for Program, for Curriculum, and for Instructional Materials Development

DAVID R. KRATHWOHL

Introduction

The frontiers of knowledge retreat before many kinds of research. The research usually reported in this column is experimental or empirical in nature. But we also learn about education when we find means to name and organize the phenomena of education more precisely. Such conceptual research, based on previous findings and thinking, is the kind described here.

This article is concerned with the use of educational objectives at several levels of detail in the educational process. The most general levels of objectives are most relevant to program planning, the intermediate level to curriculum development, and the most specific level to instructional material development. The article makes two basic points:

1. Objectives at several levels of generality and specificity are needed to facilitate the process of curriculum building and instructional development.

Reprinted from *The Journal of Teacher Education,* 16 (1): 83–92 (March 1965), by permission of author and publisher.

2. A framework or taxonomy currently exists which can facilitate the development and analysis of objectives at the intermediate level, and one is at present being developed at the more detailed level.

Analysis of Objectives—A Powerful Tool for
Educational Improvement

The emphasis upon making educational objectives specific by defining the goals of an instructional course or program has gone through many cycles since Ralph Tyler gave the topic considerable prominence in the late thirties. For some educators, careful attention to spelling out in detail the objectives of a course has become a kind of religion. Others, interestingly enough, seem to have heard of the practice of delineating objectives but, somehow or other, have been early inoculated against the notion and have so become immune. Those of us who work as advisers to various fields of higher education, particularly with our colleagues in liberal arts, home economics, etc., are impressed with the power of this simple tool to help people structure courses and view their own process of teaching with a renewed interest and from a new perspective.

Viewed both in retrospect and contemporaneously, specifying educational objectives as student behaviors seems to be a useful and powerful approach to the analysis of the instructional process. Granted it implies a particular view of the educational process. In it, "education" means changing the behavior of a student so that he is able, when encountering a particular problem or situation, to display a behavior which he did not previously exhibit. The task of the teacher is to help the student learn new or changed behaviors and determine where and when they are appropriate.

A major contribution of this approach to curriculum building is that it forces the instructor to spell out his instructional goals in terms of overt behavior. This gives new detail; indeed it yields an operational definition of many previously general and often fuzzy and ill-defined objectives. Such goals as "the student should become a good citizen" are spelled out in terms of the kinds of behaviors which a good citizen displays. There are then statements, such as, "the student shall be able to identify and appraise judgments and values involved in the choice of a course of political action"; "he shall display skill in identifying different appropriate roles in a democratic group"; or "he will be able to relate principles of civil liberties and civil rights to current events." Thus the instructor knows what kinds of behavior he is to try to develop in the classroom. In addition, the problem of assessing the extent to which he has achieved his goals becomes markedly simplified. He needs only to provide the student with a situation in which the kind of behavior he is seeking to instill should be evoked and then observe to see whether indeed it appears. Spelling out the behaviors involved in an objective such as the above frequently means specifying several pages of concrete behaviors. Such specification often gives teachers a fresh perspective on their courses and new insights into ways to teach and to evaluate their teaching. This kind of analysis of objectives is clearly a step forward.

This approach to instruction fits in very well with the behaviorist school of psychology, the well-spring from which came the recent emphasis on teaching machines and programmed instruction. It is not surprising, then, that a renewed emphasis on educational objectives resulted from the development of programmed learning. The careful specification of a step-by-step procedure for the learner calls for clearly understood objectives specified at a level of detail far beyond that usually attempted. In programmed learning, such objectives have come to bear the name of "terminal behaviors." As psychologists, physicists, systems development specialists, and others have attempted instructional programming, they have turned to education for a greater understanding of how adequately to specify educational objectives so that they concretely describe a "terminal behavior."

The Need for Objectives at Several Levels of Analysis

The renewed emphasis has given new insight into and perspective on the whole problem of the level of specificity needed in objectives. It is now clear that we need to analyze objectives to several levels of specificity depending upon how we intend to use them. At the first and most abstract level are the quite broad and general statements most helpful in the development of programs of instruction, for the laying out of types of courses and areas to be covered, and for the general goals toward which several years of education might be aimed or for which an entire unit such as an elementary, junior, or senior high school might strive.

At a second and more concrete level, a *behavioral* objectives orientation helps to analyze broad goals into more specific ones which are useful as the building blocks for curricular instruction. These behaviorally stated objectives are helpful in specifying the goals of an instructional unit, a course, or a sequence of courses.

Third and finally, there is the level needed to create instructional materials—materials which are the operational embodiment of one particular route (rarely are multiple routes included) to the achievement of a curriculum planned at the second and more abstract level, the level of detailed analysis involved in the programmed instruction movement. Just as the second level of analysis brought into concrete, detailed form the ideas of goals and purposes that were in the mind of the good teacher as he planned at the first and more abstract level, so this kind of detailed analysis brings into focus the objectives of specific lesson plans, the sequence of goals in these plans, and the level of achievement required for each goal or objective if successful accomplishment of the next goal in this sequence is to be achieved.

In realization of this, we find Gagné, Mager, and Miller [1] all writing about the analysis of objectives for programmed instruction with a plea that objectives be given a great deal more specificity so that they may be more easily turned into instructional materials. They call for a description of the situation which ought to initiate the behavior in question, a complete description of the behavior, the object or goal of the behavior, and a description of the level of performance of the behavior which permits us to recognize a successful performance.

We may note in passing that even this may not be enough specification for the development of instructional materials. There is no mention in this of the characteristics of the learner and his relation to the learning situation. Thus, not all objectives or terminal behaviors will be appropriate for all kinds and types of students. Neither will the same level of proficiency be appropriate for, nor expected of, different levels of ability. Thus a successful performance cannot have a single definition. Further, those planning instructional materials need to know where the student starts, what he brings to the situation (the "entry behaviors"). We may also need to know something about the motivation for learning (or lack of it if, for example, we are dealing with the culturally disadvantaged), and the pattern of problem solving available to us (for example, in teaching the social studies, one approach for those with rigid value patterns, another for those more flexible). While this is not a complete list, it clearly indicates that a great deal more specification is required in developing instructional materials than in laying out curricular goals.

But to return to our main theme, if we make our goals specific enough to prepare instructional materials, why use the other levels at all? Should we not, for example, discard at least the second level? Not at all! Four points need to be made.

First of all, curriculum construction requires a process of moving through descending abstractions from very general and global statements of desirable behaviors for a program, to intermediate level statements that indicate the blocks from which the program will be constructed, and finally to quite detailed statements which spell out the sub-goals, their relation to one another, and the level of achievement which results in the successful attainment of the intermediate-level behavioral descriptions. All levels of specification of objectives are needed to guide the planning of the educational process. Only as each level is completed can the next be begun.

[1] Gagné, Robert M. "The Analysis of Instructional Objectives." A paper prepared for the National Symposium on Research in Programmed Instruction, Department of Audiovisual Instruction, National Education Association, 1963.

Mager, Robert R. *Preparing Objectives for Programmed Instruction.* San Francisco, California: Fearon Publishers, 1962.

Miller, R. B. "The Newer Role of the Industrial Psychologist." *Industrial Psychology.* (Edited by B. von H. Gelmer.) New York: McGraw-Hill Book Co., 1961.

The first level guides the development of the second, the second guides the third.

To return to our example of the development of citizenship, we earlier noted three objectives at the intermediate level. Once these are specified, we can begin to think at the third level of very specific goals and their teaching sequence. For example, one would specify the different possible desirable roles in a democratic group, how these roles would build on one another, to what situations each was appropriate, and how successfully each should be displayed before passing on to the next. Each level thus permits and guides the development of the next level of specification.

Second, not all objectives lend themselves to the *complete* specification at the third level. In some instances, the universe of behaviors is completely circumscribed. For example, there are only 45 sums of two numbers 0 through 9 which need be learned, and we can specify that these must be mastered with perfect accuracy. But in many instances we cannot specify all the instances of behavior. Gagné's contrasting terminology of "mastery" objective to apply to the former and "transfer" objectives to the latter helps to illumine this difference. We cannot predict all situations the student will encounter or all the situations to which he should be able to transfer the behaviors, but we can specify a currently known sample. Nearly all our complex ability and skill objectives—application, analysis, evaluation, etc. —are "transfer" objectives. Their specification will be inexact and confined to a known sample of relevant and typical kinds of behaviors.[2] Transfer objectives seem to constitute the major *ultimate* goals for the bulk of the educational process. More exact specification of mastery goals may be possible in industrial or vocational training for specific occupations than in general education. Thus the level of detail with which educational goals can be usefully specified will depend somewhat on their nature. Again we see that several levels of specificity are needed to handle different kinds of objectives.

Third, we need to have objectives at several levels of abstraction so that we can continually examine their interrelation to one another. When developing a curriculum, we try to get those involved to agree at as detailed a level as possible. But complete agreement can probably be reached only

---

[2] Mager and others suggest that criterion performance for a successful completion be specified, e.g., "given a human skeleton, the student must be able to identify correctly by labeling at least 40 of the following bones," or "the student must be able to reply in grammatically correct French to 95 per cent of the questions put to him in an examination." (*Op. cit.*, p. 50.) It is worth noting that such levels have one meaning for mastery objectives (e.g., he should be able to give the capital and lower case letters for the entire alphabet) when the universe of behaviors is known and specified. They have a different meaning when test questions of different complexity are constructed to an indeterminate universe of behaviors in a French quiz. In the latter instance, judgment of both the level of difficulty of the problems and the matter of adequacy of sampling enter the evaluation process, and both must be taken into consideration in judging a successful performance.

at the more abstract levels. Thus we can get general agreement that students should be good citizens, but we may get some disagreement as to what this means operationally or in behavioral terms. For some teachers this may mean that all students are taught to engage in some political action—ringing doorbells at election time, writing congressmen, etc. To others this may be confined to voting and attempting to understand and to discuss issues with others. Further, such definitions will change as society and its pressures and fads change. It helps to have agreed-upon general and global objectives to which all curricula can relate. These objectives can then be redefined at the less abstract level in relation to the overall goals.

Fourth, and finally, there are many routes from the intermediate level objective to the specification of instructional materials. For example, take the objective: "The student shall be able to recognize form and pattern in literary works as a means to understanding their meaning." This is a useful objective at the intermediate or curricular-building level of abstraction, but how does the teacher translate this into a choice of instructional materials? Does he choose those literary forms and patterns which are likely to have maximum transfer to all kinds of literary materials and teach them, or does he choose those forms and patterns that will permit the deepest penetration of meaning and concentrate on them, assuming the other forms and patterns will be picked up in the course of reading? Both approaches might be acceptable. It helps to have the objective in its original abstract form to serve as a basis for judging the routes to its achievement. The routes might be thought of as sub-objectives needing evaluation to help in learning which route best achieves the intermediate-level objective.

We do not have enough psychological knowledge for the teacher and the developer of instructional materials to move with certainty from an intermediate-level objective to a single set of very detailed and concrete objectives. In the example given above, for instance, we have little theoretical basis for judging the language forms and patterns that will permit the most complete understanding of literary material. Both the instructional material specialist and the teacher precede the psychologist into an area of most-needed research. They must make choices while the psychologist is still developing the knowledge to help them.

Thus, there are at least four reasons why objectives at various levels of analysis are useful and needed in the instructional processes:

1. Each level of analysis permits the development of the next more specific level.
2. Mastery objectives can be analyzed to greater specificity than transfer objectives.
3. Curricula gain adoption by consensus that what is taught is of value. Consensus is more easily gained at the more abstract levels of analysis.

4.   There are usually several alternative ways of analyzing objectives at the most specific level. Objectives at the more abstract level provide a referent for evaluating these alternatives.

It seems clear then that objectives at several levels of abstraction are useful and important in the educational process. Let us turn now to some of the structures that have been constructed to aid exploration at these levels.

FRAMEWORKS TO FACILITATE THE STATEMENT OF OBJECTIVES

I. The Taxonomy of Educational Objectives—A Framework for Curriculum Building

The need for objectives at various levels of abstraction has given rise to frameworks or structures that assist in the analysis and development of these objectives. One of these frameworks, the *Taxonomy of Educational Objectives*,[3] appears to have proven useful in the analysis of objectives at the intermediate curriculum-building level.

Basically the taxonomy grew out of an attempt to resolve some of the confusion in communication which resulted from the translation of such general terms as "to understand" into more specific behaviors. Thus the "understanding" of Boyle's law might mean that the student could recall the formula, tell what it meant, interpret the particular meaning of the law in an article about it, use the formula in a new problem situation he had never met, or think up new implications of its relationships.

The problem of precisely identifying what is meant by particular terms plagues the evaluator as well as the curriculum builder. For one thing, these two must communicate with each other since the test constructor seeks accurately to translate the curriculum builders' objectives into situations where the student can display the behavior if he knows it. Accuracy in this translation is essential. Further, evaluators working at different institutions on similar curricula know they have something in common but frequently find it difficult to communicate accurately about it. Given precise communication, they could share and compare the effectiveness of learning devices, materials, and curricula organization. It was with this in mind that a group of college and university examiners, under the leadership of Dr. Benjamin S. Bloom of the University of Chicago, attempted to devise a framework or taxonomy that would help to hold terms in place, provide

---

[3] Bloom, Benjamin S., editor, and others. *Taxonomy of Educational Objectives: The Classification of Educational Goals.* Handbook I: *Cognitive Domain.* New York: Longmans, Green and Co., 1956.

   Krathwohl, David R.; Bloom, Benjamin S.; Masia, Bertram B. *Taxonomy of Educational Objectives: The Classification of Educational Objectives.* Handbook II: *Affective Domain.* New York: David McKay Company, Inc., 1964.

a structure which would relate one term to another, and thus provide additional meaning for a given term through this interrelationship.

The taxonomy of educational objectives is basically a classification scheme just as the biological taxonomy is a classification scheme for animals into class, order, family, genus, and species. In the educational objectives taxonomy, the kinds of behavior we seek to have students display as a result of the learning process are classified. Every behavioral objective is composed of two parts—the behavior the student is to display and the subject matter or content that is then used in the display. The taxonomy deals only with the behavioral part of the objective; the content or subject matter classification is left to the Library of Congress, the Dewey Decimal System, and such other similar classifications.

For purposes of convenience the taxonomy was divided into three domains, the cognitive, affective, and psychomotor. Handbook I, *The Cognitive Domain,*[4] has been available for about eight years. It deals with objectives having to do with thinking, knowing, and problem solving. Handbook II, *The Affective Domain,*[5] was published last year. It includes objectives dealing with attitudes, values, interest, appreciation, and social-emotional adjustment. The psychomotor domain covers objectives having to do with manual and motor skills. The feasibility of developing it is being studied by a group at the University of Illinois under Dr. Elizabeth Simpson.

> Basically the taxonomy is an educational-logical-psychological classification system. The terms in this order reflect the emphasis given to the organizing principles upon which it is built. It makes educational distinctions in the sense that the boundaries between categories reflect the decisions that teachers make among student behaviors in their development of curriculums, and in choosing learning situations. It is a logical system in the sense that its terms are defined precisely and are used consistently. In addition, each category permits logical subdivisions which can be clearly defined and further subdivided as necessary and useful. Finally the taxonomy seems to be consistent with our present understanding of psychological phenomena, though it does not rest on any single theory.
>
> The scheme is intended to be purely descriptive so that every type of educational goal can be represented. It does not indicate the value or quality of one class as compared to another. It is impartial with respect to views of education. One of the tests of the taxonomy has been that of inclusiveness— could only classify all kinds of educational objectives (if stated as student behaviors) in the framework? In general, it seems to have met this test.[6]

[4] Bloom *et al., op. cit.*

[5] Krathwohl, Bloom, and Masia, *op. cit.*

[6] Krathwohl, David R. "Taxonomy of Educational Objectives—Its Use in Curriculum Building." *Defining Educational Objectives.* (Edited by C. M. Lindvall.) Pittsburgh, Pennsylvania: Regional Commission on Educational Coordination and Learning, Research and Development Center, University of Pittsburgh, 1964.

The Cognitive Domain of the Taxonomy

Similar to the distinctions most teachers make, the cognitive domain is divided into the acquisition of knowledge and the development of those skills and abilities necessary to use knowledge. Under the heading "Knowledge," which is the first major category of the cognitive domain, one finds a series of subcategories, each describing the recall of a different category of knowledge. Each of the subheadings is accompanied by a definition of the behavior classified there and by illustrative objectives taken from the educational literature. In addition, there is a summary of the kinds of test items that may be used to test for each category, a discussion of the problems which beset the individual attempting to evaluate behavior in the category, and a large number of examples of test items—mainly multiple choice but some essay type. These illustrate how items may be built to measure each of the categories.

The taxonomy is hierarchical in nature, that is, each category is assumed to involve behavior more complex and abstract than the previous category. Thus the categories are arranged from simple to complex behavior, and from concrete to abstract behavior.

Perhaps the idea of the continuum is most easily gained from looking at the major headings of the cognitive domain, which include knowledge (recall of facts, principles, etc.), comprehension (ability to restate knowledge in new words), application (understanding well enough to break it apart into its parts and make the relations among ideas explicit), synthesis (the ability to produce wholes from parts, to produce a plan of operation, to derive a set of abstract relations), and evaluation (the ability to judge the value of material for given purposes).

Since the cognitive domain has been available for some time, perhaps this brief summary will suffice to remind the reader of its nature or to intrigue him to look into it if it has not previously come to his attention. Since the affective domain is new, let us examine it in more detail.

The Affective Domain of the Taxonomy

Though there is confusion in communication with respect to terms in the cognitive domain, those who worked on the taxonomy found the confusion much greater when they began work on the affective domain. The state of communication with respect to a term like "really understand" is nothing compared to the confusion that surrounds objectives dealing with attitudes, interests, and appreciation. When we say that we want a child to "appreciate" art, do we mean that he should be aware of art work? Should he be willing to give it some attention when it is around? Do we mean that he should seek it out—go to the museum on his own, for instance? Do we mean that he should regard art work as having positive values? Should he experience an emotional kick or thrill when he sees art work? Should he be able to evaluate it and to know why and how it is effective? Should he be able to compare its esthetic impact with that of other art forms?

This list could be extended, but it is enough to suggest that the term "appreciation" covers a wide variety of meanings. And worse, not all of these are distinct from the terms "attitude" and "interest." Thus, if appreciation has the meaning that the student should like art work well enough to seek it out, how would we distinguish such behavior from an interest in art—or are interests and appreciations, as we use these words, the same thing? If the student *values* art, does he have a favorable *attitude* toward it? Are our appreciation objectives the same as, overlapping with, or in some respects distinct from our attitude objectives?

In addition to the greater confusion of terms, the affective domain presented some special problems. For example, the hierarchical structure was most difficult to find in the affective part of the taxonomy. The principles of simple to complex and concrete to abstract were not sufficient for developing the affective domain. Something additional was needed.

By seeking the unique characteristics of the affective domain, it was hoped that the additional principles needed to structure an affective continuum would be discovered. Analysis of affective objectives showed the following characteristics which the continuum should embody: the emotional quality which is an important distinguishing feature of an affective response at certain levels of the continuum, the increasing automaticity as one progresses up the continuum, the increasing willingness to attend to a specified stimulus or stimulus type as one ascends the continuum, and the developing integration of a value pattern at the upper levels of the continuum.

A structure was first attempted by attaching certain meanings to the terms "attitude," "value," "appreciation," and "interest." But the multitude of meanings which these terms encompassed in educational objectives showed that this was impossible. After trying a number of schemes and organizing principles, the one which appeared best to account for the affective phenomena and which best described the process of learning and growth in the affective field was the process of internalization.

Internalization refers to the inner growth that occurs as the individual becomes aware of and then adopts attitudes, principles, codes, and sanctions which become inherent in forming value judgments and in guiding his conduct. It has many elements in common with the term socialization. Internalization may be best understood, by looking at the categories in the taxonomy structure:

> We begin with the individuals being aware of the stimuli which initiate the effective behavior and which form the context in which the affective behavior occurs. Thus, the lowest category is 1.0 *Receiving*. It is subdivided into three categories. At the 1.1 *Awareness* level, the individual merely has his attention

attracted to the stimuli (e.g., he develops some consciousness of the use of shading to portray depth and lighting in a picture). The second sub-category, 1.2 *Willingness to Receive,* describes the state in which he has differentiated the stimuli from others and is willing to give it his attention (e.g., he develops a tolerance for bizarre uses of shading in modern art). At 1.3 *Controlled or Selected Attention,* the student looks for the stimuli (e.g., he is on the alert for instances where shading has been used both to create a sense of three-dimensional depth and to indicate the lighting of the picture; or he looks for picturesque words in reading).

At the next level, 2.0 *Responding,* the individual is perceived as responding regularly to the affective stimuli. At the lowest level of responding, 2.1 *Acquiescence in Responding,* he is merely complying with expectations (e.g., at the request of his teacher, he hangs reproductions of famous paintings in his dormitory room; he is obedient to traffic rules). At the next higher level 2.2 *Willingness to Respond,* he responds increasingly to an inner compulsion (e.g., voluntarily looks for instances of good art where shading, perspective, color, and design have been well used, or has an interest in social problems broader than those of the local community. At 2.3 *Satisfaction in Response,* he responds emotionally as well (e.g., works with clay, especially in making pottery for personal pleasure). Up to this point he has differentiated the affective stimuli; he has begun to seek them out and to attach emotional significance and value to them.

As the process unfolds, the next levels of 3.0 *Valuing* describe increasing internalization, as the person's behavior is sufficiently consistent that he comes to hold a value: 3.1 *Acceptance of a Value* (e.g., continuing desire to develop the ability to write effectively and hold it more strongly), 3.2 *Preference for a Value* (e.g., seeks out examples of good art for enjoyment of them to the level where he behaves so as to further this impression actively); and 3.3 *Commitment* (e.g., faith in the power of reason and the method of experimentation).

As the learner successively internalizes values, he encounters situations for which more than one value is relevant. This necessitates organizing the values into a system, 4.0 *Organization.* And since a prerequisite to interrelating values is their conceptualization in a form which permits organization, this level is divided in two: 4.1 *Conceptualization of a Value* (e.g., desires to evaluate works of art which are appreciated, or to find out and crystallize the basic assumptions which underlie codes of ethics) and 4.2 *Organization of a Value System* (e.g., acceptance of the place of art in one's life as one of dominant value, or weighs alternative social policies and practices against the standards of public welfare).

Finally, the internalization and the organization processes reach a point where the individual responds very consistently to value-laden situations with an interrelated set of values, a structure, a view of the world. The taxonomy category that describes this behavior is 5.0 *Characterization by a Value or Value Complex,* and it includes the categories 5.1 *Generalized Set* (e.g., views all problems in terms of their aesthetic aspects, or readiness to revise judgments and to change behavior in the light of evidence) and 5.2 *Characterization* (e.g., develops a consistent philosophy of life).

Stripped of their definitions, the category and subcategory titles appear in sequence as follows:

1.0 Receiving (attending)
    1.1 Awareness
    1.2 Willingness to receive
    1.3 Controlled or selected attention

2.0 Responding
    2.1 Acquiescence in responding
    2.2 Willingness to respond
    2.3 Satisfaction in response

3.0 Valuing
    3.1 Acceptance of a value
    3.2 Preference for a value
    3.3 Commitment (conviction)

4.0 Organization
    4.1 Conceptualization of a value
    4.2 Organization of a value system

5.0 Characterization by a value or a value complex
    5.1 Generalized set
    5.2 Characterization [7]

Uses of the Taxonomy

The nature of the taxonomy should now be clear. What, however, are its uses? We have indicated that a prime use is the analysis and classification of objectives.

No longer should a teacher be faced with an objective like "the student should understand the taxonomy of educational objectives," or "he should appreciate the value of taxonomic frameworks." Rather the teacher can now specify whether the first of these objectives would be at the lowest level of comprehension where he would at least expect the student to be able to translate the term "taxonomy" into something like "a classification system of educational goals," or perhaps at a deeper level of understanding, classified as interpretation, where the student could restate the ideas of the taxonomy in his own words. In short, the taxonomy is a relatively concise model for the analysis of education objectives.

The taxonomy, like the periodic table of elements or a check-off shopping list, provides the panorama of objectives. Comparing the range of the present curriculum with the range of possible outcomes may suggest

[7] Krathwohl, Bloom, and Masia, *op. cit.*, pp. 34–35. Reprinted by permission.

additional goals that might be included. Further, the illustrative objectives may suggest wordings that might be adapted to the area being explored.

Frequently, when searching for ideas in building a curriculum, the work of others is most helpful. Where one's own work and that of others are built in terms of the taxonomy categories, comparison is markedly facilitated. Translation of objectives into the taxonomy framework can provide a basis for precise comparison. Further, where similarities exist, it becomes possible to trade experiences regarding the values of certain learning experiences with confidence that there is a firm basis for comparison and that the other person's experience will be truly relevant.

It is perhaps also important to note the implication of the hierarchical nature of the taxonomy for curriculum building. If the analysis of the cognitive and affective areas is correct, then a hierarchy of objectives dealing with the same subject matter concepts suggests a readiness relationship that exists between those objectives lower in the hierarchy and those higher.

The development of the affective domain has pointed up the problems of achieving objectives in this domain. For instance, a study of the relation of the cognitive and affective domains made it apparent that achievement in the affective domain is markedly underemphasized. Thus, the garden variety of objectives concentrates on specifying behavior in only one domain at a time. No doubt this results from the typical analytic approaches to building curricula. Only occasionally do we find a statement like "the student should learn to analyze a good argument with pleasure." Such a statement suggests not only the cognitive behavior but also the affective aspect that accompanies it.

In spite of the lack of explicit formulation, however, nearly all cognitive objectives have an affective component if we search for it. Most instructors hope that their students will develop a continuing interest in the subject matter taught. They hope they will have learned certain attitudes toward the phenomena dealt with or toward the way in which problems are approached. But they leave these goals unspecified. This means that many of the objectives which are classified in the cognitive domain have an implicit but unspecified affective component that could be concurrently classified in the affective domain. Where such an attitude or interest objective refers, as it most often does, to the content of the course as a whole or at least to a sizeable segment of it, it may be most convenient to specify it as a separate objective. Many such affective objectives—the interest objectives, for example—become the affective components of all or most of the cognitive objectives in the course.

The affective domain is useful in emphasizing the fact that affective components exist and in analyzing their nature. Perhaps by its very existence it will encourage greater development of affective components of cognitive objectives.

Further, in the cognitive domain, we are concerned that the student shall be able to do a task when requested. In the affective domain, we are more concerned that he *does do* it when it is appropriate after he has learned that he *can do* it. Even though the whole school system rewards the student more on a *can do* than on a *does do* basis, it is the latter which every instructor seeks. By emphasizing this aspect of the affective components, the affective domain brings to light an extremely important and often missing element in cognitive objectives.

Another aspect which came to light was the extremely slow growth of some of the affective behaviors. We saw this as having implications for both the cognitive and affective domains. Thus, every teacher attempts to evaluate the changes that he has made in his students, and it is clear that it is entirely possible for him to do so successfully at the lower levels of the taxonomy. But a teacher will rarely have the same students over a sufficient period of time to make measurable changes in certain affective behaviors. Some objectives, particularly the complex ones at the top of the affective continuum, are probably attained as the product of all or at least a major portion of a student's years in school. Thus measures of a semester's or year's growth would reveal little change. This suggests that an evaluation plan covering at least several grades and involving the coordinated efforts of several teachers is probably a necessity. A plan involving all the grades in a system is likely to be even more effective. Such efforts would permit gathering longitudinal data on the same students so that gains in complex objectives would be measurable. Patterns of growth in relation to various school efforts would be revealed. Planned evaluation efforts to measure certain cognitive objectives on a longitudinal basis are to be found in some school systems, particularly where they use achievement test batteries designed to facilitate this. Similar efforts with respect to affective objectives are quite rare. If we are serious about attaining complex affective objectives, we shall have to build coordinated evaluation programs that trace the successes and failures of our efforts to achieve them.

In particular, we noted that there was a great deal of "erosion" with respect to the affective domain objectives. When a curriculum is first conceived, affective objectives play an important part in the conceptual structure of the courses. But as time goes on, they cease to have influence on the direction of the courses or in the choice of instructional activities. In part, this results from the fact that rarely are affective objectives reflected in the grading process. Students tend to concentrate on what counts, and affective objectives rarely appear to do so. Since a part of this lack of emphasis on affective objectives in grading is due to the inadequacy of measures and ways of relating measures to objectives, it is possible that the sections of the taxonomy dealing with measurement in the affective domain may help to make these objectives more realistic parts of those courses in which affective objectives are important.

II. A Framework to Facilitate Construction of Instructional Materials

Perhaps this is enough to indicate the existence and potential usefulness of the taxonomy structure as a means of working with objectives at the curriculum-building level. What about the specification of objectives at the instructional-material-building level? Gagné writes:

> Is it in fact possible to divide objectives into categories which differ in their implications for learning? To do this, one has to put together a selected set of learning conditions on the one hand, and an abstracted set of characteristics of human tasks on the other. This is the kind of effort which has been called *task analysis*. Its objective is to distinguish, not the tasks themselves (which are infinitely variable), but the inferred behaviors which presumably require different conditions of learning. Such behavior categories can be distinguished by means of several different kinds of criteria, which in an ultimate sense should be completely compatible with each other. What I should like to try to do here, however, is to use one particular set of criteria, which pertain to the question of "What is learned?" [8]

Gagné's categories are a blending of behavioristic psychology and cognitive theory; the lowest four are related to the former, the upper four to the latter.

His categories also are hierarchical in the sense that having any one capability usually depends upon the previous learning of some other simpler one. Thus his two top categories of problem solving and strategy using "require the pre-learning of:

> *Principles*
> which require the pre-learning of:
> *Concepts*
> which require the pre-learning of:
> *Associations*
> which require the pre-learning of:
> *Chains*
> which require the pre-learning of:
> *Identifications*
> which require the pre-learning of:
> *Responses*" [9]

In more detail his categories are:

> *Response Learning.* A very basic form of behavior is called response learning, or is sometimes given other names, such as "echoic behavior." The individual learns to respond to a stimulus which is essentially the same as that produced by the response itself. . . .

---

[8] Gagné, Robert M. "The Implications of Instructional Objectives for Learning." *Defining Educational Objectives.* Lindvall, *op. cit.*, p. 21. By permission.
[9] *Ibid.*, p. 45. By permission.

Identification Learning (multiple discrimination). In this form of behavior, the individual acquires the capability of making different responses to a number of different stimuli. Of course, he does this when he identifies colors, or late model cars, or numerals, or any of a great variety of specific stimuli. . . .

Chains or sequences. Long chains of responses can most readily be identified in motor acts of various sorts. But there are many kinds of *short* sequences which are very important to the individual's performance. One of the most prominent is a chain of two acts the first of which is an *observing response.* If one is concerned, for example, with getting someone to put 17 in the numerator, this act has two main parts: (1) finding the location of the numerator (an observing response), and (2) writing in that place the numeral 17.

In establishing such behavior as part of the larger and more complex performance like simplifying fractions, one has to see to it that such a chain is learned. . . .

Association. For many years, psychologists appeared to be considering this the most basic form of learning, but such is no longer the case. It is now fairly generally agreed, and supported by a good deal of evidence, that the learning of associations involves more than an S-R connection. Instead, an association is perhaps best considered as a three-step chain, containing in order (1) an observing response which distinguishes the stimulus, (2) a *coding* response which usually is implicit, and (3) the response which is to be expected as the outcome of the association. . . .

Concepts. A concept is acquired when a set of objectives or events *differing* in physical appearance is identified as a class. The class names for common objects like chairs, houses, hats, are the most familiar examples. . . . If one can assume these more basic forms as having been acquired, then the procedure of concept learning is fairly simple. It consists mainly in establishing associations in which the variety of specific stimuli that make up the class to be acquired are represented. . . .

Principles. The next more complex form of learning pertains to the acquisition of principles. One can consider these, in their basic form, as a chain of concepts of the form If A, then B. . . . Again it is evident that the important set of conditions necessary for principle learning is previous learning, this time of the concepts which make up the principle. One either assumes that the learner already knows the concepts liquid, heating, and gas, in acquiring the principle, or else they must first be learned. . . . But when one can truly assume that concept learning has previously been completed, the conditions for principle learning become clear. The proposed chain of events is presented by means of particular objects representing the concepts making up the chain. . . .

Problem Solving. Problem solving is a kind of learning by means of which principles are put together in chains to form what may be called higher-order principles. . . . Typically, the higher-order principles are induced from sets of events presented to the learner in instruction. If carried out properly, these become the generalizations which enable the student to think about an ever-broadening set of new problems. . . .

Strategies. Are there forms of behavior which are more complex than principles, or than the higher-order principles acquired in problem solving? Some authors seem to imply another *form* of learned organization in the strategies with which an individual approaches a problem. There can be little doubt as to the existence of such strategies in problem solving. It may be that strategies are *mediating principles* which do not appear directly in the performance of the task set to the individual, but which may nevertheless affect the speed or excellence of that performance. . . . But it is possible to conceive of strategies as being principles in their fundamental nature, and of being made up of chains of concepts. . . .[10]

Important Needed Research—How to Relate the Frameworks

One may question whether either or both of these frameworks are adequate to the tasks that they have set for themselves. If nothing else, however, perhaps they have heuristic value. In fact, by their very existence, they immediately raise the question, How are the two frameworks related? and its derivative question, What instructional methods are of most value in achieving certain categories in either framework?. For example, how does Gagné's strategy development relate to the skills of the cognitive domain in applying, analyzing, synthesizing, evaluating? What instructional methods most efficiently and effectively permit achievement of these goals? These are questions that should be the focus of considerable educational research.

Summary

To sum up, we have explored the necessity for developing objectives at several levels of generality and abstraction as appropriate for different stages in the process of course and instructional material development. Increasingly, the means are becoming available to do a more thorough and precise job of working with objectives at these different levels. We have explored several frameworks: the Cognitive and Affective Domains of the Taxonomy of Educational Objectives and the classification of capabilities developed by Gagné. We have especially examined some of the implications of the former. Hopefully, as these come to the attention of those actively concerned with course and instructional material building, their heuristic value will be tested and they may be revised to the point where the process of curriculum building and instructional material development is better structured and more researchable. As this comes about, perhaps the growth we all seek in the science of education will be at least somewhat accelerated.

[10] *Ibid.*, pp. 39–44. By permission.

Behavioral Objectives in Curriculum Design: A Cautionary Note

J. MYRON ATKIN

In certain influential circles, anyone who confesses to reservations about the use of behaviorally stated objectives for curriculum planning runs the risk of being labeled as the type of individual who would attack the virtues of motherhood. Bumper stickers have appeared at my own institution, and probably at yours, reading, STAMP OUT NON-BEHAVIORAL OBJECTIVES. I trust that the person who prepared the stickers had humor as his primary aim; nevertheless the crusade for specificity of educational outcome has become intense and evangelical. The worthiness of this particular approach has come to be accepted as self-evident by ardent proponents, proponents who sometimes sound like the true believers who cluster about a new social or religious movement.

Behavioral objectives enthusiasts are warmly endorsed and embraced by the systems and operations analysis advocates, most educational technologists, the cost-benefit economists, the planning-programing budgeting system stylists, and many others. In fact, the behavioral objectives people are now near the center of curriculum decision making. Make no mistake; they have replaced the academicians and the general curriculum theorists— especially in the new electronically based education industries and in governmental planning agencies. The engineering model for educational research and development represents a forceful tide today. Those who have a few doubts about the effects of the tide had better be prepared to be considered uninitiated and naive, if not slightly addlepated and antiquarian.

To utilize the techniques for long-term planning and rational decision making that have been developed with such apparent success in the Department of Defense, and that are now being applied to a range of domestic and civilian problems, it is essential that hard data be secured. Otherwise these modes for developmental work and planning are severely limited. Fuzzy and tentative statements of possible achievement and questions of conflict with respect to underlying values are not compatible with the new instructional systems management approaches—at least not with the present state of the art. In fact, delineating instructional objectives in terms of identifiable pupil behaviors or performances seems essential in 1968 for assessing the output of the educational system. Currently accepted wisdom does not seem to admit an alternative.

Reprinted from *The Science Teacher*, 35 (5): 27–30 (May 1968), by permission of author and publisher.

There are overwhelmingly useful purposes served by attempting to identify educational goals in non-ambiguous terms. To plan rationally for a growing educational system, and to continue to justify relatively high public expenditures for education, it seems that we do need a firmer basis for making assessments and decisions than now exists. Current attention to specification of curriculum objectives in terms of pupil performance represents an attempt to provide direction for collection of data that will result in more informed choice among competing alternatives.

Efforts to identify educational outcomes in behavioral terms also provide a fertile ground for coping with interesting research problems and challenging technical puzzles. A world of educational research opens to the investigator when he has reliable measures of educational ouput (even when their validity for educational purposes is low). Pressures from researchers are difficult to resist since they do carry influence in the educational community, particularly in academic settings and in educational development laboratories.

Hence I am not unmindful of some of the possible benefits to be derived from attempts to rationalize our decision-making processes through the use of behaviorally stated objectives. Schools need a basis for informed choice. And the care and feeding of educational researchers is a central part of my job at Illinois. However, many of the enthusiasts have given insufficient attention to underlying assumptions and broad questions of educational policy. I intend in this brief paper to highlight a few of these issues in the hope that the exercise might be productive of further and deeper discussion.

Several reservations about the use of behaviorally stated objectives for curriculum design will be catalogued here. But perhaps the fundamental problem, as I see it, lies in the easy assumption that we either know or can readily identify the educational objectives for which we strive, and thereafter the educational outcomes that result from our programs. One contention basic to my argument is that we presently are making progress toward thousands of goals in any existing educational program, progress of which we are perhaps dimly aware, can articulate only with great difficulty, and that contribute toward goals which are incompletely stated (or unrecognized), but which are often worthy.

For example, a child who is learning about mealworm behavior by blowing against the animal through a straw is probably learning much more than how this insect responds to a gentle stream of warm air. Let's assume for the moment that we can specify "behaviorally" all that he might learn about mealworm *behavior* (an arduous and never-ending task). In addition, in this "simple" activity, he is probably finding out something about interaction of objects, forces, humane treatment of animals, his own ability to manipulate the environment, structural characteristics of the larval form of certain insects, equilibrium, the results of doing an experiment at the suggestion of the teacher, the rewards of independent experimentation, the judgment of the curriculum developers in suggesting that children engage in such an exercise, possible uses of a plastic straw, and the length of time for which one individual might be engaged in a learning activity and still display a high degree of interest. I am sure there are many additional learnings, literally too numerous to mention in fewer than eight or ten pages. When any piece of curriculum is used with real people, there are important learning outcomes that cannot have been anticipated when the objectives were formulated. And of the relatively few outcomes that can be identified at all, a smaller number still are translatable readily in terms of student behavior. There is a possibility the cumulative side effects are at least as important as the intended main effects.

Multiply learning outcomes from the mealworm activity by all the various curriculum elements we attempt to build into a school day. Then multiply this by the number of days in a school year, and you have some indication of the oversimplification that *always* occurs when curriculum intents or outcomes are articulated in any form that is considered manageable.

If my argument has validity to this point, the possible implications are potentially dangerous. If identification of all worthwhile outcomes in behavioral terms comes to be commonly accepted and expected, then it is inevitable that, over time, the curriculum will tend to emphasize those elements which have been thus identified. Important outcomes which are detected only with great difficulty and which are translated only rarely into behavioral terms tend to atrophy. They disappear from the curriculum because we spend all the time allotted to us in teaching explicitly for the more readily specifiable learnings to which we have been directed.

We have a rough analogy in the use of tests. Prestigious examinations that are widely accepted and broadly used, such as the New York State Regents examinations, tend over time to determine the curriculum. Whether or not these examinations indeed measure all outcomes that are worth achieving, the curriculum regresses toward the objectives reflected by the test items. Delineation of lists of behavioral objectives, like broadly used testing programs, may admirably serve the educational researcher because it gives him indices of gross achievement as well as detail of particular achievement; it may also provide input for cost-benefit analysts and governmental planners at all levels because it gives them hard data with which to work; but the program in the schools may be affected detrimentally by the gradual disappearance of worthwhile learning activities for which we have not succeeded in establishing a one-to-one correspondence between curriculum elements and rather difficult-to-measure educational results.

Among the learning activities most readily lost are those that are long term and private in effect and those for which a single course provides only a small increment. If even that increment cannot be identified, it tends to lose out in the teacher's priority scheme, because it is competing with other objectives which have been elaborately stated and to which he has been alerted. But I will get to the question of priority of objectives a bit later.

The second point I would like to develop relates to the effect of demands for behavioral specification on innovation. My claim here is that certain types of innovation, highly desirable ones, are hampered and frustrated by early demands for behavioral statements of objectives.

Let's focus on the curriculum reform movement of the past 15 years, the movement initiated by Max Beberman in 1952 when he began to design a mathematics program in order that the high school curriculum would reflect concepts central to modern mathematics. We have now seen curriculum development efforts, with this basic flavor, in many science fields, the social sciences, English, esthetics, etc. When one talks with the initiators of such projects, particularly at the beginning of their efforts, one finds that they do not begin by talking about the manner in which they would like to change pupils' behavior. Rather they are dissatisfied with existing curricula in their respective subject fields, and they want to build something new. If pressed, they might indicate that existing programs stress concepts considered trivial by those who practice the discipline. They might also say that the curriculum poorly reflects styles of intellectual inquiry in the various fields. Press them further, and they might say that they want to build a new program that more accurately displays the "essence" of history, or physics, or economics, or whatever. Or a program that better transmits a comprehension of the elaborate and elegant interconnections among various concepts within the discipline.

If they are asked at an early stage just how they want pupils to behave differently, they are likely to look quite blank. Academicians in the various cognate fields do not speak the language of short-term or long-term behavioral change, as do many psychologists. In fact, if a hard-driving behaviorist attempts to force the issue and succeeds, one finds that the disciplinarians can come up with a list of behavioral goals that looks like a caricature of the subject field in question. (Witness the AAAS elementary-school science program directed toward teaching "process.")

Further, early articulation of behavioral objectives by the curriculum developer inevitably tends to limit the range of his exploration. He becomes committed to designing programs that achieve these goals. Thus if specific objectives in behavioral terms are identified early, there tends to be a limiting element built into the new curriculum. The innovator is less alert to potentially productive tangents.

The effective curriculum developer typically begins with *general* objectives. He then refines the program through a series of successive approximations. He doesn't start with a blueprint, and he isn't in much of a hurry to get his ideas represented by a blueprint.

A situation is created in the newer curriculum design procedures based on behaviorally stated objectives in which scholars who do not talk a behavioral-change language are expected to describe their goals at a time when the intricate intellectual subtleties of their work may not be clear, even in the disciplinary language with which they are familiar. At the other end, the educational evaluator, the behavioral specifier, typically has very little understanding of the curriculum that is being designed—understanding with respect to the new view of the subject field that it affords. It is too much to expect that the behavioral analyst, or anyone else, recognize the shadings of meaning in various evolving economic theories, the complex applications of the intricacies of wave motion, or the richness of nuance reflected in a Stravinsky composition.

Yet despite this two-culture problem—finding a match between the behavioral analysts and the disciplinary scholars—we still find that an expectation is being created for early behavioral identification of essential outcomes.

(Individuals who are concerned with producing hard data reflecting educational outputs would run less risk of dampening innovation if they were to enter the curriculum development scene in a more unobtrusive fashion—and later—than is sometimes the case. The curriculum developer goes into the classroom with only a poorly articulated view of the changes he wants to make. Then he begins working with children to see what he can do. He revises. He develops new ideas. He continually modifies as he develops. *After* he has produced a program that seems pleasing, it might then be a productive exercise for the behavioral analyst to attempt with the curriculum developer to identify *some* of the ways in which children seem to be behaving differently. If this approach is taken, I would caution, however, that observers be alert for long-term as well as short-term effects, subtle as well as obvious inputs.)

A third basic point to be emphasized relates to the question of instructional priorities, mentioned earlier. I think I have indicated that there is a vast library of goals that represent possible outcomes for any instructional program. A key educational task, and a task that is well handled by the effective teacher, is that of relating educational goals to the situation at hand—as well as relating the situation at hand to educational goals. It is impractical to pursue all goals thoroughly. And it does make a difference *when* you try to teach something. Considerable educational potential is lost when certain concepts are taught didactically. Let's assume that some third-grade teacher considers it important to develop concepts related to sportsmanship. It would be a rather naive teacher who decided that she would undertake this task at 1:40 PM on Friday of next week. The experienced teacher has always realized that learnings related to such an area must be stressed in an appropriate context, and the context often cannot be planned.

Perhaps there is no problem in accepting this view with respect to a concept like sportsmanship, but I submit that a similar case can be made for a range of crucial cognitive outcomes that are basic to various subject-matter fields. I use science for my examples because I know more about this field than about others. But equilibrium, successive approximation, symmetry, entropy, and conservation are pervasive ideas with a broad range of application. These ideas are taught with the richest meaning only when they are emphasized repeatedly in appropriate and varied contexts. Many of these contexts arise in classroom situations that are unplanned, but that have powerful potential. It is detrimental to learning not to capitalize on the opportune moments for effectively teaching one idea or another. Riveting the teacher's attention to a few behavioral goals provides him with blinders that may limit his range. Directing him to hundreds of goals leads to confusing, mechanical pedagogic style and loss of spontaneity.

A final point to be made in this paper relates to values, and it deals with a primary flaw in the consumption of much educational research. It is difficult to resist the assumption that those attributes which we can measure are the elements which we consider most important. This point relates to my first, but I feel that it is essential to emphasize the problem. The behavioral analyst seems to assume that for an objective to be worthwhile, we must have methods of observing progress. But worthwhile goals come first, not our methods for assessing progress toward these goals. Goals are derived from our needs and from our philosophies. They are not and should not be derived primarily from our measures. It borders on the irresponsible for those who exhort us to state objectives in behavioral terms to avoid the issue of determining worth. Inevitably there is an implication of worth behind any act of measurement. What the educational community poorly realizes at the moment is that behavioral goals may or may not be worthwhile. They are articulated from among the vast library of goals because they are stated relatively easily. Again, let's not assume that what we can presently measure necessarily represents our most important activity.

I hope that in this paper I have increased rather than decreased the possibilities for constructive discourse about the use of behavioral objectives for curriculum design. The issues here represent a few of the basic questions that seem crucial enough to be examined in an open forum that admits the possibility of fresh perspectives. Too much of the debate related to the use of behavioral objectives has been conducted in an argumentative style that characterizes discussions of fundamental religious views among adherents who are poorly informed. A constructive effort might be centered on identification of those issues which seem to be amenable to resolution by empirical means and those which do not. At any rate, I feel confident that efforts of the next few years will better inform us about the positive as well as negative potential inherent in a view of curriculum design that places the identification of behavioral objectives at the core.

The Emerging Context
of Education[1]

ERIC F. GOLDMAN

On the occasion of Schoolmen's Week, I wish to discuss certain broad perspectives and three revolutions that have changed the context of education in the United States.

The perspective I want to emphasize focuses on the phrase, "Great Society," and I speak of it in an entirely conceptual sense, in a totally nonpartisan way and without any connection with any Administration, past or present. The Great Society, I would like to suggest, is really the culmination of our country's development from its colonial days through a number of dramatic changes and climactic shifts of opinion. Three of these shifts have been important enough to be called revolutions; they provide dividing lines in our national history.

First, the American Revolution of the eighteenth century established a free society—free in the sense of not being run by another country and soon functioning through representative popular institutions. During this period, as we peopled the continent and directed our energies to building a powerful industrial machine, a great issue arose among us, bringing on the second American revolution.

The objective of this second American revolution was establishment of the Good Society, a society that might be defined as one in which any man willing to work could provide a decent standard of living for his family. Despite a certain amount of nostalgia about America in the early 1900s, at the time this second revolution began most Americans did not have a decent standard of living. In the rituals of the day, we spoke of one nation indivisible. But in reality, we were a nation quite divided, with genuine liberty and justice only for some.

Thus, with the turn of the twentieth century, the issue emerged: Should "liberty and justice," in the social, economic, and political sense, be given to all our people? For more than fifty years this issue commanded national attention and dominated the political life of our country. The question was whether democracy of necessity had to be a leveling process—a lessening of great disparities in wealth and status in our nation. The liberal affirmed that such differences had to be ended. The conservative, while not saying

From *Educational Imperatives in a Changing Culture* (Philadelphia, Pa.: University of Pennsylvania Press, 1966), pp. 3–8. William B. Brickman, editor. Reprinted with permission of publisher.

[1] *The Emerging Context of Education* is an adaptation of Dr. Goldman's address to the opening session of the 1966 Schoolmen's Week meetings at the University of Pennsylvania.

that extreme class differences were good, did assert, passionately, that acceptance of the liberal program would destroy something more important than any amount of economic and social opportunity—American liberty.

While the conservatives and liberals battled for national control, other developments were revolutionizing the social structure of the nation: social legislation, mass production, the leadership of some businessmen, the leveling effects of a series of wars. Thus in the years immediately after World War II, the United States was already close to answering the question: "Does democracy mean a lessening of great extremes of wealth and status?" It was proceeding toward the simplest and most final of answers—the abolition of extremes in income and status.

The question in our day remains: "How far should we proceed in leveling our society?" But today, neither liberal nor conservative shows much heart for providing clear-cut answers. In recent years, the conservative has been forced to compromise—sometimes compromising himself right out of his cause—while the liberal has seen important victories. The social environment has been dramatically improved for millions in the nation, with better housing, more creature-comforts, and a lowering of many of the legal barriers of racial and religious discrimination. The two philosophies of liberal and conservative have largely ceased to sustain any genuine division in our politics. In a real sense, we are all conservatives and we are all liberals. A new consensus, on which the second American revolution was based, now calls for pushing ahead with creation of the Good Society, a society in which any man willing to work can support his family at a decent level.

Now we are on the threshold of the third American revolution—the drive for the Great Society. It is an effort to add to the good society a special lift, a special lilt, and a special vault that express and affect the spirit of human beings. This drive for a Great Society follows the tradition of all other important movements in the history of this nation. Like them, it does not urge us to take new actions just for the sake of doing something new; it calls on us to restore what we believe to be the fundamental values of our people. In the case of the third American revolution, the drive toward the Great Society is a call for the restoration of beauty in man's environment, for more brotherhood in relations with one another, and for more bounce and zest and tang in our total way of life.

More specifically, the Good Society has brought better pay for teachers and improved school buildings. The Great Society, again in terms of a nonpolitical movement, calls for a change in the quality of what is being taught by those better-paid teachers in those improved school buildings. Health programs, likewise, share the goals of the Good Society in calling for more residential housing units and better plumbing. But the Great Society requires change in the environment in which those houses are to be built and thus more civilized living.

Perhaps most dramatically, the spirit of the third American revolution is captured in the field of Negro rights. Like the second American revolution, the third revolution demands civil rights laws. But there is growing sentiment for something beyond legal protections—for a society in which civil rights laws will not be necessary.

It is in the area of understanding the democratic process that the genuine thrust of the third revolution is coming. We have not sufficiently recognized the nature of that thrust because we have not seen what is directly ahead of us. Let us remember: We are the first nation in the history of the world ever to move significantly along the road of genuine democratization, not simply of our political and economic institutions, but of our very culture. Whether it be schools, books, magazines, or television, we have placed our culture in the hands of the general population and we have given them the methods of controlling this culture. As we democratize a culture, a whole new set of problems is created.

We also may not have noticed in this nation the development of certain new forces that are contributing to the third American revolution. These forces are the boom in education and the growth of a whole new industry of major importance—the knowledge industry. It means something, and something important, to say that today, for the first time in man's five thousand years of history, a substantial part of a nation's population is being educated beyond the high-school level.

There is also the matter of the lowering of the average age of the American population. Where does this third American revolution find its strongest adherents? Among these younger age groups—people in their late 'teens, their 20's, and their 30's. One senses this revolutionary spirit everywhere, not merely in one generation's shift from another generation's attitudes, but in a fundamental change in the approach to life. We see it also in the arrival of esthetics as a serious political issue in many parts of the nation. Above all, we observe it booming among these younger people in the phenomenon called the cultural explosion. Those of you who have children reaching maturity cannot fail to notice the abyss that opens between us and them when we discuss the first and second revolutions without also touching the values of the third American revolution.

There are sound historical reasons why the third American revolution should be progressing so rapidly among these age groups. For these younger people, the old issues that once excited us are simply dead. We must face the fact that the person 20 years old today was not born until the end of World War II and did not reach maturity until after the Korean war.

Meanwhile, as the issues that moved us have died, new causes especially appealing to youth have arisen. Agitation for civil rights, for example, while important to us older people, has become for youth a commitment, not in a legal and political sense, but in a moral and emotional sense.

Each of the previous American revolutions, the first for freedom and the second for the Good Society, was impeded along the way by a genuinely deep cleavage among our people. In the battle for freedom during the eighteenth century, the patriots were on one side and on the other were the dogged and resourceful Tories. In the struggle for the Good Society, of course, there was the sharp distinction between liberals and conservatives.

One reason why I feel so strongly that the third American revolution will move ahead rapidly is that there really is no cleavage in America today comparable to the divisive forces of earlier revolutionary movements. The cleavage that one might expect to exist today would be primarily between businessmen and what might be termed the intellectual leadership. There is cleavage there, no doubt, but to nowhere near the same extent as in similar instances in the past. Again, as a result of our educational system, we have developed a remarkable group of younger businessmen, who are relatively book-minded and aware of esthetics; they are already a part of the third American revolution. At the same time, many leading educators, by being drawn into the main currents of American life, have lost to a large degree the attitude of asperity toward business that helped to create an earlier climate of opinion. Bookish businessmen and more managerial-minded educators are increasing in our society.

This, then, I would suggest, is the context in which we will be working for the next twenty, thirty, or forty years. It is not a simple context. The first American Revolution was less complex. The goals of freedom were easier to define. The second American revolution was more understandable in its demands for greater social and economic opportunities. But this third American revolution has moved into an intangible realm, which, for want of a better word, we might define as the quality of living and the quality of human relationships.

The goals of our third American revolution represent a profound change. To us as educators, it is an exciting set of goals. And I believe that the degree to which this revolution has already taken place and the force and intensity behind it refute the doleful opinion so often heard in this nation that the great adventure of being an American is over, that all of the important battles have been won. The revolution is bringing to our nation more youthfulness, more realism, more drive for a moral sense of living, more yearning for a genuine lilt in all aspects of life. The new revolution recalls the words of Thomas Wolfe, who understood our American rhythm so well. Remember, he told us that the true discovery of America lies before us and that the true fulfillment of our spirit, of our people, and of our mighty land is yet to come.

Fostering Students' Cognitive Development

It was stated in introducing the first part that educators often have different points of view about the school's major purposes or functions. To illustrate this, manuscripts were included in that part exemplifying some of these differing points of view. Without exception, though, the authors of those manuscripts did rank among the school's major purposes that of fostering students' cognitive development. No educator, certainly, would deny that task a primary place in his own hierarchy of purposes. Most, as a matter of fact, would accord it the highest place.

Knowledge of the structure of the intellect has increased significantly in recent years. Guilford points out, for example, that 80 discrete factors of intelligence, out of an hypothesized model of 120 factors, are now known and testable.[1] Knowledge of ways to promote the intellect's development has also been increasing. Although space in this part is much too limited to mention even some of those who have made and are making significant theoretical and empirical contributions to this knowledge, the part would have to have been considered incomplete had not specific attention been directed to the works of Jean Piaget, Maria Montessori, Jerome Bruner, and Benjamin Bloom. Consequently, the first three articles included here center around their work.

In the first article, Elkind pinpoints three original ideas about

[1] J. P. Guilford, "Intelligence: 1965 Model," *American Psychologist,* XXI (March 1966), 20–26.

child thought and behavior that Piaget and Montessori arrived at independently but had in common. The first of these ideas is that nature interacts with nurture in a dual way. "In the case of mental capacities, nature plays the directive role and nurture is subservient, while just the reverse is true with respect to the content of thought." [2] *The second idea is that capacity determines or sets the limits for learning. And the third idea is that repetitive behavior in children is essential to optimum cognitive functioning. Elkind analyzes the implications of each of these ideas for current educational practice.*

Although the ideas of Piaget and Montessori have attracted considerable attention during the last decade, probably no single work has captured (or alienated) the educational audience as much as Jerome Bruner's The Process of Education. *Indeed, one statement in that book has probably been footnoted more often than any in recent memory. "We begin with the hypothesis that any subject can be taught effectively in some intellectually honest form to any child at any stage of development."* [3] *And, a little later, "The task of teaching a subject to a child at any particular age is one of representing the structure of that subject in terms of the child's way of viewing things."* [4]

The question of the legitimacy of structure, or structure of the disciplines, as the cornerstone of curriculum planning is raised in Kliebard's article. On the positive side, Kliebard thinks that using structure to develop the school's curriculum accords subject matter or knowledge its rightful and important role. But, on the negative side, he believes that emphasizing structure increases the problem of achieving curricular balance. Perhaps this last point is seen best by the elementary school teacher in the area of the social studies. If structure of the disciplines is used to organize the social studies curriculum, which discipline will be used? Will it be geography or history, economics or anthropology, or sociology or psychology? And once this one discipline is decided upon, what happens to the others?

In the third selection, Jarolimek uses the six categories of objectives proposed in Bloom's Taxonomy of Educational Objectives, Handbook 1: Cognitive Domain [5] *to illustrate ways in which elementary teachers can differentiate instruction. It should*

---

[2] David Elkind, "Piaget and Montessori," *Harvard Educational Review*, XXXVII (Fall 1967), 539. (Article is included in this book.)

[3] Jerome S. Bruner, *The Process of Education* (New York: Random House, Inc., 1960), p. 33.

[4] Ibid.

[5] Benjamin S. Bloom (Ed.), *Taxonomy of Educational Objectives, Handbook 1: Cognitive Domain* (New York: David McKay Company, Inc., 1956).

be noted that the kind of differentiation Jarolimek proposes is different from the kind employed most often by teachers—for example, by varying reading requirements or by assigning different amounts of homework. The type of differentiation that is called for requires the teacher to structure learning situations at varying levels of intellectual complexity. Thus, while some students are learning factual information, others will be gathering and interpreting data, and still others analyzing a problem's fundamental elements. Unquestionably, differentiation of instruction that fails to vary the complexity of intellectual tasks has to be considered less than adequate today.

Just as no discussion of fostering the intellectual development of students would be complete without reference to the works of the people cited above, so also would it be incomplete without reference to the importance of the early childhood years, the years before school. Mukerji, in the fourth selection, states that these years are the root years for the psychosocial development of children, for their perceptual and cognitive development, language development, and creative development. The case she makes for preschool programs can hardly be questioned. About the only question that does remain is to determine what type of program is most beneficial to which kind of youngster. To date, this question continues to be debated by early childhood educators.

There also seems to be some controversy, or at least some confusion, in regard to the meanings of three terms associated with children's thinking. Do these terms, problem solving, *inquiry, and* discovery, *mean essentially the same thing, or does each term identify a unique cognitive phenomenon? In Sagl's article, the position is taken that they might best be understood if considered in relationship to one another. Her illustrations of the way she believes the processes are related should help the reader not only in differentiating among them, but also in planning teaching strategies to foster their development.*

Another cognitive process that educators are making an effort to foster is creativity. In the selection by Torrance, several cultural influences that have a debilitating effect on children's creative development are examined. Proposals are then made for a series of eleven in-service workshops designed to help teachers build the skills necessary for nurturing its development. What is most important to keep in mind is Torrance's statement that teachers do make a real difference in the creative functioning of children. His proposals, if acted upon by teachers, could do much to help make this difference a positive one.

Presented in the final article in the section are the major findings of a recent research study that was designed to measure the effects of teachers' beliefs on the academic performance of their students. It was found in the study that what teachers believed about the learning potential of students did affect significantly how much they achieved. This finding, coupled with those of several other recent studies, would seem to warrant the following conclusion: some students are going to learn, within reasonable limits of course, only as much as their teachers believe them capable of learning. Obviously, the implications of such a conclusion are many and profound.

Piaget and Montessori

DAVID ELKIND

In recent years there has been a renaissance of American interest in the work of two Europeans, Jean Piaget and Maria Montessori. Although the reasons for this rebirth of interest are many and varied, two reasons appear beyond dispute. First of all, both Piaget and Montessori have observed hitherto unexpected and unknown facets of child thought and behavior. Secondly, and in this lies their impact, both of these innovators have derived the general laws and principles regarding child thought and behavior which were implicit in their observations. In the case of Piaget, these observations led to a new philosophy of knowledge while in the case of Montessori, they led to a new philosophy of education.

Unfortunately, it is not possible, in a presentation such as this one, to do any sort of justice to the contributions of these two innovators. Under the circumstances, all that I would like to do is to describe, and to illustrate with research data, three original ideas about child thought and behavior which Piaget and Montessori arrived at independently but share in common. Before turning to those ideas, however, it seems appropriate, by way of introduction, to note some of the parallels and divergences in the Piagetian and Montessorian approaches to child study.

PARALLELS AND DIVERGENCES

Among the many parallels between the work of Piaget and Montessori, one of the most pervasive is the predominantly biological orientation which they take towards the thought and behavior of the child. This is not surprising in view of their backgrounds. Piaget, for example, was publishing papers in biology while still in his teens and took his doctorate in biology at the University of Lausanne. Likewise, Montessori was trained as a physician (she

Reprinted from *Harvard Educational Review*, 37 (4): 535–545 (Fall 1967), by permission of author and publisher. Copyright © 1967 by President and Fellows of Harvard College.

was, it will be recalled, the first woman in Italy to receive a medical degree) and engaged in and published medical research (cf. Standing, 1957). This shared biological orientation is important because both these workers see mental growth as an extension of biological growth and as governed by the same principles and laws.

In addition to, and perhaps because of, this shared biological orientation, both Piaget and Montessori emphasize the normative aspects of child behavior and development as opposed to the aspects of individual difference. Piaget, for example, has been concerned with identifying those mental structures which, if they hold true for the individual, also hold true for the species. Likewise, Montessori has been concerned with those needs and abilities that are common to all children such as the "sensitive periods" and the "explosions" into exploration. This is not to say that Piaget and Montessori in any way deny or minimize the importance of individual differences; far from it. What they do argue is that an understanding of normal development is a necessary starting point for a full understanding of differences between individuals.

The last parallel in the approaches of Piaget and Montessori which I would like to mention is of a more personal nature. Both of these workers manifest what might be called a *genius for empathy with the child*. When reading Piaget or Montessori, one often has the uncanny feeling that they are somehow able to get inside the child and know exactly what he is thinking and feeling and why he is doing what he is doing at any given moment. It is this genius for empathy with the child which, or so it seems to me, gives their observations and insights—even without the buttressing of systematic research—the solid ring of truth.

Despite these parallels, Piaget and Montessori also diverge in significant ways in their approaches to the child. For Piaget, the study of the child is really a means to an end rather than an end in itself. He is not so much concerned with children *qua* children as he is with using the study of the child to answer questions about the nature and origin of knowledge. Please do not misunderstand; Piaget is in no way callous towards the child and has given not a little of his considerable energies and administrative talents to national and international endeavors on the part of children. He has not, however, concerned himself with child-rearing practices, nor—at least until recently and only with reluctance—has he dealt with educational issues (e.g. Piaget, 1964). There is only so much any one person can do, and Piaget sees his contribution primarily in the area of logic and epistemology and only secondarily in the area of child psychology and education.

Montessori, on the other hand, was from the very outset of her career directly concerned with the welfare of the child. Much of her long and productive life was devoted to the training of teachers, the education of parents, and the liberation of the child from a pedagogy which she believed was as detrimental to his mental growth as poor diet was to his physical growth. Montessori, then, was dedicated to improving the lot of the child in very concrete ways.

The other major divergences between these two innovators stem more or less directly from this central difference in approach. Piaget is primarily concerned with theory while Montessori's commitment was to practice. Moreover, Piaget sees his work as being in opposition to "arm chair" epistemology and views himself as the "man in the middle," between the arch empiricists and the arch nativists. Montessori, in contrast, saw herself in opposition to traditional Herbartian pedagogy, which she regarded as medieval in its total disregard for the rights and needs of the child.

CONVERGING IDEAS

I hope that I will be excused if I focus upon Montessori's ideas rather than her methods, for that is where the convergence of Piaget and Montessori is greatest and where the available research is most relevant. Definitive research with respect to the effectiveness of Montessori's methods seems, insofar as I have been able to determine, yet to be completed.

Nature and Nurture

It would be easy, but unfair and incorrect, to contrast Piaget and Montessori with those who seem to take a strong environmentalist position with respect to mental development. Even if we start with writers at the extreme end of the environmentalist camp such as Watson (1928) or more recently, at least apparently, Bruner (1960), it would be a misrepresentation to say that they deny the role of nature in development. The real issue is not one of either nature or nurture but rather one of the character of their interaction. One of the innovations of Piaget and Montessori lies, then, not so much in their championing of the role of nature as in the original way in which they have conceived the character of nature-nurture interaction.

As was mentioned earlier, both Piaget and Montessori see mental growth as an extension of physical growth, and it is in the elaboration of this idea that they have made their unique contribution to the problem of nature-nurture interaction. Their position means, in the first place, that the environment provides nourishment for the growth of mental structures just as it does for the growth of physical organs. It means in addition, and this has been stressed particularly by Montessori, that some forms of environmental nourishment are more beneficial than others for sustaining mental growth just as some foods are more beneficial than others for sustaining physical growth. The "prepared environment" in the Montessori school is designed to provide the best possible nourishment for mental growth.

The relation between nature and nurture in mental growth is, however, not as one-sided as that. Not only does the child utilize environmental stimuli to nourish his own growth, but growth must adapt and modify itself in accordance with the particular environment within which it takes place. Of the many possible languages a child can learn, he learns the one to which he is exposed. The same holds true for his concepts and percepts which are, in part at least, determined by the social and physical milieu in which he grows up. Both Piaget and Montessori recognize and take account of this directive role which the environment plays in the determination of mental content. Indeed, the beauty of the Montessori materials (such as sandpaper letters, number rods, form and weight inset boards) lies in the fact that they simultaneously provide the child with nourishment for the growth of mental capacities and with relevant educational content. In short, for both Piaget and Montessori, nature interacts in a dual way with nurture. As far as mental capacities are concerned, the environment serves as nourishment for the growth of mental structures or abilities whose pattern of development follows a course which is laid down in the genes. Insofar as the content of thought is concerned, nurture plays a more directive role and determines the particular language, concepts, percepts, and values that the child will acquire.

What evidence do we have for this conception of the dual character of nature-nurture interaction? With respect to the environment as a provider of nourishment for an inner-directed pattern of structural development, there is considerable evidence [1] from Piaget-related research. In a study by Hyde (1959) for example, children of different nationalities—British, Arab, Indian, and Somali—were given a battery of Piaget-type number and quantity tasks. Regardless of nationality and language, these children gave the same responses as Piaget had attained with Swiss children. More recently, Goodnow and Bethon (1966) found little difference between Chinese and American children with respect to the age at which they manifested concrete reasoning. These cross-cultural findings suggest that children can utilize whatever stimuli are available in their immediate environs to foster their mental growth just as children all over the world can utilize quite different diets to realize their physical growth.

At the same time, there is also considerable evidence with respect to the directive role which environmental stimulation plays with respect to the content of thought. In a cross-cultural study by Lambert and Klineberg (1967) for example, there were differences even at the six-year-old level in response to the question "What are you?" Most American children thought of themselves primarily as "a boy" or as "a girl" while Bantu youngsters usually described themselves in terms of race. Furthermore, Lebanese children, frequently responded to the question in kinship terms and gave responses such as "the nephew of Ali." This study amply illustrates the role of the physical and social environment in shaping the child's self-concept.

For both Piaget and Montessori, then, nature-nurture interaction has a

---

[1] For a more complete summary of this evidence see J. H. Flavell, *The Developmental Psychology of Jean Piaget* (New York: Van Nostrand, 1963).

dual character. In the case of mental capacities, nature plays the directive role and nurture is subservient, while just the reverse is true with respect to the content of thought. It is in their emphasis upon the dual character of nature-nurture interaction that Piaget and Montessori have made their signal contribution to this age-old problem.

Capacity and Learning

Within experimental psychology, the child is generally viewed as a naive organism. That is to say, a child is one who is lacking in experience although his capacity to learn is no different from that of the adult. If differences between children and adults exist, then they reside in the fact that adults have had more opportunity and time to profit from experience than have children. For both Piaget and Montessori, however, the child is a *young* organism which means that his needs and capacities are quite different from those of the adult. This issue can be put more directly by saying that for the experimental psychologist capacity is determined by learning, whereas for the developmental psychologist learning is determined by capacity or development.

To make this point concrete, let me use a crude but useful analogy. Over the past ten years, we have seen several "generations" of computers. The early computers were relatively slow and quite limited in the amount of information which they could store. The most recent computers, on the other hand, are extremely fast and have enormous memories. Even the earliest computers, however, could handle some of the programs that the high-speed computers can. On the other hand, no matter how many programs were run on the early computers, their capacity was not altered but remained fixed by the limits of their hardware. To be sure, by ingenious programing, these early computers were able to do some extraordinary things, but their limitations in terms of hardware persisted.

As you have anticipated, the several generations of computers can be likened to the several stages in the development of intelligence. Just as the hardware of the computer determines its memory and speed, so the mental structures at any given level of development determine the limits of the child's learning. Likewise, just as the number of programs run on a computer leaves its speed and memory unaltered, so does the number of problems a child has solved or the number of concepts attained not change his problem-solving or concept-learning capacities. Furthermore, just as we can, with elaborate programing, get the computer to do things it was not intended to do, so we can with specialized training get children to learn things which seem beyond their ken. Such training does not, however, change their capacity to learn any more than an ingenious computer program alters the speed or memory of the computer. This is what Piaget and Montessori have in mind by the notion that capacity determines learning and not the reverse.

This idea is frequently misunderstood by many advocates of Piaget and

Montessori. Indeed, and here we must be frank, much of the acceptance of Piaget and Montessori in America today seems to be based on the promise which their ideas hold out for accelerating growth. Nothing, however, could be further from their own beliefs and intentions. Piaget was recently quoted as saying, "Probably the organization of operations has an optimal time . . . for example, we know that it takes nine to twelve months before babies develop the notion that an object is still there even when a screen is placed in front of it. Now kittens go through the same stages as children, all the same substages, but they do it in three months—so they are six months ahead of babies. Is this an advantage or isn't it? We can certainly see our answer in one sense. The kitten is not going to go much further. The child has taken longer, but he is capable of going further, so it seems to me that the nine months probably were not for nothing" (Jennings, 1967, p. 82). In the same vein, Montessori wrote, "We must not, therefore, set ourselves the educational problem of seeking means whereby to organize the internal personality of the child and develop his characteristics: the sole problem is that of offering the child the necessary nourishment" (Montessori, 1964, p. 70).

The view that capacity determines what will be learned has been supported in a negative way by the failure of many experiments designed to train children on Piaget-type reasoning tasks [2] (e.g., Greco, 1959; Smedslund, 1959; Wohlwill, 1959; 1960). In addition, however, there is also evidence of a positive sort which substantiates the role of capacity in the determination of what is learned. In one of our studies, for example, we demonstrated that while six-, seven-, and eight-year-old children could all improve their perceptual performance as a result of training, it was also true that the oldest children made the most improvement with the least training (Elkind, Koegler, and Go, 1962). We have, moreover, recently shown (Elkind, Van Doorninck, and Schwarz, 1967) that there are some perceptual concepts—such as setting or background—which kindergarten children cannot attain but which are easily acquired by second-grade youngsters. In the same vein, we have also demonstrated that there are marked differences in the conceptual strategies [3] employed by children and adolescents and that these strategies limit the kinds of concepts which

[2] Most of these tasks deal with conservation or the child's ability to deduce permanence despite apparent change. For example, the child might be "shown" two equal quantities of colored water in identical containers, one of which is emptied into two smaller containers before his eyes. Since the child has no way of measuring the equality of the liquid in the large container and that in the two smaller containers, he must— if he can—*deduce* the equality on the basis of their prior equality and his awareness that pouring does not change amount.

[3] In a problem-solving task, for example, once a child sets up an hypothesis, he continues to maintain it even when the information he receives clearly indicates that it is wrong. The adolescent, on the other hand, immediately gives up an hypothesis that is contradicted by the data and proceeds to try out a different one.

elementary-school children can attain (Elkind, 1966; Elkind, Barocas, and Johnsen, forthcoming; Elkind, Barocas, and Rosenthal, forthcoming). Similar findings have been reported by Weir (1964) and by Peel (1960).

There is, then, evidence that capacity does determine what is learned and how it is learned. Such findings do not deny that children "learn to learn" or that at any age they can learn techniques which enable them to use their abilities more effectively. All that such studies argue is that development sets limits as to what can be learned at any particular point in the child's life. These studies are in keeping with the positions of Piaget and Montessori. As we have seen, neither of these innovators advocates the acceleration of mental growth. What they do emphasize is the necessity of providing the child with the settings and stimuli which will free any given child to realize his capacities at his own time and pace. Such a standpoint is quite different from one which advocates the acceleration of mental growth.

Cognitive Needs and Repetitive Behavior

One of the features of cognitive growth which Piaget and Montessori observed and to which they both attached considerable importance, is the frequently repetitive character of behaviors associated with emerging mental abilities. Piaget and Montessori are almost unique in this regard since within both psychology and education repetitive behavior is often described pejoratively as "rote learning" or "perseveration." Indeed, the popular view is that repetition is bad and should be avoided in our dealings with children.

What both Piaget and Montessori have recognized, however, is the very great role which repetitive behavior plays in mental growth. In his classic work on the origins of intelligence in infants, Piaget (1952a) illustrates in remarkable detail the role which primary, secondary, and tertiary circular reactions play in the construction of intellectual schemas. Likewise at a later age, Piaget (1952b) has pointed out the adaptive significance of children's repetitive "Why?" questions. Such questions, which often seen stupid or annoying to adults, are in fact the manifestation of the child's efforts at differentiating between psychological and physical causality, i.e., between intentional or motivated events and events which are a consequence of natural law.

Montessori has likewise recognized the inner significance of repetitive behavior in what she calls the "polarization of attention." Here is a striking example with which, I am sure, many of you are familiar:

> I watched the child intently without disturbing her at first, and began to count how many times she repeated the exercise; then, seeing that she was continuing for a long time, I picked up the little arm chair in which she was seated and placed chair and child upon the table; the little creature hastily

caught up her case of insets, laid it across the arms of the chair and gathering the cylinders into her lap, set to work again. Then I called upon the children to sing; they sang, but the little girl continued undisturbed, repeating her exercise even after the short song had come to an end. I counted forty-four repetitions; when at last she ceased, it was quite independently of any surrounding stimuli which might have distracted her, and she looked around with a satisfied air, almost as if awakening from a refreshing nap. (Montessori, 1964, pp. 67–68)

The role of repetitive behavior in intellectual development is not extraordinary when we view mental growth as analogous to physical growth. Repetitive behavior is the bench mark of maturing physical abilities. The infant who is learning to walk constantly pulls himself into an erect position. Later as a toddler he begins pulling and dropping everything within reach. Such behavior does not derive from an innate perversity or drive towards destruction but rather out of a need to practice the ability to hold and to let go. What the child is doing in such situations is practicing or perfecting emerging motor abilities. Mental abilities are realized in the same way. In the course of being constituted, intellectual abilities seek to exercise themselves on whatever stimuli are available. The four-year-old who is constantly comparing the size of his portions with those of his siblings is not being selfish or paranoid. On the contrary, he is spontaneously exercising his capacity to make quantitative comparisons. The Montessori child who repeatedly buttons and unbuttons or replaces insets into their proper holes is likewise exercising emerging mental abilities. Piaget and Montessori see such repetitive behaviors as having tremendous value for the child and as essential to the full realization of the child's intelligence.

Although there is not a great deal of research evidence relevant to the role of repetition in mental growth, I would like to cite some findings from one of our studies which points in this direction. In this study (Elkind and Weiss, 1967), we showed kindergarten-, first-, second-, and third-grade children a card with eighteen pictures pasted upon it in the shape of a triangle. The children's task was simply to name every picture on the card. The kindergarten children named the pictures according to the triangular pattern in which the pictures were pasted. That is to say, they began at the apex and worked around the three sides of the triangle. This same triangular pattern of exploration was employed by third-grade children and to some extent by second-grade children. First-grade children and some second-grade youngsters, however, did a peculiar thing. *They read the pictures across the triangle from top to bottom and from left to right.*

Why did the first-grade children read the pictures in this clearly inefficient way? The answer, it seems to me, lies in the fact that these children were in the process of learning the top to bottom and left to right swing which is essential in reading English. Because they had not entirely mastered this swing, they spontaneously practiced it even where it was inappropriate. Viewed in this way, their behavior was far from being stupid, and the same can be said for older slow-reading children who read the pictures in the same manner as the first-graders.

These findings thus support the arguments of Piaget and Montessori regarding the adaptive significance of repetitive behavior in children. Repetitive behavior in the child is frequently the outward manifestation of an emerging cognitive ability and the need to realize that ability through action. It was the genius of Piaget and Montessori which saw, in such repetitive behaviors as sucking and putting insets into holes, not stupidity, but rather, intelligence unfolding.

SUMMARY AND CONCLUSIONS

In this paper I have tried to describe and illustrate with research data, three original ideas about child thought and behavior which Piaget and Montessori arrived at independently but which they share in common. The first idea is that nature and nurture interact in a dual way. With respect to the growth of abilities, nature provides the pattern and the time schedule of its unfolding while nurture provides the nourishment for the realization of this pattern. When we turn to the content of thought, however, just the reverse is true; nurture determines what will be learned while nature provides the prerequisite capacities. A second idea has to do with capacity and learning. For both Piaget and Montessori, capacity sets the limits for learning and capacity changes at its own rate and according to its own time schedule. Finally, the third idea is that repetitive behavior is the external manifestation of cognitive growth and expresses the need of emerging cognitive abilities to realize themselves through action.

The recent acceptance of Piagetian and Montessorian concepts in this country is gratifying and long overdue. It would be a great loss if within a few years these ideas were once again shelved because they failed to accomplish that which they were never designed to achieve. To avoid that eventuality, we need to try and accept Piaget and Montessori on their own terms and not force their ideas into our existing conceptual frameworks, or distort them for our own pragmatic purposes. Only in this way can we hope to gain lasting benefit from the outstanding contributions which Piaget and Montessori have made to the study of the child.

REFERENCES

Bruner, J. S. *The process of education.* Cambridge, Mass.: Harvard Univer. Press, 1960.

Elkind, D., Barocas, R. B., & Johnsen, P. H. Concept production in children and adolescents. *J. Exp. Child Psychol.*, (forthcoming).

Elkind, D., Barocas, R. B., & Rosenthal, R. Concept production in slow and average readers. *J. Educ. Psychol.*, (forthcoming).

Elkind, D., Koegler, R. R., & Go, Elsie. Effects of perceptual training at three age levels. *Science*, 1962, 137, 755–756.

Elkind, D., Van Doorninck, W. & Schwarz, Cynthia. Perceptual activity and concept attainment. *Child Develpm.*, (forthcoming).

Elkind, D. & Weiss, Jutta. Studies in perceptual development III: perceptual exploration. *Child Develpm.*, 1967, 38, 553–561.

Goodnow, Jacqueline J. & Bethon, G. Piaget's tasks: the effects of schooling and intelligence. *Child Develpm.*, 1966, 37, 573–582.

Greco, P. L'apprentissage dans une situation à structure opératoire concrète: les inversions successives de l'ordre lineaire pare des rotations de 180°. In J. Piaget (Ed.), *Études d'epistemologie genetique*. Vol. 8. Paris: Presses Universitaires de France, 1959, 68–182.

Hyde, D. M. An investigation of Piaget's theories of the development of the concept of number. Unpublished doctoral dissertation, Univer. of London, 1959.

Jennings, F. G. Jean Piaget: notes on learning. *Saturday Rev.*, May 20, 1967, p. 82.

Lambert, W. E. & Klineberg, O. *Children's view of foreign peoples*. New York: Appleton-Century-Crofts, 1967.

Montessori, Maria. *Spontaneous activity in education*. Cambridge, Mass.: Robert Bentley Inc., 1964.

Peel, E. A. *The pupil's thinking*. London: Oldhourne Press, 1960.

Piaget, J. *The origins of intelligence in children*. New York: International Universities Press, 1952(a).

Piaget, J. *The language and thought of the child*. London: Routledge & Kegan Paul, 1952(b).

Piaget, J. Development and learning. In R. E. Ripple & V. N. Rockcastle (Eds.), *Piaget rediscovered*. Ithaca, N.Y.: Sch. of Educ., Cornell Univer., 1964.

Smedslund, J. Apprentissage des notions de la conservation et de la transitivité du poids. In J. Piaget (Ed.), *Études d'epistemologie genetique*. Vol. 9. Paris: Presses Universitaires de France, 1959, 85–124.

Standing, E. M. *Maria Montessori*. Fresno: Academy Library Guild, 1957.

Watson, J. B. *Psychological care of infant and child*. New York: Norton, 1928.

Weir, M. W. Developmental changes in problem solving strategies. *Psychol. Rev.*, 1964, 71, 473–490.

Wohlwill, J. F. Un essai l'apprentissage dans le domaine de la conservation du nombre. In J. Piaget (Ed.), *Études d'epistemologie genetique*. Vol. 9. Paris: Presses Universitaires de France, 1959, 125–135.

Wohlwill, J. F. A study of the development of the number concept by scalogram analysis. *J. Genet. Psychol.*, 1960, 97, 345–377.

Structure of the Disciplines as an Educational Slogan

HERBERT M. KLIEBARD

Almost half a century ago, William Heard Kilpatrick raised the question as to whether the new and exciting term *project method* ought to be admitted into educational discourse (5). He gave it an unqualified endorsement. Ever since the publication of Jerome Bruner's influential book (3), *structure of the disciplines* has generated the same kind of excitement, not only on the part of educationists, but among academicians as well. The proposal that the structure of the disciplines can provide a workable basis for curriculum organization seems to have struck a responsive chord among many who apparently see it as a desirable substitute for such other watchwords as *core* and *life adjustment,* which are falling or have fallen out of popular and professional favor. In just a few years, *structure of the disciplines* has become a kind of rallying cry occupying about the same position that *the whole child* and *education for democratic living* have held in other times. More than any other term, it seems to reflect the new intellectual rigor which is supposed to be characteristic of such recent educational phenomena as the modern mathematics programs and the National Science Foundation's science curricula.

As with other slogans, one of the difficulties with *structure of the disciplines* is that there is some confusion as to what it means. *The Process of Education* was basically a conference report of fewer than 100 pages, less than a third of which was devoted to this topic. It was admittedly not intended to provide definitive answers, merely to state hypotheses. As a result, the problem of defining the term and resolving its implications was left open to debate and interpretation. In time, *structure of the disciplines* has been imbued with almost mystical qualities, and its stature as an educational slogan has grown, but its usefulness as an educational concept may have become somewhat obscured.

WHAT DOES IT MEAN?

The question of what is a discipline, and the question of what constitutes structure, have been central to the discussion of the new term. Several articles have been written, attempting the job of definition, which have either directly or implicitly expressed approval of Bruner's point of view

Reprinted from *Teachers College Record,* 66 (7): 598–603 (April 1965), by permission of author and publisher.

vis-à-vis the problem-centered or directly functional approach to curriculum organization. One description ascribed to disciplines the properties of analytic simplification, synthetic coordination, and dynamism (8); another the characteristics of a domain, a methodology, and a history or tradition (4); and a third sees disciplines as having conceptual and syntactical dimensions (9). These analyses were intended, at least in part, to demonstrate that the organized intellectual resources we call disciplines possess certain attributes which uniquely qualify them for teaching and learning. Unfortunately, it is easy to misinterpret these statements as implying a kind of caste system in which certain fields can be placed in a more exalted position in the academic hierarchy than others. Characteristics which have been ascribed to disciplines are taken to be criteria which in effect qualify certain fields as *bona fide* disciplines and which serve to exclude others. Certain prestigious disciplines, like mathematics and physics, become paragons which other fields of study are to emulate. As a matter of fact, a considerable amount of speculation in educational circles has taken the form of agonizing over whether education itself qualifies as a discipline or whether it has to be assigned to some kind of academic limbo. The tendency has been to use the term *field of study* for areas like education which presumably do not possess the proper set of credentials, and to reserve *discipline* for fields like mathematics and physics which are well established. One problem arising from such a distinction is that, by implication, disciplines are considered as entitled to a place in the curriculum, whereas fields of study are not.

Speculation about the term *structure* has sometimes involved the dissection of certain recognized disciplines with a view to exposing their elemental framework. This has occasionally taken the form of constructing models which are designed to illustrate graphically the complex interrelationships within a discipline. The assumption has been that once the superficial characteristics have been stripped away and the bare bones revealed, the problem of organizing the field for teaching purposes will become markedly simplified.

THE SIMPLE ORIGINS

By contrast, the examples which Bruner himself used to illustrate what he means by structure are simple and undramatic. The structure of biology, he says, may be seen through the "basic relation between external stimulation and locomotor action" to which concepts like tropism and explanations of the swarming of locusts can be related (3). In algebra, structure is related to the fundamental concepts of commutation, distribution, and association. Emphasis on these "three fundamentals" presumably will provide the basis for understanding a wide variety of algebraic operations. The structure of English involves "the subtle structure of a sentence" and the way in which variety can be introduced into the form of language without changing the meaning. Not only do Bruner's illustrations fail to suggest a kind of magical inner core of interrelated principles to which everything in that field may be related, but they all represent quite different orders of things. At one point, Bruner even suggests that structure may take the form of a kind of feeling of empathy or an ability to see parallels. Thus, in history, "If a student could grasp in its most human sense the weariness of Europe at the close of the Hundred Years' War and how it created the conditions for a workable but not ideologically absolute Treaty of Westphalia [sic], he might be better able to think about the ideological struggle of East and West—though the parallel is anything but exact" (3). According to Bruner, then, the structure of a discipline may include, but is not limited to, basic concepts, explanatory principles, generalizations, and insights. Much seems to depend on what kind of discipline it is, and to some extent, on one's individual perception of what is fundamental to that discipline. No one would claim that historians, for example, are of one mind as to what *the* structure of history is or how history should be taught.[1]

None of Bruner's illustrations, therefore, implies that the disciplines are necessarily modeled around a skeleton of interrelated principles the general form of which is common to all disciplines and which must be relentlessly sought out and exposed before that subject can be properly taught. What does seem to be implied are two simple but important propositions: The first is that the curriculum ought to be organized around certain familiar subdivisions of knowledge, which Bruner chooses to call disciplines, and not around problems, social or personal. There is no suggestion, however, that any field of study must present an approved pedigree in order to be admitted to membership as a discipline. As a matter of fact, one important matter which Bruner leaves unresolved is the question of which subdivisions of knowledge are appropriate for study in the various stages of schooling and which should be excluded. The second proposition, implied by the word *structure,* is that the curriculum in these subjects ought to reflect what is central rather than what is peripheral to the fields. It is an attempt to avoid such obvious pitfalls in the teaching of subject matter as the mechanical manipulation of formulae in mathematics and the barren teaching of history as a congeries of unrelated dates and events. The problem of organizing a field for teaching and learning, then, is not one of searching for *the* structure and then transmitting it *in toto,* but one of determining which of the basic principles, theories, concepts, and the like can be adapted for this purpose.

[1] Samuel Eliot Morison has recently criticized the approach to the teaching of history that was developed by Educational Services, Incorporated, an organization of academicians from Harvard and MIT. Recognizing that his views are outside the " 'Brunerian' frame of reference," Professor Morison nevertheless expressed a preference for the narrative tradition in history. Morison also confessed to some difficulty in understanding the aims of the group because their material was written "in 'pedagese' idiom." Apparently the scholars who worked on the program developed fluency in that dialect as a byproduct of dealing with pedagogical problems (6).

Is It Useful?

As an educational watchword, *structure of the disciplines* is certainly not without merit. The most obvious feature of the term is that it focuses the educational spotlight on knowledge in its various dimensions as the basic stock in trade of the schools. In the recent past, educationists have paid lip-service to the importance of knowledge as a fundamental factor in curriculum planning, but they have rarely given it the attention it deserves. The least that can be said is that *structure of the disciplines* may enliven the debate as to whether knowledge should be used instrumentally in the schools as a means of solving problems or whether it should be studied directly. Out of that debate a new consensus may eventually emerge, perhaps along the lines that Bellack has already suggested (1).

As has been noted, a second feature of the term is that it distinctly implies that in planning the curriculum around organized fields of knowledge, an effort must be made to emphasize what is fundamental to those fields and to minimize what is peripheral. This is not an unimportant consideration because there is reason to believe that a curriculum organized around subject-matter fields may lead to mechanistic teaching and learning unrelated to the kind of intellectual activity that characterizes the highest levels of scholarship. It is, however, not the first time that an effort has been made to plan a curriculum around what is basic to a field of study (2).

There are also some negative aspects to the way that *structure of the disciplines* has been interpreted and used, and if we are at all serious about the reevaluation of the curriculum which seems to be taking place, we ought at least to be aware of them. One of the obvious facts of life in curriculum planning is that not all of the subdivisions of knowledge can be incorporated into the curriculum. There simply is not enough time available, even assuming twelve years of schooling, to do this in any systematic kind of way. One is faced, then, with two basic alternatives: The first is to reorganize several subdivisions into broader units. This has been reasonably successful in certain instances and has met with undistinguished results in others. Botany, zoology, and physiology have been successfully combined and taught under the rubric of biology, but unresolved problems still plague the broad fields of social studies and English. The other alternative is simply to make choices from among the various disciplines, selecting those that seem more important than others.

Some Dangers

If we are to be guided by a narrow and limiting conception of *structure of the disciplines* in attempting to resolve this crucial problem, we would tend to exclude the first alternative out of hand because these broad fields have no stature as disciplines and would presumably lack well-defined structures.

In considering the second alternative, our tendency would be to favor those fields of study that can readily exhibit a network of interrelated principles as their structure. While the existence of this kind of structure may make the curriculum in that subject in one sense easier to organize, its presence does not insure that that field of study is a more desirable component of a program of general education than one that does not. If structure is interpreted this way, then the social sciences and the humanities would be relegated to a permanent position of inferiority to the natural sciences and mathematics. The danger is that the question of *how* the curriculum shall be organized will become confused with the question of *what* shall be taught.

A second danger associated with the concept of *structure of the disciplines* is that so much attention will be directed to internal investigation of each of the fields of study that the curriculum as a whole will receive only superficial consideration. The curriculum generalist, the person who is concerned with the curriculum from a broad perspective, is rarely a participant in those commissions which have sought to develop programs in the individual subject areas and have been identified with the *structure of the disciplines* point of view. As a result, there has been little attention given to questions of balance and integration in the curriculum broadly conceived. A program of general education, after all, is not a collection of independent studies. It is (or at least people try to make it) an approximation of what it is important to know.

There are signs already that this critical question may reduce itself to a power struggle among the various disciplines and will be decided on such factors as which discipline can gain enough federal and foundational support to secure a foothold in the curricula of American schools. The American Anthropological Association, for example, has succeeded in acquiring financial support from the National Science Foundation and is seeking a place for anthropology in the high-school curriculum. No major support has been forthcoming, however, for the claims of astronomy, psychology, social psychology, and philosophy. Few people would conceive of this as a desirable situation. It seems to be occurring, however, as a by-product of an extraordinary emphasis on the curriculum in individual subject fields and a corresponding lack of attention to how all of the parts fit together.

The third danger implicit in some of the proposals associated with the *structure of the disciplines* is perhaps the most subtle. It is that schooling and the world of affairs will become even more sharply disjoined than is already the case as part of an unwholesome fission between theory and practice. This, of course, is a recurring and complex problem. It has become particularly acute, however, as a result of the tendency on the part of academicians who have been developing courses of study in the various disciplines in effect to interpret structure almost exclusively in terms of theory. An academician's bias is almost inevitably toward theoretical concerns because theory frequently represents the crowning accomplishment in his field. This does *not* mean that theory ought to dominate every stage of instruction. This criticism is not intended to resurrect the old cry of "subject-matter specialist" once again as a term of opprobrium. It does recognize that a scholar's commitment to his discipline and his expertise in that field are not the only qualifications that are appropriate to planning a curriculum. It is a little late in the day to argue that the academician has no place in the development of courses of study, but it is quite another thing to hold these scholars in such awe as to preclude a useful dialogue among educationists and academicians mutually concerned with school programs.

THE ISSUE OF RELEVANCE

Paradoxically, it was a professor of physics who, in a recent interview, made the overemphasis on theory a focal point of what is perhaps the sharpest attack on some of the new "structured" courses in the sciences and mathematics. Referring to these new curricula as a form of "educational carpet baggery" and to the superintendents and school boards who implement them as "scalawags," Professor Calandra directed much of his criticism at what he considers to be a decided overemphasis on theory in programs like the ones sponsored by PSSC and CBA and an "unfortunate divorce of pure mathematics from applied mathematics" in the new mathematics programs (7). Overemphasis on theoretical abstractions and the creation of a dichotomy between theory and practice, in turn, may serve to obscure the relevance of schooling to the world of affairs. It is at least possible that intensive and continuous stress on theory will, in the mind of the student, remove that discipline from the arena of human activity out of which it arose. Structure, when equated with theory, can contribute to that unfortunate detachment.

It should be obvious that none of the dangers enumerated here is a *necessary* concomitant of *structure of the disciplines* as an educational slogan. As a matter of fact, several of the programs which are now identified with that term were under way before the publication of *The Process of Education*. Nevertheless, the phrase seems to capture the tenor of much of what has been done in the name of the new academic excellence and is presently very much in vogue. Its effect, however, is difficult to assess. On the one hand, the term has served to stimulate novel curriculum thinking and sharpen debate on certain issues; on the other, it has generated some complex problems. Each of these problems poses a potential obstacle to the development of a coherent and effective program for our schools. On balance, one must conclude that the recent emphasis on *structure of the disciplines* as the cornerstone of curriculum planning is a rather mixed blessing.

REFERENCES

1. Bellack, A. A. Selection and organization of curriculum content: an analysis. In Bellack, A. A. (Ed.) *What shall the high schools teach?* Washington, DC: Yearb. Assn. Supervis. Curric. Dev., 1956.
2. Billings, N. *A determination of generalizations basic to the social studies curriculum.* Baltimore: Warwick and York, 1929.
3. Bruner, J. S. *The process of education.* Cambridge: Harvard Univer. Press, 1960.
4. Foshay, A. W. Discipline-centered curriculum. In Passow, A. H. (Ed.) *Curriculum crossroads.* New York: Teach. Coll. Bur. Publ., 1962.
5. Kilpatrick, W. H. The project method. *Teach. Coll. Rec.,* 1918, 19, 319–335.
6. Morison, S. E. The experiences and principles of an historian. In Morison, S. E., *Vistas of history,* New York: Knopf, 1964.
7. The new science curriculums: A sharp dissent. *School Mgmt.,* 1964, 8, 76–82.
8. Phenix, P. H. The disciplines as curriculum content. In Passow, A. H. (Ed.), *Curriculum crossroads.* New York: 1962. Teach. Coll. Bur. Publ., 1962.
9. Schwab, J. J. The concept of the structure of a discipline. *Educ. Rec.,* 1962, 43, 197–205.

The Taxonomy: Guide
to Differentiated Instruction

JOHN JAROLIMEK

Discussions of differentiated instruction in the social studies ordinarily focus upon variations to be made in learning activities which the pupil is expected to perform. Most frequently the recommendations have to do with variations in reading requirements or variations in work-study activities. The teacher is advised to use more difficult reading material with the more capable pupil than with the less able one. Similarly in the case of work-study activities, the suggestion is made that the able pupil be directed toward activities which involve more independent research, more reading and elaborative thinking than his slower-learning classmate. In general, these recommendations are sound ones; but they are apt to be something less than adequate unless, in addition, careful consideration is given to the complexity of the intellectual tasks with which each of the pupils is going to concern himself.

Varying the difficulty of intellectual tasks relating to a social studies unit is a procedure which seems to have received less attention from

Reprinted from *Social Education,* 26 (8): 445–447 (December 1962), by permission of author and publisher.

teachers than it deserves. The hope is that if pupils are placed in reading materials of varying difficulty and are involved in varying types of instructional activities, this will, in itself, result in some differentiation of instruction with respect to complexity of learnings. No doubt this occurs to some extent. However, variations in complexity should be a deliberate and planned part of the teaching plan rather than be allowed to come about by a happy accident. In order to build such diversity in conceptual complexity into the program, one needs to begin with instructional objectives. The procedure under consideration here would hold general objectives constant, but would vary specific objectives in terms of the capabilities of individual pupils.

In an effort to plan deliberately for differentiated instruction in terms of the complexity of intellectual operations, the teacher may find Bloom's *Taxonomy of Educational Objectives, Handbook I: Cognitive Domain* [1] to be a helpful model. The *Taxonomy* classifies various types of educational objectives into six groups or categories as follows:

1. Knowledge	4. Analysis
2. Comprehension	5. Synthesis
3. Application	6. Evaluation

These are ordered in terms of a hierarchy representing an increasingly complex set of cognitive relationships as one moves from category one to category six. Behaviors in each succeeding category are to some extent dependent upon an understanding of related objectives in a prior category. Subheads of each of the six categories indicate that they, too, are ordered from simple relationships to complex ones. Hence, children in the primary grades need not concern themselves solely with objectives in the knowledge category but may make applications, analyses, and evaluations providing these are kept simple and clearly within the realm of direct experience.

It is perhaps true that the bulk of elementary social studies instruction concerns itself with objectives represented in category one—*Knowledge.* This includes knowledge of specifics, facts, terminology, events, etc. To a degree, an emphasis on knowledge is inevitable at early levels since pupils are rapidly building their cognitive structure. However, the knowledge category is itself spread along a continuum ranging from a knowledge of specifics to a knowledge of universals and abstractions in a field. Pupils of varying abilities might be expected to deal with different specific objectives in the knowledge category. Instruction is limiting and narrow when all pupils deal with knowledge objectives pertaining only to specifics, facts, terminology, and events.

---

[1] Benjamin S. Bloom *et al. Taxonomy of Educational Objectives, Handbook I: Cognitive Domain,* New York: Longmans, Green & Company, 1956.

The teacher must, of course, be concerned with objectives in category one—*Knowledge*—because it is fundamental to all of the others. Particularly important would be the development of a knowledge of the terminology of the social studies. Without a grasp of the vocabulary, the pupil is unable to consider problems in social studies thoughtfully. Knowledge of specific facts is important, too, not as an end in itself but because such specifics are prerequisite to the achievement of more complex intellectual objectives. Objectives in this category are relatively easy to teach and evaluate because they depend almost entirely upon recall of information. They have traditionally been a part of the social studies curriculum in most schools and consequently are familiar to teachers. While they are important, at the same time this does not give the teacher license to teach them in ways which are educationally and psychologically unsound.

In addition to knowledge of specifics, one finds in this category two other types of knowledge objectives. The first of these—"knowledge of ways and means of dealing with specifics"—would seem to have especial significance for the social studies. Included would be such knowledge of conventions as might be called for in the understanding of procedures in various affairs of citizenship—how a bill becomes a law, how government officials are elected, how laws are enforced, and so on. It deals, too, with trends and sequences such as knowledge of events which led up to more important events, steps in the production of goods, or the chronology associated with historical developments. The third large subhead entitled "knowledge of the universals and abstractions in a field" constitutes the highest order of the knowledge category. In the social studies it would call for a knowledge of major generalizations relating to the social sciences as these are forged out of the varied experiences of pupils. An example of such a generalization would be "Man's utilization of natural resources is related to his desires and his level of technology."

The second large category—*Comprehension*—requires somewhat more complex intellectual activity than recall, as is the case in the knowledge category. "Translation" and "Interpretation" are the two facets of comprehension most appropriate for elementary social studies. Data gathering brings the pupil into contact with a great variety of source materials. He uses maps, charts, graphs, encyclopedias, atlases, and others. Data so abstracted must be translated into usable form for the purpose of problem solving. Literary material, when used, requires both translation and interpretation. Much of the social studies reading material is presented in highly condensed form and has within it many possibilities for interpretation and extrapolation. If pupils are to avoid making "bookish" reports, for example, they need to be able to make a translation of the material into their own everyday language. Social studies programs could be greatly enriched, especially for the capable pupil, by directing greater attention to objectives which fall into this category—translation, interpretation, and extrapolation.

The third category is called *Application.* It means essentially that the pupil is able to use what he learns; that he can bring his knowledge to bear upon the solution of problems. Numerous authors have called attention to the need for pupils to apply what they learn. Many interesting and stimulating experiences for children have resulted in situations where imaginative teachers have provided opportunities for children to apply what they have learned to life about them. Applications of learning may be represented by some classroom activity such as dramatic play, a construction, or a report given to the class; or they may include a service project in conservation, school government, or community service. Applications need not manifest themselves in overt behavior; applications may be made wholly at the intellectual level. The pupil may, for example, apply and use knowledge previously gained in thinking creatively about new problems or situations. Perhaps most of the applications which are made are of the intellectual type.

Categories four and five—*Analysis* and *Synthesis*—represent high-order intellectual processes. In the case of analysis, the pupil must delve into the subject to a sufficient depth to perceive its component elements, relationships, or organizational principles. Such procedure enhances the development of concepts in depth, for the pupil is led to ever finer discriminations in what is relevant and what is irrelevant with reference to topics under study. Problems in the social studies oftentimes seem deceptively simple because an inadequate analysis is made of factors relating to them. It is only when one explores a problem in depth and makes a careful analysis of fundamental elements, relationships, or organizational principles that he appreciates the complexity of it. Many elementary pupils are ready for the stimulation which such analyses could provide.

While analysis calls for the isolation of relevant data, synthesis requires the bringing together of related elements and reorganizing them into new cognitive structures. In the *Taxonomy,* synthesis is further described as "the production of a plan or proposed set of operations," or the "derivation of a set of abstract relations." For elementary social studies, synthesis can be represented by the reporting of research which a pupil has conducted over a period of time. The reporting of work done on "Pupil Specialties" would be a case in point. Bright pupils find this to be an especially challenging and interesting learning experience. A capable fifth- or sixth-grade child can, through accumulated research, present an amazingly well-prepared synthesis if he has proper guidance from his teacher.

The final category—*Evaluation*—concerns itself with judgments. It assumes a considerable knowledge of the topic on the part of the pupil in order to make such judgments. To some extent it demands the use of learnings which are represented in all of the other categories. Judgments, according to the *Taxonomy,* are of two types—those based on internal evidence and those based on external criteria. Internal evidence would constitute evaluation made on the basis of clearly recognized standards with respect to internal consistency, organization, or structure. For example, a pupil looks at a map and must decide whether or not it is a correct and honest representation—rivers cannot be shown to run toward higher elevations; cities cannot be placed across rivers; colors used on the map must be consistent with those in the key, and so on. Charts, graphic material, or written reports should not contain conflicting data. A mural showing the life of the Woodland Indians should not show an Indian weaving a Navajo blanket. Judgments of this type are not especially difficult to make when one is thoroughly familiar with the material and knows what standards to apply. Judgments in terms of external criteria probably involve a level of criticism too complex and much too involved to be handled by elementary-school-age children.

It is apparent that the *Taxonomy* has much to recommend its use as a model in planning for differentiated instruction in elementary social studies. The teacher would have to become thoroughly familiar with it and with the types of objectives which might be placed in each of the categories. Perhaps the teacher would find it helpful to prepare the various categories in chart form, and in planning a unit, list possible objectives in the various categories. Use of the *Taxonomy* may also result in objectives stated more clearly in behavioral terms, as has been suggested by some authors.[2] Thus, with a knowledge of the capabilities of individual members of his class, the teacher could move pupils in the direction of those objectives which are best suited to their abilities. This would ensure that all categories had been considered and that ideas would be dealt with at varying levels of difficulty.

Thus, as the teacher plans his unit, he makes a careful analysis of the topic to be studied. Then he identifies specific, attainable objectives which could be classified in several categories included in the *Taxonomy.* In accordance with this knowledge and a knowledge of the pupils he teaches, he plans appropriate learning activities which make the attainment of those objectives possible. Combining this procedure with other generally accepted practices for individualizing instruction, the teacher would present his class with a highly diversified and stimulating attack on the study of problems in the elementary social studies. Certainly the *Taxonomy* deserves further investigation not only in terms of its usefulness in curriculum improvement but also as a guide to the teacher in differentiating instruction.

[2] Dale P. Scannell and Walter R. Stellwagen. Teaching and testing for degrees of understanding. *California Journal for Instructional Improvement,* 3:1, 13, March, 1960.

Roots in Early Childhood for Continuous Learning

ROSE MUKERJI

Early childhood education is "in." We in the field as workers, administrators or researchers are suddenly "in fashion." There is a certain logic in the new emphasis on early childhood. Some problems in our society have become urgent. Dropouts from school are not only unemployed but, in most cases, they are unemployable in the changing labor market. Democratic values are being challenged on many fronts. The effects of living in depressed urban or rural areas, in poverty, in segregated ghettos are being shown in widespread personal tragedy and waste that our conscience cannot allow.

Because we are concerned, we are now witnessing a coming together of many forces in concerted efforts to develop programs that tackle the global nature of these problems. We are seeing a ground swell of opinion which says that any program to be effective must begin with young children—younger than we thought. Sociologists, economists, political leaders, community leaders, labor and business leaders are now joining educators and other social scientists in this new trend. The focal point has moved steadily downward—from adolescence to childhood and now to early childhood which extends from primary grades down through kindergarten to children of three and four.

Because of the continuous nature of a child's development, new learning can only be rooted in previous learning and earlier learning affects that which follows. The idea of continuous learning is therefore inevitable. The logic of utilizing the educational potential of the early childhood years is self-evident.

Although it is obvious that no single agency or institution can, by itself, solve the problems mentioned earlier, it is also obvious that the schools, as an institution, have a special responsibility for tackling the problems which face our children. I am talking not only about special problems faced by disadvantaged children but also about problems *every child faces* as he struggles to make his way in our complex society: to grow up; to become civilized, if you will; to have zest for living and learning; to become independent; to become socially responsible; to feel good about himself as a person. At a time when many forces in our society are becoming

From *Childhood Education*, 42 (1): 28–34 (September 1965). Reprinted by permission of Rose Mukerji and the Association for Childhood Education International, 3615 Wisconsin Avenue, N.W., Washington, D.C. Copyright © 1965 by the Association.

increasingly (and sometimes dramatically) aware of the importance and potential power of early childhood education, the schools are becoming more involved in how to utilize these early years in nourishing later school experiences of children through continuous learning patterns.

SOME QUESTIONS

We should ask ourselves some pointed questions: Do programs for young children take into account research and empirical findings which are the bases of early childhood educational practice? Have we fallen into some comfortable ruts of familiarity? Have we been pressured to use Madison Avenue gimmicks that are purported to solve any and every problem? These are 1965 questions. We should continue to ask basic questions that were already 2,000 years old in Plato's time. What can early childhood education do? What *cannot* be expected of it? Let's not fall into the trap of expecting pre-school and early childhood education to do the impossible. But let us ask, "*In what particular and significant ways can early childhood education serve to improve the continuous learning of all children?*"

About Compensatory Programs

Putting all three- or four-year-olds from depressed areas into school will not, in itself, inevitably reverse the downward pull of failure which too often is their life story. What kind of compensatory programs will make a difference? Is it enough to provide a verbally rich environment when the content has no relevance to children's lives and problems? Does the way in which compensatory programs are organized tend to extend rather than reduce segregation in education? What do we lose by ignoring the special impact of peer models on children's learning when we limit early childhood classes to single socio-economic class groups?

About Individualizing Instruction

Fortunately we know much about the general developmental patterns through which children grow and the general sequence of levels through which they mature. We also have a substantial amount of knowledge about the wide range within each level and age group. This foundation saves us from getting trapped in the "number game": if *one* three-year-old can do a certain thing, whether it be to skip with alternating feet or to read a few words, then *every* three-year-old can do so and it is the obligation of a teacher to apply enough pressure (skillfully, of course) to make every three-year-old accomplish these tasks.

Because of the wide developmental range of children within any chronological year, it is impossible to draw a blueprint of a good program for every three-year-old, five-year-old or seven-year-old group. Even in this age of super-standardization, no amount of pressure from teachers, administrators or parents will standardize children's tempos in learning. Because this is so, we are obliged to temper and adapt teaching not only to the generalized developmental levels of children's growth and learning but also to the specific styles and tempos of individual children. Does not the very conception of the term, "early childhood education," imply that these years from three to seven or eight should be considered as a single organic unit in which learning is not only continuous but also proceeds at different tempos for different children?

About Money and Numbers

In thinking about individualizing instruction in a group setting, should not we ask, "What is a high enough ratio between teachers and young children to make the teaching-learning encounter really productive?" Some of the newer compensatory programs are following earlier high-quality programs by setting up classes with one teacher for fifteen youngsters for five-year-olds. For four-year-olds, the ratio is seven to one; for three-year-olds, five to one. Does that sound expensive? If so, then we might consider the actual cost at present which requires increased special school personnel to cope with children's failure. Just think of the present demand for remedial teachers, tutoring services, auxiliary teachers, consultants, helping teachers, and the latest designation—other teaching personnel. And what of the frustration and fragmentation which result from having to mesh the schedules of all these people?

One young first-grade teacher told me, "I'm exhausted trying to keep up with all the so-called 'help' I'm getting. Sometimes I feel I'm teaching for the clock and the auxiliary teachers instead of my children. Just give me twenty children and shut my door. I think I can do a pretty good job on the rest." Maybe the more effective way will turn out to be the most economical way in financial as well as in human terms.

About Time and Scope

Suggestions have been made to lengthen the school day for young children. Yes, we should ask, "How long should the school day be for specific children?" But even more, we need to take a careful look at what happens to children during the extended day. Aside from the amount, what is the *quality* of one-to-one interaction between teacher and child? Important as this is for all children, it is of critical importance to our large population of disadvantaged young children whose learning deficits, to some degree, stem directly from the lack of individual contact with adults who encourage, support and enrich them.

We need to ask the questions that loom larger and larger on the horizon. How can we build bridges between the school and the home? How can we build bridges among children, parents and teachers? How can we implement the multidimensional approach which includes social services, health services, community and educational agencies in the service of children who are first and foremost members of a primary family group? Is not the conception underlying Project Head Start of the Economic Opportunity program a move toward helping communities build such bridges?

POTENTIAL POWER OF EARLY CHILDHOOD EDUCATION

There is an implication in the new emphasis on three- and four-year-olds' school experience that somehow, by starting earlier, children can get to a certain point faster or that they can go further along the educational road. There are, as yet, very little data to substantiate these positions. Why, then, do so many persons envision such promise in extending downward and strengthening the earliest years of children's school experience? Why do they agree that these early years are perhaps the most fruitful in meeting the challenge of educating children effectively? I believe that the early childhood years are particularly fruitful and for four reasons have great potential power for improving education.

Psycho-Social Roots

First, these are the root years during which children meet the challenge of knowing who they are in relation to people outside special and unique confines of the family. These are the key years in which children learn how others accept them and their demands. They work through problems of getting along with others; they build their strategies of rejection, acceptance, domination, submission, abstention, leading, following, compromising, gradually putting themselves in others' shoes and thus learning empathy for the human experience.

In the early school years a child may learn to be self-confident, to strengthen inner controls and disciplines, and to see in the mirror of other children and adults that he is a worthy human being. A child may also learn that he is a failure; that he is inferior for reasons he cannot control; that somehow his family is wrong; that he cannot understand the dialect of school talk; that teachers cannot understand his home dialect; that he is not worthy of respect or of being cared for.

I do not mean to imply an "either-or" self-concept in children. I only sketch the opposite poles and leave you to fill in the continuum and complexity of feelings that more accurately describe the psycho–social experience of young children during their early school years. The implications of the continuous learning idea rest on the fact that a young child's view of himself has a profound and pervasive effect on how he functions during his elementary and later school years. The school must give him many opportunities to build on his strengths and taste frequently the sweetness and encouragement of success in privately significant and socially important events. There is need for a program that builds not on those strengths which fit neatly within our conventional concepts but on those reality-based strengths that permit a child to cope with his life's demands.

Root Years in Concept Formation

Second, the early childhood years are the root years in concept formation. According to Hunt,

> It now looks as though early experience may be even more important for the perceptual, cognitive, and intellectual functions than it is for the emotional and temperamental functions.[1]

These are the years when curiosity impels a child to reach out into his environment: to touch, squeeze, taste, ask the interminable "why"—to try to know. His primary strategy for intellectual growth is active, manipulative and sensory. He utilizes material and active intercourse to build his conceptual scheme of the world.

What are young children curious about? They are intensely curious about people and their relationships, about ages, about marriage and parenthood. We can illustrate with the following recorded by student teachers:

Three-year-old: How come you have a mommy if you're a lady?
Four-year-old: (to student teacher) Do you have any children?
Student T: No, Andy, I don't.
Four-year-old: But aren't you a teacher?
Student T: Yes.
Four-year-old: But aren't all teachers mommies?
Three-year-old: Girls don't marry girls—do they?

In this way children try to fit a new element into a previously determined category and find that it does not quite fit. However, as they meet an element of dissonance, the teacher can help them formulate a more precise category and a more accurate concept.

Young children are also trying to figure out certain quantitative measures. As one three-year-old said to another student teacher:

> You must be the oldest teacher in the room because you have the biggest feet!

Or, as one five-year-old figured:

David: When are we going home?
St. T: We'll be going soon.
David: Look at your watch and tell me.
St. T: In an hour.
David: (thinks for a moment) Oh, you mean two programs from now.

Or, as four-year-old Beverly complained:

[1] J. McV. Hunt, "The Psychological Basis for Using Pre-School Enrichment as an Antidote for Cultural Deprivation," *Merrill-Palmer Quarterly,* July 1964, Vol. 10, #3.

Beverly: I don't see why Anne is bigger than I am but she's only three and I'm four.

Teacher: Yes, Anne is taller, but you are older.

Beverly: Oh, I know. Anne is bigger than I am but I was here for more time.

Listening to various questions and comments of an individual child points up how uneven his conceptual map is at a given time. Iver, a little boy of three, verbalized these thoughts in a five-minute period:

A subway is a little house for a train and tracks are a sidewalk for a train.

Do animals grow to be people?

(When his mother wanted him to go back to sleep) The lightning is mixing with the darkning and it's almost daytime.

A single experience, no matter how successful, is not enough to build a reliable concept. A child must make many approaches from many angles over a period of time before a concept has some measure of stability. The work of Piaget, Bruner, Jersild and others supports the proposition that children cannot move ahead toward abstract structure and reasoning without a broad base of direct encounters from which to abstract and generalize. Early childhood programs are now and must continue to be rich and diversified in concrete, manipulative and sensory learning experiences. In such a setting, children will gradually develop a way to collate relevant data and a way to encompass an element of dissonance which leads them to refine previous concepts and make them more precise. The way in which conceptual growth takes place, building previous encounters into manageable sets and abstractions, underscores the necessity of a continuous learning framework within the school.

Root Years for Language

Third, the early childhood years are the root years for language development. Although there can be thought without language, many kinds of thought are intimately linked with the dependence upon language. Concepts are often coded linguistically. Language becomes an efficient way to store information, recover information and solve problems. It is a tool for organizing and structuring data according to identity, similarity, difference; according to space and time and according to cause-and-effect relationships.

Whenever comparisons are drawn between middle-class and lower social status children, a point is made of the marked differences in the way children use language. Labelling disadvantaged children as nonverbal is, I am glad to say, a cliché not substantiated by careful study. Many of these children are highly verbal in their self-structured play situations. Their language may be Spanish or another or they may use forms departing from the standard English dialect, but one could hardly call them nonverbal.

These same children may *appear* to be nonverbal when they feel inadequate and therefore may resist making verbal responses to teacher-initiated and controlled discussions.

It is true, however, that the quality of verbalization between the two classes is different. Disadvantaged children have vocabulary disabilities. The length and complexity of their sentences, their articulation and sound discrimination do not match those of the more favored group. But in expressiveness of language the distinctions are not so clear. It would be difficult to improve on the power of this exclamation about a five-year-old girl, "Man, she gotta wallop, knock you cross de moon!"

In analyzing the causes of difference in language development between children of different classes, many researchers point out that middle-class children are flooded with words in their environment and that they have many opportunities to talk with adults. Disadvantaged children, on the other hand, lack this extensive verbal stimulation. In fact, most of their conversation is with other children similarly lacking in verbal skills.

The implications are many for teacher intervention in helping children build a stronger base. There is necessity for teachers to talk with children about children's interest in a one-to-one or small group setting. There is also the necessity of providing opportunities to build meaningful vocabulary through interesting stimuli and involvement. Teachers can consciously introduce words and synonyms related to children's play; provide opportunities for children to recall these words during structured meetings when children report on their activities; make tape recordings of children's interesting experiences and provide sets of earphones for groups of children to listen to these tapes independently. The measure of success in enhancing children's language can be found in the degree to which the extended language becomes part of children's communication during their play.

Artificial word drill in a vacuum will hardly accomplish the same results. It may *seem* to take less time; but since the purpose is mainly to please the teacher (and some children readily respond to this kind of pressure), the new words and ways of speaking do not become the children's own within their play. Since reading, even in our literacy-oriented society, does not replace verbal language communication but is built on it and since language is so intimately connected with conceptualization and thinking, it is evident that there must be a continuity of teaching to develop language ability from nursery school through kindergarten, through primary grades and beyond.

Root Years for Creativity

Fourth, the early childhood years are the root years for creativity. E. Paul Torrance says,

> From the best research evidence available and the observation of many

investigators, creative imagination during early childhood seems to reach a peak between four and four and a half years and is followed by a drop at about age five when the child enters school for the first time. . . . There are now indications, however, that this drop in five-year-olds is man-made [or culture-made] rather than a natural phenomenon.[2]

If this is so, I should call it not a man-made phenomenon but a man-made tragedy. In a society that needs all the creativity it can foster to save itself from destruction and decay, we certainly cannot afford to stifle the first seeds of creativity in our young children.

There may be some room for semantic differences as to the creativity of young children. However, there is no question that a young child's free exploration and manipulation of materials and ideas are closely akin to the first improvisational and free-wheeling stage of the adult's most sophisticated and mature efforts toward creativity. The child's play, an ever-recurring creative act for him, is his fountainhead of creative experience. He not only tests himself and his ideas through play, he not only discovers relationships and truths through play, he not only practices and drills himself intensely through play, he also sustains the creative process through which he learns.

It has been found that, as the young child continues in school, not only is his highly creative behavior unrewarded but he is not looked on favorably by his teachers or his peers.[3]

Getzels and Jackson have found that teachers prefer high IQ students to highly creative students. But we must value creativity if we wish to encourage it in our children. We must develop a curriculum with many opportunities for original and self-selected work, for real problem-solving situations and for the practice of discovery techniques as ways of learning. If we really value creativity we will understand that the supportive and psychologically safe atmosphere in our classrooms must continue throughout the child's school career. The creative spirit is too tender and sensitive to be chopped off at the age of five or six or seven and then be expected to reappear on demand at nine or ten or twenty. The idea of continuous learning is indispensable to the nurturing of creativity.

Because the early childhood years are the root years for beginning self-concepts in a world of people, for beginning intellectual concepts, for a foundation of oral language and for creativity, it is no wonder that thoughtful and concerned people in education and related spheres of our society consider early childhood education an excitingly unique arena for improving the educational experience of children—providing, of course, they are seen as continuously growing in the center of a multidimensional life.

[2] E. Paul Torrance, "Adventuring in Creativity," Childhood Education, Oct. 1963, p. 83.
[3] Elliot W. Eisner, "Research in Creativity: Some Findings and Conceptions," Childhood Education, April 1963, p. 373.

Problem Solving, Inquiry, Discovery?

HELEN SAGL

> What's in a name?
> that which we call a rose;
> By any other name
> would smell as sweet [1]

What's in a name? Today, hundreds of years after Shakespeare wrote these words, this question continues to absorb man's attention. Educational writers' current preoccupation is with three terms associated with children's learning—*problem solving, inquiry* and *discovery*. Are these names for truly different phenomena? Or are they names for basically the same phenomenon? Do these names identify unique phenomena or are they "roses by any other name"?

These are no mere academic questions. On the contrary, they reflect a real need to find ways and means for improving the effectiveness of children's learning, particularly in the content areas of the curriculum; for example, in social studies. Created largely by the knowledge explosion, this concern for children's learning is taking many directions, one of which is the search for strategies that will produce an optimum mode of learning for children; hence the current anatomizing of the terms *problem solving, inquiry* and *discovery* by educators and writers.

Certainly a consensus on the meaning of these terms would go a long way toward dispelling the confusion that now exists about them. But, if anything, the microscopic scrutiny to which some writers are subjecting these terms is producing a divergence of interpretations rather than a consensus about their meaning.

RELATIONSHIP OF TERMS

What is happening as a result of attempts to anatomize the terms is that some writers are attributing singular properties to *problem solving*, to *inquiry* and to *discovery*, describing each as a more or less desirable mode of learning. Thus *problem solving*, according to some writers, is a formalized process that suffers from the dangers of stereotyping, while *inquiry*, by being open-ended in nature, avoids this pitfall. Others eulogize *discovery*,

From *Childhood Education*, 43 (3): 137–141 (November 1966). Reprinted by permission of Helen Sagl and the Association for Childhood Education International, 3615 Wisconsin Avenue, N.W., Washington, D.C. Copyright © 1966 by the Association.
[1] William Shakespeare. *Romeo and Juliet*, Act II, Scene 2.

104

contending that it puts the emphasis in the learning spectrum where it belongs—on insight. Still other writers have, indeed, called a "rose by any other name," for they use the terms interchangeably to identify essentially the same process. And this confusion is further compounded by writers who define each term—*problem solving, inquiry* and *discovery*—as a process of search.

Undoubtedly much of the confusion about the definitions of these terms is a matter of semantics rather than a dilemma that only scientific study can resolve. At least the interchangeable use of the terms by writers suggests that this may be the case. What few, if any, writers are doing, however, is defining the meaning of these terms in relation to each other. Why writers have not pursued this relationship, why they have not explored it more fully, is a moot question. To be sure, a few writers—Bruner, for one— seem to suggest that a significant relationship among them exists.

> It is evident then that if children are to learn the working techniques of discovery, they must be afforded the opportunities of problem solving. The more they practice problem solving, the more likely they are to generalize what they learn into a style of inquiry that serves for any kind of task they may encounter. It is doubtful that anyone ever improves in the art and technique of inquiry by any other means than engaging in inquiry or problem solving.[2]

Opportunities for problem solving facilitate the task of developing techniques of discovery and a style of inquiry. One approach to the meaning of these terms, then, is to consider them in relation to each other.

Using this premise as a base, a logical point of departure in exploring the nature of the relationship among *problem solving, inquiry* and *discovery* is to define the problem-solving setting. Here there is a general consensus, for most writers describe a problem-solving setting as one in which there is a blocked goal, a new or novel element that impedes progress toward the goal, inadequate or ineffective habitual or known responses with which to resolve the new element, and a resultant problem to be solved.

PROBLEM SOLVING NOT SEQUENTIAL

The task of resolving problems is often defined in relation to Dewey's five steps to complete thought or Thorndike's more specific analysis of the steps in problem solving; namely: becoming aware of the problem, clarifying it, proposing hypotheses and testing hypotheses against experiences. *But there is no mass of evidence that children always solve problems in this logical order.* In fact, *there is a growing belief that problem solving may not occur as a sequential process.*

Currently, at any rate, the sequence of learners' problem-solving ac-

[2] Jerome Bruner, "Structures in Learning." *NEA Journal* (March 1963), 52:27.

tivities receives little attention from those seeking to shed light on these activities. Rather, the focus seems to center on data-gathering and data-organizing processes involved in problem solving; on inquiry activities such as theorizing and hypothesizing; and on conditions that enable learners to discover and formulate generalizations that illumine their problems.

More specifically, problem solving is conceived by many to be a searching process in which learners engage in inquiry into possible solutions to their problems and gather data which they construct into conceptual schemes that facilitate discovery of organizing principles imbedded in the data. In this concept of problem solving, learners are guided to discover relationships among data by engaging in problem-solving experiences that facilitate this discovery. In short, by structuring data-producing experiences that lead to almost inescapable conclusions, teachers guide learners in their efforts to formulate generalizations that illumine their problems.

DISCOVERING RELATIONSHIPS

What is most important here, of course, is the fact that the learner is the discoverer of the relationships; that, even though the results of his search were predecided, he *discovers* them as he perceives the relationships among the data he gathers. Pieces fall into place at this point; the learner discovers the meaning of the relationships among the data. This is the act of discovery or, as it is sometimes referred to, the *moment of insight.* Subsequently, having made his discovery, the learner verbalizes his conclusion about the data as a principle or generalization that sheds light on the problem he sought to solve. And, most important, he can verify the generalization he has formulated.

Not all problem-solving activities result in this kind of closure, however, for to confine problem solving to controlled experiences that lead to verifiable generalizations is to limit the learner's understanding of his environment. As Suchman points out, "The pursuit of greater meaning or of new understandings is the larger purpose of education." [3] Developing a style of inquiry that adds new dimensions to the child's learning is, therefore, also a significant aspect of the problem-solving process.

PREDICTION OF WHAT WILL HAPPEN

Some problems have no certain answers. But inquiry into such problems produces insight into their causes and opens new channels of thought about them. Inquiry, in essence, is a process in which children zero in on a problem and hypothesize and formulate theories that get at the areas of why and how. The focus is not on established generalizations but on theories that predict what would happen when put to the test.

[3] J. Richard Suchman. "Inquiry." *The Instructor* (January 1966), pp. 24, 64.

In the process of formulating their theories, learners draw on their own storehouses of conceptual ideas, speculate and experiment, as well as look for data that are appropriate to their theories. And, although the teacher guides learners in this inquiry, he does not direct it toward a specific conclusion. For those teachers who consider closure essential, time spent in inquiry, in theorizing and hypothesizing may be time wasted. By the same token, however, the thinking in this aspect of problem solving must surely contribute to the development of the power of rational thought, to say nothing of adding to the dimension and meaning of learning.

How problem solving embraces controlled search, open-ended inquiry and discovery may be clarified by following a group of pupils in their pursuit of a social studies concern.

A teacher considers it important that his children acquire the generalization: *People everywhere have certain basic needs and wants; how they meet these needs depends upon their environment and cultural level.* To accomplish his purpose, he plans for and executes a series of strategic operations. He provides an opportunity for his pupils to raise significant problems bearing on this generalization. He structures a pattern of experiences that yield data that shed light on these problems, and he involves the pupils in these experiences. He engages them in frequent periods of open-ended inquiry during which they theorize about possible solutions to the problems. He helps the pupils organize the data they accumulate and leads them to discover relationships. Finally, he helps them verbalize their discovery as a generalized statement or a principle. Later he arranges new opportunities and new experiences by which the pupils test the conclusion they have verbalized.

To illustrate, the teacher regulates the classroom environment to stimulate his pupils' interest in and curiosity about man's needs for food. Among the problems that this situation generates are the following:

> Why are some kinds of foods grown in some areas of the world but not in others?
> Why are farms in the United States employing fewer workers than in the past?
> How is science changing people's eating habits?
> How can food growers meet labor shortages?
> Why are supermarkets an important community business?

As the focus of their initial data-searching activities the pupils select the problem: Why are some kinds of food grown in some areas of the world but not in others? Under teacher guidance they gather pertinent data from geography books, reference books, newspapers and periodicals; they view films and slides that provide information about food production in various parts of the world; they make study trips to observe irrigation practices and similar operations. The result of these endeavors is a body of facts—types of food grown throughout the world, rainfall, growing seasons and temperature needed to grow each type, man's efforts to modify these conditions.

Having guided the pupils to accumulate this body of facts, the teacher helps them organize the facts to find relationships among them. He asks, for example: "How does the length of a growing season influence the type of food grown in an area? Do some foods grow in tropical areas only? How does irrigation change the kind of food grown in an area?" With these and similar questions the teacher guides the pupils to find relationships among the data and to *discover* this generalization: that the food produced in an area and the geography of an area are directly related but that the relationship is not an absolute one, since man is increasingly modifying conditions by which food is produced.

Working in this pattern, the pupils pursue many avenues of search for data that illumine the problems they identified earlier. But not all of their problem-solving activities result in discovery of pre-established generalizations. Some take the form of open-ended inquiry that produces theories rather than known answers. For example, as a result of their data-gathering experiences, the pupils *discover* that farmers who use mechanical devices to harvest their crops employ fewer people than those who do not. "What of fruit and vegetable growers?" they ask. Since Congress has passed a law prohibiting employment of migrant workers who are not United States citizens, such growers are having harvesting troubles. "Could they also solve their labor shortage with mechanical devices?"

The pupils review the situations in which farmers use mechanical devices and note that, although vegetables and fruit might be more difficult to harvest than corn or wheat, soybeans or alfalfa, using mechanical devices does not seem impossible.

Drawing on their individual storehouses for conceptual ideas about the use of machines in performing tasks, about harvesting and related phenomena, they inquire into the problem and formulate theories about its solution. The following is a sample.

> "In the same way that airplanes are used to spray crops, balls could be dropped from them to knock off fruit like hail knocks it off. . . ."
> "But hail bruises fruit, doesn't it? . . ."
> "Big nets are dropped from airplanes to capture animals. A net dropped over a tree and tied around the trunk like a laundry bag would catch the fruit. . . ."
> "Instead of a net tied *around* the trunk, spread it out on stilts *under* the tree. . . ."
> "Or instead of dropping something from an airplane to knock the fruit off the tree, use a machine that shakes the trunk. . . ."
> "A corn picking machine must work something like ice tongs. Use the same idea for picking fruit. . . ."
> "But what about the many different sizes of fruits and vegetables there are? Could a machine work on all? . . ."

"Try experimenting with seeds to grow more of the fruit and vegetables the same size and shape. . . ."

"Would using mechanical devices decrease or increase how much it would cost to harvest fruits or vegetables? . . ."

"Such a machine would be very expensive. A little thing like a lawn mower costs a lot of money. . . ."

"But many farmers use the same wheat cutting machine. A big orchard owner could rent the machine to many others. . . ."

"Not if the fruit all ripens at the same time. . . ."

(These pupils did not follow through on their theories and attempt to find data to substantiate them. However, they might have decided to do so. In this event, their efforts would have led them to validate their theories, to refute them, or to conclude that there were not enough available data to test them.)

GENERALIZATION RESULTS IN BROADENED CONCEPTS

Thus, weaving in and out of problem-solving activities that generally produced the desired discovery and closure but in other instances resulted in open-ended solutions, the pupils formulated a generalization about people's need for food and the factors that control the way this need is met.

Other problem-solving activities focused on other needs such as clothing, shelter and need to express esthetic impulses, carried on in less depth and over a shorter period of time, served to verify the basic generalization and resulted in a broadened concept of man's needs.

The answer to the meaning of the terms *problem solving, inquiry* and *discovery* lies not so much in defining the discreteness of the terms as in exploring the relationship among them. In short, to know the meaning of one is first to know the relation of one to the other.

REFERENCES

Crabtree, Charlotte, and Shaftel, Fannie. "Fostering Thinking," *Curriculum for Today's Boys and Girls*. Robert S. Fleming, ed. Columbus, Ohio: Charles E. Merrill Books, Inc., 1963. Pp. 245–77.

Dunfee, Maxine, and Sagl, Helen. *Social Studies Through Problem Solving*. New York: Holt, Rinehart and Winston, Inc., 1966.

Kersh, Bert Y. "Learning by Discovery: Instructional Strategies," *The Arithmetic Teacher* (October 1965). Pp. 414–17.

Massialas, Byron G., and Cox, Benjamin. *Inquiry in Social Studies*. New York: McGraw-Hill Book Co., 1966.

Massialas, Byron G., and Zevin, Jack. "Teaching Social Studies Through Discovery," *Social Education* (November 1964). Vol. 28, pp. 384–87, 400.

Shaftel, Fannie, and Crabtree, Charlotte. "Promoting Intellectual Development Through Problem Solving," *Curriculum for Today's Boys and Girls*. Robert

S. Fleming, ed. Columbus, Ohio: Charles E. Merrill Books, Inc., 1963. Pp. 279–311.

Suchman, J. Richard. "Inquiry," *The Instructor* (January 1966). F. A. Owens Publishing Co. Pp. 24, 64.

Taba, Hilda. "Learning by Discovery: Psychological and Educational Rationale," *Elementary School Journal* (March 1963). Vol. 63, pp. 308–316.

Nurture of Creative Talents

E. PAUL TORRANCE

Plato said, "What is honored in a country will be cultivated there." He surely must have included creative talents among those nurtured by honoring them in a culture. The prevailing concept now some twenty-four centuries later, however, is that creativity must be left to chance and that outstanding creative talent will somehow flourish in spite of neglect and abuse. This erroneous idea has dominated thinking even among educators, despite contrary evidence.

No one would argue that heredity does not place limits upon creative development and achievement. Creative abilities are inherited to the extent that a person inherits his sense organs, peripheral nervous system, and brain. How these abilities develop and function, however, is strongly influenced by the way the environment responds to a person's curiosity and creative needs.

Historical evidence is compelling. How can one otherwise account for the great number of creative musicians in the period of a single century in Europe? There were Handel, Mozart, Chopin, Liszt, Verdi, Schubert, Mendelssohn, Debussy, Dvorak, Berlioz, and Wagner. How can one account for the preponderance of great artists and sculptors during the Renaissance? Why were there so many inventors in the late nineteenth century? Why does Australia produce so many good tennis players, the United States so many good basketball and baseball players, and Russia so many good women athletes? Why has the past ten years produced so many outstanding Negro athletes? As Reynolds pointed out, it is doubtful that the basic potentialities of people vary greatly from one century to another.[1] It seems that many kinds of talent, including creative talents, exist in most populations at any given time. Reynolds explains this by suggesting the principle that "talents will

Reprinted from *Theory into Practice*, 5 (4): 168–173 (October 1966), by permission of author and publisher.

[1] Reynolds, M. C. "Nurturing Talents," paper presented at Elementary Leaders Conference, Iowa State Teachers College, January 31, 1958.

develop most frequently and to the highest level in the fields that are given heroic character"—essentially what Plato said in ancient Greece.

Further evidence of the power of cultural influences in the nurture of creative development and functioning is indicated through cross-cultural studies.[2, 3, 4, 5] For example, in the United States, after about age ten, girls consistently perform better than boys on almost every kind of verbal test for creative thinking. In India, however, two investigators using independently collected data from different parts of the country and about five years apart, found that boys excelled girls in practically all of the same verbal tests.[6, 7] It was also found that children in India perform disproportionately better on verbal than on figural tests of creativity. Children in Western Samoa, Negro children in Georgia, and lower class children in Pittsburgh, Pennsylvania, performed better on figural than on verbal tests. It is difficult to believe that children in India are born with better verbal than figural creative thinking abilities and that the reverse is true in Western Samoa, among Negro children in Georgia, and among lower-class children in Pittsburgh.[8] It is also difficult to believe that in the United States girls are born superior to boys in verbal creativity and that the reverse is true in India. Differences in the nurturing influences of the cultures involved help explain these differences. In Indian cities like Delhi where data was collected, one has to know several languages. Verbal abilities are given heavy emphasis. Western Samoa has had an alphabet for only a short time and verbal skills are even now not greatly honored. In the United States, schools and middle-class culture reward verbal skills. This has not been true, however, in the Negro and lower socioeconomic class subcultures. Patterns of the developmental curves and levels of creative functioning from one culture to another can be explained logically on the basis of the nurturing influences of the cultures.[9]

If cultural and historical influences are so powerful, is it possible for teachers, educational methods and materials, and parents to make real differ-

[2] Torrance, E. P. *Education and the Creative Potential.* Minneapolis, Minnesota: University of Minnesota Press, 1963.

[3] Johnson, R. T. *The Growth of Creative Thinking Abilities in Western Samoa,* doctoral dissertation, University of Minnesota, 1963.

[4] Prakash, A. O. *Understanding the Fourth Grade Slump: A Study of the Creative Thinking Abilities of Indian Children,* master's thesis, University of Minnesota, 1966.

[5] Torrance, E. P., and Goldman, R. J. *Creative Development in a Segregated Negro School.* Minneapolis, Minnesota: University of Minnesota, Department of Educational Psychology, 1966.

[6] Prakash, *op. cit.*

[7] Raina, M. K. *A Study of Sex Differences in Creativity,* research paper, Regional College of Education, Ajmer, India, 1966.

[8] Smith, R. M. *The Relationship of Creativity to Social Class.* (U.S. Office of Education Cooperative Research Project 2250), Pittsburgh, Pennsylvania: University of Pittsburgh, 1965.

[9] Torrance, E. P. *Education and the Creative Potential, op. cit.; Rewarding Creative Behavior.* Englewood Cliffs, New Jersey: Prentice-Hall, Inc., 1965.

ences in the creative development and functioning of children? Evidence calls for a definite "Yes."

In previous works, I have summarized a variety of laboratory and field experiments indicating that the behavior of teachers can make differences in creative functioning.[10] In field experiments, instructional materials, designed to provide experiences in creative thinking and containing information about the nature and value of the creative process, proved powerful enough to make differences in creative development.[11] Dozens of experiments from kindergarten through graduate level tell the same story. The history of medical and scientific discovery tells a similar story. How else can one explain why certain teachers produced so many students who made outstanding discoveries? [12, 13]

I shall now attempt to review some cultural influences that seem important in nurturing creative talents in the United States and to propose a program for helping teachers gain the insights and skills necessary if teaching is to make a difference.

CULTURAL INFLUENCES

Success Orientation. The United States has frequently been characterized as the most success-oriented culture in the world. American education is said to prepare only for success, not frustration and failure. These must be avoided either by succeeding or in not attempting ventures where failure is a possibility. This inhibition to creative thinking occurs repeatedly in the testing of children with creative thinking tests. Many children refuse to think of what Mother Hubbard could have done when she found the cupboard bare, because "it never should have happened."

Success orientation, when greatly overemphasized, is detrimental to creative growth because creative learning involves experimenting, taking risks, making mistakes, and correcting them. If making errors is forbidden and they are severely punished, children soon give up all hope of success and stop trying to learn. To nurture creativity, teachers may have to modify their concepts of classroom success and permit children to succeed first in ways possible to them and use the resulting growth to motivate them to higher levels of creative functioning. There is a strong need for more ways in which children can succeed in school.

Peer Orientation. The United States has also been characterized as a

[10] Torrance, E. P., *Rewarding Creative Behavior, ibid.*

[11] Torrance, E. P., and Gupta, R. *Development and Evaluation of Recorded Programmed Experiences in Creative Thinking in the Fourth Grade.* University of Minnesota, Bureau of Educational Research, 1964.

[12] Gibson, W. C. *Young Endeavor.* Springfield, Illinois: Charles C. Thomas, 1958.

[13] Peterson, H., editor. *Great Teachers.* New Brunswick: Rutgers University Press, 1946.

culture in which children and young people are more concerned about the evaluations of classmates than of parents, teachers, and other authorities. Evidences of the inhibiting effects of pressures from classmates to conform emerge when we conduct sociometric studies, creative writing studies, and the like. It is likely that this powerful group orientation is largely responsible for the sharp drops in curves of creative development at about the fourth and seventh grades in most United States schools. Original ideas are common targets of pressures to conform.

The distressing thing is that many youngsters seem so concerned about these pressures that they "give up" all efforts to learn and to think. In an unpublished study I did concerning 45 seventh graders nominated by their teachers as likely dropouts, 95 per cent indicated they did not think anyone would take seriously their ideas and suggestions.

Schools can do much to lighten the tyranny of the group pressures that inhibit creative development. In creative problem-solving experiences, respect can be developed for unusual, minority ideas. Ability and interest groupings can lighten these pressures for many children. Arranging for appropriate sponsors or patrons for promising youngsters can be very powerful. Historical evidence seems to indicate that the child who starts earliest in his special efforts has the best chance of developing to the highest level in his field.[14] Sponsors can give promising youngsters a chance to develop in creative ways at an early age.

Sanctions Against Questioning and Exploration. Although teachers generally recognize the need for children to ask questions and inquire about the wonders and mysteries about them, such tendencies frequently are squelched. Forty-three per cent of those potential dropouts indicated that they were afraid to ask questions. Only 17 per cent of a large sample of fourth graders indicated they were afraid to ask questions.[15]

Misplaced Emphasis on Sex Roles. Boys and girls in different ways suffer in creative development from society's misplaced emphasis on sex role differences. Pressures resulting from this misplaced emphasis needlessly make vast areas taboo for experiencing. Creative behavior, by its very nature, requires both sensitivity and independent thinking. In the United States, sensitivity and receptiveness are feminine virtues while independence in thinking is a masculine one. Again, there is much that schools can do to reduce the tyranny of this misplaced emphasis. One way is through activities that approve independence in thinking and judgment as well as sensitivity and receptiveness. Training in the arts for boys and in science for girls through science and art camps and various kinds of cocurricular and curricular activities is one approach.

Divergency Equated with Abnormality. "Genius" and "madness" have

14 Reynolds, *op. cit.*
15 Torrance and Gupta, *op. cit.*

long been associated with one another. Almost all inventors, composers, creative scientists, and other creative persons have been regarded as insane. Although this belief was discredited long ago, the idea has persisted that any divergence from behavioral norms is unhealthy, immoral, and must be corrected. Teachers should be alert to look at behavior disapproved by the norm group for signs of creative potential. Such potentialities may not occur in the kinds of behavior valued by the school, at least not until recognized and given intelligent guidance and direction.

Other Inhibiting Influences. The foregoing are only a few of the cultural influences that seem to affect the creative development of children in the United States. We might have included emphasis upon a work-play dichotomy, a clock orientation with emphasis on speed, emphasis on appearing to be rather than actually being, and overemphasis on a limited number of talents rather than on the diversity needed. Instead of discussing these influences, I shall sketch briefly a proposed in-service education program to help teachers achieve the necessary skills and concepts to soften the tyranny of these cultural forces.

CRUCIAL TEACHER SKILLS

Almost any penetrating analysis of what is required for successful nurturance of creative talent leads to a recognition of the need for helping teachers improve certain skills. Through a series of articles in the *Instructor,* I proposed and outlined a series of learning experiences through which I believe teachers can improve the crucial skills.[16] This series of experiences is based on an analysis of skills necessary for nurturing creative talents and the status of these skills among most teachers. I have suggested that school faculties, groups of interested teachers, or individual teachers work on a different skill or set of skills each month. Participants would deliberately try to practice and improve one skill at a time, gradually integrating all of them into their behavior repertoire. For this purpose, I have suggested a number of workshops:

Workshop 1. Recognizing and Acknowledging Potentialities. One of the most important teacher skills needed in nurturing creative talents is the recognition and acknowledgment of potentialities. This skill is difficult to acquire, because recognizing potentialities of another is somehow threatening and requires imagination. One has to see a child—even one who misbehaves—not as he is, but as he could be.

There is little likelihood that teachers will do much to nurture creative talents until they become aware of these potentialities. Standardized tests are useful in becoming aware of abilities that might otherwise remain unnoticed. Teachers need not depend upon tests, however. Through the natural

---

[16] *See* the issues in Volume 74, *Instructor,* September-June 1964–65.

learning and problem-solving activities of children, there are many opportunities for observing creative potentialities. Teachers can also plan experiences that call for creative thinking and motivate children to participate in
them. One of my classes compiled a list of 230 different observable signs of
creative classroom behavior. One workshop experience might be to see how
many of the following signs abstracted from this list can be observed in a
given classroom and how these signs can be used in furthering creative
development:

> Intense absorption in listening, observing, doing.
> Intense animation and physical involvement.
> Challenging ideas of authorities.
> Checking many sources of information.
> Taking a close look at things.
> Eagerly telling others about one's discoveries.
> Continuing a creative activity after the scheduled time for quitting.
> Showing relationships among apparently unrelated ideas.
> Following through on ideas set in motion.
> Manifesting curiosity, wanting to know, digging deeper.
> Guessing or predicting outcomes and then testing them.
> Honestly and intensely searching for the truth.
> Resisting distractions.
> Losing awareness of time.
> Penetrating observations and questions.
> Seeking alternatives and exploring new possibilities.

Workshop 2. Being Respectful of Questions and Ideas. A major requirement for creative behavior is the capacity to wonder, to puzzle, to see gaps
in knowledge, and to respond constructively. Children have this capacity,
and it impels them to ask questions and seek answers. Being respectful of
children's questions is not always easy for teachers. It requires responding
with interest and curiosity rather than with threat and punishment.

To develop the skill of respecting questions and ideas, I propose that
teachers begin with the exercise sketched below:

1. Think about what it really means to be respectful of the questions
and ideas of children. Make a list of the common ways teachers respect or
fail to respect them.

2. Try deliberately to be respectful of the questions and ideas of youngsters.

3. Write detailed descriptions of one incident in which an effort was
made to be respectful of an unusual vexing question and one incident
involving an original idea by a child or young person.

4. Discuss descriptions with one another, with a friend, or with a super-

visor, trying to decide how well the effort succeeded and producing a variety of alternatives the teacher could have used.

In workshops, success depends upon the extent that the participants feel psychologically comfortable and are willing to expose their values and behavior patterns so that perceptions and reactions can be analyzed and changed.

Workshop 3. Asking Provocative Questions. Several studies have shown that over 90 per cent of the questions teachers ask call for the reproduction of information in the textbook or presented by the teacher.[17, 18, 19] To improve skills in asking provocative questions, teachers need to know the different kinds of questions. Several available schemes lend themselves to this purpose. One is presented in the paperback, *Classroom Questions: What Kinds,*[20] by a curriculum researcher who discovered that teachers in his school system rarely asked anything except memory questions. This book offers suggestions for improving memory questions—questions that emphasize the truly important facts, generalizations, and values. In addition, there are ideas for improving skills in asking questions that call for translation, interpretation, applications of information, analysis, synthesis, and evaluation. This book could be the focus of a series of workshop experiences. One week, practice could be given in making up and trying out translation questions that ask the learner to translate what he has learned from one abstraction level to another and go beyond the information to determine implications, consequences, and effects. The next week, emphasis could be given to practice with other kinds of questions. Finally, practice could be given in combining and integrating all of the different kinds of questions into a sequence of experiences.

This is one example of a scheme that could be used. Other, perhaps, equally useful schemes would be Guilford's *Structure of Intellect Model,*[21] Bloom's *Taxonomy of Educational Objectives,*[22] and Burkhart's *Divergent Power Model.*[23]

[17] Sanders, N. M. *Classroom Questions: What Kinds?* New York: Harper and Row, Publishers, 1966.

[18] Torrance, E. P., and Hansen, E. "The Question-Asking Behavior of Highly Creative and Less Creative Basic Business Teachers Identified by a Paper-and-Pencil Test," *Psychological Reports,* December 1965, *17,* 815–18.

[19] Boesen, Sister Mary Theodore. *An Analysis of the Question-Asking Behavior of Teachers in a Parochial School,* unpublished research paper, University of Minnesota, Minneapolis, 1966.

[20] Sanders, *op. cit.*

[21] Guilford, J. P. "Basic Problems in Teaching for Creativity," in *Instructional Media and Creativity,* C. W. Taylor, and F. E. Williams, editors. New York: John Wiley and Sons, Inc., 1966, pp. 71–103; "Three Faces of Intellect," *American Psychologist,* August 1959, *14,* 469–79.

[22] Bloom, B. S., editor. *Taxonomy of Educational Objectives: The Classification of Educational Goals. Handbook I: Cognitive Domain.* New York: David McKay Company, Inc., 1956.

[23] Burkhart, R. C., and Bernheim, G. *Object Question Test Manual.* Pennsylvania State University, Department of Art Education Research, 1963. Mimeographed.

After trying for a few days to ask more provocative questions, it would be useful to check progress. A class session might be taped and analyzed. Immediately after a session, the teacher could write down all of the questions he remembers asking. One member of a workshop group might write down the questions that another workshop member asks in a classroom. In classes of older children or adults, the teacher can have a student record the questions he asks. The skill has to be practiced, progress evaluated, and improvements made. Workshop members can analyze one another's questions and discuss possible alternatives.

Workshop 4. Recognizing and Valuing Originality. Teachers should make deliberate efforts to recognize and value original ideas and solutions because there is a strong tendency to ignore or discredit all unfamiliar ideas. One good way of helping teachers develop this skill is to involve them in production of original ideas and assess the degree of originality of a standard set of responses. Then participants can find out why certain responses are obvious and commonplace. The mind has not paused long enough to make the mental leap necessary for producing original responses. Such responses are not surprising, do not ring of the essence of the truth, and do not break away from the safe, easy, and ineffective.

In a series of experiences, teachers might deliberately try to recognize and encourage originality. One useful experience would be to write detailed descriptions of attempts and have them analyzed by the group. The following questions might be used as a guide:

1. In what form did the original idea occur?
2. What was the immediate reaction of the teacher?
3. What were the reactions of other pupils?
4. How was the original idea recognized and respected?
5. What were the immediate consequences of respecting the idea?
6. What do you predict that the long-range consequences will be?

Workshop 5. Developing Elaboration Ability. No idea or solution will make much difference unless some one elaborates and works out the necessary plans for its execution. Several current studies indicate that the single characteristic most differentiating the mental functioning of the juvenile delinquent and the school dropout is the inability to elaborate. Important scientific breakthroughs have frequently been postponed because the person producing the idea failed to elaborate. There is, of course, the danger of too much elaboration.

Workshop participants might focus on encouraging elaboration of some common, specific, activity: a reading lesson, a plan for a classroom or playground activity, or the like. A workshop group might see how many different and original ideas it can produce to encourage elaboration within a particular curriculum task or area.

Workshop 6. Unevaluated Practice and Experimentation. Periods of unevaluated practice and experimentation have tremendously changed what happens to students in my classes. They make far greater progress in applying course content to the solution of personal and professional problems.

Workshop participants could try at least once a week to arrange a time for some kind of unevaluated experience. They should record their experiences by trying to answer the following set of questions and discuss them with another person. They should perhaps try to avoid correcting and evaluating what was done:

1. What was the initial assignment and the nature of the situation in which it was given?
2. How did you communicate that there was freedom to experiment without being evaluated?
3. What happened during the practice period?
4. What happened immediately after the practice period?
5. What was the nature of the similar follow-up task in which the new insights or skills were applied?
6. If rewarded, how?
7. What were the immediate outcomes?
8. What do you predict will be the long-range outcomes?

Workshop 7. Developing Creative Readers. It is easier to remember and use information read creatively than things read passively or critically. When a person reads creatively, he is sensitive to problems and possibilities. He searches for new relationships, synthesizes unrelated elements, redefines or transforms known information into new uses, and builds onto what he knows. Thus, he produces multiple alternatives, looks at information in different ways and in greater depth, and fills in the gaps.

It takes effort to change from a passive, absorbent, or critical reader into a creative one. A person can become a creative reader by heightening expectations and anticipations or by doing something with what is read. These two approaches are discussed in some detail elsewhere and prove as powerful with adults as with children.[24]

Heightening expectations involves the creation of tension or warming up. Doing something with what has been read can occur at any one of four different levels:

1. Reproducing with imagination what is read, making things sound as if they're actually happening.
2. Elaborating what is read.
3. Transforming and rearranging what is read.
4. Going beyond what is read.

[24] Torrance, E. P. *Gifted Children in the Classroom.* New York: The Macmillan Company, 1965.

In workshop groups, the first week might be spent helping participants become more creative readers, heightening their expectations, and doing things with what they read. Subsequent weeks could be devoted to helping participants teach their pupils to become creative readers.

Workshop 8. Predicting Behavior. The work of Ligon has demonstrated the value of improving the accuracy of one's ability to predict the behavior of others and the practicality of doing so.[25] He has suggested the formation of "Co-Scientist Skills Clubs" and has provided the first edition of a manual for such clubs. The basic skills that would be cultivated are accuracy of observation and prediction of the behavior of others. He suggests three principles for developing improved skills in this area and a workshop program could be built around them:

1. The desire to be accurate.
2. Prediction of what the child will do in a given situation and then observation.
3. Use of the child's own words as much as possible in recording observations.

Workshop 9. Guided Planned Experiences. Investigators such as Ojemann and his associates are finding that mental development is quite different when children are provided with planned sequences of learning experiences rather than when they encounter only what the environment provides.[26, 27, 28] Application of the concept of guided learning experiences represents a deliberate attempt to assist a child in learning by developing, from an analysis of the learning task and the nature of the learner, a planned sequence of experiences for mastering the learning task by motivating him to participate in these experiences.

Workshop 10. Searching for the Truth with Methods of Research. Since the very essence of creativity is "searching for the truth," it is important that there be a series of workshops on the development of the basic concepts and skills necessary for this search. Without these skills, there will be a lack of depth in creative thinking. Attention should be given to the skills and concepts involved in different kinds of research: historical, descriptive, and experimental. For each of these kinds of research, a profitable workshop experience would be the development of at least one lesson through which a deliberate attempt would be made to develop relevant skills.

[25] Ligon, E. M. "The Co-Scientist and His Potential," *Character Potential*, October 1965, *3*, 1–26.

[26] Ojemann, R. H. "Research in Planned Learning Programs and the Science of Behavior," *Journal of Educational Research*, October 1948, *42*, 96–104.

[27] Ojemann, R. H., and Pritchett, K. "Piaget and the Role of Guided Experiences in Human Development," *Perceptual and Motor Skills*, December 1963, *17*, 927–40.

[28] Ojemann, R. H.; Maxey, E. J.; and Snider, B. C. F. "The Effect of a Program of Guided Learning Experiences in Developing Probability Concepts at the Third Grade Level," *Journal of Experimental Education*, Summer 1965, *33*, 321–30.

Workshop 11. Creative Problem Solving Skills. No program to improve the teaching skills needed to nurture creative talents would be complete without deliberate efforts to improve skills in creative problem solving. There is a variety of approaches that might be used. One of the most productive and widely used of these approaches is one formulated by Osborn [29] and Parnes [30] and their associates. It has been demonstrated that the basic concepts and skills can be developed to a useful degree through a series of workshop experiences as brief as two or three days. Such skills, of course, have to be practiced and improved.

What Teachers Believe—
What Children Achieve

J. MICHAEL PALARDY

More than three decades ago, W. I. Thomas wrote, "If men define . . . situations as real, they are real in their consequences" (1: 189). This theory has come to be known in the social sciences as the self-fulfilling prophecy. It is based on two assumptions. First, that the act of making a definition about a situation is also an act of making a prophecy about it. Second, that the act of making a prophecy about a situation is also an act of creating the conditions through which the prophecy is realized.

Recent research has presented some convincing evidence that the self-fulfilling prophecy may be at work in educational settings across the country. In a study by Rosenthal and Jacobson eighteen elementary-school teachers were told that certain of their pupils would show dramatic intellectual growth in the academic year ahead. Those pupils did make significantly greater gains in intelligence quotient than the other pupils in the same classrooms who had not been designated as "intellectual spurters." In reality, there was no difference between the two groups of pupils in their potential for "intellectual spurting." The only difference was in the minds of their teachers (2).

By using the rationale of the self-fulfilling prophecy, the study reported here investigated the effect of teachers' beliefs on pupils' achievement (3).

Reprinted from *The Elementary School Journal*, 69 (7): 370–74 (April 1969), by permission of The University of Chicago Press. Copyright © 1969 by The University of Chicago Press.

[29] Osborn, A. F. *Creative Imagination.* (Third Revision) New York: Charles Scribner's Sons, 1963.

[30] Parnes, S. J., and Harding, H. F., editors. *A Source Book of Creative Thinking.* New York: Charles Scribner's Sons, 1962.

The central purpose was to determine whether teachers' reported beliefs about first-grade boys' probable success in reading had any significant effect on the measured achievement in reading that the pupils in their classes attained. Of particular interest was the effect of these beliefs on the boys' achievement.

The major hypothesis tested was that there is no significant difference in mean scores in reading achievement between pupils classified according to sex and pupils classified according to their teachers' beliefs concerning the probable success of first-grade boys in learning to read.

In December, 1967, a questionnaire was sent to the sixty-three first-grade teachers in an Ohio city. One item on this questionnaire was designed to elicit from the teachers a report of their beliefs regarding the probable success of first-grade boys in learning to read. The item read:

> *Assume* that first-grade girls, on the average, achieve 80 per cent success in learning how to read. If this assumption were true, what per cent of success do you believe first-grade boys, on the average, achieve?

(Please check only one.)

—100%	—50%
— 90%	—40%
— 80%	—30%
— 70%	—20%
— 60%	—10%

Forty-two usable questionnaires were returned. The teachers who responded were divided into three groups. Group A consisted of the ten teachers who had checked 80 per cent. These ten teachers reportedly believed that first-grade boys on the average are as successful as first-grade girls in learning how to read. Group B was made up of the twelve teachers who had checked 60 per cent and the two teachers who had checked 50 per cent. Reportedly, these fourteen teachers believed that boys are far less successful than girls in learning how to read. Group C consisted of the eighteen teachers who had checked 70 per cent. These eighteen teachers were eliminated from further consideration because it was thought that their reported beliefs were not sufficiently different from those of the teachers in Group A or in Group B.

Five teachers in Group A were then matched with five teachers in Group B. All the teachers were women, all were Caucasian, all had at least three years of first-grade teaching experience, all had bachelor's degrees, and all were employed in schools said to be located in middle-class neighborhoods. In addition, all the teachers reportedly had three reading groups in their classes, all were using the same basal reading series, and all were teaching in heterogeneously grouped, self-contained classrooms. And, finally, in individual interviews, all the teachers made statements supporting their reported beliefs concerning the probable reading success of boys.

In early May, reading achievement scores of fifty-three boys and fifty-four girls whose teachers constituted Group A and of fifty-eight boys and fifty-one girls whose teachers constituted Group B were obtained from the reading sections of the Stanford Achievement Test, Primary Battery, Form X. Each teacher administered the test to her own pupils, and all scoring was done by the investigator.

Several of the variables that might have contributed to a difference in the achievement among the four groups were accounted for. First, no pupils who were repeating first grade were included in the sample. Second, since all the Group A and Group B teachers were teaching in neighborhood schools said to be located in middle-class areas, it was decided that most of the pupils of the ten teachers came from middle-class families.

Third, only pupils whose age, as of January 1, 1968, ranged between six years and three months and seven years and three months were included in the sample. The mean chronological age by months of the fifty-three boys in Group A was 80.4; of the fifty-four girls in Group A, 79.7; of the fifty-eight boys in Group B, 80.7; and of the fifty-one girls in Group B, 80.5. On the basis of these mean ages, it was decided that there was no marked difference in age among the groups.

Fourth, only those pupils were used as subjects who scored in the average (60–68) and the superior (69–70) ranges on Ginn and Company's Pre-Reading Test, which was administered by their teachers in late September. The mean score in reading readiness for the boys in Group A was 66.6; for the girls in Group A, 66.6; for the boys in Group B, 66.0; and for the girls in Group B, 66.0. Based on these scores, it was decided that at the beginning of the school year there was no marked difference in readiness for reading among the four groups.

A two-way analysis of variance with pupils' intelligence quotient serving as a covariable was the method used to test the null hypothesis of no significant difference in mean reading achievement scores of pupils classified according to sex and according to their teachers' beliefs concerning the probable success of first-grade boys in learning to read. Levels of significance were set at .05, and all significant values were determined by an *F* test.

Since pupils' intelligence quotient was a covariable, the four groups of pupils were equated statistically on the basis of intelligence quotient before comparisons were made between and among them. Intelligence quotients were obtained in early March from Form J of the Otis-Lennon Mental Ability Test, Elementary 1 Level. Again, each teacher administered the test to her own pupils, and all scoring was done by the investigator.

Table 1 shows the analysis of variance of the reading achievement scores of the pupils classified by sex and by the beliefs of their teachers, with pupils' intelligence quotient statistically controlled.

As shown by the 181.885 value of *F* for the intelligence quotient variation, the effect of intelligence quotient on reading achievement scores was significant at the .001 level. This result was not unexpected. It means that

TABLE 1. *Analysis of Variance of the Reading Achievement Scores of Pupils Classified by Sex and by the Beliefs of Their Teachers, with Pupils' Intelligence Quotient as a Covariable*

Source of Variation	Degrees of Freedom	Sum of Squares	Mean Squares	F
Sex	1	519.460	519.460	1.787
Group	1	347.314	347.314	1.195
Interaction for sex $\times$ group	1	1184.152	1184.152	4.075 *
Intelligence quotient	1	52860.063	52860.063	181.885 †
Error	211	61321.656	290.624	
Adjusted Total	215	114853.983		

* Significant at the .05 level.
† Significant at the .001 level.

pupils who scored high on the achievement test had high intelligence quotients and those who scored lower on the achievement test had lower intelligence quotients.

As shown by the 1.787 value of F for the sex variation, there was no significant difference between the mean reading achievement score of the 111 boys and the mean reading achievement score of the 105 girls. Similarly, the 1.195 value of F for the group variation indicates that there was no significant difference between the mean score of the 107 pupils whose teachers constituted Group A and the mean score of the 109 pupils whose teachers constituted Group B.

An inspection of the 4.075 value of F for the interaction effect, however, shows that there was a significant difference in the mean reading achievement scores of the pupils grouped both according to their sex (sex variation) and according to their teachers' reported beliefs concerning the probable success of first-grade boys in learning to read (group variation). A difference significant at the .05 level, in other words, was found among the mean scores of the 53 boys in Group A, the 54 girls in Group A, the 58 boys in Group B, and the 51 girls in Group B.

The interaction effect shown in Table 1, indicating that there was a significant difference in the mean reading achievement scores among the four groups of pupils, does not show specifically what this difference was. Consequently, an examination of the mean scores of the four groups was necessary. These scores are presented in Table 2.

TABLE 2. *Mean Reading Achievement Scores for the Four Groups of Pupils*

Teacher Group	Mean Reading Achievement Score	
	Boys	Girls
A	96.523	96.241
B	89.207	96.686

As Table 2 shows, the boys in Group B scored much lower than the pupils in the other three groups did. The scores of these three groups were quite similar. Obviously, then, the combined effect of pupils' sex and teachers' beliefs resulted in a lower mean reading achievement score for the boys in Group B, those boys whose teachers reportedly believed that first-grade boys are far less successful than girls in learning to read.

Since it was of particular interest to investigate the effect of the teachers' beliefs on the achievement of the two groups of boys, their scores were compared by an F test. This comparison revealed a difference in mean scores that closely approximated significance favoring the boys in Group A ($F = 3.124, p < .08$).

Finally, when the pupils' scores on each of the four sections of the total reading test (word reading, paragraph meaning, vocabulary, and word study skills) were analyzed by the statistical procedure described earlier, the following results were found:

1. There were no significant differences between the 111 boys and the 105 girls in their scores on any of the four subtests.

2. In word reading and paragraph meaning scores, there were no significant differences between the 107 pupils in Group A and the 109 pupils in Group B. In word-study-skills scores, however, there was a significant difference favoring the pupils in Group A ($F = 13.115, p < .01$); and in vocabulary scores, there was a mean difference that closely approximated significance favoring the pupils in Group B ($F = 3.578, p > .05$).

3. There were no significant differences in scores for word reading and vocabulary among the 53 boys in Group A, the 54 girls in Group A, the 58 boys in Group B, and the 51 girls in Group B. But there were mean differences that closely approximated significance in scores for paragraph meaning ($F = 3.271, p > .05$) and in word study skills ($F = 3.386, p > .05$). Inspection of the mean scores of the four groups on these two tests, paragraph meaning and word study skills, revealed that the boys in Group B did least well on both; and that, on both, there were no consistent differences among the other three groups.

The conclusions that can be drawn from these findings would seem to be quite clear and can be stated in two ways. The findings can be stated in terms of the major interest in the study: when first-grade teachers reported that they believed that boys are far less successful than girls in learning to read, the boy pupils of those teachers did achieve less well on a standardized reading test than a comparable group of boy pupils whose teachers reported that they believed that boys are as successful as girls in learning to read.

The findings can also be stated in terms of the self-fulfilling prophecy: when teachers in this study reported that they believed that boys are far less successful than girls in learning to read (when they defined a situation as real), the boys in their classes were far less successful than the girls (the situation was real in its consequences). Conversely, when teachers reported that they believed that boys are as successful as girls, the boys in their classes were as successful as girls.

Stated either way, the finding seems to have implications of some considerable consequence for educators.

REFERENCES

1. W. I. Thomas. "The Relation of Research to the Social Process." In W. I. Thomas, *Essays on Research in the Social Sciences,* pp. 175–94. Washington: Brookings Institution, 1931.
2. Robert Rosenthal and Lenore Jacobson. *Pygmalion in the Classroom.* New York: Holt, Rinehart and Winston, 1968.
3. J. Michael Palardy. "The Effect of Teachers' Beliefs on the Achievement in Reading of First-Grade Boys." Doctor's thesis. Columbus, Ohio: Ohio State University, 1968.

PART 3

Promoting Students' Psychosocial Health

*Fostering students' cognitive development, the theme of the pre-
ceding part, has always been the central concern, the major
focus, of the elementary school. This was never more obvious, at
least in recent memory, than during the years immediately following the successful launching of Sputnik in 1957. Indeed, during those years the concern for the education of the "whole child"
was probably at its lowest ebb since before the days of the Progressive Education Movement.*

*Recently, however, a backlash against the relative neglect
during the post-Sputnik years of the social and emotional needs
of youngsters has occurred. Although it is impossible to state
specifically when this backlash began or when it achieved significant proportions, this writer, at least, is convinced that its
zenith has yet to be reached. In this section, then, the reader is
asked to consider some of the factors that affect the psychosocial
health of children in the hope that such a consideration will result in helping shorten the time it takes to reach that zenith.
When it has been reached, when that delicate balance between
a concern for fostering students' cognitive development and a
concern for promoting their psychosocial health has been found,
it must be maintained. For one thing our students, our country,
and our world will not need is another backlash—this time
against the concept of educating the "whole child."*

*Social psychologists agree that the pressures on youth today
are alarmingly high. The Vietnam War, the bomb, the generation*

*gap, the expectations of parents, the social and racial problems—
these and other conditions of present-day life are all contributing
factors. But as McNassor points out in the first article, the schools
with their increasing emphasis on speed, competition, and academic excellence must also be held responsible. What is of greatest concern to McNassor is that the pressures the schools are
exerting on youth seem to be increasing at a rate proportional to
the efforts educators are making to upgrade the quality of the
instructional program. If this be true, then certainly a reexami-
nation of the dimensions of a quality instructional program needs
to be undertaken.*

*In the second article, Bettelheim writes about education's goal
of helping students achieve and maintain a healthy personality.
He identifies the most important ingredients of such a personality as inner freedom, personal autonomy, and the capacity to
resolve personal conflicts. But by* lecturing *about proper behavior, by* teaching *from textbooks about healthy interpersonal
relationships, by protecting children from natural conflict situations, and by allowing them only minimum autonomy in making
decisions regarding their own behavior, the schools, Bettelheim
claims, are failing in achieving that goal. If schools are a place
to learn, Bettelheim concludes, then let them be a place where
youngsters can learn the skills of emotional management needed
to live life, as it is today and will be tomorrow, fully and well.*

*Simon and Harmin, in the third article, address what to this
writer's mind is a major problem in education today, namely,
the perception of students that much of what they are required
to learn in school is irrelevant. Simon and Harmin contend that
subject matter, which can be taught at the facts level, at the concept level, and at the values level, needs to be taught in such a
way that it will help clarify students' values; that only when it
is taught in this way will it take on for students personal relevance. The two illustrations the authors use to demonstrate how
this can be done, although more appropriate at the secondary
level than at the elementary, can serve, nevertheless, as guidelines for all teachers.*

*One of the major factors affecting the psychosocial health of
children is the feelings they have about themselves, their self-
concepts. In the fourth article, the late Travis Hawk discusses
what the self-concept is, how it develops, and how it serves as
an impelling or an impeding influence on learning. Although
Hawk notes that many children enter school already having
formed negative opinions about themselves and that these opinions are amenable to only very gradual change, he does offer*

some suggestions that, if implemented by teachers, could lead to all children's viewing themselves more positively. Few suggestions should command more attention than these, for few goals of education are as important as developing the self-concept. None, in this writer's opinion, is more important.

Although every teacher is aware of the importance of the peer group in the development of such social characteristics as responsibility, adjustment, and cooperation, few teachers, if judged by current practices, take into account the peer group's potential for improving students' academic learning. In the fifth article, Elder examines the influence of the peer group along both of these dimensions, the social and the educational. The tutor-learner partnership is one little-used technique that Elder believes could improve the students' development. Here, students who would not ordinarily work with each other in the classroom setting—such as the bright and the slow, or the older and the younger—are brought together in a tutoring relationship. According to Elder, the limited data that have been gathered in regard to this practice show that social and educational benefits accrue to both partners. He is convinced, finally, that the peer group remains for educators an untapped pedagogical resource of almost unlimited potential.

In the final article in this section, Crary develops for teachers a theoretical base for discipline. He maintains that the key concept of discipline is respect: respect for each person, respect for learning, respect for the school as an institution, and respect for the basic institutions of society. If, as Crary believes, teachers would incorporate these elements of respect into their own philosophy of "proper" classroom conduct, they would find it unnecessary to use the "schoolteacherish" techniques of discipline that he says are characteristic of too many situations. For the sake of children's development, discipline is needed, but seldom, according to Crary, in its traditional sense.

This Frantic Pace in Education

DONALD McNASSOR

Frantic is a harsh word to describe this nation's effort in education and child-rearing. But no other word is more suitable for the condition I am about to describe. The word, meaning "to move wildly, in a frenzied fashion," implies bewilderment, severe mental agitation approaching distraction, an urgency to ward off imagined disaster. It means, literally, "a bit of madness." And this is exactly the state we have come to in educating children in this country. We have forgotten how children keep their good health, how they acquire a profound sense of trust in themselves as they grow toward maturity. We don't want to think too much about that! To do so in 1967 is interpreted as blatant interference with quality education and scientific and social revolutions of the time.

It is incredible that in less than a decade we should have lost knowledge about and prescriptions for mental health in the growing years so painstakingly learned in half a century. Parents and educators alike have become hysterical about achievement and competition. There is no place today for a child who underachieves in anything, no place for slowness of response, no room for gradualism in human development and individuality in learning. All children look like "underachievers" now. "Underachievement" is the watchword in child development, in homes, in schools, in the research games of the age.

Pressures on children to achieve more than they do or can, to do better even though they exhaust their resources, are universal, intense, unremitting. What is worse, the pressures as interpreted by too many children are vengeful in purpose. And we have decided that no one shall avoid the frantic pace. Even preschoolers—soon after birth, in the middle of a precarious relationship with their mothers, and all culturally different—are to be swept into this mad situation.

From *Childhood Education*, 44 (3): 148–154 (November 1967). Reprinted by permission of Donald McNassor and the Association for Childhood Education International, 3615 Wisconsin Avenue, N.W., Washington, D.C. Copyright © 1967 by the Association.

A sense of urgency that pervades education has reached ridiculous proportions. The need to be in a desperate hurry to keep children contemporary, to bring them to maturity speedily and to find weakness and close the gaps emphasizes children as objects to be manipulated and pressured into conforming to ever-accelerating production deadlines. The current argument is that the knowledge explosion produces a chain reaction that can result only in greater speed and pressure. If the situation is causing a rise in incidence of somatic tension and ulcers in children and youth,[1] no matter about that. Tranquilizers will take care of it when they are young; stronger drugs will help them forget when they reach college. And if we are going to make progress in the quantity and quality of education quickly, if in this new age we are going to make war on ignorance and backwardness, we seem quite willing to accept the heavy casualties of making war.

CHILDREN CANNOT TAKE CONSTANT PRESSURE, COMPETITION, CRITICISM

A generation of children is growing up in this high-pressure situation feeling they don't measure up, that somewhere they are failing and don't know how or why. I refer not only to underachievers but to achievers, too. This condition develops hostility in the young and contempt for traditional social values in a society. This is precisely what it is doing in more children and youth than we care to know about. Too many children psychologically are in much the same position as Joseph K. in Franz Kafka's *The Trial*.[2] He was tried and sentenced, never knowing what he was guilty of. In the course of the long trial he nearly lost his mind.

Children are pretty sturdy. They work hard to fulfill expectations in school; they can take a great deal of pressure to produce; they respond to challenges to improve. With support and encouragement, they are always ready to facilitate change and innovation. What children cannot take without ill effect is the kind of unremitting pressure and competition that imply constant criticism and weakness. Children cannot remain physically and mentally healthy by going through school with a nagging feeling that, in some way, they are not the kind of persons they are supposed to be; that no matter what they do, it is never enough. Children and youth will not become truly imaginative, affectionate and creative if they feel under pressure to be in a desperate hurry to compete for the best jobs, the top honors, the best grades, the good colleges, the better sections of classes at school, the classes most likely to yield high grade point averages. No school counselor is free from pressure by parents and children to get the right teachers.

---

[1] As claimed by Dr. Morris Wessel, of Yale University School of Medicine, and Dr. Robert McGuigan, director of School Health Services in Evanston and professor of Pediatrics at Northwestern University Medical School.

[2] Franz Kafka, *The Trial* (New York: Alfred A. Knopf, Inc., 1957).

Schools are now made up of only two kinds of teachers: the right ones and the wrong ones; the efficient and the inefficient.

HOME AND SCHOOL HAVE DEVALUED TIME TO GROW

A rich imagination and creative impulses are not produced in humans the same way we create space vehicles and cars. Children need periods of incubation, time to turn to an inner world of long thoughts, opportunities to become deeply involved with an idea or interest. Sometimes they need to hear themselves over the din of noises in the competition market. If every child has his own "Shakespeare" buried deep inside, as anthropologist Loren Eisely has said,[3, 4] I feel he has slender chance to discover it in the school of the 60's.

No matter if the world has speeded up and the rate of change enormously increased, so that each generation quickly becomes obsolete! *A child still needs time to grow up, to integrate what he learns, to consolidate what he means to himself in his time of ascendancy.* He needs time and desire to indulge in a little ordinary childlike activity that is not organized by adults. Since World War II, such activity has been increasingly prohibitive for many children. Home and school have devalued it. They make certain it is not on the program. Unorganized activity carries a penalty of guilt, of fear of getting behind in the frantic race to stay on top or to move up rapidly from the bottom.

SUICIDE MAY RESULT FROM CONTINUED PRESSURE

We have something to learn from the careful work of the physician, Herbert Hendin, who investigated *Suicide in Scandinavia* [5] over a period of years. His work is impressive because of the thoroughness with which he interviewed many youth and adults who seriously—not histrionically—attempted suicide. Their dreams were systematically analyzed. Suicide rates in Denmark and Sweden are among the highest in Europe and the world; the rate in Norway, about the lowest. Families and schools of the two high suicide countries, in contrast to Norway, place great emphasis in child development on rigid conformity, strong emotional dependence on parent and teacher, discipline through instilling guilt about letting the parents down, and a high level of performance pressure set by the society. In Denmark the child is taught to avoid standing out or showing too much individuality, another form of conformity. The Swedish child is under ceaseless pressure to get an early start, to excel, to compete, to acquire goods. And he starts

[3] Loren Eisely. *The Mind as Nature* (New York: Harper & Row, 1962), p. 50.
[4] See *All Children Have Gifts* (Washington, D.C.: Association for Childhood Education International, 1958).
[5] Herbert Hendin, *Suicide in Scandinavia* (New York: Doubleday Anchor, 1965).

the process early, for mothers are anxious to get to work as soon as possible when the child is very young.

Penalties for failing to behave in prescribed ways, according to Dr. Hendin, are loss of parental affection, hurt feelings by adults, and shaming. In Sweden and Denmark children are conditioned against showing anger and aggression.

In Norway, one of the lowest countries in suicide rate, the situation is just the reverse: more freedom for the child to grow up gradually and to develop individually, less emphasis upon competition to achieve or upon social or intellectual conformity. The Norwegian child is encouraged to find his own way and become independent—parents do not prescribe what he is to become. It is expected and accepted that he will respond to life with strong emotions of anger and quick response to unfair treatment.

The lesson is appropriate in the context of the frantic pace, despite the factor of national differences in culture and temperament. Put enough pressure [6] on children either to achieve and excel or to remain anonymous; give them early a tight performance schedule; remove unconditional love as a strong ingredient in the relations of wives and husbands and children (divorce is common in Denmark and Sweden, as in America); use guilt and shame as the principal disciplinary device; condition children to be calm, to control their anger, and a high incidence of adult and adolescent suicide is the result. This is the kind of prescription being written for many children in America.

Symptoms of Frenzied Pace

If this frenzied pace in education sounds exaggerated, a few clear symptoms can be cited. When I saw the first emergence of these I, like everyone else, was inclined to write it off as a minor penalty for attaining excellence in all spheres of American society. Our schools unquestionably needed improvement. A new age had begun and the old perceptions and solutions to human and technological problems would no longer suffice. America had to get going, schools had to get going, children had to get going. The pace had to quicken; more quality had to be built into education. As time passed, and the backwash from the pace emerged, it became clear to me that *we were not going toward a better society at all and that in the process we were laying the foundation for developing children who later would become alienated.* I am appalled at a situation where, as we become technologically more advanced, children become more suspicious, revengeful and alienated. Some of the symptoms are:

1. Increasing signs of somatic tension and illness in the young as a re-

[6] See *Don't Push Me!* (Washington, D.C.: Association for Childhood Education International, 1960).

sult of anxious parents controlling the child's responses, demanding and attacking rather than reinforcing a sense of worth. C. Henry Kempe, M.D., chief of Pediatrics at the University of Colorado Medical School, calls this "the battered child syndrome," and he sees it becoming more widespread.[7]

2. The feeling of secondary school students that they have distant, impersonal relations with teachers. There is so much to be taught in large classes, and so little time, that teachers cannot pay much attention to individuals. The growing feeling in students that teachers are not interested in the individual may not be as true as it seems, but this is the way students "read" it. The fault is not entirely due to large classes; it is also due to the pace, the desperate hurry, the acceleration all along the line. Acceleration has brought pressure to conform and to produce. This is partly what the widespread discontent on college campuses is about; why students press for more real involvement in their educational development. And it is beginning to show up in high schools.

3. Pressures on young children by parents and school to achieve excellence in every subject. There is refusal to acknowledge that a child may have a developmental temperament favorable to higher achievement in the arts or the humanities than in science or math, or the reverse. When grade cards come home, the first focus always is on the weak spots. Then there is the frantic race by everyone to raise the marks for each subject. Parents become desperate—they hire tutors; they cut out more of the child's unorganized time; they buy electric typewriters in eighth grade and type some of his papers for him. They and their children court the teachers and counselors in an effort to win better grades. Certain tough courses are avoided by some to keep the grade point average up.

4. Some high school students now talk about the importance of knowing the counselors well, saying the right things to them, for they know all too well the crucial place of the counselor's recommendation in college admission. One unenthusiastic letter can tip the balance in denial for admission to a college.

5. Increasing numbers of children and youth have a highly organized day from sunup to bedtime. To maintain this tight schedule, adults must constantly intervene to keep the level of pressure up. Quarreling and mutual distrust in the family are continuous. We are dissatisfied with our children as we have never been before. The fires of warmth, of support and affectionate ties in the home gradually become extinguished. Given the present climate, as more children compete to go to college, the situation will worsen.

6. State testing systems add pressure to the cooker. It is felt by every child, every home, every school. A state must not be far from first in the norms. A city must be toward the top of the state. School X must not fall

[7] Reported at the Los Angeles Pediatric Society's meetings, October 3, 1966.

too far down in a city. The individual teacher must show up well in this school. Now you know the logistics of this sort of thing. Many schools and children will have to show up poorly in the competition. Administrators and teachers feel the pressure. And, in the end, the children pay for not doing better. They pay by more impatience and pressure from teachers and parents whose competence is judged.

7. In the colleges, a growing group of students are reacting to the years of pressure in schools by leaving campus for a year or two. They are confused about how they got there, where they are going. They feel manipulated, pushed, controlled by their families and the colleges. A few openly fight this pressure and the value vacuum that surrounds it. Some are vigorously insisting on more involvement in deciding what is relevant in an education for this age. Read about the youth at Yale University who reject adulthood and traditional American values in Kenneth Keniston's *The Uncommitted*.[8]

Some educators fortunately recognize the unhealthy situation. Yale's President Brewster, in discussing the effects of the frantic pace, last year suggested that some youth need relief from the pressure situation by staying out of school for a year after high school graduation before starting college or between college and graduate school.

8. Reactions of younger children and their parents are well known to school counselors, administrators and physicians. Under constant scrutiny by parents are the child's every move at school; the grades he receives; the teachers he gets or doesn't get; the special class opportunities he receives or misses; his comprehension of the new math; the incessant questions by parents who are on the lookout night and day for any slippages, any discrimination. These children must sometimes feel that they are standing trial. Criticalness and doubt become the main substance of the parent-child relationship. Listen to parents as they talk and think about their children. Do they sound like people who enjoy their children?

9. The new vocabulary of educators makes it clear what they think about. A few terms of everyday conversation at school are: underachievement, below grade level, expectancy, advanced placement, upward bound, accelerated section, overachievement, honors sections, 22-minute modules, speed up, advanced introduction, enrichment, high powered, slow learner, fast learner. This vocabulary describes a new age in education, with its principal themes speed, pressure, competition.

CHANGE WAS OVERDUE

Lest there be misunderstanding, change in education was overdue. It took a war, the search for purpose and significance to life that always follows war, and a determination by the Russians to excel us in science and tech-

[8] Kenneth Keniston, *The Uncommitted* (New York: Harcourt, Brace and World, 1965).

nology to revive our critical faculties about the state of our educational system. It also took a population explosion, scientific discovery, and an increased awareness of the hollow men who inhabit the ugly, sprawling urban centers. Change had to come. Some of it has been ill advised; much of it may be for the better. Time will tell. The argument I make is that change brought a rapid increase in pressure to produce, anxiety about grades, and speed—all to the point of a frenzied condition.

Something scared the daylights out of us. Having a compulsive inferiority, we reacted and overreacted. (Not that we are different from other large nations in this trait.) More than ever, man worships at the "shrine of education and learning" as his only salvation. Every time there is presumed national disaster, threats from enemies, economic chaos, racial strife, the passing of an old order with rapid change toward an unknown one, we think education and the schools will rescue us. Then the pressure is turned up and the race is on. We think that all there is to improvement in the evolutionary process is the brain and the conditioned response. There is as much resistance to the idea of instinctual behavior in human ways as ever; ritualistic, organized learning, apparently, if there is enough quantity and quality, alone will save man from himself. This belief is bluntly rejected by Robert Ardrey in *The Territorial Imperative*.[9] The case he develops from impressive evidence, based on research on animal and man, is that man does not think because he has a brain. The brain didn't come first. It's the other way around—he developed a big brain because he thinks, because he has problems; and this makes all the difference for he still carries many of the old instinctual behaviors developed over that long period when the brain protected him from extinction. If we grasped this fully, we would not be in such a hurry, in such a frenzied state.

WHAT CAN PARENTS AND TEACHERS DO?

Parents and teachers wonder what they can do about the frantic pace that erodes the better human qualities of some children and youth. This pace as a way of life has to do with the whole of American society, with the fragmentation of personality in the twentieth century, and with explosive human conditions around the world. It has to do with urban existence; with invention, revolution and change; and with the fears and aggression of man.

Parents and teachers individually cannot get to the roots of the conditions that produce the frantic pace. But they *can* act with sensitivity and wisdom to reduce a needless amount of the sense of failure and self-criticism in children. Most of all, we are obliged, once the gravity of present trends is fully sensed, to avoid acts that increase the pressure and the pace from the present levels.

[9] Robert Ardrey, *The Territorial Imperative* (New York: Atheneum Publishers, 1966).

In large schools and large classes [10] better ways must be found to know and support the individual child [11] in his effort to meet the production schedule or to readjust it when it is unrealistic. The new flexible scheduling system in secondary schools will not be a gain unless it frees teachers to have more diagnostic and supportive conferences with pupils as individuals and in small groups.

WHAT CAN SCHOOLS AND COMMUNITIES DO?

School and community can be more cautious about introducing new programs to an ever-increasing pace. If a program clearly will not have the net effect of adding pressure on children up and down the line, and has real educational merit, so much the better. *It is common practice today to introduce new programs without critical evaluation of effects on children.*

It is time to play down speed and quantity in learning and to favor quality and individuality. Parents cannot do this alone for their child. Schools and colleges have to take the lead.

Something else can be done by parents while there is time—get off their children's backs; give children a little more free air to breathe as to what they want to become and how they are to get there.

Finally, let the impact of the frantic pace to remain contemporary become fully conscious to all of us. Assess it objectively as it affects the confidence of children. Recognize the erosion on affection that eats away the strength of a family to educate and humanize. Then we will respond to children as people reacting to unusual stress and pressure.

The quality of education had to improve. The pace had to quicken, but it did not have to engulf us all in a frenzy.

[10] See *Effective Learning and Teacher-Pupil Ratio*, by Alice V. Keliher (Washington, D.C.: Association for Childhood Education International, 1966).

[11] See *Individualizing Education* (Washington, D.C.: Association for Childhood Education International, 1964).

Autonomy and Inner Freedom:
Skills of Emotional Management

BRUNO BETTELHEIM

I have a strong conviction that the school must deal to a greater extent with the real psychological problems of our time. These problems arise both from man's susceptibility to emotional disorders and from the disintegrated behavior which often accompanies a changing society. Since ours will be an increasingly affluent society, and freedom from want will become a reality for most people, education would do well to concern itself with the development of an integrated personality. The individual with an integrated personality is able to relate successfully to other humans; he is able to analyze his past experiences and make inferences regarding his future behavior; and he has a sufficient understanding of himself so that he can develop and maintain his own sense of identity, responding to life's situations in accordance with his own interests, values, and beliefs.

In the school, we do the child a gross disservice when we surfeit him with prepared explanations of what life is about. There is, it seems to me, much to be said for developing the skill of learning from reality. Life, after all, is rarely as simple as it is made to appear in textbooks. The child who is accustomed to "prepackaged" explanations loses the capacity to produce them for himself. Conversely, the child in a secure environment analyzes the events of his life and develops increasing skill in solving his conflicts. Moreover, when the child is deprived of the opportunity to learn from reality, he becomes discouraged with his inability to find meaning in life, and he has no recourse other than to pattern his behavior on the most convenient and acceptable stereotype available.

There is much debate among educators about the best way to develop values and self-direction. We are inclined, as teachers, to tell the child too much. We are prone not only to an excess of lecturing, but to exhortation, platitudinous directive, and synthetic interpretations of "proper behavior." We would do better to saturate the school curriculum with active experiences that are prototypes of life itself. When we allow the child to experience life firsthand, we provide him with the best possible source of thinking material. If we then encourage him to interpret his experiences, gradually

From *Life Skills in School and Society*, 1969 Yearbook (Washington, D.C.: Association for Supervision and Curriculum Development, 1969), pp. 83–93. Louis J. Rubin, editor. Reprinted with permission of the Association for Supervision and Curriculum Development and Bruno Bettelheim. Copyright © 1969 by the Association for Supervision and Curriculum Development.

developing a sense of what is important and unimportant, the child can learn to decide "what is what" for himself.

Teaching of this sort requires a teacher who is himself sufficiently integrated that he does not need to take refuge in authoritarian behavior. Instead, he is able not only to tolerate and to accept, but to encourage the child's individuality. As most teachers know, meaning supplied by someone else has value only if it is internalized. If the child experiences authentic, life-like activities and is helped to analyze them and to extract useful generalizations, he will come to regulate his own behavior. For this to happen, however, he must have an opportunity to test the validity of his conclusions in practice situations. He must learn for himself which solutions work and which do not. It is only in this way that we can deal with the problem of self-direction and facilitate the development of legitimate values.

Healthy interpersonal relationships, whether between teacher and student, or between student and student, cannot be learned from books. Nor can they be developed by listening to lectures or watching television programs. They can only be learned through a succession of increasingly successful interactions with others. The school's instructional program is not my area of competence; the educational specialist will know better than I how to arrange for such experiences in the school. However, I am convinced that skill in achieving successful interpersonal relationships is infinitely more important in life than command over a collection of facts. It should also be clear that the acquisition of substantive knowledge and the development of effective interpersonal skills must be solicited through different activities.

The problem of inter-ethnic relations again serves as an example. The war between black and white has become an important social problem. The schools are expected to help alleviate matters. We must remember, however, that our educational system obeys societal norms; it does not set them. The problem will not be corrected merely by teaching children basic information on racial similarities and differences. A knowledge of racial characteristics, in and of itself, is not likely to overcome any individual's tendency toward hostile and discriminatory behavior.

For the Negro, reality cannot be swept under the rug. There is no mistaking the truth. He knows that economic success and outward appearance determine the extent to which he will be accepted in society. The poor Negro child knows that he has two strikes against him, even if the school wished to deny it. It is more realistic, and better for the child, to show him how other minorities that have faced discrimination have had to work twice as hard to progress; how unfair this is; how he can accept the challenge and succeed despite it. Because it is all so unfair, it is understandable that he wants to say "to hell with it all," but we can help him to see that such an attitude will not get what he wants for himself now, or for his children later.

There are many social problems which must be rectified with social correctives, but only those who have educated themselves well will find the right correctives. While we can and must eliminate unemployment and hunger, it is unlikely that there ever will be a society where some are not poorer than others. Those who are poor will always tend to blame it on the power structure of society. What we call the "racial problem" is really a problem of modern industrial society. Moreover, it is a problem that is restricted neither to America nor to the relationships between black and white. The fact is that in all places and in all times the children of the poor have had only limited access to good education, and their economic capabilities have therefore been severely restricted. There is, in short, a continuing and universal resentment of the rich by the poor. It is silly for whites to feel guilty because their ancestors mistreated the Negro. More properly, they should consider the fact that while some whites and some Negroes live in comfort, other whites and Negroes live in squalor, and they should reflect on what this does to each of the groups.

The relationships between black and white are heavily conditioned by the fact that most whites are more affluent than most Negroes. The widespread uneasiness over white-black relationships is of the same order as the uneasiness in the relationships between rich and poor. Put succinctly, color prejudice is based predominantly upon class differences. Lower-class whites frequently are more prejudiced than upper-middle-class whites. Each class is jealous of the class immediately above and fearful of the class immediately below. At the moment, ours is not a classless society, nor has it ever been one. Nor, with rare exceptions, have the rich and poor ever lived together amicably. If we wish to improve matters we cannot continue to confuse an economic and class problem with what seems like a race problem.

Admittedly, color differences, long used to camouflage class distinctions, have by now become a serious problem. Intolerance of any sort stems from anxiety and frustration and manifests itself in hostility. Until we are able to overcome discrepancies in our social and economic systems, we will continue to have class distinctions. And as long as class distinctions persist, it is likely that some lower-class whites and Negroes will continue to behave suspiciously, sometimes even aggressively, toward middle-class Negroes and whites, and, therefore, middle-class persons will continue to be uneasy, even suspicious of those in the lower classes.

Education can help people to learn to find life situations rewarding rather than defeating. Yet if we hope to influence basic personality, we must begin when the critical aspects of personality formation are under way. We must begin to be more specific, well before the formal school experience, and we must remain fixed on the objective throughout schooling. Interracial tolerance cannot come about unless we help children, from the very beginning, to feel secure within themselves and in their place in society. If we succeed in this, then they will be able either to store their hostility or to deal with it through integration.

A society in which the discharge of hostility and aggression—racial and otherwise—is tolerated is a bad society for all of its citizens. If we can help the child to feel protection in gratifying interpersonal relationships and provide him with opportunities for experiences which teach him successful and acceptable ways to reduce his tensions to a manageable degree, the child will gradually learn that hostility and other emotions can indeed be managed.

SELF-AUTONOMY

It has been repeatedly observed that individual autonomy is increasingly threatened by societal shifts. This diminishing autonomy stems not from the laws of man or from the media of mass persuasion, per se, but rather from the individual's failure to prize his autonomy. As his capacity to function autonomously decreases, his vulnerability to mass persuasion increases. When one examines the current social scene, it is obvious that it is becoming difficult for people to develop a satisfying intimate life characterized by spontaneity, freedom, and richness. The individual seems to be less and less able to call upon inner resources with which to countervail the growing complexity of our social and technological systems.

There is little point in bemoaning the erosion of personal freedoms since social change and technological advancements are inevitable in the course of human events. It is equally pointless to long for times past, or to try to separate one's self from reality. The constraints of mass society, the potential of nuclear destruction, poverty and unemployment, and the mounting antagonism of the world's "have-nots" are facts of life. We must deal with them as rationally as our intelligence permits. We can also help people to arrange their lives so that individual conflicts are reduced, and so that each person is able to derive maximum personal satisfaction from living. What we must avoid, to repeat an earlier point, is the illusion that we can relieve our emotional wants and discomforts with escapist tactics—whether the tactics are ignoring reality, becoming reactionary, or growing alienated. If we continue to avoid issues, we will have to invent more and more evasive tactics which ultimately will be useless in the face of inexorable social change.

The more powerful a society becomes, the less autonomy the individual is likely to enjoy. A pattern is thus established: as the individual is less able to engage in self-regulating behavior by making meaningful decisions for himself, he becomes more dependent upon external regulation and thus more open to deep-seated conflicts. Emotional disturbances result from unresolved conflicts. To resolve a conflict, the individual must have developed a well integrated personality. Coping ability comes from successful experience in solving past difficulties.

Conversely, when the individual fails to solve his conflicts, his sense of adequacy is severely diminished. In periods of rapid social change the range of alternative behaviors is substantially enlarged. The greater the range of available alternatives, the more difficult it becomes for the inadequate individual to cope. It is for this reason that periods of social change tend to increase the anxiety of people who find decision making difficult. It is highly unlikely that the growing imbalance between accelerated social transition and people's capacity to adjust to sudden change will be ameliorated unless schools pay greater attention to the enhancement of personality integration.

The elements of life which are of fundamental significance in our living are also the principal source of our fears. We can see everywhere examples of man's ambivalence between utilizing the material benefits of modern civilization and yielding the freedom and individualism which are characteristic of less highly organized societies. Moreover, it is likely that the conflict between joining the system in order to benefit from its rewards and rejecting it in order to avoid its traps will be a continuous problem for the children now in school. What is required, of course, is schooling which helps individuals learn to make use of their societal advantages without losing their individuality and autonomy; without, in brief, being consumed by the mass society which serves them. It seems to me that this constitutes another vital reason for urging that the educative process allow the child to experience life directly rather than indirectly.

With respect to the development of emotional health, it is perhaps better for a child to fight with the boy down the street—provided that some adult sees to it that nobody gets hurt and that after the fight is over they are helped to resolve their difficulty—than to read about the Civil War. The abiding disadvantage of television, similarly, is that it substitutes vicarious experience for real life. While we must deal with children in groups, the development of emotional health is a highly individual matter. Thus, the school must assist the individual within the group to understand his own emotional malaise and permit him to acquire techniques and attitudes which enable him to manage his anxieties.

Repeated success in resolving sensed threats in the home is the best assurance of later ability to cope with threats in the kindergarten. Similarly, the successful resolution of conflict situations in the third grade establishes a base from which one may ultimately deal with conflicts in college. Since humans in all societies must find a balance between self-interest and the welfare of the group, the skill of striking a balance of this sort is nurtured through repetitive experience and practice in the school. Even in the earliest school grades, the child can begin to develop skill in serving both his own interests and those of his group.

MANAGEMENT OF CONFLICT

The resolution of a conflict is a matter of reaching a decision as to the most advantageous behavior within the context of the existing circumstances. To make such a decision the individual must first rule out behavior which is

not consonant with his own values and personality. This ability to use knowledge of self in conjunction with an analysis of circumstances in order to
determine the most desirable behavior is the essence, the distinguishing
characteristic, of the integrated personality. We base our behavior on our
values, right or wrong, whether they have been learned in the school or
elsewhere.

The child whose personality is not sufficiently integrated, who has not
formed a consistent set of values, cannot test different solutions to his problems against his beliefs and interests. Thus, he is unable to reduce the
conflict to a point where it is manageable. He is literally overwhelmed by
the range of choices. Most of us recognize from experience that the greater
the number of behavioral alternatives the more difficult it is to choose the
best one. When we can reduce our options to two or three possibilities,
ruling out those which are clearly untenable, the process of decision making
becomes easier.

Out of these observations some obvious clues for education can be extracted. From the earliest point, the child's education must help him to
develop guidelines for determining the best way to gratify his instinctual
desires. As his life experience enlarges, he must acquire a corresponding
ability to resolve new conflicts by arriving at decisions which are commensurate with his developing system of values. In this manner he becomes
increasingly adept in the analytical process which facilitates decision making. The school does the child a lasting disservice when it resolves his
conflicts for him. He is similarly harmed when the school protects him from
natural conflict situations. As a matter of fact, if conflicts did not arise
routinely in the course of school life, teachers would be advised to create
artificial ones in the interest of providing the learner with crucial practice
in decision-making activity. The more natural and lifelike the school environment, the more likely that the emerging conflicts will be authentic
and useful.

Such an approach to schooling is probably the best way to ensure that
the child will eventually become "captain of his own soul," able to find
satisfaction in life and respond to his circumstances in ways which are
appropriate and satisfying. It is also the best way of reducing the danger
that he will be prey to the ready-made solutions offered by others or to the
mass rites of the society. The thoughtless acceptance of outward direction
or the mindless emulation of the behavior of others not only debilitates the
individual's uniqueness and his desire to control his own life, but it also
produces behavior which may be grossly unsuitable. The uncritical acceptance of direction in one's external life soon spreads to the internal life as
well, because, in the last analysis, the two are inseparable.

Personality integration is a continuous process. Once the person's behavior has become habitual, it can be modified only after he becomes
convinced that the required changes are worthwhile. Moreover, the unlearn-

ing of behavioral habits is in itself an exceedingly difficult pursuit. Even after the individual is willing to change, the mastery of the new behavior and its ultimate integration with his personality become a profoundly complex process. It is because behavioral change is so complex and so difficult that it behooves us to do everything possible to assure that healthy behavior is developed from the beginning.

The requirements of organizational efficiency in the school are very real, and unless great care is taken the child's sense of personal identity could easily be lost in the press of group life. While some conformity is essential to the operation of the school, educators should remember that the scope of socially acceptable behavior in our society permits a considerable degree of individuality. A feeling of individual uniqueness is extremely important to all of us. In order to find pleasure in life, one must have reasonable power over self and circumstance. All humans are impelled by conflicting motivations. The ability to balance these conflicts of interest stem from the inner freedom upon which emotional health depends.

There are, to be sure, limits to the extent to which the school can nurture each child's individuality. Nevertheless, we rarely approach these limits. Because he is anxious to please his taskmasters, even the emotionally healthy child may be seduced into excessive conformity. The schools must acknowledge that there are major differences in taste, in work habits, in the sources of pleasure, in ways of relating to others, and, generally, in the manner in which humans respond to life. It is presumptive, foolish, and dangerous to attempt to teach children the "correct" way to live. As I have suggested earlier, loss of identity is followed by loss of autonomy and by an unwillingness to be self-directive. By autonomy, it should be clear, I do not mean iconoclastic behavior or the deliberate effort to be different merely for the sake of difference. Rather, I mean man's inner ability to govern himself, and his private attempt to find meaning and relevance in life.

CONFORMITY AND INDEPENDENCE

The school must help the child to find the delicate balance between conformity and independence. The child must learn to carry on constant negotiations between his own interests and those of his group. He cannot do this, however, unless he has first learned to manage opposing tendencies within himself. In this fashion he comes to terms with his own nature and his own values. In turn, he becomes comfortable in his own inner convictions. He achieves, in sum, the consciousness of freedom which makes hypocrisy unnecessary. The child who has successfully achieved this consciousness of freedom will not need to engage in desperate and often futile behavior in order to overcome the emptiness of his life; he will not need to counteract his anxieties with drugs, promiscuity, or rebellion against authority.

The school can contribute greatly to integration of the child's personality by allowing him maximum autonomy in making decisions regarding his own behavior. Too often, it seems to me, schools approach problem solving within relatively narrow intellectual limits. While it is undoubtedly useful to know how to solve a problem by using a mathematical equation or by applying the law of supply and demand, it is, perhaps, of even greater importance to be able to solve an emotional problem by behaving appropriately. As I have repeatedly suggested, problem-solving skills thrive upon exercise and, conversely, grow fallow from disuse.

Much of the school's instruction is based on the belief that the salvation of man depends primarily upon rational behavior. While man, of course, must be motivated by rational considerations, his well-being also depends to a large extent upon his emotional life. A rational society, obviously, is no guarantee that there will not be any unhappy people. In contrast to other societies where men are still obsessed with acquiring the material necessities of life, our own society is becoming more and more preoccupied, not with the economic wherewithal for life, but with the freedom to affect and influence one's social and physical environment.

The self-direction which is so essential to free man depends upon the extent to which one can make decisions which genuinely alter the significant aspects of life. The more we encourage people to quest for practical and efficient results, the more they are likely to regard inner decisions which have no practical application as a waste of energy and as meaningless exercise. In consequence the spontaneity so important to the human spirit and the skill of inner decision making so essential to emotional health are both damaged.

Psychoanalysis helps the disturbed individual to regain fuller human functioning. Its method is to assist the individual to face a dangerous situation directly, instead of denying its existence or neglecting the dangers it poses. The method works equally well with individuals who are not seriously disturbed.

In conclusion, then, I would submit that our schools must be prototypes of our culture, posing real obstacles, real threats, and real conflicts. The overwhelming advantage of school is that the child can, under the sensitive ministrations of his teachers, survive his failures. He can have a second, third, and, if he needs it, a tenth chance. In the world outside, however, he may not survive his first failure. The school must neither be a sheltered haven nor a place where the expression of anger, hurt, fear, and other emotions is forbidden. The schoolhouse, after all, is a place to learn, and one ought to be able there to learn about life the way it is.

Subject Matter with a Focus on Values

SIDNEY B. SIMON AND MERRILL HARMIN

How increasingly irrelevant the schools seem! Social conflicts range all around us and the schools (the universities, too) go trotting down their "bland" alleys and continue to devote teaching time to grammar drills, the founding of Jamestown, and the urgent problem of how tall the flag pole is if its shadow is fifty feet at high noon.

If only we could see that the confrontation of high noon is here now, and if any drills are in order, perhaps they ought to be riot drills. If we must measure shadows, let them be the shadows of de facto segregation which cloud our land.

Of course this is not easy. Almost all of us feel tremendous ambivalence as we wrestle with that question of just how much of the standard subject matter of the school is to be set aside to make room for dealing with the current concerns of our society. We can all too quickly cite the fact that these problems are not the school's fault, and that they are too big, too all-encompassing to be tackled in school anyhow. Or we say we have other obligations, like teaching our students the inheritance of man's intellectual past.

What a school budgets time and money for, however, tells what it prizes. What and who it rewards tells what it cherishes. What the school asks on its true and false questions says more than almost anything else what it cares about, and just now, with the heavy emphasis upon college entrance, the schools care most deeply about putting in more subject matter.

We are not going into that weary either/or argument about subject matter *or* play-play-play. We have nothing against subject matter, per se. We do have an urgent need, however, to make subject matter more relevant, and to us, relevancy means that the subject matter *must* illumine a student's values. Louis Raths puts it this way: "The function of information is to inform. To inform what? To inform our values."

From *Educational Leadership,* 26 (1): 34–39 (October 1968). Reprinted with permission of the Association for Supervision and Curriculum Development and Sidney B. Simon. Copyright © 1968 by the Association for Supervision and Curriculum Development.

147

THREE LEVELS

Information which stays merely at the level of filling in the holes of a crossword puzzle, or name-dropping at a suburban cocktail party is information which we really do not need. So much of schooling is at this facts-for-facts level. There is a second level, a higher level, engagingly presented by Bruner, and this is called the concept level. We believe that there is still a higher level, a level which makes use of facts and concepts, but which goes well beyond them in the direction of penetrating a student's life. This we call the *values level*.

Let us look at an example to make this point. Take the favorite social studies topic, "The United States Constitution." We can teach this at the fact level, the concept level, or the values level.

I. *Fact Level* (U. S. Constitution)
1. Information about where and when the Constitution was drawn up
2. Who was involved and which colonies wanted what in it
3. Information about how it differed from the Articles of Confederation
4. Data on what was in the preamble and perhaps asking the class to memorize it
5. A list of the first 10 amendments and why they were called the Bill of Rights
6. The order in which the colonies ratified the document.

The above items should be fairly familiar facts to most of us, although we have probably forgotten the specifics. At one time this topic was presented to us in an organized manner, each fact building upon fact. Unfortunately, it was difficult to remember then and it still is hard to retain. It was of interest to only a few students and of little use even to them in any relevant search for values which might enlighten living in today's world.

Thus, many teachers tried to teach the Constitution at the *concept* level, encouraged by Bruner and his followers.

II. *Concept Level* (U. S. Constitution)
1. Our Constitution as a landmark in the evolving concept of democratic forms of government
2. The concept of "compromise" and how it operated in reconciling the economic forces of the period
3. The motives of the signers and the constituencies all representatives are obligated to serve
4. The social injustices which the Bill of Rights attempted to correct
5. The concept of amendment and how it has operated in state legislatures and in Congress
6. The Constitution today as seen in the actions of the Supreme Court and the American Civil Liberties Union, etc.

The above "subject matter" will be seen as the basis for good teaching.

It attempts to build relationships between random facts and to pull together generalizations supported by data. Many educators would be proud to have this kind of teaching going on in their schools, but we would argue that this approach is simply not good enough for these complex times. Let us look now at the *values* level, that third level to which subject matter needs to be lifted.

III. *Values Level* (U. S. Constitution)
    1. What rights and guarantees do you have in your family? Who serves as the Supreme Court in disputes?
    2. Have you ever written a letter to the editor of a newspaper or magazine?
    3. Many student governments are really token governments controlled by the "mother country," i.e., the administration. Is this true in your school? What can you do about it? If not you, who should do it?
    4. Should the editorial board of your school newspaper have the final say about what is printed in it? How do you reconcile the fact that the community will judge the school, a tax supported institution, by what is printed in the school paper?
    5. When was the last time you signed a petition? Have you ever been the person to draw one up? What did the last sign you carried on a picket line say?
    6. Where do you stand on wire tapping, financial aid to parochial schools, censorship of pornographic magazines, or the right of a barber to decide if he wants to cut a Negro's hair?

This kind of teaching is not for the fainthearted. It often hits at the guts, but if we are to see the school as more than a place from which we issue the press release each spring which tells which colleges our students made, then we must do more teaching at this third level, this values level.

Let us be clear that teachers are not to throw out facts and concepts. Obviously, these are essential if we are to have anything to base our values upon. On the other hand, let us say forcefully that Levels I and II, no matter how brilliantly taught, do not clarify students' values. That third level has to be consciously and consistently pushed.

To Inform Our Values

Here is another example to argue for our third level point of view. Take Shakespeare's *Hamlet*. It is a good example for three reasons. It is taught universally, it is universally taught badly, and it is a play particularly ripe with values-teaching possibilities.

I. *Fact Level (Hamlet)*
    1. Information on the year the play was written, and the sequence it occupies in Shakespeare's works.

2. What country did Rosencranz and Guildenstern come from?
3. How did Hamlet's father die? How do we know that?
4. What is the relationship between Hamlet and Queen Gertrude? Between Hamlet and Polonius? And Ophelia?
5. Identify these quotations and explain why Shakespeare put them in the play.
6. What is Hamlet's tragic flaw?
7. Who are all the people dead at the end of the play?

The above list is not meant to be all-inclusive by any means. Many other facts and details would be stressed by different teachers. Most teachers, however, feel at ease with such material. Students have been trained to feel comfortable with it, too. They know how to give the teacher what he wants on the kinds of questions which will be asked on tests. (True or False: Ophelia died from an overdose of rosemary?)

Teachers who are more aware will more often be teaching at the second level, the concept level.

II. *Concept Level (Hamlet)*
1. The concept of tragedy as opposed to comedy and how Shakespeare departed from the Aristotelian concepts of drama.
2. To understand the various thematic threads of: incest, indecision, revenge, etc.
3. To know the dramaturgy behind the "play within a play" concept.
4. The concept of "ghost" as it was understood by an Elizabethan audience.
5. Psychological concepts which motivate Hamlet, Gertrude, Laertes, etc.
6. The various ways *Hamlet* has been played by the great Shakespearean actors.

Again, our lists are merely suggestive. It should, however, be quite apparent that this kind of teaching is much more lively and meaningful as compared with the survey of routine facts or going over the play line for line. Nevertheless, it is a serious error *not* to take your teaching to that third level, the values level. *Hamlet* is so very well-suited to help students develop the skills of clarifying their values and evaluating their lives. We believe that questions like the ones below should help students to do this.

III. *Values Level (Hamlet)*
1. King Claudius supposedly killed to get ahead. How far will you go to get what you want?
2. Laertes hears his father's advice, and it comes out a string of clichés. What kind of advice do you get which falls on *your* deaf ears?
3. Part of *Hamlet* is about the obligation of a son to seek revenge for his father. Where do you stand on that kind of act?

4. Hamlet is cruel to Ophelia. In what ways have you ever been cruel to members of the opposite sex? When have you been the recipient? Is cruelty an essential part of love to you?
5. What are some things about which you are having trouble making up your mind? Where will you go for help? Whom do you trust? How will you know that you have made a wise decision?
6. What kind of son or daughter do you want to be?
7. Death is a regular happening in *Hamlet*. How close have you ever come to death? What part of you responds to a news story of death on the highway, death in Vietnam?

It might be well to take a look at the third level, the values level, questions posed here. For one thing, the questions have a heavy component of "you" in them. Among these "you" questions there are some which invite a student to examine alternatives and to follow out the consequences. Some search for elements of pride in his choices. All of them, hopefully, cause him to look more closely at his present life, to see it as related to the subject matter he is studying. Some of the alternatives show that the subject matter could be pertinent to his personal existence. This is essential, this linking of the facts and concepts to the choices and decisions in the student's real life, at least if we are serious about teaching for the clarification of values.[1]

Among these "you" questions there are several which get the student to look at what he is actually *doing* in his life. The questions about the United States Constitution at the third level illustrate this clearly. This action emphasis is very important in the search for values. Many of the social conflicts of our time rage on because so many of us have a giant gap between what we "say" and what we "do." For many of us this gap is a chasm.

These are troubled and confused times in which to grow up. To live life with integrity becomes more and more difficult for more and more people. The threads of alienation which are increasingly woven into our youth must give us all deep concern.

We must demand of the subject matter we teach that it make us more than politely erudite. We must insist that it relate to students' lives. It must pertain to the realities of life in this complex and confusing time. Subject matter which is lifted to that third level, that values level, will give us a fighting chance. We must not be guilty of ignoring Dag Hammarskjold's warning: "In modern times we are in danger of taking facts for knowledge, and knowledge for wisdom."

[1] For more on the values theory which supports this article, see: Louis E. Raths, Merrill Harmin, and Sidney B. Simon. *Values and Teaching*. Columbus: Charles E. Merrill Books, Inc., 1966.

Self-concepts of the Socially Disadvantaged

TRAVIS L. HAWK

Early American psychologists, especially William James, considered the self-concept important in behavior. Early in the twentieth century, the self-concept fell into disrepute for a number of years. This was a result of the advent of Watson's behaviorism and Thorndike's connectionism and other attempts to quantify and consider only observable acts in the analysis of human behavior. In the mid-thirties, however, as Gestalt psychology began to be well known in the United States and progressed through field theory, the self again came to be considered crucial in understanding behavior. Under the leadership of such men as Carl Rogers, Donald Snygg, Arthur Combs, and Abraham Maslow, this Gestalt-field theory movement has culminated today in a body of theory known as *phenomenology*. In phenomenology, the self is the central variable in behavior as well as in education and learning.

The purpose of the present article is to discuss some of the basic components of the self-concept, how it may be related to behavior, how it may serve as an impelling or an impeding influence on learning, and how it may be maintained or strengthened. Since there is much interest in children who have been described as culturally deprived, educationally deprived, and socially disadvantaged, I shall consider the self-concepts of these children and ways of changing them.

To understand the behavior of a person, one must understand how that person sees himself. Lecky sees all of an individual's behavior as organized into a single system, the nucleus of which is the individual's valuation of himself (1: 153). An individual cannot behave independently of the way he thinks about himself (2: 244). Many present-day authors believe that the study of human behavior begins with what a person says about himself. An individual defines his life role on the basis of values that constitute the self (3: 135).

What Is the Self?

According to Bartocci, the "self is a dynamic unity of the activities of sensing, remembering, imagining, perceiving, wanting, feeling and thinking" (4). The self includes the individual's idea of what he looks like and his

Reprinted from *The Elementary School Journal,* 67 (4): 196–206 (January 1967), by permission of The University of Chicago Press. Copyright © 1967 by The University of Chicago Press.

ideas of how he affects other persons. The self includes the meaning of one's distinctive characteristics, abilities, and unique resources. The self also includes attitudes, feelings, and values one holds about oneself, one's self-esteem or one's self-reproach or both (5: 116).

DEVELOPMENT OF SELF

The self is usually regarded as emerging from earlier learning experiences. Still, the current concept of self has a bearing on current learning experiences as it sets limits on the perception and the meaning of objects, events, persons, and symbols encountered. Thus, the self is an aspect of all one's experience and, at the same time, contributes to the quality and the form of all one's experience (6: 499). An individual's behavior is consistent with his perceptions of himself. Experience that is inconsistent with the self-concept tends to be rejected (7: 507). People who perceive or evaluate themselves as inferior or unacceptable to those around them operate under great psychological restraint (8: 236).

Dai holds that the self-concept forms the core around which all other facets of personality are organized (9: 566). Consequently, what a person thinks of himself, consciously and unconsciously, is the prime determiner of his behavior.

The importance of the self-concept in human behavior is probably demonstrated most adequately in psychotherapy. Rogers has found that psychotherapy deals, primarily, with the organization and functioning of the self (7: 40). According to Rogers, the process of therapy is to be explained with reference to a reconstruction of the self.

Although education is not and should not be perceived as psychotherapy, the educational process, by its very nature, affects a reconstruction of the self-concepts of children. Therapy is successful to the extent that the end result is a worthy, valuable, and realistic self-concept. Education has failed, regardless of the amount of knowledge imparted, when selves of pupils are inadequate, defensive, and characterized by a general feeling of incompetence in what matters to them.

The conceptions of the self described here indicate that the self-concept is learned through a gradual process of interaction with environment (7: 499). The self emerges as a consequence of learning experiences with other human beings and the introjection of their values and attitudes.

Hilgard suggests that the self emerges as a result of interpersonal relationships and becomes an object about which attitudes of approval and disapproval are organized (10). According to Mead, the self is constituted by an organization of the attitudes of other individuals toward one. The organization occurs as one engages in social behavior and participates with "significant others" (11: 186). The self, then, becomes organized with reference to the community in which one belongs or with reference to the generalized others and the social situations in which one finds oneself. The self originates and becomes organized through appraisals of "significant others" (5: 116). The phrase "significant others" means those individuals who are important to one. They have status in the life of the child because of their ability to provide feelings of security or to intensify feelings of insecurity, and "to increase or decrease his sense of well-being" (12: 6). The individual acquires and has a self only in relation to the members of his social group. The structure of his self-concept expresses and reflects the general behavior patterns of the social group to which he belongs (13: 135).

According to Anderson, the first year of life is the most important for the development of the self-image (12: 7). Each succeeding year becomes less important. The self-image, or self-concept, is seen to be structured by adolescence. After adolescence, one's self becomes less subject to modification by "significant others." Before adolescence, one's status as a child is responsible for feelings of inadequacy and a lack of confidence. As one matures and comes to feel more adequate, he becomes less subject to manipulation and modification by other people.

Apparently, there are three kinds of cultural agents, or sources of social experiences, that interact to modify and shape an individual's conception of himself. The first cultural agents are peers in the neighborhood about the same age. Later, there are peers in age-mate societies and more remote adult figures, such as teachers, who represent institutions in the community. Identification with these "significant others" probably is the major process involved in the developing self-concept. The nature of the identifications and the nature of the resulting self depend on the personalities of the individuals in the environment. This environment or social milieu is of crucial significance in the shaping of the self.

Methods of discipline used by parental figures have their influence on the self-concept that is formed in childhood. Descriptive labels used in speaking of the child form a system of rewards and punishments through which the concept of self gradually emerges. Since relationships between parents and children are characterized by a high degree of emotional content, the family is one of the major contexts in which the self-concept develops.

It is not uncommon to find individuals who regard themselves as ugly or unattractive because their parents or other cultural agents imbued them with this notion, and no amount of evidence can convince these individuals that they are anything but ugly or unattractive (12: 2). The situation is especially tragic when the individual has attributes that are valued in his present situation, but, because of the early acceptance-avoidance pattern he experienced, he finds it extremely difficult to see himself in any way but the way he learned earlier in a situation close to him. Approval by "significant others" would have led to self-acceptance and self-respect; blame and rejection by "significant others," however, have led to self-rejection.

Groups of families compose subcultures distinct from other subcultures and the mass culture. The values of these subcultures are absorbed by the child and become a part of his concept of self (14). One of these subcultures is organized around ethnicity. Typically, a child identifies with an ethnic group at an early age. When the values of an individual's subculture are unique, and when there is great cleavage around these values, there is early and definite identity with that subculture (5). Awareness of social-class differences is fairly well established during elementary-school years. Awareness of these differences becomes a major basis for forming social groups by the time children attain junior high school age.

Are there discriminable differences between the self-concepts of the socially disadvantaged and the socially advantaged that may be responsible for differences in the behavior of these two groups? Recent writings have attributed many characteristics to the socially disadvantaged (15). I submit that the self-concept is formed through assimilation of external labels that are applied to the person. If this proposition is valid, we would expect that counterparts of these external labels would be represented in the self-concepts of children from disadvantaged cultures. In fact, several investigators have found the self-concepts of disadvantaged children to be characterized by low self-esteem, self-deflation, and self-depreciation (16, 17). These characteristics of the self are manifest in behavior as difficulty in interpersonal relationships, difficulty in accepting responsibility, and a general pattern of behavior that tends to be fearful and passive.

Disadvantaged children tend to aspire to ideals of personal beauty and fame, not to the moral and the intellectual qualities that are characteristic of the middle-class child (18). Maas found the relationships of lower-class parents and their children to be rigid, and the children were found to exhibit fear of parental authority (19). Frequently lower-class children come from strong mother-dominated environments and from large families, which tend to be a handicap to verbal development. In lower-class families there are fewer interactions between mothers and children than in middle-class families.

Not only does lower-class family life tend to differ from middle-class family life, but also the school life of the disadvantaged child is different from that of the advantaged child. For instance, Coster found that children from higher-income families are twice as likely as children from low-income families to get grades of A and B (20). Heintz found that the pupil from a lower socioeconomic class was given a mark four points lower than his higher-status classmate for work of equal quality (21). A child's socioeconomic status influences his academic success as much as his intelligence quotient does when grades are used as the criterion of success. The self-concept of the disadvantaged child, therefore, usually depreciates, and he has less self-esteem as a result of the educational process.

Teachers in culturally deprived neighborhoods feel uncomfortable about their inability to cope with the problems of cultural deprivation. Davidson and Lang found that children become aware of the teachers' attitudes toward them, and the self-concept depreciates as a result (22).

Disadvantaged children fare worse with their peers than with their teachers. Peers have described disadvantaged children as dirty, poorly dressed, bad mannered, unpopular, not good looking, unfair in play, and given to fighting (23, 24). With the exception of disadvantaged males participating in athletics, extracurricular activities largely include only middle-class pupils.

Battle and Rotter found lower-class children to be more externally controlled than middle-class children. People with internal control accept personal responsibility for what happens to them; people with external control attribute responsibility to circumstances outside themselves (17).

A word of caution should be added at this point. Children we classify as *socially disadvantaged* cover a wide range of abilities and backgrounds. General labels may be appropriate for some of these children, but not all of them. We do a grave injustice to these children when we expect all of them to be a certain kind of person. Each child is an individual with unique characteristics and deserves to be treated so.

This application of descriptive labels is one aspect of the current concern for the culturally disadvantaged that may have detrimental effects. Children tend to be seen as a class, and behavioral expectations are set up for a class. The child who has some but not all the characteristics expected of the class may be forced into a kind of behavior seen as appropriate for him because of his assignment to a classification.

Many children, otherwise socially disadvantaged, enjoy wholesome, affectionate relationships with their parents and siblings, and these children have favorable and healthy self-concepts. By the same token, some middle-class children suffer from negative labels, rejection, and unwholesome relationships with their parents and "significant others," and these children are handicapped by their unwholesome self-picture. I might add that regardless of external appearances and characteristics, any child who has an unfavorable picture of himself is a socially disadvantaged child.

CHANGING THE CONCEPT OF SELF

I have described the significance of the self-concept in behavior, and the development of the self-concept. We come now to the most difficult questions of all: Can one's concept of self be changed—be made more adequate? What educational practices appear to be most appropriate for this purpose?

I shall begin with two propositions: first, that the self is difficult to change; second, that when change does occur, it is very gradual. Once a self-image has been formed, behavior becomes somewhat compulsive and predictable. The individual expects people in subsequent environments to treat him the way original significant people treated him (12). When the child goes to school, he expects his teacher to behave toward him as his mother has. The teacher, in turn, may believe certain labels are appropriate to describe socially disadvantaged children. The teacher may not apply these labels verbally, but he may very well communicate them to the child through his behavior toward him. What I am saying is that the child and the teacher have preconceived notions about each other. The more nearly these expectations are met, the greater the likelihood that the child's concept of self will not change. The familiar role that both the child and the teacher have been playing becomes the most probable one, even though objective observation would indicate that it is uncomfortable.

People have a tendency to compulsively maneuver themselves into situations that are natural and habitual for them (12). A child strives to be himself in any situation and to live in accord with his concepts about himself (5).

Further, the concept of self serves as a censor for one's perceptions. An individual does not perceive what is actually in his physical and social environment. He perceives those aspects that relate to, enhance, and maintain the self. According to Rogers, as an individual moves toward a more positive view of self, he becomes more open to his experience (25). That is, he can be less defensive and does not have to distort what he perceives. He is able to perceive his world more realistically. The more unworthy an individual feels, the more defensive he has to be, and the more he has to distort his perceptions to maintain the person he thinks he is. The more unworthy an individual feels he is, therefore, the more difficult it is to change his self-concept.

Combs says that "it is people who see themselves as unliked, unwanted, unworthy, unimportant or unable who fill our jails, our mental hospitals, and our institutions" (26: 52). He describes the individual who has a positive view of self as one who expects to be successful, as one who behaves courageously, is less disturbed about criticism, is free to pay more attention to events outside the self, behaves unselfishly, does not have to be concerned about whether he is conforming. In summary, a positive view of the self permits openness and freedom.

To help an individual gain a more positive view of self, one first has to see the person as the person sees himself. This is the deepest way to know and respect him (27). It is wrong to substitute the world of the teacher for the world of the child. Much sympathy may be wasted on the disadvantaged child, who, according to our standards, is in pitiable circumstances. We evaluate his circumstances according to our own backgrounds rather than according to his. He may be quite comfortable, even though ragged, and would feel uncomfortable any other way. Moustakas wrote "correspondence of perceptual experience is perhaps the best basis for understanding what an experience means to another individual" (27). It is extremely difficult for one who has not been disadvantaged himself to view the world of a disadvantaged child from the child's vantage point. Possibly the only sub-stitute for a common background of experience is to listen with objectivity and warmth and to get to know the other person so well that we can feel with him, not about him.

The schools face a dilemma today in this important task of developing the self of disadvantaged children. Is the self of a disadvantaged child best developed when he is placed with other disadvantaged children or when he is placed with advantaged children? The trend is toward multicultural schools in the belief that the disadvantaged can overcome the ill effects of disadvantagement by associating with middle-class children. In fact, several studies have shown that upward social mobility is more probable when the lower-class child has access to the behavior patterns and the value standards of the middle-class child.

Yet, children formulate their self-concepts by comparing themselves with those around them. Is the disadvantaged child more likely to develop feelings of self-depreciation in a situation where there are many cultures than in a situation where there is one culture? Hawk compared culturally deprived boys and girls in schools attended predominantly by culturally deprived pupils with equally deprived boys and girls attending schools in predominantly middle-class neighborhoods (28). She found that the children in predominantly deprived schools received more friendship choices and leadership choices from their classmates. This finding suggests that the current emphasis on multicultural schools must consider the social relation-ships of children and their effect upon their self-concepts.

Probably the key word in improving one's concept of self is *acceptance*. An individual learns that he is adequate by being treated as if he were adequate. An individual learns that he is competent by performing success-fully on tasks that are appropriate to his level of competence. Combs suggests that "to produce a positive self, it is necessary to provide experi-ences that teach individuals they are positive people" (26).

In the literature two conflicting statements were encountered about acceptance. Combs says, "it is possible to distinguish between accepting an individual and accepting his behavior" (26:121). Moustakas says that it is not possible to accept a person and reject his values and ideals. One cannot separate an individual from his behavior. "Behavior is self" (27: 44). I agree with Moustakas' statement. If we accept the proposition that an indi-vidual's behavior is linked with his view of himself, I would think we would have to accept behavior as self.

In passing, however, I would suggest that when a teacher has to make negative comments, he make them about behavior, not about the person.

The child may differentiate between his person and his behavior. A negative statement about behavior may not have the self-depreciating effects that negative comments about the person might have. Ignoring a child may be even more damaging than negative statements. It is more threatening to be overlooked than to be punished (12).

SCHOOL AND SELF

Growth of the self is facilitated by understanding and acceptance. *Perceiving, Behaving, Becoming,* the 1962 Yearbook of the Association for Supervision and Curriculum Development, serves as the major basis for the ideas about education that are expected to lead toward a more worthy and more positive view of the self (26).

Warmth and acceptance in the classroom are essential to growth of the self. A pupil learns best in a situation where he feels he is respected. In such a situation he does not have to be defensive about his self because it is not under attack. Under situations of threat, the self is less open to spontaneous expression (27). In a warm atmosphere the child can express his feelings and experience acceptance instead of the rejection to which he has been accustomed.

A classroom climate that is high in challenge and low in threat provides self-discovery and appreciation through success experiences. The most significant learning occurs in a situation where threat to the self of the learner is at a minimum and the individual is free to explore the resources available to him (27).

Respect for uniqueness and the individualization of instruction require that each child be given tasks appropriate to his level of competence. If tasks are matched with levels of competence, success is assured, and a positive view of self is the result. If tasks are too easy, there is no challenge and no sense of satisfaction from completing them. If tasks are too difficult, failure, which adds to negative feelings about the self, is inevitable.

Emphasis on persons and feelings should be added to emphasis on knowledge, with emphasis on persons being the more important. Research indicates that emphasis can be placed on persons without any loss in learning of subject matter (29).

Assessment should be based on individual accomplishment rather than on group comparisons. The deprived child should be able to say with some satisfaction, "I am gaining. I can now read material or work arithmetic problems that I couldn't before." Isn't this preferable to "I was last in the class last time, and I am still last," when both statements may be true?

Encouragement and positive remarks should replace negative ones. In a recent study by Page, pupil performance improved to a statistically significant degree when teachers wrote encouraging comments on pupils' papers (30). A control group given a conventional mark without comments lost ground in performance during the same time.

Communication to each child that he belongs and that he is an important member of the group helps the disadvantaged child overcome negative views of himself. Each person must realize that "it is all right to let other people see the real *me*." He does not have to fabricate a *me* for others to see, a *me* that he feels will be more acceptable than the real *me*. An individual must know that he is in a situation in which it is comfortable for him to reveal the real *me* and not have to develop a *me* that he feels others will approve.

In the atmosphere I have described, the individual's evaluation of himself should improve. Krugman reports an experimental program in the New York City schools where self-concepts of deprived children were changed by giving them "the feeling that the school cared" and by arranging school tasks at such levels of difficulty that the children enjoyed continuous success experiences instead of accustomed failure (31). In this situation the changes in self-concept were accompanied by higher levels of achievement and better personal and social adjustment. Deutsch suggests that success experience is the key to a positive view of the self: "The lower-class child enters the school situation so poorly prepared to produce what the school demands that initial failures are most inevitable, and the school experience becomes negatively rather than positively reinforced" (32).

The value of positive regard by the teacher is attested by the research of Davidson and Lang (22). These authors investigated the relationship between children's perceptions of their teachers' feelings toward them and their own self-perception. A check list of objectives was administered under two conditions: "My teacher thinks I am" and "I think I am." A high positive relation (.82) was found between children's perceptions of their teachers' feelings toward them and the children's perceptions of themselves. The findings of this study suggest that children are aware of the way their teachers feel about them and that they see themselves in the same way the teacher does. The moral to this story is a simple one. If you want a child to feel positive about himself, feel positive about him.

One other study illustrates that what has been said here is not just theory but actually works in practice. Staines thought that teachers may be reliably distinguished by the frequency with which they use words that are likely to mold the self (29). Two pairs of teachers agreed to permit an observer to record and classify all that they said. The four teachers varied widely in the number of positive comments used. Most of the comments stressed performance and status. It was hypothesized that teachers who differ in the frequency of their self-referential comments would produce significantly different self-pictures. During a twelve-week period an experimental teaching method was used. Situations were arranged in which the child could see himself in various ways—as a planning, purposing, choosing individual who was responsible and accountable. During this period, positive comments were made that paid particular attention to preserving the children's status. All negative comments were avoided. An attempt was made to build adequacy by success and appreciation and caring for status. Teachers accepted the children's behavior in an effort to teach acceptance of self. To help the children develop an appropriate ideal self, the teachers helped establish suitable levels of aspiration directly by commendation or indirectly by allusion or suggestion.

These free methods made pupils more sure of what they were and more accepting of what they wanted to be and more accurate in their judgments of what others thought of them. During this twelve-week period a control teacher used typical high pressure methods and placed great stress on correctness, on passing examinations, and on the serious consequences of failure—all of which led to greater signs of insecurity and more negative views of the self. The two groups—the free group and the high-stress group —were compared on reading and number tests. The free group made slightly greater gains.

Considerations about the self present both hope and despair. Self-concepts are relatively stable entities, changing only very slowly through the experiences that are provided. No end product of education is more important, however, than one's concept of self. If an individual can look in the mirror and take pride in what he sees, his chances of success and happiness are good. As the ill effects of social disadvantagement are alleviated, the major advantage will lie in the way individuals view themselves.

REFERENCES

1. P. Lecky. *Self Consistency*. New York: Island Press, 1951.
2. W. Stephenson. *The Study of Behavior: Q-Technique and Its Methodology*. Chicago: University of Chicago Press, 1953.
3. M. Sherif and H. Cantril. *The Psychology of Ego Involvements*. New York: John Wiley and Sons, 1947.
4. P. A. Bartocci. "The Psychological Self, the Ego, and Personality," in D. E. Hamachek (editor), *The Self in Growth, Teaching and Learning*, 14–26. Englewood Cliffs: Prentice-Hall, Inc. 1965.
5. A. T. Jersild. *Child Psychology*. Englewood Cliffs: Prentice-Hall, Inc., 1960 (fifth edition).
6. G. Murphy. *Personality: A Biosocial Approach to Origin and Structure*. New York: Harper and Brothers, 1947.
7. C. R. Rogers. *Client-centered Therapy*. New York: Houghton-Mifflin, 1951.
8. D. Snygg and A. W. Combs. *Individual Behavior*. New York: Harper and Brothers, 1949.
9. B. Dai. "Some Problems of Personality Development among Negro Children," in C. Kluckhohn and H. A. Murray (editors), *Personality in Nature, Society, and Culture*. New York: Alfred A. Knopf, 1954.
10. E. R. Hilgard. "Human Motives and the Concept of Self," *American Psychologist*, 4 (September, 1949), 374–82.
11. G. H. Mead. "Language and the Development of the Self," in T. M. Newcomb and E. L. Hartley (editors), *Readings in Social Psychology*. New York: Henry Holt, 1947.

12. C. M. Anderson. "The Self-Image: A Theory of the Dynamics of Behavior," D. E. Hamachek (editor), *The Self in Growth, Teaching, and Learning.* Englewood Cliffs: Prentice-Hall, Inc., 1965.
13. G. H. Mead. *Mind, Self and Security.* Chicago: University of Chicago Press, 1934.
14. S. M. Jourard and R. M. Remy. "Perceived Parental Attitudes, the Self and Security," *Journal of Consulting Psychology,* 19 (October, 1955), 364–66.
15. F. Reissman. *The Culturally Deprived Child.* New York: Harper and Brothers, 1962.
16. D. P. Ausubel and P. Ausubel. "Ego Development among Segregated Negro Children," in H. A. Passow (editor), *Education in Depressed Areas,* 109–41. New York: Bureau of Publications, Teachers College, Columbia University, 1963.
17. E. S. Battle and J. B. Rotter. "Children's Feeling and Personal Control as Related to Social Class and Ethnic Group," *Journal of Personality,* 31 (December, 1963), 482–90.
18. R. E. Carroll. "Relation of School Environment to the Moral Ideology and Personal Aspirations of Negro Boys and Girls," *School Review,* 53 (January, 1945), 30–38.
19. H. S. Maas. "Some Social Class Differences in the Family Systems and Group Relations of Pre- and Early Adolescents," *Child Development,* 22 (June, 1951), 145–52.
20. J. K. Coster. "Some Characteristics of High School Pupils from Three Income Groups," *Journal of Educational Psychology,* 50 (April, 1959), 55–62.
21. E. Heintz. "His Father Is Only the Janitor," *Phi Delta Kappan,* 35 (April, 1954), 265–70.
22. H. H. Davidson and G. Lang. "Children's Perceptions of Their Teachers' Feelings toward Them Related to Self-Perception, School Achievement, and Behavior," *Journal of Experimental Education,* 29 (December, 1960), 107–18.
23. W. L. Warner. *Democracy in Jonesville.* New York: Harper and Brothers, 1949.
24. A. B. Hollingshead. *Elmtown's Youth.* New York: John Wiley and Sons, 1950.
25. C. R. Rogers. "Toward Becoming a Fully Functioning Person," in A. W. Combs (editor), *Perceiving, Behaving, Becoming,* 21–33. Washington: Association for Supervision and Curriculum Development, 1962.
26. A. W. Combs (editor). *Perceiving, Behaving, Becoming.* Washington: Association for Supervision and Curriculum Development, 1962.
27. C. E. Moustakas. "True Experience and the Self," in D. E. Hamachek (editor), *The Self in Growth, Teaching and Learning.* Englewood Cliffs: Prentice-Hall, Inc., 1965.
28. J. Hawk. "A Comparison of Academic and Social Factors of Culturally Deprived Children Attending Deprived and Nondeprived Schools." Unpublished Master's thesis. Knoxville, Tennessee: University of Tennessee, 1965.
29. J. W. Staines. "The Self-Picture as a Factor in the Classroom," *British Journal of Educational Psychology,* 28 (June, 1958), 97–111.
30. E. B. Page. "Teacher Comments and Student Performance: A Seventy-four Classroom Experiment in School Motivation," *Journal of Educational Psychology,* 49 (August, 1958), 173–81.

31. M. Krugman. "The Culturally Deprived Child in School," *National Education Association Journal,* 50 (April, 1961), 22–23.
32. M. Deutsch. "The Disadvantaged Child and the Learning Process," in A. H. Passow (editor), *Education in Depressed Areas,* 163–80. New York: Columbia University, 1965.

Peer Socialization in School

GLEN H. ELDER, JR.

Although the student group is a valuable educational resource, it remains an untapped potential in the curriculum of most primary and secondary schools. Recognition of this potential is frequently obscured by concern over the peer group's contra-influence on student achievement and conduct. Considering the influence of peer groups on the social development of youth, Bronfenbrenner concludes that it is

> . . . questionable whether any society, whatever its social system, can afford largely to chance the direction of this influence, and realization of its high potential for fostering constructive development both for the child and society.[1]

The primary objective of this article is to examine structures and inter-action patterns in the classroom which promote the utilization and development of student resources within the peer-group setting.[2] Unlike the stress on social adjustment and conformity in earlier writings in education, the following discussion emphasizes the development of individual talents as well as social responsibility, cooperation, and tolerance through processes of social exchange, observational learning, and social reinforcement.

The first part of the article—on socialization as a transactional process—establishes a perspective for the analysis of classroom socialization.[3] This section is followed by an examination of the learning experiences afforded

From *Educational Leadership,* 26 (5): 465–473 (February 1969). Reprinted with permission of the Association for Supervision and Curriculum Development and Glen H. Elder, Jr. Copyright © 1969 by the Association for Supervision and Curriculum Development.

[1] Urie Bronfenbrenner. "Responses to Pressure from Peers vs. Adults Among Soviet and American School Children." *International Journal of Psychology* 2: 206; 1967.

[2] A longer version of this paper has been written by the author: Department of Sociology, Alumni Building, University of North Carolina, Chapel Hill.

[3] For a recent review of peer socialization in the elementary schools see: John C. Glidewell, Mildred B. Kantor, Louis M. Smith, and Lorene H. Stringer. "Socialization and Social Structure in the Classroom." In: Martin and Lois Hoffman. *Review of Research in Child Development* 2: 221–56; 1966. Russell Sage Foundation.

by inter-age and interracial relationships. The article is primarily restricted to children in elementary school for reasons of available data and brevity.

Socialization as a Transactional Process

Socialization entails social learning which prepares the individual for membership in society and in groups within the society; it facilitates transitions from one status to another by conditioning behavior for the new requirements of specific roles and group life. Such learning is influenced by the degree of coordination among socializing agents in goals and practices, and by particular training techniques and ecological contexts.

There are three *time emphases* in the socialization of children: (a) on the past—molding the young in the image of the older generation by transmitting the cultural heritage and by reinforcing traditional behavior; (b) on the present—orienting the child toward the standards of membership and role performance in his current groups, such as the family, age-group, and classroom; and (c) on the future—preparing the child for the anticipated requirements of future roles, groups, and transitions.

Socialization agencies are concerned to some extent with all three emphases, especially the contemporary demands of group membership, but schools in particular have major responsibilities in the preparatory task. In American society, the dominant time-perspective—toward the future—is most characteristic of the middle class, while an emphasis on the past and present is found in the upper and lower classes respectively.[4]

The influences to which a child is exposed include explicit training and a broad range of social conditioning which might be described as the unconscious patterning of behavior. Instruction and learning through observation are potential examples of these two types of influences.

Socialization is most commonly viewed as a one-way process which stresses the effect of the social agent on the child. Reliance on this framework has had the unfortunate effect of obscuring a basic source of socialization for authority figures—the young. Like parents, teachers partly learn their role, develop teaching skills, and acquire language patterns from the young.[5] A transactional perspective is sensitive to the way in which students socialize their teachers and each other, as well as to the influence of teacher on students.[6] Student and teacher are defined in terms of each other and behavior is a consequence of the reciprocal influence of each person on the

---

[4] See: Florence R. Kluckhohn and Fred L. Strodtbeck. *Variations in Value Orientations.* Evanston, Illinois: Row Peterson and Company, 1961. pp. 27–28.

[5] On language patterns, see: Emil J. Haller. "Pupil Influence in Teacher Socialization: A Socio-Linguistic Study." *Sociology of Education* 40: 316–33; Fall 1967.

[6] For a thoughtful analysis of classroom behavior from a transactional perspective, see: Ira J. Gordon. *Studying the Child in School.* New York: John Wiley & Sons, Inc., 1966.

other in a particular situation. A satisfying social exchange in this relationship generally creates conditions favorable to similar transactions among students in the classroom. Elementary school classrooms, in which the teacher encourages student participation in problem solving and decision making, are generally distinguished by a high level of interaction and cooperation among students, minimal conflicts, tolerance for divergent opinions, and responsible initiative in school work.[7]

In a teaching relationship that is truly reciprocal, the teacher at times is also a student, and the student—especially in adolescence—is also an instructor. The teaching role of the child is especially relevant to the situation of youth in a rapidly changing society, for as Erikson observes,

> . . . no longer is it merely for the old to teach the young the meaning of life, whether individual or collective. It is the young who, by their responses and actions, tell the old whether life as represented by the old and as presented to the young has meaning.[8]

Teaching becomes effective when the materials presented possess or acquire such meaning for the learner. Since teachers typically have relatively limited authority, this restricts the authority which they can reinvest in their students and contributes to the negligible control which students exercise over their education.[9] This handicap to meaningful teacher-student exchange is seen on all levels of formal education.

Up to mid-adolescence, the presence of children in school is a compulsory requirement, and thus the principles which govern social exchange in a voluntary relationship are not entirely applicable to teacher-student transactions.[10]

Nevertheless, it is apparent that social exchange with teachers is not a profitable experience for many students, and although restraints may keep their bodies in school, aggressive or passive responses to injustice and relative deprivation diminish the value of classroom experiences for other students. These consequences suggest that an equitable exchange of services, knowledge, and rewards should be an intrinsic objective in teacher-student transactions.

Teaching opportunities provide a basis for social exchange among students. The child who excels in a particular subject has the opportunity to gain competence and a sense of social responsibility by tutoring a slower student. Thus the slower student gains encouragement, understanding, and academic assistance from a person who is not socially removed by a large age difference and evaluative authority. The learning benefits achieved by

[7] Glidewell *et al.*, *op. cit.*, p. 232.

[8] Erik H. Erikson. "Youth: Fidelity and Diversity." *Daedalus* 91: 24; Winter 1962.

[9] James G. Anderson. "The Authority Structure of the School: System of Social Exchange." *Educational Administration Quarterly* 3: 145; Spring 1967.

[10] On social behavior as exchange, see: George C. Homans. *Social Behavior: Its Elementary Forms.* New York: Harcourt, Brace & World, Inc., 1961.

students in the teaching role generally affirm the principle that teaching is a valuable developmental experience. Student tutors gain as much or even more in academic learning than the students they work with.[11] When students are used as instructors of other students, aptitude heterogeneity within the classroom may be transformed from a teaching handicap to an educational asset. Both age and ability groupings can be viewed as consequences of a teacher-centered model of instruction. Such groupings facilitate the instructional task for the adult teacher, but limit teaching-learning possibilities within the student group. Systematic incorporation of tutoring relationships in the curriculum may help to reduce student indifference associated with the passive role of the learner.

SOCIALIZATION IN THE CLASSROOM

Socialization is a continuing process for the individual. Thus an understanding of peer influences and learning at one point in time requires an examination of the student's past, especially of his reinforcement history in family and classroom experiences.

One of the first tasks the child faces as he enters a new classroom in elementary school is to gain an understanding of his role, of where he stands in relation to classmates and the teacher. This cognitive map or perspective is associated with the child's developing status as defined by his peers.

In the first few days or weeks of class, students tend to sort themselves out on three status dimensions: (a) liking or social acceptance, (b) the ability to influence other students, and (c) competence in schoolwork.[12] One should note here the resemblance between these status dimensions among children in the classroom and those in the larger society, such as prestige, power, and wealth or accomplishment. Accuracy of the student's perception of his classroom status is generally greater among children of high versus low status (defense mechanisms are a factor here) and in classrooms with a clear status hierarchy. This determinant of status perception is likewise operative in the larger community.

In the elementary school, a child's status on these dimensions remains moderately stable from one grade to another. Although a causal sequence among these status factors cannot be confidently determined, the success of a child in working out friendships or accepting relationships with other students appears to have a very significant effect on his perceived ability to influence his classmates and to achieve.

The peer system in most elementary school classrooms includes several

[11] Robert D. Cloward. "Studies in Tutoring." *Journal of Experimental Education* 36: 14–25; Fall 1967; and Glen H. Elder, Jr. "Age Integration and Socialization in an Educational Setting." *Harvard Educational Review* 37: 594–619; Fall 1967.

[12] This paragraph and the next are indebted to a review of research by Glidewell *et al.*, *op. cit.*

subgroups, some dyads, and a few isolates. While there is little need to recite the widely recognized consequences of social rejection, studies of peer-group socialization have found that these effects vary in relation to the status structure of the classroom. Possession of low status in the eyes of classmates is most strongly correlated with negative attitudes toward school, low self-esteem, and under-utilization of mental ability when this status is correctly perceived by the student.[13] As noted earlier, clarity of the status structure increases the accuracy of this perception. More detailed information on the determinants and content of social exchange in elementary school classrooms is needed.

Conditions which foster beneficial exchange and learning among students are also those which lessen prejudice: equal status in the situation, pursuit of common goals, cooperative interdependence, and support from the main authorities, structures, and norms.[14] As individuals interact with one another under favorable conditions, they are likely to acquire common perspectives and more positive feelings toward each other.

While status equality and similarity in values, background, or skin color are significant bases of interpersonal attraction, there are tasks within the classroom which bring together children who would not ordinarily choose each other—such as the bright and dull, or older and younger students. The tutoring relationship is a good example. Rewards for tutor and learner are contingent on cooperative rather than competitive interdependence. Relatively equal rewards for progress on the teaching-learning task serve to reinforce cooperative behavior.

School Composition, Student Relationships, Learning

Social stratification and segregation in a complex society limit a child's knowledge and understanding of himself and of others from different life situations. In schools, the composition of the student body on sex, race, and family status specifies a particular type of learning environment, as do age-grades and ability groups. If the social composition of the classroom resembles that of the larger community and society, children have the opportunity to acquire an understanding and appreciation of social and cultural variation through observation, exchange, and instruction. Instead of reinforcing uniformity in the children of diverse groups in society, schools could utilize this diversity for broadening the knowledge and understanding of the students. Age-heterogeneous and inter-racial relationships are two examples of such diversity. The educational and social relevance of these experiences are suggested by the results of several recent studies.

[13] Richard G. Schmuck. "Some Relationships of Peer Liking Patterns in the Classroom to Pupil Attitudes and Achievement." *School Review* 71: 337–59; 1963.
[14] Gordon W. Allport. *The Nature of Prejudice.* New York: Doubleday Anchor, 1958. p. 267.

Cross-Age Relations

At the University of Michigan's Institute for Social Research, a series of exploratory investigations have been conducted on relationships between children of different ages in two elementary schools and in a summer camp for children from 4 to 14 years of age.[15] The main objectives of the project are to develop and implement a constructive program of cross-age interaction, and to assess the impact of inter-age perceptions and attitudes on both younger and older children.

The inter-age program among elementary school children included the following elements. Children in the sixth grades were assigned as academic assistants in the first four grades, where they helped the children with their course work. The effectiveness of the older students and the response of the younger children were contingent on the following training procedures.

The teachers were first oriented to the potential of cross-age interaction among students and teachers. The use of academic assistants was described as requiring the teacher to "lend the resources" of his children. At several points during the school day, older children were given special training in relating to younger children, and in teaching content material. In order to counter peer-group norms which did not reward interaction with younger children, the investigators asked a small group of seventh graders, who had high status among their peers and were experienced in working as helpers, to talk to the sixth graders about the benefits of the helping relationship.

The importance of these training procedures was reinforced many times in initial sessions with the older helpers. When asked, "What sorts of things have you observed at school or at home between youngers and olders?" the children reported few constructive encounters. It was common that "some bigger kids" were taking something away from, bossing, or shoving "little kids." One potential source of this dominance pattern is the process by which children learn age-norms in the family. The behavior of younger children is frequently derogated when adults attempt to reinforce age-appropriate behavior in their offspring.[16] "Don't act like your little brother" is a mild example of this practice.

The results of this experiment in cross-age interaction show that younger boys and girls perceive older children positively when the latter include them in activities, display friendliness, or offer help and recognition. The younger children tended to learn how to cope with adults and older chil-

[15] Peggy Lippitt and John E. Lohman. "Cross-Age Relationships: An Educational Resource." *Children* 12: 113–17; 1965; Jeffery W. Eiseman and Peggy Lippitt. "Olders-Youngers Project Evaluation." Report prepared for the Stern Family Fund and the Detroit Board of Education, 1966; and Ronald Lippitt *et al.*, "Implementation of Positive Cross-Age Relationships." Chapter 5 in unpublished manuscript, 1966.

[16] For a more detailed discussion of this point, see: Glen H. Elder, Jr. "Age Groups, Status Transitions, and Socialization." Prepared for the Task Force on Environmental Aspects of Psycho-Social Deprivation, National Institute of Child Health and Human Development, June 19, 1968.

dren; became aware of the abilities, freedoms, and limitations of older children; developed conceptions of the meaning of different levels of "grown-upness"; and gained an opportunity for greater reciprocity and autonomy than is possible in relations with an adult teacher.

The ability of the older children to communicate with younger children, coupled with their other services, greatly enriched the educational experience of both groups. Most of the older students were enthusiastic about the program, especially the low-achievers from low-status families, whose desire to learn and relation to authority figures in the school generally improved. The older children were given a chance to assume responsibility; to test and evaluate their knowledge, teaching, and social skills; and to work through personal problems encountered with age-mates and siblings.[17] In a number of cases, attitudes and skills acquired in the cross-age experience were transferred to relationships in the family.

Similar opportunities for cross-age interaction and exchange are available in nongraded elementary schools, but competent research on these processes is sadly lacking.[18] One searches in vain among countless reports on the nongraded school for any sophisticated examination of cross-age interaction, or even for any recognition of its educational potential. Reliable evidence on the academic effects is also lacking. In view of the social learning potential of age-heterogeneous groups, the need for well-designed research on cross-age interaction in this setting is compelling.

Interracial Friendships and Learning

The accumulation of research findings on interracial contact provides a preliminary appraisal of the social and academic effects of desegregated schools and classrooms. In the nationwide Coleman study,[19] academic performance and a sense of mastery among Negro students were related to the proportion of white students in their schools. Much of this effect is a consequence of the higher social class background and scholastic ambitions of the white students. More recently, studies supported by the U.S. Commission on Civil Rights show that close friendships with white students have a positive effect on the academic performance and attitudes of Negro students over and above the influence of student social class.[20]

Although observational research is needed to fill in the intervening proc-

[17] The results of this research are similar in many respects to the findings of a study of cross-age interaction in an adult-adolescent school. See: Glen H. Elder, Jr. "Age Integration and Socialization in an Educational Setting," *op. cit.*

[18] John I. Goodlad and Robert H. Anderson. *The Non-Graded Elementary School.* Revised Edition. New York: Harcourt, Brace & World, Inc., 1963; and Frank R. Dufay. *Ungrading the Elementary School.* New York: Parker Publishing Company, 1966.

[19] James S. Coleman *et al. Equality of Educational Opportunity.* Washington, D.C.: Superintendent of Documents, U.S. Government Printing Office, 1966.

[20] U.S. Commission on Civil Rights. *Racial Isolation in the Public Schools.* Washington, D.C.: Superintendent of Documents, U.S. Government Printing Office, 1967, Volume 2. Findings reported in the following paragraphs were drawn from this volume.

esses through which interracial friendships have their effect, a clue to such processes is suggested by available data on classroom social structure; emotional acceptance is related to leadership status, self-esteem, and the utilization of abilities. Among Negro students in the study, possession of close white friends was correlated with their involvement in extracurricular activities and a preference for desegregated schools regardless of the racial composition of the classroom.

On the other hand, interracial tension—which was inversely related to the length of time students were enrolled in a desegregated school—had a negative effect on the attitudes and performance of Negro students. Desegregated schooling in childhood has also been found to be related to positive interracial attitudes among Negro adults.

The interracial consequences of desegregated schooling and close Negro friends were similar among white students. White students with close Negro friends were less likely than other white students to prefer an all-white school, regardless of the proportion of Negro students in their classroom. Length of time in a desegregated school—a crude index of exposure to the socializing influence of a biracial setting—was related both to having Negro friends and to a preference for desegregated schooling.

These limited findings are a mere step toward an understanding of interracial contact and learning in the schools. Classroom observations and laboratory research,[21] in particular, are needed to supplement the findings of survey research.

The educational resources present among students in a classroom may either be utilized within the curriculum or ignored. The challenging task for teachers with biracial or age-heterogeneous classrooms is to use these resources creatively in furthering the social and academic learning of their students.

What task in the classroom can effectively bring children differing in age, race, and aptitude together for exchanging services, ideas, and experiences in a mutually rewarding relationship? Equally important, what conditions sustain an equitable social exchange between teacher and students?

[21] An example of the kind of experimental work needed is described in: Irwin Katz. "The Socialization of Academic Motivation in Minority Group Children." In: *Nebraska Symposium on Motivation* 15: 133–91; 1967. David Levine, editor. Lincoln: University of Nebraska Press.

Discipline as Curriculum

RYLAND W. CRARY

Discipline is not a "bad" word; it is an educational necessity. The necessity in educational discipline is the maintenance of a learning situation. But it is necessary to beware of appearances. The appearance of perfect order need not mean that learning is taking place; neither need disorder mean that dynamic learning is in the making. Schoolteacherishness and hooliganism are both equally productive as springs of bad discipline.

"Schoolteacherishness" is our term for most of what is wrong—of what is unprofessional—about instruction in the schools. Two factors in schoolteacherish discipline are tradition and insecurity. Most adults, if told to perform the role of a teacher, would exhibit schoolteacherish discipline. Children also know the role well, and when playing school, they parody the classroom from time immemorial: "That was the bell. Quiet now. Johnny, are you chewing gum? Spit it out. You know very well we don't chew gum in school. Now, class, let's all turn our books to page 111. We don't speak without raising our hands. Did you have permission to speak? Nice little girls don't whisper; do they, Mildred?"

A realistic analysis of the disciplinary problem also includes "hooliganism." We shall use the term as a descriptive label for customarily destructive or disruptive models of behavior. A student may exhibit hooliganism but is not necessarily a hooligan. The mode of behavior should not be used to stereotype the individual or generalize overconfidently on his essence.

The romantic would tell us that "there are no bad boys," but even he must admit that there are boys who behave badly. Challenge rather than theory confronts two million teachers daily. Often this challenge is in the form of a personal or organized attempt to resist the establishment of a learning situation. The challenge must not be minimized; it is a challenge to the institution of the school itself. The school does not solve its problem by labeling its students "bad," but it should begin by acknowledging and defining bad conduct.

Bad conduct is part of the culture of the school, and not all of it is grim. The school as an academic institution has often taken itself too seriously, and this has invited comic perceptions quite often. Students tramp in unison while visitors walk the aisles of study halls; sneezing fits run epidemic through assemblies when dull speakers hold forth; a dozen students exhaling through old pipestems turn a library into the atmospheric counterpart of a corner pool hall; snakes, toads, and mice still appear in surprising places;

whole classes resist efforts to be brought to order; erasers, books, dough-balls take wing; paper gliders float lazily in somnolent classrooms in late September afternoons; and we can recall a day after Halloween when a live horse was found in a third floor room, a legend that will endure as long as the author's alma mater stands. Such deeds scarcely facilitate learning, but they wrench the school from grimness; they remind the schoolteachers that people are around; they assert that the drama of the school, like that of life, is incomplete without comedy. The school very often can control overextensions of such correctives by joining in the laughter. Let one teacher join the burlesque of sneezing fits and the epidemic ceases in appreciative laughter.

Not all bad conduct derives from philosophy. Students may steal, lie, betray, attempt rape or mayhem, commit arson, and burglarize. They may blackmail, bully, and extort; they may serve as agents in the peddling of dope and pornography among their fellows. Students have even murdered within the school. These deeds are too serious to be funny, and they do not contribute to constructive learning. Fortunately, such deeds are not typical of the school, although they are brought to the school. Their incidence should rule out sentimental conclusions or retention of the thesis that discipline is a term somehow inappropriate to the modern or humane educational vocabulary.

Conduct that is bad in the societal sense is criminal behavior and is sometimes brought to the school. Even this behavior must be understood as well as policed, but it is beyond the school's capacity to cope with criminality. School discipline must be such that it competently copes with the challenge to maintain a learning situation. Students come to school "damaged," and sometimes the school contributes to this damage. The damaged personality presents a real danger to the school because of four basic misperceptions that such a person brings to the classroom:

1. A damaged view of human worth and dignity
2. An inadequate view of what learning means to the particular individual
3. A hostile or disparaging view of the school
4. A disregard for and a sense of disaffiliation from the institutions of society

The school does have an obligation to help the damaged individual, but it also has an obligation to prevent such students from denying others the right to learn. Thus, there is a real necessity for discipline.

To attain discipline, it is necessary to establish a solid theoretical base derived from the necessities of the learning situation. This done, the disciplinary function will be exercised educationally. Sound theory will divest the disciplinary function of the schoolteacherish, the personal, the crotchety, and the arbitrary. It will bulwark against extremes of neurotic or dogmatic self-indulgence on the part of students or teacher.

Respect is the key concept of discipline. It is fundamental to the learning situation in four aspecfs: (1) respect for the *person* (each person), (2) respect for *learning*, (3) respect for the *school* as an institution, and (4) respect for the *basic institutions* of society. This then is the foundation for solid disciplinary theory.

Respect is not an authoritarian concept. Respect derives from internal directives, self-knowledge, appraisal, participation, and consent. It may be sought but not commanded. Allegiance may be bought, coerced, duped, or traded. Respect does not exist without freedom and understanding.

In our construct there is no statement on respect for authority, nor is there need for it. What is sought is a source of functional order to maintain a learning situation, but respect for authority is a tired appeal of tyrannies too febrile to make sense. Not infrequently statements of school "philosophies" include the development of respect for authority as a primary objective. Such an objective would be more appropriate to the schools of Hitler, Mussolini, or Stalin than for those of a free society.

False coin, too, is made of the appeal to respect the teacher. In a true community of respect the teacher as a person and as an agent of learning needs no special status. The other side of the schoolteacherish desire for special tokens of regard is the teacher's traditional willingness to treat students with arbitrary indignities and tokens of disrespect, in the name of respect for adult and authority alike.

The source of discipline is *not* personal. The notion that power resides in teacher prerogative is an antieducational tenet that lies at the root of many unnecessary classroom problems. The source of the teacher's disci-

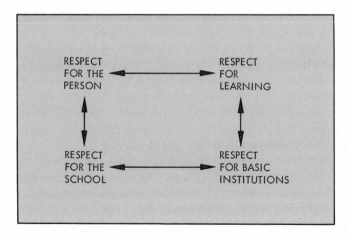

THE CONSTRUCT OF RESPECT
IN THE CLASSROOM

plinary force is official and resides in his role. His obligation is to conduct learning situations. Professionalization of teaching simply means an ability to establish and to maintain learning situations. Functional discipline is essential to learning, and the teacher has no need to personalize this function. To insist upon irrelevancies of conduct or manners that neither obstruct nor advance learning is personalizing discipline and is unprofessional. To allow conduct to persist that interferes with the basic learning situation, whether from indolence, good nature, laissez-faire attitudes, or sentimental permissiveness, is again to personalize discipline and constitutes dereliction of duty. The dictate of discipline is not what teacher likes or dislikes, tolerates or detests, but simply what the learning situation necessitates.

This concept alters the very vocabulary of the classroom. "I don't like that sort of thing" or "not in my classroom," in terms of functional discipline becomes, "We are here to learn, not to fool around," or "Can't let you sleep, John; we'd be cheating you and the taxpayers."

Obviously, the function of discipline varies with the individual activity. It cannot be the same pattern for the multiplicity of arrangements and involvements that make up the normal day's work within the new model. In the classroom, even as in architecture, form follows function. Rows of empty houses are orderly enough, but they lack function. If a vital learning situation is complex, then the forms around or within which students structure their efforts will be as varied or complex as the purposes of their learning.

THE ELEMENTS OF RESPECT

Respect for the person. The classroom can only be well disciplined for learning if it is grounded on the principle of human dignity. Indignities visited upon persons by other persons deny respect; they destroy functional discipline. Intrusions on personal dignity have been common, even conventional, in the classroom. The classroom has too often included class-oriented patterns of teacher preference and favoritism, psychologically cruel and unusual punishments (such as exposing a student to ridicule in his most vulnerable attributes), corporal punishment, ridicule of error (by teacher or fellow students), suppression of dissent and free discussion, neglect of any, many, or a few on personal or preferential grounds. Respect for the person implies acceptance of each student's weaknesses as well as strengths, and these often masquerade in one another's togs.

A free climate of expression is the first requisite of respect, and all effective social intercourse should contain relevance of comment. However, teachers often err in cutting off comment before a student has established relevance while they are more generous anent their own discursiveness.

Treatment of error is the acid test of respect. Freedom is based on the assumption of mortal fallibility. It follows that error deserves correction rather than punishment or ridicule. Indeed, the good teacher seizes upon and emphasizes the one correct statement in ten from a poor contribution; the weak teacher gloats upon the missing 2 percent of a 98 percent sound statement. Error maltreated becomes stubborn, loyally defended. In a good learning situation student and teacher alike recognize that they have no stake in being wrong. Correction is a favor, not a rebuke. These are essential although not painless lessons for maturity, but growing up is never easy.

Respect for the teacher is adequately secured in the concept of respect for the individual. A new, inexperienced, or insecure teacher should remember that respect must be reciprocal if learning is to take place. The teacher is accorded the same respect that is extended and maintained among and for the students, each of whom is responsible to the learning situation.

Respect for learning. Respect for learning begins with professionalized teaching. A classroom ought to be a place characterized by well-mannered, reciprocal human behavior because it is a place where people associate, because it is in a school, and because it is a part of the larger community. Such a classroom presupposes *functional discipline,* and it is a necessary component for learning to take place. In fact, the expectation and raison d'être of the school are learning, but it is not easy to assure that learning takes place. It is not evidenced by simply assigning, reciting, praising, scolding, quizzing, and grading.

It would be sentimental to assert that the opportunity to learn compels respect. It does for a few, but learning is not effected by throwing either a ball or a textbook to a group of students. For teachers to move from the pillar of strength that respect for learning is, they must know what learning is all about. A sterile pretense of learning compels disrespect! Indeed, student rebellion against sheer boredom should not be construed as a result of bad discipline. On the contrary, it may be a responsible expression of respect and even hunger for learning.

Respect for the school. The school is an institution created by man. Candor compels its officers to admit its errors and absurdities. Honest self-criticism is a sign of confidence, but the school may become debilitated by morbid introspection on its shortcomings. Even the poorest schools represent man's best hopes. To criticize the school is an act of loyalty, but to permit damage to its basic function is to sit passively and contribute nothing.

Respect for the school comes more readily when it is broadly based. A democracy stands on firmer grounds than an autocracy. A school may be forgiven its inadvertencies but gains respect from its achievements. There must be consonance among the four pillars of respect. Respect for the school cannot endure when the school abuses persons or neglects learning.

To deserve respect the school must study justice within the academic setting. This includes the study of equality, due process (fair procedures), participation in enactments by which one is governed, rights of petition and appeal, freedom from coerced testimony, absence of cruel or unusual punishments, presumption of innocence, no mass punishments to get at the guilt of a few. These hard-earned principles have served free men well. The school should examine its disciplinary system in relation to constitutional principles of justice.

Respect for the basic institutions of society. Respect within the school does not stand alone. The school that neglects the development of respect betrays not only itself but society as a whole. Those roads that lead to school, the homes from which its students come, the regulations which affect students and their parents are the products of a long, historic achievement. A school contributes to much more than the solution of its disciplinary problems when it gives its students some sense of value for a man's achievements. Let the school bolster itself by teaching children the worth of their heritage. And let the school also teach a corollary obligation: he who betrays one basic institution betrays all.

The school's insistence on respect for basic institutions does not mean pious verbalism or dereliction of civic responsibility. Schools cannot endure, or expect respect for long, in a community of corrupted basic institutions. The school must teach students to recognize community betrayal, whether it be by labor leaders who connive with hoodlums, industrialists who defraud the government, bankers who embezzle, or public officials who raid or carelessly guard the public treasury.

Without doubt, professional insecurity has been a source of much *bad* discipline. Bad discipline does not describe any particular pattern of order or disorder; it implies social incoherence that obstructs or detracts from the realization of a learning situation.

Parents also contribute to bad discipline. Parental relationship to bad curricular practice warrants exploration, but for our purposes, the three listed here include the basic problem:

1. Parents are often baffled by their children; they too need to be educated.
2. Parents are often the products of authoritarian subcultures: one or both dominant parents, closed-circle ethnic groups, dogmatic definitions of evil nature, antique notions of child-rearing and family life.
3. Parents are often in pursuit of their own youth and refuse to give up their games. They often refuse the responsibilities of maturity. When they are aware of their limitations, guilt debilitates their efforts to create responsible standards of behavior for themselves and their children.

With an understanding of its four pillars of respect, the school will stand beside responsible parents in developing the pervasive respect upon which the human community depends. When necessary, the school will not hesitate to move into the social vacuum occasioned by parental insecurity or abdication. Here, equal opportunity means that the school will make its civilizing impact available to all.

One further insecurity sometimes debilitates the teacher's will to assert the disciplinary obligation. This is the notion that good discipline is somehow undemocratic. Primitive progressivism suffered from this misconception. It abhorred classroom tyranny, and it was right. It maintained that authoritarianism in the schools of a democracy was an anachronism and a contradiction. But the fallacy that weakened this premise was the prevalent assumption that anything not authoritarian must be democratic. Too often the lid was off, and harassed teachers found themselves defending constant chaos in the classroom because it was not authoritarian.

Neither was it a democracy. Laissez-faire permissiveness is neither authoritarian nor democratic, but it does move toward tyranny. The classroom without functional discipline becomes chaotic, and chaos invites tyranny. The alternative to tyranny need not be anarchy. Teachers are obligated to maintain learning. Learning rests upon the pillars of respect, and these are the pillars of democracy as well. The teacher need not feel that by serving one well he is in great hazard of neglecting the other. Discipline that maintains the learning situation is the foundation of curriculum itself.

PART 4

Organizing Students
for Learning

Patterns of elementary school classroom organization vary from school district to school district and even, within the same district, from school to school. Generally, though, five characteristics apply to most schools. First, classes are graded rather than non-graded. Second, students are taught most subjects by a single teacher rather than by a series of teachers. Third, students from any single grade level are assigned to classrooms on a random basis rather than according to preestablished criteria. Fourth, classes are attended by students who come generally from a small geographic area and from similar socioeconomic conditions rather than from a large geographic area and from diverse socioeconomic conditions. And fifth, students generally remain in the elementary school for six years rather than for four or five, or seven or eight years.

The potential advantages and disadvantages of this particular pattern of organization have long been the subject of considerable debate among educators. Although most now think that organizational improvements could and should be made, few have identical views of what the most desirable alternative is. In this part, then, attention is given by eight writers to some of the most frequently mentioned of these alternatives. As the reader will soon discover, not all the writers favor the alternatives they present and discuss. The readings selected for this part reflect, as much as anything else, a biased point of view on the part of this writer in terms of his own thinking about desirable organizational change. In this highly controversial area, however, with pros and cons abounding on every proposal and with space in this part limited, the biased perspective seemed unavoidable.

In Anderson's article, the first in this part, twelve patterns of classroom organization are contrasted. Each of the patterns has three variables. It may be graded or nongraded; it may have unit-age groupings (all six-year-olds, for example) or multi-age groupings; and it may be self-contained or taught by a teaching team. Anderson's thesis is that the most desirable of these patterns is the one that combines team teaching and nongradedness and employs some form of multi-age grouping. The least desirable is the graded, self-contained, unit-aged pattern. Unfortunately, from Anderson's perspective, this latter pattern is most characteristic of elementary school organization at the present time.

Nongradedness is also the subject of the second article. In it McLoughlin makes two major points. The first is that current research shows little, if any, superiority for the nongraded pattern as opposed to the graded plan. This holds true in the area of students' achievement as well as in the area of their social and emotional development. McLoughlin's second point, however, is that much of this research may be invalid because many schools purporting to have nongraded programs in fact do not. Although McLoughlin seems to support the idea of nongradedness, he cautions, "Every grade label can be cleansed from every classroom door in the school without influencing the school's attainments with children as long as graded instructional practices prevail behind these doors." [1]

Subject-matter specialist and departmentalization and their opposites, subject-matter generalist and the self-contained classroom, are two sets of concepts that are usually contrasted when thought is given to ways of organizing students for instructional purposes. Or are they, in fact, opposites? In the selection by Howard, a new way of looking at the distinction between specialist and generalist is presented. She argues that the usual way of differentiating between these concepts is no longer valid in the light of today's new organizational patterns and instructional roles. As one alternative, she proposes that some elementary school teachers be content generalists, but that they specialize at the same time in some particular phase of teaching, for example, in role playing, inquiry training, or evaluating.

[1] William P. McLoughlin, "The Phantom Nongraded School," *Phi Delta Kappan*, IL (January 1968), 250. (Article is included in this book.)

Following Howard's article are two that have as their central focus the issue of homogeneous versus heterogeneous grouping. Neither Wrightstone nor Olsen, the authors, respectively, of these articles, appears to favor homogeneous grouping. Each, however, emphasizes different reasons. Wrightstone points out that research generally shows little or no difference in achievement between students grouped homogeneously and those grouped heterogeneously. Olsen, on the other hand, expresses concern about the social and emotional effects on students, particularly the dull ones, of being intellectually segregated.

Another grouping pattern, although certainly not so well known as either of the above, is what Thelen refers to in the sixth article as teachability grouping. Essentially, this form of organization attempts to place with each teacher the types of students who, in the past, seemed "to get a lot out of his classes." Thelen contends, because the image of the preferred student differs from teacher to teacher, that personal compatibility between teachers and students ought to constitute the most important grouping criterion. As the research cited in the article indicates, this pattern of organization is not without disadvantages, but in this writer's opinion it does offer educators another organizational alternative, albeit one that needs much further investigation.

The final articles in this part deal with two organizational patterns that have deep-seated implications not only for the elementary school, but for the total school program as well. These are the middle school and the educational park. The middle school, as Compton points out, is designed specifically for the "in-between-agers," the students in the fifth through eighth grades. Her premise is that neither the self-contained classroom of the elementary school nor the departmentalized junior high school now meets the needs of these youngsters very effectively. Establishing middle schools to facilitate the task of better meeting their needs would mean replacing the traditional 6-3-3 organizational pattern with a 4-4-4 plan.

The educational park concept, as Fischer defines it in the last article, "is a scheme under which several thousand ghetto children and a larger number from middle-class white neighborhoods would be assembled in a group of schools sharing a single campus."[2] The campus would be large, covering between fifty and

[2] John H. Fischer, "School Parks for Equal Opportunities," *The Journal of Negro Education*, XXXVII (Summer 1968), 301. (Article is included in this book.)

one hundred acres and enrolling about sixteen thousand students in a K-4-4-4 pattern. Because of the park's unprecedented size, Fischer sees in its creation many potential educational advantages, including the obvious one of integration. But he also warns against the possible concomitant of mass student mistreatment and dehumanization. It need hardly be said, finally, that the creation of educational parks would require massive federal, state, and local funding, strong community support, and exceptional educational planning.

Some Types of Cooperative Teaching in Current Use

ROBERT H. ANDERSON

Under the general heading of "cooperative teaching" may be found dozens of different patterns of school and staff organization. Some of these derive from, or are associated with, attempts to achieve greater flexibility in pupil grouping. Others are associated with efforts to eliminate the administrative and instructional characteristics of rigid, lock-step graded school structure. Still others involve the use of nonprofessional or paraprofessional assistants in the schools, and a few are the result of experimentation with mechanical devices, programed materials, and other technological resources. Most, however, have stemmed from a growing interdependence among teachers in the face of the increasing complexity of teaching responsibilities and the need for greater specialization in the professional ranks.

Woodring notes that team teaching might be more appropriately "called 'team organization and planning' because the teaching, at any given moment, usually is done by an individual rather than by a team." [1] Certainly this is often the case: a group of teachers may be joined together in a partnership concerned with instructional planning, coordination of schedules and resources, and general evaluation, but each teacher retains his essential sovereignty and performs teaching functions in privacy. If each teacher also deals primarily with "his own class" of pupils throughout the school week, and has a minimum of contact with the pupils of his teaching colleagues, then the label of "team teaching" would indeed be somewhat erroneous. Sometimes, however, the aforementioned teachers do in fact have

Reprinted from *The National Elementary Principal*, 44 (3): 22–26 (January 1965), by permission of author and publisher. Copyright © 1965, Department of Elementary School Principals, National Education Association. All rights reserved.
[1] Woodring, Paul. "Reform Movements from the Point of View of Psychological Theory." *Theories of Learning and Instruction*. Sixty-Third Yearbook, Part I, National Society for the Study of Education. Chicago: University of Chicago Press, 1964. Chapter 12, p. 292.

183

a shared teaching responsibility for a good many children, so that many teaching decisions and outcomes are constantly examined by the total staff. It would seem that in such situations a more definite merging of sovereignties and an increase of side-by-side teaching activities may be expected to develop.

THE THEORETICAL IDEAL

One model of cooperative teaching, then, requires an extensive co-involvement of a number of teachers (let us say between three and six) in the entire range of instructive-related functions: planning, actual work with the same children, and evaluation. In this model, which some regard as the ultimate or ideal, all team members (including the children when appropriate) share jointly in the formulation of broad, over-all instructional objectives and in the weekly or daily determination of the more immediate teaching goals. The model requires all team members to be at least minimally conversant with each other's specific daily plans and to be given at least periodic (e.g., weekly) opportunity to contribute to and criticize the plans of colleagues. Each team member, at least several times weekly, should carry on teaching functions in the actual presence of a colleague, whose own role at the moment might involve co-teaching, or assisting, or observing—it being the colleague's subsequent obligation to offer constructive advice or criticism in an evaluative session. This model, therefore, implies that arrangements can be made for extensive intra-team communication, and it obviously makes heavy demands upon the time, energies, and emotions of the teachers involved.

At this stage of development, this idealized model does not exist full-blown in any project known to the author. In all probability, hierarchically structured teams such as those in Lexington, Massachusetts, and Norwalk, Connecticut, come the closest to fulfilling the ideal model, yet even these have not yet solved all of the various problems that are involved.

Hierarchical structure, in which leadership is formally assigned and in which the leader enjoys a salary supplement or equivalent recognition, has not yet become very widespread. However, it now seems that there is a trend toward the formal assignment of leadership to the best qualified person in the team. The relatively superior teacher, who also has a significant professional specialty and the talent and appetite for carrying leadership responsibility, can expect in a growing number of communities to be assigned as "team leader" with a salary supplement up to $1,000 or more. In the minds of some proponents, this feature of team teaching organization promises to attract and retain a greater number of outstanding persons in the teaching profession.

Formal hierarchical organization in some instances calls for more than one level of responsibility and competence above the regular role of teacher.

The title of "senior teacher" or "specialist teacher" may be used, for example, to denote a professional with above average qualifications and an assigned leadership role under the team leader. This arrangement tends to be found chiefly where there are fairly large teams (e.g., five to eight members) or where an effort is being made to provide leadership experience for future team leaders.

LESS FORMAL PATTERNS

Perhaps the most typical teaching teams pattern in current use is the semi-hierarchical structured team. Here, the members of the team are officially joined together in a close working relationship, the administration having designated various roles for the members (e.g., each member providing leadership in a given curriculum area) but all members having an essentially equal status. The person designated as "leader" is seen primarily as a parliamentary chairman or coordinator, without any unusual authority and without salary supplement or other tangible recognition of responsibilities carried. The leadership may actually rotate from member to member over a period of time, or the school principal may in effect be the team leader. An example of the latter is an outstanding project underway in the Hamilton School, a small elementary school in Newton, Massachusetts. Sometimes, the semi-hierarchical team is a good pattern to use in a school where there is apparent resistance to full-fledged hierarchy and/or where the administration is unsure as to which of the teachers have the talents and the temperament for leadership. In such situations, a gradual move can be made toward hierarchical structure as the staff becomes more accepting of the idea.

Many so-called team operations represent at best what might be called a voluntary federation of sovereign teachers. Membership in the team is not a formal obligation of the teacher, and his involvement in the professional planning and activities of his colleagues tends to be relatively minor. Nevertheless, this arrangement can be fruitful if the federated teachers take sufficient advantage of the flexibility and sharing that is possible. Leadership tends to be very informal, each teacher being in effect a free-lance participant.

In both the semi-structured and the federated patterns, examples can be found that are "departmental" in flavor. Although such arrangements are far more common in secondary schools, some elementary schools have lately turned to the use of subject matter specialists as one way of providing more competent instruction across the curriculum. Some schools have, in effect, discarded the self-contained classroom organization, wherein each teacher as a generalist taught in all curriculum areas, and rearranged teaching assignments along departmental or subject matter lines. Since departmentalization has for some time been in general disfavor in elementary education, it is therefore a source of concern in some circles that such a trend is discernible.

DEPARTMENTALIZATION

It may be helpful to point out that conventional departmentalization, with which the so-called "self-contained" classroom has long been contrasted, is itself a form of self-contained organization. That is to say, the teachers in conventional departmentalization are almost literally autonomous in their various roles, each as independent of the other as are "self-contained" classroom teachers. The chief difference between the two conventional patterns, then, is explained less by the meaning of the phrase "self-contained" than by the distinction between generalist and specialist. Most authorities would probably concede that more competent instruction *area by area* is characteristic of the departmentalized pattern, but it is generally believed that this advantage is countervailed by the uncoordinated, fragmentary experiences the child receives at the hands of independent teachers, each unaware of his colleagues' work and each seeing only a certain aspect of the child's growth and performance.

With the emergence of team teaching, a fresh impetus has been given to the idea of specialist teaching. A significant difference, however, may be found in some of the current plans involving the use of subject matter specialists in the elementary school: the team-oriented concept of communication, coordination, and cooperation. "Cooperative departmentalization," then, is a term we may use in cases where separate specialists join together in a federation under conditions somewhat resembling team organization.

NONGRADING AND MULTI-AGE PATTERNS

By now the reader is aware of numerous variants of team organization and staff cooperation that may be found across the country at the present time. Some of these are primarily modifications of the old pattern of literal self-containment (generalist or specialist), while others are more valid examples of cooperative teaching ranging from loose federations all the way to formal, hierarchical team structure.

Two other trends in school organization may be identified, both having to do with the types of group memberships arranged in the school for children. The first of these is multi-age or inter-age grouping: the assignment of children to teams, classes, or instructional groups in which they associate with children of two or more age levels. One example is the multi-grade, multi-age grouping plan such as that developed about eight years ago in Torrance, California, where a primary class might include six-year-old, seven-year-old, and eight-year-old children, and an intermediate class might include nine-, ten-, and eleven-year-old youngsters. A second trend, closely related to the use of multi-age classes, is the abandonment of graded structure in favor of more flexible patterns of arranging and defining the vertical progress of pupils through the elementary school. It is not the purpose of this article to elaborate on multi-age and nongraded patterns, although this author is convinced of their merit and sees their acceptance and development as one of the important goals of American public schools in the years ahead.

One of the principal advantages of team teaching, and variants thereof, appears to be that it stimulates and fosters the further development of flexible grouping patterns and of the nongraded school itself. In many places where cooperative teaching has flourished, attitudes and practices associated with nongraded organization have tended also to flourish. Probably this is due to the more careful analysis that team teachers tend to make of their responsibilities and also to the increased flexibility they enjoy in responding to pupils' needs. We are tempted to argue, therefore, that experience with cooperative teaching is a useful strategic preparation for the adoption of a nongraded plan. Team teaching and nongradedness in combination, especially where multi-age groupings are also employed, appears to represent an ideal or ultimate form of elementary school organization.

Twelve Patterns

In actual practice, at least twelve combinations of these organizational features and their opposites may be found at present in the United States.

In our chart, boxes 1, 2, 7, and 8 refer to self-contained classes in which there is either graded or nongraded vertical organization and in which the children are either of the same age or of different ages. In boxes 3, 4, 9, and 10, the same factors exist except that there is some form of multiple-adult cooperative staff organization in effect. In boxes 5, 6, 11, and 12, the same variables are now combined with full-fledged team teaching organization.

POSSIBLE PATTERNS OF
SCHOOL/CLASS ORGANIZATION   (Key)

1	2	3	4	5	6
NG	NG	NG	NG	NG	NG
SC	SC	MSC	MSC	TT	TT
UA	MA	UA	MA	UA	MA

7	8	9	10	11	12
G	G	G	G	G	G
SC	SC	MSC	MSC	TT	TT
UA	MA	UA	MA	UA	MA

G   Graded vertical organization (promotion/failure)

NG   Nongraded vertical organization (continuous progress)

UA   Unit age grouping (6-year-olds, 7-year-olds, etc.)

MA   Multi-age or inter-age groupings (6-7, 6-7-8, etc.)

SC   Self-contained horizontal organization (1 autonomous teacher)

MSC Modified self-contained: cooperative departmentalization, semi-departmentalization, informal cooperation (several autonomous teachers)

TT   Team teaching horizontal organization

Our previous argument in effect supports box 6 (nongrading combined with team teaching and inter-age grouping) as representing the theoretical ideal. By implication, box 7 represents the theoretically least desirable combination. Probably boxes 5 and 8 are, in turn, the next best and next worst, respectively, although both strategic and value considerations make this a very difficult judgment. As an interesting exercise, the reader might ask himself which boxes represent in fact the next best and the next worst arrangements.

If one believes with this author that nongradedness is the most precious and desirable of the organization forms we may consider, then boxes 12, 11, 10, and 9 seem to be useful avenues in the direction of box 6. Experience to date does not offer much advice as to how best to proceed from box 7 to the Utopia of box 6, although it may be that one or another form of cooperative teaching is easier to understand and to implement than is the more ambiguous and complicated concept of nongrading. If this is the case, perhaps a concerted effort to develop team teaching will be a useful step toward the eventual achievement of a workable nongraded structure.

Nonprofessional Aides

Some team teaching projects involve the extensive use of teacher aides and clerical aides. The Norwalk model reserves a fairly major role for the aide, and the Lexington model calls for two full-time aides supplementing a full complement of six or seven teachers. Many projects call for a more limited use of aides, e.g., a half-time aide serving six teachers. In the new Granada Elementary School in Belvedere-Tiburon, California, the staff positions for a team serving 100 pupils include one team leader, one senior teacher (five or more years of experience), one junior teacher (little or no teaching experience), one full-time intern, two student teachers, a half-time teacher aide, and several volunteer instructional aides (parents who help with health, library, and various aide functions).

Perhaps the most prevalent pattern, for financial reasons, is the one involving *no* aides, or at most a small allotment of a school secretary's time. In fact, team teaching is not dependent upon the availability of nonprofessional assistants; but it is rather disappointing that American schools have been so slow to recognize the crying need for supporting services, and those teams fortunate enough to have aides seem to be making more rapid progress in improving instruction.

Pupil Groupings

Team teaching is frequently associated with the use of varying sized instructional groupings, including large groups of 40, 75, 100 or more children on the one hand and small seminar groups (12–15 pupils) and working groups (5–8 pupils) on the other. Some critics have deplored large group instruction, especially for young children, and protested that teams seem not to arrange for seminar and working groups as often as would be desirable. This may well be a valid complaint, since most teams have been slow to develop small group instruction patterns. Regarding large groups, the critics have probably exaggerated both the extent to which large group instruction is actually carried on and the educational hazards of such instruction. Large group lessons, in part because they are usually prepared more carefully, are often superior in quality to lessons under conventional circumstances. It seems unlikely that teams will overindulge in this form of teaching, however, and in many existing team projects such lessons play only a minor role in the scheme of, things. The great preponderance of team teaching is still done in class groupings of 20–30, although this may be due more to the habits of teachers and the influence of the architectural environment than to valid theories of educational grouping.[2]

Team teaching is not totally dependent upon flexibility in school design, although it is extremely helpful to have school spaces that lend themselves to various types of groupings. Existing school buildings usually have at least some flexibility, and sometimes they can be modified at reasonable cost. Especially urgent, it would seem, is alerting school boards and administrators to the need for flexibility in all *future* school construction.

Sub-groupings within the total team may be based upon some presumed similarity among the youngsters, so that the students tend to reinforce each other in the learning process, or upon some presumed dissimilarities as in the case of deliberate heterogeneous grouping. Academic history and potential, social or personal factors, age, interests, learning styles and personalities, and many other factors may serve to explain the various sub-groups that are formed. Increasingly, the varying talents and teaching styles of the adults in the team are also being taken into account.

Much Yet to Learn

Cooperative teaching in the 1965 setting finds its origins in century-old trends, yet it has a special currency in this time of fundamental ferment and change. That so many patterns exist is a reflection of the American system of decentralized schools, each community having the freedom to shape its educational program (within broad limits) along its own lines.

At the same time, certain team teaching models in particular have tended to influence the general trend to date because they were among the first to be widely described in the literature, both professional and popular. Whether the influence of these early pilot programs will diminish as re-

[2] Anderson, Robert H. "The Organization and Administration of Team Teaching." *Team Teaching.* (Edited by Judson T. Shaplin and Henry F. Olds, Jr.) New York: Harper & Row, 1964, pp. 208–09.

search and theory become more highly developed is a matter for speculation. Suffice here to say that cooperative teaching is still in a formative, even
primitive, stage. Yet despite its newness, most observers are agreed that
cooperative teaching represents an extremely promising and challenging
field for further exploration.

OTHER REFERENCES

Blair, Medill, and Woodward, Richard G. *Team Teaching in Action.* Boston:
Houghton Mifflin Co., 1964. 229 pp.
National Education Association, Project on the Instructional Program of the Public
Schools. *Planning and Organizing for Teaching.* Washington, D.C.: the Asso-
ciation, 1963. 190 pp.
Herbert, John. *Team Teaching. A Working Bibliography.* (Mimeographed.)
Horace Mann-Lincoln Institute of School Experimentation, Interim Reports.
New York: Teachers College, Columbia University, August 1964. 39 pp.

The Phantom Nongraded School

WILLIAM P. McLOUGHLIN

Few propositions for educational change have generated and sustained as
much interest as the nongraded school. It is discussed at nearly every major
educational conference, and symposiums on the nongraded school are increasing in popularity. Furthermore, the body of available literature is increasing rapidly; most leading professional journals have published several
articles on this topic. Through these and other means, educators have
learned more of the promises of the nongraded school than they have of its
accomplishments.

This is understandable, for nongrading appears to be preached more
than practiced and practiced more than appraised. In fact, few dependable
estimates on the present status and anticipated growth of the nongraded
school are currently available and sound studies on its accomplishments are
even more difficult to come by. From what is available one would be hard
put to determine just how many schools have nongraded their instructional
programs and how many are seriously contemplating the change. If findings
in these areas are obscure, the outcomes of the evaluations of existing nongraded programs are even less definitive.

The available estimates of the number of schools with nongraded pro-

Reprinted from *Phi Delta Kappa,* 49 (5): 248–250 (January 1968), by permission of author and publisher.

grams fluctuates from 5.5 percent [1] to 30 percent.[2] These, it must be pointed out, are unqualified estimates; they do not consider the quality of the programs purporting to be nongraded. When this element is added, estimates of the number of schools with *truly* nongraded programs shrink considerably. Goodlad, in 1955, estimated that less than one percent of the schools in the country were nongraded [3] and in 1961 he felt there were probably fewer than 125 schools to be found with *truly* nongraded programs.[4]

If uncertainty marks present estimates of the number of schools operating nongraded programs, certainly forecasts for future growth are dubious. In 1958 the NEA reported 26.3 percent of the respondents to its survey saying they intended to nongrade their schools.[5] Five years later, however, this estimate had dwindled to 3.2 percent.[6] On the other hand, the USOE's pollings reverse this trend. Of schools queried in 1958, only 13.4 percent expected to become nongraded,[7] but two years later this estimate doubled and 26.3 percent of the respondents reported considering nongrading their schools.[8] With these conflicting findings it is difficult to know if the nongraded school is coming into its own or passing out of existence.

One thing seems clear from these surveys, however: nongrading is related to district size. Nearly all available surveys confirm this; the larger the district, the more likely it is to have one or more nongraded units. Here we should stress that this does not mean that nongrading is the principal organizational pattern in large school districts. It simply means a nongraded unit is operating in one or more of the district's several elementary schools.[9]

Studies of the influence of nongrading on students are rare, too, and their composite findings somewhat bewildering. Thirty-three empirical studies of the influence of nongrading on student academic achievement have been identified. Not all of these, however, consider the same variables. About half of them assess the influence of nongrading on reading achieve-

[1] Lillian L. Gore and Rose E. Koury, *A Survey of Early Elementary Education in Public Schools, 1960–61*. Washington, D.C.: U.S. Department of Health, Education and Welfare, 1965.

[2] National Education Association, *Nongraded Schools*. Research Memo 1965–12. Washington, D.C.: Research Division, NEA, May, 1965.

[3] John I. Goodlad, "More About the Ungraded Plan," *NEA Journal*, May, 1955, pp. 295–96.

[4] National Education Association, *Nongrading: A Modern Practice in Elementary School Organization*. Research Memorandum 1961–37. Washington, D.C.: Research Division, NEA, October, 1961.

[5] National Education Association, *Administrative Practices in Urban School Districts, 1958–1959*. Research Report 1961-R10. Washington, D.C.: Research Division, NEA, May, 1961.

[6] NEA, *Nongraded Schools, op. cit.*

[7] Stuart E. Dean, *Elementary School Administration and Organization: A National Survey of Practices and Policies*. Washington, D.C.: U.S. Department of Health, Education and Welfare, 1963.

[8] Gore and Koury, *op. cit.*

[9] William P. McLoughlin, *The Nongraded School: A Critical Assessment*. Albany, N.Y.: The University of the State of New York, The New York State Education Department, 1967.

ment, while 25 percent look at its influence on arithmetic performance. Only 11 percent of the studies question the impact nongrading has on the student's development in language arts. Nine percent report on the total achievement scores of children. The remaining studies are spread so thinly through the other curricular divisions that a detailed consideration of their findings is hardly profitable.[10]

Judged by these studies, the academic development of children probably does not suffer from attending a nongraded school; there is some evidence, admittedly sketchy and tentative, to indicate it may be somewhat enhanced. One thing is certain; children from graded classes seldom do better on these measures than children from nongraded classes. More commonly, children from nongraded classes excell their contemporaries from graded classes.

For example, 15 studies considered the influence of nongrading on the general reading achievement of children. Seven of these report no significant difference between children from graded and nongraded classes. In other words, nothing is lost by having children attend nongraded classes. But only two studies found children from graded classes outscoring children from nongraded classes, while six studies found the general reading attainments of children from nongraded classes superior to that of children in graded classes.

Similar though less distinct outcomes are attained when the reading subskills of comprehension and vocabulary development are examined. Again, the principal finding of 14 studies is that there are no marked differences in the accomplishments of children in these areas regardless of the type of organization in which they learn to read. Furthermore, for every study showing greater gains for children from graded classes, there is an equal number of studies counterbalancing these findings.

The mirror image of this picture emerges when the arithmetic attainments of children from graded and nongraded classes are contrasted. Eleven studies considered the influence of nongrading on children's general arithmetic achievement, and their findings are inconclusive. Three report differences favoring children from nongraded classes, five found differences favoring children from graded classes,[11] and three found no difference.

But when the arithmetic subskills of reasoning and knowledge of fundamentals are examined, different outcomes appear. Of the 12 published studies in these areas, one reports differences favoring children from graded classes but six report differences favoring children from nongraded classes. The remaining five show no real difference in the achievement of children in these areas, regardless of the type of class organization.

In language arts, too, there is scant evidence to demonstrate that or-

10 *Ibid.*
11 *Ibid.*

ganization influences achievement. Seven of the 10 studies in this area report no true differences in the language skills developed by children from graded and nongraded classes. One reports achievement test scores of children from graded classes as superior to those of children from nongraded classes, while two studies found the observed differences in the achievement of children from nongraded classes indeed significantly superior to that of controls in the graded classes. Apparently, nongraded classes are no more effective in developing language arts skills than are graded classes.

Total achievement test scores, too, seem remarkably immune to change because of changes in organizational pattern. Half of the eight studies using them to measure the efficacy of the nongraded school found no significant differences in the achievements of children from graded and nongraded classes. The remaining studies divide equally: Two reported differences favoring children from graded classes while two found differences favoring children from nongraded classes. So here, once again, the influence of nongrading on the academic development of children is indeterminate.

Better student achievement is not the only claim put forth for the nongraded school. Its advocates maintain, implicitly or explicitly, that superior student adjustment is attained in the nongraded school. Certainly student adjustment and personality development are crucial concerns of educators and, quite reasonably, they are interested in developing learning settings which foster this goal.

Unfortunately, studies assessing the influence of nongrading on student adjustment are even more rare than studies assessing its influence on their academic achievement. Moreover, the diversity of procedures utilized in these studies to measure adjustment lessens their cumulative value. Sociograms, adjustment inventories, anxiety scales, and even school attendance records have all been used as indices of pupil adjustment. But no matter how measured, there is scant evidence to support the contention that superior student adjustment is realized in nongraded schools. On the 32 separate indices of adjustment used in these studies, the overwhelming majority, 26, indicate that there is no significant difference in the adjustment of children from graded and nongraded classes. Only four of the measures (general adjustment, social adjustment, social maturity, and freedom from age stereotypes) showed differences favorable to children from nongraded classes, while the remaining two (social participation and freedom from defensiveness) were favorable to children from graded classes.[12]

Research, then, finds little to impel or impede practitioners interested in nongrading. Under either organization children's adjustment and achievement appear to remain remarkably constant. For those to whom the nongraded school is a magnificent obsession, these findings must come as a

[12] *Ibid.*

numbing disappointment. Taken at face value, current research on the non-graded school seems to say that its contribution to the academic, social, and emotional development of children is marginal.

But should these findings be taken at face value? It might be naive to rest the fate of the nongraded school on past research. The validity of these studies should be rigorously tested, for they depend on one tacit but critical assumption: that the experimental schools, those purporting to be non-graded, are *truly* nongraded. If this assumption is not met and the experimental schools are not nongraded, then research has told us nothing about the efficacy of the nongraded school.

Too often, on close inspection, one finds that schools credited with operating nongraded programs are not nongraded at all. Homogeneous grouping and semi-departmentalization of instruction in reading and arithmetic are frequently passed off as nongraded programs. These techniques must be recognized for what they are. They are administrative expediencies developed to make the *graded* school work. They are not nongraded instructional programs.

If these are the "nongraded" programs represented in these studies, then researching their effectiveness is an exercise in futility, for the *experimental* schools are as graded as the control schools and no experimental treatment is being tested. Research has done nothing more than contrast the performances of children from graded schools called graded schools with the performance of children from graded schools called nongraded schools. Essentially, we have simply researched the age-old question: "What's in a name?"

The nongraded school is defensible only because the graded school is indefensible. Its justification flows from its efforts to correct the instructional errors of the graded school. It is reasonably unlikely that any amount of manipulation of the physical arrangements of schools will produce discernible differences in the academic or psycho-social development of children. Every grade label can be cleansed from every classroom door in the school without influencing the school's attainments with children as long as graded instructional practices prevail behind these doors.

Nongrading begins with significant alterations in instructional, not organizational, procedures. As long as schools seek practices designed to group away differences they are *not* nongraded. The nongraded school never held this as a goal, for it is impossible. Rather, nongrading says: "Accept children as they are, with all their differences, and teach to these differences. Don't try to eradicate them!" Until educators develop instructional programs that will meet this challenge they are not nongrading. They are simply masking their old egg-crate schools with a new facade.

A Look at Specialization

ELIZABETH Z. HOWARD

Concerns about specialization are not new. They have been voiced for more than a decade in curriculum matters and at times have been the subject of heated debate.

The locus of these concerns has been the elementary school. As the knowledge explosion has become an obvious reality, and as more and more learning occurs outside of school, teachers must examine their own adequacy in the realms of knowledge. The old complaint, "They keep adding things to the curriculum and never take anything away," has changed to a new one: "We can't possibly know enough about everything to teach what is expected." In almost every classroom there are now children who know more about something than the teacher knows.

Specialization has seemed like an answer. At least three major forces have taken this position: the national curriculum projects, the teacher certification agencies of the various states, and a large group of scholars in the disciplines. Interestingly, though, all three of these forces are "outside" the professional groups of common school educators; yet their opinions and deliberations are having a potent effect on developments within schools.

Specialization for an elementary school teacher has typically been defined as a strong subject-matter background in one discipline. The national curriculum projects, for example, have been almost entirely built around single subjects—mathematics, physics, anthropology. Each curriculum project has presented convincingly an image of its own importance in the total curriculum.

State certification bodies, too, have pushed for excellence in the only way they knew how—by demanding higher standards of subject-matter preparation prior to achievement of a license to teach. Thus they have strengthened this same definition of specialization.

Scholars in the disciplines have become involved in the specialization concern by extending their advice to the field of elementary and secondary education. Bestor, Koerner, and Conant have been among the loud voices calling for scholar-teachers in both elementary and secondary schools.

From *Educational Leadership*, 26 (6): 547–550 (March 1969). Reprinted with permission of the Association for Supervision and Curriculum Development and Elizabeth Z. Howard. Copyright © 1969 by the Association for Supervision and Curriculum Development.

NEEDED: A NEW DEFINITION

Where, meanwhile, does the teaching profession fit into the stress on specialization? What voices are being raised to indicate teachers' feelings about this issue? What major contributions are the curriculum leaders making? What are we doing to bring back "inside" the profession a consideration of these major concerns about specialization that have so strongly been espoused by forces "outside" the profession?

It is true that a few voices have been heard within the teaching profession protesting the pressure for scholar-teacher specialization in elementary school and arguing for strong generalist teachers. It is also true that some teachers and curriculum workers have spoken out in favor of more specialist-teachers. The debates, however, have generally been based on outmoded concepts of "coverage," "departmentalization," "prescribed curriculum," "teaching," and the kind of school that has too long been familiar to us.

In 1969 these concepts are no longer valid. The school must be a different kind of place, and the definition of specialization in that school must be appropriate for education in today's world.

CHANGING PATTERNS OF SCHOOL ORGANIZATION

Change in the way schools are organized is finally occurring, and already the implications for the specialization debate are evident. One example is team teaching. This pattern was initially introduced as a means of improved staff utilization, an opportunity for each teacher to be viewed as a specialist in some phase of the curriculum. In adopting team teaching, unfortunately, many schools reverted to the old practice of "departmentalization," without adopting the real essence of teaming (shared planning, shared teaching, shared evaluation) among teachers.

Some elementary schools, however, have found that team teaching offered possibilities for other kinds of specialization not tied to subject-matter departmentalization. Each teacher on a team can be a generalist in the content of elementary education; but each teacher may also be a specialist in some phase of *teaching*. For example, Teacher A has a particular skill in using role playing, simulation, elaborative thinking. Teacher B is a student of concept development and inquiry training. Teacher C has a strong interest and ability in diagnosis of learning needs in skill development.

Together these team members plan teaching strategies for all curriculum areas and for all the children in their team. These teachers are truly specialists, but theirs is a specialization quite different from the subject-matter-depth definition. These teachers contend that their sort of specialization makes sense in today's changing elementary school and contributes more appropriately to more children than departmentalization was able to do. It prevents the curriculum fragmentation that has so often resulted from subject-matter specialization.

A second example of a changing organizational pattern is represented by the World of Inquiry School in Rochester, New York (part of Project UNIQUE, a federally-funded project dealing with a variety of urban-sub-urban educational problems). In this school, children are assigned to heterogeneous interage "family" groups. For example, a family group may include children with an age range from 7 to 9, or from 5 to 8, or even from 5 to 10 years. The "family teacher" provides individualized instruction in math and reading skills. Each child, in addition, plans his own schedule to take advantage of interest areas staffed by specialists in science, art, social studies, technology, music, library, and "shop" (which may include such interests as photography, cooking, electricity, and a host of other activities).

In addition, many kinds of specialists are brought in, or children are taken to them outside the school, as community resource specialists in such interests as urban problems, fine arts, medicine, human relations, and Negro history. Again, the function of specialization in this school represents a far broader definition than the one so typically ascribed to specialization in the departmentalized school organization. It provides subject specialists but utilizes them within a framework of a truly individualized program.

In these examples, then, we see newer ideas of school organization— ways of organizing both teachers and learners—and a new definition of specialization. Without rejecting the validity of subject-matter-depth specialization, we can also use a broader range of specialties to good advantage. The primary need in any new plan is that teachers make use of the possibilities available to them, rather than to think of departmentalization as the only way to utilize specialists.

CHANGING ROLES OF TEACHERS

Class size has long been a focus of teacher complaint. Yet until recently much of the teacher's "teaching" could be done as well with large groups as with small. The real urgency of reducing class size is related to our increasing attempts to individualize and personalize instruction.

Every classroom teacher, in any kind of school organization, must be a specialist in the art of providing a flexible environment for learning. (It may help if each teacher, in addition, is a specialist in one particular discipline, if only to provide a model to children of the excitement of "digging into" history or earth science or mathematics in depth!)

It is important for us to realize, though, that the knowledge explosion has made obsolete or irrelevant much of what teachers "know"; that many curriculum guides are designed for "coverage" of the wrong knowledge for tomorrow's world; and that we have reached a stage when we must abandon the curriculum notion of a sacred body of content to be "learned" by all children.

Consequently, the new teaching roles require that each staff member be a lifelong learner as well as a teacher. The science specialist in a school cannot relax in his knowledge of science gleaned from past study; he must be a continuing learner of science and a continuing student of instructional materials and procedures. He must be sure that the instructional materials center provides a wide range of science materials, and he must be available for individual children and teachers who are pursuing science interests in their learning. A teacher who is a student of history can help other teachers and some of the children to understand how a historian approaches learning.

Each teacher must still be a generalist in elementary education—generalist in the sense of concern for diagnosing children's unique learning needs, selecting appropriate materials for individual children, and opening up new doors to learning—but serves his specialist function within the total school staff through his availability to all other teachers and to individual children.

Obviously, the definition of specialist suggested here is quite different from the departmentalized teacher definition used for a long time in education. The old arguments of "specialist *versus* generalist" are no longer valid, in the light of new patterns of school organization and new teaching roles.

USING OUTSIDE SPECIALISTS

Just as new kinds of specialization are emerging within the school, so we are more acutely aware of new kinds of specialists available outside the school. It is not improbable that these persons will eventually become school staff members, full or part time, to the advantage of both children and teachers. We can visualize, for example, the group process or systems analysis specialist as a part-time staff member of a school, like the artist-in-residence or (noncertified) foreign language teacher or guidance counselor now found as specialists in some schools. It is quite possible that a computer specialist will be part of the instructional staff, available not only to teachers and administrators but also to children who elect the study of data processing and computer analysis as part of their individualized school program. Old ideas of teacher preparation and certification will undoubtedly need to be reexamined as new specialties become essential.

Schools do need specialists, but the old departmentalized approach cannot survive within a philosophy of individualized instruction. Schools do need subject-matter specialists, but the old notion of sacred content for all cannot survive in today's knowledge explosion. Schools will need specialists in ways that cannot yet be visualized. If the teaching profession argues either for or against specialization in the old terms, it will be standing in the way of needed change toward new definitions and new kinds of specialization in tomorrow's schools.

Ability Grouping and
the Average Child

J. WAYNE WRIGHTSTONE

Children in the typical school population represent a wide range of aptitudes and have diverse educational needs. Is ability grouping—placing together children who, on the basis of intelligence tests, achievement tests, and teachers' judgments appear to have similar capacities for learning—the best means of meeting these diverse needs? Opinions differ on this matter as, indeed, they have ever since ability grouping made its American debut in Detroit, in 1920.

Proponents of ability grouping say that it is easier to teach a group whose abilities are in the same range, pointing out that materials suitable for one member of the group will tend to be suitable for all and that the same will be true of instruction. They claim that the majority of teachers and many parents prefer ability grouping. As their clincher, they submit that the system protects children with high ability from the risk of being held back by those of lower ability.

Opponents of ability grouping counter by citing teachers who prefer to teach classes composed of children who represent a broad range of ability. They add that in any case children grouped homogeneously on the basis of one factor or school subject will not necessarily be homogeneous in other ways and that ability grouping really causes only a slight reduction in the wide range of pupil achievement. They claim that such grouping is basically undemocratic and encourages snobbish attitudes, and quote parents who feel that for their children to be in classes for children of average or low ability stigmatizes them. These foes of ability grouping warn that low-achieving classes run the danger of becoming dumping grounds for disruptive children.

To date, administrators have based most of their arguments pro and con on doctrine rather than on research. What does research say?

Some studies have shown that while having three ability groups at each level reduced the variability of pupil achievement by about 15 to 17 percent, the teacher is more important in the educative process than the device of organizing classes according to ability.

One investigator claims that ability grouping doesn't work because it is based on two erroneous assumptions: that achievement in most school subjects is almost entirely dependent upon intelligence and that the relationship between intelligence and achievement doesn't change. This investi-

Reprinted from *NEA Journal*, 57 (1): 9–11 (January 1968), by permission of author and publisher.

199

gator cites facts and figures to show that in a given school, boys and girls who score the same in an intelligence test vary widely in their achievement in reading, math, social studies, and science. The variations occur despite identical IQ's because the relationship between intelligence and achievement, influenced as it is by pupil motivation, attitudes, interests, and teaching practice is not static, but dynamic.

In 1966, the Horace Mann-Lincoln Institute of School Experimentation reported results of a comparative study of broad, medium, and narrow range ability grouping in 86 classes organized at the beginning of the fifth grade and remaining intact to the end of sixth grade. After being divided into five ability levels on the basis of IQ scores, some pupils were assigned to homogeneous classes, others to heterogeneous ones.

The general conclusion from this study is that narrowing the range of ability in a class on the basis of some measure of academic aptitude does not produce greater achievement of pupils at any ability level. Average pupils in classes with narrow ranges of ability learned no more than those in classes with the wide ranges. The effect of both kinds of grouping was similar with regard to aspirations and attitudes toward school.

Studies such as these suggest that no plan of grouping makes teaching and learning a simple matter. Any group of 30 or more average pupils, no matter how alike they seem, shows individual differences sufficient to challenge the ingenuity of the most competent teacher.

Classification by ability cannot remove individual differences or the need for adapting instruction to them. Indeed even if all the physical and intellectual factors were equal, the progress of average children in a homogeneous group would be equal only if each of them received exactly the same motivation under exactly the same circumstances with the same material in equal quantity. Even though children seemed to have the identical achievement at the beginning of the school year—in reading, for example—within a month or two, different rates of progress would have widened the range of achievement.

The research discussed so far bears out the thesis that the simple solution called ability grouping cannot meet the varied abilities and needs of the average child. What ammunition does research offer to the opposite viewpoint?

Standard tests of academic achievement, particularly where adaptations of standards, materials, and methods are made, show that pupils make slightly larger gains under ability grouping. The evidence in support of ability grouping indicates that it yields best results in academic learning for dull children; next best, for average children; and least, for bright children. (This conclusion must be regarded as tentative. Some experts claim that the differences may arise because test scores of higher ability pupils, unless carefully controlled, tend to regress toward lower ability levels; hence, the differences reported may not be as significant as they appear at first glance.)

In one study a reading test given to a sixth grade class revealed a range from below fourth grade to above twelfth grade. An intelligence test was then administered to estimate the degree to which pupils were reading above or below their general ability level.

On the basis of the achievement and intelligence tests, pupils were organized into four groups. The first group read from one to four grades above grade level and possessed above average to superior intelligence. The second group read at grade level and possessed a range of intelligence from slightly below average to superior. The third group read from one to two grades below grade level and ranged from below to slightly above average in intelligence. The fourth group read three or four grades below grade level and ranged in intelligence from below average to average.

These basic groups were organized into other subgroups within the class for such specific reading instruction objectives as word analysis, word meaning, rate of reading, and comprehension of paragraph meaning. Later tests showed that this pattern of refined grouping resulted in accelerated and enriched learning for most of the pupils.

Grouping of average children within a classroom may serve several purposes. One purpose is to provide direct instruction of a specific skill needed in reading, writing, spelling, or math. Another purpose is to build on the children's interests. Such groups may be formed within the class when new projects are undertaken or when new interests arise. This type of temporary grouping is frequently found in social studies, science, home economics, or health education. In these areas, effective learning comes through discussion, group planning, and research assignments undertaken by small groups.

Grouping may be arranged for social purposes, on the basis either of sociometric techniques or of the teacher's observations of "who likes whom or who likes to work with whom." Such groups are formed when problems involving social living exist within the classroom and when assignments are so informal that friendship choices are more important than academic abilities or curriculum interests.

Although research shows that classroom teachers have differences of opinion about ability grouping, several studies reveal that a majority of teachers prefer it.

Data regarding the effects of ability grouping upon the personal characteristics of pupils are so inadequate or subjective that no valid conclusions can be drawn.

Parent reaction to ability grouping is sharply divided: Some parents are all for it, but others apparently abhor it.

In my opinion, ability grouping for the average child is neither a cure nor a calamity. Its value appears to depend upon the teacher who uses it. When it is used without a clear knowledge of the specific learning needs of each average pupil and without the recognition that it must be articulated with carefully planned adaptations in curriculum, grouping can be ineffective or even harmful. It can be harmful when it lulls teachers and parents into believing that ability grouping is providing differentiated education for average pupils of varying degrees of ability, if such differentiation is non-existent.

Ability grouping is dangerous when it leads teachers to underestimate the learning capacities of pupils at the average ability levels. It can also be harmful when it does not provide flexible channels for moving children from average to higher groups and back again, either from subject to subject or within any one subject as their performance at various times in their school careers indicates.

On the other hand, ability grouping for average children may be used effectively when it grows out of the needs of the curriculum and when it is varied and flexible. Average pupils can be assembled in subgroups for special work, such as advanced content or remedial instruction in a given subject. Teachers can more easily carry out specific plans appropriate for an achievement level without having to provide for other widely divergent pupils for whom the particular content may be inappropriate.

The average child comprises the middle 50 to 60 percent of the pupil population. This represents a wide range of abilities, achievement, attitudes, and skills. No ability group of average pupils will be homogeneous in growth and development in such characteristics as height, weight, intelligence, or academic achievement. An average child's learning is not even; he may achieve well in one area and poorly in another.

For this observer, the answer that research gives is: The effective teacher with excellent pupil-teacher rapport and effective instructional materials will supersede ability grouping in producing effective learning for the average child.

Should We Group by Ability?

JAMES OLSEN

To a very large extent, ability or homogeneous grouping based on intelligence and/or achievement scores is still widely practiced in the public schools of this country (8). This practice rests on the assumption that bright children learn more when they are separated from their slower peers and grouped for instructional purposes with other bright children. We assume

Reprinted from *The Journal of Teacher Education,* 18 (2): 201–205 (Summer 1967), by permission of author and publisher.

that when we place together children who are more nearly alike in achievement and intelligence the instruction they receive will thereby be more
individualized. The argument for ability grouping is that if we narrow the
range of ability and achievement within an individual class we can increase
the quantity and quality of learning in that class.

Today, the validity of this hypothesis is a major issue, not only because
it affects the organization of the schools and the kinds of social and intellectual experiences to which students are exposed but also because the
practice of ability grouping involves broad social questions. With the bussing
of children, the locating of many new schools in border areas, and the
redefining of neighborhood boundaries, we can be assured that in the immediate future our students will have heterogeneous backgrounds socially,
racially, and intellectually. If we look at the issue of ability grouping from
a social standpoint, therefore, it takes on a new and important significance.

I think that most teachers and administrators would agree that when a
child is confined to a particular ability group he is committed, whether we
like to admit it or not, to an education of a very definite caliber. The
student who has been placed in a slow class quickly learns that he is in the
"stupid" class. In a study investigating the effects of ability grouping on
the self-concept of 102 fifth-grade children who had been grouped throughout their school career, Maxine Mann found that, when the children in the
lowest group were asked why they were in this particular class, they replied:
"I'm too dumb," "I can't think good," "We aren't smart," "We don't think
good," etc. Apparently these children felt they were intellectually inferior;
any negative feelings they had of themselves as learners when they entered
school were simply reinforced by their grouping assignments (17). An
analogous study made by Abraham and Edith Luchins of 190 sixth-grade
children in a New York City school came up with the same evidence (15).

There is also overwhelming sociological evidence that ability grouping
offers a way in which we can create *de facto* segregation in the classroom
after we have integration of the schools (20). Low-income children are
almost always assigned to the lower-ranking groups, and upper-income
children to higher-ranking groups. This is mainly because the lower-income
child comes to school with many cultural disadvantages, such as lack of
readiness for reading, lack of school know-how, etc., with the result that
he gets a low score on the middle-class-biased I.Q. test (20). Even though
we know that these tests do not measure native ability (6), we are still
using them to categorize students into low, average, and superior classes.
And we do this in spite of the fact that we know that intelligence is not a
static entity, genetically predetermined, and that a child's environment and
schooling have a profound effect on his mental functioning. As long as
educational and social opportunities are unequal, test results will be unequal;
yet, through these tests, educators help to strengthen the segregation and
class barriers they profess must be overcome.

When students are placed or segregated into ability groups, an intellectual ghetto is created which parallels the social ghetto from which they come, whether that ghetto be Park Avenue or Harlem. In the lower-ability groups, the teachers' expectations of the students' academic performance are inevitably lowered (7). How many teachers truly believe in the academic potential of students with low I.Q.'s who are often, according to their standardized test scores, "retarded"? This set of expectations must necessarily affect the learning process. The child himself comes to accept his own intellectual inferiority: if the school authorities do not consider him to be very bright, are they not right? Thus students in the lower-ability groups or tracks develop a sense of intellectual inadequacy which they can carry with them for the rest of their lives.

There are other kinds of psychological reverberations for the students in the top classes. In the Luchins' study already cited, the top students admitted they felt snobbish and superior to students in the lower-ability classes. As the superior students put it, "People would think we were dumb if we played with dumbbells." Thus our schools help to perpetuate the social-class stratification that exists in the larger society.

In addition, the better teachers are usually assigned to the better classes, with the result that those children who most need the best teaching do not receive it. Inexperienced teachers are always most heavily concentrated in lower-income schools, and since seniority usually counts when class teaching assignments are made, experienced teachers get the higher-ability classes and the new, inexperienced teachers get the left-over assignments, or the lower-ability classes (20). It would seem that simple justice and common sense would dictate that the lower-ability classes would get the best teachers so that they would have the best teaching available to compensate for their academic deficiencies. But apparently this type of adjustment is not generally preferred.

In the face of the social and psychological price we pay for ability grouping, it is ironic that the research clearly indicates that ability grouping in itself does not improve achievement in children (5, 8, 9). Not only this, but bright children grouped according to ability and taught separately do *not* learn more. Ruth Ekstrom, in her review of the literature on experimental studies of homogeneous grouping, concluded that there is no consistent pattern for the effectiveness of homogeneous grouping by age, course content, or ability level (9). David Abramson's study bears out this point (1). In other words, the research generally shows no significant differences in school achievement because of ability or homogeneous grouping.

Why? I.Q. and standardized test scores do not provide a valid qualitative index of individual differences in instructional needs, abilities, motivational levels, or learning styles of pupils. We may group students according to intelligence, but any psychologist will tell you that two 110 I.Q.'s on a Wechsler Intelligence Scale is an arithmetical accident because their scores represent different kinds of subtest scatters (5). Or take two students with the same reading score. One child may have excellent comprehension skills in spite of the fact that he is deficient in certain word attack skills. Another child, with the same score, may be competent in his word attack skills but be unable to read for main ideas; in other words, one student's liabilities may be the other's assets. Thus, even though these students have identical standardized test scores, their specific instructional needs are really quite different.

When we multiply these differences by the thirty or forty children in a classroom, we can readily see that our homogeneously grouped class is a statistical myth, not a pedagogic reality. In short, grouping does not solve the problem of meeting individual differences. Rather the practice of ability grouping actually militates against a true differentiation of teaching according to a student's need because we use it to rationalize what we really do in our schools: teach the class as an undifferentiated unit. We may talk about individualized differences, but the real differences in experiential background; academic abilities; verbal, perceptual, and auditory skills; differences in interests and in previous educational background are glossed over and ignored in daily classroom practice.

Soviet schools do not use either I.Q. tests (11) or ability grouping (12, 20); teachers feel that the use of I.Q. tests tends to retard the academic progress of students with low scores. Instead, in the Russian school, the child who finishes his work first helps the child who is having trouble with his lesson; and since the Russians feel that teaching is a very good way to learn, the child who teaches is not being penalized. But pupil cooperation and mutual help are not emphasized in American schools. Indeed, we seem to retreat in horror at the suggestion of other ways of meeting the problem of individual differences—of how we can adjust what we do in the classroom to each individual (18). Certainly, ability grouping does not solve this problem. What we must do is *construct a program which makes it possible for teachers to individualize instruction* on the following levels: the content of learning, the level of content, the kind of methodology, and the speed of learning.

Such a program will require the teacher to measure and diagnose continually so that the student can learn according to his needs. But the prime responsibility of the learning process will be on the student, not the teacher. Thus, the program would have self-teaching and self-directing aspects that would decrease the teacher's continual participation (team-learning techniques, for example, would be used); the learner would move at his own pace and in the direction of his interests and needs. In a classroom with this self-instructional emphasis, the teacher's role would be modified: he would initiate activities, work with individual students, diagnose, and supervise the overall direction of the learning process. Above all, he would teach pupils to teach themselves, and he would group and regroup students according to their special needs at a given time in a given content. This large-group instruction would be deemphasized and a methodology based on individual, team, and small-group learning would be employed.

Such a structured learning environment would make the practice of initiative and decision making on the part of students a reality rather than a fond dream. The focus of the program would not be, as it is now, upon the extrinsic reward of the mark or grade but upon the intrinsic rewards of the learning process. Students could risk behavior change; the teacher would be working *in conjunction with the student* and not in a judgmental capacity.

To create such an environment for learning is indeed a formidable task. But if we truly believe in our students' ability to grow and realize their potentialities, then I believe we must begin to break through the lockstep methods of grouping and the rigidities of the class lesson and make our programs adjustable to individual pupils rather than adjusting the pupils to the programs. In this way, perhaps we can begin to resolve some of the inconsistencies between what we say and what we, in fact, do.

BIBLIOGRAPHY

1. Abramson, David A. "The Effect of Ability Grouping in the High School upon Achievement in College." Doctor's thesis. School of Education, New York University, 1958.
2. _____. "The Effectiveness of Grouping for Students of High Ability." *Educational Research Bulletin* 38: 169–82; October 14, 1959.
3. Bettelheim, Bruno. "Segregation: New Style." *School Review* 66: 251–72; Autumn 1958.
4. Clark, Kenneth. "Disadvantaged Students and Discrimination." *The Search for Talent.* College Admissions 7. Princeton, N. J.: Educational Testing Service, 1960. pp. 12–19.
5. Cohen, S. Alan. "Reading: Large Issues, Specific Problems, and Possible Solutions." Paper given at meeting of Mobilization for Youth, 1964.
6. Davis, Allison. "Socio Economic Influence upon Children's Learning." Speech given at the Midcentury White House Conference on Children and Youth, Washington, D. C., December 5, 1950.
7. Deutsch, Martin. "Aspects of Ability Grouping." *Integrated Education* 2: 48–49; February-March 1964.
8. Eash, Maurice J. "Grouping: Some Implications from Research." Paper given at the ASCD Conference, October 1960.
9. Ekstrom, Ruth. *Experimental Studies of Homogeneous Grouping: A Review of the Literature.* Princeton, N. J.: Educational Testing Service, 1959.
10. Getzels, Jacob W., and Jackson, P. W. "The Meaning of Giftedness: An Examination of an Expanding Concept." *Phi Delta Kappan* 40: 75–77; November 1958.
11. Giles, G. G. T. "Why Soviet Teachers Oppose Intelligence Tests." *Anglo-Soviet Journal* 14: 1–13.

12. Grant, Nigel. *Soviet Education.* Baltimore, Md.: Penguin Books, 1964.
13. Henry, Jules. "Attitude Organization in Elementary Classrooms." *American Journal of Orthopsychiatry* 27: 117–33; January 1957.
14. Husen, Tortsen, and Svensson, N. E. "Pedagogic Milieu and Development of Intellectual Skills." *School Review* 68: 36–51; Spring 1960.
15. Luchins, A. S., and Luchins, E. H. "Children's Attitudes Toward Homogeneous Groupings." *Pedagogical Seminary and Journal of Genetic Psychology* 72: 3–9; March 1948.
16. MacKinnow, Donald W. "What Do We Mean by Talent and How Do We Test for It?" *The Search for Talent.* College Admissions 7. Princeton, N. J.: Educational Testing Service, 1960. pp. 20–29.
17. Mann, Maxine. "What Does Ability Grouping Do to the Self Concept?" *Childhood Education* 36: 357–60; April 1960.
18. Rabb, Herb. "Grouping in the Classroom." *Mobilization for Youth Newsletter* 2: 1; April 1964.
19. Rudd, W. G. A. "The Psychological Effect of Streaming by Attainment." *British Journal of Educational Psychology* 28: 47–60; February 1958.
20. Sexton, Patricia Cayo. *Education and Income: Inequalities of Opportunity in Our Public Schools.* New York: The Viking Press, 1961.

Grouping for Teachability

HERBERT A. THELEN

Common experience, reinforced by a very large number of studies, gives us every reason to believe that the particular combination of teacher and pupils in the classroom has significant consequences for education. However, there is increasing use of such devices as ability grouping that in no way depend on what the teacher is like. It may be well to discuss the idea that the "right" class for one teacher may not at all be the "right" class for another. In this paper I shall present some experiences that throw light on the problem of composing the "right" class for each teacher.[1]

Teachers differ markedly in the ways they teach, in the ways they respond to children, and in the ways they want and expect students to respond to

Reprinted from *Theory into Practice,* 2 (2): 81–89 (April 1963), by permission of author and publisher.

[1] One can imagine two conditions under which grouping would make no sense at all: (a) When the teacher's operation is in no way dependent on the composition of the class—some lecture courses, presented the safe way year after year, appear to approach this condition, although audience response would always have *some* influence on the teacher's feelings of adequacy and success; and (b) When the differences between teachers are such that the students can adapt readily as they move from one teacher to the next—consider, for example, the students who seem to get along in school more by studying the teacher than by studying the subject.

them. It seems unreasonable to suppose that all students would be equally well able to meet a teacher's needs and expectations. But to carry the discussion further, we have to describe more specifically just how profound the differences are, how "deep" the demands, how different the roles the students must take from one classroom to the next.

In our recent study of "teachability grouping," our research team attempted to examine twenty-eight classes from an anthropological point of view. From this study, four major classroom types emerged:

1. The overarching purpose of the class—its reason for existence—is to be exploited by the teacher. What the teacher seeks always is love, respect, or fellowship. The students quickly learn not to give him any feedback that would make the teacher see that he is not, in the students' eyes, the lovable person, the expert, or the delightful "one of the gang" that he wants to be. This teacher's ego ideal seems to be the autocratic boss, the kindly grandmother, the cute adolescent—almost anything, in fact, except an educator.

2. The overarching purpose of the class is to be comfortable. Don't rock the boat; avoid all conflict; there is no need to be unpleasant. During those first few weeks while the class is getting "shaken down," a process of negotiation is going on: the teacher agrees not to make uncomfortable demands on the class provided the class will give up its wish to learn anything. The dominant activity is an agendaless discussion—a running bull session.

3. The overarching purpose of the class is to be toilet trained into such values as punctuality, quiet, orderliness, and respect for adults. The class exists to be quiet, punctual, and all the rest—not as conditions required for productive educative activity, but as ends in themselves. The teacher in this class has two theories to guide him: one, a theory of classroom management; the other, a theory of learning. He thinks, "First I must manage the class—only then can I teach it." Somehow he never quite gets around to teaching it.

4. The overarching purpose of the class is to "achieve," as the public and administrators commonly understand that term. The class perpetually reenacts the achievement ritual: the reading of the sacred text; the daily catechism over the assigned parts; and the confirmation ceremony through which the elders, by suitable rituals of examinations, decide who are the true believers ("A" students). The learning outcome depends a good deal on the spirit in which the ritual is followed. The spirit can be enthusiastic, warm, incisive—or it can be indifferent, hostile, meandering. It is probable that the learning is determined by the spirit rather than the ritual; that is, the enthusiastic, incisive teacher would get better results than the other kind, no matter what procedures they both used.[2]

Most teachers are, of course, a blend of such "types." Although the types

[2] Thelen, H. A. "One Small Head—," *Educational Leadership,* December, 1962, *20,* 203–209.

might be described differently by different observers, all observers would undoubtedly find different types.

One interesting thing about these descriptions, beyond their portrayal of differences, is the implication that subconscious factors are dominant. For it is most unlikely that the teachers we observed were aware of these dominant qualities in their classrooms. In fact, it is highly probable that most of them would vigorously resist these characterizations. We do not for a minute suppose that teachers intentionally create these climates. The climates emerge as a reflection of the total personality of the teacher; and the fact that the personality of the teacher can color a year's work with thirty children demonstrates how tremendously influential the teacher is—whether or not he knows it or likes it.

DIFFERENTIAL PREFERENCES AMONG TEACHERS

Differences among teachers are found at conscious, as well as subconscious levels. When asked, teachers give different answers to specific questions about how they teach or about what sort of students they can teach best.

In one study, forty teachers were asked to indicate from a list of fifty student behavioral traits the ones that best described the kind of student they considered superior and productive. The teachers placed markedly different emphases upon critical thinking, social adequacy and co-operation, and personal maturity. The image of the preferred student—presumably the kind the teacher beams his instruction to—differed from teacher to teacher.

Then we asked one of the teachers, many of whose students had already been tested on an assessment battery, to give us the names of several who, in her opinion, "got a lot out of class," and several who "got very little out of class." We analyzed the tests to see what differences they revealed between these two groups of students. We discovered, first, that the successful and unsuccessful students did not differ very markedly on specific scores, but that they did show slight patterns of difference among many scores. This was of considerable interest, because it suggested that no one or even several factors like IQ, age, interest in working in groups, etc., could be used by themselves as selection factors. Second, the more successful students were in many ways quite unlike the teacher. Complementation rather than congruence may well have been the more important principle.

The importance of the "fit" between teachers and classes was evident in the generally inconclusive results of studies of ability grouping. Ruth Ekstrom, for example, studied all the published accounts of ability grouping over the last fifty years. In each study she compared student achievement in homogeneous groups of high, medium, or low ability with achievement in the usual heterogeneous group. She concluded that each condition produced the better results about a third of the time. She interpreted this inconclusiveness in this way: When the teacher "knew what to do" with the high-ability class, for example, he achieved better results; but better results could not be expected unless the teacher adapted his instruction to the particular group in front of him. Two-thirds of the teachers were unable to do this. In short, the critical factor is the teacher's ability to adapt instruction to the actual group before him. There may be some teachers who can adapt their instruction most effectively to a homogeneous high- or low-ability group, but the number of such teachers is undoubtedly very small. This is true because the ability of the student does not have much to do with the effectiveness of the teacher. Although teachers generally perceive their good classes as brighter than their difficult classes, a check of the actual IQ's of the students may reveal no difference.

When teachers are asked to *name* their good and bad students (e.g., the ones who they think get a great deal or very little out of a class), they seldom agree on the same students. In one project we had three teachers working with the same fifty students for three hours each day. One teacher selected seven, and the other two teachers selected nine students as getting a great deal out of class. But the three teachers agreed on only three students.

We conclude from these and other experiences that classroom climates, standards, and values differ significantly among teachers, and that personal "compatibility" between teachers and students is the most important basis for placing students in effective classes.

An Investigation of "Compatibility" Grouping

In the spring of 1960, fifteen teachers agreed to participate in an experiment on teachability grouping.[3] These teachers were located in eight elementary and junior-high schools in Illinois, Wisconsin, and Indiana. The grades ranged from 8 through 11; the subjects taught were English, American literature, social studies, geometry, advanced algebra, biology, world history, and American history.

For the academic year 1960–61, each of the fifteen teachers was given two classes. In one the students were carefully chosen, on the basis of a 405-item assessment battery, to be most "like" those the teacher had said "got the most out of" previous classes; in the other (the control class) the students were chosen by the school officers using their regular selection procedures.

During that year, the thirty classes were studied in detail. Each class was observed from three to five times by a team of at least two observers. From one to three sessions in each class were tape-recorded, and the tape

---

[3] This account includes material from the Summary and the Final Report of the Cooperative Research project—"Development of Different Methods of Teaching for Different Types of Students." The Final Report is available from the U.S. Office of Education. Within a year, it will be published as a book.

record analyzed and coded, statement by statement. Diagnostic conferences pooled the impressions of all the observers. Ten post-meeting reaction sheets filled in by the students at the end of the class sessions were selected randomly from the larger number administered during the year. The students also took a student-opinion survey, and sociometric and Guess Who tests during the spring of 1961. The teachers took the sociometric tests and furnished grades, achievement records, and lesson plans. They also were interviewed for from two to five hours by the observers on different occasions.

Some of the findings from the study follow. Data for two of the teachers were incomplete; thus, the report is based on results with thirteen teachers.

1. What can be said about "teachable" students? The 405-item assessment battery provided about 1600 responses. Of these, 140—less than 10 per cent—significantly differentiated between students who got a great deal out of class (hereinafter referred to as "teachable") and those who got little out of class. Of these 140 items selected, 66—47 per cent—were found common to a significant majority of the thirteen teachers. These 66 items did not cluster around any one major characteristic, such as brightness, independence, or achievement. Nevertheless, these items do produce a pattern which indicates a high degree of personal adequacy; striving to realize one's capabilities; uneasy control over this striving; and the effort to develop such control through acceptance of social values, development of cooperative ways of working, adoption of a strong orientation to "work," and preference for a "firm" teacher with whom one can identify. But note that this pattern accounts for only about 4 per cent of the item responses. Thus, it represents only a rather mild tendency; however, this is about all that the teachable students had in common among the thirteen teachers.

2. How did the operation of teachable classes compare with the regular classes? There were 95 categories of observation used by observers and students. Thirty-six per cent of these discriminated significantly between teachable and regular classes. These core items portray the teachability classes as having *higher solidarity*. The five subthemes that emerge are: a more work-oriented, less inattentive, less distractable, more manageable class; more work-solidarity among the students; more enthusiasm in the teacher's approval of work; less rigidity, more flexibility in the teaching; and greater permissiveness with respect to disruptive behavior which, however, occurs significantly less frequently. The teacher "gives more of himself" and is "more of a person" in the teachable classes. But note that the differences described here again represent only a mild common tendency. They seem to be mostly subconscious changes in the responses of the teachers to the high-solidarity, more manageable class. Certainly the teachers did not consciously plan differently, nor did they knowingly follow different strategies.

3. What were the results of having teachability classes? Of the thirteen teachability classes, eleven received higher grades from the teacher, one received lower grades, and one received the same grades (as compared to the corresponding regular classes). Moreover, when the twenty-six classes are divided into top and bottom halves by means of the teachability scores of the students, three-quarters of the students in the top halves got better grades than the average student in the bottom halves.

In respect to pre-post gain on achievement tests (as compared to over-all grade for the total year's work), only five of the teachable classes made greater gains than the regular classes, whereas eight of the regular classes gained more than the experimental classes. Thus, the teachers seemed to be saying that their educational purposes as shown by final grades were better achieved by the teachable classes even though they gained less on whatever it is that achievement tests measure.

As for interpersonal feelings, nine of the thirteen teachers preferred the students in their teachable classes to "work with" or to "chat with," and six preferred the teachable class for both purposes. On the other hand, the students in nine of the regular classes preferred the teacher to "work with" and to "chat with" more than did the students in the corresponding teachable classes. When rating preferences among themselves, students in eleven of the thirteen teachable classes had higher preferences than regular students for "chatting with" one another; and in eight teachable classes they indicated higher preferences than the regular students for "working with" one another.

4. *What were some of the differences among teachability classes?* One long case study and four short case studies, based on all the data for five teachers and their ten classes, show that the teachers wanted and got very different things in their teachable classes. (a) One teacher appeared to want more vigorous, personally involving interaction with his students; (b) another wanted a class that could penetrate more deeply into principles of his subject; (c) another wanted a class he could move faster with; (d) another wanted a pleasant, friendly, non-work oriented class that would make him feel more adequate; (e) another wanted a class in which he could combine "counseling" with teaching. In these five situations, varying in the extent of their psychological exploitation of students, all except (d) were successful in the eyes of the teacher. In case (d) the teachable class started off well but rapidly deteriorated, because neither the teacher nor the students he selected as teachable were able to give the group the leadership it needed.

CONCLUSIONS

1. Teachability grouping, which gives each teacher a class full of students "like" those who, he believes, "got a lot out of class" in the past, results in more "manageable" classes and in higher attainment of the teacher's purpose.

2. The teacher tends to be more satisfied with his teachable class, to like the students better, and to give them higher grades. The students tend to be more orderly and manageable, more cooperative, and more satisfied with the activities. They do not necessarily like the teacher better as a person, nor do they tend to rate the course as a whole higher (as compared to other courses). They do tend to like each other better, and their class appears to be more cohesive than the control class.

3. The changed behavior of the teacher in his teachable group seems to be due mostly to his responding differently to the class. He does not consciously plan differently nor execute different strategies.

4. The students, although operating more to give the teacher what he seeks, may gain less satisfaction in the teachable class. This appears to be the case when the teacher is concerned primarily with meeting his own psychological needs rather than with educating the class. The resulting exploitative situation may produce negative reactions in the students—even though they still perform better in the teacher's eyes.

5. If the personal need of the teacher is strongly dominant and is antithetical to group development, his teachable class may in fact deteriorate rapidly and become chaotic. (This occurred in the case of one teacher.)

6. The teacher's grades appear to reflect attainment of his purposes. They reflect "achievement" only insofar as "achievement" is central among the teacher's purposes. In half of the cases we studied, achievement, while sought through procedures presumably planned for it, was secondary to such things as enabling the teacher to play some role he wanted or developing a particular quality of interaction among the students.

7. The teachable class facilitates the execution, through teaching, of the teacher's purposes, but *teachability grouping per se does not make him a different or better educator*. This problem has to be approached through tactics of training and re-education of the teacher.

8. To make teachability grouping possible, there must be a choice of teachers available to teach a subject. The more differences that exist among the styles of these teachers, the greater the range of students that can be accommodated.

9. The preceding statement implies that beyond a general orientation to inquiry, the teachers who are employed should have quite different styles of teaching. The further implication is that, defined procedurally, there is no one "right" way to teach.

10. The teacher has to help by selecting the children who are to be placed in teachable groups. In fact, grouping ought to be considered among the professional responsibilities of the faculty and should not be left solely in the hands of the administration.

Whatever sort of person and pedagogue the teacher happens to be, he will be both of these more effectively when given a room full of students like those he thinks "got a lot out of his previous classes." If he is exploitative, he will be more exploitative; if he is a clown, he will be more of a clown; if he wants to "cover the ground," he will cover more ground. Hopefully, if he likes to inquire with the class, he should be able to get more and better inquiry going.

The teacher is more effective with a "compatible" class, but note that compatibility is determined on the basis of students the teacher says get more out of class—this may mean that the teacher likes them better, can jump on them with fewer feelings of guilt, is stimulated by them, or simply feels that they are more vital and alive. The model for the teachable student is developed from other students selected by the teacher, and the basis of his selection is not very clearly defined. Note that the model is *not* the teacher's description of the sort of student whom he describes as teachable; it is taken from the actual students whom he designates.

Teachable classes are not more homogeneous than regular classes. In some cases one would have to observe for quite a while to decide which was which. The differences are many but small, and they are distributed over a wide gamut of measurable traits. It is as if there is some sort of pervasive bias in the students' general way of life; it is not a question of one or two outstanding characteristics (like IQ, past achievement, submissiveness, independence, outgoingness, etc.). The finding of greater "maturity" exists, but only as a small common tendency not at all obvious in overt behavior.

I find an analogy the best approach to thinking about these matters. Suppose you attend a lecture given by a person who has a foreign accent. This accent means different things to different members of the audience. Some persons simply will not understand what the man is saying; others will not listen because they don't like foreigners; still others will be more interested in studying the man and imagining his background than in listening to the lecture; and so on through a wide range of possible reactions. The one thing we can say confidently is that those members of the audience who have lived abroad will probably get more (of whatever they want) from the lecture. In other words, the common factor is an ability to cope with a way of life that is generally similar to other ways of life, but that has some unique but small particular differences from them. The pattern of attitudes, information, and skill that is called on is but a small part of the person's total capability and personality, *yet it importantly determines* what he will get from the lecture. We certainly would not see those who get a great deal from the lecture as essentially different in "type" from those who get little out of it; yet the fact that some get more than others do is significant.

Possibly the child may regard teachers as "foreigners," and he may react in much the same way as members of the lecture audience. Thus, the unique personality components of both teacher and pupils must be considered in developing teachable groups.

The Middle School: Alternative to the Status Quo

MARY F. COMPTON

The most neglected age group in the schools today is that which is becoming known as the "in-between-ager." This group includes students in the later years of the elementary program and those in the first two years of the junior high school. These are the youngsters who have needs quite different from their younger and older counterparts. Indeed, one of the characteristics which unites this group is that they are so different from one another—the differences between students during these years are much more numerous and varied than during any other period of public education.

These children in the middle years have been neglected under the present 6-3-3 plan of school organization. Neither the self-contained classroom of the elementary school nor the subject-centered program of the junior high school adequately meets their needs.

ELEMENTARY SCHOOL INADEQUACIES

In most elementary schools, whether a child is six and just beginning formal schooling or twelve with at least five years' experience in school, it is highly probable that the teaching is the same—ten-, eleven-, and twelve-year-olds are being taught like the younger children in the school. One need not have training in educational psychology to recognize the wide gulf between the characteristics of first grade children and those in the fifth or sixth grades. The differences are evident. Many eleven-year-old girls are already pubescent, and boys of the same age are approaching this stage of development. These children resent being treated like "little children," for their needs, interests, and desires are quite different from those of the first grader who, nonetheless, shares with them a similar instructional program.

The predominant pattern of organization for the elementary grades is the self-contained classroom, with one teacher responsible for instruction for one group of children during most of the school day. The failure to provide for the in-between-ager in the elementary school is not so much because of the theory of this approach, as its practice.

Champions of the self-contained classroom argue that it alone of the various alternative modes of horizontal school organization provides a uni-

Reprinted from *Theory into Practice*, 7 (3): 108–110 (June 1968), by permission of author and publisher.

215

fied and integrated approach to the numerous subject areas taught in the elementary school. Actually, the self-contained classroom offers a program segmented by subject areas to the same degree as the departmental program. However, the departmental approach offers instruction by specialists in the various subject areas; the self-contained classroom does not.

No educator can be a specialist in all areas of the curriculum—a role expected of the teacher in the self-contained classroom. Usually, this teacher emphasizes and does a fairly creditable job of teaching the subjects in which he has the greatest amount of preparation and with which he feels most secure, usually the language arts. Instruction in other curriculum areas may be incidental (or accidental) because the teacher feels insecure in teaching them, and they may take a back seat in the daily program.

Evidence indicates that specialization of instruction is needed for the student in the upper elementary grades. Proponents of the self-contained classroom argue that departmentalization tends to fragment the curriculum, oblivious to the fact that the program they support is itself extremely fragmented. They further argue that the fifth- and sixth-graders lack the psychological maturity to benefit from instruction by subject area specialists.

Studies conducted in Tulsa, Oklahoma by Broadhead [1] and Livingston [2] indicate that semi-departmentalization may have a *positive* effect on the social adjustment of children in the upper grades. In the two studies, students in semi-departmental programs demonstrated better social adjustment than students in self-contained classrooms.

The use of special teachers in science and mathematics in grades 5 and 6 was studied by Gibb and Matala.[3] They found that students taught by specialists achieved at a higher level in science than youngsters taught by the teacher in the self-contained classroom, but achievement in mathematics was about equal. The children themselves expressed a preference for departmentalized instruction.

JUNIOR HIGH SCHOOL DEFICIENCIES

The name given to the institution for the three years between elementary and high school was unfortunate—"junior" implies a scaled-down version of a "senior" counterpart. The major fault of the junior high school is that it has become a mimic of the senior high school, complete with varsity athletic teams, pep rallies, marching bands, cheerleaders, class proms, and

[1] Broadhead, Fred C. "Pupil Adjustment in the Semi-departmental Elementary School," *Elementary School Journal,* April 1960, *60*, 385–90.

[2] Livingston, A. H. "Does a Departmental Organization Affect Children's Adjustment?" *Elementary School Journal,* January 1961, *61*, 217–20.

[3] Gibb, E. Glenadine, and Matala, Dorothy C. "Study on the Use of Special Teachers of Science and Mathematics in Grades 5 and 6," *School Science and Mathematics,* November 1962, *6*, 565–85.

even graduation exercises. A great deal of pressure is exerted on the junior high school student to excel physically, and this may present emotional danger for youngsters who cannot at this age measure up to the ideal.

The junior high school program of studies, as well, tends to parallel that of the high school. With the exception of a few junior high schools in which vestiges of the core-type program remain and others using true team teaching (not merely "turn teaching"), the separate-subject program with one subject per period is well entrenched. There is likely to be little relationship between the various subjects to which the student is exposed during the course of a school day unless interdepartmental planning has occurred. In most instances, the opportunity for the student to explore is usually quite limited. Too often, the student's choice may be restricted to only one or two subject areas.

The pressure exerted by the high school often actually determines the offerings of the junior high school—the granting of Carnegie-unit credit in grade 9 is to a great extent responsible for this. The high school must either accept the Carnegie credits of the junior high school or attempt to control the granting of these credits in grade 9. When the ninth grade is included in the high school, the senior institution does not feel compelled to dominate the program of the junior high school.

Also contributing to the problems of the junior high school is the teacher assigned to teach this age group. Few teacher education programs differentiate the preparation for junior high school teachers from that designed specifically for elementary or high school teachers. Some teachers work with junior high school students by choice, but most, unfortunately, have no aptitude for teaching this age group, lack an understanding of them and their needs, and find themselves on the junior high staff because junior high schools are difficult to staff. All too often, the junior high school staff is recruited from among dissatisfied and/or unsuccessful teachers at either the elementary or senior high levels.

THE MIDDLE SCHOOL

When the junior high school appeared on the educational scene some sixty years ago, the decision to separate the seventh, eighth, and ninth grades from the elementary school and the high school was a consequence of a concern of representatives of higher education for the introduction of high school subjects earlier in the school program.

The purposes of the junior high school later became to provide (1) a bridge between the elementary school and its self-contained classroom and the specialized subject-field program of the high school, (2) exploratory experiences to aid youngsters in selecting a specific program in the high school, and (3) academic, vocational, and personal guidance. Had the junior high school fulfilled these purposes and the elementary school recognized the need for a program for its older students, there might have been no need to challenge the 6-3-3 plan as educators now are doing.

The middle school, which many school systems across the country are adopting, appears to be a promising alternative to this inadequate 6-3-3 organization—it focuses attention on a portion of the school population too often treated as second-class citizens in the public schools.

Because the middle school varies from school district to school district (as well it should), describing *the* middle school specifically is just as impossible a task as attempting to describe *the* elementary school or *the* junior high. However, they do share elements in common:

1. Articulation with the elementary school to assure easy transition for youngsters. This may necessitate a pseudo self-contained classroom approach during a portion of the school day for the first year of middle school education.
2. Team teaching by subject-matter specialists in areas of general knowledge which are closely related—English language, literature, history, geography, economics, anthropology, science, art, and music.
3. Skills laboratories staffed by technologists with subject-matter competencies to provide remedial, developmental, and advanced instruction in such skills as reading, listening, writing, mathematics, science, foreign language, art, music, and physical education.
4. Independent study for *all students*, commensurate with the topic selected for study and the student's needs, interests, and abilities.
5. A home-base group assigned to a teacher with special training in guidance and counseling, as well as the time and the opportunity to aid children with personal and academic problems on a regularly scheduled basis.
6. A program of activities in which each student will be able to participate—based on the personal development of students rather than on enhancement of the school's prestige or the entertainment of the public.
7. A plan of vertical school organization providing for continuous progress of students.
8. Evaluative techniques in light of individual progress, rather than the prevalent punitive system of assigning grades in terms of some elusive "average" for a particular chronological age group.
9. A program tailored to the needs of each student, with individualized student schedules.
10. An instructional and administrative staff with an understanding of the in-between-ager, competence in teaching at least one subject area, and a genuine desire to provide the best possible program for these youngsters.

CONCLUSION

As a new institution, aimed at articulating programs to meet the needs, interests, and abilities of the specific students it serves, the middle school may serve as a vehicle for change for the entire spectrum of the public school program.

However, the middle school should not be viewed as a panacea for all the ills of the present school program, for the success of any plan of school organization depends on the extent to which it meets the needs—cognitive, affective, and psychomotor—of the students it serves. If the middle school does not meet these needs, like the junior high school before it, it too should be replaced.

School Parks for Equal Opportunities *

JOHN H. FISCHER

Of all the plans that have been put forward for integrating urban schools the boldest is the school park. This is a scheme under which several thousand ghetto children and a larger number from middle-class white neighborhoods would be assembled in a group of schools sharing a single campus. Placing two or more schools on one site is not a new idea, but two other aspects of the school park are novel. It would be the largest educational institution ever established below the collegiate level and the first planned explicitly to cultivate racial integration as an element of good education.

A small community might house its entire school system in one such complex. A large city with one or more large ghettos would require several. In the most imaginative and difficult form of the proposal a central city and its neighboring suburban districts would jointly sponsor a ring of metropolitan school parks on the periphery of the city.[1]

The characteristic features of the school park—comprehensive coverage and unprecedented size—are its main advantages and at the same time the chief targets of its critics. Is the park a defensible modern version of the

Reprinted from *The Journal of Negro Education*, 37 (3): 301–309 (Summer 1968), by permission of author and publisher.

* This chapter is excerpted from a paper entitled "The School Park" prepared by Dr. Fischer under contract with the U.S. Commission on Civil Rights. It was undertaken independently from the Commission and is the responsibility of the author alone.

1 Thomas B. Pettigrew, "School Desegregation in Urban America," unpublished paper prepared for NAACP Legal Conference on School Desegregation, October 1966, pp. 25–33.

common school, perhaps the only form in which that traditionally American institution can be maintained in an urban society? Or is it a monstrous device that can lead only to the mass mistreatment of children? Whatever else it is or may in time turn out to be, it is neither a modest proposal nor a panacea.

Since even one such project would require a substantial commitment of policy and money, it is obvious that the validity of the concept should be closely examined and the costs and potential benefits associated with it carefully appraised.

The purpose of this paper is to assist that process by considering the relevance of the school park to present problems in urban education and by analyzing, although in a necessarily limited way, its potentiality.

THE PROBLEM

Twelve years of effort, some ingeniously pro forma and some laboriously genuine, have proved that desegregating schools—to say nothing of integrating them—is much more difficult than it first appeared. Attendance area boundaries have been redrawn; new schools have been built in border areas; parents have been permitted, even encouraged, to choose more desirable schools for their children; pupils from crowded slum schools have been bused to outlying schools; Negro and white schools have been paired and their student bodies merged; but in few cases have the results been wholly satisfactory. Despite some initial success and a few stable solutions, the consequences, for the most part, have proved disappointing. Steady increases in urban Negro population, continuing shifts in the racial character of neighborhoods, actual or supposed decline in student achievement, unhappiness over cultural differences and unpleasant personal relations have combined to produce new problems faster than old ones could be solved.[2]

Underlying the whole situation are basic facts that have too seldom been given the attention they merit. Some of these facts bear on the behavior of individuals. Few parents of either race, for example, are willing to accept inconvenience or to make new adjustments in family routines if the only discernible result is to improve the opportunities of other people's children. A still smaller minority will actually forego advantages to which their children have become accustomed merely to benefit other children. Most parents, liberal or conservative, hesitate to accept any substantial change in school procedures unless they are convinced that their own children will have a better than even chance of profiting from them. While prejudice and bigotry are not to be minimized as obstacles to racial integra-

[2] Jeanette Hopkins, "Self Portrait of School Desegregation in Northern Cities," unpublished paper prepared for NAACP Legal Conference, October 1966, pp. 1–3.

tion, resistance attributed to them is often due rather to the reluctance of parents to risk a reduction in their own children's opportunities.

. . . .

The controversy over what constitutes viable racial balance in schools or neighborhoods remains unsettled, for the data are far from complete. There is abundant evidence, however, that few middle-class families, Negro or white, will choose schools enrolling a majority of Negro children if any alternative is available. Additional complications arise from social class and cultural relationships. Although borderline sites or school pairing on the periphery of a ghetto may produce temporary racial desegregation, these devices rarely bring together children of different social classes. As a consequence, the predictable antagonism between lower class white and Negro groups increase the school's burden of adjustment problems and diminish the benefits of cultural interchange.

. . . .

The moral and legal grounds for desegregating schools are clear and well-established. The factual evidence that integration can improve the effectiveness of education is steadily accumulating.[3] For the purposes of this paper there is no need to review either. But it will be useful to examine what is now known about the conditions that must be met if schools are to be well integrated and effective.

The first requirement is that the proportion of each race in the school be acceptable and educationally beneficial to both groups.[4] This means that the proportion of white students must be high enough to keep them and, more importantly, their parents from feeling overwhelmed and to assure the Negro student the advantage of a genuinely integrated environment. On the other hand, the number of Negro students must be large enough to prevent their becoming an odd and isolated minority in a nominally desegregated school. Their percentage should enable them to appear as a matter of course in all phases of school life. No Negro student should have to "represent his race" in any different sense than his white classmates represent theirs.

Many efforts have been made to define a racially balanced school, but no "balance," however logical it may be statistically, is likely to remain stable and workable if it results in either a majority of Negroes, or so few that they are individually conspicuous. This suggests in practice a Negro component ranging from a minimum of 15 to 20 per cent to a maximum of 40 to 45 per cent.

School districts with small Negro minorities, even though they may be concentrated in ghettos, can ordinarily devise plans to meet these conditions

---

[3] James S. Coleman, *Equality of Educational Opportunity* (Washington, D.C.: U.S. Department of Health, Education, and Welfare, 1966), p. 332.
[4] Pettigrew, *op. cit.*, p. 17.

without large scale changes in the character of their school systems. Central cities with sizeable ghettos and smaller cities with larger proportions of Negroes will usually be required to make substantial changes in order to attain integrated schools.

But even when such acceptable racial proportions have been established, an effectively integrated school can be maintained only if a second condition is met: The school must respond to the educational needs of all its students better than the schools they might otherwise attend. The school must possess the capacity, the physical facilities, the staff strength, the leadership, and the flexibility required not only to offer a wide range of programs and services, but also adapt them to the special circumstances of individual students.

THE PARK AS A POSSIBLE SOLUTION

In school districts where redistricting, pairing, open enrollment, and busing offer little hope of producing lasting integration and high quality school programs, the school park may well offer a satisfactory solution. School parks (called also educational parks, plazas, or centers) have been proposed in a number of communities and are being planned in several. The schemes so far advanced fall into several categories. The simplest, which is appropriate for a small or medium-sized town, assembles on a single campus all the schools and all the students of an entire community. As a result the racial character of a particular neighborhood no longer determines the character of any one school. All the children of the community come to the central campus where they can be assigned to schools and classes according to whatever criteria will produce the greatest educational benefits. The School Board of East Orange, N. J., has recently announced a 15-year construction program to consolidate its school system of some 10,000 pupils in such an educational plaza.[5]

Another variant of the park is a similarly comprehensive organization serving one section of a large city as the single park might serve an entire smaller town. Where this plan is adopted the capacity of the park must be so calculated that its attendance area will be sufficiently large and diversified to yield a racially balanced student body for the foreseeable future. Merely to assemble two or three elementary units, a junior high school and a senior high school would in many cities produce no more integration than constructing the same buildings on the customary separate sites.

Less comprehensive schemes can also be called school parks. One, applicable to smaller communities, would center all school facilities for a single level of education—e.g., all elementary schools, or middle schools,

---

[5] "Desegregation. Ten Blueprints for Action," *School Management,* X (October 1966), 103–105.

or high schools, on a single site. Single-level complexes serving less than a whole community are also possible in large cities. . . .

A fourth, and the most comprehensive, type of park would require a number of changes in school planning and administration. This is the metropolitan school park designed to meet the increasingly serious problems posed by the growing Negro population of the central cities and the almost wholly white suburbs that surround them. The proposal, briefly stated, is to ring the city with school parks that would enroll the full range of pupils from the kindergarten to the high school and possibly including a community college. Each park would be placed in a "neutral" area near the periphery of the city. Each attendance area would approximate a segment of the metropolitan circle with its apex at the center of the city and its base in the suburbs. Since many students would arrive by school bus or public carrier, each site would be adjacent to a main transport route.[6]

The potentialities of school parks in general can be explored by projecting what might be done in such a metropolitan center. We can begin with certain assumptions about size and character. In order to encompass an attendance area large enough to assure for the long term an enrollment more than 50 per cent white and still include a significant number of Negro students from the inner-city ghetto, the typical park, in most metropolitan areas, would require a total student body (kindergarten to Grade 12) of not less than 15,000. It would thus provide all the school facilities for a part of the metropolitan area with a total population of 80,000 to 120,000. The exact optimum size of a particular park might be as high as 30,000, depending upon the density of urban and suburban population, the prevalence of nonpublic schools, the pattern of industrial, business, and residential zoning, the character of the housing, and the availability of transport.

The site, ideally, would consist of 50 to 100 acres but a workable park could be designed on a much smaller area or, under suitable circumstances, deep within the central city by using high-rise structures.[7] Within these buildings individual school units of varying sizes would be dispersed horizontally and vertically. On a more generous plot each unit could be housed separately with suitable provision for communication through tunnels or covered passages.

The sheer size of the establishment would present obvious opportunities to economize through centralized functions and facilities, but the hazards of over-centralization are formidable. To proceed too quickly or too far down that path would be to sacrifice many of the park's most valuable opportunities for better education.

Because of its size the park would make possible degrees of speciali-

[6] Pettigrew, *op. cit.*, pp. 25–33.

[7] Harold B. Gores, "Education Park; Physical and Fiscal Aspects," in Milton Jacobsen (ed.), *An Exploration of the Educational Park Concept* (New York: New York Board of Education, 1964), pp. 2–7.

zation, concentration, and flexibility that are obtainable only at exorbitant cost in smaller schools. A center enrolling 16,000 students in a kindergarten-4-4-4 organization, with 1,000–1,300 pupils at each grade level, could efficiently support and staff not only a wide variety of programs for children at every ordinary level or ability, but also highly specialized offerings for those with unusual talents or handicaps.

Such an institution could operate its own closed circuit television system more effectively, and with lower cable costs than a community-wide system, and with greater attention to the individual teacher's requirements. A central bank of films and tapes could be available for transmission to any classroom, and the whole system controlled by a dialing mechanism that would enable every teacher to "order" at any time whatever item he wished his class to see.

The pupil population would be large enough to justify full-time staffs of specialists and the necessary physical facilities to furnish medical, psychological, and counseling services at a level of quality that is now rarely possible. Food service could be provided through central kitchens, short distance delivery, and decentralized dining rooms for the separate schools.

The most important educational consequences of the park's unprecedented size would be the real opportunities it would offer for organizing teachers, auxiliary staff, and students. In the hypothetical K-4-4-4 park of 16,000, for example, there would be about 5,000 pupils each in the primary and middle school age groups, or enough at each level for 10 separate schools of 500 pupils.

Each primary or middle school of that size could be housed in its own building, or its own section of a larger structure with its own faculty of perhaps 25. Such a unit, directed by its own principal, with its own complement of master teachers, "regular" teachers, interns, assistants, and volunteers, would be the school "home" of each of its pupils for the 3, 4, or 5 years he would spend in it before moving on to the next level of the park. A permanent organization of children and adults of that size employing flexible grouping procedures would make possible working relationships far superior to those now found in most schools. Moreover, since a child whose family moved from one home to another within the large area served by the park would not be required to change schools, one of the principal present handicaps to effective learning in the city schools would be largely eliminated.

While not every school within the park could offer every specialized curriculum or service, such facilities would be provided in as many units as necessary and children assigned to them temporarily or permanently. Each child and each teacher would "belong" to his own unit, but access to others would be readily possible at any time.

The presence on a campus of all school levels and a wide range of administrative and auxiliary services would present the professional staff with opportunities for personal development and advancement which no single school now affords. The ease of communication, for example, among the guidance specialists or mathematics teachers would exceed anything now possible. It would become feasible to organize for each subject or professional specialty a department in which teachers in all parts of the park could hold memberships, in much the way that a university department includes professors from a number of colleges.

For the first time, a field unit could justify its own research and development branch, a thing not only unheard of but almost unimaginable in most schools today. With such help "in residence" the faculty of the park could participate in studies of teaching problems and conduct experiments that now are wholly impracticable for even the most competent teachers.

Much would depend, of course, on the imagination with which the park was organized and administered and how its policies were formed. Since the metropolitan park, by definition, would serve both a central city and one or more suburban districts, its very establishment would be impossible without new forms of intergovernmental cooperation. At least two local school boards would have to share authority, staffs, and funds. The State educational authority and perhaps the legislature would be required to sanction the scheme and might have to authorize it in advance. Public opinion and political interests would be deeply involved as would the industrial and real estate establishments of the sponsoring communities.

The planning of a metropolitan park would have to be viewed as a concern not merely of school people, parents, and legislative or executive officials. It would have to be approached from the outset as a fundamental problem in metropolitan planning. Its dependence on quantitative projections of population and housing data is obvious, but equally important is its relation to the character of the housing, occupancy policies, and ethnic concentrations. To build a park only to have it engulfed in a few years by an enlarged ghetto would be a sorry waste of both money and opportunity. No good purpose, educational or social, would be served by creating what might become a huge segregated school enclave. A school park can be undertaken responsibly only as part of a comprehensive metropolitan development plan. Where such planning is not feasible, the establishment of a metropolitan school park would be a questionable venture.

It may be reasonable in some circumstances to project a park within the limits of a single school district. Where the analysis of population trends and projected development justify a single district park, the intergovernmental problems disappear, but agreements within the municipal structure will still be important and may be quite difficult to negotiate. The need for comprehensive community planning to assure the future viability of the park is certainly no less necessary within the city than in the metropolitan area.

Once the park is authorized, the question of operating responsibility must be addressed. In a sense that no individual school or geographic subdivision possibly can, the school park permits decentralized policy development and administration. Because of the natural coherence of the park's components and their relative separation from the rest of the district—or districts—to which it is related, the park might very well be organized as a largely self-contained system. The argument for placing the park under a board with considerable autonomy is strong whether it is a metropolitan institution or a one-city enterprise. For the first time it could thus become possible for the citizens in a section of a large community to have a direct, effective voice in the affairs of a school serving their area. . . .

Citizen participation would have to occur at points other than the board, however. If the park is to be strongly related to its communities, and integrated in fact as well as in principle, parents and other citizens would have to be involved, formally and informally, in many of its activities. These might range from parent-teacher conferences to service on major curriculum advisory groups. They could include routine volunteer chores and service as special consultants or part-time teachers. The specific possibilities are unlimited but the tone of the relationships will critically affect the park's success.

. . . .

Obtaining the necessary cooperation to build a metropolitan park will not be easy but the financial problems will be equally severe. A park accommodating 16,000 pupils can be expected to cost in the neighborhood of $50 million. The financial pressures on cities and suburban districts make it clear that Federal support on a very large scale will be required if school parks are to be built. But it is precisely the possibility of Federal funds that could provide the incentive to bring the suburbs and the central city together.

While categorical support through Federal funds will continue to be needed, effective leverage on the massive problems of urban education, including, particularly, integration, can be obtained only through broadly focused programs of general aid, with special attention given to new construction. Little can be done toward equalizing opportunities without a sizeable program of school building expansion and replacement. Such aid, moreover, must be available for both the neglected child and the relatively advantaged.

If much of this new assistance were expressly channeled into creating metropolitan parks, on a formula of 90 per cent Federal and 10 per cent State and local funding, it would envision equalized, integrated schools of high quality in most cities within a period of 10 to 15 years.

Would such a program mean abandoning usable existing school buildings? Not at all, since most districts desperately need more space for their present and predictable enrollment, to say nothing of the other uses that school systems and other government agencies could readily find for buildings that might be relinquished. The impending expansion of nursery school programs and adult education are only two of the more obvious alternate uses for in-city structures.

Is the school park an all-or-nothing question? Is it necessary to abandon all existing programs before the benefits of the park can be tested? Short of full commitment, there are steps that can be taken in the direction of establishing parks and to achieve some of their values. The "educational complex" put forward in the Allen Report for New York City is one such step. As described in that report, the complex is a group of two to five primary schools and one or two middle schools near enough to each other to form a cooperating cluster and serving sufficiently diversified neighborhoods to promote good biracial contact.

An educational complex should be administered by a *senior administrator,* who should be given authority and autonomy to develop a program which meets appropriate citywide standards but is also directly relevant to the needs of the locality. Primary schools within the complex should share among themselves facilities, faculties, and special staff, and should be coordinated to encourage frequent association among students and parents from the several units. Within the education complex teachers will be better able to help children from diverse ethnic backgrounds to become acquainted with one another. Parent-teacher and parent-school relations should be built on the bases of both the individual school and the complex. The children—and their parents—will thus gain the dual benefits of a school close to home and of membership in a larger, more diverse educational and social community. The concept of the educational complex arises in part from the view that the means of education and much of their control should be centered locally.

Although it may not be possible to desegregate all primary schools, ultimately most of them should be integrated educationally. This will aid the better preparation of students for life and study in the middle school; it will more nearly equalize resources; and it will give the staff in the primary schools new opportunities for innovation and originality in their work.[8]

Experimental projects on a limited scale might also be set up between city and suburban districts to deal with common problems. The Hartford and Irondequoit projects transporting Negro students to suburban schools are examples of what can be done.

Additional efforts could include exchanging staff members; involving students, particularly at the secondary level, in joint curricular or extracurricular activities; setting up "miniature school parks" during the summer in schools on the city-suburban border; conducting work sessions in which board and staff members from metropolitan school systems examine population changes, common curriculum problems, and opportunities for joint action.

[8] State Education Commission's Advisory Committee on Human Relations and Community Tensions, *Desegregating the Public Schools of New York City* (New York: New York State Department of Education, 1964), p. 18.

Establishing school parks would mean a substantial shift in educational policy. In addition, as has been pointed out, the metropolitan park would require concerted action among governmental units. New forms of State and Federal financial support and sharply increased appropriations would be essential. . . . Parents and other citizens, school leaders, public officials and legislators will be justified in asking for persuasive factual and logical support for such radical proposals.

The response must be that critically important educational, social, and economic needs of a large part of urban America are not being met by our present policies and practices and that there is no reason to think that they will be met by minor adjustments of the present arrangements. The evidence is irresistible that the consequences of racial segregation are so costly and so damaging to all our people that they should no longer be tolerated. Through bitter experience we are learning that the isolation of any race is demeaning when it is deliberate and that it is counterproductive in human and economic terms, no matter how it is caused or explained. The elimination of this debilitating and degrading aspect of American life must now be ranked among the most important and urgent goals of our society. The task cannot be done without concerted action among many forces and agencies. Participation by private agencies and by government at every level will be needed. But central to every other effort will be the influence and the power of the public schools. Those schools, which have served the nation so well in achieving other high purposes, can serve equally well in performing their part of this new undertaking—if the magnitude of the task is fully appreciated and action undertaken on a scale appropriate to a major national purpose.

The steps that have heretofore been taken to cope with segregation have been of no more than tactical dimensions. Most of them have been relatively minor adaptations and accommodations requiring minimal changes in the status quo. It should by now be clear that we cannot integrate our schools or assure all our children access to the best education unless we accept these twin goals as prime strategic objectives.

. . . .

Establishing rings of school parks about each of our segregated central cities would, to be sure, require decisions to invest large sums of money in these projects. The prior and more important commitment, however, must be to the purpose to which the money will be dedicated: effective equality of educational opportunity at a new high level for millions of our young people.

The school park is no panacea. In itself it will guarantee no more than a setting for new accomplishment. But the setting is essential. If we fail to provide it or to invent an equally promising alternative, we shall continue to deny a high proportion of our citizens the indispensable means to a decent and productive life.

5

Using Instructional Resources

The nearly infinite number of instructional resources available to teachers today is in most ways a highly desirable condition. But the condition itself is no panacea. For it is becoming increasingly difficult for teachers to choose from all the resources that are available those best suited to meet specific instructional criteria. It is no easy task to learn the skills necessary to use the resources effectively. And it is no easy task to learn the new teaching roles that many resources require. Indeed, even as the number of instructional resources has increased, so has the level of professionalism demanded of teachers kept pace.

The eight articles presented in this part are devoted to an examination of several of these resources. As will be seen, some of them, such as computers, are still largely in the developmental and field-testing stages; others, such as programmed learning materials, are already being used by significant numbers of teachers across the country; and still others, such as textbooks, remain unchallenged as the most common instructional tool. Regardless of their present usage, however, the relative merits of each of these resources must be critically analyzed now so that future decisions regarding their adoption and deployment will be based on the soundest of criteria.

The first two articles have as their central focus the textbook. In the first of these, English contends that as an educational tool the textbook is expensive, outdated, and inefficient. And in the second, which was written in response to the English article, Soghomonian takes to task not the textbook itself, but the use many teachers make of it. Together, these articles should raise for the reader some serious questions about the legitimacy of "textbook teaching."

In the next three articles, the reader's attention is directed to what may indeed be a significant part of education's future. Certainly, on a small scale it is already a part. Dale, in discussing in general terms the topic of educational technology, does not see the various forms of electronic media's ever replacing teachers, but does see their providing teachers with additional time to serve in different kinds of roles, namely, as guides, counselors, and organizers.

A description of one type of educational facility that is designed to house much of the new technology is given in Brick's article. Known as the learning center, this facility has several unique features. First, it functions as a resource center for such items as audio-visual equipment, reference materials, science labs, diagnostic materials, and electronic teaching devices. Second, it is easily accessible to students for individual, small-group, and large-group work. And third, it is staffed by a coordinating teacher whose major responsibilities include scheduling students, coordinating the center's activities, and working with both teachers and students on specific instructional problems. As described by Brick, the learning center concept does seem to have the potential for providing teachers with one means of individualizing instruction.

Another means of individualizing instruction is the subject of the fifth article. In it Suppes analyzes some of the problems and promises of computer-assisted instruction. He points out how computer programs are now used both to supplement the regular curriculum and to present in toto certain basic concepts and skills. He foresees the day when computer technology will be perfected to the extent that genuine dialogue can be held between students and computers. And finally, Suppes is of the opinion that the problems of computerized instruction, of which at both the technological and the ideological levels there are several, are far less serious than many believe.

At the present time, of course, few teachers have ready access to computers for instructional purposes. On the other hand, there are few teachers who do not have access to programmed learning materials. In the sixth article, then, Arnstine's discussion of programming should not only be timely, but should also serve as a contrast to certain ideas expressed in the Suppes article. In brief, Arnstine believes that the use of programmed materials can only foster rote forms of learning. He denies that programming can assist in the development of the more complex intellectual operations. Although the reader in the final analysis may not agree with the reasoning underlying Arnstine's convictions, he will be hard pressed to arrive at conclusions much different from Arnstine's in regard to the specific example of programming that is used.

Some of the principles of programmed learning are often used in another type of instructional resource, called the instructional package. This particular resource is described by Loughary in the seventh article. He points out how the instructional package differs from earlier materials, such as practice sets, and how it differs also from what is now known as the systems approach to curriculum planning. These terms, and the rationale underlying them, need to be clearly understood by the reader because they are increasingly becoming integral parts of most of the new curriculum programs.

The final article in the section differs significantly from the others in that it does not focus directly on an instructional resource per se. Rather, it deals with an approach to teaching that utilizes all types of resources, both personal and physical, in an effort to maximize student involvement in the learning process. The unit of work as an approach to teaching is not, as Tomlinson points out in the article, a new idea. It neither guarantees success nor purports to be "teacherproof." But for the creative teacher it is replete with instructional opportunities. In this writer's opinion, Tomlinson's concluding comment that the unit of work frees the good teacher to do his best and the poor teacher to do his worst serves amply as both a challenge and a warning.

The Textbook—Procrustean Bed of Learning

FENWICK ENGLISH

One of the cherished and hallowed idols of public education is at last exhibiting signs of decay and falling into well-earned disrepute: the textbook. For generations it has been the Procrustean bed to which we have subjected students. Like Procrustes, we have either stretched our students' legs or cut them off to fit the textbook.

According to *The Rand McNally Handbook on Education*,[1] "The role of the textbook in instruction is a major issue in education." The handbook also noted that as late as 1956 "textbooks continued to be the core of instructional materials in this country." The trend away from the textbook began with three contemporary phenomena, which I shall discuss.

It has been estimated by Claude Fawcett [2] that it takes 10 years for a textbook to be born. This would include the writing, editing, adopting, printing, evaluating, purchasing, and distributing. Glass says of our newest science textbooks that they will be out of date, like a new car, in five years and need revision.[3] We are all familiar with the fact that because of the pace of our modern industrial and technological society, we are roughly doubling man's accumulated store of knowledge each decade.

In California $9 to $15 million was spent last year, according to Caspar Weinberger,[4] to prepare outdated, and in some instances, false information for students to learn as established truth because the "text says so." As students, we may remember physics books which showed the atom as a permanent structure. We memorized this structure as immutable fact. Today it is

Reprinted from *Phi Delta Kappan*, 48 (8): 393–395 (April 1967), by permission of author and publisher.

[1] Arthur W. Foshay (ed.), *Rand McNally Handbook of Education*. Chicago: Rand McNally, 1963.

[2] Claude W. Fawcett, "Technological Change and Education," *Journal of Secondary Education*, January, 1961.

[3] H. Bentley Glass, "What Man Can Be." (Address at the February, 1967, Convention of the American Association of School Administrators, Atlantic City.)

[4] Caspar W. Weinberger, "Lack of Coordination Seems at Root of Textbook Trouble," *Los Angeles Times*, March 30, 1966.

233

a false picture of the nature of the atom. Thus it is not only impossible for a textbook to be contemporary, but equally impossible for it to be authoritative.

Any book which after the time it is published and placed in the hands of students fails to include half of man's total experience in that field cannot be authoritative.

The problem of increasing knowledge and the inability of traditional texts in coping with it has been highlighted by Lawrence Metcalf.[5] In the area of history the buildup of detail has led to the practice of "easy familiarity." This is the result of having more and more to say in about the same space of previous textbooks. Metcalf summarizes that "the only solution is for the writer to express himself in generalities, leaving out the detail that would give these generalities meaning." Metcalf reiterates William James' law that "no one sees any further into a generalization than his knowledge of detail extends."

Whitehead [6] dealt with such hollow generalizations as "inert ideas," that is, ideas learned "without being utilized or tested, or thrown into fresh combinations." The "facts" or "concepts" of the text learned in the abstract can only be remembered in the abstract. This is what makes the practice of cramming inevitable, and the loss of that information equally inevitable. The lack of application or rigorous examination of text concepts deludes students into thinking they may really understand something when the text is "merely clever in its language and phrasing." [7]

Research and investigation into the nature of learning have revealed many fallacies upon which previous assumptions about learning have been based. One of these identified by Walker [8] is the "whole class concept of teaching." Walker explains that this is the notion that "groups of 30 or more students are expected to learn the same thing at the same time and at approximately the same speed."

Richard Suchman [9] has attacked this concept on the following basis. "Any teacher who takes the time to determine the level of conceptual readiness and intrinsic motivation of each of his pupils before and during his teaching activities finds that it makes no sense to teach an entire group of children as a group. He can never presume that any two children start from the same set of concepts and move with equal speed and along parallel lines of conceptual growth."

Because the textbook is based upon the "whole-class concept" and the

[5] Lawrence E. Metcalf, "Research on Teaching the Social Studies," *Handbook of Research on Teaching*, N. L. Gage (ed.). Chicago: Rand McNally, 1963.

[6] Alfred North Whitehead, *The Aims of Education and Other Essays*. New York: The Macmillan Company, 1929.

[7] Metcalf, *op. cit.*

[8] A. Reed Walker, "Education and Individuality," *The Bulletin of the National Association of Secondary School Principals*, December, 1965.

[9] Richard J. Suchman, "Learning Through Inquiry," *Childhood Education*, February, 1965.

idea that all students will begin and end at the same point, it confines students to one level. It acts as the Procrustean bed. By narrowing thinking and learning to this level it bores the student who wishes to forge ahead, and leaves behind those with little interest, reading difficulties, or the inability to pursue further study. It is the result of the idea of "gradedness."

Many teachers rely upon the textbook as the authoritarian block upon which to chop off student inquiry. A teacher who hides between the covers of the text finds safety by confining learning to within its scope. In this way it is very easy to conceal one's own ignorance; it is a tacit refusal to keep abreast of the times. Student learning is similarly confined, if we can believe the notion that effective instruction increases the differences and levels of achievement of the learners.

Ben Bloom [10] has illustrated that cognition occurs on many levels. If we apply his *Taxonomy of Educational Objectives* as a criterion to judge the caliber of typical questions at the end of a chapter, we find that few, if any, are outside of category one, or "the recall of specific facts, principles, classifications, and categories." When a student answers a question involving who, what, when, or where, and copies directly from a passage in the preceding chapter, it is possible for him to have a correct answer without comprehending the meaning of the answer. Thus Bloom's cognitive category of "comprehending" is only rarely touched. It is usually the case that no question enters into the higher levels identified in the *Taxonomy*, such as analysis, application, synthesis, or evaluation. If most of our classroom time is spent in having students regurgitate items in Bloom's area one, we have tapped only the most shallow and superficial of human mental talents: the ability to memorize. Memorization does not necessarily include understanding or the ability to apply information or learned skills to a problem; in short, the questions at the chapter's end are too often examples of "inert ideas." William Burton [11] has labeled a parallel practice of the page assignment in a single text followed by a formal verbal quiz as "grossly ineffective" and "calculated to interfere with learning."

An equally absurd idea that many teachers and administrators fret over is the idea that one must be sure and "cover" the text content within a given period of time. We have shown that no two children ever begin together in even one dimension of learning, let's say the quality and quantity of information acquired. What we really mean by "cover" is that the teacher exposes the group to a certain sequence of ideas, continuity of material, lists of categories, etc. The assumption expressed in this idea is that a given amount of exposure equals a given amount of learning. But we all know better.

[10] Benjamin S. Bloom, *Taxonomy of Educational Objectives. Handbook I Cognitive Domain*. New York: David McKay Co., 1956.
[11] William H. Burton, "Implications for the Organization of Instruction and Instructional Adjuncts," *Learning and Instruction*, 49th Yearbook of the National Society for the Study of Education. Chicago: University of Chicago Press, 1950.

A half-century ago John Dewey [12] challenged the continuity notion when he said, "The most scientific matter arranged in most logical fashion loses this quality, when presented in external, ready-made fashion, by the time it gets to the child. It has to undergo some modification in order to shut out some phases too hard to grasp, and to reduce some of the attendant difficulties. What happens? Those things which are most significant to the scientific man, and most valuable in the logic of actual inquiry and classification, drop out. The really thought-provoking character is obscured, and the organizing function disappears. . . . So the subject matter is evacuated of its logical value, and, though it is what it is only from the logical standpoint, is presented as stuff only for 'memory.'"

Further examination of text questions will reveal the degree to which they demand the convergent type of thinking to arrive at the "right" answer. Hilda Taba [13] has labeled such "right" answers as those depending on "authority rather than on rational judgment." Taba's remarks, while directed toward the teacher, take the textbook into account for producing acts which "control and limit the responses of students and thereby inhibit their mental activity beyond that which is necessary for orderly development of thought."

The textbook has reduced student interests and abilities to one level. It has promoted mediocrity, apathy, and the continuance of generations of passive learners. The exercises, questions, drills, etc., center primarily on convergent answer-giving behavior. Rarely are students challenged by textbooks to produce divergent, creative acts or perform analysis on the logic of the ideas or organization of the content. Research on cognition and the need to produce and accentuate differences have relegated the textbook to the era of the hornbook and the duncecap. It is a relic in the educational museum of obsolescence.

The impact of instructional technology and the systems approach to education have also imperiled the textbook's future. A. A. Lumsdaine [14] revealed the epitome of the highly analytical approach in his definition of the word instruction, "a generic term referring to any specifiable means of controlling or manipulating a sequence of events to produce modifications of behavior through learning. It is applicable whenever the outcomes of learning can be specified in sufficiently explicit terms to permit their measurement. These outcomes may include changes in attitudes, interests, motivations, beliefs, or opinions as well as in knowledges, skills, and other performance capabilities."

Lumsdaine drops the textbook as a valid instructional material because "The usual textbook does not control behavior of the learner in a way which

[12] John Dewey, *The Child and the Curriculum*. Chicago: University of Chicago Press, 1902.

[13] Hilda Taba, "Teaching Strategy and Learning," *California Journal for Instructional Improvement*, VI, No. 4, December, 1963.

[14] A. A. Lumsdaine, "Instruments and Media of Instruction," *A Handbook of Research on Teaching*, N. L. Gage (ed.). Chicago: Rand McNally, 1963.

makes it highly predictable as a vehicle of instruction or amenable to experimental research. It does not in itself generate a describable and predictable process of learner behavior. . . ." The textbook will eventually be replaced by programmed materials and a new array of factual handbooks.

Virgil Herrick [15] has succinctly stated the limitations of the textbook as an instructional aid. Paraphrased arguments are:

1. The textbook cannot think or discover. This has to be done by the student.

2. The textbook should not be the sole instrument for organizing and developing the major ideas, or for relating this pattern of ideas to the problems and experiences of a particular group of students.

3. The textbook should not be the sole determinant of what is to be taught.

4. A textbook cannot determine the speed with which a student moves through his learning activities or the speed with which they move past him. A textbook can do very little to help a child pace his learning according to his purpose and the nature of the content being studied.

5. Learning, if it is to be valuable, must be evaluated and then applied to future learning and behavior. A textbook has very little to do with this problem.

In summary, the textbook in its present form is outdated, expensive, and inefficient. The assumptions underlying its present usage are false; they do not explain or foster learning in depth or promote student inquiry. Educators must now begin the task of informing the public and lobbying for a change in state textbook laws which require "uniform use" of texts provided free by the state. The removal of legal straitjackets will provide the freedom necessary to arrive at modern education in a time when "modern" is woefully out of date.

The Textbook—Tarnished Tool for Teachers?

SAM SOGHOMONIAN

Mr. English has gone and done it. He has come right out and said the textbook is obsolete. Moreover, it is useless, false, and less than authoritative, he thunders. What awful allegations! Does he mean *all* textbooks? Does

Reprinted from *Phi Delta Kappan*, 48 (8): 395–396 (April 1967), by permission of author and publisher.

[15] Virgil E. Herrick, *The Elementary School*. New Jersey: Englewood Cliffs, 1956.

he include the fifth-grade geography, the seventh-grade arithmetic, and the ninth-grade social studies text?

Now, comparing the traditional textbook to the Procrustean bed is a cute analogy, but it's faulty, like most analogies. Iconoclast English completely misses the point. He blames the textbook for the ills of education. It's rather like blaming this typewriter for my spelling errors, or the automobile for the more than 50,000 annual deaths, or the rifle for missing the bullseye. He would, in short, blame the laws because some men violate them. Methinks Mr. English is asleep on the Procrustean bed of learning.

There are good and bad textbooks, easy-to-read ones, and hard-to-understand ones. But the major fault, the core of the problem, is not the text per se, but that too many teachers have made the text an icon. Therein lies the monster. The text is not protoplasm; the teacher is. The classroom text is inert, as is any tool. It hardly seems fair to criticize the tool and not the operator.

The problem is that too many teachers lean too heavily upon the textbook. These teachers we must help, or do without. If public education is no more than the classroom teacher directing the inventorying of meaningless data for unmotivated students, better to keep the kids at home and mail them the texts—their parents could do little worse, and millions of dollars could be saved in personnel and construction costs.

The major criticism made of the text itself is that with the knowledge explosion no textbook can be very contemporary. If it contains less than half of the available data in a given field, we are told, it cannot be considered authoritative. There is an answer to this charge: If books are guilty of perpetuating outdated and inadequate knowledge, why and how will other media be guiltless? Will they provide better information? If there *is* better information, I say, let's put it into a textbook.

I have always complemented basic texts with collateral ones, plus the daily newspapers, weekly magazines, germane television presentations, field trips, guest speakers, filmstrips, and tapes. Neither I nor my students ever consider the textbook more than bare bones. The flesh we put on together.

And what teacher does less? Oh, a few, maybe. And a student confronted daily by no more than teacher and text is being shortchanged. But to throw out the textbook because some of them are dated and others superficial is (pardon me, please) to throw out the baby with the bath.

The emergence and influence of programmed instruction and the educational hardware that American businesses have suddenly made so available will inevitably change the status of the public school textbook, but before you exchange old lamps for new ones make sure you're getting something better.

If innovation and an instructional technology will add quality and meaning to America's classrooms, then so be it. Rewrite the text. Bring it up to

date. But don't underrate it. Barney Grossman [1] says that the actual possession of a textbook, a personal textbook, provides a psychological dimension
not afforded by a school-owned machine. How cozy can your students get
with hardware, Mr. English?

I grant that most of today's school texts use the "once over lightly"
approach. The only alternative that makes sense is for the teacher to provide
depth, in courses and at levels where it is required. I kind of thought
that was the teacher's function. He is the only "organic" part of the curriculum; he provides the "post-holing."

To the charges that the class concept of learning is outmoded, that kids
cannot be taught in groups, that they are limited to the knowledge included
in the text, that teachers find security in the text and feel they must cover
it, etc., I say this: Individual instruction is the optimum arrangement, but
with the present system and level of financial support its feasibility is dim.
If one text seems to limit learning, get another one, a better one, or get
two. The world's basic knowledge can still be found in books. The focus
of education is not to obtain encyclopedic knowledge, it is to teach the
younger generation how to learn, how to locate knowledge necessary for
wisdom in dealing with life's problems. And wisdom is the ability to make
choices in one's own and society's best interest.

With the burgeoning of the world's knowledge (it now doubles each
eight years, we hear, not 10), serious questions are raised regarding which
and how much knowledge is needed to give school children their cultural
heritage and to equip them for the future. How much knowledge does one
need to learn to make wise choices, to make prudent use of leisure time, to
learn tolerance and compassion? Only as much as he can translate into
wisdom.

Language labs, overhead projectors, closed-circuit television, and other
educational hardware don't by themselves spark excellence.[2] Nor does a
portfolio of new curricula. It is the teacher who must do much of the
igniting.

Mr. English's passion (or is it a fetish?) for the metallic classroom is
not atypical of the new breed's headlong rush into the space age. But in
his galactic galloping Mr. English fails to attack the real enemy of public
education—which is local control. But that's another topic.

Before we follow any plausible Moses to the promised land, let's make
sure it's not a wasteland. Closed-circuit television is already passé. The Ford
Foundation spent $23 million to launch instructional TV and is disappointed
in its progress.[3] One reason: machinery is only as good as the educational
material it presents. Everyone now knows the meaning of GIGO (if not,

[1] Barney Grossman, "A Book of One's Own," *NEA Journal*, January, 1967.
[2] "The New Breed of Teachers: Igniting the Individual Pupil." *Newsweek*, September, 1966.
[3] *Ibid.*

"garbage in, garbage out"). It is much easier to install a machine than it is to create learning. No computer, however magnificent its information storing capacity, is as flexible, as imaginative, or as subtle as a good teacher. Children can learn with the simplest tools, by themselves, at their own speed, *if teachers use imagination.* Innovation will not produce better teachers or better students unless the innovation comes from within the teacher.

Electronic Education

EDGAR DALE

Educational technology is a means, not an end. But what is the end—the goal we are trying to achieve?

We face the age-old question: What knowledge is of greatest worth? My answer would be: That knowledge is of greatest worth which enables us to learn our worth; which enables every man, woman, and child to achieve his potential.

We are a long way from achieving that goal. But something new has happened. Modern media of communication have enabled the disadvantaged to learn that their potential is underdeveloped and caused them to look longingly at any form of governmental or economic arrangement which promises to help them achieve that goal. Further, among the affluent today in the United States, and especially among the young, there is a feeling that they, too, have not achieved their potential; that perhaps the goals they have tried to achieve were not the most worthwhile. They are asking: Instead of trying to get ahead of the others in school, college, business, or professional life, wouldn't it make more sense to try to get ahead with the other fellow? They are asking: Wouldn't the circle of friendship and cooperation which helps everybody be better than the ladder of competition where it is every man for himself?

It is in such an atmosphere that we discuss the topic, educational technology. The problem really is not whether we shall use film, filmstrip, radio, recordings, computers, overhead projectors, television, simulation devices, etc. That issue is settled. We are going to use every possible means to help learners achieve their potential. The problem is how and when you combine their use with a live teacher.

Electronic media, including programmed materials, will not replace teachers but will help replace them, enable them to play the important role of guide, counselor, motivator, organizer, integrator, critical questioner,

Reprinted from *Ohio Schools,* 46 (1): 20–22+ (January 1968), by permission of author and publisher.

intellectual gadfly—the things that only a live and lively teacher can do in personal, face-to-face communication. The teacher can become a model of the thinking man or woman instead of being the administrator of learning tasks easily handled by a mediated teacher. The teacher can spend more time designing and programming the learning environment of the student so that he can become an independent learner.

A teacher is one element in a learning situation—sometimes an indispensable one. But sometimes the learner doesn't need a classroom teacher at all. Indeed, our best, most creative learning will not take place in the presence of a teacher. Furthermore, all instruction aims to prepare the student to learn outside the physical presence of a teacher.

The able teacher tries to make himself dispensable. He helps his students move from dependence to independence. We should let the teacher perform the uniquely human tasks that require mature, compassionate guidance. The teacher should not spend time or energy on those aspects of learning which can be efficiently learned by other means. If a book or filmstrip can really substitute for a teacher, let's use these ways of communicating with students.

Another question that we must face as we try to think through the problem of educational technology is the place where learning should take place. We have a stereotyped notion that most learning will take place in the school and college in a formal learning atmosphere. But the places where we learn informally are legion.

We can get our instructions on what to learn, how to learn, and why we learn from a live teacher or instructor. But some of these instructions may be secured by telephone, telelecture or closed circuit television to homes or dormitory rooms—from a distant teacher. The learning may take place in the Museum of Natural History in Dayton, at a Shakespearean play at Antioch, or in many other settings.

It is clear that the conditions of learning are going to change a great deal in the next few years. What we must do is to make much greater use of our teaching staffs to program this learning. In such a program we would not wait until the child came to nursery school or kindergarten before we worked with the parents on a language development program. The teacher would become a consultant to parents and help them set up an effective learning environment in the home.

As we try to program this instruction, we shall have to face some tough, hard questions about goals and objectives. We need a basic educational taxonomy; a classification of the kind of behaviors we want. Do we expect the student to memorize what the teacher or book says, or do we want the learner to discover the implications and the applications of this knowledge? When we decide on the whole range of behaviors we shall try to reach, we have committed ourselves to a radical change in our educational program.

We also need a radical change in the entire testing programs of our schools. Most school and college tests are largely on questions of fact, but they contain very little questioning of fact. Students are usually required to answer questions they never asked. They are told to answer questions but less commonly are they taught to question answers.

The author visualizes the time when our testing program will be a functioning part of the learning program. Now it is an after-piece. We now discover what students don't know at the end of the unit instead of having them discover at the beginning what they don't know and then remedy their ignorance.

I see a testing program which will be so simple and so easily available that any child or any adult could take a test on a computer or by some other means almost any time he wants to and discover his attainments on any of several phases of a subject. He could take a vocabulary test and discover those aspects of important life experience where he is weak and where he is strong. Further, the computer may actually print study materials for him or refer him to books, pamphlets, recordings, or programmed instructional materials.

It follows that we must have easily accessible sources of learning materials which fit the needs and abilities of a wide range of children. Here we turn to a new type of library—the learning materials center.

These centers are concerned with all the media which carry important messages—print, film, filmstrip, computer, photograph, painting, radio, recording, videotape, television, radiovision, telelecture. The Meadowbrook Junior High School in Newton, Mass. has four major learning centers, one each for math, science, and language, and a large combined center for English and social studies.

ALL FIVE SENSES

In a classroom of tomorrow now being built in the Centennial School District, Warminster, Pa., there will be a special experiences center to be used for teaching through all five senses—sight, sound, smell, feel, and even taste.

Some of these learning materials centers will have built in dial access systems. At Ohio State University, for example, a student can dial in from 368 different locations, 27 of which are in fraternity and sorority houses. A catalogue indicates what is found in the center. The magnitude of this service is indicated by the fact that an average of 40,000 calls is received each week. Video is being tied into the center and it is no exaggeration to say that eventually a dial access system will put the world's best ideas at the learners' finger tips and present it in a form that they can easily understand.

New systems of distributing ideas are also available in the amplified telephone lecture, the radiovision program which can be tied in with telephonic feedback.

Properly programmed, the computer can present varied and flexible experiences to the individual learner. It can diagnose his level of learning and fit the new experiences to this background. It can give him messages by a typewriter, by a film, a television sequence, a slide, or a recording. It can receive or react to messages by pressing knobs, by a light pencil, a cathode ray tube, or by a typed message. Computers are being developed that react to spoken stimuli.

We may mistakenly conclude that the computer will convey only rote and drill material, and nothing dealing with the higher mental processes. This need not happen. For example, certain elements in learning to write expository prose will be taught by computer. By means of the light pencil on the cathode ray tube, the learner can rearrange the structure of a "disorganized" paragraph. The computer could ask the learner to analyze and discriminate between various paragraphs and pick the best one.

No one expects the computer to make a brilliant writer out of a learner. But the computer can present and juxtapose writing choices which require increasing levels of discrimination. Computer-assisted instruction can provide more quickly, and perhaps more effectively, some of the basic background of skills and insights needed for the complicated higher mental processes involved in effective writing and reading.

Professor O. K. Moore has experimented with the use of a computerized typewriter as the first tool which children use in writing the letters of the alphabet. The children freely explore the computerized typewriter and when they strike the key, the computer calls the name of the letter or the symbol struck.

Modern life is too varied and too complex to meet and understand all of it at first-hand. In curriculum-making, we must study those educational situations most likely to help us solve our basic personal and social decisions and be most generative of new ideas. Following this selection, we can then set up learning programs which stimulate these situations and then evaluate how well students can solve these problems.

Simulation is being used in an administrative training program developed by the University Council for Educational Administration which simulates and checks the decisions of an elementary school principal in a suburban community. The simulations provide the necessary reality by including filmstrips, sound motion pictures, and tape recordings.

Donald R. Cruickshank and Frank W. Broadbent have developed what is called *Teaching Problems Laboratory* where "real" situations are presented to teachers in training or in-service. This is available from Science Research Associates.

RASH OF SIMULATIONS

We may now expect a rash of simulations to be available at all levels of education. One is called *Inter-Nation Simulation*. Another is titled the *Game of Farming* and presents problems faced by the Kansas farmer in three sharply varying historical periods.

Teachers will have to make some important decisions about learning by simulation. The critical question is this: does the simulation teach the intended learning economically and efficiently? How elaborate must the equipment be to give a feeling of reality, to avoid the feeling of merely play acting? Since simulation will play a large part in the education of the future, we should now put a number of task forces at work to evaluate this new approach to instruction.

In summary, I would present these conclusions:

—Progress in the use of certain media has been widespread but our students and teachers do not yet have easy access to the excellent films, filmstrips, and recordings already produced. Nor do we have access to the best that has been printed—the kinds of materials that should be found in learning materials centers.

—The programming of instruction and the developing of instructional systems are still undeveloped fields. There is much yet to do in helping students learn how to learn and to develop a taste for learning. Our taxonomies are inadequate. We do not have the necessary tests to determine whether learning has taken place and to provide a diagnosis and remediation for what has not been learned.

—There is too sharp a disparity, too great a lag, between what we know how to do in education and what we are actually doing. We need to use the new media to help us shorten this lag.

—The great revolution going forward today in our schools means a shift in the role of the teacher from a Jack or Jill-of-all-trades to taking on the role of a sophisticated organizer, administrator, counselor, guide, and simulator of learning. The new role promises to be more complex but certainly more professional. We have the choice of staying where the inaction is or moving into the excitement and challenge that always faces the pioneer.

Learning Centers: The Key to Personalized Instruction

E. MICHAEL BRICK

The greatest problem facing educators today is one of preparing children for a world that will exist in an entirely different form when they are responsible adults. Even though the last few years have been a time of educational research, reforms that might be expected have as yet only touched a small portion of our schools.

Reprinted from *Audiovisual Instruction*, 12 (8): 786–792 (October 1967), by permission of author and publisher.

It is becoming conspicuous to practitioners, as well as observers, that our *electronic technology* is precluding the status quo in education. And yet, with the exception of the lighthouse districts across the nation, the facilities, teaching methodology, and content of instruction continue to resemble the classroom of decades ago. By comparison, stable business organizations have moved rapidly into the realm of putting theory into practice.

Perhaps the first casualty to the traditional theories and methods is the concept of teacher-centered instruction. An identifiable trend to shift from the *teaching* act to the *learning* processes is emerging in school districts that are attempting to personalize the instructional program. As a point of reference, the Aborigines have managed to exist for more than 20,000 years in a desolate environment. Anthropologists claim that their secret to survival has been teaching. They pass on to the young every shred of knowledge about how to find their way in a trackless desert. Such knowledge is conveyed to the young as being *the* way to behave, and any innovation is frowned upon.

The teaching process has provided the Aborigines with a way to survive in a hostile and relatively unchanging environment. Teaching and the imparting of knowledge make sense in an unchanging environment, but our society lives in an environment which is *continually changing*. We know that knowledge imparted in the area of physics will be outdated in a decade; that the so-called "facts of history" depend largely upon the current mood and temper of the culture; and that chemistry, biology, genetics, and sociology are in such flux that a firm statement might become outmoded by the time the knowledge is ready to be used.

The significance of this analogy is that education is faced with a new goal of *facilitating change and learning*. It is conceivable that the majority of our citizenry would accept the concept that the only man who is educated is the man who has *learned how to learn;* the man who has learned how to adapt to change; the man who realizes that only the process of *seeking* knowledge gives a basis for security.

Do we as educators know how to achieve this goal of *facilitating learning* in education, or is it a will-of-the-wisp which sometimes occurs, sometimes fails to occur, and as such offers little real hope?

FOUNTAIN VALLEY SCHOOL DISTRICT POINT OF VIEW

The Fountain Valley School District has analyzed solutions for these perplexing problems to keep its program in step with a fast changing world and believes that the following questions must be answered to plan for the future:

1. Will the program be one that is life-oriented and therefore geared toward the development of problem solving, analysis, inquiry, and decision-making skills?

2. Is it one in which the student is actively and intimately involved as a participant rather than an observer?

3. Is it built on a student's successes as an individual rather than on his failure at a rigid norm?

4. Will it be in step with the requirements of the community and parental awareness of the need for innovation?

One of the innovations that the Board of Trustees and educators have established to resolve the questions presented is the *Learning Center concept.* The Learning Center functions as an *extension* of the regular classroom and operates as a teaching and resource learning center for a cluster of six or eight teachers, depending upon the building design. The educational process in these clusters is personalized through techniques of pupil *placement,* academic *diagnosis, prescription,* and continuous *evaluation.* The prime effort of the program is to integrate the classroom and Learning Center functions to cope with the knowledge explosion; to match students with necessary and appropriate materials, concepts, and people to provide for *individualized instruction.*

CLASSROOM PROGRAM

In order to understand the significance of the Learning Center, it is appropriate to describe the regular classroom program in that the processes involved are integrated.

Working in a nongraded school district, the teacher may be operating with single age level, flexibly grouped, or a multigraded class, but with multilevel books, basal systems, materials, reading labs, science labs, and electronic equipment.

1. The *class grouping* arrangement allows the teacher to spend more than one year with the children in order to *expand* and *personalize* the instructional program. In the diagnostic process, children can be scheduled into the Learning Center for more individual work.

2. Such *equipment* as tape recorders with headsets are used as "a second teacher" in the regular classroom to provide skill lessons in phonics or mathematics, spelling or enrichment materials. Tapes are prepared by the teacher for immediate skill needs, prepared by the District Curriculum Materials Center for more general needs, or purchased commercially.

Film projectors designed as a self-contained projector and screen unit with headsets allow for additional individualizing of instruction. Students can take a self-selected or teacher-prescribed film or filmstrip to these projectors and view them in the classroom without disturbing the other children.

3. *Pupil-teacher conferences* are conducted during class time for the purpose of identifying academic successes or problems and to prepare a record for individual and small-group assignments or lessons.

These individual conferences permit personal evaluations and interaction for growth. These analyses are then converted into an ongoing profile for each child to continue effective personalized prescriptions.

This process is not only essential for individualization in the regular classroom but is also the foundation for scheduling of students into the Learning Center for individualized skill lessons and learning activities.

4. *Cooperative teaching* provides for additional grouping of children to capitalize on the teacher's strengths for in-depth instruction and encourages cross-fertilization of ideas and social maturation among students.

The Learning Center, because of its size and space arrangement, becomes an ideal location for special groups or classes to gather.

5. *Self-directed* learning activities include individual contracts for work at the student's level, self-selective reading with follow-up and evaluation by the teacher, small-group discussions with summary and evaluation, research, experimentation, creative dramatics, projects, and debate. These types of learning experiences place more responsibility for learning *with the individual student*. The Learning Center is completely integrated with these activities in such a way that many are conducted in the Center itself.

BUILDING PROGRAM

The educational program in Fountain Valley is one that utilizes everything under its control, even the building program, to facilitate the learning process. School buildings as such are not merely protective shelters; they are educational tools designed to provide the flexibility so precious to a diverse and creative instructional program.

The 11 schools in the district, all constructed since 1963, have reorganized the use of space so that six or eight classrooms are clustered about a core room called a Learning Center. The architectural firm of Carmichael-Kemp from Los Angeles has worked with the community, Board of Trustees, and educators in developing this concept to fulfill the instructional needs as indicated by professional staff.

In each building, provisions have been made for movable walls, sliding chalkboards in front of glass windows for control purposes into the Learning Center, vinyl-covered cork walls, movable desks, cabinets, and case work on casters to provide for flexibility in organizing special centers in both the classrooms and the Learning Center.

Learning Center: The Learning Center functions as a resource center for diagnostic materials, electronic teaching devices, tape banks, test banks, science centers, rotating library systems, use and storage of audiovisual equipment, and reference and resource materials.

It also operates as a teaching center supervised by a *Coordinating Teacher* who conducts individual, small-group, and cooperative teaching programs.

The Center is organized so that several activities can continue at once.

In one corner of the room ten-year-olds might be working with microscopes analyzing and reporting on minute animal life; alongside, a group of seven-year-olds could be working on phonics with tape recorder and headsets; students from various classrooms are working independently in study carrels; in the back of the room, several children are watching a film about sets and numbers while another group watches an American Heritage presentation on educational television; other students are completing reading assignments in the library or checking out books from the Teacher Aide. At the same time, the Coordinating Teacher might be working with children to develop geographical concepts.

Coordinating Teacher: The Coordinating Teacher is selected on the basis of being a master teacher and an expert in interpersonal relations. Ten percent additional salary is paid for assuming this responsibility.

The Coordinating Teacher is not assigned to a regular classroom and works either in the Learning Center or with the teachers and children in the classroom cluster. The following is an outline of the Coordinating Teacher's major tasks.

1. Coordinating the use of the Learning Center with teachers as to materials, equipment, personnel, and programs.

2. Scheduling children for instructional purposes after planning sessions with the teachers.

3. Cooperatively evaluating the academic progress of the children with the teachers.

4. Developing and working in cooperative teaching programs.

5. Working on curriculum development projects independently or in planning sessions.

6. Conducting orientation for teachers to new methods and special programs.

7. Holding conferences with teachers individually or in teams for planning and problem solving.

8. Conducting in-service education programs.

The type of instruction the Coordinating Teacher provides in the Learning Center is based entirely upon a cooperative diagnosis of the specific needs and interests of each student. It is the Coordinating Teacher's function to fill the *prescriptions* and forward an evaluation to the classroom teacher regarding the effectiveness of the learning experience. This teaching includes requests for instruction in every area of the curriculum and is requested for students who range from gifted to slow in mental ability and academic achievement. *No ability group* or specific type of instruction is emphasized to the exclusion of others. This attitude prevails in that it is important for all children to have access to the opportunities provided by the Learning Center.

Regularly scheduled planning time for staff is important if the Learning Center is to function properly. While teachers may meet at all times of the day to handle problems as they arise, scheduled planning sessions are provided for through the use of paid Teacher Aides for lunch-time supervision and other large-group outside activities.

Building Educational Leader: The responsibility of the Building Educational Leader (Building Principal) for several Learning Centers at his school becomes one of assistance in the *teaming* sense and one of supervision in terms of suggesting the type of curriculum strategy to be developed. It is also his task to provide guidance for formal planning sessions with the Coordinating Teachers, and other special staff service with the classroom teachers.

A main concern of the Building Educational Leader is to provide direction so that the Center does not become a departmentalized situation which would lessen the responsibility of each professional to work with children on the basis of *diagnosis* of academic and social needs, *prescription* at individual levels, and *evaluation* to insure continuous pupil progress. The primary goal of this total team effort is to provide an atmosphere of cooperation, flexibility, good communication, and to promote the teachers' primary responsibility for the academic and social progress of students.

Auxiliary Personnel: Additional staffing for the Learning Center is the paid Teacher Aide who serves as a secretary and noninstructional assistant to the Coordinating Teacher and the regular teachers in the cluster. Her responsibilities include clerical work, filing, duplicating, circulating and retrieving materials, record keeping systems, and operating audiovisual equipment. Each Learning Center is staffed with at least one salaried Teacher Aide.

In addition to this Teacher Aide program is a volunteer group of approximately 1,000 parents who work in service capacities to the schools once a week for four hours.

1. The Curriculum Materials Center Aides fill requests from the Learning Centers and classroom teachers by making visual aids, teaching devices, and instructional media using hand tools.

2. Library Aides devote time by assisting in the central library with such tasks as shelving books, filing catalog cards, checking books out, and circulating requested books to the Learning Center.

3. Health, Welfare, and Safety Aides assist the nurses at the school level with hearing tests, immunization programs, safety programs, and puppet shows for primary children.

DISTRICT PROGRAM

Special Services Staff: The special services staff offers a wide range of technical competency by providing direct service within the Learning Center and classrooms which aid pupils directly. The psychologist, teacher of the educationally handicapped, the speech therapist, and the nurse function as resources of diagnostic information, special materials, and techniques which contribute to the variety of instructional alternatives available to the co-ordinating and regular classroom teacher.

Curriculum Materials Center: In order for the classroom teacher and Learning Centers to meet the needs and interests of individual children, it is most important to have a centralized storehouse of ideas, materials, equipment, and available personnel. In Fountain Valley, the Curriculum Materials Center functions as a distribution center for these areas and also provides a laboratory in which teachers can work. It is staffed with technicians and coordinators (one of whom is a professional AV person) who work with the teachers at the Center and in each of the schools.

The Center provides for in-service programs directed by the district and universities, library services, audiovisual services, teaching aids, study prints, films and filmstrips, transparencies, tapes and records, and "idea" booklets. The full-time consultants provide specialized assistance to teachers in that their recommendations are assessed at weekly in-service education meetings.

SUMMER SEMINARS

Seminars are conducted each summer for new and experienced teachers. These separate seminars are designed to explore the practical and theoretical application of new teaching techniques and methods. The emphasis for these programs is placed in five major areas:

1. The mechanics of a classroom organization and planning to individualize instruction

2. Use of materials and audiovisual equipment in individualizing instruction

3. "Theory to practice" of how children learn

4. Organization and techniques for cooperative teaching

5. Use of the Curriculum Materials Center, service personnel, functions and use of the Learning Center.

A 12-month school year with two four-week summer sessions also provides an opportunity for new teachers to observe demonstrations given by regular classroom teachers.

Fountain Valley's Board of Trustees, teaching staff, administration, and community hold for their children's education a *total* commitment to placing proven educational theory into practice. Research studies have gathered together a large amount of data concerning the individuality of the *learner,* the prominent role of the *teacher,* and the necessity for the development of a *total curriculum* to meet the individual learner's needs and interests. These educational processes do not take place in a vacuum but demand an extension to the classroom—the *Learning Center.*

The desirable input areas, when put into practice, are most conspicuous in that the Learning Center concept is really an extension of teaching space, instructional materials, electronic equipment, and teaching and supporting personnel.

Computer Technology and the Future of Education

PATRICK SUPPES

Current applications of computers and related information-processing techniques run the gamut in our society from the automatic control of factories to the scrutiny of tax returns. I have not seen any recent data, but we are certainly reaching the point at which a high percentage of regular employees in this country are paid by computerized payroll systems. As another example, every kind of complex experiment is beginning to be subject to computer assistance either in terms of the actual experimentation or in terms of extensive computations integral to the analysis of the experiment. These applications range from bubble-chamber data on elementary particles to the crystallography of protein molecules.

As yet, the use of computer technology in administration and management on the one hand, and scientific and engineering applications on the other, far exceed direct applications in education. However, if potentials are properly realized, the character and nature of education during the course of our lifetimes will be radically changed. Perhaps the most important aspect of computerized instructional devices is that the kind of individualized instruction once possible only for a few members of the aristocracy can be made available to all students at all levels of abilities.

Because some may not be familiar with how computers can be used to provide individualized instruction, let me briefly review the mode of operation. In the first place, because of its great speed of operation, a computer can handle simultaneously a large number of students—for instance, 200 or more, and each of the 200 can be at a different point in the curriculum. In the simplest mode of operation, the terminal device at which the student sits is something like an electric typewriter. Messages can be typed out by the computer and the student in turn can enter his responses on the keyboard. The first and most important feature to add is the delivery of audio messages under computer control to the student. Not only children, but students of all ages learn by ear as much as by eye, and for tutorial ventures in individualized instruction it is essential that the computer system be able to talk to the student.

A simple example may make this idea more concrete. Practically no one learns mathematics simply by reading a book, except at a relatively advanced level. Hearing lectures and listening to someone else's talk seem to be almost psychologically essential to learning complex subjects, at least as far as

Reprinted from *Phi Delta Kappan*, 49 (8): 420–423 (April 1968), by permission of author and publisher.

ordinary learners are concerned. In addition to the typewriter and the earphones for audio messages, the next desirable feature is that graphical and pictorial displays be available under computer control. Such displays can be provided in a variety of formats. The simplest mode is to have color slides that may be selected by computer control. More flexible, and therefore more desirable, devices are cathode-ray tubes that look very much like television sets. The beauty of cathode-ray tubes is that a graphical display may be shown to the student and then his own response, entered on a keyboard, can be made an integral part of the display itself.

This is not the place to review these matters in detail; but I mean to convey a visual image of a student sitting at a variety of terminal gear—as it is called in the computer world. These terminals are used to provide the student with individualized instruction. He receives information from audio messages, from typewritten messages, and also from visual displays ranging from graphics to complex photographs. In turn, he may respond to the system and give his own answers by using the keyboard on the typewriter. Other devices for student response are also available, but I shall not go into them now.

So, with such devices available, individualized instruction in a wide variety of subject matters may be offered students of all ages. The technology is already available, although it will continue to be improved. There are two main factors standing in our way. One is that currently it is expensive to prepare an individualized curriculum. The second factor, and even more important, is that as yet we have little operational experience in precisely how this should best be done. For some time to come, individualized instruction will have to depend on a basis of practical judgment and pedagogical intuition of the sort now used in constructing textbook materials for ordinary courses. One of the exciting potentialities of computer-assisted instruction is that for the first time we shall be able to get hard data to use as a basis for a more serious scientific investigation and evaluation of any given instructional program.

To give a more concrete sense of the possibilities of individualized instruction, I would like to describe briefly three possible levels of interaction between the student and computer program. Following a current usage, I shall refer to each of the instructional programs as a particular system of instruction. At the simplest level there are *individualized drill-and-practice systems*, which are meant to supplement the regular curriculum taught by the teacher. The introduction of concepts and new ideas is handled in conventional fashion by the teacher. The role of the computer is to provide regular review and practice on basic concepts and skills. In the case of elementary mathematics, for example, each student would receive daily a certain number of exercises, which would be automatically presented, evaluated, and scored by the computer program without any effort by the classroom teacher. Moreover, these exercises can be presented on an individualized basis, with the brighter students receiving exercises that are harder than the average, and the slower students receiving easier problems.

One important aspect of this kind of individualization should be emphasized. In using a computer in this fashion, it is not necessary to decide at the beginning of the school year in which track a student should be placed; for example, a student need not be classified as a slow student for the entire year. Individualized drill-and-practice work is suitable to all the elementary subjects which occupy a good part of the curriculum. Elementary mathematics, elementary science, and the beginning work in foreign language are typical parts of the curriculum which benefit from standardized and regularly presented drill-and-practice exercises. A large computer with 200 terminals can handle as many as 6,000 students on a daily basis in this instructional mode. In all likelihood, it will soon be feasible to increase these numbers to a thousand terminals and 30,000 students. Operational details of our 1965–66 drill-and-practice program at Stanford are to be found in the forthcoming book by Suppes, Jerman, and Brian.[1]

At the second and deeper level of interaction between student and computer program there are *tutorial systems,* which take over the main responsibility both for presenting a concept and for developing skill in its use. The intention is to approximate the interaction a patient tutor would have with an individual student. An important aspect of the tutorial programs in reading and elementary mathematics with which we have been concerned at Stanford in the past three years is that every effort is made to avoid an initial experience of failure on the part of the slower children. On the other hand, the program has enough flexibility to avoid boring the brighter children with endlessly repetitive exercises. As soon as the student manifests a clear understanding of a concept on the basis of his handling of a number of exercises, he is moved on to a new concept and new exercises. (A detailed evaluation of the Stanford reading program, which is under the direction of Professor Richard C. Atkinson, may be found in the report by Wilson and Atkinson.[2] A report on the tutorial mathematics program will soon be available. The data show that the computer-based curriculum was particularly beneficial for the slower students.)

At the third and deepest level of interaction there are *dialogue systems* aimed at permitting the student to conduct a genuine dialogue with the computer. The dialogue systems at the present time exist primarily at the conceptual rather than the operational level, and I do want to emphasize that in the case of dialogue systems a number of difficult technical problems must first be solved. One problem is that of recognizing spoken speech.

[1] P. Suppes, M. Jerman, and D. Brian, *Computer-assisted Instruction at Stanford: The 1965–66 Arithmetic Drill-and-Practice Program.* New York: Academic Press, 1968, in press.

[2] H. A. Wilson and R. C. Atkinson, *Computer-based Instruction in Initial Reading: A Progress Report on the Stanford Project.* Technical Report No. 119, August 25, 1967, Institute for Mathematical Studies in the Social Sciences, Stanford University.

Especially in the case of young children, we would like the child to be able simply to ask the computer program a question. To permit this interaction, we must be able to recognize the spoken speech of the child and also to recognize the meaning of the question he is asking. The problem of recognizing meaning is at least as difficult as that of recognizing the spoken speech. It will be some time before we will be able to do either one of these things with any efficiency and economy.

I would predict that within the next decade many children will use individualized drill-and-practice systems in elementary school; and by the time they reach high school, tutorial systems will be available on a broad basis. Their children may use dialogue systems throughout their school experience.

If these predictions are even approximately correct, they have far-reaching implications for education and society. As has been pointed out repeatedly by many people in many different ways, the role of education in our society is not simply the transmission of knowledge but also the transmission of culture, including the entire range of individual, political, and social values. Some recent studies—for example, the Coleman report—have attempted to show that the schools are not as effective in transmitting this culture as we might hope; but still there is little doubt that the schools play a major role, and the directions they take have serious implications for the character of our society in the future. Now I hope it is evident from the very brief descriptions I have given that the widespread use of computer technology in education has an enormous potential for improving the quality of education, because the possibility of individualizing instruction at ever deeper levels of interaction can be realized in an economically feasible fashion. I take it that this potentiality is evident enough, and I would like to examine some of the problems it raises, problems now beginning to be widely discussed.

Three rather closely related issues are particularly prominent in this discussion. The first centers around the claim that the deep use of technology, especially computer technology, will impose a rigid regime of impersonalized teaching. In considering such a claim, it is important to say at once that indeed this is a possibility. Computer technology could be used this way, and in some instances it probably will. This is no different from saying that there are many kinds of teaching, some good and some bad. The important point to insist upon, however, is that it is certainly not a *necessary* aspect of the use of the technology. In fact, contrary to the expectations sometimes expressed in the popular press, I would claim that one of the computer's most important potentials is in making learning and teaching more personalized, rather than less so. Students will be subject to less regimentation and lockstepping, because computer systems will be able to offer highly individualized instruction. The routine that occupies a good part of the teacher's day can be taken over by the computer.

It is worth noting in this connection that the amount of paper work required of teachers is very much on the increase. The computer seems to offer the only possibility of decreasing the time spent in administrative routine by ordinary teachers. Let us examine briefly one or two aspects of instruction ranging from the elementary school to the college. At the elementary level, no one anticipates that students will spend most of their time at computer consoles. Only 20 to 30 percent of the student's time would be spent in this fashion. Teachers would be able to work with classes reduced in size. Also, they could work more intensely with individual students, because some of the students will be at the console and, more importantly, because routine aspects of teaching will be handled by the computer system.

At the college level, the situation is somewhat different. At most colleges and universities, students do not now receive a great deal of individual attention from instructors. I think we can all recognize that the degree of personal attention is certainly not less in a computer program designed to accommodate itself to the individual student's progress than in the lecture course that has more than 200 students in daily attendance. (In our tutorial Russian program at Stanford, under the direction of Joseph Van Campen, all regular classroom instruction has been eliminated. Students receive 50 minutes daily of individualized instruction at a computer terminal consisting of a teletype with Cyrillic keyboard and earphones; the audio tapes are controlled by the computer.)

A second common claim is that the widespread use of computer technology will lead to excessive standardization of education. Again, it is important to admit at once that this is indeed a possibility. The sterility of standardization and what it implies for teaching used to be illustrated by a story about the French educational system. It was claimed that the French minister of education could look at his watch at any time of the school day and say at once what subject was being taught at each grade level throughout the country. The claim was not true, but such a situation could be brought about in the organization of computer-based instruction. It would technically be possible for a state department of education, for example, to require every fifth-grader at 11:03 in the morning to be subtracting one-fifth from three-tenths, or for every senior in high school to be reciting the virtues of a democratic society. The danger of the technology is that edicts can be enforced as well as issued, and many persons are rightly concerned at the spectre of the rigid standardization that could be imposed.

On the other hand, there is another meaning of standardization that holds great potential. This is the imposition of educational standards on schools and colleges throughout the land. Let me give one example of what I mean. A couple of years ago I consulted with one of the large city school systems in this country in connection with its mathematics program. The curriculum outline of the mathematics program running from kindergarten to high school was excellent. The curriculum as specified in the outline was about as good as any in the country. The real source of difficulty was the magnitude of the discrepancy between the actual performance of the students and the specified curriculum. At almost every grade level, students were performing far below the standard set in the curriculum guide. I do not mean to suggest that computer technology will, in one fell stroke, provide a solution to the difficult and complicated problems of raising the educational standards that now obtain among the poor and culturally deprived. I do say that the technology will provide us with unparalleled insight into the actual performance of students.

Yet I do not mean to suggest that this problem of standardization is not serious. It is, and it will take much wisdom to avoid its grosser aspects. But the point I would like to emphasize is that the wide use of computers permits the introduction of an almost unlimited diversity of curriculum and teaching. The very opposite of standardization *can* be achieved. I think we would all agree that the ever-increasing use of books from the sixteenth century to the present has deepened the varieties of educational and intellectual experience generally available. There is every reason to believe that the appropriate development of instructional programs for computer systems will increase rather than decrease this variety of intellectual experience. The potential is there.

The real problem is that as yet we do not understand very well how to take advantage of this potential. If we examine the teaching of any subject in the curriculum, ranging from elementary mathematics to ancient history, what is striking is the great similarity between teachers and between textbooks dealing with the same subject, not the vast differences between them. It can even be argued that it is a subtle philosophical question of social policy to determine the extent to which we want to emphasize diversity in our teaching of standard subjects. Do we want a "cool" presentation of American history for some students and a fervent one for others? Do we want to emphasize geometric and perceptual aspects of mathematics more for some students, and symbolic and algebraic aspects more for others? Do we want to make the learning of language more oriented toward the ear for some students and more toward the eye for those who have a poor sense of auditory discrimination? These are issues that have as yet scarcely been explored in educational philosophy or in discussions of educational policy. With the advent of the new technology they will become practical questions of considerable moment.

The third and final issue I wish to discuss is the place of individuality and human freedom in the modern technology. The crudest form of opposition to widespread use of technology in education and in other parts of our society is to claim that we face the real danger of men becoming slaves of machines. I feel strongly that the threat to human individuality and freedom in our society does not come from technology at all, but from another source that was well described by John Stuart Mill more than a hundred years ago. In discussing precisely this matter in his famous essay *On Liberty*, he said, the greatest difficulty to be encountered does not lie in the appreciation of means towards an acknowledged end, but in the indifference of persons in general to the end itself. If it were felt that the free development of individuality is one of the leading essentials of well-being; that it is not only a co-ordinate element with all that is designated by the terms civilization, instruction, education, culture, but is itself a necessary part and condition of all those things; there would be no danger that liberty should be undervalued, and the adjustment of the boundaries between it and social control would present no extraordinary difficulty.

Just as books freed serious students from the tyranny of overly simple methods of oral recitation, so computers can free students from the drudgery of doing exactly similar tasks unadjusted and untailored to their individual needs. As in the case of other parts of our society, our new and wondrous technology is there for beneficial use. It is our problem to learn how to use it well. When a child of six begins to learn in school under the direction of a teacher, he hardly has a concept of a free intelligence able to reach objective knowledge of the world. He depends heavily upon every word and gesture of the teacher to guide his own reactions and responses. This intellectual weaning of children is a complicated process that we do not yet manage or understand very well. There are too many adults among us who are not able to express their own feelings or to reach their own judgments. I would claim that the wise use of technology and science, particularly in education, presents a major opportunity and challenge. I do not want to claim that we know very much yet about how to realize the full potential of human beings; but I do not doubt that we can use our modern instruments to reduce the personal tyranny of one individual over another, wherever that tyranny depends upon ignorance.

Rote or Reasoning: Some Cautions on Programming *

DONALD ARNSTINE

As investment mounts in the new educational industries, spokesmen for programmed materials become unbounded in their enthusiasm. An ad in *The New York Times* reads:

Reprinted from *The High School Journal*, 51 (8): 353–364 (May 1968), by permission of author and publisher.

* For critical discussion of some of the arguments in this essay, I am grateful to Professor Robert M. Gordon of the Department of Philosophy of the University of Wisconsin.

Your youngster need not be gifted or particularly interested in the subject— he will learn it at a rapid pace, absorbing information swiftly from his UNIVOX course, and moving on. And he'll have a whale of a time doing it.

Government appears to share the enthusiasm of the industries. Richard Louis Bright, director of educational research for the U. S. Office of Education (a former Westinghouse employee with a doctorate in electrical engineering) visualizes "completely computerized classrooms taking over the nation's schools in 10 or 15 years, each pupil seated at an individual console, absorbing information prepared by the country's best teachers" (*The Cleveland Plain Dealer,* March 14, 1966). Even in the more scholarly pages of the *Harvard Educational Review,* one may read that, if teachers tend to resist the promise of educational technology, "it will be necessary to direct the sales pitch also to the prospective user." [1]

In education no less than in the field of cosmetics, salesmanship seldom offers good grounds for buying the product. Even before examination, we would not expect machinery or programs to make our children brilliant any more than we would expect bath soap to make them beautiful. The incapacity of soap to produce beauty does not discourage us from using it to keep clean; in like manner, the limitations of programmed materials should not keep us from using them for what they can do. Final decisions about the use of programming in educational settings may be political and economic ones, but they should in turn be based on careful analyses of educational utility. The intention in this paper is to pursue the question, for what can we use programs? The focus will be on what programs can do, and, in the course of that discussion, reasons will be offered for believing that the form in which programmed materials are cast is best suited to rote forms of learning which preclude more complex intellectual operations.

The analyses that follow focus on educational means, not ends. Thus the issues raised here must always be taken as subordinate to the question, what do we want to teach? That question, of course, must be dealt with on its own grounds, and independent of considerations of hardware. To do otherwise is to risk allowing the nature of the hardware to influence one's notion of what is worth teaching:

Surely, if one uses teaching machines he commits himself to a philosophy of education that endorses goals compatible with the use of these machines. There seems something backward about adjusting one's goals to fit his tools, rather than devising tools to fit his goals. [2]

[1] G. Howard Goold, "Discussion: the Education Industries," *Harvard Educational Review,* 37 (1967), 117.

[2] James A. Jordan, Jr., "Teaching Machines and Philosophy of Education," *The School Review,* 71 (1963), 156, 157.

I

(It is well to be clear at the outset that the results of empirical testing of instructional programs do not offer a clear-cut answer to the question, what can programs do?) If we try to determine whether programs foster outcomes more like the rote acquisition of simple facts, or more like the operation of complex and critical skills, empirical research is peculiarly silent. Experimental studies have, for example, shown the relative efficacy of covert as compared with overt responses (and usually found them to be equally effective),[3] and they have shown the relative efficacy of logical as compared with scrambled frame sequences (and again, there has been little difference in the accuracy of students' responses).[4] Other studies have correlated achievement scores subsequent to using programs with a variety of student personality characteristics,[5] and many studies have compared the achievement scores of two student groups, one of which (the control group) was subject to conventional teaching procedures, and the other of which (the experimental group) used programmed instruction.[6] But in all the studies with which this writer is familiar, the measure of achievement has been the number of correct responses on an achievement test. Were the responses indicative of the simple acquisition of facts, or of the acquisition of complex intellectual skills? The studies do not tell us this.

Since we must arrive at a judgment about what programs can do if we are to consider how they might be used, and since empirical studies of programmed instruction are limited in the help they can give us, another mode of analysis will be adopted. First, we will examine some representative sections, or frames, of a typical instructional program, in an effort to see what one could reasonably expect a student to learn from it. Then a critical examination will be made of the claim that, while many existent programs do present material in a rather doctrinaire, rote manner, programs could be constructed to teach more complex intellectual skills such as, for example, the adducing of reasons. On the basis of these analyses, suggestions will be made for the possible school uses of programmed materials.

---

[3] See L. M. Stolurow and C. C. Walker, "A Comparison of Overt and Covert Responses in Programmed Learning," *Journal of Educational Research,* 55 (1962), 421–429.

[4] See V. Roe, H. W. Case, and A. Roe, "Scrambled Versus Ordered Sequence in Auto-Instructional Programs," University of Southern California, Department of Engineering, Report No. 61-48 (1961).

[5] See B. A. Doty and L. A. Doty, "Programmed Instructional Effectiveness in Relation to Certain Student Characteristics," *Journal of Educational Psychology,* 55 (1964), 334–338.

[6] See, for example, Joseph Spagnoli, "Experience with Programmed Materials," *Journal of Educational Research,* 58 (1965), 447–448.

II

Machines vary in complexity, from cardboard viewers sold in supermarkets to costly electronic computers. The heart of programmed instruction, however, is the program, which consists of a series of closely related items or frames to which the student must respond and which immediately afterward inform the student of the correctness of his response. Below appear the initial frames of a programmed textbook in chemistry.[7] The underlined words are those that had been left blank in the text. The student responds by filling in the blank, whereupon he turns the page, finds the correct answer (and is thus said to be reinforced), and is presented with a new sentence to be completed.

1. This is a pile of pebbles (there is a picture). The pebbles are large, so it is easy to see them. If you make them smaller (another picture) you have sand. If you make them still smaller (another picture) you have powder.
2. Why is it difficult to see powder particles? They are too small to be seen easily.
3. Each powder particle is made up of millions of even smaller particles, called atoms. Why can't you see an atom? It is too small.
4. A chair, a book, and a piece of fruit are all made up of atoms. As you might guess, everything is made of atoms.

With these four frames the student is launched into the study of atomic structure. Has he been asked to reason? Has he learned any complex intellectual skills? Surely, not yet. What he has done, in filling in the blanks, is simply to repeat a word or phrase that he read moments earlier. It might be added that he has been given a very unsophisticated impression of what an atom is. One could infer from the above frames that, with a powerful lens, he could see the little particles called atoms. But this is simply false. Electrons get the same treatment: they too are too small to be seen (frame 12).

After completing a few simple diagrams, the student learns about the nucleus of the atom; it may be noted that in the following three frames, what the student acquires is no more than a convention for word usage:

8. The nucleus is the center of the atom.
9. The plural of nucleus is nuclei. If one atom has one nucleus, then two atoms have two nuclei.
10. Write the word that means more than one nucleus. nuclei.

Soon afterward appear three frames that deal with the "movement" of electrons:

13. Electrons move about the nucleus in complicated ways and paths we do not completely know and understand.

[7] Charles R. Dawson (editorial supervisor), *Chemistry 1: Atomic Structure and Bonding* (New York: Appleton-Century-Crofts, 1962).

14. Do electrons travel around the nucleus in neat circles? <u>no.</u>
15. In the diagram (which is pictured), the path of an electron about the nucleus is shown by a <u>circle.</u> Does this mean that we think the path is exactly this shape? <u>no.</u>

The student is told that the path of electrons is not circular, yet in every diagram in the text, the path is represented as circular. He is given no reason why (a) the actual path is not circular, or (b) the diagrammed path is circular. The student, of course, has no problem in filling in the blanks. But it is not possible to conceive what sense he could make of them. Like the earlier frames on the atom and its nucleus, these frames, too, are exemplary of what is called rote learning.

Further on in the program, the concept of force is first explained and then used:

59. A force is a push or a pull. Whenever something is pushing or pulling we say that it is exerting a force. What are the man and the dogs (pictured) in the last two frames doing? (Use the new term.) <u>They are both exerting a force.</u>
60. Whenever something is pushed or pulled we say that a force is exerted on it. On what were the dogs exerting a force? On what did the man exert a force? <u>the sled, the crate.</u>
61. What is a force? <u>A force is a push or a pull.</u>
62. When a proton and an electron are near each other a force pulls them together. We say that a proton and an electron attract each other. Do objects which attract each other tend to move together or apart? <u>together.</u>
63. Protons <u>attract</u> electrons.
64. (Circles representing a proton and an electron are presented, and the student is asked to draw arrows indicating the direction in which they would move.)
65. What do we mean when we say that two particles attract each other? <u>We mean that they exert a force on each other that pulls them together.</u>

In these frames the student is presented a gross definition of force, after which he is shown how the concept apparently explains the attraction between protons and electrons. As before, the student's response involves only his repeating what he has just been told, and again it is difficult to suppose that any complex intellectual skills are operating. But more needs to be said than this, for it is doubtful that even much of an explanation is being given. Do the frames afford an understanding of why the particles attract one another? In frame 59, "force" is defined as "a push or a pull." Frame 65 calls for a meaning, and if we simply substitute in it the definition given earlier, we get, "we mean that they (the particles) exert a push or a pull on each other that pulls them together." This may be the meaning of the term attraction, but a student doesn't need a chemistry text to learn it; all he needs is a dictionary. For this reason, one might surmise that the student, while acquiring some minimal understanding of definitions, is acquiring very little understanding of chemical processes. The same preoccupation with language is exhibited in the following frames:

170. Sometimes the chemical symbol for an atom consists of the first two letters of the atom's name. Thus, the symbol for lithium is Li and the symbol for neon is <u>Ne.</u>
171. Chemical symbols always start with a <u>capital</u> letter.
172. What is wrong with this symbol for a berryllium atom? be <u>It does not begin with a capital letter.</u>
173. For what atom does the following symbol stand? H <u>A hydrogen atom.</u>

Throughout the program, definitions are presented and facts are asserted, but the student is never told how the facts are discovered, how they are verified, or what sorts of observations could be made if the facts were true. For example, he is told (frame 397) that when an atom gives or loses an electron, a charged particle (ion) is formed. But he is not told how electrons are gained and lost until, at frame 441, he learns they are donated among atoms. The serious student must either take donation to be some form of charity, or accept the program on faith. A few frames later (frame 446) the student is told, "The force which holds two oppositely charged ions together in an ionic compound is called an ionic bond." The next several frames offer specific examples of the point, and restate it in several ways. Yet recalling that force was earlier defined as "a push or a pull," the student again has only an expanded definition, and not an explanation. It would make just as much sense had the push or pull in question been called a marriage bond. To cite a final example, several frames beginning at number 700 tell the student how two hydrogen atoms can share each other's electrons and thus gain a stable structure. In this discussion, as is also the case throughout the program, no reference is made even to the most obvious of related observable events. Hydrogen explosions have been frequent and sometimes disastrous, but the student would never guess this from studying hydrogen in the program.

On an analysis of this program in chemistry, one must conclude that very little chemistry is taught or learned. The student is given no hint of how hypotheses are tested or even conceived. He will not understand why anyone should bother to inquire into chemistry in the first place, for he is not told what difference it would make (in terms that he could understand) if all the material in the program were true (which, because of its gross oversimplification, it is not). I would suggest, then, that the student learns not chemistry, but rather a form of language game. This is a game in its generic sense: a pastime or amusement, the outcome of which is not intrinsically related to anything else of significance in the player's life. The chief reason for such a lack of relation is the fact that the game is one of definitions. The definitions have little meaning in themselves, but the object of the game is to remember them and to remember the ways they are related to one another within the context of the game. This program, then, so far from presenting anything for the exercise of complex intellectual skills, instead presents only rules for the use of unfamiliar terms. As such, it teaches in a rote manner, and the only use it might have in the classroom would be to free the teacher from the drill aspects of teaching.[8]

III

The chemistry program under consideration is only one of many available programs, and it could be argued that better ones can be written—programs that would avoid the oversimplifications and rote features noted here.[9] This argument cannot be met by simply analyzing more programs. Not only would both analyst and audience eventually wear down from exhaustion, but the claim, "but a better program could be written" would always be ready to greet each new analysis. Thus we must consider the question, how could a better program be devised, such that a student might learn to exercise reason—that is, to acquire complex intellectual skills?

One attempt to propose the programming of complex intellectual skills [10] —largely taken to be verbal ones—argued that what a person says is governed in part by what he anticipates saying. Since these anticipations are themselves based (partly) on an understanding of syntactic patterns, it was suggested that those patterns be programmed. A critic pointed out that anticipated responses—if indeed they can be called responses at all—are covert, and that if covert or unseen events are to be included among the factors that control behavior, then the idea of external control (by means of an instructional program) is impossible.[11] It would appear, then, that this attempt to program complex intellectual skills was purchased at the high price of giving up the very principles on which programmed instruction is based. The outcome of such an attempt might be an educationally

---

[8] See Fred Guggenheim, "Curriculum Implications and Applications of Programmed Instruction," *School Review,* 73 (1965), 59. Also apparently in support of this view is James J. Muro, "Programmed Instruction: A Positive Point of View," *Clearing House,* 40 (1966), 493.

[9] Writing in support of programming, George L. Geis notes that, because the construction of a program is both costly and arduous, it would be foolhardy simply to teach "inane reflexes." Instead, programmers must focus on "crucial concepts rather than a myriad of facts. Though it is true that most available programs are little more than texts on which surgical removal of words has been done, we look forward to programming as an instrument of concept formation rather than one of information passage." Geis, "Variety and Programed Instruction or, What Can be Programed?" *A V Communication Review,* 14 (1966), 115. What the author does not make clear is, what *is* concept formation? Might not the writers of the chemistry program cited above deny that they were programming "inane reflexes," and insist they were facilitating concept formation?

[10] Lauren B. Resnick, "Programed Instruction and the Teaching of Complex Intellectual Skills: Problems and Prospects," *Harvard Educational Review,* 33 (1963), 451, 466.

[11] Peter S. Rosenbaum, "Discussion," *Harvard Educational Review,* 34 (1964), 84.

valuable sort of workbook, but it would not be a program as that term has been discussed and described for more than a decade.

If a program could enable students to give reasons for their beliefs, it could not be said that only simple rote learning was being facilitated. It has been noted that when a student is simply caused to answer items or complete frames correctly—which the selective reinforcements of programmed materials can easily do—he does not know why he answered.[12] It has thus been proposed that the rote learning of conclusions can be avoided "when the reasons are built right into the causal sequence for changing behavior, i.e., the frames of the program itself."[13] But is it possible to do this?

Build the reasons into the program itself is a proposal much like (for those who would learn to hunt lions) find the beast and shoot it between the eyes. The advice is well meant, but it is not clear how we are to go about acting on it. Indeed, the proposal to build reasons into the program itself cannot be acted upon at all, for it is based on a misunderstanding of what a reason is. In what follows I do not propose to analyze comprehensively the nature of reasons, but only to direct a little light on one feature of reasons which is relevant to the present inquiry.

Is the assertion, "It is going to rain" a reason? It seems an odd thing to ask. If, at breakfast, I look out the window and remark to my wife, "It is going to rain," then that is simply a judgment or prediction based on observation. But if I say, "We'd better call off the picnic," and my wife asks, "Why?", I may answer, "It is going to rain." In that context, "It is going to rain" functions as a reason. Thus whether or not a sentence constitutes a reason depends on the context of its utterance. The same sentence may serve as a reason in one context, but not in another. And it would follow that there is no class of reasons waiting to be drawn upon and plugged into the sequence of frames in an instructional program.

What would happen if we tried to build reasons into a program? The question is better understood if translated into a more precise question: if sentences which served as reasons in certain contexts were included within the frames of a program, how would they then function for a student? The student's task when confronting the program is to complete a sentence correctly. In theory, the material in each frame builds on the content of the previous frame, and leads to the next frame. As the student deals with each frame serially, one might well ask, how is he to tell which blanks call for conclusions, and which call for reasons? No answer is forthcoming. The student is not seeking reasons at all: his task is to find the correct response to each frame. Correct responses, not reasons, are what pay off for

[12] James E. McClellan, "Automated Education: A Philosophical Approach," in Alfred de Grazia and David A. Sohn (eds.), *Programs, Teachers, and Machines* (New York: Bantam Books, 1964).
[13] *Ibid.*, 112.

the student. Thus regardless of the fact that certain frames in the program may have functioned for the programmer as reasons within his frame of reference, they do not so function for the student. He who does not seek reasons does not find them.

Again, it must be concluded that the form of programmed materials turns every effort to facilitate complex intellectual skills into but another technique for the promotion of rote-learned responses. It might be added that the small step format practically guarantees this outcome. In order to avoid student errors, the information in each frame is so slightly greater than that found in the previous frame that only the feeblest effort of thought is called for. The effect on students has been summarized by Herbert Thelen and John R. Ginther, reporting on the use of programmed materials in Chicago schools:

> Two striking reactions turned up on our data: first, the elaborate and ingenious ways of short-cutting the program (called "cheating" by the teachers); and second, the oft-noted phenomenon of going through the program, apparently satisfactorily, and then being unable to pass tests or answer questions about what it is that one has been reading or answering. The alleged reward from immediate feedback, telling the student that he has made the right response, is simply inadequate.[14]

Small steps, in short, promote boredom. People (including students) normally seek to avoid it, and when they have succeeded, they seldom have a clear recollection of what went on.

IV

Programmed materials foster only a rote form of knowledge acquisition. The form in which programs are constructed precludes any form of learning other than this. How, then, can they be used in an educational context, and especially that of formal schools?

Industry and the military have successfully used programmed materials in achieving their own training purposes. As long as the concern is only that the student make the correct responses (if the light turns red, then pull switch A; if the pointer remains within the green band, then pull switch B . . .), the program is an efficient way to get results. All that is wanted is an operative who performs his assigned tasks correctly; others are available who can do the thinking. There may be good reasons to regret an economic and industrial system that calls upon people to behave in ways such as this, but in the military and in industry, what is held to be important is the outcome or the product—not the effects which processes may

[14] H. Thelen and J. R. Ginther, "Experiences with Programed Materials in the Chicago Area," In *Four Case Studies of Programed Instruction* (New York: Fund for the Advancement of Education, 1964), 60.

have on the people who contribute to those ends. In schooling, on the other hand, matters are different, for what is important is just the quality of students' thoughts and actions. The school aspires to help students acquire "reasoned grounds for thinking as they do." [15] On the basis of the analyses undertaken here, programmed materials will not be helpful in this regard. The rote acquisition of discrete responses is simply irrelevant either to having reasons or being able to reason.

How and how much programs might be used in schools must depend largely on what teachers think is worth teaching. Programs will not foster intellectual growth, nor are they likely to help develop any desirable attitudes (they are much too dull for that), but they can help to familiarize students with the meanings of terms and to assist in drill work. The extent to which a teacher might have recourse to programs would then depend on how much importance he attached to such ends.

While there may be few teachers who would wish to use programs as the sole or the chief materials in their instruction, they may still be considered as possibly useful adjuncts to instruction, or as resource or reference materials. There would seem to be little reason why a program should not serve as an instructional unit within a wider course of study if, after the teacher has carefully analyzed it, he judges that the program's content offers a treatment of the subject taught compatible with his own. If on the other hand there is an incompatibility between program content and the teacher's understanding of the subject, the program (or the teacher?) had better be abandoned. Programs, in giving only answers, do not raise questions for the students to think about. Thus a program alien to the teacher's perspective can only confuse the students and overburden the teacher. The incompatibilities and rote-learning aspects of programmed materials might be forgiven, however, if the teacher is called upon to prepare his students for external examinations, such as those of the College Entrance Examination Board.

Considered as reference or resource materials, programs appear rather awkward. Since they are standardized in form, they are not well suited to students with special needs or special interests in a field of study. And lacking indexes, programs cannot easily be utilized at the point where students might need particular kinds of information. Programs are quite unlike libraries, encyclopedias, films (which can have an immediate appeal wholly lacking in programs), or dictionaries. Consulting a program would be like consulting a dictionary that was not alphabetized.

There is something about technology that smacks of magic, even though some technologists charge that only they have been disabused of the crudities and rites of a pre-technological age. An advertisement for the journal *Educational Technology* recently asserted, "In place of the semi-mystical 'art' of teaching, educational technologists are formulating a science of

[15] McClellan, *op. cit.*, 108.

education, in which teaching is virtually always effective and learning is assured." Effective teaching that results in genuine learning is hard to come by; it will always require great effort and good judgment—often performed on the spot, when confronting students. A world in which teaching were virtually always effective, and learning always assured, might be a benign one in which to live (even if men, with no further problems to solve, might throw down roots and turn into vegetables). But it is not the world that we live in. In our world, we try to do better what we think is worth doing, and our potential means and instrumentalities must be judged in that light. Programmed materials will not perform miracles; they must be judged in the same way in which we judge workbooks, filmstrips, and pencils. Nor are any of these things simply neutral—equally capable of being used for good or ill. If a pencil were neutral, we should have no qualms about giving one to an infant. Programs, too, may cause some damage if swallowed indiscriminately.

Instructional Systems—Magic or Method?

JOHN W. LOUGHARY

The term "instructional systems" first began appearing with some noticeable regularity around 1960. During the intervening years it has come to be a part of the "new education" jargon, along with other words such as input, output, monitor, and de-bug. A growing number of instructional systems companies have been founded and many established firms have created instructional systems departments.

More and more, school districts refer to their instructional systems, and it is no longer uncommon to find the position of systems analyst listed in school district personnel classifications. Perhaps the clearest evidence that "instructional systems" refers to something real are the employment advertisements for educational systems specialists placed in many metropolitan newspapers. Several years ago such ads were unheard of.

Nevertheless, there is sufficient historical reason to justify skepticism regarding the validity and uniqueness of the instructional systems concept. Education has a history of old wine in new bottles, and many professional

From *Educational Leadership*, 25 (8): 730–734 (May 1968). Reprinted with permission of the Association for Supervision and Curriculum Development and John W. Loughary. Copyright © 1968 by the Association for Supervision and Curriculum Development.

educators and laymen alike wonder whether instructional systems are another case, so to speak. The question is especially important, it seems to me, in light of the many claims, both stated and implied, made for the systems approach in education. These claims include: individualized instruction responsive to differences in pupil background, interests, and ability; decreased clerical tasks for teachers; better use of facilities and materials; more precise measurement of achievement; and, in many instances, increased relevancy of instruction to the real world of the learner. Let us take another look at the reality of instructional systems.

CHARACTERISTICS OF INSTRUCTIONAL SYSTEMS

One should begin, I suppose, by asking, "What is an instructional system?" and "What is new or unique about its construction and operation?" Usually, such a system involves a complexity of procedures, several media, and has relatively specific objectives. It seems obvious that a temporal reference point is needed, as is some statement of scope. School systems of one hundred years ago would fit the general definition just stated, but this is a different use of the term.

Instructional systems, in the current sense, are almost without exception concerned with a particular body of knowledge suggested by what has been historically labeled a course. There are certainly innovations in subject matter organization, but in some general manner an instructional system is concerned with a subject matter content which is something less than the total subject matter of a greater curriculum.

In my opinion, the traditional course consisting of a single text, supplementary reading, lectures, possibly a workbook, and several examinations is not a fair point of comparison. I can recall, however, something which at least at first look appears similar to modern instructional systems, and is illustrated by the bookkeeping practice sets which many of us did in high school, in my case during the mid 1940's. These exercises and current instructional systems have several similar aspects.

One thing which the procedures illustrated by the practice set and recent instructional systems have in common is the integration of a number of specific skills and competencies into a comprehensive and systematic package, including some representation of the real world environment. In other words, both use simulation as a teaching-learning procedure. Both also require careful planning and coordination in the development of the materials and procedures involved, and can be distinguished from many other kinds of instruction by the field test (de-bugging) which precedes large-scale use.

Another common feature is the operational concern for student motivation via active student participation in the learning process. In the practice set, as in current instructional systems, the student must do more than read. Most instructional systems are based, among other things, on the "principles" of programmed instruction, and an obvious question is: do the authors of practice sets and similar exercises, without stating so explicitly, use the same concepts? These are usually stated as: (a) organize materials in small units of instruction, (b) provide for active student participation, (c) provide constant feedback for the student, and (d) provide immediate positive reward. At least the practice sets which I completed when I was a student and similar exercises which I later used as a high school teacher seemed consistent with such principles.

I conclude that the instructional systems being developed are not entirely new. Whether they are an outgrowth or refinement of earlier materials, I cannot say. But it is clear that some teachers of at least a generation ago used instructional procedures much more complex and dynamic than textbooks and lectures.

What, then, are the distinctive characteristics of instructional systems? It seems to me that a distinction needs to be made between instructional systems in the sense of teaching-learning packages, and instructional systems as a set of procedures for developing and implementing curriculum and materials. In the first case, instructional systems seem to be extensions of earlier learning exercises, as we have seen above. There are, however, some important differences. Instructional systems in the second sense involve what I think can justifiably be called a scientific approach to education. At least in theory, it is an attempt to design curriculum and develop instructional procedures and materials which reflect what research has revealed about the teaching-learning process. For purposes of convenience, I have considered the two kinds of instructional systems separately.

INSTRUCTIONAL PACKAGES

Instructional packages which I have looked at recently emphasize individualization. There is an attempt to account for differences in pupil learning rate, past achievement, interest, and aptitude. When systems developers are successful, pupils need only be concerned with what they do not know, and are given credit, and more important, respect for prior learning. In the older systems all pupils were expected to complete all of the procedures. Usually there was no choice. The instructional package could not be modified, and it was an all or nothing proposition.

Another difference is in regard to the comprehensiveness of systems. The earlier instructional exercises usually were intended to be supplementary instructional materials. It was expected that students would learn the "basics" by the textbook-lecture route, and use the exercise to practice what was "learned." While many instructional packages or systems still are intended as supplementary materials, there is a growing interest in developing comprehensive systems which encompass all of the substance and materials of a defined area of study. While such a system might be developed and conceptualized as a set of modules, it would be closely coordinated.

Another difference which would appear to be important is the multimedia characteristic of new instructional systems. The concept goes beyond using several media in a given unit of instruction. Some instructional systems attempt to provide the pupil with a choice of media for each "lesson" in a unit. To the extent that people differ in the capacity to learn from different media, and to the extent that media differ in effectiveness with certain kinds of learning tasks, the multi-media aspect of instructional systems can be a major innovation.

Two additional characteristics of recent instructional systems are especially important. First, some systems are developed to minimize the dependence on the teacher for their operation. While not totally teacher-independent, they are to varying degrees capable of being operated by the pupil himself. The significance is in the changed role of the teacher, whose function as a presenter of information is lessened considerably. Ideally, he is then free to give greater emphasis to instructional plannning, trouble-shooting, and enrichment for individual pupils.

Second, it is clear that in one way or another the instructional systems characteristics noted so far all aim at increasing individualization of instruction. Individualized instruction results in the need for current and responsive instructional management systems. Two important functions that such a system must perform are monitoring pupil learning behavior and coordinating instructional personnel facilities and materials. Historical reporting of pupil achievement and once-a-term scheduling of facilities, personnel, and materials are totally inadequate for an individualized instruction system. Sometimes daily flexibility of scheduling and real time information about pupil behavior are essential for comprehensive individualized instruction systems. It is becoming apparent that at least with large groups, nothing short of a computer-assisted management system can meet these requirements. Several such systems are under development, including one at the U.S. Naval Academy in Annapolis; another being developed by the American Institutes for Research; and a joint Duluth, Minnesota Schools-URS Corporation project, to name only three. When operating, the management system would provide for on-line instructional management as well as being a research and evaluation vehicle.

The instructional packages or systems, it seems to me, do represent something new in education. In theory their attention to individualization, perception, and specificity of learning goes beyond anything in the past.

EDUCATIONAL RESEARCH AND DEVELOPMENT

The second meaning of instructional systems refers to the use of systems concepts and procedures as both tools and as a model for developing instructional programs. The general steps involved are: (a) defining learning objectives; (b) determining specifications for a system which would meet the objectives; (c) designing a system based on the specifications; (d) developing the system (for example, instructional materials and routines, physical plant, training of personnel); (e) system de-bugging (i.e., a trial run and necessary corrections); and (f) system implementation and evaluation.

How much of this is educational nonsense and how much a useful approach? This probably depends on whether two major conditions are met. First and most essential is the careful defining of learner objectives in behavioral or performance terms, and the second is the careful and imaginative work which must go into system design.

The difficulty in preparing performance objectives differs immensely, of course, with both the nature of the subject and the kind of learning involved, e.g., facts versus learning to apply a concept. Nevertheless, those who have attempted writing performance objectives, in the humanities for example, find they can increase the specificity of objectives. Without carefully defined objectives, the use of a systems approach is likely to be educational nonsense, and one had better limit instruction to textbooks and lectures.

But given adequate performance objectives, there is still no guarantee that an effective instructional system will emerge. A superficial and unimaginative approach to systems development results in a mechanical-like system with which learners usually become bored quickly, or in a set of procedures which have questionable relevancy to the objectives.

There is nothing magical about the instructional systems concept. A systems approach to education, whether it be used to design instructional packages, or as a basis for operating instructional programs, is neither easy nor does it guarantee effective learning. Not infrequently, both the ardent supporters and severe critics ignore the latter point.

There are too many instances of individualized instruction which differ from traditional instruction only in regard to more machines and brightly colored boxes of what are essentially cut-up textbooks. A disappointing proportion of what are labeled behavioral objectives fails to qualify, and much of what is claimed to be flexible in the new education actually appears to increase the rigidity of schools.

Excluding (but not discounting) the important early work in programmed instruction, a systems approach to education was first used by researchers, who began to borrow this tool developed by industry and the military. In brief, the systems approach was first used in education as a research procedure, and it is probably still used with greater skill and understanding primarily by researchers. There are, of course, exceptions.

I would suggest, then, that the eventual contribution of instructional systems depends on how well educators learn to use a systems approach. The essential difference between using this particular tool and others in education is the multi-functional nature of systems analysis, and the difference is one which should not be overlooked. A screwdriver, for example, can be used in a clumsy manner and still be of some value. In contrast, the minimum level of efficiency needed to render a wood lathe useful is considerably greater. Analogously, multiple choice exams, for example, are useful to most teachers, even when they possess only the crudest of test construction skills. In contrast, the point where a systems approach will be useful entails both a more complex set of skills and a higher level of proficiency in their use.

In conclusion, my chief concern at this point is not whether educational systems represent a new and useful development. I think they do, at least potentially, and the experiences to date justify a major effort to find out. What is most important is for educators, especially those in teacher education, to achieve the necessary system development competencies so that comprehensive and precise instructional systems can be developed and tested in a number of areas.

The Unit of Work as an Approach to Teaching

LOREN R. TOMLINSON

It should be made clear at the outset that the intention here is not to present or to discuss the unit of work in any comprehensive way. Rather it is to focus on the unit of work as an approach to teaching and to pay particular attention to the traits that seem to account for its acceptance in education.

Over the years the unit of work frequently has been the center of bitter controversy in education. The basic idea was conceived early in this century as a part of the broad, general revolt against the barren and irrelevant school practices that prevailed at the time. Originally called "the project method," it represented a decided departure from conventional practices in that traditionally organized subject matter was abandoned in favor of child-oriented projects that were designed to assist pupils in achieving both intellectual and ethical goals through the procedures employed, as well as through the substantive content.

The term *unit* came into use in the 1920's and since that time has been widely used and variously modified to label a variety of ideas and prac-

An original paper written especially for this volume.

tices. We speak not only of units and units of work but also of subject-matter units, experience units, process units, pupil-centered units, teaching units, resource units, and so on. Although such terms have no precise meanings, they do represent attempts to designate a particular interpretation, emphasis, refinement, or dimension of the basic concept itself. Of course, the term in its variations has also been grossly misused at times and applied to practices that deny the concept in every respect.

DEFINITIONS AND DESCRIPTIONS

It would appear that more explicit definitions and authentic, detailed descriptions would result in greater uniformity in the development of units of work. But definitions invariably need clarification and the most detailed descriptions are never complete. And too, the unit of work is essentially theoretical. As such, its true nature is not to be discovered in definitions and descriptions, but rather at the operational level as the teacher, in planning and working with children, makes the innumerable decisions that ultimately determine the quality of their learning experiences. Obviously, all of the factors that must be weighed before decisions are made cannot be anticipated, especially without references to a particular situation. Consequently, definitions, descriptions, and suggestions can at best provide only the guidelines for the teacher.

A Definition

The unit of work can be defined as an organization of content and procedures into a broad learning experience that has significance for both the children and the teacher. Various interpretations are given to the unity that is implied in the term *unit*. Some conceive of the unity as residing in the organization of the content or subject matter. Others see it in terms of the coordinated series of procedures that go into the development of the unit of work. Still others take the position that the unity can exist only in the learner's experience. There is much to be said for each of these points of view. Taken separately, however, each is incomplete.

Although it is sometimes done, it is probably fruitless to discuss the relative importance of procedures and of content in the unit approach to teaching. Both are essential elements, closely interrelated and often indistinguishable. Attempts at units of work that are carefully developed from the standpoint of procedures, but that deal with content of questionable worth, seldom satisfy either the children or the teacher. On the other hand, the most challenging and worthwhile content can be dissipated through procedures that ignore sound principles of teaching. Indeed, the effectiveness of the unit of work experience suffers from the neglect of either of these two just as certainly as it does from not providing learners with the kind of experiences that result in cognitive and affective behavioral changes.

A Description

The description that follows, abbreviated as it must be, does provide an overview of the fundamental procedures involved in the development of the unit of work. Adaptations, of course, would have to be made in consideration of specific circumstances, such as the maturity of the children, their familiarity with unit-of-work procedures, and the learning resources available. It must be pointed out, too, that most units of work require a considerable block of time in the school day and are usually carried out over a period of several weeks. As they are developed units of work move through three phases: initiation, development, and culmination.

Initiation. This phase is concerned with preplanning. It begins with the selection of a topic either by the teacher alone or by the teacher and the children together. The selection is usually made within some established curriculum framework to ensure coordination and to avoid unnecessary repetition from grade level to grade level. Following this selection the teacher proceeds to prepare a statement of practicable purposes specifying understandings, attitudes, abilities and skills, and behavior changes as expected outcomes. This statement, in effect, outlines the scope of the study and serves as a guide as the unit is developed in detail with the children.

Major effort is devoted during the initiation phase to helping the children become acquainted with the learning possibilities inherent in the topic and to helping them gain a broad overview from which they can raise informed, intelligent questions. As the questions are raised, they are listed and grouped categorically and then plans are made as to how the work is to be pursued. Involved here are decisions regarding what is to be done by the whole group, by small groups, and by individuals.

Development. After the purposes have been determined and the procedures decided upon, the children are ready to enter into the developmental phase of the unit of work, in which the first concern is with gathering and organizing information and sharing findings with others.

In carrying out the research, use is made of as many types of informational resources as feasible. Field trips may be taken. Some resource people may be asked to visit the class, whereas others may be interviewed outside the classroom by small groups or by individual children. A variety of audiovisual resources may be employed, as well as books, magazines, newspapers, encyclopedias, and other types of printed materials.

After the research is well under way and the children have acquired information and developed understandings, consideration can then be given to dramatization, illustrations, demonstrations, and similar activities that enable them to apply and express what they have gained. If they are to be of real value, such activities should be carefully planned and should reflect the thinking and the work of the children. They have questionable educational value, of course, if they are undertaken just for the sake of having activities or if the children's efforts are used solely for the purpose of preparing a polished product.

Culmination. The culminating phase of the unit of work follows naturally out of the others. It is a time for summarizing and reviewing important aspects of the study, for clearing up misconceptions, for consolidating gains, and for evaluating. Perhaps the most satisfactory type of culminating activity is that in which children share their experiences with an audience of parents or with other classes. Although dramatizations, displays, and other such activities may have an important place in the presentation, emphasis should be given primarily to what the children have learned and how and why the work was done. Here again the genuine expressions of the children should be respected and not exploited for entertainment values.

THE POTENTIAL OF THE UNIT OF WORK

Among other things, the preceding definition and description indicate that the role of the teacher in unit teaching is essentially that of a guide and that deliberate efforts are made to take into consideration the purposes of the children. The flexibility of the unit of work permits a variety of practices and procedures. It can be adapted in some form to differing conditions, perhaps to all but the most extremely structured situations. But its essence lies with the control of a teacher who is sensitive to the concerns of the children and who helps them discover for themselves what they need to know. To the extent to which there are departures from this, the basic concept is compromised.

Also suggested by the definition and description are some of the potential advantages and disadvantages of the unit of work as an approach to teaching. It should be clear that there is nothing intrinsically good or bad in the procedure itself. The potential that is to be realized depends upon several factors, such as the availability of suitable materials, equipment, facilities, supervisory help, and the like. But most of all, of course, it depends upon the teacher and his understandings, skills, and inclinations.

Some Difficulties

Unit teaching can fail for any number of reasons. But given adequate support by way of resources the major difficulties center around the types of demands placed upon the teacher and the children that are different from those ordinarily made of them in more traditionally structured programs. Insofar as the teacher is concerned, first and foremost among these demands is the added responsibility he must assume for what happens in the teaching-learning situation. The extensive preplanning involved, the need to search out, collect, and organize resource material, and the necessity of extending his own knowledge of the content area—all require additional effort of the teacher. But undoubtedly even more demanding than this is the obligation to guide the learning process and to become accountable for learning outcomes.

The children, too, may have their difficulties with the unit of work. They are at liberty to participate more actively in the teaching-learning process, but unless they are quite young, their work in school has often conditioned them to a more passive role. Many have become comfortable in the routine of having someone tell them exactly what to do and when to do it. At first, many children resist the new freedom the unit of work affords them, but most respond, eventually, to the challenges it presents.

Some Opportunities

The same conditions that account for a good many difficulties also account for a good many of the advantages of units of work. There is evidence to support the contention, for example, that when a good teacher becomes seriously engaged in selecting and organizing learning activities for the children in his class, and when the children are actively involved in the learning process, the quality of learning improves. The earnest commitment to learning that can develop on the part of both the teacher and the children is a distinguishing characteristic of a sound unit of work and basic to any advantages that are to be realized. Some of these potential advantages can be reviewed in the context of certain familiar challenges that are encountered in the elementary school classroom.

Providing for Individual Differences. There is no question but that the unit of work as an approach to teaching can go a long way toward accommodating the spread of individual differences found in the typical classroom. Working with a wide range of abilities and interests is seldom simple for the teacher under any circumstances, but it presents an impossible situation for the teacher who restricts himself to common learning activities and inflexible requirements for all. Because the content may range broadly and the activities vary, the unit of work can provide many opportunities for meeting the different interests and abilities of the children. For example, the child who is intellectually gifted can undertake an assignment in conjunction with the unit that may go far beyond the abilities of the group as a whole. At the same time, as he reports back and shares his information and understandings with his classmates, he can serve as a valuable resource to them. On the other hand, the child with limited ability need not be constantly frustrated with intellectual tasks that are beyond him. If he has difficulty with reading, he may gather information from audio-visual materials, from educational trips, and from interviews to supplement what is available to him in print. Both the gifted child and the less able child can find satisfying and stimulating work and, at the same time, contribute to the success of the unit in progress.

Much of the same holds true for the variety of interests ordinarily found among a group of children. The role children's interests play in the development of the unit of work is sometimes misunderstood and often a point of controversy. It is not considered advisable to permit the fluctuating, transitory interests of the children to dominate a unit of work. When the

real and abiding interests of individuals and groups of children are identified, however, there is usually no great difficulty in providing for them.
Genuine interests can often serve as a point of entry into a study and very
often will sustain efforts throughout. Of course, a sound unit of work will
open up new areas of interest, as well as accommodate the old.

Enriching Skills, Subject Matter, and Aesthetics. A complementary relationship can exist between the unit of work and all of the curriculum areas.
In the development of the unit any or all of the skill, subject-matter, and
aesthetic areas of the curriculum may be drawn upon and used. This is
not done deliberately but follows naturally in the pursuit of a study that is
not restricted to a particular curriculum area. Cutting across subject-matter
lines accentuates the interrelatedness of different subject matters and may
help children come to view subject-matter categories for what they are:
useful, logical arrangements devised as a convenient means of classifying
and storing knowledge.

A continual responsibility faced by the elementary school teacher is
that of developing activities that provide children with opportunities to
use academic skills in functional ways. The awkward, contrived situations
in which children are so often expected to use skills are only too familiar.
For the children such situations have little or no meaning outside the context of the school.

To the extent that the unit of work is in keeping with the purposes of
the children, it offers abundant opportunities for them to make practical
use of their skills. The purposes that impel children vary. At one time they
may be reading for the personal satisfaction of learning more about a
given topic; at another time they may be making notes for a report to other
members of the group; at still another time they may be trying to bring
about a division of responsibilities in a group. The point is that they have
some purpose that lies beyond the skills that are involved. Instead of being
an end in themselves, the skills become a means to an end.

Much the same can be said with regard to the aesthetics areas. Here
children can make use of art, music, and aspects of physical education to
convey understandings, appreciations, and feelings that may be beyond
their facilities with spoken or written language.

It bears repeating that the unit of work draws upon the various curriculum areas as they are needed. The phrase "draws upon" correctly implies that subject matter, skills, and aesthetics are used as materials, tools,
and vehicles to achieve the children's purposes and through them the
purposes of the unit of work as established by the teacher. This is not to
say that the skills, subject matter, and aesthetics are not important in their
own right, but that insofar as the unit of work is concerned, they perform
a service function.

In their own turn the skills, subject matter, and aesthetic areas can be
enhanced through the unit of work. Because they are used by the children
in a meaningful context they may be viewed in a new light. Arithmetic

can become important to the child who wants to compare travel times in different modes of transportation; the table of contents and the index become helpful devices if he is seeking specific information in a book; or the use of historical resource material becomes a necessity if he is responsible for organizing facts to support a dramatization. Many of the activities of the unit of work can also provide the experiential base so necessary for aesthetic and creative expression.

In the course of the study, there are opportunities for the teacher to identify individual and group deficiencies that need attention. At times it may be best to attend to these immediately, but it is generally wiser to avoid disrupting the work in progress to do so. If the disability appears in the area of the language arts, for instance, the teacher may defer instruction and then take time later during the language arts period to deal with the matter. One advantage here is that the need for the particular skill may be as apparent to the children as it is to the teacher. This, of course, then becomes a most opportune time to work on it.

Providing for Quality Learning. It is widely accepted that the ultimate test of the quality of learning is whether that learning influences behavior. There are two points about the relationship between learning and behavior that seem to be pertinent here. One is that in order to have a lasting influence upon behavior the learning must have a strong impact upon the learner. The other is that changes in the behavior brought about by learning may take various forms, depending upon the type and level of learning. These may be reflected in the learner's action in general, his performance on a specific task, the ideas he expresses, the attitudes and values he reveals, and so on.

The changes in behavior that result from different types and levels of learning may be simple and quite obvious, or they may be complex and difficult to discern. Children who really learn to spell, not only spell the words correctly on spelling tests, but also do so in all of their writing. They have developed a level of spelling proficiency, and one aspect of their behavior with respect to written communication has been changed in a very direct and observable way.

But the changes in behavior that grow out of the broad understandings and appreciations that are the goals of the unit of work are not always so evident. For example, in a study of foods, certain learnings that the children acquire may have a direct bearing upon their food choices in the school cafeteria. But in the same study the children may come to understand firmly that people are largely interdependent in meeting their food requirements. The effect that this particular learning would have on the children's behavior would be less conspicuous, but certainly no less substantial. This important understanding has wide reference and transfer value. It could lead to an appreciation on the part of the children of the essential interdependence of mankind and could have far-reaching influence upon their attitude toward the social world in which they live.

But, obviously, the manifestations of this behavior would not be so readily apparent as in the case of food choices.

Providing for Learning That Endures. Unrelated bits of information and the meaningless performance of a skill are not conducive to desirable behavioral change. In the sound unit of work, the teacher's primary concern is that the children develop concepts, broad generalizations, attitudes, and skills and abilities. This is not to belittle the importance of specific information. The unit of work deals extensively with detailed facts, and makes use of them. They are the specifics of content that lead to and support the broad understandings. It is not a matter of learning of facts so much as it is the learning from facts.

It is evident that these broad outcomes are not likely to be achieved if the teacher feels pressed to rush children over material and through activities within a rigid time schedule. Children need time to learn. The broad and flexible block of time in the unit of work gives the children ample opportunity to discover and entertain ideas, to extend and build upon concepts, and to formulate generalizations. They also have time to apply and test the understandings and abilities that they are developing.

In addition to those learnings that are associated with the content of the study, there are concomitant learnings that relate more closely to the instructional procedures used in the unit of work. Children have opportunities to explore and to satisfy their curiosity, to share information with others, to gain aesthetic satisfactions from creative experiences, and to engage in individual and group activities through which they can have congenial work experiences and gain the satisfactions of work well done. And, of course, the children's enjoyment of the work does not mean that it is any less demanding of them. Motivated by their own purposes, they become their own task masters, and frequently set higher goals and a stiffer pace for themselves than would otherwise be required of them. What is most important is that they can come to view learning as an agreeable and satisfying experience.

Providing for Problem Solving and Critical Thinking. Our society demands that individuals seek solutions to their own problems. Although the process of solving problems can be formulated into a sequence of logical steps, in practice it is not always an orderly procedure that can be taught or learned directly. Indications are that it may be best to present children with problem situations and give them guidance in developing their own methods of attack.

The procedures followed in the unit-of-work approach to teaching are especially appropriate for affording children problem-solving experiences. The three phases of the unit of work are roughly equivalent to the series of steps in problem solving: questions or problems are raised or identified, answers or solutions are sought from all available sources, and action is taken on the basis of the findings.

In the unit of work children are expected to scrutinize critically the opinions, ideas, and facts that they gather. They have a stake in what goes on, and because they expect to make use of what they are learning, they seek organized, congruent information as a basis for their actions. Typically, they consult a variety of resource materials, and it is not unusual for them to encounter different points of view and sometimes find contradicting data. All of this can help children see the necessity of learning to discriminate among sources of information and to approach all types of resources with a wholesome doubting attitude. For instance, when in the books they read children discover conflicting opinions and discrepancies, they may be on the road toward becoming critical readers. After a few such experiences they may never again stand in quite so much awe of the authority of the printed word. They may come to the important realization that books and other forms of printed material are written by human beings, and, therefore, are subject to human error and vagary.

Providing for Personal Social Development. Perhaps the most widely acclaimed potential advantage of the unit of work is its contribution to the personal and social development of children. Not only does the content of many studies deal directly in this area, but the basic procedures followed in developing the study do afford the children first-hand experiences with social interactions and with self-control. As they engage in group and independent work, children can learn in practical ways the necessity of accepting and discharging responsibilities, of meeting obligations, of being cooperative, and of showing concern for the welfare of others. Through the clashes and conflicts that normally accompany attempts at working together, the children can sharpen group work skills and develop an appreciation for cooperative behavior.

It is also the usual practice for the teacher to arrange for the children to participate in the planning and evaluating of learning activities and in the establishment of standards for guiding behavior in different situations. When the teacher does this, he is sharing authority and responsibility with the children, an essential condition for developing their self-management capacities. As the children mature through their experiences in sharing authority, they can assume increasing responsibility for making and carrying out plans, for developing and living up to agreements, and for managing their behavior in general.

These, then, are what seem to be some of the outstanding characteristics of the unit-of-work approach to teaching. Because of its firm philosophical and psychological foundations, it has persisted and evolved over the years, and in the minds of many today continues to be the most appropriate and sophisticated means available for helping children achieve the broad objectives of the elementary school. There is no formula for the unit of work and there are no guaranties, only possibilities. To a considerable degree, control of the teaching-learning situation is relinquished to the teacher and herein lies its potentialities. It frees the good teacher to do his best and the poor teacher to do his worst.

PART 6

Understanding and Teaching the "Different" Student

Understanding and teaching students who come from middle-class backgrounds, who are of average ability, who achieve in ways consistent with their ability, and who are socially and emotionally well adjusted is in itself no easy task. But the task assumes greater proportions when students are "different." The purpose in this part is to reacquaint the reader with some of these students in the hope, first, that they will be better understood and, second, that curricular and instructional strategies better designed to meet their needs will be developed. Neither hope will be easily realized. But it is becoming increasingly clear that both hopes must be if our society is to prosper—even, in fact, survive.

The initial three articles have as their central focus the disadvantaged. Ornstein, in the first article, reveals that there are approximately 28 million school-age children living in the United States today at or below a minimum subsistence level—living, in other words, in poverty. In addition to the economically deprived situations in which these children live, Ornstein identifies other areas of deprivation that seem to him to be concomitant conditions of their poverty. These children are deprived socially, environmentally, hygienically, experientially, and educationally. Many of them, in addition, have injured personalities, face various forms of racial prejudice and discrimination, and live in unstable family situations. Ornstein can present no magic formula for negating the effects of this vicious cycle of poverty on chil-

dren's development, but he does see, as others do, the crucial role education must play in the attempt.

In the second article, Riessman does not deny that disadvantaged youth experience certain socializing influences that make the typical kind of school experience for them less than satisfactory. He points out, however, that educators must pay greater attention to some of the positive characteristics of these children. Disadvantaged youth, for example, may be slow in learning but not necessarily dull. They may have deficiencies in the use of formal language, but they are very articulate when using informal language. And although they might harbor resentment against the school, they value highly the need for relevant education. If relevant education is to be provided them, Riessman claims, new school programs and educational techniques must be designed using these positive characteristics as basic guidelines.

Passow, in the third article, takes to task the professional educator for at least some of the ills of inner-city education. He maintains that too many teachers and administrators in this setting are racially biased; that they unwillingly accept appointments to inner-city positions; that they expect and accept inferior standards of student behavior and achievement; and that they spend an inordinate amount of time in monitoring students and too little in teaching them. Rectifying these conditions, according to Passow, will require sweeping changes in teacher education at both the pre-service and the in-service levels. Several of the more promising of these changes are enumerated.

In the fourth and fifth selections, McCandless points out various ways of providing for students who fall at both ends of the intellectual continuum, the gifted and the slow learning. He states that schools typically use one of four techniques, if any at all, in making special provisions for their gifted students. These are acceleration, segregation, early admission, and enrichment. Although most educational practitioners today believe that the first three of these are generally undesirable, the research Mc-Candless cites indicates that if used judiciously their effects on students are usually more beneficial than harmful. On the other hand, McCandless believes for several reasons that enrichment is not an adequate means of providing for the gifted.

In dealing with their slow-learning students, McCandless states, schools most frequently employ one or a combination of three strategies. The first, deceleration or failure, has generally proved unsatisfactory. Its opposite, "social promotion," tends to be a more common practice and is thought to be more desirable.

Its major limitation is that many slow learners who are socially promoted during the elementary grades often find the transition to the more highly structured junior high school very difficult. The third strategy is segregated classes. Although in this practice, too, there are obvious limitations, McCandless believes it might be the most realistic of the three, both in terms of fostering the mental health of slow learners and in terms of increasing their academic performance.

A different picture of the slow learner is presented in the sixth article. In it Laurita expresses his belief that many students who are labeled as slow learners are frequently labeled falsely. He includes among these: many who come from lower-class socio-economic environments, some who have visual and auditory impairments, and others who for various reasons are simply unwilling to meet the school's demands. Laurita contends, finally, that many so-called slow learners are students who have fallen victims to an educational system that has no built-in mechanism for dealing with unique personalities and individual learning styles and needs.

In the final article in the section, Morse gives a general over-view of those children who are probably the most difficult of all to understand and teach. These, of course, are the disturbed youngsters. As might be expected, Morse offers no simple cure-alls for the problems these children have. He gives no pat for-mulas to teachers for succeeding with them. However, he does distinguish between types of disturbed children, and he does examine some of the more usual causes underlying various be-havior problems. In concluding, Morse elaborates on certain critical areas of organization, instruction, and special services that need to be either changed or implemented if in the regular school setting the social and emotional needs of disturbed young-sters are to be effectively met.

Who Are the Disadvantaged?

ALLAN C. ORNSTEIN

INTRODUCTION

The President's Council of Economic Advisors, using the 1962 price index, reports that a family of four is poor if its annual income is $3,000 or less. A single person is considered poor if he earns less than $1,500. With this in mind, the Administration maintains that between 33 and 35 million Americans scrape along in poverty.

Harrington's *The Other America* contends that the same family earning $4,000 in 1960 is poor. The amount for an unattached individual is $2,000. He believes that between 40 and 50 million Americans are living in poverty. (25)

In addition to the poverty level, I am of the opinion that a subsistence level exists. An individual earning between $2,000 and $3,000 falls into this category, so does a two-person family earning between $3,000 and $4,000, and so does a four-person family earning between $4,000 and $5,000. Applying these figures to the 1960 census, and adding it to those who live in poverty, it is estimated that 70 million Americans live in one or the other low income groups. (16)

The populace of both income groups, to be sure, is financially disadvantaged. This means that they cannot afford many goods and services which are essential to the majority of Americans. It also means that they are subject to a whole chain of other disadvantages. In a vicious, stubborn cycle, the fact that they are financially disadvantaged causes other disadvantages, and the fact that they have so many other disadvantages gives rise to and increases their financial deprivation.

The majority are white, although non-white minorities suffer the most intense and concentrated number of disadvantages. In a spectrum of grim blight, they stretch across the country, from North to South, from coast to coast, hidden in rural waste lands and submerged in urban squalor.

Reprinted from *Journal of Secondary Education*, 41 (4): 154–163 (April 1966), by permission of author and publisher.

Although the magnitude and the number of their disadvantages vary with the level of their income, many live on the fringe, in a bleak no-man's land, human exiles from the rest of America.

Now the disadvantaged youth, and by this I mean about 40 per cent of the 70 million Americans, (16) seem doomed to become the next generation of disadvantaged Americans. Although their only real chance of changing their fortune is by taking advantage of educational opportunities available to them, most of them drop out of school or graduate as functional illiterates. (40)

The problem is the same everywhere. The schools have been unable to educate or equip these children for today's world. (40) Their access to occupational opportunity and a better life is impossible, because they do not have "the vocational training and background of skills and knowledge to get and keep a job." (38) Since these youngsters cannot obtain a job except of the most inferior quality, they never get a chance to break away from their misfortune. It is foolish, therefore, to hope for a brighter future where every indication leads us to expect a worsening trend. Midway through the sixties, then, the nation is confronted with a most dangerous problem: As Harrington puts it, "An enormous concentration of young people who, if they do not receive immediate help, may well be the source of a kind of heredity (deprivation) new to American society." (25, p. 183)

It is now appropriate to consider more specific aspects of this deprivation; perhaps, then, we will be able to surmise a solution to this foreboding crisis.

Self Deprivation. Disadvantaged children often have injured personalities. Many lack a sense of self-esteem, self-praise, and self-importance. Many have low and unrealistic aspiration levels. "They feel," according to Kvaraceus, "like nothing and nobody, unwanted and unnecessary." (32) They have feelings of guilt and shame, and have limited trust in adults. (31)

Disadvantaged children are usually too demoralized and frustrated, and too powerless to combat the forces that confuse and ensnare their lives. (22) They "know" they are failures, and they are convinced they always will be. They live in defeat and despair, and feel inferior and exiled from the prevailing society. The majority are too disillusioned and dispirited to care. They have been rejected and discouraged too many times to have any ideas of hope or ambition. (39) They will not even try to do what is necessary to escape their deprivation—stay in school, for instance.

Also, the disadvantaged cannot cope with humiliation, nor can they assimilate an attack on their dignity or values. Resentment, intense anxiety, and often direct hostility are manifested among these adolescents. (21) Any aspect of authority: their parents, their teachers, the law, the school, is a direct target for their anger. Similarly, emotional disorders requiring specialized treatment are common among many of these children. (31, 39)

One of my colleagues described these children: "They know they are being left out of the mainstream. They're sophisticated and naive at the same time. They know they have little opportunity and yet they want the American dream—a job, a car, a T.V., a little recognition." Another colleague added, " 'The Star-Spangled Banner' doesn't mean a thing for these children, and when they say 'liberty and justice for all' they know damn well they're not getting their full share."

Social Deprivation. Disadvantaged youth are often uncommitted to the larger society and uncontrolled by its values. Unable to participate successfully in the life of the larger society, they feel unwanted and rejected, and often turn to delinquent sub-cultures. "In these sub-cultures," writes Olsen, "the youngster's need for status and acceptance is satisfied." (38) Here he is respected, and his lack of a sense of identification with the general American culture is reinforced to the point that he is all but lost to his society. (38, 44)

In this connection, Richard Cloward and Lloyd Ohlin have set forth a theory that explains juvenile delinquency essentially as a response to deprivation. Given a society with a certain core of values shared by all which emphasizes achievement and status, and given certain classes of youth that are deprived of the means to participate or obtain success, and there is a high manifestation of antisocial behavior. (7)

The negative values evidenced by these children begin to develop at an early age. Tenenbaum (49) and Cavan (4) maintain that it is not surprising to find disadvantaged children of six or seven smoking and sniffing airplane glue, and young teenage boys and girls openly engaging in sex play, drinking, gambling, and stealing. By the same token, Salisbury is of the opinion that many by their early teens make excellent prospects for dope and vice; in fact, both go hand in hand. "First the girl is 'hooked' to drugs," he writes. "Then, she is put into prostitution to earn money for her drugs." (45, p. 79)

What makes matters worse is that the parents are often tolerant and uncritical of such behavior. Some are too busy working or caring for a host of other sons and daughters, but others are engaged in the same activities as their children. For example, Cavan asserts that "the free sexual activities of the adolescent girl may simply repeat the activities of her mother; the girl herself may be illegitimate." (4)

The outcome is that disadvantaged youth accept and often boast of their deviant behavior. Many are proud of, rather than disturbed by their actions. In reacting as they do, then, these children are merely expressing contempt and striking out against those who reject them. For this reason, it is not uncommon to find depressed areas saturated with gangs. Writes Salisbury, "There is only one place where the youngsters can star. It's not at home, not in school. It's in the street." (45, p. 52)

To be sure, these are the same boys who turn schools into blackboard jungles, who extort protection money from younger children, who rape a thirteen-year-old girl in the bathroom, who make zip guns in shop, who knife the monitor in the hallway, and who attack the teacher who tries to bring them order. (39, 45)

Environmental Deprivation. The disadvantaged are hidden along the rural countryside in wooden shanties over the hills and out of sight from major turnpikes. They are also submerged in the garbage-strewn ghettos of our large cities. Indeed, the physical conditions are depressing in both areas.

In rural and urban slums, whole families are boxed into one or two rooms, paying high rentals to a landlord they never see. There is no running water, no bath or inside toilet, no heat in winter, except what the kitchen stove delivers, no refrigerator, no icebox. (33, 45) Two or three children may sleep on the same bed. Living space is cramped and overcrowded, denying any form of privacy and sensitizing children to adult sexual behavior. Maintains Crosby, "Often young girls are victims of adults. They become mothers when they are children. Illegitimacy is accepted." (9)

Not rarely, children three or four years old sit out on their front stoops late at night. In the backwoods of Georgia or on the streets in Harlem, the reason is the same. They cannot go to bed. Someone is sitting on it. Until the adults are ready for bed, there is no place for them to sleep. Consequently, many school children will fall asleep in class because they have not fully slept at night.

Here it is important to add that many city slums have been ripped down and replaced by low-cost housing projects. In many cases, however, this practice has made the environment worse, concentrating it almost exclusively with the most crippled and deviant segment of our population.

By screening the applicants to eliminate those with even modest wages, the community becomes a receptacle for the poorest and most deprived elements in our society. (45, 52) Fort Greene, for instance, the largest low-income (Negro and Puerto Rican) housing project in the United States, has almost 50 per cent of its families on welfare. (24) As soon as a family income rises above a minimum figure, it is forced to leave, replaced by a needy family, more than likely on relief and incapable of helping itself, with probably one or more of its members engaged in some type of anti-social behavior. The whole community is a reservoir for what Conant characterizes as "social dynamite," and there are hundreds of urban communities like this across the country.

Thus it is that the home and street of the ghetto are despairing complements. Few successful adult models are available for the children to emulate. Deviant behavior and social problems also are frequent, and are worsening at a frightening pace. This is reflected in statistics on delinquency and crime, unemployment, welfare, alcoholism, prostitution, drug addiction, illegitimacy, illiteracy, disease, and broken homes.

Parental Deprivation. Most disadvantaged children are members of families with many problems: divorce, desertion, unemployment, chronic sickness, mental illness, delinquency, and alcoholism. Their parents or the adults they live with regard as normal and natural such things as poverty, dependence on relief agencies, free sex relations, illegitimate children, and physical combat. (4, 26, 34). Not surprisingly, the children reared in these homes also accept these conditions, all of which are marginal to delinquent behavior.

Most damaging to the child is family instability. "Children in the same family group," declares Crosby, "sometimes have a number of different fathers. These youngsters are accustomed to seeing a succession of men in the home whose relations with the mother are transitory." (3) In the same vein, Cavan writes, "Many children live within several families during their lives. Many have never lived with both parents." (4)

Frequently, the mother assumes the male role, as breadwinner and as the one who metes out harsh and suppressive forms of punishment. (15) She usually works even when the family is not split. The children are denied the benefits of her affection and love. (17, 23) The atmosphere at home is indifferent and hostile. There is little kindness or supervision. The children, therefore, are free to roam the streets. The images of their parents are images of despair, frustration, and enforced idleness. They detach themselves from their parents, and they acquire independence outside the home. They rebel against teachers and the rest of the adult world, and they adopt interests in conflict with those of the school.

Hygienic Deprivation. There is a high rate of illness and malnutrition among disadvantaged groups. Many are ignorant of good health practices and are unable to pay for any type of medical care. (15) Their standards of sanitation and cleanliness are atypical with respect to the dominant society. (14) Medical and dental checks will show hundreds of children who have never brushed their teeth or bathed regularly. (20)

A large number of these children are also improperly and irregularly fed. They go to bed hungry, they get up hungry, and they go to school hungry. They do not know what it means to go for one day with a full stomach. Their only complete meal is obtained in school; in fact, the school serves as a broadway for free lunch.

One study of low-class children indicated that 30 per cent of the group under 13 years of age had no milk. In another study, one-quarter of the children had no vegetables or fruits in the vitamin C category. More than half were suffering from vitamin A deficiencies. Similarly, a large number of the children were suffering from one form of malnutrition or another; gum and tongue conditions, rickets, and acne, for a few examples. (50)

It is depressing. The majority of the children who enter my classroom come with shabby and spoiled clothing. Their shirts and blouses are torn; buttons are missing; zippers do not work. When it rains some of them do not come to school, because they have holes in their shoes. On Fridays there are some who do not come to school, because they have no white shirt or blouse, and cannot be admitted to the assembly.

Thus there is a common denominator among these children; not enough proper medical care, not enough proper food, and not enough clothing.

Racial Deprivation. Besides being faced with an intricate number of disadvantages, non-white minorities suffer from discrimination and prejudices. This, in turn, intensifies their other disadvantages and institutionalizes their financial deprivation. In most instances, minority groups must accept a lower or inferior position because of norms and vertically imposed definitions the larger society sets up. Furthermore, they conform to expectations of the society although conformity is directly opposed to their own self-interest. Asserts Hines, "An acquiescence in degradation takes place which becomes internalized and accepted wholly or in part by the discriminated group as part of its own way of life." (27)

With regard to Negro children, numerous tests indicate negative consciousness and unmistakable rejection of their skin color in preschool years. (6, 13, 28) Other tests also show that preschool white children ascribe inferior roles and low status to Negroes. (1, 2) At a very young age, then, Negro children learn that they belong to the wrong group and are worth very little according to the standards of the larger society.

Negro children have some contact with the world outside their ghetto, through mass-media communication: movies, radio, television, newspapers, magazines, and comic books. From these and other sources, they learn that they are considered by the prevailing society to have a second-class status. (38) In this connection Jefferson says, "They would like to think well of themselves but often tend to evaluate themselves according to standards used by other groups. These mixed feelings lend to self-hatred and rejection of their group, hostility toward other groups, and a generalized pattern of personality difficulties." (29)

Their attendance at a segregated school also adds to their "inferiority." (5) It should be noted, however, that many large cities spend extra money on these schools. New York City, for example, spends an extra $65 million yearly on "special services" for its 400 thousand disadvantaged children. (51) Nevertheless, segregated schools are generally inferior; more important, the children realize that they are being rejected and prevented from associating with children in the larger part of the community.

Corresponding problems exist among other minority groups. Spanish-speaking children, for example, are subjected to perhaps more discrimination. In addition, first-generation Mexican and Puerto Rican children have linguistic problems. Many are torn between two opposing cultures; therefore, suffer from "anomie." (3, 43, 52) Their whole life situation, too, encourages the conviction that they cannot improve their condition very much by school or hard work.

Experience Deprivation. For the greater part, the disadvantaged are handicapped by a lack of information and awareness about any part of the world except their own limited one. From his study, Deutsch found that 65 per cent of the slum children have never been more than twenty-five blocks away from home, that half reported their homes were not supplied with writing pens, and the majority had no books, except for some comic books and magazines. (18) Similarly, many of these children have never been to the movies, eaten in a restaurant, or ridden in a bus except to school. Some have never had a birthday party, some do not even know their own birthdays; likewise some begin school without knowing their own names. (15, 20, 31)

It should be noted that the youngsters' physical surroundings are also impoverished, thus retarding all types of cultural stimulus and background. As Deutsch points out, most disadvantaged children have limited experiences, a scarcity of objects to manipulate, and a limited number of colors and forms to discriminate. (19)

This stimulus and background deficiency is a primary cause for the child's learning and school retardation. Writes Deutsch, "A child . . . who has been deprived of a substantial portion of the variety which he is maturationally capable of responding to is likely to be deficient in the equipment required for learning." (19) In the same vein, Piaget's developmental theory makes clear that the more limited a youngster's experiences are, the less he is likely to be interested in learning. (30, 41, 42)

Education Deprivation. Besides lacking the requisite experience for learning basic skills, most disadvantaged youth are handicapped by numerous other factors which foster their school failure. Their depressed conditions have a deleterious effect upon their mental health. (19, 39) The fact that many come from crowded and noisy homes inhibits the development of their auditory and visual discrimination, and causes inattentiveness in school. (19, 42) Also, the combination of their impoverished environment and limited experiences hinders the development of their memory and language skills. (10, 35, 36, 41)

In many instances the assumption is made that when these children begin school they have developed skills necessary for learning. The truth is, however, many are unable to speak in whole sentences and are unable to find sense in their teacher's statements or in the stories in their primer. (36) Many cannot perceive the difference between letters and numbers. Ordinary concepts, such as near and far, or even the difference between red and blue, are meaningless. To attempt to teach these children how to read before they can visualize different letters is absurd. The assumption, then, that they are ready for learning, is the cause for more frustration, and when continued and compounded year after year, it is the cause of school failure.

True, the parents of most disadvantaged youth have been unable to provide the background and initial experience for formal learning; nonetheless, the parents are not against education. At worst, they see no need for it and are indifferent. Writes Mitchell, "Many have hope for their children but have little formal education themselves and know very little about studies or how to help their children. Most parents care a great deal; but care without knowledge. . . . (34)

Thus the experience deprivation of these children is compounded by the inadequacies of their parents. By the third grade, a large number are retarded one or more years in the basic skills. Their failure manifests a change in behavior. When they enter junior high school, they are openly defiant and their minds are closed. Passed from one grade to another, without any basis in knowledge or achievement, many lose interest in school; moreover, the longer they stay in school the more discouraged they become.

The outcome is that the majority of disadvantaged youth leave school or are suspended at an early age. In the poorest areas of the large cities about 60 to 70 per cent of the pupils drop out from school before graduation. (8) In discussing this point, Sexton found in her study that the dropout rate for low-income urban children is six times higher than that of middle-class children. (47) Rural areas have even higher dropout figures. (12, 37) Among Texas Mexicans, for example, the average education limit is six years of schooling, and the chances are that it is constantly interrupted, and inferior. (3, 25)

SUMMARY

Although no one program can itself lead to a solution to deprivation on a mass scale, education is most important, because without it there is no hope that the disadvantaged will ever acquire skills to hold a decent job so that they can break from their complex web of impoverishment. Unquestionably, more money is needed to be spent, more on elementary schools than in college, and more money in slum and rural schools than in suburban schools. Right now the situation is reversed. (46) Nevertheless, the political and economic power structure on all governmental levels is at present willing to spend large sums of money on the experimentation and research for the education of the disadvantaged. They are willing not because they have suddenly become humanitarian, but because they are afraid of the consequences if they do not. (40) For this reason, almost any school system or college can obtain today a federal grant which is focused on the educational needs of disadvantaged children.

But money is not enough, unless it is channeled wisely. The fact that the disadvantaged have an integral chain of handicaps means that the whole child must be considered. Higher Horizons' type of programs, prekindergarten education, after-school-study centers, and the like, have very rarely, if ever, been fully effective. In the next few years, we will spend billions of dollars on similar educational programs. Unless all the integral number of disadvantages of these children are taken into account our new efforts will also fail.

Indeed, time is running out. "This is our last chance," writes one educator. "We cannot afford another generation as ignorant as we are." The demands of our society necessitate that we educate our disadvantaged youth. As Shaw put it, "The preservation of our democratic way of life, the demands of our economy, and the mental health of our people all require that we learn how to educate these children effectively." (48)

REFERENCES

1. Ammons, R. B., "Reactions in a Projective Doll Play Interview of White Males Two to Six Years of Age to Differences in Skin Color and Facial Factors." *Journal of Genetic Psychology.* Vol. LXXVI (1950), pp. 323–341.
2. Blake, Robert; Dennis, Wayne, "The Development of Stereotypes Concerning the Negro," *Journal of Abnormal and Social Psychology,* Vol. XXXVIII (1943), pp. 525–531.
3. Burma, John H., "Spanish-Speaking Children," in Eli Ginsberg, *The Nation's Children,* Vol. III (New York: Columbia University Press, 1960), pp. 78–102.
4. Cavan, Ruth S., "Negro Family Disorganization and Juvenile Delinquency," *Journal of Negro Education,* Summer 1959, pp. 230–239.
5. Clark, Kenneth B., *Prejudice and Your Child* (Boston: Beacon Press, 1936).
6. Clark, Kenneth B.; Clark, Mamie J., "The Development of Consciousness in Negro Pre-School Children," *Journal of Social Psychology,* Vol. X (1939), pp. 591–599.
7. Cloward, Richard A.; Ohlin, Lloyd E., *Delinquency and Opportunity* (Glencoe, Illinois: Free Press, 1960).
8. Conant, James B., *Slums & Suburbs* (New York: McGraw-Hill, 1961).
9. Crosby, Muriel, "A Portrait of Blight," *Educational Leadership,* February 1963, pp. 300–304.
10. Cutts, Warren G., "Special Language Problems of the Culturally Disadvantaged," *Clearing House,* October 1962, pp. 80–83.
11. Dai, Bingham, "Some Problems of Personality Development among Negro Children," in C. Klucholn and H. A. Murray, *Personality in Nature, Society and Culture* (New York: Knopf, 1956), pp. 545–566.
12. Daniel, Walter G., "Problems of Disadvantaged Youth, Urban and Rural," *Journal of Negro Education,* Summer 1964, pp. 218–224.
13. Davis, Allison, "The Socialization of the American Negro Child and Adolescent," *Journal of Negro Education,* July 1939, pp. 264–275.
14. Davis, Michael M.; Smythe, Hugh H., "Providing Adequate Health Services to Negroes," *Journal of Negro Education,* Summer 1949, pp. 283–290.
15. Della-Dora, Delmo, "The Culturally Disadvantaged: Educational Implications

of Certain Social Cultural Phenomena," *Exceptional Children,* May 1962, pp. 467–472.

16. Department of Commerce, Bureau of the Census, *Current Population Report,* Series 1-227, No. 96; Series 1-601, No. 225; Series 1-604, No. 226.

17. Deutsch, Martin, "Some Considerations as to the Contributions of Social Personality and Racial Factors to School Retardation in Minority Group Children," paper read at the American Psychology Association, Chicago, September 1956.

18. Deutsch, Martin, "Minority Group and Class Structure as Related to Social and Personality Factors in Scholastic Achievement," Mimeographed, No. 2, Ithaca, New York: Society for Applied Anthropology, 1960.

19. Deutsch, Martin, "The Disadvantaged Child and the Learning Process," in A. Harry Passow, *Education in Depressed Areas* (New York: Columbia University Press, 1964), pp. 163–179.

20. Ford Foundation Reprint, "Stirrings in the Big Cities: The Great Cities Project," Mimeographed, New York: Ford Foundation, 1962.

21. Friedenberg, Edgar Z., *The Vanishing Adolescent* (New York: Dell Publishing Co., 1962).

22. Galbraith, John K., *The Affluent Society* (Boston, Houghton Mifflin, 1958).

23. Goff, Regina M., "The Curriculum as a Source of Psychological Strength for the Negro Child," *Education Administration and Supervision,* May 1952, pp. 299–301.

24. Guidance Department, Sands Junior High School, Fort Greene, Brooklyn, New York.

25. Harrington, Michael, *The Other America* (Baltimore: Penguin Books, 1964).

26. Health and Welfare Council of the Baltimore Area, Inc., A Letter to Ourselves; A Master Plan for Human Redevelopment, Mimeographed. Baltimore: The Council, January 18, 1962, p. 3.

27. Hines, Ralph, "Social Expectations and Cultural Deprivation," *Journal of Negro Education,* Spring 1964, pp. 136–142.

28. Horowitz, Ruth E., "Racial Aspects of Self-Identification in Nursery School Children," *Journal of Psychology,* Vol. VIII (1940), pp. 91–99.

29. Jefferson, Ruth, "Some Obstacles to Racial Integration," *Journal of Negro Education,* Summer 1957, pp. 145–154.

30. Hunt, J. McV., *Intelligence and Experience* (New York: Ronald Press, 1961).

31. Krugman, Judith I., "Cultural Deprivation and Child Development," *High Points,* November 1956, pp. 5–20.

32. Kvaraceus, William C., "Alienated Youth Here and Abroad," *Phi Delta Kappan,* November 1963, pp. 87–90.

33. Masse, Benjamin L., "Poverty, U.S.A.," *America,* July 20, 1963, pp. 73–75.

34. Mitchell, Charles, "The Culturally Deprived Child—A Matter of Concern," *Childhood Education,* May 1962, pp. 412–420.

35. Newton, Eunice, "The Culturally Deprived Child in our Verbal Schools," *Journal of Negro Education,* Fall 1962, pp. 184–187.

36. Newton, Eunice, "Verbal Destitution: The Pivotal Barrier to Learning," *Journal of Negro Education,* Fall 1960, pp. 497–499.

37. O'Hara, James M., "Disadvantaged Newcomers to the City," *NEA Journal,* April 1963, pp. 25–27.

38. Olsen, James, "Children of the Ghetto," *High Points*, March 1964, pp. 25–33.
39. Ornstein, Allan C., "Effective Schools for Disadvantaged Children," *Journal of Secondary Education*, March 1965, pp. 105–109.
40. Ornstein, Allan C., "Program Revision for Culturally Disadvantaged Children," to be published, *Journal of Negro Education*, Spring 1966.
41. Piaget, J., *The Language and Thought of the Child* (New York: Humanities Press, 1926).
42. Piaget, J., *The Origins of Intelligence in Children* (New York: International Universities Press, 1952).
43. *Puerto Rican Profiles* (New York: Board of Education of the City of New York, July 7, 1964).
44. Redl, Fritz, *Children Who Hate* (Glencoe, Illinois: Free Press, 1951).
45. Salisbury, Harrison E., *The Shook-Up Generation* (Greenwich, Connecticut: Fawcett Publications, 1959).
46. Sexton, Patricia, "Comments on Three Cities," *Integrated Education*, August 1963, pp. 27–32.
47. Sexton, Patricia, *Education and Income* (New York: Viking Press, 1961).
48. Shaw, Frederick, "Educating Culturally Deprived Youth in Urban Centers," *Phi Delta Kappan*, November 1963, pp. 91–97.
49. Tenenbaum, Samuel, "The Teacher, the Middle-Class, the Lower-Class," *Phi Delta Kappan*, November 1963, pp. 82–86.
50. "The Nutritional Status of Negroes," Study by Nutrition Branch and Program Analysis Branch, Division of Chronic Disease, Public Health, F. S. A., *Journal of Negro Education*, Summer 1949, pp. 291–304.
51. *The Public Schools of New York City Staff Bulletin*, Vol. III, January 11, 1965.
52. Wakefield, Dan, *Island in the City* (New York: Corinth Books, 1965).

The Overlooked Positives
of Disadvantaged Groups *

FRANK RIESSMAN

I have been interested in the problems of lower socio-economic groups for about 15 years, during most of which time there has been a lack of concern for the educational problems of children from low-income families. In the last five years, however, this attitude has changed markedly. There is

Reprinted from *The Journal of Negro Education*, 32 (3): 225–231 (Summer 1964), by permission of author and publisher.
* This is a revision of an opening address at the Conference on Education of Disadvantaged Children, held by the Office of Education, May 21–23, 1962, Washington, D.C.

now an enormous interest on the part of practitioners and academic people in this problem. I think we are on the point of a major breakthrough in terms of dealing with this question.

After appraising a good deal of the recent work that has been done on the education of disadvantaged children, I feel that there is a considerable agreement regarding many of the recommendations for dealing with the problem, although there are some very different emphases. What is missing, however, is a theoretic rationale to give meaning and direction to the action suggestions. I should like to attempt to provide the beginnings of such a rationale.

I think that a basic theoretic approach here has to be based on the culture of lower socio-economic groups and more particularly the elements of strength, the positives in this culture. The terms "deprived," "handicapped," "underprivileged," "disadvantaged," unfortunately emphasize environmental limitations and ignore the positive efforts of low-income individuals to cope with their environment. Most approaches concerned with educating the disadvantaged child either overlook the positives entirely, or merely mention in passing that there are positive features in the culture of low socio-economic groups, that middle-class groups might learn from, but they do not spell out what these strengths are, and they build educational programs almost exclusively around the weaknesses or deficits.

I want to call attention to the positive features in the culture and the psychology of low income individuals. In particular, I should like to look at the cognitive style, the mental style or way of thinking characteristics of these people. One major dimension of this style is slowness.

Slow vs. Dull

Most disadvantaged children are relatively slow in performing intellectual tasks. This slowness is an important feature of their mental style and it needs to be carefully evaluated. In considering the question of the slowness of the deprived child, we would do well to recognize that in our culture there has probably been far too much emphasis on speed. We reward speed. We think of the fast child as the smart child and the slow child as the dull child. I think this is a basically false idea. I think there are many weaknesses in speed and many strengths in slowness.

The teacher can be motivated to develop techniques for rewarding slow pupils if she has an appreciation of some of the positive attributes of a slow style of learning. The teacher should know that pupils may be slow for other reasons than because they are stupid.

A pupil may be slow because he is extremely careful, meticulous or cautious. He may be slow because he refuses to generalize easily. He may be slow because he can't understand a concept unless he does something physically, e.g., with his hands, in connection with the idea he is trying to grasp.

The disadvantaged child is typically a physical learner and the physical learner is generally a slower learner. Incidentally, the physical style of learning is another important characteristic of the deprived individual and it, too, has many positive features hitherto overlooked.

A child may be slow because he learns in what I have called a one-track way. That is, he persists in one line of thought and is not flexible or broad. He does not easily adopt other frames of reference, such as the teacher's, and consequently he may appear slow and dull.

Very often this single-minded individual has considerable creative potential, much of which goes unrealized because of lack of reinforcement in the educational system.

Analysis of the many reasons for slowness leads to the conclusion that slowness should not be equated with stupidity. In fact, there is no reason to assume that there are not a great many slow, gifted children.

The school in general does not pay too much attention to the slow gifted child but rather is alert to discover fast gifted children. Excellence comes in many packages and we must begin to search for it among the slow learners as well as among the faster individuals.

My own understanding of some of the merits of the slow style came through teaching at Bard College, where there is an enrollment of about 350 students. There I had the opportunity of getting to know quite well about 40 students over a period of four years. I could really see what happened to them during this time. Very often the students I thought were slow and dull in their freshman year achieved a great deal by the time they became seniors. These are not the overall bright people who are typically selected by colleges, but in some area, in a one-track way, these students did some marvelous creative work. It was too outstanding to be ignored. I discovered in talking with students that most of them had spent five or six years in order to complete college. They had failed courses and made them up in summer school. Some had dropped out of college for a period of time and taken courses in night school. These students are slow learners, often one-track learners, but very persistent about something when they develop an interest in it. They have a fear of being overpowered by teachers in situations where they don't accept the teacher's point of view, but they stick to their own particular way of seeing the problem. They don't have a fast pace, they don't catch on quickly and they very often fail subjects.

At the present time, when there is a measure of public excitement for reducing the four-year college to three years, I would submit that many potentially excellent students need a five or six year span to complete a college education.

The assumption that the slow pupil is not bright functions, I think, as a self-fulfilling prophecy. If the teachers act toward these pupils as if they were dull, the pupils will frequently come to function in this way. Of course, there are pupils who are very well developed at an early age and no teacher can stop them. But in the average development of the young person, even at the college level, there is need for reinforcement. The teacher must pick up what he says, appeal to him, and pitch examples to him. Typically this does not occur with the slow child. I find in examining my own classroom teaching that I easily fall into the habit of rewarding pupils whose faces light up when I talk, who are quick to respond to me and I respond back to them. The things they say in class become absorbed in the repertoire of what I say. I remember what they say and I use it in providing examples, etc. I don't pick up and select the slower pupil and I don't respond to him. He has to make it on his own.

In the teacher training program future teachers should be taught to guard against the almost unconscious and automatic tendency of the teacher to respond to the pupil who responds to him.

HIDDEN VERBAL ABILITY

A great deal has been said about the language or verbal deficit supposedly characteristic of disadvantaged children. Everybody in the school system, at one time or another, has heard that these children are inarticulate, non-verbal, etc. But is not this too simple a generalization? Aren't these children quite verbal in out-of-school situations? For example, that the educationally deprived child can be quite articulate in conversation with his peers is well illustrated by the whole language developed by urban Negro groups, some of which is absorbed into the main culture via the Beatnick and the musician, if you dig what I mean.

Many questions about the verbal potential of disadvantaged children must be answered by research. Under what conditions are they verbal? What kind of stimuli do they respond to verbally? With whom are they verbal? What do they talk about? What parts of speech do they use? Martin Deutsch of New York Medical College is doing some very significant research trying to specify these factors and I surveyed some of his findings in my book, *The Culturally Deprived Child.* I think Deutsch is getting at some very interesting things. One technique he uses is a clown that lights up when the children say something. "Inarticulate" children can be very verbal and expressive in this situation.

Disadvantaged children are often surprisingly articulate in role-playing situations. One day when I was with a group of these youngsters, sometimes mistaken for a "gang," I asked them, "Why are you sore at the teachers?" Even though I was on good terms with them, I could not get much of a response. Most of them answered in highly abbreviated sentences. However, after I held a role-playing session in which some of the youngsters acted out the part of the teachers while others acted out the parts of the pupils, these "inarticulate" youngsters changed sharply. Within a half-hour they were bubbling over with very verbal and very sensitive answers to the questions I had asked earlier. They were telling me about the expressions on the teachers' faces that they did not like. They reported that they knew the minute they entered the room that the teacher did not like them and that she did not think they were going to do well in school. Their analyses were specific and remarkably verbal.

However, the quality of language employed has its limitations and I think herein lies the deficit. As Basil Bernstein indicates, the difference is between formal language and public language, between a language in a written book and the informal, everyday language. There is no question in my mind that there is a deficit in formal language. Since this deficit is fairly clear, the question might be asked, why make such an issue of the positive verbal ability to these children.

The reason is that it is easy to believe, that too many people have come to believe, that this formal deficit in language means that deprived people are characteristically non-verbal.

On the other hand, if the schools have the idea that these pupils are basically very good verbally, teachers might approach them in a different manner. Teachers might look for additional techniques to bring out the verbal facility. They might abandon the prediction that deprived children will not go very far in the education system and predict instead that they can go very far indeed because they have very good ability at the verbal level. In other words, an awareness of the positive verbal ability—not merely potential—will lead to demanding more of the disadvantaged child and expecting more of him.

Education vs. the School

There is a good deal of evidence that deprived children and their parents have a much more positive attitude towards education than is generally believed. One factor that obscures the recognition of this attitude is that while deprived individuals value education, they dislike the school. They are alienated from the school and they resent the teachers. For the sake of clarity, their attitude towards education and toward the school must be considered separately.

In a survey conducted a few years ago, people were asked, "What did you miss most in life that you would like your children to have?" Over 70 per cent of the lower, socio-economic groups answered, "Education." The answer was supplied by the respondents, not checked on a list. They could have answered "money," "happiness," "health," or a number of things. And I think this is quite significant. Middle-class people answer "education" less frequently because they had an education and do not miss it as much.

A nation-wide poll conducted by Roper after World War II asked, "If you had a son or daughter graduating from high school, would you prefer to have him or her go on to college, do something else, wouldn't care?"

The affirmative response to the college choice was given by 68 per cent of the "poor," and 91 per cent for the more prosperous. The difference is significant, but 68 per cent of the poorer people is a large, absolute figure and indicates that a large number of these people are interested in a college education for their children.

Why then do these people who have a positive attitude towards education, hold a negative attitude towards the school? These youngsters and their parents recognize that they are second-class citizens in the school and they are angry about it. From the classroom to the PTA they discover that the school does not like them, does not respond to them, does not appreciate their culture, and does not think they can learn.

Also, these children and their parents want education for different reasons than those presented by the school. They do not easily accept the ideas of expressing yourself, developing yourself, or knowledge for its own sake. They want education much more for vocational ends. But underneath there is a very positive attitude towards education and I think this is predominant in the lower socio-economic Negro groups. In the Higher Horizons program in New York City the parents have participated eagerly once they have seen that the school system is concerned about their children. One of the tremendously positive features about this program and the Great Cities programs is the concern for disadvantaged children and the interest in them. This the deprived have not experienced before and even if the programs did nothing else, I believe that the parents and the children would be responsive and would become involved in the school, because of the demonstrated concern for them.

SOME WEAKNESSES

A basic weakness of deprived youngsters which the school can deal with is the problem of "know-how." Included here is the academic "know-how" of the school culture as well as the "know-how" of the middle class generally. Knowing how to get a job, how to appear for an interview, how to fill out a form, how to take tests, how to answer questions and how to listen.

The last is of particular importance. The whole style of learning of the deprived is not set to respond to oral or written stimuli. These children respond much more readily to visual kinesthetic signals. We should remodel the schools to suit the styles and meet the needs of these children. But no matter how much we change the school to suit their needs, we nevertheless have to change these children in certain ways; namely, reading, formal language, test taking and general "know-how."

These weaknesses represent deficiencies in skills and techniques. However, there is one basic limitation at the value level, namely the anti-intellectual attitudes of deprived groups. It is the only value of lower socio-economic groups which I would fight in the school. I want to make it very clear that I am very much opposed to the school spending a lot of time teaching values to these kids. I am much more concerned—and in this I am traditional—that the schools impart skills, techniques and knowledge rather than training the disadvantaged to become good middle-class children.

However, I think there is one area indigenous to the school which has to be fought out at some point with these youngsters; that is their attitude toward intellectuals, towards knowledge for its own sake, and similar issues.

These children and their parents are pretty much anti-intellectual at all levels. They do not like "eggheads." They think talk is a lot of bull. I would consciously oppose this attitude in the school. I would make the issue explicit. There would be nothing subtle or covert about it. I would at some point state clearly that on this question the school does not agree with them and is prepared to argue about the views they hold.

OTHER POSITIVE DIMENSIONS

In my book, *The Culturally Deprived Child,* and in various speeches, I have elaborated more fully on these and other positive dimensions of the culture and style of educationally deprived people. A brief list would include the following: cooperativeness and mutual aid that mark the extended family; the avoidance of the strain accompanying competitiveness and individualism; the equalitarianism, in informality and humor; the freedom from self-blame and parental over-protection; the children's enjoyment of each other's company and lessened sibling rivalry, the security found in the extended family and a traditional outlook; the enjoyment of music, games, sports and cards; the ability to express anger; the freedom from being word-bound; an externally oriented rather than an introspective outlook; a spatial rather than temporal perspective; an expressive orientation in contrast to an instrumental one; content-centered not a form-centered mental style; a problem-centered rather than an abstract-centered approach; and finally, the use of physical and visual style in learning.

SUMMARY AND IMPLICATIONS

I have attempted to reinterpret some of the supposedly negative aspects—e.g., slowness—that characterize the cognitive style of disadvantaged individuals. I have given particular attention to the untapped verbal ability of these individuals and have indicated the basic weaknesses of the disadvantaged child which the school must overcome, such as the lack of school know-how, anti-intellectualism, and limited experience with formal language. Others which should be noted here are poor auditory attention, poor time perspective, inefficient test-taking skills, and limited reading ability.

The school must recognize these deficiencies and work assiduously to combat them. They are by no means irreversible, but even more important, because neglected, the positive elements in the culture and style of lower socio-economic groups should become the guide lines for new school programs and new educational techniques for teaching these children.

There are a number of reasons why it is important to emphasize the positive:

1. It will encourage the school to develop approaches and techniques, including possibly special teaching machines, appropriate for the cognitive style of deprived children.

2. It will enable children of low income backgrounds to be educated without middle-classifying them.

3. It will stimulate teachers to aim high, to expect more and work for more from these youngsters. Thus, it will constrain against patronization and condescension, and determinate, double-track systems where the deprived child never arrives on the main track.

4. It will function against the current tendency of over-emphasizing both vocational, non-academic education for children of low-income background.

5. It will provide an exciting challenge for teachers if they realize that they need not simply aim to "bring these children up to grade level," but rather can actually develop new kinds of creativity.

6. It will make the school far more pluralistic and democratic because different cultures and styles will exist and interact side by side. Thus, each can learn from the other and the empty phrase that the teacher has much to learn from deprived children will take on real meaning. General cultural interaction between equal cultures can become the hallmark of the school.

7. It will enable the teacher to see that when techniques, such as role-playing and visual aids are used with deprived children, it is because these techniques are useful for eliciting the special cognitive style and creative potential of these children. All too often these techniques have been employed with the implicit assumption that they are useful with children who have inadequate learning ability.

8. It will lead to real appreciation of slowness, one-track learning and physical learning as potential strengths which require careful nurturing. The teacher will have to receive special training in how to respond to these styles, how to listen carefully to the one-track person, how to reward the slow learner, etc. Special classes for slow learners will not culminate in the removal of these youngsters from the mainstream of the educational process on a permanent second track, and longer periods of time in school and college can be planned for these students without invidious connotations.

Dr. Irving Taylor, who has been concerned with various types of creativity in our American society, has observed that the mental style of the socially and economically disadvantaged learners resembles the mental style of one type of highly creative persons. Our schools should provide for the development of these unique, untapped national sources of creativity.

Diminishing Teacher Prejudice

A. HARRY PASSOW

"By all known criteria, the majority of urban and rural slum schools are failures." This judgment by the President's Panel on Educational Research and Development grew out of five indictments of current school practices: the severe scholastic retardation which progressively worsens as children grow older; a dropout rate which exceeds 50 percent; fewer than five percent of this group enrolling for some form of higher education; deteriorating I.Q. scores, and a distressing picture of adolescents leaving schools "ill-prepared to lead a satisfying, useful life or to participate successfully in the community."

The plight of the inner-city school is a pulsing tangle of academic retardation, pupil and staff transiency, racial imbalance, alienation, personnel and staff shortages, and general inadequacy of resources. The tough question raised by social psychologists such as Goodwin Watson is, "To what extent has the school itself cultivated the apathy, lack of self-confidence, absence of persistent effort, the evasions, the suspicions, defensiveness and hostility of slow learners? Are the attitudes and biases of professional educators—conscious or not—responsible for the inferior attainments and expression of problems in inner-city schools, or are teachers being made scapegoats for the ills of school and society?"

Increasingly, educators are beginning to understand the meaning of this background which the Negro child (and his counterpart in every other minority group) brings into the classroom from the time he enters. The young Negro is fully aware of racial differences long before he enters school, and much of what goes on in the classroom extends and reinforces his feelings of inferiority. This is so, even when the teachers are basically sympathetic to the problems stemming from discrimination. However, too often teachers and administrators are consciously or unconsciously racially biased, lack understanding and insight into the bases for the child's reactions and behavior, are hostile and frustrated, and think and act in terms of stereotyped images.

On the other hand, Joseph Lohman maintains that most Negroes, as well as whites, think in terms of stereotypes. The Negro child and his parents view the teacher "not as an individual, but as a representative of the group which has treated them as inferior and has discriminated against them." While the teacher may in fact be unprejudiced, unless he can accept the pupil's right to these feelings of suspicion and hostility as valid and respond without becoming defensive, he will not be able to serve effectively.

Reprinted from *New York State Education*, 55 (5): 6–10 (February 1968), by permission of author and publisher. Copyright © 1968 by New York State Teachers Association.

303

MIDDLE CLASS ORIENTATION

Since the studies of the 1930's, the charge has been made that the school is a middle-class institution. As William Burton puts it, "The school has generally been geared to the aims, ambitions, moral or ethical standards of the white, prosperous, middle-class, Protestant, Anglo-Saxon population." Further, Burton observes, "many lower-class children simply do not value the objectives and the processes of the school, hence do not try. The school immediately dubs these children unintelligent, uncooperative, or stubborn."

Martin Deutsch's study indicated that as much as 80 percent of the school day in the experimental classes went to disciplining and organizational details (i.e., collecting milk money, cookie funds, reports). In contrast, this figure never exceeded 50 percent in the control classes. Deutsch suggests that these data imply that the lower-class Negro child is getting one-half to one-third the exposure to learning that children from more favored environments receive and, in all probability, does not get the same help or support at home that is common in the middle-class family. If these findings are consistent, Deutsch speculates, the teacher's role and self-concept are probably transformed from that of an instructor to that of a monitor, who is likely to ask for transfer out of the lower-class school as soon as possible.

That the social origin of the classroom teacher influences his attitudes toward his pupils, their parents, his colleagues, and the administrators is backed up by several studies. Howard Becker's analysis of social-class variations in teacher-pupil relationships reveals that, by reacting to cultural differences, teachers "perpetuate the discrimination of our educational system against the lower-class child." Becker found that the amount of work and effort the teacher requires varies inversely with the pupil's social class. This aggravates the problem and widens the gap between what the child should know and what he does know in each grade. Children from lower-class families are considered more difficult to control, "being given to unrestrained behavior and physical violence." However, it is in the area that Becker calls "moral acceptability" that the slum child's actions and appearance are most distressing, managing "to give teachers the feelings that they are immoral and not respectable. In terms of physical appearance and condition, they disgust and depress the middle-class teacher."

Examining children's perceptions of their teachers' feelings toward them and their self-concepts, scholastic achievement and behavior, Helen Davidson and Gerhard Lang found a direct relationship between children's social class and teachers' ratings. Also, they found that children clearly sensed their teachers' attitudes toward them. Those who felt their teachers ranked them low seemed to have lower self-perceptions, achieved less well, and behaved less well in the classroom than did more favored classmates.

By Allison Davis' reckonings, 95 of every 100 teachers are from middle-class origins, a way of life that differs sharply from that of the majority of their pupils. They often undergo an emotional trauma when beginning teaching in situations with lower-class pupils:

> Many new (and old) teachers find it impossible to understand the attitudes and values of these pupils; they are puzzled by the students' reactions to the material and to the instructor, and by their often sullen, resentful behavior. . . . The result in many cases is bewilderment, followed by disillusionment and apathy.

David Gottlieb reports on the differences and similarities between 36 Negro and 53 white teachers in outlook toward their work and their students (approximately 85 percent Negro, from low-income families) in six inner-city elementary schools. More than 80 percent of both groups were female, with the Negro teachers tending to be somewhat younger, more likely to be married, with fewer divorcees or widows. The Negro sample tended to come from larger communities and were twice as likely to have attended public colleges in urban centers. While the white teachers were generally raised in middle-class families, the Negro teachers came from lower-class families in primarily manual occupations. To Gottlieb, the fact that the Negro teachers, more often than the white, came from lower socioeconomic strata, and from families headed by a woman, possibly explains the differences in the attitudes and perceptions of the two groups. Gottlieb concluded that white teachers are less well prepared than their Negro counterparts to work in the inner-city school. With respect to job satisfactions, the Negro teachers seemed less likely to voice their gripes. They tended to mention factors associated with "the system" (i.e., related to the physical or organizational structure), while the white teachers were more often critical of either students or their parents.

When selecting from a list of 33 adjectives those which most accurately described their pupils in the inner-city schools, Negro and white teachers differed in their choices. In order of importance, white teachers most frequently selected talkative, lazy, fun-loving, high-strung, and rebellious. Negro teachers selected fun-loving, happy, cooperative, energetic, and ambitious. The white teachers tended to omit adjectives which are universal attributes of children and related to successful learning. Thus, the Negro teacher is less likely to list shortcomings which might be attributed to Negroes generally and point to deficiencies in the system to explain his dissatisfactions.

Dissonant Standards and Exceptions

The effects of social stratification and segregation on the academic attainments of elementary school children have been studied by Alan Wilson, who analyzed achievement records of elementary school pupils in a district characterized by socio-economic residential segregation. Expecting different achievements among children from varying ethnic and socio-economic strata, Wilson found also that "the normalization of diverging standards by teachers" crystallized different levels of scholastic attainment. Teachers apparently adapt their norms of success and their concepts of excellence to the composition of their student bodies. They accept much less from the low-income children. The normalization of lower standards of performance in the less favored socio-economic group provides the same kind of circular reinforcement for the group that normalization of past performance does for the individual student.

Students who are considered outstanding in less favored schools do not achieve as well as the average student in the more favored school, yet receive higher marks. However, as the students progress into secondary schools and junior colleges, uniform achievement criteria are applied to all, and those who have been over-evaluated in the past fall behind and often drop out. Wilson observed that students from the "Hills" (more favored) schools tend to be assigned to the academic streams, while those from the "Flats" (least favored) schools are assigned almost automatically to the general or vocational programs. He also found that although many of the working class, and especially Negro, students entered the so-called open-door junior colleges, even at this late point they are "counseled or 'cooled out' into terminal vocational training."

Thus, by accepting and expecting lowered standards, teachers must bear some responsibility for the sharp differences between the disadvantaged youth's aspirations and achievements. Arguing that these low expectations and standards on the part of teachers and administrators account for inferior achievement, Kenneth Clark asserts:

> A normal child who is expected to learn, who is taught, and who is required to learn will learn. . . . A single standard of academic expectations, a demanding syllabus, and skillful and understanding teaching are essential to the raising of the self-esteem of disadvantaged children, increasing their motivation for academic achievement and providing our society with the benefits of their intellectual potential.

But this matter has a second sharp edge. It is easy to see vindictiveness in high standards, as Eleanor and Leo Wolfe caution:

> The dilemma is reflected in the plaint frequently heard from teachers who work in schools in changing neighborhoods. They often report that if they adhere to the same grading standards they used with previous (more privileged) populations, they may be accused of prejudice, or at least of harshness, as demonstrated by a larger number of failures and poor grades. But if they alter their grading system they may be accused of relaxing standards to the detriment of their new pupils.

Perceiving the Job

The unwillingness of new teachers to accept appointments to inner-city schools and the tendency of experienced teachers to seek transfers or to leave teaching have been characterized by Harry Rivlin as a subtle, nationwide teachers' strike which cannot be stopped by a court injunction. The major reason for this condition, Rivlin maintains, is fear:

They (young teachers) are afraid they will be trapped in a blackboard jungle; they are afraid of possible physical attack; they are afraid that they cannot deal with the situations they will meet in the schools; and they are afraid that they will have to spend their days being policemen rather than teachers.

The high rate of rejection of appointments to depressed area schools by beginning teachers is due, Vernon Haubrich suggests, to the "inability to comprehend, understand, and cope with the multiple problems of language development, varying social norms, habits not accepted by the teacher, behavior which is often not success-oriented, lack of student cooperation, and achievement levels well below expectancies of teachers."

Becker found that the typical Chicago teacher's career consisted of shifting from one school to another, seeking a position where basic work problems—stemming from relationships with children, parents, principals and other teachers—were least aggravated and most susceptible of solution. Teachers felt that the nature and intensity of problems vary with the social class background of the pupils. What comes out by implication is that teachers praise discipline and pliability above their pupils' other traits. The lowest group (slum children) is perceived as "difficult to teach, uncontrollable and violent in the sphere of discipline, and morally unacceptable on all scores, from physical cleanliness to the spheres of sex and 'ambition to get ahead.'" Children from the better neighborhoods, on the other hand, are viewed as quick learners, easily taught, but spoiled and lacking such traits as politeness and respect for elders. The middle group (lower-middle and upper-lower class) is perceived as hardworking but slow learning, easy to control, and most acceptable to the teachers on the moral level.

The new teacher in the Chicago system, Becker found, typically begins her career in the least desirable kind of school and then follows one of two paths: she applies for a transfer to a better neighborhood school as soon as possible, or she adjusts resignedly over a period of years to the unsatisfactory conditions and work problems of the lower-class school. Adjustment in the second pattern erases the teacher's restlessness and efforts at transfer. A change in the ethnic or racial composition of the neighborhood or in the administrative structure (e.g., arrival of a new principal) may result in the position becoming unsatisfactory and the teacher seeking a transfer to a nicer school.

Teaching in the inner-city school is perceived as an undesirable assignment, even as a "type of punishment or an initiation ritual that must be survived if one is to succeed in the city school system." Yet, some teachers do stay and some spend their entire careers there. To find out why, William Wayson studied a sample of 42 teachers (27 white and 15 Negro) who had remained in slum schools, and 20 teachers (16 white and 4 Negro) who had transferred from these schools. The most apparent difference between white stayers and leavers was that a greater proportion of the former tended to be inert, rooted in the situation, and unwilling to change jobs and face an unknown situation. The second greatest difference was in the liking for the autonomy enjoyed in the slum school—freedom from pressures or interference from outside the classroom, either from parents or administrators. Eighty-nine percent of the stayers also expressed altruism and loyalty to an accommodating principal who catered to the needs and desires of the staff, while only 19 percent of the leavers gave responses in one or more of these categories. All Negroes felt constrained by organizational rules and other external pressures, and their responses tended to agree with those of the white stayers more than the white leavers.

Simply staying in a slum school cannot be construed as success, Wayson points out, for other criteria are needed to judge this. Unfortunately, some of the sources of satisfaction for the teacher in the slum school and some of the reasons for staying seem negative and unhealthy.

A Better Focus

The foregoing survey of literature gives a bleak montage of teachers and administrators who are blinded by their middle-class orientation; prejudiced toward all pupils from lower-class, racial, and ethnic minority groups; culturally shocked and either immobilized or punitive in the classroom; and groping constantly for safer berths where success, in terms of academic achievement, is more likely. Some, not all, teachers are hostile, vindictive, inept or even neurotic, but many more are compassionate and skillful. Many disadvantaged children *do* achieve; many *do* have healthy self-images, high aspirations, and positive motivations; for many, the classroom is the most supportive element in their lives.

The picture of the biased teacher in a school system heavily stacked against the lower-class, minority-group child is both distorted and incomplete. It implies courses of action for the teacher which may be, to some extent, contradictory: to make the classroom a haven from the problems of depressed-area living while giving full play to elements of the lower-class culture, to provide many essential social-welfare benefits while still increasing the time devoted to academic instruction. The picture ignores or dismisses as irrelevant the growing body of research which details the impact of poverty and unemployment, of segregation and discrimination, of all other aspects of the inner-city ghetto living on the mental, emotional, and physical development of the disadvantaged child. Having little or nothing to do with policy decisions regarding racial balance and desegregation, for instance, the teacher is called on to implement these policies and to effect integration within the classroom. It is obvious that schools alone cannot deal satisfactorily with all the forces and factors which affect inner-city life—but it is equally clear that the schools (meaning teachers, administrators, and other personnel) have a central role and a catalytic function to perform.

It does little good to belabor the middle-class teacher for having middle-class values; instead, the emphasis must be on knowing about and understanding the lower-class culture, especially where it collides with the culture that permeates our schools. Many of the differences involve relationships with peers, adults, authority figures, and culturally different individuals.

These relationships, involving apathy and withdrawal, aggression and hostility, test the teacher constantly. Joseph Lohman suggests that the teacher must expect and be able to take either rejection or hostility without returning it:

> She is the adult and can expect a little more of herself than of a still maturing student. She must learn to live with frustration and not let it keep her from continued effort. She cannot expect results too soon, either in her own increased awareness of our culturally divergent children or in their reactions to her. She can demand certain standards of behavior; she cannot demand that children trust her or believe in her when they have had too much experience to the contrary.

Social and behavioral scientists, together with insightful teachers, have provided analyses of the problems of the inner-city child. But, they have also identified variations from middle-class patterns which can be assets rather than liabilities. Leon Eisenberg advises that "the key issue in looking at the strengths of the inner-city child is the importance of not confusing difference with defect." Teacher education programs must provide experiences to enable personnel realistically to understand and accept various subcultures, recognizing strengths and positive aspects on which to build.

The Preparation of Teachers

Clearly, teacher education at both the pre-service and in-service levels needs modification if we are to recruit, train, and keep dedicated teachers who have the know-how, insight, and commitment to extend educational opportunities to disadvantaged children. Changes are already being initiated in many teacher preparation programs.

Involvement of subprofessionals, teacher aides, and indigenous persons from the inner city in projects designed to help disadvantaged children has opened up new training programs, some of which have been as helpful for the trainers as for the trainees in altering attitudes toward the culturally different. With support of federal and foundation funds, numerous institutes and workshops have focused on helping staff plans for integrated education, for pre-school programs, and for remedial projects of various kinds.

No radical innovations in teacher preparation programs have yet emerged, although some patterns seem to be forming. These include:

(a) Early and continuous contact with children and adults in disadvantaged areas in a variety of school and non-school related activities. These range from one-to-one tutoring of pupils to supervising after-school activities to classroom observation and intensive classroom teaching. These experiences are carefully supervised and often analyzed in seminar or small group sessions afterward.

(b) Intensive involvement of behavioral and social scientists who apply research and theory from their disciplines to the specific needs and problems of the disadvantaged area. These include cultural anthropologists, social psychologists, architects, city planners, historians, and political scientists—many of whom are actively involved in field experiences with students.

(c) Intensive involvement of successful school practitioners—classroom teachers, principals, counselors, and others—in working with the teacher education staff in planning, supervising, and evaluating experiences. The two-way flow of college and school staffs has been of considerable benefit to both. Rivlin has urged the use of affiliated schools as laboratories for urban teacher education.

(d) Opportunities for pre-service teachers to work with non-school agencies, government and agency-sponsored, and to become actively involved in on-going projects for overcoming poverty, extending civil rights, and generally "reversing the spiral toward futility." Aside from the insights acquired into the life styles of the inner-city families, such experiences are apparently instrumental in more positive attitude formation to the problems faced in such areas.

(e) Modification of college courses to develop techniques and skills essential to teaching in depressed areas. These include help with diagnostic and remedial procedures, with methods and materials for individualization of instruction, with strategies for classroom control, and with personnel and material resources.

(f) Opportunity to examine, discuss, and plan local program adaptations to known situations, current research, and experimentation being reported by education centers.

(g) Establishment of internships and other means for continuing relationships between the college and the teacher in service, so that the teacher has continuing supervisory aid as well as support.

Leon Eisenberg maintains that the effective teacher of inner-city children is one whose concern for their welfare goes far beyond the four walls of the classroom: "to have citizen participation in efforts to upgrade the neighborhood, to abolish discriminatory practices, to provide more recreational facilities, and to support social action for human betterment." Education in the inner-city school has dimensions which are less crucial in more favored schools with better advantaged children.

Teacher education must offer experiences which will help the teacher, both in preparation and in-service, to modify his behavior and attitudes for the sake of his pupils' healthy development and successful learning. In doing so, the teacher will truly teach.

The Gifted

BOYD R. McCANDLESS

Intensive studies of the characteristics of bright and dull children have been made. As a group, the bright are taller, handsomer, stronger, healthier, show fewer behavior problems, are less likely to have cavities in their teeth, and do better work in school. Although a higher percentage of children from "good" families belong to the bright group than is true for families in the middle and lower classes, in terms of absolute numbers the majority of gifted children are middle-class, and vast numbers of children from lower-class families also classify as gifted. Children toward the lower end of the intellectual scale can be characterized in terms opposite to those we have used for the gifted: they are less popular, less healthy, do less well in school, and so on. But both the bright and the dull achieve below their capacity and the academic achievement of the bright in United States public schools is far lower than we would expect on the basis of their IQ.

Ketcham (1957) reports on a group of forty gifted boys as they progressed from 6 to 12 years of age, and from the first to the seventh grade. At age 7, for example, their mental age averaged 9 years, 3 months, but their over-all educational age only 7 years, 2 months. The same figures for forty-two gifted girls similarly followed were also 9 years, 3 months and 7 years, 2 months. At 12 years of age, the boys averaged 17 years, 11 months in mental age, and 15 years, 8 months in educational age; the girls, 17 years, 5 months in mental age, and 15 years in educational age. These youngsters were relatively accelerated in reading, lagged most markedly in arithmetic.

Paradoxically, this same tendency typifies public-school children at the opposite end of the intellectual spectrum. It is probable that the phenomenon of underachievement, occurring in two such different groups, has very different causes. The bright are victims of underexpectation and understimulation; the slow learners are victims of frustration, defeat, and overexpectation.

Historically and currently, United States schools have used the following techniques with the gifted: they are accelerated, segregated, admitted early to school (a special form of acceleration), or given an enriched curriculum.

It has been widely held that *acceleration* is bad for a child. Pushed ahead a grade or two, he may be with children of similar mental age, but will lag behind his classmates in physical maturity and social development. To some degree and in extreme cases, this is undoubtedly true. But discreet acceleration of children whose physical size and social maturity is in line with their intellectual ability and reading achievement appears to do them good rather than harm. In the United States the most extensive work with the intellectually gifted has been done by Terman and his associates (Terman and Oden, 1947). Terman has found that the most successful gifted adults were those accelerated a year or more in school. No social-emotional disadvantages seemed to result from this acceleration.

Worchester (1959) should be quoted in this context:

> It is interesting that, although acceleration has undoubtedly been used far more than any other method of providing for the rapid learner, and although there has been more research as to the outcomes of acceleration than there has been for any other method, and although almost all of the research has shown results favorable to acceleration with hardly any study showing negative values, still a large proportion of teachers and administrators will have little or none of it. (p. 1)

Worchester comments that acceleration is "a sort of daylight saving. We get the chores of the world done early in the day so that there may be more opportunity for the real joys of living a little later" (p. 3), and estimates that "if we got the top 3 percent of our gifted into their life work a year earlier, the country would have the advantage of some million years' additional use of its best brains, and it could probably find use for them. Only good effects, in general, have been found for up to two years of acceleration" (p. 4).

Segregation into special classes has often been tried for gifted children. Where research on the results has been carried out (Albers, *et al.*, 1947; Ausubel, 1951; Bonsall, 1955; Carlson, 1947; and Havighurst *et al.*, 1955) positive results have usually been reported. Both teachers and children enjoy the classes, and the children typically accomplish twice as much or more schoolwork than in their regular class. But for reasons that are logically not very clear, segregation has been condemned as undemocratic. Is it not better for the very bright child to encounter stiff competition from his intellectual peers than to coast along with his regular class, always getting the top A yet never really having to work for it? Does the child third from the top bitterly resent having the two gifted children in his class removed to a special class? Probably not; when they were in the regular class, he could *never* be first, no matter how hard he worked. With them gone, he may often be tops.

United States schools segregate in many ways. The best contact athletes are segregated into football or basketball teams; the best musicians are segregated into glee clubs and bands. No one argues that this is particularly undemocratic (although many are concerned about a school tendency to produce observers rather than participants in the performing arts and sports). Why then do we argue that segregation of the intellectually gifted group is undemocratic?

Such segregation, of course, presents school administrators with very real problems. Many parents whose children are *not* gifted secretly or publicly believe that they *are*, and often exert strong pressure on school authorities to place their youngsters in classrooms for the gifted. Such pressures, when they come from influential citizens, are hard to counter. It can be surmised that many a school superintendent has abandoned the practice of segregated classes for the gifted with a sigh of relief.

If superior children are to be placed in special, segregated classes, this placement should of course be made only after full consideration of *all* the child's needs. A simple measure of IQ does not provide enough information. We must know how efficiently the child is using his IQ, obtain an estimate of his social maturity, find out how placement in a special class will affect his relations with friends, parents, brothers and sisters. All these things should be known and taken into account before placement is made. If they are, one might predict outstanding success for special classes.

A common United States practice in education for the gifted is *enrichment*. Ideally, every class should be small enough to permit the teacher both to plan for and attend to the individual needs of each child in the group. Every teacher should be trained so that she can make such plans efficiently. Every classroom should have, among its books and equipment, materials simple yet interesting enough to appeal to its slowest-learning child and give him some feeling of mastery and success, yet complicated and difficult enough to challenge the brightest youngster. This represents a surprisingly wide range of material. It is not at all uncommon, for example, for a fourth-grade class in an ordinary middle-class neighborhood to include some children who do not read at all—who are *literally* functioning at a kindergarten or early first-grade level—and other children who are achieving at a college-freshman level as far as reading is concerned, and as high as eighth- or ninth-grade level in number skills.

The average classroom does not include such a range of teaching aids, and its class enrollment is so large that even the most dedicated and skilled teacher lacks the time to do careful individual planning for any but the "problem" children in her class. Far too few teachers are thoroughly trained to do individual planning, aside from having to spend a disproportionate amount of time on the "squeaking wheels" of the class—the children in the bottom fourth or fifth academically, and those with behavior problems. Since, in general, the very bright are relatively self-sufficient, manage at least to do all right with their schoolwork, and rather infrequently present serious behavior problems, they tend to be neglected.

Even well-trained teachers can pick out only about half the children in their classes with extremely high IQ's. Reasons for this lie partly in the nature of teacher-training, and partly in the characteristics of United States children. For rather nebulous reasons, Americans distrust "eggheads." It is not particularly fashionable to be "the best student in the class." More emphasis is put on being popular or good at games than on intellectual achievement. This may be true of boys even more frequently than it is of girls. Consequently, very bright children may "hide their light under a bushel" and simply do not try very hard. The present author has related elsewhere in a discussion of this topic (McCandless, 1957) an anecdote about an 11-year-old friend of his who, during her first five grades of school, had consistently been the best in her class in work with numbers. During the sixth grade her arithmetic standing plummeted to about the class median. Asked how this had happened, she shrugged and said, matter-of-factly, "Girls are just not *supposed* to be that good in arithmetic."

These points illustrate some of the difficulties confronting teachers when they cry enrichment. They cannot enrich the program of a gifted child if they do not know who he is; if they must spend too much time on children who, for one reason or another, are school problems; if gifted children, for cultural reasons, are dragging their heels; or if the classroom does not include appropriate types and ranges of material.

Another method that has been tried with the very bright child is *early admission* to school. This is a special form of acceleration, and many of the same reservations have been expressed concerning it. Few of these reservations are buttressed by facts. One of the most ambitious studies of the question has been done by Hobson (1956), concerning children in the Brookline, Massachusetts, public schools. For twenty-five years preceding his evaluation, these schools had been admitting to kindergarten children with mental ages of 5 or more years, but who were as young, chronologically, as 4 years on October 1 of the year they entered school. Criteria in addition to IQ were employed in admitting such children.

Hobson's sample is impressively large. His subjects include 550 underage children and 3891 regularly admitted children (to whom he refers as "others"), all of whom graduated from the Brookline schools between 1946 and 1955. Included in his "others" group were many underage children who had transferred to Brookline from other schools. These children in general did better than their older classmates, although they did less well than the carefully screened early-admitted children who had begun school in Brookline. Some of the representative findings are listed below.

"Graduation with honors" from Brookline high school demands a solid A and B average for all subjects taken in the last two years of school. Hobson's underage boys exceeded the "other" boys in better than a 2:1 ratio of 18.75 percent to 8.43 percent. Corresponding figures for the girls were 25.46 percent and 15.04 percent.

A second criterion of school success was broader than graduation with honors. Election to Alpha Pi in the Brookline schools depends on the student's accumulation of points, one third of which come from participating in extracurricular activities. Such items as election to class offices are included. Of the underage boys, about 13 percent received this honor; less than 6 percent of the "other" boys did. Corresponding figures for girls were 19 percent and 9 percent.

Hobson also studied two classes more intensively, obtaining about the same results as those given above. As a group, underage boys and girls averaged 18.8 extracurricular activities during their school years; the "other" group averaged only 12.1. The only category in which any possible disadvantage appeared for early admissions was boys' contact sports (such as football and basketball), where more of the "others" took part. But in other sports, such as tennis, the underage group was somewhat superior to the "others." Underage children were also more frequently accepted into serious, highly rated four-year colleges and universities.

This careful study offers a strong argument against those who say that moderate acceleration handicaps children in the areas of social and motor skills.

In justice to United States public education, it should be added that attitudes toward training the gifted are currently becoming more flexible, that the major methods of furthering their progress are being reevaluated, and that new adaptations of these major methods are being developed. For example, many school systems now have "enrichment" consultants; in many schools the first three or four years of school are ungraded, and children are allowed to progress through them as fast as they can master the work; and so on.

Other Exceptional Children

BOYD R. McCANDLESS

Segregation and highly specialized training are taken more or less for granted for other groups of exceptional children, such as the cerebral-palsied, deaf, and blind. There is some tendency, the full merits of which are not yet clear, to incorporate into regular classrooms all children who can possibly succeed. In one situation, blind children are provided with both intensive and extensive preschool experiences (to facilitate socialization); then, at an appropriate developmental age, are placed in the regular grades. Results are tentative, but encouraging. For the most part, however, such groups, including the low-grade mentally defective (below about 50 IQ), receive specialized and segregated training.

Controversy exists, however, about education for high-grade mentally defective and borderline children (with IQ's from about 50 to about 85), whose educational attainments by the middle of the elementary-school years are ordinarily below even the modest level that would be predicted from their IQ. *Deceleration* (failure to promote) and *segregation* have been the most frequent educational measures used by the public schools, at least in those systems where special procedures have been tried at all.

Convincing evidence exists (Goodlad, 1954; Sandin, 1944) that failure to promote a child is accompanied on his part by discouragement, pro-

From Chapter 7, from *Children: Behavior and Development,* Second Edition, by Boyd R. McCandless. Copyright © 1961, 1967 by Holt, Rinehart and Winston, Inc. Reprinted by permission of Holt, Rinehart and Winston, Inc.

gressive retardation, hostility (active or latent) toward the school, and symptoms of general maladjustment. But it is not clear whether this cluster of socially maladaptive behaviors and attitudes is the result of failure to promote or whether it accompanies the academic difficulties that lead to the child's not being promoted. In any event, the presence of large, physically mature, surly, older children (a majority of whom are usually boys from lower socioeconomic classes) in classes of younger boys and girls presents very real problems in the school situation. Probably a majority of United States schools now practice what is sometimes called "social promotion," that is, regardless of the child's academic achievement, an effort is made to keep him with his age group. The results of this practice are particularly striking (and troublesome) when a child moves from elementary to junior high school. Typically, at this time, a child changes from a class that revolves almost entirely around one teacher to a platoon system, where different teachers teach different subjects; formal academic requirements ordinarily become more stringent. Where, in the first six grades, a child may have been limping along, in the seventh grade he becomes immobilized, with severe accompanying disturbances of all sorts.

There is no easy way out of this dilemma. Speaking very tentatively and without solid conviction, the author favors special or segregated classes, placement in which is made on a broader basis than an IQ test. Segregation of the slow-learning has been vociferously attacked as undemocratic and out of line with the philosophy of "developing the whole child." Anyone who has observed in the public schools knows that there is discrimination against pupils in "opportunity rooms." Common parlance for such classes by school children is "dummy rooms," and certainly some school systems make them little more than baby-sitting arrangements. However, clever and devoted teachers can produce remarkable results. One teacher (E. McCandless, 1943), working for two successive years with slow-learning children newly admitted to an institution for borderline mentally defective problem children, produced an average academic gain of nearly three grade levels per year. Prior to their commitment to the institution, these children, who averaged about 13 years of age at the time of commitment, had averaged a gain of only about .3 grade levels per year. Most of them had attended the generally very adequate schools of Detroit, Michigan.

Since academic achievement tests were administered independently of the teacher, there was no contamination of results in this study. The techniques used were those of individual diagnosis, strong personal interest in and attention to each child, and moderate firmness, although disciplinary techniques appeared to be milder and more democratic than those prevailing in other classrooms in the institution.

One interesting but tragic study (G. O. Johnson, 1950) charts the academic progress and social acceptance of mentally retarded children (average IQ, about 64) in regular public-school classes. The picture is a hopeless one. During each year of school attendance, the youngsters fell further and further behind academically. First-graders lagged 4.7 months behind their classmates academically (for a combination of arithmetic and reading); second-graders 9.5 months; third-graders 12.7 months; fourth-graders 17.6 months; and fifth-graders 27.8 months! This picture of progressive frustration and defeat holds true despite the fact that the mentally retarded children averaged almost two years older than their normal classmates.

Although these children comprised less than 6 percent of the total group of children studied, 40 percent of the most rejected children in the twenty-five classes included in the research came from the mentally defective group. Other children characterized them by such phrases as "rough, mean, teases, bullies, fights, misbehaves in school, poor sports, cheats, is dirty, smells." Not only were they actively rejected, but few children named them as friends. In these classes, social acceptance mounted steadily with intellectual level, the low (below 59 IQ) mental defectives being less acceptable than the highs, the borderline children more accepted than either group, the normal children still better accepted, and the superior youngsters (above 130 IQ) having the highest acceptance and the lowest rejection scores as determined by votes of their classmates.

Even though the number of mentally defective children in this study is relatively small, the picture the study presents is brutally clear. The life of the slow-learning child in the regular class is a miserable one of academic failure, increasing in severity year by year and compounded by social rejection. It seems that he *could not be worse off* in a special class, either academically or socially, even though other children in the school called it the "dummy class." In the special class he is at least competing with other children of his own level, and can occasionally taste success. From a mental-hygiene point of view, it is perhaps better for him to have some victory and some acceptance from his peers, even though the majority of children derogate his class, than to be integrated but rejected.

The Slow Learner: A Convenient Label

RAYMOND E. LAURITA

Education today is beset by a host of problems resistant to solution. Prominent among these is the nagging question of what to do with the "slow learner." This twentieth century anomaly is the subject of countless research

Reprinted from *New York State Education,* 55 (2): 14–17 (November 1967), by permission of author and publisher. Copyright © 1967 by New York State Teachers Association.

studies concerned with finding a successful method of dealing with these children. Those placed in this nebulous category need not spring from the slums nor live in the midst of poverty. The slow learner resides in all stratas of society and his presence in every school is an educational fact of life.

Why do these children arouse such trepidation in our schools? How do they manage to earn the title "slow learner?" More to the point, are slow learners really slow or are they rather the innocent victims of a convenient label attached because modern education has failed to make provision for their particular problems?

Finding an answer to these questions poses an important challenge to responsible laymen and educators for at least two reasons. First, the undeniable presence of children who learn slowly in almost every classroom offers seemingly insurmountable obstacles to quality education for the majority. Second, if in fact these children have been mislabeled, we are doubly guilty, both of unconscionable discrimination and failure to discover and provide educational programs needed by "all" children to develop their fullest potential.

The slow learner has been described, characterized, and profiled by numerous writers, yet a precise definition of the condition is difficult to pin down. Ostensibly he is the child, be he in the primary or secondary school, who is unable to perform at the same rate as those of his class and consequently needs specialized treatment.

To understand the reason for the chaos the slow learner causes by the mere fact of his presence, it is necessary to understand the nature of current educational theory. Children today learn everything from reading to home economics in a progressive series of gradual, carefully arranged stages. Each stage, as it is thought out and incorporated in the curriculum, is dependent on a prerequisite knowledge of the preceding steps or learned skills. Attached to this process is the appellation "developmental education."

An example will serve to explain how this almost universal theory of education is applied. In learning to read, the children in our schools undergo a preparation period, sometime during the kindergarten or first grade, referred to as "getting ready to read." Each day they are exposed to exercises considered to teach skills and evoke responses similar to those used in the intuitive reading process. The child examines figures in a variety of shapes, sizes and arrangements, thought to develop the ability to recognize word shapes. He goes through a wide range of planned exercises to improve his understanding of left and right sidedness.

Objects in the room are labeled in an effort to help him discover that words are really symbolic representations for both concrete objects and abstract concepts. A whole industry caters to the development, sale and distribution of gimmicks, and shortcuts to prepare the child for what may be the most difficult undertaking of his life.

After a period considered suitable by the experts, the child learns a number of words at sight to be used over and over until they are quickly recognized. As these words are learned, they begin to appear repeatedly in the primers or first books of the first grade. Sometime during this process, as new words continue systematically to be introduced, he is exposed to techniques designed to make him independent. It is presumed he will become less reliant on learning words by rote and more able to discover new words by himself. Sequence and orderliness are the aim of the system.

In theory the approach is sound for it is based on the findings of educational theorists who have attempted to break the inductive-deductive learning process into a simple, almost mathematical series of graduated steps. Yet the existence of millions of education's failures lends credence to the doubts many in and out of education express concerning the practical impossibility of creating and carrying out a program based on such a philosophy. The distinct possibility exists that developmental education has a serious flaw. Within its structure is no built-in mechanism to successfully cope with the atypical, unusual child who fails to respond like an automaton but reacts rather as a flesh and blood, unique personality.

Attempts to deal with the problem of individual difference have been hastily incorporated into the system of "developmental education," but have generally proved cumbersome and unworkable. Grouping or segregating children with similar problems has been a twofold failure. First because this process neglects coming to grips with the basic causes underlying individual student difficulty and secondly, it fails to recognize the interrelationship and overlapping of problems in the educational and personal lives of the afflicted students.

Programs designed to correct impaired ability in a specific subject area without reference to the basic source of difficulty are poor medicine. Many problems that become gross by the time the child reaches high school began as small but unmet needs in the lower grades.

It is entirely possible a child labeled the "slow learner" may be a victim of the system, included in the ranks of those who do not fit the patterns envisioned by abstract thinkers. The student who cannot keep up, who is disinterested, who is lacking in the attributes measured by verbal, culture-oriented intelligence tests does not fit into the scheme of developmental education.

The assumption generally drawn is that his failure places him in the category of slow learner. If intelligence and individual ability are to be measured solely by a student's capacity to keep pace with those of a particular group, then educators are correct and a slow learning child is indeed a misfit. This view isn't the only possible alternative, however, nor is it in any case a positive approach to adopt in attempts to solve a pervasive problem.

Developmental education has, in fact, an extremely narrow, artificial perspective for it tends to treat individuals as faceless statistics. According to educators espousing the theory, there must inevitably be a predictable number of slow, average and superior students. Acceptance of this view is tantamount to a dehumanization of man.

Belief in the existence of other explanations for a child's inability to learn skills and understandings at a predictable rate offers a more human, more realistic answer for the failure of so many to keep pace with their peers and learn at rates differing from predicated norms. Human personality is diverse, complex and in a state of constant change. Understanding the interplay of factors in the personality is a study of infinite variety. Precise statistical studies may arrive at expectations of behavior and performance, but precision or even accurate predictability in the case of the individual is a contradiction.

Individual difference and the capacity for growth are the very factors differentiating man from machines and which hopefully will always differentiate him. Children entering school are unique and no amount of pedagogical double-talk will ever change that. If we wait for the child to arrive at the school door and then expect him to respond in an almost prearranged manner, education will continue to be plagued by the slow learner, the dropout, the defeated individual rebelling against society's insistence on his learning what it considers to be "good."

By the same token, if we insist on making success in school and consequently in life dependent on the acceptance of values, ideals and expectations established by majority consensus as being acceptable, we are likewise likely to fail. Those who cannot find satisfactory outlets for their own basic needs will find avenues in conflict with society. The statistics on juvenile crime, drug addiction and delinquency tend to support this conclusion.

For the system of education presently practiced in the United States to succeed optimally, it will be necessary to make provision for those who cannot, or will not, conform. Revisions and adaptations need to be made to assist these youngsters to profit from democratic education. Dr. Francis Keppel, former United States Commissioner of Education, has stated we need "a revolution in thinking and attitude," if we are to cope with the problems facing the schools. Dr. Keppel feels that education "must make good on the concept that no child within our society is either unteachable or unreachable—that whenever a child appears at the doors of our schools he presents a direct challenge to us and to all our abilities. . . . For educators, the question is not the environment that children bring to the school from the outside, but the environment the school provides from the inside."

By far the largest and most resistant group of education's problems are the culturally deprived. It is from their ranks the overwhelming majority of slow learners are enlisted. Again it is Dr. Keppel who cites a figure of thirty percent of the school age population in this category for whom the schools are "failing dismally" to provide adequately.

Writing in the *Reading Teacher,* Millard Black, a Los Angeles elementary supervisor, attempted to define those who comprise the culturally deprived. "They live not only in the central areas of our great cities. One southern governor in January, 1964, declared that 20 per cent of the citizens in his state can neither read nor write, that 50 per cent of the state's young people fail to complete high school. The disadvantaged child is of no single race or color. Poverty, delinquency, and failure to achieve the goals established by the mainstream of society are shared by peoples of all colors and national origins. . . . He is no stranger to failure and the fear that continued failure engenders. He knows the fear of being over-powered by teachers who are ignorant of the culture and mores of his society, and who may not expect success of him. He fears lack of recognition and understanding from teachers whose backgrounds are totally dissimilar and who either misinterpret or fail to recognize many of his efforts to achieve and to accommodate himself to demands which are basically alien."

Attempting to deal with a problem of this magnitude is unbelievably complex. The most logical and realistic solution to preparing the deprived child for the experiences of the school is a massive program of federally supported pre-school education. These children need to be exposed to the culture, language and expectations of those who are to teach them if the present system is to succeed. The aim of such preparation should not be to denigrate or extirpate any rich and colorful traditions of these children but rather to enable them to develop self-esteem and independence—to permit them to integrate their own cultural heritage with that of society to the betterment of all.

Another group of children often falsely labeled as slow learners are many suffering from insufficient physical well-being or maturity. All in education pay lip service to the principle that a child needs the best possible health. Yet at present there are very few schools making any more than a token effort at discovering and treating physical disabilities capable of causing difficulty in the initial learning experiences.

In order to even begin to perform the tasks of the school adequately the child must have near perfect vision. He must not only be able to see objects clearly, he must also be able to discriminate minute differences existing in the relatively exacting visual work he performs daily. Reading instruction, for instance, makes demands on the child's vision that cannot be underestimated; the slightest inadequacy in visual excellence can lay the groundwork for confusion that will make the job of learning to read difficult for some and impossible for others.

How possible is it that the spiral of failure which typifies the slow learner began not because of inferior mental ability but results from impaired vision instead? The American Optometric Association estimates "four out of every ten children in the United States are visually handicapped for adequate school achievement." Considering this figure encompasses almost nine million children, it is safe to assume at least some slow learners have been unfairly categorized.

Another area of the child's total physical well-being almost universally overlooked as a possible cause of slow learning is inadequate hearing ability. It is imperative not only to be able to hear the spoken word but also to have the ability to differentiate between sounds of great similarity. The increasingly verbal nature of education makes efficient auditory ability a prerequisite for success. One expert on this subject, Dr. Albert Harris, states, "Auditory perception skill is an important element in reading readiness and in some studies has out-ranked all others in its contributions to success in reading."

Since poor auditory ability is such a significant factor, it is inconceivable why schools continue to pay attention to gross, obvious cases of hearing difficulty and totally neglect less apparent but equally inhibiting minor problems. How many slow learners are really only children who were unable to hear adequately and develop basic understandings essential for the construction of a secondary education?

In a recent book dealing with the brain injured child, *A Teaching Method for Brain Injured and Hyperactive Children,* the authors pointed out the need for a better understanding of this problem. The need they considered most pressing was the implementation of programs of therapy and instruction. They stated that the brain-injured child constitutes a proportion of the school population "apparently much larger than had been anticipated," and requires specialized diagnosis and treatment.

As programs for the identification of the brain injured improve there is a growing realization among educators that many children identified as slow learners in the past were indeed mislabeled because of their disturbed, unusual response to the demands of mass education.

The possibility of alternate reasons for slow learning are in reality unlimited. Despite the obvious need for early diagnosis and remedial care, a major response continues to be the designation of children as slow learners. Instead of developing an apparatus for detection and a corps of trained personnel to deal with early school difficulty, education continues to deal ineffectually with the debris of neglect.

American schools have much to crow about but they have utterly failed to understand the need for comprehensive pre-school medical examinations with resulting diagnosis and treatment as a cure for the ills of the slow learner. Action must be preventive before the child is caught in a trap of frustrating defeat, not after.

Somehow society has allowed itself to accept the fallacious principle that success in the tasks of the school is the sole determinant of individual ability. Conversely, failure to achieve has become the indicator of lack of ability. Educators have developed a pseudo-sophisticated jargon to identify, to pigeon-hole all those who do not measure up to the artificial, narrow standards a middle-class society deems desirable.

Educationists toss around terms like sociometry, standard deviation and intellectual status index with a smug facility but with little understanding of the humanity of the statistics to which they refer. Where concern for the individual was once the central focus of education it has now become clever to discuss cross-sections and percentile groups. The victim in this tragic process of dehumanization is the individual child, especially the one who may or may not have accurately been designated a slow learner.

Slow learner is actually a meaningless term. It does little except indicate the child who for any of a thousand reasons finds it difficult to learn at the rate or in the comprehensive manner demanded by the school. Instead of seeking out constructive means of prevention and correction, our schools have managed only to become more narrow and conforming in their demands and less tolerant of the atypical, unusual child. We have made them social lepers by labeling them with odious stigmas that carry degrading connotations in our school-conscious society.

To be labeled a slow learner in a poor school is bad enough, but to be placed in that category in a school of higher socio-economic status is tantamount to being ostracized. It effectively destroys the child's self-concept, restricts his opportunity for the best teaching and forces him to accept the unhappy cubby-hole he has been assigned.

Surely there is a more humane, more enlightened method for dealing with this problem of difference. How long will education continue to be plagued by those who insist on pragmatic, short-range treatment of the manifestations of defect instead of finding long-range solutions, aimed at eradicating the causes which create and nourish basic educational and human defect?

We in America are perhaps the most pragmatically successful people who ever lived. We have an uncanny facility for seeing expedient cures with almost intuitive insight.

Yet it is this very approach of practicality bringing us to the brink of disaster in education. The time for applying expedient cures for every situation has gone past. We must somehow learn to direct our attention to making changes that will hurt. Answers must be found for basic problems and remedies applied that aren't going to work overnight or please everyone. The time for greater concern for those in need is at hand and unless it is attended to at once, the consequences may be calamitous.

Thus the problem of the slow learner appears in its true perspective as but a part of the overall conflict in education. The expedient solution devised to ameliorate the problem of the child unable to stay with his group was solved temporarily by resorting to remedial classes. Neglected, however, was any concern for the prevention of more and more slow learners. Instead of bringing the problem under control and instituting suitable programs for the atypical child, we are stuck with a crazy-quilt pattern of special classes, remedial groups, classes for the disturbed, for the slow learner, etc.

Is there a solution to the problem? The answer has to be yes or the outlook for education would indeed be bleak. The first requirement in any program designed for success will have to be a change in our local, national and personal attitudes.

It isn't necessarily more spacious and ornate schools we need but increased concern for the children within the schools.

Finally, we need to learn how to take the hard, less convenient road.

Disturbed Youngsters in the Classroom

WILLIAM C. MORSE

"John can make a shambles of my classroom. The only way I can get anyplace talking with him is away from the group. Then he explains very clearly why he does various things. He usually admits that they were dumb things to do, but there is no carryover. He already has a court record.

"And then there are Beth and George. Beth is so quiet and dreamy that she seems here only when I press her with questions and then she drifts away. George is another story. His conversations are non sequiturs. He asks the strangest questions—and always with a worried look. The psychologist has referred him for intensive treatment, but there is a long waiting list. Most of the time I can almost keep on top of the situation, but there are days when I don't seem to be getting anywhere."

An experienced teacher was describing her classroom. Almost any teacher in almost any school could paint a similar picture, and although the percentage of Johns, Beths, and Georges in the typical classroom is small, it does not take huge numbers of disturbed youngsters to create a critical mass that can confound a teacher and convert a classroom to chaos.

What can a teacher do that will be helpful to the disturbed children in the classroom and at the same time will keep them from disrupting the rest of the class? Source books are not available for teaching attitudes, values, identification, or empathic behavior. Advice ranges from the assured behavior modifiers who direct the teacher to "train" the pupils to the proponents of a leave-them-alone-and-they'll-all-come-home-to-Summerhill philosophy.

These answers are too simple. If the schools are to meet their responsibility toward all children, teachers and schools must change. Teachers need to understand what causes the disturbed children in their classes to be that way. They need to develop new teaching skills and to find new ways of

Reprinted from *Today's Education, NEA Journal,* 58 (4): 30–37 (April 1969), by permission of author and publisher.

using resources. School systems need to look for new ways to use the resources—the time, space, techniques, and personnel—now available and to add new resources.

UNDERSTANDING DISTURBED PUPILS

Some children are disturbed both in their home-community life and in school. Their difficulties are pervasive—with them wherever they go. For example, many a youngster who is rejected and unwanted in his family feels the same way in school.

In other children, disturbance shows up at home or at school but not in both situations. Ralph, for instance, is a skilled leader on the playground and in his neighborhood and gets along reasonably well in his fatherless home. He chafes under the pressure of school routines, however. He is in constant contest with conformity demands and has no interest in school learning. Generally speaking, he is happy-go-lucky and forgets a school disciplinary episode almost before it is over.

Other children who feel supported and do very well in school have difficulties elsewhere. The school is sometimes central in problem behavior and somtimes peripheral, but the aim is to make the school compensatory whenever possible.

The behavior symptoms a child displays are not an automatic revelation of the causes of that behavior. To plan effectively for a disturbed child, the teacher needs not only to see accurately what the youngster does but to understand why he does it. This requires the teacher to do some diagnostic thinking and to gain the ability to see life through the eyes of the pupil.

Let us apply diagnostic thinking first to pupils who are aggressive toward peers, perhaps toward the teacher, and even toward school requirements—pupils who display what is called "acting-out behavior." Children with this broad range of symptoms are the most frequent referrals to special services and special classes. They may provoke fights, break rules, and generally defy the teacher. Older youngsters often turn sullen and hostile. Acting-out children prevent others from working, may react with an outburst if required to conform, and are ready to rebel at a moment's notice.

Since this type of behavior can make conducting classes impossible, no one should be surprised that teachers find it the most vexing difficulty.

When teachers explore beyond the generalized acting-out symptoms, they find some common patterns.

Sometimes aggressiveness results from a lack of adequate socialization. Our culture is producing increasing numbers of children who have never developed social concerns for others, who still function on an impulse basis, doing what they want to do when they feel like it. For one reason or another they lack a suitable prototype for basic identification. Sometimes they take on an omnipotent character—"No one can make me." At best they are narcissistic, bent on following their own desires; at worst they are without the capacity to feel for others. They practice a primitive hedonism.

Sometimes, these children come from indulgent, protective families and become embittered when crossed. When one is asked why he did something, he is likely to say, "I felt like it," until he learns it goes over better to say that he doesn't know why.

Because his delinquent and destructive behavior may stem from a lack of incorporated norms and values, the child with a defect in socialization needs a benign but strong surveillance, so that he is held accountable for misbehavior. He requires clear and specific limits, enforced without anger or harshness. At the same time, he needs models, such as a "big brother," teachers, and older youths, to set an example of proper behavior.

The process of rehabilitation of the unsocialized child is slow and rough, with many periods of regression, because the school is asking the child to give up immediate gratification for long-term goals and to replace self-seeking with consideration for the rights of others. Frequently these youngsters make their first attachment to a single strong teacher and will comply only with his demands. Generalized trust builds slowly. Substantial correction, especially at adolescence, is most difficult. Since the school is the major conformity agent of society, it becomes the natural battleground.

A subgroup among the aggressive children is composed of youngsters who lack social skills but have the capacity to learn them because they have been cared about and loved at home, even though their families have been too disorganized to teach adequate behavior. They are not so much anti-conforming as they are untutored in social skills. Role playing and demonstrations by models are useful to show such children the behavior expected of them.

While the reduction of acting-out behavior through teaching basic socialization is difficult, teachers still must try. Learning to value the rights of others is essential for members of a democratic society and recent follow-up studies indicate that neither individual treatment nor institutional custody is a satisfactory approach for such youth.

Another common cause of acting-out behavior is alienation. Estrangement from the educational establishment is occurring more and more frequently. Sometimes, from their very first day, these students find no gratification in the school experience, and their disinterest turns to hostility. The teacher sees these youngsters as problems in motivation. "They just don't seem to care about anything they should be doing."

For the most part, these are not weak children, and they are often well-accepted by peers outside of school. Having found life engaging elsewhere, they can't wait to get at it. One sixth grader had already figured out the number of days until he could quit school. Cars, money, the opposite sex, jobs—these are high demands of the alienated adolescent.

Youngsters like this are usually first admonished, then suspended to "shape them up." Suspension actually works in reverse, since they want out in the first place. If the youngsters are not suspended, too many teachers handle the problem by demanding nothing and letting them do just about as they please.

The better way of resolving the difficulty would be to undertake a thorough examination of the curriculum to see what could be altered. A junior high school pupil, already conducting a profitable business of his own, found nothing in classes with any meaning to him. With visions of establishing himself as an adult, he finally ran away with his girl friend.

Education is turning off an increasing number of able and intellectual youths. Such disenchantment was evidenced first at the college level, but it has already seeped down to the junior high. Many young people feel that school is a meaningless scramble for grades and graduation instead of the authentic education experience they seek. What often needs to be done is to make over the school rather than the pupil, but some teachers still rigidly follow the current curriculum as though it were sacred.

In some children, acting-out behavior in school is reaction to failure. No one wants to fail or even be in a marginal position, and yet thousands get failure messages every school day. The child comes to hate the establishment that makes him a failure, so he strikes back. Some failed first at home, where nothing they did was as good as what a sibling did—where no matter how hard they tried, they failed. The hatred such children feel for adults at home may transfer to their teachers, who may never have been in the least unfair.

The amount of defiling and belittling, to say nothing of direct abuse, that children suffer in our supposedly child-favoring culture comes as a shock to many a protected teacher. If the cause of acting-out behavior is in the home, then acting out in school is merely a displacement, but the acting-out child gets a reputation that is passed along ahead of him and he lives up to it.

School can be too taxing for certain children, grading too severe, and teacher's help too scarce. Although they get along well at home, children with mild learning disabilities or limited academic ability frequently drift into frustration at school. Some of the slow-developing early primary pupils or late-blooming adolescents in junior high are too immature to meet expectations. The solution is for the school to adjust to the pupil by proper pacing. Many of these pupils change surprisingly when a perceptive teacher builds in success.

Still other children who act out are anxious about their lives in general. Often they are hyperactive, driven to release tension through physical activity. They are oversensitive, easily distracted, and given to disruptive behavior. After misbehaving, they feel guilty and promise never to repeat the offense, but in a subsequent period of anxiety they do repeat it, acting out in order to dissipate tension.

Some of this group actually seek punishment because they feel they are bad and should pay the penalty. This feeling of guilt may stem from wrong things they have done or merely thought of doing. For instance, one boy, who was being stimulated by a seductive mother, used to blow up in math class, where concentration was required. He could do the math, but not when he was upset. It took the social worker a long time to help him work this out.

A special category of anxiousness, found with increasing frequency in suburbia, is achievement neurosis. In order to meet overt or covert expectations, pupils who have this affliction feel compelled to be on top. They have lost the satisfaction of learning as its own reward; grades are to prove they are as good as their parents want them to be. These youngsters are frequently tense and driven and overvalue the academic. Their parents are forever inquiring, "How well is John doing?"

Children who are driven in this way need to be made to feel better about themselves. Some of them demand much attention, always seeking resubstantiation by adult approval. If the source of the damaged self-picture is an overdemanding home or neighborhood, it is often difficult to provide enough compensatory success in school to allay it. This is where counselors, psychiatrists, psychologists, school social workers, or referral agencies play their part.

By now it is easy to see why any two acting-out children may not need the same type of help from the teacher. But teachers' concerns are not limited to those who directly disrupt the educational process, for the profession is equally attuned to pupils who have given up. While withdrawn children may not cause the teacher managerial difficulty, they, too, are in need of special assistance.

Many unhappy, depressed youngsters are in school today. Basically, these youngsters have very low self-esteem; they have somehow been taught by life that they are good-for-nothing and important to nobody. Often, internal preoccupation takes over, and they drift into a world of fantasy. They absorb the support sensitive teachers give, but often this is not sufficient to strengthen them to a point where they can sustain themselves.

Sometimes students are confirmed losers. They just know they will fail and usually contrive to make their anticipations come true. Others come to rely on fate rather than on their own efforts. As one youngster put it: "Fifty-fifty, I pass or I flunk. It depends on the breaks." So why put forth any effort?

Another group of the withdrawn children are the lonely ones. The loner drifts by himself at recess or eats alone in the junior high cafeteria or has no one to talk to about his high school lessons. Because he feels that nobody would care, he sees no point in trying to make friends. Many youngsters who are scapegoats in their peer group come from among the lonely ones, especially if they have some physical problem such as overweight, a tic, or odd looks. In these cases, the way the teacher manages the group life in the classroom is just as important as individual attention and counseling.

DEALING WITH DISTURBED PUPILS

No magic, no single cure, no shortcut will solve the problems of disturbed children in the schools. The job demands an extension of the individualization that is the essence of good school practice. This calls for teacher time and specially planned curricular experiences. To provide these, many school systems will add a new resource—the psychological, social-work, or psychiatric consultant. Conflict between specialists and regular classroom teachers used to be commonplace, but teachers have now discovered a new way to use the specialists' help, replacing long discourses on "how Johnny got that way" with discussions of what can be done now, in the classroom.

Frequently, a curriculum expert and the principal should join the teacher and the special consultant in discussions about a disturbed child. Remedial action should be based on study of the deviant youngster's classroom behavior and of his basic personality. Clinical insights provide the backdrop for practical planning.

When the problem is caused not by the school but by the child's home situation, the remedial goal is to have the school provide a supportive environment that will compensate, in part, for what is lacking or negative. Referral services to agencies that can offer individual therapy are vital also. They are not enough, however. Group work agencies, boys' clubs, and big brothers can help the unsocialized child who does not have serious internal conflicts. Such a child is in dire need of basic identification building.

Many disturbed children who can function within normal bounds and utilize the regular classroom much of the time lapse occasionally into disruptive behavior that throws the classroom into chaos. Some schools—secondary as well as elementary—deal with this problem by having a special teacher, trained to work with the disturbed in both academic and behavioral spheres, to whom such a child goes during a crisis. This teacher works with him in a special classroom where he can receive assistance on both individual and small group bases.

While the issue is still current, the crisis teacher and the child discuss the matter, much after the fashion of crisis intervention in community mental health. Close liaison with the regular teacher is, of course, mandatory. Referrals to a school or community service for intensive individual work may be needed, but the crisis teacher is the key person to support the regular classroom teacher and the pupil and to coordinate the entire effort in time of stress. When the pupil has gained control and/or is able to do the task in question, he returns to the regular classroom.

NEEDED CHANGES

The task is to examine the classroom environment and the teacher's role. What changes will improve the helping index?

No one has any idea of making the teacher into a psychotherapist, although many disturbed students form a profound relationship with their teachers. The function of the teacher is to provide pupils with a reasonable human relationship (in itself therapeutic) and the opportunity to grow through academic accomplishment and social learning.

Achievement is therapeutic for a child, especially when he has achieved little or nothing in the past. Having an adult who cares about him and who helps him when he falters instead of getting angry and rejecting him is certainly helpful. Peer acceptance in the classroom has lasting significance for the lonely child.

In this sense, therapeutic intervention has always been a part of school, but some children need much more. Providing that more will require three things:

1. The schools will have to reexamine how the curriculum, methodology, and experiences can be bent to enhance growth and minimize failure.

2. Teachers will have to learn new skills.

3. Teachers will have to become more open about their feelings toward disturbed children, because externalizing attitudes is a necessary step in changing negative feelings.

Since the school operation itself provokes a considerable amount of school difficulty, what is taught and how it is taught will require adjustment. Pupils need short assignments that interest them and that they are capable of doing. Not only the level of difficulty but the rate of learning should be attuned to the child, with provision for remedial teaching of what he has missed.

Individualization for the alienated youngster requires new subject matter that is relevant rather than merely different. Some children with learning disabilities require the use of self-tutoring devices. Iconoclastic curriculums, such as cooperative work programs for older youths, are needed.

Although most behaviorists avoid considering disturbed children in any but symptomatic terms, they offer the teacher two most useful guidelines.

First, they tell teachers to study what the child actually does. Observation of how and to what the pupil responds often shows that much of what the teacher is doing is quite beside his intent. Many disturbed children are adept at controlling teachers by getting them to make inappropriate responses, thus reinforcing just what the teacher wishes to eliminate. If the pupil cares more about having *some* kind of relationship with the teacher than he does about *what* kind of relationship he has, he can get teacher attention by misbehavior. Thus, a teacher encourages repeat performances of an undesirable behavior even as he tells a pupil not to behave that way.

Second, behaviorists emphasize that many pupils do not operate on the basis of high-level gratifications, such as love of learning. Teachers must deal with them on their own motivational level. For example, the attention span and motivation of some who need concrete rewards suddenly improves when the teacher recognizes this need. Free time earned for work done or proper behavior may help get children started who have never had any real success before. They forget their "can't do" to earn free time. Behavior that approximates being acceptable is worth rewarding at first.

Punishment, the major reward many disturbed children receive, is a poor teaching device. Low grades seldom work as a challenge. Emphasis needs to be on accomplishments rather than on failures. Many teachers, wedded to the illusion of homogeneity, have a hard job learning to help these children achieve by accommodating to the special range they present in ability, rate, motivation, and interests. Sometimes the range can be narrowed. In junior and senior high, for example, a student can be assigned in every course to the teacher and the content best suited to him.

When nothing else works, something may be gained by asking a child to do only what interests him. One pupil studied nothing but the Civil War. Another drew pictures. This was no real solution, but the teacher survived and the other students could do their work. Desperate conditions require desperate measures, and it is better to have a student reading about the Civil War than conducting a war with the teacher.

Teachers of classes that include disturbed children need to be particularly skilled in group management. The capacity to establish a work orientation for the class as a whole that will provide psychological insulation is one of the most critical skills in a class that includes disturbed children. Jacob Kounin and his associates have found out that the same teachers are successful in managing both disturbed and normal students.

These teachers focus on the group and its learning activities, actively solicit feedback, concentrate on more than one thing at a time, and select the proper targets for their interventions. The high degree of involvement reduces negative contagion from the disturbed pupils and provides the needed reserve for the teacher to work out the marginal situations that develop.

The first questions a teacher needs to ask are, "How meaningful is the work to these pupils? Can they do it? Do I understand the various roles and relationships in the class well enough to be able to emphasize the things that will maintain stability instead of reacting in a haphazard way to everything that happens?"

The successful teacher knows how to use grouping itself as a tool.

1. Some classroom groups are particularly stable and constitute a reservoir of peer help for the distraught pupil; other groups have such a thin shell of control that one acting-out pupil means a breakdown. If most members of a class offer support, they can calm down a lot of misbehavior as well as serve as models of proper action.

2. Pupils whose behavior frightens their own age peers and makes them anxious may not bother slightly older children, so upgrouping a disturbed child may reduce negative group effects.

3. Sometimes the size of the group is important. Classes with several disturbed pupils should be smaller than others. In fairly large schools, three or four teachers of the same grade or course can arrange to have one small class for those who need it by making the other classes somewhat larger.

4. When a class needs relief from a pupil's disturbing antics, sending the offender to another class for a visit may be helpful. The teacher needs to make advance provisions for doing this. He also needs to know when to intervene in this way and to find out what the child does that makes his classmates anxious and angry.

Of course, any kind of exclusion must be used with extreme care. It would be ill-advised for a youngster who wanted out in the first place, or one who was so fearful as to be traumatized. Sometimes, however, planned exclusion can produce controls in a youngster.

Teachers need to develop skill in talking productively with children. They spend a great deal of time in verbal interaction with their students and, unfortunately, the typical verbal interplay is largely a waste. Fritz Redl has pioneered with what he calls "life-space interviewing," a technique that is particularly well suited to helping the teacher of disturbed children put an end to the undesirable behavior or at least to take steps in that direction.

The content of life-space interviewing focuses on the ego level and the behavior experience in the "life-space" shared by teacher and student. The technique provides an opportunity for diagnostic exploration, mild probing, and planning for the future on the basis of realistic appraisal. First the teacher asks the pupil for his perception of what happened, and then, step by step, examines what can be done to clarify reality. This leads to specific strategies which can serve to reduce recurrences. Of course, not all students will respond, but this style prevents moralizing on the one hand and passive acceptance on the other. The same principles can be used with groups for classroom problem solving.

Classroom problem solving brings up the concept of crisis intervention. Youngsters are most teachable at a time of conflict, when they are searching for a resolution. Being able to use the crisis at hand and knowing how to talk effectively to children are two skills basic to any classroom management of disturbed pupils. Behind this rests a new concept of acceptance. Psychological acceptance means responding to the student in order to facilitate his adopting more acceptable patterns of behavior. This may mean more strict enforcement of regulations, more listening to his concerns, or doing whatever is relevant to his self-concept and nature.

Three qualities seem to be critical in order for a teacher to develop the right interpersonal relationship with disturbed students: strength to stand testing without giving in or becoming hostile, a belief that the youngster can change (this eliminates the self-fulfilling prophesy of failure that many teachers imply, if only on the unconscious level), and a recognition that the classroom is a good place for helping youngsters. Of course, certain teachers seem to have natural talent with particular types of disturbed children. Definitive teachers, for example, are most successful with insurgent pupils, while a quiet teacher may get closer to frightened youngsters.

Disturbed children require an inordinate amount of teacher time, so there is never enough to go around. Several plans have been used to add teacher power. Frequently, children low in confidence and self-esteem benefit from one-to-one sessions, cause no disruptions during them, and focus on the task. Sometimes, with a mature class, a teacher can borrow a little special time for such students, but in most cases this is just not possible. Often the only feasible learning condition for them is a tutorial, manned by a community volunteer, a teacher aide, or an older student, with the teacher supervising and designing the lesson material.

Other means of stretching the busy teacher's time include the use of a self-tutoring device, task cards setting up individual projects, and prerecorded tapes with lessons and answers. A peer may serve as tutor-listener if proper pairing can be arranged.

Parents are a teacher's resource more often than we have believed. Programs for disturbed students, particularly the alienated ones, are reaching out to include the home. Rather than letting behavior difficulties continue to a point where a student must be excluded, the schools now, at an early stage of a difficulty, schedule conferences in which parents, student, teacher, and a mental health specialist participate. The assumption is that all parties really want to solve the difficulty, and the support of the home may be critical. When parents are hostile to the pupil, the hostility is less likely to provoke unfortunate behavior if the matter can be talked out and plans drawn up to meet the difficulties. While no punches are pulled, the issue is to teach the child what he *must* learn rather than revert to punitive handling.

Help may be needed outside the classroom. Here a "big brother" or "big sister" may be most important in providing not only reasonable recreation but identification as well. Assistance with homework, especially at the junior and senior high levels, may be the only road to survival.

A wise teacher keeps time flexible in planning for the disturbed youngster. Some children may be able to benefit from one hour of school but no longer. Some can make it through the morning but fall apart before the afternoon is under way.

Wise use of space is important. For example, some disturbed students benefit from having offices or study cubicles to reduce distraction. On the other hand, some need to see others and observe what is going on in order to feel less anxious.

The more flexible the concept of space in the teacher's mind, the more he can use this resource to serve the disturbed student. Dividing the room into work centers for various subgroups is one technique. Using the hall not as a punitive place but as a stimulus control may be appropriate. Some older youngsters can do their work better in the library, while others would roam the halls if not under surveillance.

Above all, the teacher and the school need to bear in mind that, for a disturbed child being able to escape temporarily from group pressures is often the key to survival. Each school should have a place and, if possible, a person for a disturbed child to go to at a time of crisis.

Even with the most able consultation and highly skilled teaching it may not be possible to help a child in the regular school setting, and unless he can be helped—not merely contained—in the classroom, he should not be there. The teacher's survival and the other children's welfare, as well as his own, are at stake.

For children who still fail to respond in the regular classroom after everything feasible has been done, the next step is the special class. Such classes provide relief for the whole school system and, generally speaking, they offer the disturbed pupils more individualized planning, with the result that pupil behavior and achievement improve. Some recent research, however, suggests that the improvement tends to disappear when the pupil returns to the mainstream. Indeed, the special class is far from being a panacea. It often helps least the unsocialized youngster, who needs so much, and sometimes it includes very disturbed children, even though the general consensus is that psychotic children need more help than a special class can give.

The special class falls short of the mark for other reasons. Frequently, special class curriculums do not include individual work and family contacts, although classroom work alone is usually not enough. Further, many public school teachers do not have the assistants they need to conduct a special class successfully.

And the special class bears a stigma. Students seldom see the value of being "special" and attitude is a critical part of the impact. Particularly at the secondary level, they resist being set apart. To adolescents, the stigma is so oppressive to their whole quest for a self (and a normal self) that it generates a great deal of friction. The stigma is strengthened because teachers and school administrations are seldom eager to welcome back a "cured" student. Nevertheless, special class provisions, if properly handled and staffed, are part of the sequence of support needed in every school program.

When all is said and done, most disturbed children are, and will continue to be, in the regular classroom, and, like it or not, classrooms and teaching will have to change if the schools are to fulfill their ever-increasing responsibility for the social and emotional development of children.

PART 7

Evaluating Pupils and Programs

Evaluation in education is frequently equated with measuring students' achievement. This is analogous to measuring the length and width of a table top and from the measurements determining that the table is oak or maple, that its craftsmanship is excellent or poor, that its style is provincial or contemporary, and that its appearance is appealing or harsh. Evaluation, in other words, is more than measurement just as appraising a table is more than finding its dimensions. Or stated in another way, measurement is a legitimate and necessary part of evaluation, but only a part.

Evaluation can be defined here as making judgments about the value of every phase of the school's program—from its goals to its program of studies to the learnings its students acquire. This is no easy task in terms of the insight and skills needed to do it well. But it is a task absolutely essential to the maintenance and improvement of quality education.

The first article in this part illustrates well how one evaluative tool, tests, can assist the teacher in improving his own instructional program. In the article, Dyer points out that the teaching-learning process is a continuous experiment that can be successful only if appropriate feedback is obtained. Basically, feedback enables the teacher to keep readings on his students much as a thermostat keeps readings on a room's temperature. The more feedback the teacher has, and the better it is, the better chance he'll have to structure appropriate learning situations. Tests, obviously, provide the teacher with one means of obtaining feedback. They are not, Dyer emphasizes, peripheral to the instructional process—something to be done after the fact; rather, they are central to the process—something to be done before additional steps can be taken.

In the second article, Ebel takes a critical look at five of the concerns many have about the growing use of objective tests. He lists these concerns as the inadequacy of tests for evaluating attitudes and values, the often ambiguous nature of test items, the negative influence of tests on teaching, the pressure of testing on students, and the harmful social and psychological consequences of intelligence and aptitude testing. Ebel admits that each of these concerns has an element of justification. But he argues that the alternative, to discontinue or cut back the use of objective tests, would be professionally irresponsible.

Allen, in the third article, describes how knowledge that is gained from evaluation can be used in two different ways. Knowledge can be used externally to determine how well the school's objectives are being met and to enable teachers to communicate with others about students' progress. And it can be used internally to give students the kind of feedback they need for self-evaluation. Allen contends that both types of evaluative information are legitimate, but that the latter is probably needed more and, to date, is less effectively gathered.

Most educators agree that the traditional marking system, which depends largely on comparing the performance of each student with the others in his class, is pregnant with flaws. And yet to abolish all school marks at this time would be virtually impossible. As an alternative to the norm-referenced mark, Trow in the fourth article proposes that educators use a mark or score that "is a point along a continuum of subject-matter knowledge or skill that indicates the degree of proficiency achieved by an individual without reference to anyone else." [1] This type of mark, which Trow calls criterion-referenced, would have several immediate advantages. Not the least of these is that it would enable the student over a period of time to judge, in absolute rather than relative terms, the progress he is making in any given area. In addition, Trow's proposal would seem to be consistent with education's goal of fostering self-evaluation.

The traditional marking system Trow refers to as norm-referenced, along with the graded pattern of classroom organization,

[1] William Clark Trow, "On Marks, Norms, and Proficiency Scores," *Phi Delta Kappan*, XLVII (December 1966), 172. (Article included in this book.)

has been a chief contributor to the perennial dilemma faced by all but a few teachers—that of whether to promote or to retain the student who is achieving below par. Mouly, in the fifth article, points out that three reasons are generally given as justification for failing a student. The first is that failure or the threat of it will motivate him; the second is that by failing him classroom standards will be maintained; and the third is that the nonpromoted student will do better academically in succeeding years. None of these reasons, according to Mouly, is tenable. Because of this, and also because of the psychosocial consequences of failure, it would seem that the decision not to promote a student must be made very, very cautiously.

National Assessment, a long-range project aimed at measuring the nationwide effectiveness of educational programs, is the subject of Moellenberg's article. At the time it was written, the decision to begin the assessment had not yet been made. But at the time of this writing, the first year's assessment had been done; and by the time these words are published, the first three-year cycle will have been completed. Moellenberg's analysis of National Assessment, however, remains current, for much of it centers around the potential abuses that could be made of the results of the assessment. This is no small problem, but one that Moellenberg believes the concerted efforts of the profession can resolve.

In the final article in the section, Frymier contends that as a social system education has a serious conceptual flaw because there is no systematized, discrete mechanism within education for generating evaluative data. Because there is no systematic mechanism, the schools cannot depend regularly on evaluation for corrective feedback. And because there is no discrete mechanism, those same people who set the policies, design the programs, and carry out the instruction end up evaluating their own efforts. These two conditions, Frymier points out, prevent the schools from utilizing the real power inherent in evaluation for upgrading the quality of their programs. Ultimately, basic structural changes in the educational system will have to be made if that power is to be fully employed.

Needed Changes to Sweeten the Impact of Testing

HENRY S. DYER

There are no doubt a good many things that can and should be done to promote right thinking and proper conduct among the users of tests. This paper considers two approaches that might be helpful. The first has to do with getting people to look behind the numbers commonly associated with tests, and the second with getting them to see tests as an integral part of the educational process.

To suggest that it is important to get behind the numbers is to suggest that the kind of pupil performance a test score stands for runs the risk of being lost from sight under the statistical superstructure of scales and norms and other interpretive data that get erected upon it. This is not to say that the superstructure is unnecessary or that a firm grip on the meaning of the numbers can be dispensed with in trying to understand students or in trying to get them to understand themselves. On the contrary, the art of statistical thinking and careful inference is absolutely fundamental to the proper use of test results, and the neglect of this art or the failure to exercise it constitutes a serious failure of professional responsibility.

But a thoroughgoing awareness of the probabilistic nature of the numbers that go with tests is not in itself sufficient for obtaining a full sense of what they mean. A test score, however expressed, points in two directions at once. Through norms, scales, contingency tables, and the like, it points *outward* to populations with which the student may be compared and to situations in which the level of his performance may be predicted or estimated. But a score also points *inward* to the processes that lie behind it, that is, to the specific mental operations that have generated the score. In the practical application of tests, the pragmatic tradition, which has had

Reprinted from *The Personnel and Guidance Journal*, 45 (8): 776–780 (April 1967), by permission of author and publisher. Copyright © 1967 by the American Personnel and Guidance Association.

such a strong effect on educational developments of all kinds in this country, has led to a neglect of the meaning to be derived from that aspect of a test score that points inward. We have been so concerned with using test scores to classify students in one way or another or to predict how they will make out, academically or otherwise, that we have, I think, paid far too little attention to the details of behavior that a test score presumably summarizes.

This is particularly true in the case of tests of general intelligence. Piaget (1963, pp. 153–154), referring to Binet's work, has called attention to the problem in these words:

> It is indisputable that these tests of mental age have on the whole lived up to what was expected of them: a rapid and convenient estimation of an individual's general level. But it is no less obvious that they simply measure a "yield" without reaching constructive operations themselves. . . . Intelligence conceived in these terms [i.e., in mental age terms] is essentially a value-judgment applied to complex behavior.

To put it another way, the normative score—that is, the single number that we call a mental age—may be a quick and easy way of seeing how a child's test performance compares with that of other children, but, in itself, it tells nothing at all about the nature of the performance on which the children are being compared.

This kind of blind comparison, with its implication of a value judgment, has had much to do with making test scores unpleasant to many recipients. It slaps a label on a child and leaves him and his parents with the impression that there is nothing that he or his teachers can do about it. It regards mental age—or worse still, the IQ—as an unmodifiable *condition* of achievement rather than as a "yield" of the educational process that can itself be affected, in part at least, by what happens in the classroom. It overlooks the fact that, if the school is to be something more than a device for sorting pupils into convenient categories, it must take some part of the responsibility for developing pupils' intelligence, instead of relying on the genes and the accidents of the environment to do the whole job. If it is to assume this responsibility, it will have to go behind the numbers on tests to try to understand in detail *how* pupils are thinking and *what* in detail might be done to help them think better.

We speak glibly of "abstract thinking," but we too rarely look at how children handle the specific tasks on tests so as to get a feeling for the actual mental operations that are involved in their thinking. A small study by Connolly and Wantman (1964) has demonstrated not only how one can get behind the numbers, but also what a wealth of information can be found there. They simply asked students to talk their thoughts into a tape recorder while reasoning their way through items on an aptitude test. They show that playbacks of the material can be assigned with reasonably good reliability to descriptive categories of mental behavior that can do much to give a student's score substantive meaning.

THE PERCEPTION OF TESTING AS PART OF THE EDUCATIONAL PROCESS

If a school is to perceive itself as engaged in educating pupils, and not just housing them while they grow up, it needs to acquire the view that testing taken in the broadest sense, is indispensable to teaching. For years we have been giving lip service to the notion that testing is an "integral part of the educational process," but in fact a considerable part of the testing that goes on in schools is divorced from teaching. It has become a part of the mystique of the school psychologist and the guidance counselor, and usually yields only incidental information for use in the actual management of instruction. This may explain why many teachers perceive standardized tests as either threatening or irrelevant.

What is needed is some sort of conceptual model of the teaching-learning process that puts testing right in the middle of that process. The model proposed is based on a conception of education as a comprehensive system of control and communication in which those responsible for instructing and guiding the pupil—teachers, counselors, administrators—are provided with a continuous flow of information about the needs of students, the relevant factors in their life situations that affect their development, and the day-to-day effects of the educational program on their growth as persons and as citizens. The kind of control system implied is an extension to education of the system of control and communication in animals and machines that Norbert Wiener (1948) described 19 years ago in *Cybernetics*. In that revolutionary book, Wiener brought into general usage the notion of *feedback*. Testing can be usefully thought of as the means for providing feedback in the process of instruction.

Wiener cites the ordinary thermostat as a simple example of a control device that supplies self-correcting feedback. When the temperature of a room drops, the thermostat flashes a signal to the heater to get going; when the temperature rises to a certain level, the thermostat tells the heater to cease firing. Education does not have communication and control devices as efficient and as dependable as a thermostat. And the reason is obvious: educational systems are a billion times more complicated than heating systems. In a heating system the controls can be automatic and mechanical; in an educational system the controls must be largely voluntary and must depend upon frequent and intelligent human intervention. The feedback required to keep a heater responsive to the needs of a household is of one kind only—temperature readings. The kinds of feedback needed to keep an educational system responsive to the needs of the learner are practically infinite: they include readings on the hopes, aspirations, frustrations, fears, physical condition, attitudes, values, interests, skills, abilities, past accomplishments, and current levels of achievement of every student a teacher faces in his classes. They should provide usable information on how all of these qualities, traits, characteristics, and behavior tendencies are changing from moment to moment, from hour to hour, from week to week, and from year to year. They should tell how students are interacting with each other, with their teachers, and with the materials of instruction, so as to make possible reasonably dependable inferences about what procedures and what materials are producing what kinds of effects on what kinds of youngsters. They should tell what is happening in the home and elsewhere that may be facilitating or impeding the student's development as a person and as a functioning member of society.

Of course, such complex varieties of feedback are not now available and are unlikely to be available for a long time to come, if ever. Testing (and its first cousin, programmed instruction) is still a couple of light years away from the instrumentation necessary to furnish the kinds of feedback required to keep the educational process fully effective at all times for all pupils. As a systems analyst would say, it is scarcely sufficiently refined to "close the feedback loop" in all particulars. But the inadequacy of tests is hardly an argument for their abandonment as tools of teaching, as some of the critics of testing seem to imply. It is an argument, rather, for extracting all the information there is in the instruments available and supplementing as best one can by looking and listening for any clues to be had about what is going on "out there" in the minds of students.

This conception of testing as part of a communication and control system is shown schematically in the chart labeled "Testing in the Educational Process" (Figure 1). The chart attempts to show how tests can or should function in any kind of instructional system, whether one conceives of such a "system" as the total collection of activities that constitute the school system of an entire state, or as the collection of activities that go on in a single classroom, or as something between the two.

The model has five elements: I for the instructor, S for the student, E for the student's environment, F for the feedback, and t for points in time. The student environment (E) is between the horizontal lines. It is not to be thought of as static, but as a continuous stream of events impinging on the life and growth of the student, changing as he changes during the course of time. The four boxes labeled S stand for a single student at successive points in time. The four boxes labeled I may represent a single instructor or a succession of different instructors, depending on how long the time intervals happen to be and on how the educational program may be organized. If the interval between t_1 and t_2 is 10 minutes, say, then presumably the instructor at both points is one and the same person who is getting the feedback (F) from his own efforts with the student. If the interval between t_3 and t_4 is two years, then the instructor in the first instance may be a high school teacher and the instructor in the second instance a college teacher, in which case the feedback is the possible information link that, it is hoped, will prevent the student from becoming a lost soul as he crosses the Great Divide between high school and college.

The arrows pointing from the instructor to the student are meant to

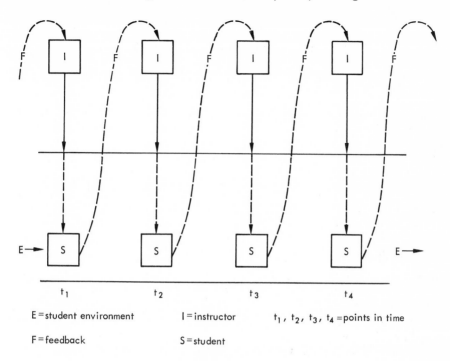

E = student environment   I = instructor t_1, t_2, t_3, t_4 = points in time

F = feedback   S = student

Figure 1. Testing in the educational process

suggest that the essence of instruction consists in manipulating the environment so as to provide the student with maturing experiences. This is to say
that the most any instructor can do is to try to create the appropriate conditions for learning and then hope that something favorable will happen to
the student as a consequence.

Whether the hope is fulfilled depends, of course, on whether the instructor hits upon the *right* conditions for each student. This in turn depends
on two things: (1) the quality of the information about each student that
a teacher has to start with—that is, the information supplied by the feedback
from a previous occasion, and (2) the validity of the hypothesis that the
instructor develops in light of this information about what will work and
what will not work to produce learning. According to this scheme of things
the teaching-learning process is a continuous experiment. Its effectiveness
is conditioned absolutely by the amount and quality of the feedback available for generating and checking hypotheses about what to do next. In other
words, good teaching depends on good testing.

There is nothing really new about this conception. As far back as 1895
John Dewey was preaching it (McLellan & Dewey, 1895). In his words:

> Education is precisely the work of supplying the conditions which will enable
> the psychical functions, as they successively arise, to mature and pass into
> higher functions in the freest and fullest manner, and this result can be secured
> only by knowledge of the process. . . .

CONCLUSION

The primary task of those of us who are persuaded of the ancient truth that good testing really is essential to good teaching is to get others to see it in the same light, for the impact of testing on education is a function of the perceptions of the consumers of tests. If tests are perceived as peripheral to the educational process, their impact will be peripheral. If they are perceived as devices for putting constraints on the curriculum, they will indeed put constraints on the curriculum. If they are perceived as instruments for sorting children into ironbound categories, they will be used for that purpose. But if they are perceived as supplying basic data needed for helping children learn to cope more and more effectively with the world into which they are growing, then they will be used to provide that kind of help.

At present there is a certain woodenness about the use of test results that fails to take account of the fact that scores can point inward as well as outward. The main problem seems not to be that tests are having a bad impact on education, but that they are having *insufficient* impact.

What are the chances that this deficiency can be overcome? Perhaps the answer can be found in the history of testing. It has taken just about 50 years for standardized tests to win general acceptance as aids in assessing and predicting academic performance. If one holds with the late Paul Mort's 50–50 theory concerning the diffusion of new ideas about education (Mort, 1964), it will take another 50 years before the full possibilities of testing will be brought to bear as an aid in the educational process. These possibilities will be realized only as more and more people work at the notion that the use of tests as predictors is not enough, that tests have a very large role to play in helping us to see the student's mind in action *here and now* so that we can help him upset the predictions. On this point, the advice of Alfred North Whitehead in his famous essay on the aims of education (1949, p. 18) is still good:

> The mind is never passive; it is a perpetual activity, delicate, receptive, responsive to stimulus. You cannot postpone its life until you have sharpened it. Whatever interest attaches to your subject matter must be evoked here and now; whatever powers you are strengthening in the pupil, must be exercised here and now; whatever possibilities of mental life your teaching should impart, must be exhibited here and now. That is the golden rule of education, and a very difficult rule to follow.

The right use of tests should help make the rule a little easier to follow and thereby sweeten their impact on the school and the community.

REFERENCES

Connolly, J. A., & Wantman, M. J. An exploration of oral reasoning processes in responding to objective test items. *Journal of Educational Measurement*, 1964, *1*(1), 59–64.

McLellan, J. A., & Dewey, J. *The psychology of number and its applications to methods of teaching arithmetic.* New York: D. Appleton, 1895.

Mort, P. Studies in educational innovation from the Institute of Administrative Research. In M. B. Miles (Ed.), *Innovation in education.* New York: Bureau of Publications, Teachers College, Columbia Univ., 1964. P. 318.

Piaget, J. *Psychology of intelligence.* Paterson, N. J.: Littlefield, Adams, 1963.

Whitehead, A. N. *The aims of education and other essays.* New York: New American Library, Mentor Books Edition, 1949.

Wiener, N. *Cybernetics, or control and communication in the animal and the machine.* Cambridge, Mass.: MIT Press, 1948.

Prospects for Evaluation of Learning

ROBERT L. EBEL

What of the prospects for educational evaluation? Will present practices and trends continue or will they be reversed? Will current issues and problems continue to perplex us or will they be resolved?

The long history of education suggests some answers. It is safe to predict that changes will come in evaluation as in other aspects of education. But it is also safe to predict that the enduring changes are more likely to evolve slowly than to explode suddenly. There will be no dearth of revolutionary suggestions, but few of them will be put to the test of extensive practical application. And of these, few will enjoy more than temporary popularity. Those who proclaim that current educational practices are incredibly wrong-headed may be applauded even by teachers, but they are unlikely to initiate many enduring advances in education.

That these things are so, as I believe they are, should not be deplored or blamed on the stubborn conservatism of teachers. Rather they should be accepted as convincing evidence that embodied in current educational practices is a great deal of practical wisdom, accumulated over a great many years from the experiences of a great many good teachers. A new idea today must be very good indeed to be better than the hosts of good ideas that have preceded it. It is not surprising that few of today's new ideas make the grade. It is not surprising that significant changes come slowly.

But changes do come. The changing social scene brings changes in educational emphases. Developing techniques bring change in the process of evaluation. Let us survey three of the changes that have been occurring or seem likely to occur in response to social and technological changes.

A. Increased emphasis on education and its evaluation

Reprinted from *The Bulletin of the National Association of Secondary School Principals,* 52 (332): 32–42 (December 1968), by permission of author and publisher.

B. Development of versatile test scoring devices
C. Misgivings about the adequacy of some present tests and testing programs.

A. EMPHASIS ON EDUCATION AND ITS EVALUATION

Our descendants may look back on the decades following World War II as the golden age of education. Never before had it been valued more highly. Never before had so much of it been made available so easily to so many. Never before had it been supported so generously. Never before had so much been expected of it.

Many aspects of this emphasis on education have led to increased emphasis on evaluation. The rush of students to college, in numbers far greater than most good colleges could accommodate effectively, has led to the enormous expansion of college admissions testing programs. The flow of dollars to support the education of students who are able but not affluent has led to the development of various scholarship testing programs.

Although it is unlikely (indeed it is demographically impossible) that participation in these programs will grow as rapidly in the future as it has in the recent past, there is no good reason to anticipate that it will decline substantially. The needs these programs have served will remain to be served, and no better alternative seems likely to develop. But we can hope, and we ought to expect, that tests will improve and that test results will be used with increasing wisdom.

Another aspect of the emphasis on education in recent years has been concern for quality in education and for equality of educational opportunity. These have led in turn to greatly increased expenditures for education, and to increasing federal involvement in education. All of these developments lead, sooner or later, to recognition of the need for valid and reliable assessments of the result of our educational efforts. How much of what are our children learning? How wide is the gap between slum and suburb in educational attainment? Are the extra dollars we spend today yielding better educational results? Where do the greatest needs exist for federal support to local educational efforts?

Although the standardized tests given in many schools and the state-wide testing programs conducted in some states provide partial answers to the first of these questions, the others call for more specific efforts on a broader scale. Explorations of the feasibility of a national assessment of educational progress that have been conducted recently represent attempts to meet these needs.

As state support of local educational efforts has increased in recent years there has been increasing interest among state legislators and administrators in obtaining evidence supporting and justifying these increased expenditures. This has resulted in numerous proposals and several enactments relating to mandatory testing and reporting of test results in the public schools.

There is no reason to suppose that any of these motivations for increased testing of educational attainments is likely to diminish or disappear in the years ahead. On the contrary it seems likely that they will spread and grow. Few if any of us would wish to see public interest in education or public support of education diminish. But if that interest and support remain strong, then support of efforts to evaluate the outcomes of education is also likely to remain strong.

B. High Speed Test Scoring Machines

The growth of wide-scale programs for testing educational achievement, and for college admission and scholarship testing, have led to the development of high speed, high capacity, highly automatic machines for scoring objective tests. Typically these machines translate marks on an answer sheet into electronic impulses which are then fed into a computer, to be evaluated, converted, analyzed, and reported. Other test scoring machines, smaller, cheaper, and less complex in structure or function, have been designed to lighten the test scoring burdens of the classroom teacher.

The development of these diverse and versatile test scoring devices represents the major technological advance in the evaluation of learning since 1950. While it does not seem reasonable to expect an indefinite continuation of the recent rapid pace of development of scoring devices, it is reasonable to suppose that the years ahead will see rapid growth in the utilization of such devices. Their influence on education in the years ahead may be far greater than it has been during the years of their development.

C. Misgivings About Educational Testing

So educational testing has grown in response to growing concern for education. So too the technology of testing, at least in so far as it is reflected in test scoring devices, has developed in response to growing demands for testing. But there are those who believe that all is not well with the evaluation of learning today, despite the current popularity of objective tests and mass testing programs. Among the concerns they have expressed are these:

> That the tests currently used to evaluate learning are inadequate to the task, measuring only imperfectly the less important educational outcomes.
>
> That objective tests are spuriously attractive because of the ease with which they can be scored en masse, but are seriously deficient as tools for the evaluation of learning because of their inherent ambiguities, their tendency to emphasize superficial factual information, and their reward of successful guessing.
>
> That wide-scale testing programs and the use of standardized tests place teachers in curricular straitjackets, preventing them from meeting local needs or making use of unique local opportunities, suppressing their creative ideas and their individualities as teachers, and rewarding routine, mechanical teaching.

That testing places students under undue pressure and exposes them to unnecessary experiences of failure, diminishing their confidence in themselves and destroying the natural joy of learning.

That testing, particularly intelligence and aptitude testing, leads to the labeling of particular pupils as bright or dull, in both cases adversely affecting their expectations, their efforts and their whole self-concepts; denying and thus tending to destroy the almost infinite potential for development that is inherent in every human being.

Concerns such as these are expressed most often, not by the enemies of education, but by its friends; not by outsiders but by members of the educational profession itself. Some have been expressed, or supported, even by those whose specialty is the evaluation of learning. I propose to take a closer look at five of these concerns.

1. The Adequacy of Tests for Evaluation

One's opinion of the adequacy of current tests for the evaluation of learning is likely to depend largely upon his notions concerning the task of the schools. If his ideas of what the schools ought to be doing coincides with what most schools spend most of their time trying to do, that is, to help students gain command of useful verbal information, then he is not likely to consider tests, which require a student to demonstrate his command of useful verbal information, as intrinsically inadequate.

The extensive involvement of most schools in verbal information is easy to illustrate. The subject matter of most studies—history, literature, science, geography, even mathematics (if its symbols are regarded as essentially verbal symbols)—is verbal information. What gets communicated between teacher and pupils is also largely verbal information. If verbal information is extracted from formal education there is very little if anything left.

But many educators are unwilling to admit that their aims are so prosaic, so limited (?), so attainable (!). They prefer to claim objectives that are more spiritual than material—vast, indefinite and hence largely immeasurable. We can not deny their right to such a preference. But we can point out the difficulty they have in demonstrating that the pursuit of such objectives is a good way to spend the taxpayers' money. And we can assert that, so far as anyone knows for sure, the peculiar excellence of man is his ability to produce, to communicate, to store, and to use verbal knowledge.

Are we saying that verbal knowledge is all that matters where man is concerned? Certainly not. How a man feels is always more important *to him* than what he knows. How he behaves (i.e., the ethical and social choices he makes) is often more important *to others* than what he knows. For some men (e.g., bricklayers or violinists) non-verbal skills may be more important than those that are verbal. But verbal knowledge is relevant, often highly relevant, to all of these other "goods."

While schools can not afford to ignore muscular skills, or attitudes, or values, or character, or overt behavior, neither can schools afford to give any of these things priority over command of knowledge in specifying its mission. And if it should choose to give other things priority, it will almost certainly find that cultivation of command of useful knowledge is the best, if not the only, means it can use to attain the ends it seeks.

If this is true about man and about the process of educating him, tests can do much of the job of evaluating learning. In the years ahead they are likely to do more of it than they have done in the past. This is not to say that current tests leave nothing to be desired. None is flawless, and some are quite imperfect. They reflect our own imperfections as teachers and as testers, the inadequacies of our perceptions of what knowledge is likely to be of most use, and our lack of skill in testing precisely and meaningfully the degree of a student's command of that knowledge. Many tests in current use are inadequate, but the faults lie less in the direction they point than in the distance they travel.

2. The Usefulness of Objective Tests

One of the attractive features of the objective test form is the ease with which it can be scored. But there are others also, such as definiteness in scoring and extensiveness in sampling various aspects of achievement. The scorer of an objective test indicates unequivocally which answer he considered correct to each question. Each student's performance is judged against the same standard. Thus an objective test score is likely to be fairer to the students than an essay test score. Because more questions are asked in the usual objective test than in the usual essay test, a more extensive sample of the student's command of knowledge is obtained. Both fairness in scoring and extensiveness in sampling operate to make objective test scores typically more reliable than essay test scores.

But what of the charges of superficiality, ambiguity, and guess-work that critics lay against objective tests? That test questions, either in objective or essay form, are sometimes trivial and superficial is beyond dispute. But that objective test questions can probe the student's command of essential ideas and his ability to use these ideas to solve complex problems and make important decisions is also beyond dispute. If an objective test question is trivial, the fault lies less in the form than in the content of the question.

Yet it is surely the case that objective test questions appear to be trivial more often than do essay test questions. This is due in part to the fact that an objective test ordinarily includes many more questions than an essay test. If a test can include only a few questions the tendency is to make each one general and comprehensive. If it can include many, the tendency is to make each question more narrowly specific.

Objective test questions also tend to be more "factual" than essay test questions because it is easier to defend one particular answer as the correct answer if the question is factual than if it involves inference, explanation, problem-solving or prediction. But it is important to remember that a fact in this sense is a verifiable truth, which need not be trivial. There are a great many important facts, such as universal gravitation, and $e = mc^2$.

Indeed, if a subject for study in school or college is not loaded with important factual truths of these kinds, the value of studying it would seem open to serious question.

Yet another reason why objective test items are sometimes thought to be superficial is that answers to them apparently could be learned by rote, without real understanding. And so they could, but for a number of reasons they seldom are so learned. For one thing, it is always possible to pose questions on an objective test that the examinee has never encountered before, and thus to require answers from him that he could not possibly have learned by rote. For another, rote learning is a difficult, ineffective, and unsatisfying method of learning most things that students study. The student who has difficulty in understanding a subject is unlikely to find rote learning an attractive or effective alternative.

That test questions, either in objective or essay form, are sometimes ambiguous is also beyond dispute. Indeed, the separateness of human beings, the uniqueness of their experiences, and the indefiniteness of language make the total elimination of ambiguity in human communication impossible. Ambiguity hampers our teaching as well as our testing. We need always to seek to avoid it or to minimize it. With reasonable skill and care in test construction it can be reduced to the point where it no longer interferes seriously with the evaluation of learning.

Like ambiguity, guessing is more of a bogey than a genuine menace in the use of objective tests. Well-motivated students do very little blind guessing on tests that are appropriate for them. The correctness of their informed guesses is related substantially to the amount of relevant information they command. Thus their "guesses" provide valid indications of achievement. A student who does a great deal of blind guessing is likely to get a very low score on a good test. For all these reasons, the influence of guessing on objective test scores is far less than it is commonly assumed to be.

Finally, the effects of both ambiguity and guessing is to make test scores unreliable—that is, to make repeated measurements yield inconsistent results. If a test constructor succeeds in building a test that yields reliable scores, and many objective tests do yield reliable scores, it is safe to conclude that supposed defects related to ambiguity and guessing were not serious on those tests.

Thus despite the criticism of objective tests, it seems likely that their popularity will continue to grow. The supposed deficiencies of these tests are not inherent in the form, and do not seriously detract from their value. With growing recognition of the fairness and dependability of objective tests, and with growing skill in using them, their popularity is likely to grow also.

3. The Influence of Tests on Teaching

If students and teachers know in advance that a particular kind of test is going to be used to evaluate learning, they will almost certainly be influenced in what they study and what they teach by what they expect the test to require of them. Students are seldom likely to know, and usually ought not to know, the precise questions they will be asked. But if students and teachers know the general nature of the questions to be asked and the general areas of content to be covered, they will direct their study and teaching toward these kinds of capability.

If the tests that exert this kind of influence of teaching and learning are good tests, with appropriate curricular coverage and emphasis, and if they are not the sole basis for the evaluation of learning, they are likely to do much more good than harm. Those who warn against such influence seldom do so on the ground that every teacher ought be free to teach whatever he chooses. What concerns them most is their belief that the wrong people —i.e., the testmakers—are exerting the influence. But who are the testmakers? In most cases they are master teachers. In most cases what their tests aim to cover is what is currently being taught in good schools. In most cases the tests they build aim to follow rather than to lead curricular innovations.

The teachers most likely to behave as if the testmakers have placed them in a curricular straitjacket are the teachers who are least secure in their positions because they are least competent. It is these who are most likely to make the review of old tests or similar current tests a major part of their instructional program.

External tests have been influencing what is taught in particular classrooms for nearly 40 years. Can anyone honestly claim that as a result we now have too much uniformity among various classrooms in what is being taught? Or is it not true, in view of the increasing mobility of our people, that a considerably greater degree of uniformity could be tolerated?

The influence of tests on teaching is likely to continue in future years. If it develops along the paths that it has followed in the past it is likely to continue to be an educational asset.

4. The Pressure of Testing on Students

What of the pressure tests allegedly put on students? What of the feelings of inadequacy and of failure they may engender? In considering these questions, it may be helpful to remember that test scores themselves neither reward nor punish, neither praise nor blame. They simply report levels of achievement. If the reports are sometimes disappointing the blame may rest on ineffective learning (or teaching). Or it may rest on unrealistic, over-ambitious expectations. It is not the measure of achievement but the aspiration to achievement that places students under pressure. It is not the steam gauge that causes the boiler to explode.

The evidence supporting a belief that the typical student today operates under too much pressure for his own good is by no means clear. No doubt some students do feel too much pressure to achieve. No doubt others feel too little. But the suggestion that the way to deal with cases of excess pressure is to stop paying so much attention to achievement makes very little educational sense. Instead we need to pay more attention to the setting of realistic goals, and to the recognition of individual differences in interests, abilities, and avenues for self-fulfillment. We have made progress in this direction in the past. We have reason to expect that in the hands of reasonable educators, the progress will continue.

5. *The Consequences of Intelligence and Aptitude Testing*

Consider finally the belief that the social and psychological consequences of intelligence and aptitude testing are harmful. In some hands they undoubtedly have been harmful. Too many educators have accepted a child's IQ as the major determinant of his educational potential. Although the items in most intelligence and aptitude tests are clearly measures of developed ability, too many educators have been willing to believe that they provided direct and dependable measures of his innate capacity for learning. On too many occasions a child's low IQ score has been used to explain his failure to learn instead of being used to help him to learn.

But intelligence and aptitude tests have sometimes been interpreted properly and used constructively. It is hard to beat a good intelligence test as a convenient measure of a young child's general educational development. Since all learning builds on prior learning, effective teaching requires information on each child's level of educational development.

While some school systems have abandoned the use of intelligence tests because of serious abuses of them and because of local political pressures, and while other school systems may follow their lead in the years ahead, it is not likely that intelligence testing will disappear. We can hope and expect, however, that intelligence and aptitude tests will be interpreted more realistically and used more constructively.

PROSPECTS, PREDICTIONS, AND PROGRESS

These are some of the prospects we see for the evaluation of learning. Teachers are likely to continue to do it, for to teach without testing is unthinkable. They are likely to do more of it, and to do it better as they become more skilled in the techniques of their craft. Above all they are likely to use the results of testing more wisely and more constructively.

These forecasts are not made with the assurance of certain expectation. The freedom men have to mold their own destinies, as well as the limitations of any man's wisdom, preclude certainty in the prediction of human developments. These predictions reflect a mixture of what we expect and what we hope. If they are desirable, we can work to make them come true. . . .

The Student Evaluation Dilemma

PAUL M. ALLEN

Evaluation is inevitable. It is also exasperating, frustrating, and extremely humbling.

Nearly every teacher has, at some time, experienced a painful twinge of guilt as he has sneaked into the classroom clutching an examination made in haste the night before. Many teachers have been bewildered by the maze of percentile ranks, stanines, and Z scores they find carefully recorded in students' files. And what teacher, sitting down to make out report cards, has not cried out for an escape from the seasonal task of playing god?

Probably two factors explain why evaluation, which is so completely a part of a teacher's daily life, is frustrating or exasperating. First, the teachers find themselves in the center of an intellectual tug-of-war. And, second, the existing evaluation programs require teachers to play a role that they either don't understand or can't accept.

For the last 15 to 20 years, behavioral scientists and other educational pundits have been choosing sides and bombarding teachers with apparently conflicting truths. Stimulus-response associationists and operant conditioners trade theories and insults with perceptual and field psychologists. The stimulus-response associationists and the operant conditioners claim that behavior can best be explained by a concept of *external causation*. Perceptual and field psychologists, in contrast, espouse a theory of human behavior that might be called *internal causation*. And in between stands the teacher.

In addition, the day-by-day evaluation activities required of the teacher can't help but cause consternation. He is required to sit in judgment on others, even though he realizes that his knowledge about them is fragmentary—probably a close approximation at its best and downright nonsense at its worst. Teachers recognize the potential inaccuracies and frailties of grades and yet they find too many administrators, parents, and students accepting grades as gospel. Testing programs and courses of study require them to do things *to* students, yet they are supposed to teach in such a way that students will become self-realizing, self-actualizing individuals.

Teachers are confronted with a dilemma—a dilemma made up of apparently conflicting theories of human behavior and apparently conflicting demands on a teacher's daily activities. For better understanding, it is necessary to examine this dilemma more completely.

The first of two apparently conflicting explanations of human behavior has been called *the theory of external causation*. To put it over-simply,

Reprinted from *Today's Education, NEA Journal,* 58 (2): 48–50 (February 1969), by permission of author and publisher.

people who subscribe to this theory believe that human behavior is simply a kind of observable human movement and that environment consists of all of the individual's physical and social surroundings.

The basic premises underlying the concept of external causation are:

1. Man's behavior is initiated by external forces. For example: A student would say, "The *teacher made* me study," or "My *sister made* me angry."

2. Man *reacts* to external forces and consequently his form and function are the results of environmental influences. Man is a passive receiver of stimuli. When he receives a stimulus, he reacts in accordance with the conditioned or innate reflexes it calls into play.

3. The environment is judged good or bad depending on the resultant behavior. The slum environment that produced a medical researcher could be judged "good." The slum environment that produced a criminal would be classified as "bad."

Using this theory as a basis for evaluation, what a man does can be measured against external criteria. Even more important, his behavior can be changed by manipulating his environment, and the success of this manipulation can be judged by measuring the resultant behavior.

Most traditional programs of evaluation stand foursquare in the camp of external causation. The basis of nearly every evaluation plan since 1850 has been a program of testing and measuring. We are told that the test data are important—that with complete knowledge about a student, it is possible to predict how he will behave in every possible situation. As a result, the educators observe, measure, record, and predict. They plan and administer programs of standardized testing. They carefully record in grade books students' scores on teacher-made tests and collect written observations of student behavior in cumulative records. In short, the entire evaluation program is other-person-oriented.

Of course, such information is important. It is necessary in order to discover if valued educational objectives are being reached. This kind of feedback is essential for curriculum development and educational policy making. And finally these data are needed for the record keeping that enables teachers to write letters of recommendation and administrators to send transcripts to future employers and university placement offices. More significantly, these records enable educators to communicate, with some understanding, about students' achievements.

Appearing to be in complete contrast with the concepts just examined is *the theory of internal causation.* People who accept this theory believe that an individual's environment is psychological and consists of what he perceives it to be and not what others describe it to be. Behavior then becomes psychological movement and may or may not be observable.

The basic premises underlying this theory of human behavior are:

1. Man's behavior is initiated internally. For example: A student might say, "The teacher didn't make me study; *I decided* it was a good idea," or "My sister was reading my book and now *I am* angry."

2. Man *interacts* with his environment rather than reacting to it. Behavior is not a matter of a simple stimulus-response; rather it is a state of the total organism. This concept of interaction implies a relationship between an individual and his environment in which he interprets and uses his environment for his chosen purposes.

3. Environment is neither good nor bad. Each person's environment is unique, for it is basically what he perceives it to be. Environment can be a vast dynamic vista of opportunity with which each individual interacts in a unique way.

According to the theory of internal causation, change in man's behavior is self-initiated. Evaluation then would turn toward an inner state of being and the criteria would become personal. An individual's feelings and attitudes would probably be used in the process of making judgments.

Few, if any, existing programs of evaluation are consistent with the theory of internal causation. This theory implies that the primary purpose of evaluation is self-evaluation—for both students and teachers. The process of self-evaluation would provide the feedback to enable the individual to make the changes necessary to keep him on the track toward his chosen goals.

Since change is initiated from within, only the individual can change his behavior. But to change his behavior, he needs the objective data of his own learning. If these data are made available to each individual in a nonthreatening manner, he can compare his action with his intent and his results with his objectives. By this process, he can discover not only the existing gaps in his mastery and understanding but also the personal meaning of his learning.

Self-evaluation has not yet gained acceptance as the most fundamental, the most important outcome of evaluation programs. Even assuming that the importance of this outcome were accepted, the knowledge is not yet available on just how to gather the data that would have pertinence to each individual—or on how to make it available to students and teachers in a nonthreatening manner. The point is not whether self-evaluation should occur, for it is occurring every moment of every day. The point is—what data gathered in what way should be made available? Even more basic— should self-evaluation become the fundamental, structuring purpose of an evaluation program?

Now the dilemma has another dimension. It seems essential that the school system have the information that the traditional evaluation program provides. And for purposes of self-evaluation, a new program of evaluation based on the theory of internal causation must be developed. Can two apparently conflicting goals in education be accomplished? *If it is necessary to make a choice, which program should be chosen?*

A parallel to this question arose in the field of modern physics. Since Newton's time, scientists had believed it possible to observe and track a particle, whether grains of dust or a planet, to determine its speed, and to predict its position for any moment of time. This is the doctrine of causality —the certainty that cause produces effect. If the laws and relationships among observable phenomena should be discovered, the state of the universe would be known, for an observable cause will produce a predictable effect.

Surprisingly, such certainties collapsed in observations of the world of the atom. If an electron started out on its rounds at a certain speed, it would be impossible to predict its time of arrival at a given point. The reason is that it is not possible to observe the electron without disturbing it. The observer's beam of light will actually change the electron's course and speed.

Niels Bohr, world-famous Danish physicist, has said that any observation regarding the behavior of the atom will be accompanied by a change in the state of the atom. Interaction with unpredictable results takes place between the observer and the phenomenon observed. Yet without disturbance, there can be no measurement and no knowledge. Heisenberg called this *the theory of uncertainty*.

The implications of all this for the dilemma in human behavior are apparent. The proponents of operant conditioning have presented ample evidence in support of external causation. The perceptual psychologists and the field psychologists are proposing and competently defending the theory of internal causation.

The manner in which the physicists resolved their dilemma is a milestone in man's intellectual development. Niels Bohr did not see helplessness in the quandaries. Instead, he proposed *the concept of complementarity*, a new way of looking at the problems. This concept recognizes the existence of two explanations rather than one. Both theories are valid and useful for a better understanding, but they are mutually exclusive if applied simultaneously. The knowledge of the position of the particle is considered complementary to the knowledge of its velocity, but the two cannot be computed simultaneously.

In our own camp, human behavior can be explained by both external causation and internal causation. The two theories together complement each other and offer us a more complete view and understanding of human behavior, education, and evaluation. So, like a house of cards, our dilemma has collapsed. *We don't need to make a choice.* Instead we need to learn how to build an evaluation program that will utilize as completely as possible the potential of both theories.

If we listen to teachers for 10 minutes, we will hear more complaints about evaluation than any other aspect of education. When teachers discover themselves spending hours gathering data for the purpose of marking and grading and additional hours recording these data, frustration results. When they are placed in the role of sitting in judgment on others, they feel deeply their inadequacies and their misgivings about playing such a role. And still both teachers and students cry out for the objective feedback essential for making the profoundly important, personal decisions in teaching and learning. But because evaluation programs do not produce these data, guesses, biases, and the opinions of the uninvolved and the uninformed too often form the basis for decisions.

Teachers are now becoming aware of what is missing—*the data for self-evaluation.* By knowing what is missing and by recognizing that what seems to be conflicting is not necessarily so, perhaps teachers can channel the energy now expended on frustration and exasperation into a search— a challenge. The challenge then is to devise the ways to gather the data of self-evaluation, discover how these data are to be used, and find a way of doing something about them at the classroom level.

And one more challenge. The data justified by the concept of external causation are also needed. Find a way to combine the two. Fortunately, it is possible to have both.

On Marks, Norms, and Proficiency Scores

WILLIAM CLARK TROW

I am not a school administrator, but if I were and saw the headline, PRO-FESSOR WOULD ABOLISH SCHOOL MARKS, I would emit the old "ho-hum" and turn on television to the ball game.

Not that marks do not deserve to be abolished. Anyone who has not lived his life in the ivory tower, however, knows that trying to abolish them would be like trying to abolish money. Sometimes a school or college deplores the over-emphasis on marks and decides to do without all but the essential "pass" and "fail." But soon such variations appear as "pass plus" and "pass minus," and these are soon followed by "honors," to which plus and minus signs are shortly added, and the same old system is back again.

And in the schools, when a superintendent is daring enough to make the attempt, formerly ill-attended PTA meetings are crowded with protestors, news articles discuss competition as the American way of life, and teachers favoring the status quo explain that "he" is working for a degree at the university or trying to make a name for himself. Even some of the

Reprinted from *Phi Delta Kappan*, 47 (4): 171–173 (December 1966), by permission of author and publisher.

students, for whose benefit the move was undertaken, want to know where they stand in comparison with others in their classes.

USES FOR SCHOOL MARKS

Of course marks do have their place, such as it is. They represent a teacher's evaluation of a student's performance on a limited academic task or on an extended series of such tasks. But they are in reality a multiple-purpose system. Their general utility is revealed by even a partial list of their functions. They serve:

To inform teachers, students, and parents of how well individual students are doing in comparison with the others in their grade or class; and at year's end to designate those destined for promotion and non-promotion.

To provide data for academic and vocational counseling and guidance.

To reward good performance—except for those who cannot do very well. (The rewards are not quite the same as reinforcement, and as a rule not efficiently manipulated.)

To punish poor performance whether or not the student could do better. (If he could not, such action is at least ethically questionable.)

To motivate learning—but students are motivated to compete for marks rather than to attain the more substantial values.

Although marks do serve useful purposes, the good and bad are almost hopelessly mixed in the traditional marking system, and the side effects are mostly on the negative side. The superior are not challenged but are often rewarded for a performance that for them is mediocre; they will "pass" anyway. The retarded are discouraged, as are the disadvantaged, for they are unfairly asked to do things they cannot do, and so get farther and farther behind ("cumulative ignorance"). There is no assurance that anyone, even those in the middle range of ability, are learning as well as they might.

In addition to the functions listed, marks serve as a basis for communicating with the home, for giving special attention to exceptional children, and for such tasks as promotions, award of prizes, and job recommendations. But even for these purposes, taken by themselves marks are dubious criteria for professional judgments.

For the time being, the solution seems to lie not in abolishing marks but in reducing their unwholesome influence by also employing a different form of appraisal.

MARKS THAT DEPEND ON NORMS

Like achievement test scores, marks that depend on norms are based on a comparison of the performance of each student with the others in his grade or class. If the student is in a bright class, he is liable to get a lower mark than he would if he were a member of a slow group.

Even the standardized tests are stacked against him; for they are designed to produce a normal curve, with hard questions included that a large proportion of the students cannot answer—and there may be no good reason why they should. It is uneconomical to spend time and money trying to teach pupils what it is known beforehand they will not learn. If they *should* learn such items, they can and should be taught. But if they are taught, the whole class will be able to answer all (or nearly all) of the questions correctly, and "the curve" goes out the window. Or else the teachers would hold to it as an article of faith and conclude either that the test on which everyone gets a good mark is not a good test, or that the students cheated.

As a matter of fact, what has been termed a "mastery test" has been tried out here and there. It is a test to discover whether pupils have really mastered a given content. If, as in most subjects, there are areas of knowledge about which students should know something but not everything, they might properly receive the top score for answering, say, half the questions correctly, and given no more credit for memorizing further details, which they will soon forget. This would be done on the assumption that their time would be better spent doing something else; e.g., taking a field trip or working on some project.

The current marking system presents an anomalous situation, one up with which we would not put, to paraphrase Winston Churchill's famous declaration, if we had not long assumed that it was the proper procedure. But this is not the end. Raw scores are practically meaningless, so they are transposed into the relative terms of age or grade norms. There is some paper convenience in this arrangement, but it tells us little or nothing of what a student actually *knows* or can *do*, and no one is likely to inquire. Instead, it only tells which students of the same age or in the same grade answered more or fewer questions correctly. To some people "fifth-grade arithmetic ability" may mean something; but what of fifth-grade French ability, or tenth-grade violin, or twelve-year-old typing, or even college algebra?

Marks or scores based on such concepts as those, dependent as they are on the student's relative standing, have been called "norm-referenced."[1] This term is sufficiently awkward to be sure of incorporation into the current technical jargon of education. What we lack and need badly is a content or "criterion-referenced" score based directly on proficiency in subject matter.

MARKS DEPENDING ON PROFICIENCY

The criterion-referenced score is easiest to use when there is some absolute unit of measurement as, for example, in track and field sports. The most accurate mark for ability in running is time in minutes and seconds for a

[1] Robert Glaser, "Psychology and Educational Technology," *Educational Technology*, May 15, 1966, pp. 1–14.

certain distance, and for jumping or throwing it is distance in feet and inches. Similarly, the most accurate mark for typing or shorthand is letters or words per minute. Such measures can be easily converted into a scale, say, of zero to 100, zero being just no ability and 100 that of the top-level professional. Other abilities could be placed along such a scale as this, the ability to play a musical instrument or use a foreign language. In some subjects—social studies, for example—it would be more difficult, but not impossible, to obtain a reasonable consensus on such a sequential arrangement. But almost any planned continuum would result in a more meaningful score than we now have.

The criterion-referenced score, then, is a point along a continuum of subject-matter knowledge or skill that indicates the degree of proficiency achieved by an individual without reference to anyone else. Whatever grade he is in, or whoever else is in it, the student's score is the same and indicates *his* level of proficiency. If he is to be instructed, his performance would start at this point and would be expected to move on from there. Sequentially scaled achievement tests to measure his abilities and record his progress remain to be devised.

Some skills might have two or three or more continuums, language skills, for example, having such items as handwriting, spelling, vocabulary, pronunciation, and verbal fluency. Similarly for musical skills, such matters as tone quality, technique, reading, and musical feeling might be included. A composite score might be of value under certain circumstances.

OBJECTIVES

It will soon be discovered that to define points on the zero-to-100 continuum the content of instruction in the form of objectives must be clear and definite. And this is the most important reason for moving over to a criterion-referenced marking system. It tends to force attention to the problem of objectives. Just what are students expected to learn?

It is in the formulation of objectives that our educational practice is perhaps weakest. General statements are good enough as far as they go, but they do not go far enough. Specifically, what should young people be taught when the stated objective is "knowledge of history," "understanding of geographical concepts," "appreciation of art," or "realization of the meaning of democracy"?

Actually, every teacher teaches specific concepts and generalizations without raising the question of agreement or disagreement with every other teacher. Basic agreements on objectives could be used as a starter. Finer demarcations would be subject to modification based on further research. If instruction is to be effective, the statements of successive objectives should be much more specific than is customary and should indicate just what at different stages the students will be expected to know and be able to do,[2] e.g., to identify, differentiate, solve, construct, list, compare, contrast, etc.

A sequential statement of content objectives has many advantages, among them the following:

It clarifies for a teacher the successive competencies he should expect of a student in progress, and the goal or terminal behavior sought.

It clarifies for the student what is expected of him and so reduces the strain of uncertainty about "what will be asked on the examination."

It places the emphasis on learning and teaching, where it belongs, and not on school marks.

It provides a succession of check points showing the progress made in the successive attainment of objectives which for the student is rewarding, reinforcing, and motivating, and tends to reduce irrelevant conduct.[3]

In summary, some of the advantages of criterion-referenced marking may be noted:

It gives each student an absolute rather than a relative measure of his achievement or performance that does not depend on what others do.

It provides the opportunity for each student to compete with his own prior record. Over a period of time, a succession of measures reveals the progress that he is making.

It facilitates temporary groupings of students who have actually reached the same level for discussions, TV showings, field trips, etc.

It encourages arrangements by means of which students may proceed at their own rate: They do not have to be held back or pushed ahead.

It makes it easier to adapt instruction to those students who transfer from other schools, since grade standards vary so widely, and to help those who have been absent, since they can go on from the point where they left off.

It furnishes data for obtaining averages and deviations in proficiency for different age groups, and correlations may be found with whatever variables one may be interested in.

It forces attention on content objectives and individual differences in

___

[2] See Robert F. Mager, *Preparing Objectives for Programmed Instruction*. San Francisco: Fearon Publishers, Inc., 1962. The excellent suggestions in this little book apply not only to programming but to instruction and testing generally, but they need to be carried further. See also, *Taxonomy of Educational Objectives*, Handbook I, *Cognitive Domain*, by Benjamin S. Bloom *et al.* New York: Longmans, Green, 1956; and Handbook II, *Affective Domain*, by David Krathwohl *et al.* New York: David McKay, 1964. Unfortunately, the third handbook on the psychomotor domain has not yet been compiled.

[3] After completing the first draft of this manuscript, I learned that this procedure is being tried out by the Learning Research and Development Center at the University of Pittsburgh. It is briefly reported in the following mimeographed articles: "The Role of Evaluation in Individually Prescribed Instruction," by C. M. Lindvall and Robert Glaser; "The Project for Individually Prescribed Instruction (Oakleaf Project)," by C. M. Lindvall; and "The Development of a Sequentially Scaled Achievement Test," by Richard C. Cox and Glenn T. Graham.

the progress of students. Hence criterion-referenced marks would be useful now and will be even more so in the future when needed for computer-assisted instruction now being developed.

DUAL ASSESSMENT

Should the traditional norm-referenced marking system be continued? For the present, probably yes; partly because it would be more than one's life is worth to try to get rid of it, and partly because it provides a convenient comparison of the performance of pupils with that of others in the same grade or class, though proficiency scores would be more satisfactory for this purpose. It is quite possible that the old norm-referenced system will gradually wither away as the new criterion-referenced individual scores come into common use. The process of development can begin in a small way with the skills that are now measurable in absolute units; gradually we will move out to the other subject-matter areas.

When a number of influential school administrators and teachers become aware of the possibilities and begin to apply pressure, then and only then will the makers of standardized tests evince an interest. As one wrote, "The idea is a good one and practicable. But it took us 20 years to get norms and the curve across to the profession, so why start all over again?" Perhaps this brief paper will suggest reasons for making a fresh start.

Promotional Policies

GEORGE J. MOULY

The oldest attempt at dealing with individual differences in the classroom revolved around what might be called rigid standards of grade placement. A child was retained in a given grade until he had mastered its content and, conversely, he could get a double promotion if he had already mastered enough of the content of the grade following that which he had just completed.

Acceleration was particularly common in the old one-room school where a gifted child could go through the first eight grades in perhaps four or five years. In fact, repeated double promotions could result in college graduation perhaps as early as age fifteen. It has been frowned upon in recent years on the argument that it overemphasizes the intellectual and the academic at the expense of the other phases of the child's all-round de-

From Chapter 10 from *Psychology for Effective Teaching*, Second Edition, by George J. Mouly. Copyright © 1960, 1968 by Holt, Rinehart and Winston, Inc. Reprinted by permission of Holt, Rinehart and Winston, Inc.

velopment and that the accelerated child may become a misfit from the standpoint of physical, social, and emotional adjustment.

At the other end of the continuum are those whose work is below par and who, according to the older view on the subject, needed to be retained lest they got hopelessly bogged down and interfered with the progress of students in the next grade. Before we proceed to a discussion of the validity of this position, let us consider the question: "Why fail students?" Whereas the specific answer to that question varies, the policy of failure "where warranted" is said by its advocates to serve three important functions:

[a] To motivate students who apparently will work only when the threat of failure is kept constantly before them. This is not true. Otto and Melby (1935), for example, found no difference in the achievement of children threatened with failure and those assured of promotion—and fortunately so, for it would be a sad commentary on the appropriateness of our curriculum and our methods if it were. Failure is a last-ditch attempt at motivation and it ought to be possible for the few teachers who still rely heavily on fear of failure as a motivational device to locate more positive measures.

[b] To maintain standards. Some people feel that the high school is losing its academic reputation by graduating students who have been carried along for years, and community groups have on occasions demanded a return to the "good old standards" where one did not graduate without a certain amount of knowledge. They overlook the fact that the solution in those days consisted of forcing the student to drop out, sometimes long before he got to high school.

[c] To reduce the variability within the classroom. It is argued that his increased mental development and the general overview of the work will enable the child who is retained to do much better as he repeats the grade. This has not been realized in practice. As early as 1911, Keyes showed that repeaters do worse, rather than better, than they did the first time. Cook (1941) and Klene and Branson (1929) likewise showed that potential repeaters profited more from being promoted to the next grade than from being retained. Thus, Cook, in his comparison of schools with rigid standards as represented by an average retardation of nearly two years in Grade 7 with a matched sample of schools having liberal promotional policies with a corresponding average retardation of only .17 of a year, found a significant difference in achievement favoring the schools with lenient promotions; but he found no difference in the range of individual differences in the two sets of schools. Coffield and Blommers (1956) found that children who reached Grade 7 in eight years (because of failure) knew less than comparable children who had been promoted. Evidently, the standards of the school cannot be raised by accumulating the dullards any more than the standards of a ball team can be raised by keeping the unfit for an extra year or two. Of course, emphasis in school must be on the individual child but, if our concern *has* to be for the standards of the school, let us at least be logical and eliminate, not retard.

Also to be considered, in view of the modern emphasis on the total child, are the effects of retention on his personality. Although the evidence is not entirely conclusive, the consensus supports the statement by Goodlad (1952, p. 449) that "throughout the body of evidence runs a consistent pattern: undesirable growth characteristics and unsatisfactory school progress are more closely associated with nonpromoted children than with promoted slow-learning children." In view of his need to maintain a consistent self-image, the child who is retained is likely to see himself as dumb, tough, or unconcerned, as many teachers who have repeaters in their class can readily attest. Having been separated from the group to which they belong and being out of step physically, socially, and emotionally with the new group, these children find it difficult to get accepted and often react to the whole situation with discouragement, hostility, and misbehavior.

Evidence points to the fact that retention is not effective in reducing the range of individual differences and that it tends to have negative effects on academic achievement and personality development. It does not follow, however, that children should never be retained; no doubt a child who is retarded physically, socially, and emotionally as well as mentally and academically, may profit from being put into a somewhat younger age group; each case must be evaluated on its own merits. The decision to promote or to retain should be made only after consideration of all the factors— not just the academic—and generally the teacher should have to show cause why the child should be retained in terms of how he can be helped more by retention than by promotion. The important thing is not to promote or to retain but rather what the teacher does after having made this decision, for the element of failure is not eliminated by universal promotion. Unless the teacher is prepared to take the child at his level—as he must do with all the other children in the class—and make the necessary adjustment and adaptations of instructional methods and materials to bring the curriculum down to his level, the child had better be retained, for otherwise classwork will become progressively more baffling to him. If he has to be frustrated, it is debatable whether it is more devastating to be frustrated once a year or continually throughout each day of the year.

Retention should not be thought of as a form of punishment but rather as a matter of optimal grade placement for maximum growth. At all times, the child's instructional needs should take precedence over the teacher's convenience and, if by special help and remedial procedures, he can be kept with his group without taking too much of the teacher's time and energy away from the other children, he should be promoted. Furthermore, if he is to be retained, he should be prepared for the decision; it is especially important that the parents be in on the decision for their opposition might well render unwise an otherwise wise decision to retain.

To avoid the objections to complete failure, various compromises have been suggested, e.g., partial failure or even conditional failure where the child is given the option of attending summer school. A proposal that seems to have merit is that of having fewer promotion periods. A number of schools operating on a nongraded basis have a primary block consisting of six semesters which can be shortened or extended by two semesters before the child moves into Grade 4. There is no passing or failing: the child simply covers the material of the first three grades at his own speed. The effectiveness of these solutions varies from case to case but none can be considered a cure-all.

National Assessment: Are We Ready?

WAYNE P. MOELLENBERG

Once again, the halls of learning echo to the sounds of impassioned debate as educators attempt to reach a degree of consensus on a weighty issue. That issue, national assessment, has probably stirred more controversy than any other, with the exception of professional negotiations, since those dark days when Sputnik challenged the American educational establishment. Indeed, it seems likely that the matter of assessment may produce even more heat and less light, if that is possible, than the debates about the shortcomings of American education which followed the Russian feat.

The former issue presented educators with a "fait accompli" which required reasonable explanation, an area of considerable expertise among us. However, decisions about a question requiring a choice are not so easily arrived at, and one may expect that ponderous committee deliberations will go on for some time before the question, "to assess or not to assess," is settled.

A critical factor in such circumstances is that decisions may be made by others about these matters while educators are still deliberating. In the case of national assessment, it seems likely that hard-pressed legislators and school boards, seeking a way of evaluating the needs of education, may become increasingly insistent that some objective measures of condition and progress be soon forthcoming. If nothing else is advanced, it seems very likely that such groups will embrace national assessment as the best available means of evaluation.

To avoid such "decision by default," it seems that educators must overcome the emotional considerations that have clouded the issue and take a hard look at some probable outcomes. Then, if this consideration seems to demonstrate the advisability of assessment as presently proposed, it can be chosen with reason. If not, alternative modes of evaluation can perhaps be devised in time to be substituted.

Reprinted from *The Clearing House,* 43 (8): 451–454 (April 1969), by permission of author and publisher.

A first consideration is the question of whether the evaluation of schools must indeed become more systematic than it has been in the past. There are several indications that it must. The increasing mobility of our population, the growing involvement of the federal government in education, and the increasing importance of education in modern life would all point toward the need for a systematic way of determining what is happening educationally at all times and in all parts of the country.

Education is no longer local in nature, and can no longer be evaluated adequately on a purely local basis. However, this certainly does not mean that it can or should be evaluated strictly on a national basis either, since there are still local variations which *must* be imposed on the national picture for valid evaluation.

For these reasons, it seems evident that whatever is done must have both national and local perspectives. Perhaps this could be accomplished by the adaptation and use of a common core of basic instruments in local districts, with local control, interpretation in terms of local conditions, and the development of good local norms to supplement the national norms. This would provide a degree of the commonality so badly needed for broad evaluation on a national level, but would still provide for autonomy and meaningful interpretation at the local level.

A second concern, closely related to the first, is the matter of accountability. Certainly educators share with most other professionals the position of being accountable to the public they serve. We should be able to produce demonstrable results which would show what we have been doing. Further, we should be able to show that the results under conditions which we call desirable are better than those under conditions we term undesirable. However, we cannot let ourselves be put into the position of saying that our results must show up at a given time and place on a given set of objective test scores.

Like the medical profession, we must reserve the prerogative to decide what the symptoms mean and what should be done about them. Also, we share with our medical colleagues the situation of the advanced or chronic disability for which the prognosis is not good with the present state of the art. In other words, no one, including educators themselves, can stretch the very limited range of measuring instruments to cover all, or even a large majority, of the important educational outcomes. We cannot deny accountability, but we cannot accept it based only on certain very limited criteria.

The matter of what these criteria shall be and who shall develop them is another aspect of the question requiring the most careful attention. If the measures are going to provide the means for analyzing education on a nationwide basis, then it seems certain that there would need to be batteries of objective tests with demonstrated reliability and extensive, nationwide norm groups. These requirements would certainly rule out any shoestring operations, since the development of tests on such a scale requires heavy investments of capital and the resources of an extensive organization. It seems likely that very few institutions in the country could even attempt the task, and probably none of them could surpass the resources and personnel of the group currently developing national assessment materials.

All of this seems to indicate that the materials planned for the national assessment project will probably be as good as any objective measures of that type which could presently be developed. However, the development of the materials is only one of the critical phases of the process, and since this phase is in the hands of some well-qualified professionals, it may be a smaller source of danger than later phases.

Once the materials have been developed and the decision has been made to use them, then the next phase of the process is initiated. It is at this point that the tests pass out of the hands of the relatively small group of highly trained specialists and into the hands of a large group of users with diverse backgrounds and purposes. In terms of administering the tests, this part will probably present no special problems, since the directions will undoubtedly be made sufficiently clear that appropriate testing conditions can be maintained by persons with reasonable training in test administration. However, it is in the later *usage* of the test results that the greatest abuses are likely to occur, if past experience is any indicator, for it is here that widespread preparation is needed but lacking.

One of the things that experience with other tests might lead us to expect is that some teachers will "teach to the test" and that some administrators will attempt to attach survival value to such action. The measures being taken to avoid these problems are appropriate, but it is doubtful whether they will be sufficient.[1] So long as some teachers and administrators regard test results as a direct and comprehensive measure of teaching effectiveness, without due consideration for all of the dozens of variables which contribute to those scores, we will have a high likelihood that the subject matter of the tests will become a curriculum guide for many classrooms.

The point will be made by some that this situation is not altogether undesirable if the tests really measure what the youngsters need to know, but such arguments overlook the fact that any test can sample only a small portion of the content in a given subject area. Further, such practices undermine the validity of norms and the meaning of scores made by children without such "coaching."

All of this points toward a deeper-lying problem, however, which concerns the subtle effects of testing programs on educational goals.[2] There is a persistent temptation to expand the reasoning that "anything which exists can be measured" to include also the idea that "if it cannot be mea-

[1] Ralph W. Tyler, "Assessing the Progress of Education," *Phi Delta Kappan*, September, 1965, pp. 13–16.

[2] An excellent expansion of this point can be found in the article by Harold C. Hand, "National Assessment Viewed as the Camel's Nose," in the September, 1965, issue of *Phi Delta Kappan*.

sured, it is not very important anyway." Such reasoning could well lead us toward a new emphasis on specific skills, which lend themselves rather readily to measurement, and away from emphasis on divergent processes which are more difficult to measure. The retrogressive nature of such teaching, in an age which requires increasing diversity and flexibility rather than greater conformity and mastery of specifics, would seem particularly unfortunate.

The preceding discussion obviously deals with what might happen and not with what must happen. Educators who are aware of appropriate uses and limitations of test scores would be far less prone to allow their school programs to be dominated by the content of tests. They would recognize that scores deal with only certain aspects of educational outcomes, and that even these aspects are greatly influenced by many kinds of variables besides quality of instruction. The implications of this situation are very clear: if assessment is to work on a wide scale, then it must be preceded and accompanied by an intensive campaign to educate potential users on the meaning of the tests and their results.

This campaign should include classroom teachers, administrators, school boards, legislators, and parents, with the purpose of providing a sufficiently broad base of conceptual understanding so that specific test results could be interpreted meaningfully by these groups. The task of providing such education would need to involve educational laboratories, colleges and universities, and public school personnel with adequate backgrounds in the areas of measurement and evaluation. In connection with the process of providing understanding of the measurements, there would also need to be an extensive program of public relations to convince the public of the need to use the results in the most constructive ways.

To briefly summarize the points which have been made:

(1) The pressures for some form of evaluation on a broad scale are building rapidly, for a number of reasons which seem very valid.

(2) Such broad-scale evaluation should involve significant effort at the local level in the assessment of local conditions and the development of local norms.

(3) The instruments to be used in the broad-scale evaluation involve such heavy demands in development that it would seem necessary to entrust it to an organization with extensive resources similar to those of the group presently engaged in the national assessment planning.

(4) Special preparations will need to be made to facilitate appropriate use of the tests and their results by persons both inside and outside the educational establishment.

The analysis of these factors seems to lead to some rather clear implications. For one thing, if some form of broad-scale evaluation is necessary and coming, and if it requires the kind of organizational resources which are presently planned for national assessment, then it seems evident that educators would do well to work *with* rather than *against* the movement. Their efforts would seem much more beneficial if they were aimed at minimizing the dangers and possible abuses that accompany the widespread use of tests. With proper leadership from the educational profession, it seems that assessment may well be a boon rather than a bane.

Curriculum Assessment: Problems and Possibilities

JACK R. FRYMIER

Every model for curriculum development includes the concept of assessment or evaluation. From the theoretical point of view, evaluation plays an important part in improving program in several ways. Purposes can be selected, for example, on the basis of good data about the nature of society or the nature of the learner. Or, content, experiences, organization, and methodology can be set forth in testable form.

For instance, rather than assuming that any particular selection of content or sequence of experiences or methodological approaches or organizational stratagems is effective, responsible leaders in curriculum development can hypothesize about these things, then put their hypotheses to empirical test. Over a period of time such evaluative and assessment techniques should enable curriculum workers to make steady progress in terms of improving program.

Two major developments have forced the concepts of assessment and evaluation into special prominence. Talk of national assessment in education, on the one hand, and the requirement for evaluation built into the Elementary and Secondary Education Act program, on the other, are forcing curriculum workers to reexamine these notions as they apply to curriculum development today.

Any view of the educational scene suggests that programs are changing dramatically. At no time in the history of American schools have curricular changes been so widespread or so intensive as in the past decade. Modifications of course content, organizational structures, methodological approaches, evaluation procedures, and even purposes themselves have been instituted. Unless one is willing to accept change for its own sake, however,

From *Educational Leadership*, 24 (2): 124–128 (November 1966). Reprinted with permission of the Association for Supervision and Curriculum Development and Jack R. Frymier. Copyright © 1966 by the Association for Supervision and Curriculum Development.

he is forced to ask: "Are the curriculum changes really significant?" Or to ask in another way, "Do children learn better in the new programs than they did in the old?"

This, of course, may be the wrong question. Some persons maintain that since the old purposes were not themselves appropriate, it is unreasonable to compare the new efforts today in terms of objectives which are actually obsolete. On the other hand, it may very well be that some kind of accumulated curriculum wisdom has been reflected in the decades of activity which have gone into what we generally describe as "conventional program." If this is true, comparisons of new efforts with previously existing programs may be perfectly legitimate.

NEW QUESTIONS NEEDED

The fact is, these questions are academic. Even though changes in curriculum have been extensive, and many of these changes have been positive, few people are satisfied with the state of affairs in American curriculum today. The inadequacies are so obvious that thoughtful curriculum workers are continuously struggling to find new and more powerful ways to improve the program.

This dissatisfaction arises in part because of a kind of gnawing professional perspective which says: "No program is perfect. We must improve." Part of the dissatisfaction, however, stems from the very real fact that inappropriate and ineffective curricula can be found in almost any district or any building without difficulty at all. Too many children hate the very thought of having to learn in school. Too many find school a boring, unexciting place to be. Too many are unsuccessful in acquiring those ways of behaving which seem desirable to those in charge.

Why is this so? Many factors probably account for such a state of affairs today. I would like to suggest two. In my opinion, we have tended to ask the wrong questions in curriculum, and secondly, assessment has been ineffectively utilized as part of the total educational scheme.

If we ask the wrong questions we always get the wrong answers. In curriculum development we often ask the *frequency* question or the *efficiency* question, for example, rather than the *effectiveness* question. We say, "How many schools are using language laboratories?" or "How many schools have PSSC physics this year?" "How many classrooms are nongraded?" "How many teachers utilize generative grammar or structural linguistics in their language arts programs?"

The assumption underlying these questions is that if more schools are using a particular program, it must be better. Obviously that is the wrong assumption. Frequency is not an appropriate criterion at all.

This fall, for instance, more than half of the youngsters who study physics in our secondary schools will be studying the PSSC physics program, but the proportional enrollment of high school students taking physics has steadily decreased during the same period of time that the new program has come into being. If we assume that the number of programs in use is important, we pose for ourselves the absurd possibility that the time might come when all of the schools would teach a particular course and none of the children would take it, that we would then be doing a perfect job.

Consider another example. Curriculum workers frequently make judgments about program in terms of money. "How much will it cost?" "How efficient will it be?" "Can we afford such an innovation?" These questions presuppose that the basic purpose of education is to save money. No one is willing to agree with that aloud, of course, but the fact remains that if we ask an economic question, we can only get an economic answer. But that is the wrong question.

If schools exist to save money, there are many ways in which expenditures can be reduced. We can lower teachers' salaries, we can increase class size, or we can eliminate expenditures for instructional materials, for instance. These will all save money. The purpose of education is not to save money, though. It is to help children learn.

Curriculum workers must always focus upon the effectiveness question. Does the new program, do the new materials, will the new techniques enable students to learn more, better, faster, than some other approach? Does it make a significant difference in the lives and minds of those we teach? If it does not, the program is ineffective. Whether it costs more money or less or whether it is widespread or is not evident in any other school at all is immaterial. Frequency questions or economic questions simply get in the way. We must learn to ask the effectiveness question every time.

A CONCEPTUAL FLAW

A deeper, more elusive problem affecting program development, however, stems from the fact that education is a social system with a conceptual flaw. Every social system represents a human undertaking designed to fulfill human needs. Government, science, industry, education—these are all illustrations of different kinds of social systems in evidence today. Looked at in terms of systems theory, every effective social system reflects three phases of operation which accomplish separate functions, and these functions enable the system to maintain itself in an ongoing, dynamic, improving way.

Phase one includes the intellectual activities, the planning, policy making, hypothesizing function. Phase two involves the doing, accomplishing, effecting function. Phase three is the evaluating, assessing, reflecting, judgmental function. Taken together they represent various aspects of social undertakings which are designed to allow the system to accomplish the objectives toward which it is aimed, and at the same time keep changing for the better.

These three phases of any social system are most clearly illustrated in our concept of government. The planning phase is represented by the legislative branch. The doing phase is represented by the executive branch. The evaluating or assessing phase is represented by the judicial branch. In industry, however, the model still holds. Somebody plans, somebody produces, and somebody judges the effectiveness of those activities in a realistic way.

Any careful study of social systems other than education suggests that these three functions have been made relatively discrete and that they are accomplished by different groups, each one of which has power. That is, the Congress is different than the President, and the Supreme Court is different still. The same notion holds at the state and local level, too. From the functional standpoint, our system of government has been conceptualized in such a way that these different functions are accomplished by separate groups.

Another point, however, rests on the fact that social systems in an open society actually depend upon the third phase of the operation to assure improvement and intelligent change. That is, when the courts decide that a particular law is constitutional or unconstitutional or that a particular action by the President either is or is not appropriate, they feed back into the system new data which guarantee that the enterprise will be able to change itself and to improve. In industry the same thing is also true.

Planning and producing a new product or service represent the first and second phases of that social system in operation. Once the product goes on sale, however, evaluation must occur. Judgments are made by those who buy. If the general public buys the product or service, what they really do is feed back into the system new data which tell those responsible for planning and production that they have done the job well. Or, if the product or service becomes available and the public refuses to buy, this too, constitutes corrective feedback. It tells those responsible that something about their operation is not satisfactory and it must be changed. In either event, evaluation plays the critical role of providing corrective feedback to the other parts of the system so that the entire operation can be improved.

ROLE OF FEEDBACK

Two things are important about our discussion thus far. One is that the concept of corrective feedback, which is performed during the evaluation phase of the social systems operation, represents the precise point at which improvement can be assured. Second, in these illustrations it is also evident that the assessment or evaluation effort is best accomplished by a separate group which has appropriate influence of its own. Congress is not allowed to pass judgment on the constitutionality of its own laws, for example, nor are manufacturing companies permitted to have the ultimate say in the worthwhileness or value of the products they produce. These decisions are reserved for other groups.

In other words, feedback is imperative if the system is to operate at the highest possible level of effectiveness; yet, at the same time, it is probably not possible to assume that those who plan or those who implement can also accomplish the evaluation role. The power of evaluation rests in part upon the nature of the feedback information which is generated by the process, but in part upon the fact that the evaluation group has an authority of its own. Said still another way, our system of government and our system of economics, at least, presume that when the evaluation group makes its decision known, the rest of the system will have to pay attention to the feedback. The rest of the system is not free to ignore the data, whether they are positive or negative in form.

Looked at in terms of such a social systems model, education obviously has a conceptual flaw. School boards accomplish the policy making role. Professional persons undertake the effecting, implementing, doing role. But there is no special group whose responsibilities encompass the assessment function in any meaningful way. The general public passes judgment on the effectiveness of schools, of course, but seldom do they have a way of communicating their concerns with precision to assure improvement in schools. They may vote down a bond issue, for instance, but often as not no one really knows what the negative vote means.

On the other hand, advisory councils or curriculum councils often attempt to perform the evaluation role. In the first instance the fact that their activities are advisory—no one has to pay attention to the feedback—illustrates the fact that the system is not assured of information in such a way that it has to improve. Likewise, curriculum councils may very well study a particular problem in program carefully and creatively, only to find that their recommendations go completely ignored. That such recommendations may be accepted and used only serves to reinforce the fact that they may also be ignored. There is no rigor in the system which insists that we utilize the best that we know.

Theoretically, education has this conceptual flaw. There is no aspect of the system which regularly generates evaluative data, nor is there anything in the concept which requires that the system pay attention to the feedback if it should appear.

Do we need curriculum evaluation? Is assessment important? On these questions everyone agrees. Of course! Where should evaluation occur? Who should accomplish the assessment role? How should these persons be selected? How can we assure ourselves that the system will be able to use and profit by the feedback data which are obtained? These are difficult problems.

Several alternatives seem to be available, but what is needed most now is a thoughtful consideration of analyses such as the one presented here, then extensive discussion of both the problems and possibilities which are involved. We may be on the verge of a genuine breakthrough in education, if we can muster the creative genius to explore the implications inherent in a consideration of the real power of assessing carefully everything we do.

Keeping Current/
Looking Ahead

It requires little foresight to predict that the elementary school of the future will be markedly different from what it is today. As a matter of fact, many of the trends identified in previous parts of this anthology are even now setting the parameters for this new school. In this part the reader is asked to take another look at some current trends, for it is believed that only by knowing them and understanding their implications can he develop the new skills and competencies that will be prerequisites to working effectively in the elementary classroom of the future.

In the first article in the section, Corwin reflects on the sources and prospects of what has become in recent years a common phenomenon in United States education—teacher militancy. Corwin does not deny that the desire for better wages and working conditions was originally the incentive underlying most cases of militant teacher action, but he does believe that another factor is now assuming equal, if not greater, importance. This factor, the demand of teachers for more decision-making authority, has far-reaching implications for the already tenuous relationship that exists between many administrative and teaching personnel. Corwin believes that ultimately administrators must relinquish some of their decision-making prerogatives to teachers and, until that happens, that the incidence of strikes, walkouts, and sanctions is not likely to decline.

In the second article, Rand and English describe a way of organizing a teaching staff that purportedly facilitates involving its members in the decision-making process. In this approach, known as differentiated staffing, all teachers and paraprofessionals, based on training, experience, and merit, are given differentiated instructional responsibilities (including decision-making authority) and are remunerated accordingly. The responsibilities may range from translating educational research into classroom practice, at the higher end of the continuum, to keeping records and duplicating materials at the lower end. In implementing one form of differentiated staffing in Temple City, California, Rand and English have found that the merits seem to far outweigh any disadvantages. They caution, however, that the concept has not met with as much acceptance at the elementary level as it has at the secondary.

Over the years many methods have been used to evaluate teacher behavior, but only recently have techniques been devised to analyze it scientifically. In the third article, Waetjen briefly reviews the format of four systems for analyzing the behavior of teachers and presents some major findings from studies that have employed these systems. Although the picture of teaching that emerges on the basis of the findings is far from encouraging, the very fact that the act of teaching can now be analyzed in a more scientific and less haphazard way means that an important breakthrough to the eventual improvement of instruction has been made.

Krech, in the fourth article, points out that science may be on the brink of making another important breakthrough, one that could lead eventually to the improvement of man's cognitive functioning. He cites several recent research studies that demonstrate that the intellectual performance of rats, mice, and goldfish has been successfully modified through the use of drugs. The same drugs, Krech projects, may someday be used with human subjects with similar results. When and if they are, the educational, ethical, and social implications will be numerous.

Another contemporary phenomenon, which Shane discusses in the fifth article, is the reawakening of interest in early childhood education. Several factors are mentioned as being responsible for this renewed interest. Perhaps chief among them is the growing recognition that the early years are the critical years for a person's intellectual, psychosocial, and linguistic development. There seems to be little doubt, as Shane notes, that educational programs for the two- to five-year-old will soon abound. That these programs will play a significant role in reshaping the nature of elementary education in the 1970's and 1980's is also beyond doubt.

An event that has probably received less notoriety than the others mentioned in this section has been the emergence of big business into education. But this event is no less significant than the others in terms of its implications for education. In the sixth article, Muller examines the present relationship between industry and education and points out that some of the concerns and fears educators have about the business-education combine are not totally ill-founded. He concludes, on the one hand, by cautioning his colleagues in the business world not to usurp those tasks best left to education and, on the other, by expressing his hope that educators will not underestimate the potential of business for helping education achieve its goals.

In the seventh selection, Eisele describes and analyzes selected current developments in the field of educational technology as they are and will be affecting the school's curriculum. The author divides these developments into three broad categories: (1) tutorial systems for independent learning, (2) information storage and retrieval systems, and (3) management systems for instruction. Each of them has tremendous educational potential, but none, Eisele admits, is likely to result in substantial, across-the-board improvements unless certain prerequisites are met. The first prerequisite listed by Eisele, the systematic planning of curricula that are replete with teaching and learning alternatives, is perhaps most appropriately mentioned here. For this prerequisite will require of educators a more thorough understanding of the purpose and methods of curriculum planning than most now possess.

In Frazier's article, the last in this part, are presented three conceptual models of the elementary school teacher of the future —the first as a specialist, the second as an executive, and the third as a professional. Frazier believes that as a specialist this new teacher will need specialized competencies in one or more curriculum areas; as an executive he will need planning, managerial, and supervisory skills; and as a professional he will need methodological expertise as well as curriculum development know-how. These models, as developed by Frazier, will require substantive alterations in the pre- and in-service education of teachers as well as in the types of supportive services that are provided them. It is noted, finally, that there will be problems in initiating and implementing these changes, but that the problems will seem minuscule when compared with the curricular and instructional improvements that such changes should make.

Teacher Militancy in the United States: Reflections on Its Sources and Prospects

RONALD G. CORWIN

Everyone knows that teaching is a troubled occupation. But few people are probably fully aware of just how widespread are its problems—certainly they are more pervasive than the recent rash of well-publicized strikes, walkouts, and sanctions would indicate. These visible and covert indications of unrest have been bred within a much broader context of discontent that has swept this country in recent years. Existentialism, with its doctrine of personal commitment and decisive action has finally come of age; this generation blames most of its problems on a self-conscious sense of alienation rooted in the failure of existing social arrangements—large segments of the population complain of feeling a loss of a sense of meaningful control over their destiny. Group militancy represents an alternative for people not content with this fate.

With the assistance of mass media, the problems of urban America, especially the voices of the Negro and the alienated adolescent, have finally broken through; other partially disenfranchised groups are following suit. Militancy has become a common response to pervasive sociological tensions and a generic symptom of the failure of existing social institutions. Teacher militancy must be understood in this context.

SOURCES OF CONFLICT

While the aggressiveness of teachers may be stimulated in the context described, the context in itself is not a sufficient explanation for this aggressiveness. The plain fact is that, in many respects, educational bureau-

Reprinted from *Theory into Practice*, 7 (2): 96–102 (April 1968), by permission of author and publisher.

cracies are not working very effectively. People will not feel constrained to accept the authority of a system that fails to come to grips with the pressing problems of the day, nor obliged to administrators who are no more able than they to cope with the ailments of their occupation—inadequate financing, competing objectives and cross pressures, educational failures, dropouts, and student discipline problems. School systems have become so complex and have had to adapt to such a wide range of situations that administrators no longer can maintain centralized control over educational practice—although in view of their legal responsibility, many administrators have vainly attempted to preserve the fiction of doing so. This persistent effort, on the part of both administrators and teachers, to maintain customary routines and traditional evaluation standards in a climate of failure, has only aggravated the tension. As teachers have specialized and systems have become larger, teachers have been thrust into positions from which they can exert considerable influence over day-to-day policy. The problem is that most existing systems do not give adequate recognition to the increased influence of teachers and offer few viable ways by which they can resolve their grievances within the existing authority structure. As a consequence, the domains of teachers and administrators have become blurred. Positions of authority in school systems at best have become precarious. We are now witnessing the precipitant shift in this power structure.

This general situation helps to explain some of the findings from a study of staff conflicts in the public schools.[1] The single most frequent type of conflict identified (one in every four) concerned authority problems between teachers and administrators. Much of this tension was associated with a school's professional climate and some of it with the characteristics of the school itself. Professional responsibility requires that some of the traditional administrative decisions be delegated to teachers, and, by and large, administrators have not relinquished their authority willingly. The instability of the authority structure seemed to increase in relationship to a school's size, number of levels of authority, degree of specialization, and its overall complexity. The rates of many types of disputes increased with the amount of authority a faculty member exercised over routine classroom decisions, probably because those teachers with some authority have more to fight about and have more occasions for doing so. Even in these situations, however, there was a lower rate of the more severe, "major incidents" (in which several parties were eventually drawn into heated discussions about an issue).

Much of the conflict is a by-product of the fact that schools are reorienting themselves from sheer obedience to routines to more problem-centered approaches to education. This shift is requiring greater delegation in recognition of the fact that no one group has a full grasp of the existing

[1] Corwin, Ronald G. *Staff Conflicts in the Public Schools.* (USOE Cooperative Research Project No. 2637, 1966.) This report will be published soon by Appleton-Century-Crofts.

problems. Although innovation and experimentation have become watchwords in education, little fundamental change has occurred in the wake of scores of new programs—a fact which merely calls further attention to the crisis. Paradoxically, this climate of innovation has generated an atmosphere of defensive conservatism on the part of both administrators and teachers anxious about imminent status changes. Since the official position of administrators has given them the upper hand in controlling the direction of change at the local level, most of the proposed changes are aimed at improving classroom teaching through inservice programs for teachers and modified teaching procedures and curricula, rather than involving fundamental alterations in the system itself. The proposals being suggested seem to imply that teachers are responsible for many of the existing problems, and the teachers are understandably apprehensive about accepting the blame. At the same time, of course, opportunities have arisen for new positions of leadership and realignments of groups. People who have long been in positions of subordinate status are becoming sophisticated about organizations, learning to manipulate the existing system and creating organizations of their own to facilitate their purposes. New leaders in time of change do not feel bound by traditional authority nor peaceful means of settling disputes—indeed, the very moral order itself is being disputed.

Some teachers can be expected to capitalize on these opportunities to improve their position. There are several factors in their favor. One of the most apparent examples is the disproportionate number of lower-class people who seem to be attracted to teaching as a way of improving their status.[2] In a society where a person's status is closely linked with his occupational status, his own position rises and falls with the fortunes of his occupation. Also, the lack of opportunity for individual mobility in teaching encourages the efforts of teachers to achieve collective mobility. And, at the same time, they are gaining strength, both in number and in concentration. Given the projected growth of teachers in the work force and the trend toward urban concentration, their absolute power is bound to increase whether or not the proportion of militants grows.

The power of teachers is further enhanced by their responsibility for evaluating the achievement of children, which, in this society, is tantamount to determining their life chances. This power brings teachers into direct confrontation with parents of all social class levels.

Probably the most important basis of teachers' new sense of power is the growing specialization within teaching. Because of specialization, teachers' level of education is likely to increase in the long run; although, until recently, their rate of increase in education has barely kept pace with that of the general population. Of more immediate importance are the educational gains of a small segment of teachers, a marked increase in the specialization in the use of teaching techniques for distinct populations, and the

[2] Davis, James. *Undergraduate Career Decisions.* Chicago: Aldine Press, 1965.

beginnings of separate career lines for teachers of various classes and types of students. Skill at teaching the new math, i.t.a., working with the handicapped, and successful experience in slum schools can not only provide the basis for challenging the conventional authority of laymen, but also ultimately place teachers in positions of superior information compared to the administrators who hire and evaluate them. The traditional role which line administrators have played as "curriculum leaders" has already become unfeasible, and even the effectiveness of the curriculum specialists is limited by pressures on them to achieve system-wide uniformity.

Professionalization represents one very effective means by which members of an occupation can utilize their special knowledge as a leverage for improving the relative position of their occupation, while, at the same time, protecting themselves from the attacks of their adversaries. Hence, professionalization represents both a defense of, and a quest for, status. Without denying the economic interest and material gain undoubtedly involved in the incentive behind some forms of militancy, the distinctive significance of militant professionalism is the shift that it represents from interest politics to the politics of status.[3] In fact, a correlation could not be found between teachers' salaries and their conflict rates in the study of staff conflicts—the only economic variable related to conflict was a positive association between a system's total financial receipts and the rate at which major incidents occurred in high schools. Conflict is probably more closely related to the way existing economic resources are allocated (i.e., the relative deprivation) than to the absolute level of income of a system. It is precisely the satisfactions omitted from material rewards, namely decision-making power, which seem to underlie much of the discontent in teaching.

However, professionalization, itself, is the source of additional tensions, for teachers do not agree among themselves on appropriate standards, and professional principles are incompatible with bureaucratic principles of school organization in many crucial respects. In particular, according to professional principles, teachers would be granted more decision-making authority over the classroom, especially over curriculum content, than they have received within most school systems. To become more professional, teachers will have to gain more power, which will mean challenging the existing system of administration. Hence, in the study of staff conflicts, the incidence of most types of conflict (with an important exception to be noted) in a school increased with the faculty's average level of professionalism. The significant point is that this association was more prominent in the more bureaucratic schools compared to the less bureaucratic ones. In other words, it is in the most bureaucratized schools that a strong commitment to the professional orientation is most likely to lead to conflict. On the other hand, conflict did seem to diminish when the less professionally oriented faculties were bureaucratized.

[3] Hofstadter, Richard. "The Pseudo-Conservative Revolt," in *The Radical Right*, Daniel Bell, editor. New York: Doubleday and Co., Inc., 1964, pp. 75–96.

ALTERNATIVE INTERPRETATIONS

In reviewing closely related alternative interpretations, most people would probably be inclined to start with the assumption that conflict simply represents another phase of the Hobbesian war of "all against all," especially among certain belligerent types of people having *deviant personality traits,* i.e., abnormal degrees of vanity, drive for recognition, inability to adjust to others, emotional instability, etc. Without denying the relevance of such factors, it seems more important to recognize that certain *situations* apparently produce tensions which are easily kindled largely independently of the particular people who are part of the situations. For example, in nearly every school interviewed in the study of staff conflicts, teachers of academic subjects had some complaint against teachers in the extracurricular programs because of the class disruptions created by activity practices and special events. Similarly, vocational teachers often expressed antagonism toward academic teachers and counselors who monopolized the good students and sent them the castoffs. And, schools with high rates of faculty turnover were simply more conflict-prone than more stable schools. Moreover, so important a characteristic as a person's age did not completely account for his conflict rate; the correlation between professional orientation and conflict rate held for all age categories tested.

The most belligerent professionally oriented teachers, far from being marginally "deviant" people, were better integrated into their peer groups, better educated, and more respected and had more group support from their colleagues. While teachers who were both professional and militant did represent only a small proportion of all teachers, it was a group with backing from a broad base of teachers.[4] Yet, it is important to note that while administrative personnel policies have traditionally been based on assumptions about individual psychology, in fact personnel problems in the public schools today seem to be basically sociological in nature.

The personality deviance hypothesis underlies several variants on the *frustration-aggression* theme. In this case, however, conflict is portrayed as a generic human response to social constraints rather than the product of unique personality traits. From this perspective, it appears that teachers have become belligerent because they have been prevented from obtaining their objectives. This may be true, but such an interpretation is rather mechanistic, since in itself it accounts for neither the origin of the objectives frustrated nor the sources of frustration. The *alienation* thesis, which has become so popular, in some respects amounts to a more elaborate frustration-aggression hypothesis. But, in this case, the sources of frustration usually have been traced to social roots, such as disenfranchisement, marginality, and powerlessness, and the objective usually has been more explicitly iden-

---

[4] Our analysis also suggests that the debate over whether militancy and professionalism are more characteristic of the NEA or AFT affiliates may be misplaced. The differences which were found do not easily lead to a clear-cut answer, and the informal leaders seem to have more influence than the officers of either organization.

tified as the search for identity and control over one's destiny or more meaningful participation in life. It is possible that engaging in conflict provides some people with a sense of meaningful participation in their society. This could help to explain our finding that both the personal job satisfaction of teachers and the overall faculty morale increased with individual and faculty conflict rates.

The alienation theme suggests that the militant leadership in teaching is coming from its youngest members who are closest to the current generation of alienated youth. However, the backgrounds of the most belligerent professional teachers indicated that, while it was true that the young males do not seem to be among the most loyal of employees, the middle-aged men most frequently became involved in conflict; apparently it takes time for even the militantly inclined to develop the respect, the group support, and the margin of security necessary to nurture the capacity for militant leadership.

The alienation theme, however, seems to focus on only the negative side of a larger equation, for while alienated people are in some sense in a state of rebellion against something, at least some of them also seem to be positively identifying with alternative standards, including in some cases, professional standards. It is difficult to believe that teachers who are well integrated into their professional groups are entirely alienated or that these teachers are simply opposed to "the system." It seems more accurate to say that they are caught between competing parts of the system and forced to choose between divergent standards.

Once the dynamics of the interplay among competing alternatives has been introduced, the full complexity of the situation comes into better focus, and some of this complexity is faintly captured in the notions of *relative deprivation* and *reference group theory*. Relative deprivation alludes to the differences between a person's present situation and some outside standard, often either a former state of his own being or the achievements of his contemporaries. Reference group theory capitalizes exclusively on the social basis of standards by which one compares himself, indicating that they are usually advocated by, or are exemplified in, some social group to which he may or may not belong. Teachers, then, can be expected to compare their station in life with that of persons of equivalent education, income, or work. They are likely to expect rewards at least equivalent to those obtained by people with similar levels of education. Moreover, even when they are making progress, they may become discontented if they are not progressing as rapidly as the groups with which they compare themselves. Hence, although in recent years teachers' average income has increased faster than that of industrial workers (over a 20 per cent increase during the last five years alone), they still lag behind other professional groups. Similarly, more than half of today's high school teachers have over five years of education, but even with this educational progress they have barely kept pace with the general society and still lag far behind other professional groups. Also, the proportion of all teachers with an M.A. has not increased during the past decade (perhaps partly because of the influx of new teachers).[5]

Although not explicit in any of the foregoing concepts, *status congruency* is still another comparative dimension of status which is essential for understanding the complex set of forces behind teacher incentive. It is important to recognize that there are several dimensions of teacher status, each of which may change at variable rates—the status congruency framework explicitly focuses on this element of convergence and divergence among a person's present statuses. Incongruence among statuses has become a critical feature of our society. Where there is no longer a close connection between various dimensions of status, such as salary, authority, and level of education, winning salary increments, for example, does not in itself provide access to power. It can be assumed, then, that a group compares its achievements in one area not only with the achievements of other people, but with its own achievements in other areas. Hence, teachers are likely to consider their standing in education relative to their salary, occupational prestige, and authority. The consistency of expectations which others have of them, and the demands which can in turn be made, depend upon the consistency of their ranking on the various dimensions of status. Congruent statuses mutually reinforce their position, whereas incongruent ones are likely to lead to confusion and precariousness of status, their lower statuses detracting from their achievements. Therefore, we can expect that people with incongruent statuses will be prompted to increase their respectability in those areas in which they have not yet become respectable enough. A significant advance in one form of status merely illuminates the disparities in the overall status pattern. Consequently, progress in one respect, far from satiating the status quest, can in itself encourage a group to increase its efforts to improve in other respects as well.

Increases which teachers may have made in their authority do not seem to have kept pace with their advances in salary and education in recent years. Such a discrepancy could be an important incentive behind their recent efforts to achieve new levels of authority. Significant in this connection is Goffman's finding that, for people occupying middle- and upper middle-class positions, there was an inverse relationship between the consistency of their statuses and their preference for extensive change in the distribution of power in the society.[6]

The *equilibration* of a *total* system is a product of the mutual congruencies among interdependent positions. Looking at the total system, advances in any one position may threaten counterpositions. In public education, for example, the changing relationship of teachers to administrators, to parents, and to students has played a part in producing the current state of tension. Administrators, for example, have good reason to feel defensive toward

[5] *NEA Research Bulletin,* October 1967, *45,* 87.

[6] Goffman, Irwin W. "Status Consistency and Preference for Change in Power Distribution," *American Sociological Review,* June 1957, *22,* 275–81.

teachers. The subordination of teachers developed during an era when they were poorly trained and when administrators had already taken significant steps toward professionalization. But, since that time, teachers have become better trained, and the supply-demand ratio for trained teachers has become more favorable. At the same time, consolidation has reduced the demand for administrators at the highest levels, and the larger role of technical decision and the increasing magnitude of public school systems have inevitably made administrators more dependent upon the judgments of teachers.

Teachers, too, have reason to be defensive about the recent efforts of laymen from all strata to reassert their authority in the wake of the crisis in education. For a time it seemed that, in the big cities especially, administrators had gained the upper hand and communities were content to let the professional administrators run things. However, middle-class parents appear to be more anxious than ever before about the education of their children and the civil rights movement has mobilized previously lethargic lower-class parents, who are also demanding a greater voice in the schooling of their children. Plans to decentralize inner city schools, such as those proposed for New York City, will bypass teachers and increase the authority of laymen at precisely a time when teachers want more authority for themselves.

Finally, the adolescent revolt, reflecting a new level of power for children, poses another threat to teachers. Children have gained leverage through a variety of devices ranging from innocuous forms of intimidation *via* their parents to slowdowns and outright violence against teachers. In most schools teachers complain about discipline problems, often casting some of the blame on what they believe to be feeble administration.

Given the quest of teachers for power and the mutual defensiveness of teachers, students, and administrators, their relationship assumes more of the character of naked bargaining than of clear-cut subordination. *Exchange theory* provides one way to analyze bargaining relationships systematically. From this perspective, it would appear that as an occupational group comes within sight of the upper occupational bracket, it develops a margin of security which, in turn, alters its ratio of investment to reward. The extended period of training of teachers and the current affluence of this country increase the teachers' career alternatives and reduce the cost of losing. As teachers achieve their own leverage, they can afford to rely less on administrators to do their bargaining for them—especially since administrators are likely to bargain low, operating as they do under different constraints.

Administrators probably are accustomed to thinking in terms of the bargaining model. Therefore, it is important to note that the exchange and congruence models provide different answers to a crucial question. For example, from a strictly bargaining point of view, one might have expected that the recent salary increments compensate teachers for their low authority and prestige; however, we have seen that within the congruence framework, a salary increase may simply encourage employees to achieve other forms of advancement. The shortcoming of the bargaining model is that, in itself, it does not indicate what a group will and will not be willing to bargain away. Less well-educated groups seem more willing to settle for salary as a compensation for their lack of authority, while better educated groups appear to be less willing to tolerate extreme discrepancies between income and authority. The bargaining model, then, must be interpreted against the background of status congruency.

CONSEQUENCES OF MILITANCY

Turning from the sources of teacher militancy to its consequences introduces several other considerations. First, in order to think clearly about the probable consequences, it is necessary to distinguish the element of militant professionalism from the broader development of teacher militancy. Militancy has many sources, and professionalism is only one. While the most professional schools in our sample had the highest conflict rates, there were some schools with higher conflict rates which were not very professional. Unlike some forms of militancy, militant professionalism represents more than a negative reaction to the existing system. For example, we found that the most professionally oriented militants in our sample were more concerned about student welfare than their adversaries.

The distinction between militancy and militant professionalism can suggest some very practical points of departure. For one thing, the incidence of "major incidents" diminished rather than increased with professional orientation, even though other types of conflict generally increased with the latter orientation. The one exception was in the most bureaucratic schools, where all types of conflict increased with the faculty's professional orientation. Indeed, conflict seemed to be most prevalent where professional faculties were also highly bureaucratized; bureaucratic controls seemed to be much more effective in the less professional schools. This means that administrative principles which are effective in one situation can backfire in another. The important point it suggests is that administrators may have to put up with some friction if they want to maintain professionally oriented faculties; supporting professionally oriented teachers may be a more effective way to control major forms of conflict than attempting to suppress them by imposing more bureaucratic control. But, it is precisely where militant professionalism is strongest that administrators are probably most tempted to impose additional control. If instead, administrators were to support teachers, teacher militancy could provide them with an effective leverage against community pressures.

Second, when we refer to the militancy of "teachers," we are in fact speaking of a small minority of all teachers. However, their numbers are less important than their potential influence. Opposing professional militancy in effect means opposing the most respected teachers with strong backing from their peers.

Third, the clash between the teaching profession and the bureaucracy is only part of the story. More tension between teachers and lay communities interested in reasserting their control also can be anticipated. Teacher militancy seems to be on a collision course with the civil rights movement in the big cities as lower-class parents begin to assert their authority. It is possible that this latter development will entail more radical modifications in the system than those ever contemplated by middle-class parents. It may be prophetic that the teachers union in New York City has not supported desegregation plans and has been resisting experimental projects leading to greater community control. This defensiveness is probably partly a reaction to the fact that teachers are bearing the brunt of criticism for poor quality education in inner city schools, even though the problem goes far beyond the factors that teachers are able to manipulate from within their classrooms. In any event, the defensiveness probably will persist until big-city teachers have gained a greater measure of control and status security. Yet, looking further into the future, we can expect that even people who otherwise steadfastly oppose change will be prepared to initiate it if they are sufficiently in charge to control some of its effects and are rewarded for their efforts.

Generally speaking, social conflict reflects the fact that there already have been changes in societal needs and demands which have not as yet been incorporated into the social structure. The concessions that are likely to be made as a result of teacher militancy are therefore likely to involve some basic changes in the structure of public school systems. One need not romanticize the motives of teachers to admit that the problems of education and the interests of American people are so varied and intricate that no one group will be permitted to dominate the system for long without being subject to attack. We are well beyond the point where school policy can be equated to the proclamations of administrators, but this is the myth we have inherited and by which we continue to live.

The only apparent basis for stability is to recognize the growing power of teachers and include them more centrally in the decision-making process. Given the severity of problems under the existing system, it will be difficult to defend any other course. Historically, in this country we have had to learn either to include the excluded or live with strife. Until teachers create a more central place within the system for themselves they will continue to go around it.

Ultimately, the direction which teacher militancy takes will depend upon the answers to two fundamental theoretical and practical questions: First, how quickly will educational bureaucracies be able to accommodate the professional roles of employees? The answer to this question will determine whether the militant professionals or the more extreme, less-professional militants will eventually hold the balance of power, and this can have dire implications for the severity of conflict, as well as for the welfare of students. Alternatives are needed to the industrial-military models of organization, with their chain of command, system-wide uniformity, and universal evaluation standards and incentive systems. We are only beginning to learn that bureaucratization is not equivalent to centralized control, but, rather, promotes subgroup autonomy. The immediate problem is not how to preserve central control but how to harness the potential of this autonomy.

Second, is *power* a limited quantity, or is it possible for teachers to increase their power without diminishing the power of administrators and laymen? It is possible that distinct domains of decision-making authority can be developed for administrators, teachers, and the public in such a way that the total power of any one group will not be sacrificed. This in turn will require that administrators, in particular, find new roles as teachers assume some of their traditional functions. One option open to them is to leave most of the internal matters to teachers, while administrators become more skillful at managing the sociological problems inherent in their relationships with the community and all levels of government. Clearly, the present crisis faced by the public schools has occurred because the external sociological problems have been neglected too long.

However, regardless of the answers to these questions, perhaps we need not be too alarmed about the prospects of militancy. Militancy sows the seeds of its own demise. The fact that teachers are segmentalized (by the very specialization that is the source of their strength) is a constant source of constraint. And as teachers gain concessions they will become more incorporated into the system. Eventually, the existing disparities among the various statuses of teachers will diminish with these gains. We can take some consolation in the practice which history has of converting the value-laden ideological issues of one era into the institutions of the next.

Towards a Differentiated Teaching Staff

M. JOHN RAND AND FENWICK ENGLISH

The acute shortage of teachers and the growing movement toward teacher professionalization are placing unbearable strains upon the present organizational structure in education. The shortage is worst in the nation's largest metropolitan areas, where organizational structures are most rigid and inner-city children in greatest need of good education. In suburban districts

Reprinted from *Phi Delta Kappan*, 49 (5): 264–268 (January 1968), by permission of authors and publisher.

there is growing constituent dissatisfaction. Taxpayers are balking at increasing education costs without some proof that the pudding will be better.

Rising militancy and mass "resignations" last fall are signs that teachers are dissatisfied with their roles as mere implementers of administrative decision. Their demands are certainly more inclusive than simply a raise in pay. Teachers are telling us something we should have known or predicted long ago. When a group of people increase their technical competence close to that of the top members of the hierarchy, lines of authority become blurred. The subordinate position begins to rest more upon arbitrary and traditional distinctions than upon competence to perform the job.

Teachers are demanding inclusion in the decision-making process in education. As Corwin says,[1] professionalism is associated positively with militancy. Rather than arouse hostility in administrators and lay boards, it should be welcomed as one sign that the teaching profession is coming of age.

Increasing teacher specialization and competence mean that roles within the present educational structure are in the process of change. Teachers are recognizing that to break out of the ceilings imposed by the single salary schedule they must reexamine the assumptions which support it. The increasing need for high specialization and advanced training means that some teachers should be paid between $20,000 and $25,000 per year, as are specialists in other fields. So long as we have the single salary schedule, however, no one will get this amount. The money simply cannot be raised without a complete (and in the short run completely impossible) overhaul of tax structures, school financing, and public value systems.

Hence the dissolution of the single salary schedule is a must if the teaching profession is to advance. Teachers will generally admit that not all of them possess the same abilities or strengths. They reject the onus of "merit pay," however, as "unprofessional" or otherwise undesirable. Merit pay plans offer the advantage of dissolving the single salary schedule, but ordinarily make no distinction in job responsibilities of teachers. Added pay is for "merit," not for added responsibility. As long as teaching is considered an art, one man's "superior" teacher is another's "average" teacher. Judgment of teaching "excellence" must be based on careful research just beginning to emerge at some universities. We have a long way to go before we can specify on the basis of empirical evidence what teaching excellence consists of. Hence we do not have the foundation for merit pay.

The Temple City plan approaches the problem from a different perspective. Teachers are not treated the same. They may receive additional remuneration for increased professional responsibilities, which means change in their roles as teachers. These new responsibilities imply increased training and time on the job, and implicit in the concept of advancement is professional

[1] Ronald G. Corwin, "Militant Professionalism, Initiative and Compliance in Public Education," *Sociology of Education*, Vol. 38, pp. 310–31, Summer 1965.

competence as a teacher, however it is measured. Teachers are not chosen to be paid more simply for continuing to perform the same functions; they are paid more for assuming increased responsibilities in the instructional program. They are selected on the basis of their experience and qualifications for the job by a professional panel and are retained only as they are able to perform adequately in their capacities. The Temple City Differentiated Staffing Plan, almost wholly designed by teachers, offers a way for teachers to receive remuneration of $20,000 per year by differentiating teaching roles and systematically enlarging their authority and decision-making powers to shape the instructional program.

The Temple City plan is not a brand new idea. Aspects of the plan have been espoused by Myron Lieberman,[2] J. Lloyd Trump,[3] and Robert Bush and Dwight Allen [4] at Stanford University. Allen was instrumental in developing the Temple City project, funded by the Charles F. Kettering Foundation of Denver, Colorado, for for an 18-month study. The TEPS program of the NEA has also been active in proposing differentiated roles for professional personnel. The strength of the Temple City concept of differentiated staffing resides in a high degree of staff participation in its development. Indeed, the process of development is every bit as important as the product, i.e., an acceptable organizational design to implement the ideas of the professional staff.

The original model of differentiated staffing was developed by Allen and presented to the California State Board of Education in April of 1966 (see Figure 1). Later it was altered in the work done by Temple City teachers (see Figure 2). At the present, this model is undergoing further revision as a result of financial studies and further staff feedback. A brief sketch of the job descriptions follows.

TEACHING RESEARCH ASSOCIATE

The teaching research associate (TRA) is the "self-renewal" unit of the organization. His primary function is to introduce new concepts and ideas into the schools. He is well versed in research methodology and evaluation of instruction. The TRA may conduct field studies, but his major purpose is to translate research into instructional probes at the school level. The TRA functions in the present structure as a classroom teacher, as do all of the other personnel in the differentiated staffing plan, although in a limited capacity. In this way he does not lose sight of the receivers of his efforts. The TRA represents the apex of professional advancement for the aspiring teacher.

[2] Myron Lieberman, *The Future of Public Education*. Chicago: University of Chicago Press, 1960.

[3] J. Lloyd Trump and Dorsey Baynham, *Guide to Better Schools*. Chicago: Rand McNally, 1961.

[4] Dwight Allen and Robert Bush, *A New Design for High School Education*. New York: McGraw-Hill, 1964.

Figure 1. The proposed teacher hierarchy based on differentiated compensation and responsibilities. (This model of a differentiated staffing plan was developed by Dwight Allen and was presented to the California State Board of Education in April, 1966.)

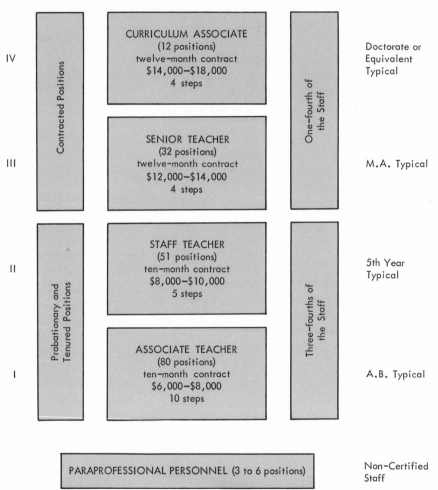

The teaching research associate meets all of Rogers'[5] criteria for initiating planned change in education. These are: (1) base the topics investigated on felt needs of practitioners; (2) create an educational structure to facilitate change; (3) raise the practitioners' ability to utilize the research results. Part of the TRA's responsibilities are implied in the third criterion mentioned by Rogers. Much of his liaison work with staff and current research will be to increase the sophistication level of teachers and help them use it in practice and evaluate its effectiveness.

[5] Everett M. Rogers, "Developing a Strategy for Planned Change," paper presented at a Symposium on the Application of System Analysis and Management Techniques to Educational Planning in California, Orange, California, June, 1967.

Teacher Job Analysis Task Force:

Allan Shuey, Temple City High School (Chairman)
William Schmidt, Oak Avenue Intermediate School
Tad Root, Elementary Schools
Janice Peet, Elementary Schools
Fenwick English, Administration

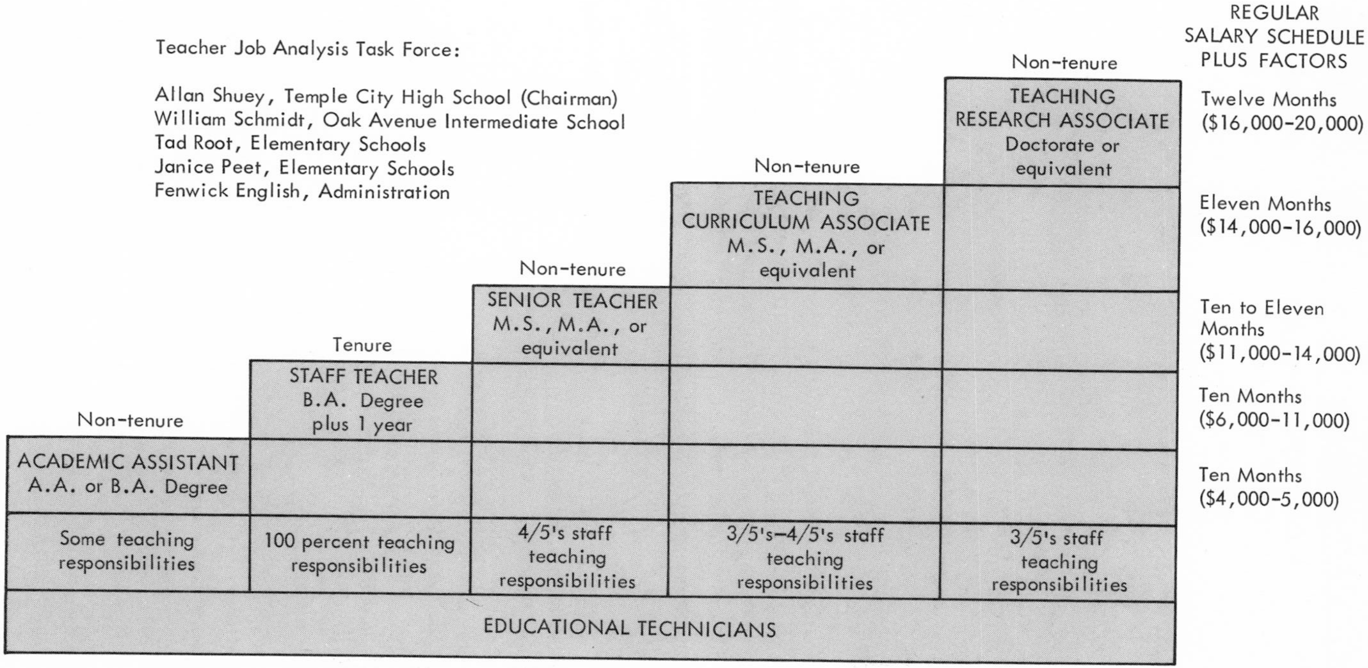

REGULAR SALARY SCHEDULE PLUS FACTORS

Position	Tenure status	Teaching responsibilities	Salary
ACADEMIC ASSISTANT — A.A. or B.A. Degree	Non-tenure	Some teaching responsibilities	Ten Months ($4,000–5,000)
STAFF TEACHER — B.A. Degree plus 1 year	Tenure	100 percent teaching responsibilities	Ten Months ($6,000–11,000)
SENIOR TEACHER — M.S., M.A., or equivalent	Non-tenure	4/5's staff teaching responsibilities	Ten to Eleven Months ($11,000–14,000)
TEACHING CURRICULUM ASSOCIATE — M.S., M.A., or equivalent	Non-tenure	3/5's–4/5's staff teaching responsibilities	Eleven Months ($14,000–16,000)
TEACHING RESEARCH ASSOCIATE — Doctorate or equivalent	Non-tenure	3/5's staff teaching responsibilities	Twelve Months ($16,000–20,000)

EDUCATIONAL TECHNICIANS

Figure 2.   Temple City unified school district: a model of differentiated staffing.

Teaching Curriculum Associate

The teaching curriculum associate (TCA) also must possess knowledge of research methodology, except that his knowledge is more applicable to curriculum theory, construction, and evaluation. In addition, the TCA would be adept at modifying national curriculum studies to meet local needs and local teacher proclivities.

The TCA also works at raising the level of teacher specialization in specific subject areas. He is more of a communications specialist than the TRA. However, due to the overlap in some functions, and because it is difficult to separate research from curriculum and instructional improvement studies, these two functions will probably be combined into one position: the Teaching Research-Curriculum Associate.

The Senior Teacher

The senior teacher is primarily responsible for the application of curriculum and instructional innovations to the classroom. The senior teacher is an acknowledged master practitioner, a learning engineer, a skilled diagnostician of the learning process. He is the teacher's teacher.

The senior teacher as an instructional advisor heads a subject group and represents this area on the school academic senate. He shares with the school principal the selection, performance, and evaluation of his colleagues in that subject specialty. In a team teaching situation, the senior teacher would function as a team leader. At least one-half of this teacher's day would be with students.

The Staff Teacher

In a sense, all teachers in the differentiated staffing plan are staff teachers. A full-time staff teacher spends his school hours with students. He performs the same professional functions as most teachers in typical school districts. In a differentiated staffing plan the staff teacher is relieved of semi-professional and clerical duties by employment of the following assistants:

The Academic Assistant

The academic assistant is a skilled paraprofessional, or a teacher intern (associate teacher) from a nearby college or university. He works with students and may instruct in special or skilled areas. He may also maintain physical materials, grade papers, and supervise resource center activities or student study.

The Educational Technician

The educational technician assumes many of the clerical and housekeeping tasks that consume so much professional time in the present organization.

The technician keeps records, duplicates material, types, supervises student movement on campus, takes attendance, etc. The technician has little, if any, instructional responsibilities.

THE ACADEMIC SENATE

Teachers are formally involved in school decision making through the organization of an academic senate on each campus. One of the responsibilities of senior teachers is to represent the staff in the establishment of school policies relating to the educational program and its improvement.

THE SCHOOL MANAGER

In addition, the principal's role is differentiated by establishing a position called school manager. The school manager assumes responsibility for most of the business functions of school operation and thus relieves the principal for attention to the instructional program. It is hoped that eventually the principal will also refurbish his image as a teacher by assuming some direct teaching responsibilities with students. Most principals would find this impossible now, since they too are overburdened with paperwork and administrivia.

This combination of teacher specialists and administrator generalists would provide the school with the best judgments of all the professionals occupied with shaping a dynamic instructional program. School leadership is clearly enhanced with teachers exercising judgment as to how the instructional program should be improved. The principal's role is strengthened, since he can count on the specialized expertise of his senior teachers in the hiring and evaluation of the instructional staff. Teachers are intimately involved in professionalizing and disciplining their own ranks through the academic senate. This is crucial for full-fledged maturity; effective professional regulation can only occur when teachers assume responsibility for each other's performance. Administrators should welcome this desire for more responsibilities and assist their staffs in learning how to develop and exercise the leadership concomitants to fulfill this important professional role.

A discussion of differentiated staffing would not be complete without mentioning some of the problems the district has encountered in studying this concept. Differentiated staffing challenges a basic assumption inherent in the organizational structure of education. The myth that all teachers are equal exercises a powerful influence upon our thinking. The present organizational structure which assumes that one teacher can be all things to all students is a barrier of the first magnitude, especially at the elementary level.

One way of avoiding change and protecting oneself is for the teacher to shut his door and isolate himself with his 30 children. The position of the teacher in his classroom fortress is easier and more secure without the scrutiny of his colleagues. To differentiate teacher roles is contrary to the standard organizational pattern of elementary education for the last 100 years. When teachers perform different functions and assume new responsibilities they cannot be with children all day long. They must have time during the school day to plan with colleagues and conduct studies or meet with individual students. This implies some type of flexible scheduling, plus dual use of instructional models and resource facilities. This in turn means that teachers must delegate to paraprofessionals many nonprofessional responsibilities that do not demand a high degree of skill and training.

We have found a greater resistance at the elementary level to concepts of differentiated staffing than at the secondary. Some teachers fear that team teaching, use of paraprofessionals, resource centers, and flexible scheduling will permanently "damage" their children. They fail to recall that the present organizational structure established in 1870 at the Quincy Grammar School was organized for administrative convenience and that critics pointed out even then that it rather callously ignored the needs of continuous educational progress for each individual student.

Also we noted that a greater proportion of women than men object to teachers assuming a professional disciplinary role with their colleagues. This is especially true at the primary level, where a traditionally protective environment shields both students and teachers from decision making and colleague interaction.

At the secondary level, the idea of differentiated staffing was received more warmly. Here more teachers are men and the tradition of subject area specialization and leadership through department chairmen has been well established. However, some teachers at the secondary level are just as immobilized in their six-period day, self-contained classrooms as their elementary counterparts.

Some administrators will be uncomfortable in sharing the decision-making process with their staffs. Fear of losing status is an important consideration when proposing new roles for teachers. One must remember that almost all other roles in a school district hinge upon that of the teacher. If the teacher base is expanded upward, a shift is required in functions all the way to the superintendent. This means that in the Temple City plan teachers (teaching research associates) will sit with principals in an academic coordinating council headed by the superintendent. This district-wide group plans and anticipates district movement. Teachers (teaching curriculum associates) will also be a part of the curriculum coordinating council headed by the assistant superintendent. This group articulates curriculum development through the grades. Teacher specialists form an integral part of the decision-making machinery with the administrators of the district.

The Temple City plan of differentiated staffing offers a way to emancipate the teacher. It changes and enlarges the roles of teachers, increases their autonomy and decision-making powers, offers career advancement, and places them in a position to assume a regulatory function of their own profession. From the point of the administrator it enhances the leadership potential of his staff and builds in some guarantee that the instructional program will indeed remain vital and strong in all areas. A board of education and community should be encouraged when their teachers are willing to assume a corporate responsibility for the quality of education in their schools. The fact that teachers are disciplining themselves, are constantly in the self-renewal process, and have the freedom to rise as teachers to the top of their abilities and willingness to work means that the collective human resources which lie fallow in every organization are more fully tapped. In the short time our project has been operative we have been amazed at the talent which has emerged from our staff.

The most difficult barrier of all is not physical or financial but the subtle limitations in our vision, attitudes, and expectations, conditioned by one organizational structure for over 100 years. The validity of this structure may have been eroded, but its form has been firmly implanted in our psyches. The ability to rise above our own conditioning and previous expectancy levels is the most difficult problem, for solutions cannot be devised until problems are accurately perceived. Perception is limited when assumptions cannot be questioned. Our inability to see that some of our frustrations stem from traditional assumptions is a tragic dilemma. Differentiated staffing is a concept which challenges a whole host of notions about how American education should be organized and operated. At the moment it may be heresy; in a decade it may be practice.

Recent Analyses of Teaching

WALTER B. WAETJEN

My plan is first to review several researches, and then sweep together the crumbs of these researches to see whether there are some patterns in the findings. I shall not try to review all the studies of teaching, for if I were to do so, you and I would be here more than a week because of an increasing volume of such research in the past two decades.

H. H. Anderson was one of the first to try to find out what goes on in classrooms. He divided the teacher behaviors he identified into two major categories: *dominative* behavior and *integrative* behavior. By dominative behavior he meant the ways in which a teacher controls the classroom situation; by integrative behavior he referred to the ways in which a teacher tries to get youngsters to synthesize and to integrate what they learn. In the late 40's, John Withall developed a rather complex technique for assessing

Reprinted from *The Bulletin of the National Association of Secondary School Principals*, 50 (314): 17–29 (December 1966), by permission of author and publisher.

the social-emotional climate of the classroom. These initial, pioneering attempts to assess the teaching act were rather gross, as would be expected. As these assessment efforts went on, however, there came to be greater differentiation and better discrimination in the way teaching was measured.

Following up on Withall's work, Medley and Mitzell developed an instrument which they called the Observation Schedule and Record. (oscar for short.) Some of you have probably seen it or used it. oscar is simply a list of behaviors of teachers and of pupils. By charting what occurs in the classroom on this checklist, one can identify three major factors: (1) the emotional climate of the classroom; (2) the emphasis on verbal discourse; and (3) the social organization. At first blush it may seem that a classroom's emotional climate and its social organization are the same thing, but they are not. Climate refers to the feeling tone; social organization refers to the way in which the people are related, one to another.

OLD ASSUMPTIONS BLASTED

The past six or seven years have been especially profitable in terms of research on the teaching act. If nothing else, recent research has certainly blasted—and I mean blasted to smithereens—some of our assumptions. The major casualty has been the idea that we can evaluate teaching by "watching" a teacher teach. It is patently clear that one cannot evaluate teaching simply by going into a classroom without any scheme or schedule or checklist in hand and just watching what goes on. I know this raises all kinds of questions, and well it should, because what it discredits is still the most prevalent means of evaluating teachers. In fact, many principals and many supervisors use a major portion of their time in watching teachers teach.

Nevertheless, honesty forces us to face the fact that the research of the past half-dozen years raises serious questions about present modes of evaluating, not only of teachers in service but of student teachers as well. Schools of education have been no better than the public schools in heeding the findings of research. With very few exceptions, the professor or the critic teacher simply walks into a student teacher's classroom, sits down, and "watches" what goes on—despite the demonstrated fact that the evaluation which results is anything but trustworthy.

So much by the way of general introduction. Now I wish to take up a few specific pieces of research. I used three criteria in making my selection:

1. They were done in public school classrooms, not contrived laboratory situations
2. The subjects in the study were typical of those found in public school classrooms
3. They were done on the teaching act just as it occurs in the classroom, without any attempt on the part of the experimenter to change the behavior of the teacher.

Unfortunately, these criteria eliminated two excellent studies, which I commend to you. One of them was done by Hilda Taba, who tried to find out whether one can train teachers in such a way that they have a significant impact on the level of cognition or of conceptualization in the classroom. The other was done by Mary Jane Aschner with highly gifted youngsters, using Guilford's structure of the intellect as the basis for determining just how teachers might help youngsters by structuring the classroom; in this instance, by answering questions to achieve different kinds of outcomes.

HUGHES' STUDY OF ELEMENTARY TEACHING

The first study I shall review was done by Marie Hughes, under the title, "The Development of Means for the Assessment of the Quality of Teaching." It grew out of an in-service investigation in Provo, Utah, designed to determine sound bases for a merit pay system. The feeling was that the usual criteria of degrees earned, years of experience, and involvement activities had little relevance to quality of teaching to justify merit pay distinctions. It seemed logical to look at teaching itself, to see whether the "goodness" of teachers could be measured.

The objective of Hughes' study was to present a description of teaching as it is found in elementary schools from kindergarten through sixth grade. The study was carried on by analysis of the interaction of teacher and child, teacher and group, and teacher and class. One group of subjects in this study were 25 teachers who were judged to be "good," selected from a list of 40 teachers recommended by a county office staff. There was another group of 10 teachers from one school, selected as representative of the 25 professional employees in that school, two teachers from each grade.

Two observers were placed in each classroom to record actual teacher behavior and pupil response. They worked on the basis of the "Provo Code," developed by Hughes and her associates when they were first working in Provo. It categorized 31 specific teacher functions or pupil functions. These can be subsumed under three broad classifications. Let us look at these categories a moment, starting from the bottom. *Negative affectivity* stands for those times when a teacher reprimands, admonishes, threatens, punishes, et cetera. *Positive affectivity* stands for the very opposite, when the teacher uses supportive statements or offers help to a pupil. Another category of particular interest is the *development of content*. This refers to occasions when a teacher responds to a pupil's activity by accepting, by clarifying, by evaluating, etc.

One particular teacher function that appears to be especially important from the Hughes study is *control*. This includes such things as the teacher's setting standards, structuring, or in some other way organizing the classroom so that it has focus and purpose. Hughes included negative affectivity as part of control, because when a teacher is reprimanding, admonishing, or threatening, he is controlling.

Analysis revealed, further, that the most frequent and pervasive functions performed by the teachers were in this first category, *controlling*. Hughes finally wrote, "The teachers directed the children in what they should do and how they should do it, what they should answer and how they should answer. There was little evidence of discipline problems."

RARE USE OF PERSONAL RESPONSE

Another significant finding revealed the teacher's extremely low use of functions that develop content. From my point of view this is important—and I should like to dwell on it. Information which children placed in the situation was often ignored, overlooked, or not considered by the teacher. More importantly, the kinds of teacher responses which seek expansion and association of ideas, which ask for comparison and inference, and which relate to personal experience and opinion occurred rarely.

Personal response functions include acts which develop rapport between teacher and child, teacher and group, or teacher and class on a personal basis. This accounted for a relatively small number of the total teaching functions that a teacher performs. Personal response, Hughes found, was correlated significantly but negatively with the category of negative affectivity. In general, teachers use more functions of positive affectivity than of negative affectivity. From a mental health point of view, this is encouraging.

Hughes, you recall, studied two groups of teachers, 25 in one and 10 in the other. In comparing these groups it was found that there were no significant differences between the 25 teachers who were judged as being good and the other teachers representative of one school. There were some differences that were not statistically significant, but one difference was striking enough to deserve mention: primary teachers are more controlling and more negative than intermediate grade teachers. They also performed a larger number of total teaching functions than the intermediate teachers did during the experimental period.

When the six best records were compared to nine records clustering around the median, there were significant differences favoring the good group on controlling functions and on functions that develop content, personal response, and that demonstrate negative affectivity. There were no differences between the groups on positive affectivity. Something that runs through the research on teaching, no matter whether a teacher is judged as being excellent, mediocre, or poor, is that all teachers seem to use about the same degree of positive affectivity.

BELLACK STUDY OF HIGH SCHOOL TEACHING

A study conducted by Arno Bellack and associates included 15 high school teachers and 345 students in the New York City area. The teachers and students were from classes in Problems of Democracy in grades 10 and 12.

Bellack's study called for more than merely classroom observation and an assessment of what was seen. He developed, with the teachers, a unit of instruction on international economic problems, which was to run over a two-week period. The teachers were very carefully rehearsed in terms of the actual concepts or substantive meanings that were to be developed during this period. As in most researches on teaching, a system for categorizing pupil behaviors was developed.

1. *Structuring* refers to focusing attention on subject matter or procedures. It's a launching of interaction, getting a group or class started on something, having them attend or give attention to something.
2. *Soliciting* refers to eliciting a verbal or a physical response. Soliciting may be present when a pupil or a teacher asks a question. It may consist of giving a command or of making a request.
3. *Responding* is reciprocal to soliciting and occurs only in relation to soliciting.
4. *Reacting* comes about as a result of structuring, soliciting, and responding, but it is not produced directly by them. For example, when either a teacher or a pupil accepts, rejects, modifies, or expands on what has occurred in the classroom, reacting is taking place. A good example might be when a teacher evaluates a student's response.

The objectives of Bellack's research were to describe the verbal events that occur in the classroom; to discover similarities and consistencies in the teaching pattern or discourse; to define the distinctive aspects of the roles played by teachers and pupils; and to find out how to provide some estimate of the variability among teachers and classes along each of these dimensions. I want to call your attention to some of the major findings of this research.

One of his major findings has to do with the teacher-pupil ratio of lines spoken. The ratio was three to one, teachers to pupils. In this study, at least, teachers were considerably more active verbally than pupils.

It was also found that the teaching roles of the classroom are clearly delineated for both teachers and pupils. Teachers are responsible for structuring the lesson, while the pupils' primary task is to respond to teachers' solicitations. More specifically, structuring and soliciting were teacher functions, responding was a pupil function. And, very significantly, reacting was primarily a teacher function.

VARIANCE IN SUBSTANTIVE MEANINGS

In most classes, structuring accounted for about 10 percent of the total number of lines spoken. Soliciting, responding, and reacting each accounted for between 20 and 30 percent. Further, approximately 75 percent of the total discourse in the classroom was concerned specifically with substantive meanings; that is, with curriculum content. But of all the categories, classes varied most widely in the substantive meanings that were expressed. It must be remembered in this connection that there had been a training period for the teachers along the lines of specific concepts or generalizations to be developed during the research. Nevertheless, to repeat, classes varied most widely in the substantive meanings that were expressed rather than their being clustered around the specific concepts that were to have been developed. Bellack states it this way: "This finding was not anticipated, in view of the fact that the major restriction imposed on teachers by the research procedure was the specification of the particular substantive meanings to be covered."

If learning is interacting with ideas and with people, then one would expect to find a fairly high degree of expression of substantive meanings by the learners as well as the teachers. But in this study it developed that approximately 25 percent of the total discourse involved instructional meanings, and all of these were expressed by teachers rather than by pupils.

Bellack made these comments on his findings:

> One way of conceptualizing the results is in terms of the language game of teaching and learning. Despite the fact that the rules of this game are not explicitly stated for any of the players, this sample of teachers and pupils obviously followed a set of implicit rules, with very few deviations. These rules define the teaching game, although classes differ somewhat in details. The classroom game involves one person called the teacher and one or more persons called pupils. The object of the game is to carry on a linguistic discourse about subject matter, and the final payoff of the game is measured in terms of the amount of learning displayed by the pupils after a given period of play.
>
> In playing the game, each player must follow a specific set of rules. If one plays the role of teacher in this game, he will follow one set of rules. If one plays the role of pupil, he will follow a somewhat different, although complementary, set of rules. One is permitted some deviations from these rules, and the subsequent pattern will characterize one's individual style of play. These deviations, however, are infrequent and are relatively minor in comparison to the general system of expectations. In fact, the first rule of the game, which might be called "the rule of rules," is that if one is to play the game at all, he will consistently follow the rules specified for his role.

College teaching provides a good example of playing the game. There is a clear-cut expectation in college that the professor will determine what is to be covered in the course and the pace at which it is to be covered. Should a professor not prescribe what is to be taught, his students are at a loss. Why? Because the professor is not playing his part of the game. The rules students have learned through experience have taught them that the professor sets forth content, and, if he doesn't, students are upset. In like manner, the professor expects that the student will turn in his papers on time and that he will respond in certain ways but not in other ways. Should he not, then the professor is upset, and he knows that the students are not playing the game properly.

FLANDERS' STUDY OF TEACHER INFLUENCE

Another major study on teaching was done by Flanders, who tried to develop a system by which he could measure the teacher's influence in the classroom. He developed a category system which takes into account each interaction in the classroom. It enables one to determine whether the teacher controls students in such a way as to free them for action, or, on the other hand, whether the teacher acts to decrease students' freedom of action. The procedure runs something like this: There is an observer in a classroom who, at the end of each three-second interval, records the observed acts of the teacher. This continues at the rate of 20 or 25 observations per minute. When there is a major change in the class formation or in the communication pattern, or if the teacher shifts from lecturing to giving a test, the observer draws a double line and notes the change. Flanders developed ten groupings of behavior, which I shall describe briefly. The first seven of these categories cover teacher behavior. Categories eight and nine are what Flanders calls "pupil talk," and the last category is "noise."

1. *Accepts feelings:* The teacher accepts or clarifies the tone of the student, but does so in an unthreatening manner.
2. *Praises or encourages:* Student action is taken into account. Jokes that relieve tension, but not jokes that are at the expense of an individual, are recorded in this category.
3. *Accepts and uses students' ideas:* Ideas offered by students are clarified, built, or developed.
4. *Asks Questions:* The teacher asks questions about either curriculum content or procedures the pupils are to follow in the classroom. This teacher action obviously requires a pupil response.

These first four categories of teacher behavior are what Flanders refers to as indirect influence. An indirect influence increases the freedom of action of the pupils. It is referred to as the "I" (indirect) part of the scale.

5. *Lecturing:* The teacher gives facts, opinions, or expresses his own ideas.
6. *Giving directions:* This category includes the teacher's commands, orders, and directions.
7. *Criticizing or justifying authority:* These are teacher behaviors intended to change pupil behavior from being unacceptable to acceptable. This might consist of reprimanding a youngster or it might be an occasion where the teacher uses his position as a way of justifying authority.

Categories five, six and seven are referred to as the "D" (direct) part of the scale and serve to increase the control of the teacher by concentrating authority in the teacher while decreasing pupil participation.

8. *Pupil response:* A pupil responds to a teacher in either a verbal or physical manner.

9. *Initiation:* Questions and statements are initiated by the pupil, quite independent of direct teacher influence.
10. *Silence, noise, or confusion:* This group is used when an act cannot be placed in one of the other nine categories.

INFLUENCE PATTERNS VARY

The teacher influence pattern may vary according to the way the class is organized. Different patterns of organization might be seen, for example, when a class is settling down to work; when the teacher is introducing new material; when there are periods of evaluation; and when the teacher is supervising seat work. These are noted on the interaction analysis to determine if there is a difference in the ID ratio as the classroom situation or activity periods change.

This study in question was done with 16 eighth-grade mathematics teachers and 16 seventh-grade social studies teachers. In selecting the teachers, Flanders chose those who had what we might call natural teaching styles. However, some of them used an above-average amount of direct influence on their students, while others had an above-average amount of indirect influence.

Flanders found that the students in the indirect classes (classes where teachers used indirect methods extensively) achieved more than students in direct classes in both mathematics and science. He also found the differences were even greater between classes consistently exposed to indirect and direct patterns of teaching. In other words, the most indirect teachers were associated with higher academic achievement by students, while the most direct teachers were associated with lower pupil achievement.

A third finding was that indirect teachers are more flexible. They tend to begin their teaching of a topic or unit with a higher proportion of indirect influences, and they become more direct in their approach as progress toward the goal of the learning occurs. In contrast, this variation is not present in the direct classes. Students who achieved most and had significantly high scores on attitude tests were in classes exposed to flexible patterns of teacher response. To say that differently, the greater the teacher's repertoire of teaching styles, the more likely there was to be greater student achievement and high scores on attitude tests.

PERKINS' STUDY OF CLASSROOM ACTIVITY

Hugh Perkins at the University of Maryland developed a procedure for measuring student behavior, learning activity, and teacher behavior as these may be related to differential achievement. For his study he chose some students who appeared to be achieving satisfactorily and others who were underachievers, and then tried to find out how teaching behaviors and various learning activities influenced student achievement. Two-minute samples of classroom behavior and learning activities of 72 fifth-graders and 72 teachers were used. The observations were made in one or more of four academic subjects: language arts, science, mathematics, and social studies. Altogether there were 2,410 two-minute samplings, totaling about 80 hours of observation over five months.

Perkins used three scales to distribute his data. One of these classified teachers in five groups: *leader-director*, when the teacher is conducting a recitation, a discussion, is lecturing, or works with small groups; *resource person; supervisor; socialization agent*, which means that the teacher would point to the right thing to do, the social expectancies, or criticize a youngster's behavior; and *evaluator*, when the teacher listens or gives a mark for an oral report to either an individual or a group.

In addition, Perkins had a series of student classes, describing what students actually did. There were eight of these:

1. The student is interested in ongoing work; he listens and watches.
2. He is reading or writing or doing other appropriate work in the assigned area.
3. He shows high activity or involvement; for example, reciting or carrying on a physical activity associated with the learning activity.
4. He is intent on work in some other subject or area; that is, he is doing school work of some kind, but not of the kind or in the subject he is supposed to be occupied with.
5. He is work-oriented in a social respect; an example would be discussing school work with one or more of his peers.
6. He is work-oriented socially toward the teacher; he is discussing some problem or procedure with the teacher.
7. He is social-friendly oriented; he is carrying on conversation with classmates about something other than school work.
8. The student withdraws; he seems detached and out of touch with ideas or activities present in the classroom.

Perkins found that approximately 75 percent of the time, behavior of both achievers and underachievers was academic work-oriented, listening or watching, reading or writing, high activity, or working with peers. Note that these mean that for 75 percent of the time both the achiever and the underachiever were focused on the presumed learning task. A second finding was that the achievers engaged in significantly more social work with peers than did the underachievers. Third, the underachievers more frequently withdrew from learning activities. Fourth, about 75 percent of the time, seat work and recitation were the dominant learning activities. Discussion, individual work, group work, or oral reports were used infrequently.

LOW INCIDENCE OF PRAISE

Perkins' fifth finding is of interest in terms of Marie Hughes' findings: there was a low incidence of praise. Only four percent of the time was taken up by pupils' ideas, pupils' answers, or personal experiences of pupils. Finally, the teacher used the leader role and/or the supervisor role almost exclusively. Eighty-eight percent of all the teaching acts were in those two categories. This paralleled the high incidence of seatwork and recitation as pupil activities.

RECURRING PATTERNS IN THE RESEARCHES

The picture of teaching that has been presented from these researches is vastly different from that picture of teaching which is expressed, hoped for, desired or striven for in our curriculum guides. There is a great difference between what and how we profess to be teaching, and what is actually going on in classrooms.

It is very clear that in all of these studies the teacher was in a dominant position, and, contrarily, the pupils played a passive role in the classroom. Bellack said that, in terms of the total number of lines spoken, there was a three-to-one ratio, teachers to pupil. Perkins stated that the leader-supervisor role was played by the teacher 88 percent of the time. What all this adds up to is the "rule of the two-thirds." At least two-thirds of the time the teacher is either dominant, controlling, or speaking in the classroom.

Teachers, regardless of grade level, subject taught, or supervisors' ratings, make very little use of pupil behavior in helping to develop curriculum content. This means that personal data, placed in the learning situation by either the teacher or by the learner, are practically nonexistent. Perkins found that this occurred only one percent of the time. Marie Hughes stated it differently. She said that when a pupil attempts to bring personal information into the picture, he is either cut short, ignored, or overlooked.

LEARNER IN PASSIVE ROLE

Another recurring theme that I see is that in all of these researches we find the learner cast in a passive role. (Perkins commented that there was a high incidence of seat work. Bellack commented that the pupil's primary task is to respond to the teacher's solicitation.) I would argue that some learning is essentially passive. But I would argue that more of it is an active process.

Another generalization the data consistently support is that the level of cognition, or thinking, in the typical classroom is low. Hughes says, "The most common mental operation found in the classroom was simple memory and recall."

Finally, by far the largest portion of the meanings expressed in the classroom are substantive, and most of the meanings are expressed by the teacher. What a proper teacher-pupil ratio in this respect should be I can't say, but I do believe that students should be encouraged or permitted to be more expressive.

Psychoneurobiochemeducation

DAVID KRECH

I am a rat-brain psychologist with a weakness for speculation. Now time was when rat research was a fairly harmless activity, pursued by underpaid, dedicated, well-meaning characters. The world took little note and cared even less about our researches on how rats learned to thread their way through mazes. Oh, occasionally a misguided educator would take us seriously and try to fashion an educational psychology out of our rats-in-a-maze studies. But the classroom teachers—once removed from the school of education—would quickly see through such nonsense, and, forsaking all rats, would turn to the serious and difficult task of teaching children—unencumbered and unaided by our research and theory.

But time no longer is. Our psychology—especially when combined with educational practice and theory—must now be listed among the Powerful and, even perhaps, the Dangerous sciences. I refer specifically to the recent research developments in brain biochemistry and behavior—to some of which research I now turn.

The research I will discuss really concerns itself with the venerable mind-body problem beloved of philosophers and theologians. For brain biochemistry and behavior research seeks to find the *physical* basis for memory. In essence it asks the following question: In what corporal forms do we retain the remembrance of things past? What are the chemical or neurological or anatomical substrates of the evocative ghosts we call "memories"? Over the centuries of thought and decades of scientific research we have gained but very little on this question. Today, however, there is a feeling abroad that we are on the verge of great discoveries. Indeed, some researchers believe that we already know, in the rough, the form the final answer will take to the question I have raised. And it is this: The physical basis of any memory, whatever else it may be, involves either the production of new proteins, the release of differentiated molecules of ribonucleic acids (RNA's) or the induction of higher enzymatic activity levels in the brain. In a word, for every separate memory in the mind we will eventually find a differentiated chemical in the brain—"chemical memory pellets," as it were.

What warrant do we have for such a prophecy? To begin with, we have reason to believe that the storage of memory in the brain is a many-splendored, multi-phased, actively changing affair. That is, any single memory is not merely "deposited" in a completed form in the brain. Rather, it goes through a complex developmental history in the brain in which it changes from a short-term into a long-term memory. And each stage in this consoli-

Reprinted from *Phi Delta Kappan*, 50 (7): 370–375 (March 1969), by permission of author and publisher.

dation process seems to be dependent upon different although interrelated chemical mechanisms. Let me indicate to you one set (of quite a number which are now available) of speculative hypotheses concerning this developmental transformation of memories.

First we can assume that immediately after every experience, a relatively short-lived reverberatory process is set up within the brain. This process continues for a time after the stimulus disappears and permits us to remember events which occurred moments or minutes ago. But this reverberatory process fairly quickly decays and disappears—and as it does, so does the related memory. However, under certain conditions, the short-term reverberatory process, before it disappears completely from the scene, triggers off a second and quite different series of events in the brain. This second series of events involves the release of new RNA's or the production of new proteins and other macromolecules. And these chemical changes are relatively long-lasting and serve as the physical bases of our long-term memories.

Now it can be supposed that if we increased the robustness or the survival time of the initial reverberatory process we might increase the probability of converting the short-term memory into a long-term memory. There are several ways one could do that. Through the repetition of the same stimulus one could presumably prolong or continually reinstate the reverberatory process and thus, perhaps, make it more effective in inducing permanent chemical changes in the brain. The old-fashioned term for this procedure is "drill" or "practice," and drill and practice are indeed effective techniques for helping the conversion of short-term memories into long-term ones.

But James McGaugh, at the University of California at Irvine, got the bright idea that he could achieve much the same results chemically. His argument—very much simplified—went something like this: A drug which would increase neural and chemical activity within the brain might either increase the vigor of the reverberatory process, or the ease with which the long-term chemical processes would "take off," and thus facilitate the conversion of short-term memories into long-term ones. Apparently his idea was a sound one, for with the use of chemical compounds like strychnine and metrazol, which are central nervous system stimulants, McGaugh has been eminently successful in raising the intellectual level of hundreds of southern California mice.

In one of his experiments which is most pregnant with social implications and promises and forebodings for the future, McGaugh tested the maze-learning ability of two quite different strains of mice. One of the strains was, by heredity, particularly adept at maze learning; the other, particularly stupid at that task. Some animals from each strain were injected with different doses of metrazol after each daily learning trial to see whether there would be an improvement in their ability to retain what they had learned on that trial—and some were not. The findings pleased everyone—presumably even the mice. With the optimal dosage of metrazol, the chemically treated mice were 40 percent better in remembering their daily lessons than were their untreated brothers. Indeed, under metrazol treatment the hereditarily stupid mice were able to turn in better performances than their hereditarily superior but untreated colleagues. Here we have a "chemical memory pill" which not only improves memory and learning but can serve to make all mice equal whom God—or genetics—hath created unequal. May I suggest that some place in the back of your mind, you might begin to speculate on what it can mean—socially, educationally, politically—if and when we find drugs which will be similarly effective for human beings.

But let me continue with my story. What chemistry can give, it can also take away—as Agranoff and his now notorious goldfish at the University of Michigan have shown. Agranoff argued that if we could prevent the brain from manufacturing the chemicals involved in the long-term memory process, then we would create an animal which might have normal short-term memories, but would be incapable of establishing enduring memories. Agranoff trained his fish to swim from one side of an aquarium to another, whenever a signal light was turned on, in order to avoid an electric shock. Goldfish can learn this task within a 40-minute period, and once it is learned, they remember it over many days. Now Agranoff varied his experiments. Immediately before, and in some experiments immediately after, training, Agranoff injected puromycin or actinomycin-D (two antibiotics which prevent the formation of new proteins or nuclear RNA) into the brains of a new group of goldfish. His findings were most encouraging (to Agranoff, that is, not necessarily to the goldfish). The injected goldfish were not impaired in their *learning* of the shock-avoidance task since, presumably, the short-term reverberatory process which enables a fish to remember its lesson from one trial to another—a matter of a few seconds—does not involve the synthesis of new proteins or nuclear RNA. But when tested a day or two later the fish showed almost no retention for the task they had known so well the day before—indicating that the long-term process *is* dependent upon the synthesis of these compounds in the brain. Here, then, we find not only support for our general theory but we have a suggestion that there exist in antimetabolites whole families of chemical memory preventatives which seem not to interfere with the individual's immediate capacity to obey immediate orders, but which do prevent him from building up a permanent body of experiences, expectations, and skills. Conjure up, if you are of that mind, what evils such weapons can wreak in the hands of the Orwellian authorities of 1984—but I must hurry on to our next set of experiments.

A number of years ago, James McConnell at the University of Michigan threw all the brain researchers into a tizzy by reporting that he had succeeded in teaching planaria—a fairly primitive type of flatworm—to make a simple response to a light signal, that he then ground up his educated flatworms, fed the pieces to untrained fellow worms—and lo and behold, the uneducated flatworms wound up with the *memories* of the worms which they had just eaten, and, without any training, could perform the response of the late-lamented and digested "donor" worms!

But then all hell broke loose when other workers in other laboratories and in other countries reported that they could train a *rat*, make an extract from its brain, inject this extract into an untrained rat, and by so doing cause the recipient rat to acquire the memories of the now-dead donor rat. It is one thing to claim this for the primitive planaria, which, after all, do not have very much in the way of a structurally differentiated and organized brain. It is a very different thing to claim it for the rat, which *is* a serious mammal, with a highly developed brain, not too different in complexity, in differentiation, and in organization from our own.

The dust raised by these reports has not yet settled. Indeed, most scientists are definitely on the side of the nonbelievers—but the work goes on, and we cannot predict the final outcome of these experiments, many of which have given negative results. However, as a result of this work, a number of brain researchers have been moved, over the last two or three years, from the position of stiff-necked disbelief to the position of "well, maybe—I don't believe it, but well, maybe." And this is where *I* stand at the moment—fearless and foursquare proclaiming "well, maybe. . . ." Now, if it should come to pass that McConnell and his fellow believers are right, then we will indeed have made a huge jump forward. For we would then have a most effective behavioral assay method which should enable us to zero in on this marvelous brain-goulash which can transfer information from one brain to another, and isolate and identify in detail all the "memory" proteins, enzymes, RNA's, or other macromolecules. After that—the world of the mind is ours! But that day is not here yet. Let me leave these brave new world experimenters and go on with another question and another set of experiments.

Does the research I have reviewed mean that if and when we will have developed get-smart pills (*a la* McGaugh), or chemical erasures of wrong mental habits (*a la* Agranoff), or specific knowledge pills (*a la* McConnell), we will be able to do without Head Start programs, educational enrichment programs, school supervisors, educational research, and, indeed, without most of our educational paraphernalia? The answer to this question, gentlemen, is a most reassuring "NO." I might even say, *"Au Contraire."* Precisely because of the advances in brain biochemistry, the significance of the educator will be greatly increased—*and just as greatly changed.* Let me tell you why I think so by describing to you the results of some of our own work in the Berkeley laboratories.

Some time ago we set ourselves the following problem: If the laying down of memories involves the synthesis of chemical products in the brain, then one should find that an animal which has lived a life replete with opportunities for learning and memorizing would end with a brain chemically and morphologically different from an animal which has lived out an intellectually impoverished life. For almost two decades, now, E. L. Bennett, Marion Diamond, M. R. Rosenzweig, and I, together with technical assistants, graduate students, and thousands of rats, have labored—and some of us have even sacrificed our lives—to find such evidence. Let me tell you some of what we found.

At weaning time we divide our experimental rats into two groups, half of the rats being placed in an "intellectually enriched" environment, the other half—their brother—in the deprived environment. While both groups receive identical food and water, their psychological environments differ greatly. The animals in the first group live together in one large cage, are provided with many rat toys (tunnels to explore, ladders to climb, levers to press), and they are assigned to graduate students who are admonished to give these rats loving care and kindness, teach them to run mazes, and in general to provide them with the best and most expensive supervised higher education available to any young rat at the University of California. While these rats are thus being encouraged to store up many and varied memories, their brother rats, in the deprived group, live in isolated, barren cages, devoid of stimulation by either their environmental appurtenances, fellow rats, or graduate students. After about 80 days of this differential treatment, all the animals are sacrificed, their brains dissected out and various chemical and histological analyses performed. The results are convincing. The brain from a rat from the enriched environment—and presumably, therefore, with many more stored memories—has a heavier and thicker cortex, a better blood supply, larger brain cells, more glia cells, and increased activity of two brain enzymes, acetylcholinesterase and cholinesterase, than does the brain from an animal whose life has been less memorable.

We can draw several morals from these experiments. First, the growing animal's psychological environment is of crucial importance for the development of its brain. By manipulating the environment of the young, one can truly create a "lame brain"—with lighter cortex, shrunken brain cells, fewer glia cells, smaller blood vessels, and lower enzymatic activity levels—or one can create a more robust, a healthier, a more metabolically active brain. If it should turn out that what is true for the rat brain is also true for the human brain, and that by careful manipulation of this or that group's early environment we can develop among them bigger and better brains or smaller and meaner ones, the wondrous promises of a glorious future or the monstrous horrors of a Huxlian brave new world are fairly self-evident.

The second conclusion I draw from our experiments is this: Since the effect of any chemical upon an organ is, in part, a function of the beginning chemical status of that organ, and since—as we have just seen—the chemical and anatomical status of the individual's brain is determined by his educational experience, then the effectiveness of the biochemist's "get smart pill" will depend upon how the educator has prepared the brain in the first instance. Indeed, a review of all the data indicates that manipulating the educational and psychological environment is a more effective way of inducing long-lasting brain changes than direct administration of drugs. Educators probably change brain structure and chemistry to a greater degree than any biochemist in the business. Another way of saying this is: The educator *can potentiate or undo the work of the brain biochemist.*

But there is still more to report, and more lessons to draw. Consider the experimental problem we faced when we tried to create a psychologically enriched environment for our Berkeley rats. We did not really know how, so we threw everything into the environment, including, almost the kitchen sink, and called it "a psychologically enriched environment." The cages were kept in brightly lighted, sound-filled rooms; the rats were given playmates to relate to, games to manipulate, maze problems to solve, new areas to explore. They were fondled and tamed and chucked under the chin at the drop of a site-visitor. In other words, we provided our happy rats with almost every kind of stimulation we could think of—or afford. And it seems to have worked. But of course it is quite possible that in our "kitchen-sink design," many of the things we did were not at all necessary—indeed, some may have had an adverse effect. And so we undertook a series of experiments to discover which elements of our environment were effective and which were not. I shall not bore you with the details of the many experiments already run and the many more which are now being run in the Berkeley laboratory. Let me list, however, some of the tentative conclusions which one can already make:

First: Sheer exercise or physical activity alone is not at all effective in developing the brain. A physical training director seems not to be an adequate substitute for a teacher.

Second: Varied visual stimulation, or indeed any kind of visual stimulation, is neither necessary nor sufficient to develop the brain, as we were able to demonstrate by using rats blinded at weaning age.

Third: Handling, or taming, or petting is also without effect in developing the growing rat's brain. Love is Not Enough.

Fourth: The presence of a brother rat in our intellectually deprived rat's cage helps him not a whit. *Bruderschaft* is not enough.

Fifth: Teaching the rat to press levers for food—that and only that seems to help somewhat, but only minimally. Not every problem-set will do, either.

The only experience we have thus far found really effective is freedom to roam around in a large object-filled space. From a recent experiment in Diamond's laboratory there are some suggestions that if the young rat is given continuous and varied maze-problems to solve—that and little else—the rat will develop a number of the same brain changes (at least the morphological ones) which we had observed in our randomly "enriched" environment.

It is clear, then, that not *every* experience or variation in stimulation contributes equally to the development of the brain. But of even greater interest is the suggestion in the above data that the most effective way to develop the brain is through what I will call *species-specific enrichment experiences.* Here is what I mean: The ability of a rat to learn its way through tunnels and dark passages, to localize points in a three-dimensional space full of objects to be climbed upon, burrowed under, and crawled through is, we can assume, of particular survival value for the rat as he is now constituted. Presumably, through the selective evolutionary process, the rat has developed a brain which is peculiarly fitted to support and enhance these skills. The "effective rat brain," therefore, is one which is a good "space-brain"—not a lever-pressing brain or an arithmetic-reasoning brain. The effective stimulating environment, correspondingly, would be one which makes *spatial learning* demands on that brain—which "pushes" that particular kind of brain in that particular way. To generalize this hypothesis, I would suggest that *for each species there exists a set of species-specific experiences which are maximally enriching and which are maximally efficient in developing its brain.*

If there be any validity to my hypothesis, then the challenge to the human educator is clear. For the educator, too, you may have noticed, has been using the kitchen-sink approach when he seeks to design a psychologically or educationally enriched environment for the child. Some educators would bombard the child—practically from infancy on—with every kind of stimulus change imaginable. His crib is festooned with jumping beads and dangling colored bits and pieces of wood (all sold very expensively to his affluent parents); he is given squishy, squeaking, squawking toys to play with, to fondle, to be frightened by, to choke on. He is jounced and bounced and picked up and put down. And when he goes to school— he finds the same blooming, buzzing confusion. He is stimulated with play activities, with opportunities for social interaction, with rhythmic movements, with music, with visual displays, with contact sports, with tactual experiences, and with anything and everything which the school system can think of—or afford. But it may be that a "stimulating environment" and an "enriched environment" are not one and the same thing. It is not true that a brain is a brain is a brain. The rat is a rat and he hath a rat's brain; the child is a child and he hath a child's brain—and each, according to my hypothesis, requires its own educational nutrient. What, then, are the species-specific enrichments for the human child?

Of course I do not know the answer to this question, but let me share with you my present enthusiastic guess that in the language arts will you find part of the answer.

I can start with no better text than a quotation from my teacher, Edward Chace Tolman, who was a completely devoted rat psychologist. "Speech," he wrote, ". . . is in any really developed and characteristic sense, the sole prerogative of the human being. . . . It is speech which first and foremost distinguishes man from the great apes." (1932) [1] In my opinion, it is in the study of language, above anything else, that the psychologist will discover the psychology of man, and that the educator will discover how to educate man.

In the first place, and we must be clear about this, human language, with its complex and *abstract structure*, has *nothing* in common with animal communication. Language is probably the clearest instance of a pure species-specific behavior. This is true whether you study language as a neurologist, or as a psychologist. Let us look at some brain research first.

Recently Robinson, at the National Institute of Mental Health (1967), attempted to discover which areas of the monkey's brain controlled its vocalizations.[2] Now the monkey most certainly uses vocalization for communication, but principally for communications with emotional tone such as threat, fear, pain, and pleasure. In Robinson's study 15 unanesthetized animals, with brains exposed by surgery, were used. Some 5,880 different loci or spots in the brain were stimulated by electrodes to see whether such stimulation could bring forth vocalization. The loci explored included neocortical areas as well as areas in the limbic system, that older part of the mammalian brain which is most intimately involved with motivational and emotional responses.

Robinson's results were clear-cut: First, despite his exploration of several hundred different neocortical sites he was unable to raise a single sound from his animals by stimulating their *neocortex*. Second, stimulation of the limbic system brought forth regular, consistent, and identifiable vocalizations.

These results differ sharply from those found with the human brain. While there is some evidence that human cries and exclamations—uttered in moments of excitement—are also controlled by the limbic system, *speech and language clearly depend upon neocortical areas*—areas for which there simply are no analogues in the brain of any other animal. These areas are, of course, the well-known Broca and Wernicke areas in the left hemisphere of the human brain. It seems clear, as Robinson puts it, that "human speech did not develop 'out of' primate vocalization, but arose from *new tissue* [italics my own] which permitted it the necessary detachment from immediate, emotional situations." Man's brain, *and man's brain alone*, is a language-supporting brain.

Corresponding to the neurological picture is the psycholinguist's view of language. Almost every psycholinguist is impressed not only with the unique nature of language itself but with its unique mode of achievement by the child. Whatever value so-called reinforcement or stimulus-response theories of learning may have for describing acquisition of motor skills by

[1] Edward Chace Tolman, *Purposive Behavior in Animals and Men*. New York: The Century Company, 1932.
[2] B. W. Robinson, "Vocalization Evoked from Forebrain in *Macaca Mulatta*," *Physiology and Behavior*, 1967, No. 2, pp. 345–54.

people, maze-learning by rats, and bar-pressing by pigeons—these theories are assessed as completely trivial and utterly irrelevant when it comes to understanding that "stunning intellectual achievement" (McNeill, 1966),[3] the acquisition of language by the child. Indeed, in reading the psycholinguist's work one is left with the impression that we will have to develop a species-specific learning theory for this species-specific behavior of language. I must confess that I agree with them. And if we ever achieve an understanding of language development, and if we learn how to push the *human* brain with this *human* experience, then will we indeed be on our way.

I know that other people have proposed other ways with which to enrich the child's education. Some plug for what are referred to as "cognitive" experience or "productive thinking" experiences, etc. Let me hasten to record that I quite agree with them. As a matter of fact, I am not at all certain that I am saying anything other than what my cognitive friends propose. For I hold with McNeill's judgment that ". . . the study of how language is acquired may provide insight into the very basis of mental life." And, I would go on, being human *means* having an effective mental, cognitive life.

It is for these and many, many other reasons that I would urge the educator to turn to the psycholinguist—as well as to Piaget and Crutchfield and Bruner—for his major guides in designing a rational educational enrichment program.

Whether my guess merits this enthusiasm or not will perhaps eventually be determined by research. But here is the challenge and here is the promise for the educator. Drop your kitchen-sink approach, and specify and define for us the species-specific psychologically enriching experiences for the child—and we will be off and running!

Where will we run? Let me speculate out loud. It is perfectly reasonable to suppose that we will be able to find specific biochemical boosters and biochemical inhibitors for different kinds of memories and imagery, or for different kinds of abilities, or for different kinds of personality or temperament traits. With such chemical agents in hand, and with appropriate educational and training procedures, we may use them as supplementary therapy for those failing in this or that trait and thus will we be able to rectify and heal some of the mentally retarded and the senile. Of course we may use these agents for evil—to create docile, intellectually limited, but efficient human beasts of burden without memories beyond the order of the day (remember Agranoff's fish?).

But above all, there will be great changes made in the first and foremost and continuing business of society: the education and training of the young. The development of the mind of the child will come to rest in the knowledge and skills of the biochemist, and pharmacologist, and neurolo-

---

[3] D. McNeill, "The Creation of Language," *Discovery*, 1966, No. 27, pp. 34–38.

gist, and psychologist, and educator. And there will be a new expert abroad in the land—the psychoneurobiochemeducator. This multi-hybrid expert will have recourse—as I have suggested elsewhere—to protein memory consolidators, antimetabolite memory inhibitors, enzymatic learning stimulants, and many other potions and elixers of the mind from our new psychoneurobiochemopharmacopia.

There is a grievous problem here, however. Experts, whatever else they may be, are notorious ordertakers. *Who* will direct our psychoneurobiochemeducator where to work his expertise, and *what* shall we tell him to do? Here we are talking about goals, values, and aims. Shall our expert raise or lower docility, aggressiveness, musical ability, engineering ability, artistic sensitivity, effective intellectual functioning? Shall different ethnic or racial or national or social groups receive different treatments? In past centuries, and even today, this differential group treatment is precisely what our relatively primitive but quite effective medical and educational experts have been ordered by us to carry out. And lo, they have done so! On one side of the town they have created enclaves of the sickly, the weak, the ignorant, the unskilled—in a word, the brutalized social vanquished. On the other side of the town they have created the social victors—the healthy, the strong, the knowledgeable, the skilled. Will we continue to do this in the future with our much more sophisticated and effective psychoneurobiochemeducators? Who, in other words, will control the brain controllers—and to what ends?

I have thought and worried about these questions, and I must confess to you that I cannot avoid a dread feeling of unease about the future.

At the same time I keep whistling the following tune in an attempt to cheer myself up: If there be any validity at all to my speculations this afternoon, they add up to this: The biochemist, neurologist, psychologist, and educator will eventually add to the intellectual stature of man. With this in mind, and clinging to a life-long faith in the virtues of knowledge and the intellect (for certainly, at this stage I can do no less), I find myself believing that man who by taking thought will have added cubits to his intellectual stature, will also acquire the added bit of wisdom and humaneness that will save us all. Let me stop on this note—before I scrutinize this faith and this hope too carefully.

The Renaissance of
Early Childhood Education

HAROLD G. SHANE

A major contemporary development in education—one which seems certain to influence public schools in the 1970's—is the widespread reawakening of interest in the very young child. It is important at this juncture for educational leadership to be aware of some of the factors and events which have led to this new concern for early childhood. In particular, thought needs to be given to the practices and policies which will be introduced, studied, and evaluated as a downward extension of the public schools occurs in the coming decade.

A LONG HISTORY

For centuries great educators such as Comenius, Pestalozzi, Froebel, Basedow, and Montessori intuitively sensed the importance of children's experiences before the age of six. Also, during the past 40 years, nursery and pre-school specialists have made a strong case for the guidance of boys' and girls' early learning. Rose Alschuler, James Hymes, and Laura Zirbes are representative of the many contemporary figures who, beginning in the 1920's, made important contributions to pre-school practice.

Sometimes this was accomplished through research, but more often through reasoned conjectures based upon empirical study and personal insight.

In years past, children were, of course, also made the object of quite careful medical and psychological research. For example, the writings of Arnold Gesell and Frances Ilg provided useful longitudinal child-growth data. Willard Olson and Robert Havighurst, respectively, made "organismic age" and "developmental tasks" standard pedagogical phrases, while Jean Piaget for a quarter century has been respected for his developmental-cognitive studies.

But despite enthusiastic supporters and a substantial literature before 1960, no priority and frequently little heed was given by the public schools or the general community to the development of programs for children in the four-year span beginning at two and extending through age five. True, the Lanham Act expediently provided money for the care of children of working mothers during World War II, and some districts began to offer

Reprinted from *Phi Delta Kappan*, 50 (7): 369+ (March 1969), by permission of author and publisher.

kindergarten programs for two or three hours a day. But for the most part, the importance of early childhood was honored more by words than by actions in the schools. Even today in many states considerable parental pressures (or tuition) is required before kindergarten programs are launched for four-year-olds. In wide areas there are no kindergartens at all.

Let us now look at the confluence of events and circumstances that have led to the present renaissance of interest, which holds promise for the long delayed provision for education of two-to-five-year-olds.

FACTORS IN RENAISSANCE

The renaissance of interest in the very young has been stimulated by many things. An inventory of some of these elements and events follows.

Political decisions. To be both blunt and succinct, it seems rather obvious that policies and "politics" at the federal level have had a distinct bearing on the funding of educational programs begun prior to the kindergarten level. By the earlier Sixties it was becoming clear that there was much social dynamite in the ghettos of the city and in Appalachia-type rural slums. One of a number of ways of postponing or precluding explosions was providing educational programs for the children of the poor.

Current social commentaries. Recent attention-capturing books that focus on the complex challenges and appalling conditions of ghetto education have helped to convince many citizens of the importance of an early, problem-preventive approach to educating our children of poverty. Although they vary appreciably in quality and insight, this genre of book includes such titles as *Education and Ecstacy, Our Children Are Dying, Death at an Early Age, How Children Fail,* and *The Way It 'Spozed To Be.*

The great national concern which has developed for the problems of rural areas and the inner city has quickened interest in the young child and lent support to providing for education of the culturally different.[1] Educators have begun to point out that it is short-sighted and wasteful to have so-called compensatory education in elementary and secondary schools to repair damage done to boys and girls before they enter kindergarten or the primary school.

Head Start. Operation Head Start, as part of the war on poverty, is both a result of the new recognition for the importance of children's early experiences and a cause of the current awareness of these early years.[2]

Environmental mediation. One important influence in developing programs for very young children is the concept of environmental mediation—

---

[1] The January, 1969, KAPPAN contains a number of provocative and relevant articles on the inner city and segregation. Also cf. Edward T. Hall's article in this issue, pp. 379–80.

[2] For a succinct assessment see Keith Osborn, "Project Head Start," *Educational Leadership,* November, 1965.

the idea that during the child's early life wholesome forms of intervention in his milieu can help him become more effective in his transactions and interactions with others. While a sentimental interest in improving the environment of children has existed for centuries, the concept of a deliberate, planned intervention is, for practical purposes, a phenomenon of the Sixties.

Creating intelligence. Closely related to the point above is the accumulating evidence suggesting that the young child's intelligence is modifiable, that we can in effect "create" what we measure as an I.Q. The old "ages and stages" concept simply does not correspond with new information about childhood, the ways in which children learn, and the ways in which they develop. Benjamin Bloom, Ira Gordon,[3] and J. McVicker Hunt[4] are among writers who stress the significance of a facilitating environment for the optimal development of children and emphasize the importance of children's early years. Research done by David Krech[5] with infrahuman subjects strongly suggests that glia (memory) cells, brain size, and the blood supplied to the cerebral hemispheres actually can be increased by intervening in the milieu to create stimulating surroundings. His article on page 370 is especially provocative in that it implies that we may have been losing out on the best years of the learner's life by postponing his in-school education—until the ripe old age of six.

Psychoneurobiochemeducation. The rapidly developing field which Krech has called "psychoneurobiochemeducation" has implications for early contacts with children. Specialists in certain disciplines such as biochemistry have conducted experiments with both subhuman and human subjects that are beginning to demonstrate the use of drugs (such as pipradol, or magnesium pemoline) in influencing mind, mood, and memory. While pharmacies and surgical suites operated by boards of education seem unlikely to dominate our schools, there is reason to believe that very early school contacts for children having personality and learning problems may permit chemical therapy to reclaim these boys and girls who would otherwise become liabilities to society.

Experiments in early learning. Experiments in early learning, although not unique to the present decade, have fueled discussions and provided relevant—and sometimes disputed—data to the process of creating educational policies which will govern school practices in the 1970's.[6] O. K.

---

[3] Cf. Ira Gordon's article in this issue, pp. 375–78.

[4] The following references are helpful: Benjamin S. Bloom, *Stability and Change in Human Characteristics.* New York: John Wiley and Sons, 1964; Ira J. Gordon, "New Conceptions of Children's Learning and Development," in *Learning and Mental Health in the School.* Washington, D.C.: Association for Supervision and Curriculum, 1966, pp. 49–73; and J. McVicker Hunt, *Intelligence and Experience.* New York: The Ronald Press, 1961.

[5] David Krech, "The Chemistry of Learning," *Saturday Review,* January 20, 1968, p. 48–50. Also cf. Krech's article in this issue, pp. 370–74.

[6] Cf. Bernard Spodek's article in this issue, pp. 394–96.

Moore's [7] inquiries into responsive environments, Dolores Durkin's [8] exploration of pre-school reading instruction, and Bereiter and Engelmann's [9] controversial work on early academic learning through predominantly oral methods at the University of Illinois as they attempted early cognitive training are illustrative of contemporary projects.

Improved understanding of subcultures and group membership. Cultural anthropologists such as Edward T. Hall [10] have begun to point out the implications of membership in a given U.S. subculture. Accumulating evidence suggests that it is during the first four or five years of life that many personal behaviors—in language, attitude, values, even ways of learning—begin to take on the form they will retain for a lifetime. We now spend billions for remedial work, for penal and mental institutions, and for belated compensatory or supportive education necessitated, in a number of instances, because schools have not had early contacts with the children who will become their clientele.

The early influences of social class. Research by Jerome Kagan [11] has begun to suggest that social class membership—closely related to subculture group membership—begins permanently to influence personality, for better or worse, by the age of five or before.

Ethnicity as a mediating factor. Gerald Lesser [12] and his associates convincingly state, as a result of several replicated studies, that ethnicity (i.e., ethnic, subculture group membership) apparently causes children to learn in different ways.

Language development. For years now, Basil Bernstein's [13] work, which demonstrates that social class and one's linguistic characteristics are intimately related, has been widely accepted. The research cited, as well as analogous studies, which space precludes listing, are beginning to form a mosaic of data suggesting that these years of early childhood are more critical than any other stage of human development. In other words, if society, through its educational planning, does not vigorously begin to foster facilitating environments for very young children, it may be too late or immensely expensive to remove the psychological scar tissue that has long

[7] O. K. Moore, "Autolectic Responsive Environments for Learning," in *The Revolution in the Schools,* Ronald Gross and Judith Murphy (eds.). New York: Harcourt, Brace, and World, 1964, pp. 184–219.

[8] Dolores Durkin, *Children Who Read Early.* New York: Teachers College Press, Teachers College, Columbia University, 1966.

[9] Carl Bereiter and Siegfried Engelmann, *Teaching Disadvantaged Children in the Preschool.* Englewood Cliffs, N.J.: Prentice-Hall, 1966. 299 pp.

[10] Cf. Edward T. Hall, *The Silent Language* (1959) and *The Hidden Dimension* (1966), both published by Doubleday.

[11] Jerome Kagan, "The Many Faces of Response," *Psychology Today,* January, 1968, pp. 60–65.

[12] Cf. the article by Fort, Watts, and Lesser in this issue, pp. 386–88. Also cf. Susan S. Stodolsky and Gerald Lesser, "Learning Patterns in the Disadvantaged," *Harvard Educational Review,* Fall, 1967, pp. 546–93.

[13] Basil Bernstein, "Language and Social Class," *British Journal of Sociology,* November, 1960, pp. 271–76.

since formed on the personalities of certain young children before they enter school at the age of six.

Educational technology. A number of other elements have made educators more acutely interested in the initial years of childhood.[14] Improved technology has produced "talking" typewriters, "talking" books, and other teaching aids that can be used by boys and girls of three and four if they are in a school setting where they are available. Also, the progress made in developing Stage III computers promises to provide equipment that can be used in four- and five-year-old kindergartens.

Mass media: the phantom curriculum. The "phantom curriculum" to which mass media daily expose the child also has a bearing on early childhood education. By the time the child is enrolled in kindergarten or the primary school, he has an ill-assorted but important array of information.[15] There are those who not only contend that the massive sensory input of mass media is making children educable sooner, they also contend that the schools have a responsibility to help children at an early age acquire more coherent input. The problems here have been widely recognized, although much remains to be done in coping with them.

The rediscovery of Montessori, Piaget, and Vygotsky. While it is difficult to determine whether it is a cause or a result of the renaissance in early childhood education, the rediscovery of the work of Montessori, Piaget, and Vygotsky certainly has helped to enliven the instructional scene. These distinguished persons focused their work on aspects of methods, cognition, human development, and language growth at age five or below.

A decline in the elementary school population. Finally, a small group of prescient educational leaders, persons who are of a pragmatic turn of mind, are casting a speculative eye on the two- to five-year-old group because of the widespread use of the "pill." In view of the drop in the U.S. birth rate in the last few years, there will be an inevitable decline in the gross elementary school population by 1975. One way of utilizing the staff and the space that are likely to become available will be to extend the school's responsibility downward.

21st Century Education

Interest in the very young has great educational promise if we succeed in developing psychologically sound, socially contributive programs for the two-through-five age group. The authors who appear in this special issue of the Kappan do an excellent job of providing the kind of input which professional leadership and the general public need to have in the 1970's when far-reaching educational decisions seem likely to be made.

[14] Cf. article by Meierhenry and Stepp in this issue, pp. 409–11.
[15] John McCulkin, "A Schoolman's Guide to Marshall McLuhan," *Saturday Review,* March 18, 1967.

But absorbing information input is only one aspect of the many decision-making tasks with which tomorrow is already confronting us. There is the equally important matter of *value*-input. The young children with whom we are concerned in many instances will spend the larger part of their lives in a new century.

As we study innovations we must ask ourselves as often as necessary the questions: For what kind of a world are we preparing our children and, in view of current trends, does it promise to be a good world? If not, what can we do through our policy decisions to shape society so that tomorrow will be better?

Let us begin our contemplation of programs for the youngest by first sweeping away some of the intellectual smog that continues to obscure many of our goals. The projects we initiate should be based not just on better knowledge of early childhood but on rationally examined values as well. These are values that should reflect a reasoned quest for a twenty-first century in which life has become more humane and secure, is marked by outreaching friendship for others, and is less confused and violent than the era through which we have been groping our way.

Industry's Role in Education

L. A. MULLER

Although lacking the drama of an international news event, I believe the sudden emergence of big business into education will rank among the significant events of this decade.

It is too early to measure the implications of this event, but we do know that business has developed an impressive array of techniques and technological devices which hold tremendous promise for education.

The new technological devices, born of large-scale research and development programs, take the form of highly complex media.

What characterizes the new media is that they would not normally be available in the traditional classroom experience. There are, for example, the audio-visual capabilities of movies, television, video tape and language laboratories. There are film strips, sound recordings, microfilm and a number of laboratory and model devices.

As an example, you have no doubt seen time-lapse photography which, in effect, compresses time and illustrates the growth of a plant or the meta-

Reprinted from *Educational Technology*, 7 (10): 8–11 (May 1967), by permission of publisher.

morphosis of a butterfly. These media can often convey knowledge with more force and meaning than a verbal description.

Also, there are teaching machines based on programmed instruction. And finally, there is possibly the most promising and probably the least understood of educational aids: the computer.

On the one hand we have this new media. On the other we have an educational system of great organizational complexity which is now under intensive pressures: the demands for equality, the appeal for excellence, and the need for better use of human resources.

It is clear that one of today's most challenging problems is the creative use and orchestration of these media within this complicated and changing environment.

I am enthusiastic about the promise of computers and other technologies at all levels in education. But I stress the word promise.

I am gravely concerned that we may never realize the full potential these technologies hold for our school systems. Or, at least we may experience a generation of delay before doing so.

Why?

Because, unfortunately, there appear to be serious misunderstandings growing up between the worlds of business and education. It is just conceivable, if this situation continues, that many of the benefits which might evolve from technology will be forfeited before they are ever enjoyed.

For example, I have read where some educators fear that business will ultimately attempt to shape the objectives of education:

1. that course content will be written and controlled by corporations;
2. machines foisted on reluctant teachers;
3. that the role of the teacher will be diminished;
4. students dehumanized;
5. and that all of this is just around the corner.

Unfortunately, I believe these attitudes are in small part a creation of our own making. In the past few years there has been much talk in certain quarters about how technology is going to revolutionize education, that it holds out some kind of panacea for all problems. I have heard people talk enthusiastically about how technology will provide a Socrates for every student and freedom from routine for every teacher. What's more, these people tell us, this too is just around the corner.

Obviously these are extreme positions and we are fortunate that few people subscribe to them. Nevertheless, they are dangerous, for they deprive us of a basis for discussion and disguise the real problems we face. We may not always agree, but we are surely obliged to first clear the air of myth. For only then can we begin building bridges on which to meet and discuss mutual problems.

In my brief association with education, I have developed an appreciation for the concerns of educators.

I appreciate the attitude of the local educator who feels that the control he has traditionally held is slipping from his grasp. He does not want to become a tool of government policy. Nor should he. From his vantage point he does not normally see his pupils as potential creators of gross national product or trainees in the race for space. He sees them as individuals.

There is an instinctive, and legitimate, fear that one day someone at the top will have the power to manipulate education: to use it as a valve that can be turned by a master planner, to automatically produce, say, 3000 more electronics engineers or somehow alter the output of the educational system without consideration for the differences and diversity in human values.

Then, too, I appreciate the attitude of the teacher who sees big business intruding into his world. He is suspicious that the profit motivation of business may be incompatible with the ends of education. Business can normally define its objectives and measure results in quantitative terms. Profit is a measure of success. Not so in the classroom. The teacher's job is to produce a better person, not a better product or process.

As a corollary to this, the educator fears business will be a centralizing force in education, that it will tend to diminish diversity and concentrate decision making. This is surely a legitimate concern.

I appreciate also the attitude of the educator who is concerned that certain management techniques which have proved enormously successful in business may be misapplied in education. The success of the systems approach in science and defense does not necessarily mean it can be automatically transplanted to the environment of education. Although these techniques appear to hold promise, the fact is, we really don't know with certainty where and how these techniques are applicable in the instructional environment.

Again, I appreciate the attitude of the educator who suggests that we are enchanted by technology. He asks whether technology and technique are shouldering aside the traditional humanistic values. He questions whether this new preoccupation may not be detracting from other important needs of education. Finally, he is conspicuously unimpressed by the talk of speed, efficiency and productivity.

As a corollary, the teacher is concerned about the very complexity of technology. Will he be able to control it or will he be transformed into a technician?

WHAT CAN BUSINESS DO?

I ask: what do these concerns mean to us? To all of us who are intensely interested in seeing our country's educational system benefit from science and technology? First, I think an appreciation of these problems provides at least a platform for discussion. Second, I think we are obliged to speak out and define our position on what business can and should do in the face of these problems. I suggest the following as a point of departure.

In the first place, I believe that industry must proceed with a large measure of modesty and humility, embracing the principle that the aims of education are best left to educators. They must draw up the blueprint as to how technology will fit into their objectives. No salesman can perform such a task.

We must be dedicated in our efforts to assist educators, but we must do so within a framework of self-discipline and restraint. After all, we are heirs to a remarkably successful system whose history is rooted deeply in local responsibility.

Second, course content must remain the responsibility of educators. Industry should contribute by supplying products and technical assistance which will help the educator attain his objectives. There are many valuable services that industry can offer which do not diminish the role of the educator.

Third, business must recognize and make clear that much of the advanced technology is not yet fully validated. Particularly with such methodologies as computer assisted instruction, we are still in a stage of experimentation. There isn't sufficient evidence to advocate large-scale adoption, and I believe unfounded claims can only raise barriers between business and education.

As a corollary to this, we must recognize that it would be unwise, at best, to introduce complex equipment without the understanding of teachers and administrators. Speaking to this point, a colleague and respected competitor, Frank Keppel, put it very nicely when he said that teachers, after all, have an effective pocket veto over innovation.

On the other hand, business should assist education through research testing techniques, to accelerate the educational validation of its products. But even this is a responsibility which business must assume hand in hand with the educator.

Fourth, technology can only be an aid, not an end, in education. We must never permit technology to dictate ends.

The great challenge is to use technology with imagination and creativity, while recognizing its limitations. Machines can obviously never substitute for the essential interpersonal exchange between student and teacher. Furthermore, we must recognize, as the educator already does, that technology is only a small part of a much larger system.

Fifth, no discussion of this subject would be complete without acknowledging the fundamental importance of course material—so often referred to as "software." As Dean Sizer of Harvard has pointed out, "In the education industry we have technical devices of great sophistication before we have clear aims, much less material for them, better educational equipment than ideas on how to use it."

Educational Technology
and the Curriculum

JAMES E. EISELE

"MODERN TECHNOLOGY CREATES DOMESTIC DISCORD" reads a recent story title in the newspapers. The story describes how officials were applying technology to the study and analysis of traffic patterns in and around a major United States city. Automatic cameras were set up around the city to photograph automobile license plates during certain periods of the day. Following the identification of the owners of several photographed plates, officials made contact with them in order to gather other kinds of information about their travel. The discord spoken of in the title of the story occurred when the wife of one of the photographed-license-plate owners discovered, through the home contact, that her husband was in the city at 8:00 A.M. on a day when he was ostensibly on a business trip in another city.

This story helps illustrate two major points about technology that should be kept in mind. The first point is that *technology* refers to the scientific and systematic treatment of a subject and is not necessarily synonymous with machinery or equipment used to this end. In other words, the technology referred to in the story above was the study of traffic patterns and not the use of the automatic cameras by themselves. The same technology might have been employed using only visual sighting and recording of data without the use of automatic camera equipment. At the same time, there is no reason at all why equipment, automated or not, would not often be used for other than technological purposes. Applying the same principle to education, R. Louis Bright (1) recently made a similar distinction:

> Educational Technology is not synonymous with hardware, as many people seem to think; rather it is, as I see it, an instructional theory or approach which may or may not involve hardware.
>
> The way in which motion picture projectors, single concept films, instructional TV, language laboratories, overhead projectors, and other hardware are used in most cases has no relation to the current instructional theory of educational technology.

On the other hand, a more specific definition of technology, especially educational technology, is necessary to distinguish it from its origin—science or the "scientific method." This distinction is generally accepted as technology's being the application of science to the practical, whereas science, in general, may or may not relate directly to any contemporary prac-

An original paper written especially for this volume.

tices except, perhaps, the accumulation of new knowledge. Applying this essential distinction between science and technology, Unwin (10) defines educational technology in this way:

> Educational Technology is concerned with the application of modern skills and techniques to the requirements of education and training. This includes the facilitation of learning by manipulation of media and methods, and the control of environment in so far as this reflects on learning.

This, then, illustrates the scope of this paper as dealing with some salient developments in the application of science (technology) to the curriculum (instruction) of the past, the present, and the future.

The other point to be remembered from the story in the opening is that there may be vast ramifications resulting from the utilization of technology in present human endeavors with which we are not prepared to cope, or with which we are unwilling to live. The significance of this point is that an essential concomitant to the use of technology must be the developing of human preparedness for the implications that may be the result of desirable and necessary technology. No matter how mundane the newspaper story may appear to the scientific community, the impact of technology upon the family involved is hardly inconsequential.

Some of the more serious consequences of employing technology are well known. Air and water pollution, traffic congestion and safety, crime increase, and unemployment can all be traced, at least in part, to changes introduced into society via technology (2). Mary Alice Hilton (8) has suggested that counting votes, using them for the prediction of results, and broadcasting this information from the East, after the polls have closed, to the West, where the polls still remain open, may affect the outcome of elections by influencing the way people vote in the West.

This paper does not propose any solutions to the consequences of technology in education, by any means. However, the subject is broached because of the author's conviction that these consequences must be taken into account by all those who look to technology as the hope for the future of education. Good or bad, the consequences of technology will be with us and we must be aware of them and prepare for them wherever possible.

With the foregoing definition of educational technology, and with the admonition to be aware of the possible consequences of technology, only a definition of curriculum remains necessary in the introduction. The term *curriculum* is better understood today than ever before since it was first defined as something other than simply courses of study. For many people, however, the definition of *curriculum* as, "all the experiences of the learner under the direction of the school," is much too broad. Nevertheless, the common view of curriculum, today, and the interpretation to which technology must address itself, is that curriculum includes the planned (and sometimes unplanned) experiences that are designed, implemented, and evaluated for the achievement of the stated purposes of the school. This definition includes instructional objectives, the subject matter to be taught, the teaching and learning activities to be performed, the materials and media to be used, and the evaluation techniques and devices to be employed by teachers and learners, to achieve those goals of the school that are determined by society, by human needs, and by what is believed about the nature of man.

BACKGROUND

Man has always been an adventuresome animal and, as a result, has continually searched for "a better way." Only sheer speculation could describe what life might be like, if it were to exist at all, without this constant search. There have been conservative elements of society that have attempted to retard some of the progress that man has made, to be sure. However, through his efforts, man has extended his life span by several years, has done much to improve his environment (although, at the same time, he has done much to damage it), has generally improved his health, has created and applied tremendous amounts of knowledge, and has even set foot on the moon. The beginnings of these achievements can only be dated from the beginning of man. And the history of technology is best traced from this point with the identification of landmarks along the way. Certain of these landmarks can be recognized as part of the developing technology of education.

Finn (5) was probably accurate in dating the earliest known educational technology at about 3000 B.C. with the invention of cuneiform writing and clay tablets. To be sure, the discovery of a method of communicating more effectively must have been pivotal in facilitating the processes of education.

The concept of improved communications can be traced through the period from 500 B.C. to 1500 A.D. with the invention of man-made roads, paper, printing, glazing, and passenger vehicles; the use of horses and camels; ship building and navigation developments; and the use of pictorial art (9). It seems only fair to note, however, that these developments did little to alter education between the previous period and the nineteenth century.

The nineteenth century must truly mark the beginnings of educational technology as it is known today. The significance of this period of history is recorded by Alfred North Whitehead in his *Science and the Modern World* (New York, the Macmillan Company, 1925), where he states that "The greatest invention of the nineteenth century was the invention of the method of invention." He was, of course, referring to what has commonly become known as "the scientific method." Cremin, too, has confirmed the importance of this era to education and science (3, p. 90):

> Henry Steel Commager has likened the nineties to a great watershed in American history, a decade in which "the new America came in as on flood tide." His metaphor is as apt for pedagogy as for any other realm.

The nineteenth century was distinguished in educational history as the period of Herbart and Pestalozzi, who sought to develop a scientific "method" of education; G. Stanley Hall, who is remembered for his pioneer work in applying psychology to education; Herbert Spencer and his emphasis on evolution and science; William James and his *Principles of Psychology;* Edward L. Thorndike with his experimental psychology; and, of course, John Dewey for his experimentalist philosophy and dedication to science (11).

Often overlooked as a milestone in the development of an educational technology is an event that nearly changed the face of curriculum and instruction in America and stands, in fact, as the forerunner of most of what has been accomplished in the past ten years. This event began in 1932, ran until 1940, and was appropriately coined "The Eight Year Study." The Study, an outgrowth of the Progressive Education Association Convention of 1930, can be credited with at least three significant contributions to the emergence of a technology of education. First, it represents one of the first, and best, attempts at systematic, longitudinal study of education. Second, there is no doubt that the curriculum revision procedures employed in the Study resulted in one of the earliest attempts at a multimedia approach to teaching and learning. Third, the resource unit, invented by the participants in the Study, is an obvious prototype of many of the curriculum innovations of the 1960's.

Following World War II, education saw the rise of many mechanical aids to instruction. These devices—projectors, visuals, paperback books, television, and so on—were a result of a technology developed for the war effort. Educational testing received a great deal of impetus from research and experimentation directed toward developing a more effective war machine. These tools have played a substantial role in educational technology, although their effect on classroom teaching and learning is not at all clear.

The 1950's spawned what nearly became one of educational technology's greatest fiascos—the teaching machine and programmed learning. Although traceable directly to Pressy's invention of a machine to test students in 1926, and even to Thorndike's principles of animal learning, B. F. Skinner is generally credited with "inventing" programmed learning. Certainly, based as it was upon principles of psychology, programmed learning was a significant step toward an effective educational technology, even though it failed to have a substantial impact on learning in the classrooms of most schools.

At the same time that programmed learning techniques were being tried out in the schools, teachers began to experience the "machine age" of education. For the first time, in many cases, schools became the proud possessors of 8mm film projectors, tape recorders, language laboratories, overhead projectors, and opaque projectors. Little is known about the quantity or quality of use to which these machines were put during this period, but it is known that much that had formerly been written on chalkboards was written on overhead projectors—probably in a much less readable form.

Popular in the sixties were at least three significant developments in educational technology that are difficult to date relative to one another. The three, which will be discussed in the next section, are "curriculum packages," computers, and "the systems approach." These three developments are illustrative of the present state of educational technology, and they represent much of the work of educational innovators of the present decade. As such, they can best be discussed under the rubric, "Current Developments."

CURRENT DEVELOPMENTS

Although the brief history that has been presented is merely skeletal, it illustrates that educational technology is not a product of the current decade alone. However, though the roots are deep, the results of technology applied to education have barely been felt in the typical American classroom. Still, the developments of the past decade are substantial and will, in time, have tremendous effects upon teaching and learning. Some of these developments have already affected greater numbers of classrooms, or appear to have the potential to, than others and will be briefly discussed in this section. In some cases it is necessary to identify developments for discussion that are representative of many other developments. This is done for the sake of brevity and not through oversight.

It is convenient to divide the major developments in educational technology into three categories that, with some overlap, seem to account for most of the efforts and products of workers in the field. These categories are tutorial systems for independent learning, information storage and retrieval systems for providing resources of teaching and learning, and management systems for facilitating instruction. It can be seen in this section that these categories each contain both mechanical and manual techniques and devices, some automated and some not. These factors appear to be independent of the category in which they fall.

Tutorial Systems for Independent Learning

Because all learning is individual in the sense that a group does not possess behavior independent of the persons who constitute the group, making the distinction between group learning and independent learning is not a simple task. To make such a distinction really requires a knowledge of the primary intent of the activity. For example, it is possible to show a film to thirty pupils with the intention of affecting individual behavior within the group without changing the group behavior at all. In this case, the learning that takes place could be termed independent as presently defined. On the other hand, the activity is, in itself, accurately described as a group one.

These distinctions for many current media are beyond the domain of this paper for the simple reason that they are deserving of more thorough analysis than can be attempted here. The emphasis will be, instead, on the transition from media for independent learning to media that are developed as integral to total systems of instruction. In this section the paper will deal exclusively with technological devices that are intended for use by individuals independent of the group—i.e., whether the group exists or not. Therefore, the devices or techniques discussed are those that may often be used in a group setting, but the existence of the group is essentially irrelevant to their use.

The Textbook

The textbook, one of the oldest technological devices for teaching and learning, is still the most popular among most classroom teachers. The value of the textbook has been undisputed for over a century in America and has been widely adopted by classroom teachers as almost the sole determinant of what to teach, and how to teach it, as well. There have been, and continue to be, attempts to woo educators from their heavy reliance on the textbook but these efforts have failed, largely, for two reasons. First, no other technology has yet been made as readily available and convenient to the classroom teacher as is the standard text. Second, few efforts have been made that concentrate on bringing about changes in the total educational system that would accommodate the utilization of newer techniques and devices. If teaching and learning are to realize substantial improvement as a result of technology, and it is clear that instruction can and should benefit greatly from it, future efforts will have to take cognizance of these two factors.

Programmed Instruction

Programmed instructional (P.I.) materials and teaching machines are almost as readily available to the classroom teacher as the textbook. Linear and branching programmed materials have enjoyed some limited success in gaining acceptance and use in the classroom. Because P.I. employs small, incremental steps of learning, with reinforcement built in, it has been demonstrated as an effective way to allow individual pacing and learning of certain kinds of behaviors (notably cognitive recall).

Recently, the principles of P.I. have been utilized in conjunction with electronic data-processing equipment. Program frames are presented to the learner by the computer with various kinds of interface, the learner's response is compared with many alternative correct ones, and the program is advanced to the frame that his response would indicate is appropriate. The use of the computer in this way has introduced a tremendously increased capability of programs to branch into many more alternative paths, determined by what the learner needs to know, than is possible with a program in book format. This use of the computer and programmed learning is widely known as Computer Assisted Instruction, or C.A.I. Essentially, its value to the teacher is the same as that of P.I.—individual pacing and immediate reinforcement. At present, the use of the computer may enjoy additional benefits because of its novelty to the learner, though this effect is not likely to be lasting.

Simulation

Another tutorial technique that may or may not be computer based is simulation or gaming. The principles of simulation are not original to this decade but their systematic application is very recent. Wing (11), for example, has developed sophisticated economic games that allow the learner to make economic decisions, and experience (via 35mm slides) the likely consequences of his decisions.

Simulation has been applied to the preparation of elementary school teachers without the use of computers but with a modified multimedia approach. Cruickshank, Broadbent, and Bubb (4) have developed a kit that contains situations (filmed or written) that the student uses to identify problems and to work toward their solution. Other material provided in the kit includes bibliographies of related literature, references on curriculum (a handbook), a faculty handbook, and data on learners. This program, like other simulation games, has the advantage of bringing the student much closer to experiencing reality than do either textbooks or programmed learning.

Gaming and simulation have been utilized in several other aspects of education, such as politics, logic, business, and administration. Information about specific games can be obtained from many sources today but one of the best is the *Occasional Newsletter* published by Project SIMILE of the Western Behavioral Sciences Institute (1121 Torrey Pines Road, LaJolla, California).

Self-instructional Kits

Currently available are several versions of self-contained and self-instructional kits for independent learning activities. Two examples of such devices are Science Research Associates' (Chicago: S.R.A., Inc.) reading kits and Follett Publishing Company's (Chicago) "Spelling and Writing Patterns" kit. In kits of this type, the learner finds complete directions for performing the suggested activities as well as for determining progress and moving from level to level.

These kits have been generally well received by classroom teachers and are quite widely used. This is perhaps because of a number of reasons, among which may be that they are not exorbitant in cost, they require a minimum of the teacher's time to direct, they are self-contained, and they are not "threatening" in appearance as are some types of equipment, such as teaching machines or remote computer terminals.

Information Storage and Retrieval

The development of information storage and retrieval systems is a logical extension of the human memory, just as electronic data-processors and computers are the extension of other human cognitive processes. When man realized that more data was available than he could remember, he was compelled to find a way to store that data in some retrievable way if he was ever again to make use of it. Hence, we have seen the rapid growth of massive structures for housing all kinds of printed matter containing information known to man. It soon became inevitable, though, that as man used this knowledge to uncover more knowledge, the increase was geometric and would exceed the physical capability of standard means of storage and retrieval. This probability led to the development of a more advanced information technology that has tremendous implications for education if one major purpose of education is viewed to be the use of knowledge to uncover more knowledge.

Microphotography

One fascinating technique for increasing storage capabilities is to reduce the physical size of the data to be stored. This is accomplished with many kinds of documents by the photographing of the material with small film—usually 8mm or 16mm—which can be viewed with several types of enlargers. This technique was used as long as a full century ago, which would appear to disqualify it as a current development. However, as a teaching device, its potential has only begun to be explored with the development of practical enlarging and viewing devices.

Another factor that may have previously inhibited the use of microphotography was the problem of retrieval. Although great amounts of data could be stored on extremely small areas, the problem of filing this film for later use remained a vexing one. Much of this difficulty has been eliminated through the use of microfiche (4″ x 6″ film "cards") containing several strips of microfilm. The cards, along with a national clearinghouse of data—Educational Resources Information Center (ERIC)—now provide an economical, practical, and useful system for storing and retrieving data on microphotographs.

Library Resource Storage

Short of recording library resource material directly on microfilm, ways have been sought to catalogue these materials so that their location can be ascertained quickly and with a minimum of effort. Techniques for accomplishing this have now been developed so that a document can be indexed by a number of its characteristics, which, when requested by a user, will allow the retrieval of bibliographic data along with some indication of where the document is stored.

Of course, systems have also been developed for using reduced images (microphotography, for example) in connection with data processors to further facilitate the filing, indexing, and retrieval of the tiny documents. Also, documents in printed form can be stored on punch cards, magnetic tapes, or discs that can be retrieved in printed form via data processors by the use of appropriate indices.

Anyone familiar with contemporary education will quickly recognize that the systems described here have not been widely used to date. This, of course, is primarily because of cost factors and should soon become more affordable as more rapid, economical equipment becomes available.

Dial Access Retrieval

One of the most exciting technological developments in the area of information storage and retrieval is the progress being made toward locating data and making it almost instantly available on some display mode when the code numbers of the desired documents are dialed. At present, dial access systems are operational for both audio-recorded data and audio-video recorded data.

This system operates by the recording of data on magnetic tape and the indexing of the various items of information with magnetic impulses. When the code for any given piece of information is dialed, electronic signals are sent from the remote dialing and display terminal to the centrally located tape recorder/playback. The recorder/playback is activated by the electronic signals and begins searching for the section of the tape reel containing the code that has been dialed. This, then, is transmitted back to the display device at some remote location.

Although dial access retrieval systems may be a most exciting venture, many difficulties must be eliminated before large-scale implementation is possible. One major difficulty that remains is that no feasible way has yet been found to create random access. Rather, present systems require a great deal of programming, scheduling, and manual operation. Another difficulty lies in the present cost of such systems. Nevertheless, dial access appears to be the wave of the future in information storage and retrieval.

Management Systems for Instruction

The so-called curriculum reform movement of the 1960's seemed to hold the national spotlight more than any of the previously described trends in educational technology in this decade. Perhaps this attention has been justified in terms of the effect that the products of the movement have had upon teaching and learning. Perhaps not. At this point, it appears safe to say only that the results of the curriculum reform seem to have found their way into more classrooms, and have been more effectively used, than many of the other available innovations. Only a few of these systems can be described here, and the attempt will be made to select those that are illustrative of the entire field.

The uniqueness of management systems for instruction is that they have been developed around some comprehensive view of teaching and learning. Although there are significant differences in the views to which they adhere, each project has been built upon a systems approach to instruction or, again, a total view of the instructional process. This view includes an analysis of the components of instruction and consists of some combination of objectives (expected outcomes), evaluation, and instructional strategies.

"Science: A Process Approach"

Developed by a commission on science education of the American Association for the Advancement of Science, this curriculum project contains seven levels of science instruction for elementary grades. Each level consists of a discrete number of lessons that specify the skills necessary for problem solving determined by subject-matter specialists and science educators. Each pupil is expected to acquire each behavior specified at a level before moving to the next level. His competency in the behavior is determined by pre- and post-testing. For each level there are accompanying kits of instructional materials to be used in acquiring the requisite behaviors.

Much of the success of this project must be attributed to the provision of most of the necessary instructional aids: behavioral objectives, tests, and instructional materials. There is reason to believe that *Science: A Process Approach* has had considerable effect on science instruction in elementary schools in this decade.

"Individually Prescribed Instruction (I.P.I.)"

Not drastically unlike the preceding curriculum project, I.P.I. represents curriculum "packages" for individualizing instruction in selected subjects in the elementary schools. The mathematics program, for example, consists of units of instruction on specific arithmetical concepts, such as "numeration." Each unit consists of a discrete number of cognitive objectives, curriculum-embedded tests for use during instruction, posttests for use after instruction, and instructional materials for working on each objective.

In this program each child is tested for his knowledge of the unit and assigned to objectives that he has not already met. The teacher then prescribes an instructional exercise to fit the child's objective. In theory, the learner progresses through the predetermined sequence of objectives in the unit and then moves to the next unit in sequence.

Computer Systems

Computer systems for instruction have been developed primarily to help the teacher organize and manage individually tailored curriculums, at the same time allowing for more freedom of choice and flexibility than is possible in most other management systems. Only two such programs are known by the author to exist on a scale that makes them relatively well known. Many others, to be sure, must be in existence, but these two seem large enough in their present influence to be singled out for inclusion here.

Project PLAN is currently under development by the American Institute of Research in Palo Alto, California. In addition, fourteen school districts throughout the United States are cooperating with A.I.R. in the development and implementation of what the system developers call teaching-learning units. Because of the complexity of systems of this type, it may be best to let its originator speak for himself in describing the program.

In September, 1967, John C. Flanagan gave this account of Project PLAN (6):

> The functional model being developed begins with tentative plans for the educational objectives to be attained by each individual, assists him in attaining these objectives through the use of specially-designed modular segments of learning activities, and continuously monitors his progress with respect to the attainment of these objectives. . . .
>
> The computer will . . . store a complete list of instructional materials in the form of modules or manageable segments which may be called "teaching-learning units." These will be systematically indexed in terms of what the student is expected to learn from them, what the prerequisites are, and for what type of student and situation this unit is especially well suited.

Apparently, students in classes where PLAN is to be employed will pursue their individualized lessons independent of other members of the class. No mention has been made in the literature about providing assistance with the management of large-group and small-group instructional activities. Rather, the intent of the project seems to be to provide sufficient teaching-learning units for all individuals in the group and, thereby, to give the teacher assistance in managing numerous independent instructional activities.

Computer Assisted Curriculum Planning (7) has been in existence since 1964, although its origin goes back much further than that date. This project probably represents the most substantial effort, to date, actually to utilize a computer-based instructional system in classrooms. This is partially accounted for by the fact that the date of 1963 is merely the date of the first externally funded project. The planning and conceptualizing of the system go back as far as 1955 and can be traced back even further if the visions of progressives in the 1930's are considered.

This project consists of vast collections of teaching-learning suggestions organized around relevant topics (thirty-six at present and the task of adding new ones will never be complete) on all levels, including college, and in many subject areas. Each topic includes a large list of related behavioral objectives, an extensive listing of relevant subject matter, instructional activities for independent, small-group, and large-group study (these are also divided according to introductory, developmental, or culminating activities), instructional materials of all kinds, and evaluation procedures related to the expected outcomes.

Each item in the collection is coded to three sets of variables. Subject matter, activities, materials, and evaluators are coded to the *behavioral objectives* to which they relate. All of these, plus the behavioral objectives, are coded to certain specified *learner characteristics* and to *instructional variables.*

A teacher can select objectives from a given topic, describe the characteristics of each learner in the class, make certain instructional choices (such as audio materials only), and he will receive from the computer a printout of suggestions for large-group and small-group instruction for each objective, suggestions for independent instruction for each objective chosen for each learner, and, if desired, the names of all learners with common objectives and a total listing of materials in the collection.

Many other combinations of suggestions can be generated for printout by the computer. Among them are specific types of printouts, such as mini-packs, which are integral to a sophisticated feedback system for updating the data bank. These consist of all the suggestions in the collection related to a given behavioral objective.

This project seems to have unlimited potential and shows great promise as an educational technology. It portends, in fact, a future when curriculum and educational technology are wedded for mutual purposes, although what has been described is already, in fact, a reality.

THE FUTURE

The future use of educational technology must continue to be addressed to the developing of techniques for helping researchers to determine behavioral objectives, subject matter, instructional activities and materials, and means for evaluation for individual learners in the classroom. To date, technology has come a long way toward that end from the early development of hardware, especially for tutorial purposes, to increased utilization of software with new storage and retrieval systems, to the use of a systems view of teaching and learning that incorporates many of the earlier developments. There is even evident a trend from a narrow systems view of instruction, which called for highly prescribed packages, to a more comprehensive, liberalized view of the total process that provides for greater decision-making through increased numbers of choices of equal value. This trend should continue.

In fact, the direction that educational technology takes is a most critical issue. In terms of know-how and hardware, educators are well on their way to an advanced technology of instruction. However, the course can take either of two distinct directions. If technology is used to narrow the available choices and to deemphasize decision making, Orwell's *1984* could be a reality by approximately that date. If technology is used, on the other hand, to increase and enhance choices and decision making, education can help assure that society will never resemble Orwell's *1984* or his *Animal Farm.*

Taken to its ideal, then, a curriculum of unlimited choices can be visualized for the future. The curriculum would be determined through intelligent decision-making by learners with expert guidance from teachers. These decisions would include the selection of objectives as well as strategies for accomplishing them. Upon this base the curriculum of the future can be built. This can be done, however, only with the use of technology and there is every indication that educators are on their way to doing it. However, certain prerequisites are already plainly apparent and these must be achieved before an ideal can be approached.

PREREQUISITE TASKS FOR EDUCATORS

As mentioned, certain prerequisites must be achieved by educators if the use of technology is to result in substantial improvements in education. For these, the term *prerequisite tasks* seems to be appropriate. The need to accomplish these tasks is great, for on them depends the future of the curriculum through the use of educational technology. If these tasks are not accomplished, it remains highly doubtful that technology will ever make a difference in what is taught or how it is taught in the schools.

The first prerequisite task is the immediate systematic planning of the curriculum. This step must be taken on a universal scale if educational technology is to make a substantial impact on the curriculum. Educators have been told this fact for over twenty-five years and now the reality exists that technology has far surpassed their readiness for it. A static, subject-matter–centered curriculum does not require, or even benefit substantially from, the utilization of technology for optimum implementation. This type of curriculum can be aided some by linear programs, which, like the curriculum, tend to narrow the number of alternative choices for both teachers and learners. As long as this type of curriculum prevails there will not exist a great need for technology, or even a willingness to utilize it. A dynamic curriculum, however, that requires vastly expanded alternative choices and that will of necessity involve the use of technology for its implementation will evolve only through the systematic planning of the curriculum.

The next prerequisite task for educators is the improvement of procedures for the preparation of teachers. Teachers prepared to teach a narrow range of choices within a narrowly defined discipline or field will not be prepared for the advent of educational technology. The recommendation, therefore, is that teachers-in-training be provided with experiences related to their own realistic needs in becoming teachers. This will require moving beyond the college classroom and into the classrooms of the youngsters that they will one day teach. It further requires that teachers of teachers utilize systematic planning in their own curriculum, and emphasize the development of skills of decision making rather than restricting it through telling the prospective teachers "how it should be."

Another prerequisite task is the use of expert knowledge in the design, development, implementation, and evaluation of educational technology.

By expert knowledge is meant the knowledge of persons who have studied and researched in the areas of education and technology. This is hardly the place in which to cite examples, but it would not be difficult to point out several technological innovations that have failed miserably because of the lack of educators' involvement in their development. And often this neglect is the fault of educators, themselves, for not taking the lead in this endeavor.

A fourth prerequisite task is for educators to take the initiative in discovering new and better ways of financing education and, in turn, educational technology. Technology, in particular, cannot be bought at bargain prices. However, for years one major data-processing firm was known to grant "educational" discounts to institutions of higher learning, but not to public schools. Educators did take the lead here and this practice is rapidly changing—though not fast enough. Educators must "sell" their work to their clients and communities; and they must also sell their efforts to the supportive industries, for neither can do without the other. And it is becoming increasingly important for educators to have primary responsibility for making decisions that require professional expertise.

A final prerequisite task to be discussed here is the need to consider the host of support systems that must accompany any technological innovation. Programmed learning will not work without programs, microphotography is of little use without display devices, and management systems require extensive collections of instructional materials. These and many other supports must be taken into consideration and provided for, or educational technology faces certain delay and maybe even permanent alienation.

Conclusions

1. Educational technology is more than hardware; it is the application of science to curriculum and instruction.

2. The consequences of employing technology in the improvement of curriculum may have tremendous consequences, of which educators must be aware.

3. Educational technology began with the invention of cuneiform writing and has progressed through the invention of the printing press, the development of a method of science, and the use of hardware and multimedia, programmed learning, and finally, systems for instruction.

4. Prerequisite to widespread implementation of technology to curriculum and instruction are certain tasks for educators, which include the use of systematic planning, the improvement of teacher preparation, the use of expert knowledge through involvement, the improvement of educational financing, and the development of adequate support systems.

Above all, educational technology can carry curriculum and instruction a long way in more than one direction. Careful consideration must be given as to which way education needs to go in a democracy—to a narrow, linear interpretation or to a broad base for increasing the number of viable alternatives and improving the use of decision-making skills.

REFERENCES

1. Bright, R. Louis, "Educational Technology as an Approach," *Educational Technology* (January 15, 1968).
2. Chipley, Donald R., "Technology and Educational Change," A Paper Delivered to the Southeastern Region Conference of the Philosophy of Education Society (Statesboro, Ga.: Georgia Southern College, February 3, 1968).
3. Cremin, Lawrence A., *The Transformation of the School* (New York: Alfred A. Knopf, 1952).
4. Cruickshank, Donald R., Frank W. Broadbent, and Roy L. Bubb, *Teaching Problem Laboratory Simulation Directors Guide* (Chicago: Science Research Associates, Inc., 1967).
5. Finn, James D., "The Emerging Technology of Education," *Instructional Process and Media Innovation*, ed. Robert A. Weisgerber (Chicago: Rand McNally and Company, 1968), pp. 289–327.
6. Flanagan, John C., "Functional Education for the Seventies," *Phi Delta Kappan*, XLIX, Number 1 (September 1967), pp. 27–32.
7. Harnack, Robert S., "Use of the Computer in Curriculum Planning," *International Review of Education* (A Special Issue on "Uses and Values of the Computer in Education"), ed. Richard Wolf (Hamburg, Germany: UNESCO Institute for Education, 1968), XIV, Number 2, pp. 154–169.
8. Hilton, Mary Alice, "Cybernation and Its Impact on American Society," *Technology and the Curriculum*, ed. Paul W. F. Witt (New York: Teachers College Press, Columbia University, 1968), pp. 1–33.
9. Singer, Charles, et al. (eds.), "On Evaluating Technology in History," *Technology, Industry, and Man* (New York: McGraw-Hill), pp. 14–16.
10. Unwin, Derick, "Applying Educational Technology," *Educational Technology* (January 15, 1968).
11. Wing, Richard L., "Computer Controlled Economics Games for the Elementary Schools," *Audiovisual Instruction*, 9 (December 1964), pp. 681–682.

The New Elementary School Teacher

ALEXANDER FRAZIER

Some ideas about what the new elementary school teacher will look like are beginning to take shape. These ideas, to be presented here in terms of three more or less competitive models, deserve our thoughtful study but must

From *The New Elementary School* (Washington, D.C.: Association for Supervision and Curriculum Development, 1968), pp. 96–112. Alexander Frazier, editor. Reprinted with permission of the Association for Supervision and Curriculum Development and Alexander Frazier. Copyright © 1968 by the Association for Supervision and Curriculum Development.

be understood to be incompletely developed. The reconceptualization of instruction from which the models derive will continue. But as we move from the 'sixties into the 'seventies we can be certain that as agreement comes on the functions to be ascribed to the new teacher, these will be defined more precisely and fully than in the past. In consequence, we shall need to have much in mind how best to prepare the new teacher and how better to support and serve him on the job.

THREE MODELS OF THE TEACHER

Let us first, then, examine the dimensions within which the functions of the new teacher are being currently tested or tried out. These dimensions may be considered in terms and models of the teacher as specialist, the teacher as executive, and the teacher as professional.

The Teacher as Specialist

The extent to which specialization of the teaching function should exist in the elementary school has long been a question for discussion and debate. The assumption has sometimes been made that the triumphs of the virtues of the self-contained classroom in the literature on elementary education after 1930 disposed of the matter and that reconsideration of the merits of specialization requires, first of all, an attack on these virtues. However, in practice the value of the specialist teacher has seldom been denied; the real problem has been one of establishing relationships between special and general teachers in order to provide the benefits of both advanced training and intimate association. In the past, our will to resolve the problem of balance was frequently weakened by our inability to finance an adequate staffing of our schools. But today we seem to be agreed that children deserve to have more specialized competencies available to them, and we are trying to supply these in several patterns that look promising to most of us.

Regular teacher. Some degree of specialization within the staff of a school organized largely as self-contained classrooms is to be expected as teachers exercise their right to choose among varied and increasingly available opportunities for further education in the content areas.

The uses of general teachers with specialized competencies are several. They may serve as consultants to the other teachers in their building, not only the new teachers, but also to older colleagues who seek help in presenting a puzzling concept in mathematics or enlarging the science component in a social studies unit. The school may organize a portion of the week so that children with particularized interests and talents may have some access to the specialists among the staff. Such teachers may also serve as contact or key teachers in system-wide undertakings, representing their buildings and carrying new ideas back to them.

Working together, a school staff may agree to encourage the development of varied competencies among its members and to seek complementary competencies in the selection of newcomers to the group.

Team member. The rapid development of the concept of team teaching during the past ten years reflects the concern we have for using specialist teachers more effectively. Team teaching arrangements provide ways that seem to maximize the availability of these teachers and yet ensure more unity in the life of the child, as well as more knowledge of and association with him by the teacher or teachers to whom he is assigned than may usually have been found under the departmentalized programs of the past.

An attempt to describe all the patterns that pass for team teaching today will have to be foregone. Yet we may note that in most situations in which the team functions well, the unit of children ceases to be 25 with a teacher ratio of 1 to 25 and becomes a larger unit—one, let us say, of 100, with a teacher ratio of 4 to 100 (or, in the most richly staffed situations, of 5, 6, or 7 to 100).

The devices by which a multiple staff plans for this larger unit to provide for individual and group needs; for common, remedial, and enrichment experiences; and for sustained as well as periodic contacts with children— these deserve our closest attention and analysis.

Special teacher. Historically, the elementary school with self-contained classrooms has had available the services of teachers from some of the more highly specialized fields—art, music, physical education, homemaking, and industrial arts.

Plans for the use of these specialists have differed, of course, in terms of grade level, competency of the regular teacher, curriculum outlook, space and facilities, and the like.

As a reflection of current public expectations, the ranks of the special teachers as such have been augmented by the addition of teachers in modern languages and sometimes science and mathematics. Occasionally the addition has come via television.

Auxiliary teacher. Similarly, auxiliary teachers with specialized competencies have long been available in elementary schools. Remedial reading teachers have been provided for thirty years or more by some school systems. In the early and mid 'fifties, numerous schools set up enrichment opportunities for gifted or talented children as adjuncts to the regular program.

Today, often under provisions of the Elementary and Secondary Education Act, school systems are adding many remedial and enrichment teachers to work with children from disadvantaged backgrounds. Although we may feel that the call for specialists in remedial reading, remedial mathematics, and language development has outrun the supply and that the relationship of specialized to regular teachers needs to be considered more carefully, we can agree that the role of the auxiliary teacher specialist is being newly appreciated and supported.

The most remarkable fact about the growth in the number of such teachers may well be the assignment of the auxiliary person to a new base of a few teachers, in what is sometimes termed a "plus"-teacher relationship.

Resource teacher. Another type of specialist teacher being currently added to the staffing mix in greater numbers is the resource teacher who serves as a consultant to the regular teacher.

The pattern of relationship is not new, but the role sometimes may be. When school systems were going through the period of implementing the new mathematics program, it was not unusual for them to release a teacher considered to be more expert than the others to serve on call as a counselor to his colleagues. The practice being pursued by some districts today of piloting a new venture with a few teachers and then providing for its gradual extension each year to additional classrooms has brought pioneer teachers out of their classrooms to help others in getting under way with i/t/a or one of the other new beginning reading programs.

The resource teacher is generally regarded as a helper whose value comes from competence out of the ordinary, a colleague without more authority than comes from such competence.

The elementary school teacher as a specialist of one kind or another is thus becoming well-developed as a model for the new teacher of children. The variety of roles and relationships being tested out as well as the growth of new concepts of teacher-pupil ratio distinguish our present from our earlier thinking about the teacher specialist. If or as this model prevails, we will certainly need to address ourselves freshly to the preparation of teachers; most of our present preservice programs are obviously not geared to this model.

The Teacher as Executive

What are the essential functions of the teacher of children? We must return to this question if we are to understand the developing model of the teacher as an executive. The nature of teaching is currently under study as it has not been for half a century. This scrutiny includes close attention to the problems of planning for learning in an environment freshly rich in resources and personnel, in which the teacher may be confronted with new responsibilities and attendant new roles.

Manager of resources. Several aspects of the current educational scene work toward the definition of the teacher's functions as those of manager of resources.

The union of scientific analysis of content and scientific preparation of teaching materials promises to provide us with an increasing array of devices that will enable learners to enter some kind of self-regulating encounter with what is to be learned. Diagnosis and evaluation, as a result, will become even more important teaching tasks, while presenting content through dialoguing with individuals and groups will be less important, at least in those parts of the curriculum that respond to the arts of educational technology.

The very rapid growth of materials centers in elementary schools promises to move the base of more teaching from the textbook to a range of resources. Organizing for the use of such collections calls for skills that may not have been so widely needed in the past.

The emphasis on the need for more opportunities for independent study and personal inquiry can be added to the picture to complicate the prospect that the teacher of tomorrow will need to be a kind of manager of the learning environment, expert in selecting and assembling resources of many kinds, assessing needs, and setting up and supervising situations maximizing the time spent by children with the newly varied materials for study.

Team leader. The executive demands on the leader of a teaching team or the chairman of a cooperative teaching venture are plainly apparent.

Because of the great variety of ways in which teaching teams are organized, it is difficult to spell out the duties required of leaders. In the prototype found in the early literature on team teaching, the leader was identified as one selected because of his competence as a master teacher and rewarded by extra pay as well as charged with additional responsibility. One of the justifications of the team structure was that it made it possible to retain in teaching situations persons who might otherwise be attracted to administration by higher pay. Recently a midwestern state superintendent of public instruction has proposed that master teachers carrying executive functions of this sort be paid from $12,000 to $15,000.

More realistically perhaps, the team or cooperating teaching unit has to develop among its members the skills of planning and leadership needed in order to function effectively, skills that have not in the past been included in programs of teacher preparation.

Coordinator of aides and auxiliaries. The regular teacher in many elementary schools now has so many persons available to help him that he can be thought of as having to function in part as an executive.

The number of teacher's aides, auxiliary teachers in the school, and ancillary personnel available on call forces the teacher to plan for and with his own team, so to speak. In a report of one prekindergarten program, the role of the teacher, who has two fulltime aides to assist with 22 pupils, is defined as that of "a coordinator and supervisor as well as a teacher," charged with organizing and planning "activities for all the adults working in the program." For this situation, the adults include many persons representing health and social services as well as the parents of the children.

A report from an inner-city school program of a sizeable school district lists these persons as available full or part time to the regular teacher: enrichment teacher, reading improvement teacher, mathematics improvement teacher, elementary counselor, nurse, physician, dentist, visiting teacher, psychologist, and persons staffing an after-school study center. General and special consultants are also available from a regional service center.

As we are all aware, these are not unusual situations; they are cited simply as samples. In some schools the problem of handling additional personnel is less familiar than it long has been in other more favored schools or school systems. The regular teacher who is to use the full staff provided for him may well need to think of himself as coordinator or supervisor and to be educated specifically for his executive duties.

Again, the model of the new elementary school teacher as an executive of sorts arises in part out of the proliferation of resources and personnel and also perhaps from the effort to analyze the variety of functions or roles subsumed in the concept of teaching and to assign them more directly to cooperating staff members, as found in the classroom itself, in team relationships, or in auxiliary and ancillary relationships. If the prime teacher is to be thought of as carrying these larger responsibilities of manager, organizer, leader, coordinator, and supervisor, then he may well require new kinds of experiences in his preservice education.

The Teacher as Professional

Another model for the new elementary school teacher is to be found in the definition of the teacher as a fully functioning professional person. The model is based largely on the historic conception of the professional as one who is expected to make use of new knowledge on his own terms and who is held to be obligated to contribute to new knowledge as well as he can. This conception has not been widely accepted in the past as appropriate to the functioning of the precollegiate teacher. However, there are indications that it may now be regarded as reasonable and desirable to think of the teacher of children and youth as increasingly self-directing and independent. We may examine this prospect from several points of view.

Curriculum maker. The teacher has the ultimate responsibility for the development of curriculum as he works with learners in his classroom.

This generalization, long familiar in the literature on curriculum development, has been given new meaning by the experience of the national curriculum projects of the past ten years. A recent book reporting on some of these is entitled, *Curriculum Improvement and Innovation: A Partnership of Students, School Teachers, and Research Scholars* (edited by W. T. Martin and D. C. Pinck; Cambridge, Massachusetts: Robert Bentley, Inc., 1966). The focus in the implementation of the new programs has been primarily on teacher reeducation; principals and supervisors have sometimes had to find out what was going on from their teachers already inducted into a new program by its sponsor.

In most of the new programs, the original design or selection of curriculum content has been seen as the province of the scholar. But there has been a new importance assigned to the function of the teacher as the person who must test the program for teachability. In addition, the emphasis on the reeducation of the teacher to handle new content has highlighted again his role as the ultimate curriculum maker and has given rise to the mammoth federal programs of subsidized teacher reeducation.

The renewed recognition of the importance of the teacher in developing the curriculum may cause us to review the nature of his preparation and also the kinds of services we provide him after employment.

Innovator. The teacher can create new knowledge through what he does in his classroom, in his own personal laboratory for professional learning.

We have granted this possibility in the past. In the early 'fifties, we attempted to combine action research and in-service education. But we are newly aware of the opportunity and indeed the obligation of teachers to engage in innovative ventures. We welcome teachers who offer to try out something so that we all may study the results. Perhaps we ask several teachers to test a variety of new approaches to science. We may formalize a situation by designing an experimental set-up in which competing programs for the teaching of beginning reading are compared. Or we may organize for the development of a new oral language program that we hope will be better than anything that has come to our attention.

The growth or reorientation of research services in the public schools reflects the urgency we all feel to become more competent in testing, experimenting with, and developing new ideas. The role of the teacher as innovator is likely to be further supported as the Research and Development Centers and the Regional Educational Laboratories begin to supply us with their output.

What does the teacher as innovator need to know? This is a question to which all of us may need to address ourselves.

Specialist in methodology. The unique province of the teacher is teaching; his professional capital is his competence in methodology.

The validity of this sensible contention is currently buttressed by theorization and research into the nature of teaching. The revival of interest in methodology is providing new dignity to teaching as teaching. At present, this interest ranges from analysis of the verbal behavior of teachers to the identification of the stages of concept development through which the teacher must guide learners. In the largest sense, the new concern for methodology encompasses many aspects of educational technology; it accounts for the revival of interest in the work of Maria Montessori; it is reflected in the proposals for doing more with inquiry, discovery, and independent study.

In short, a new content of methodology is being developed. The question for us may be how to help prospective and experienced teachers to advance their knowledge of this content.

The model of the teacher as a professional has these several components. Much of what is behind the model has to do with the rise in status of precollegiate teachers, particularly elementary school teachers, from the subordination that may have been appropriate when teachers were poorly prepared to a new level of responsibility more nearly analogous with that generally enjoyed by their college colleagues. The essence of professionalism in teaching is independence in decision-making about what is taught and how. For the elementary school teacher so to function, what must he know and how should he be supported in his teaching situation?

WHAT THE NEW TEACHER MUST KNOW

Each of the three models of the new teacher is an attempt to put the broadened dimensions within which the precollegiate teacher is now operating into a set of ordered relationships. Each model attempts to account for some, if not all, of the same dimensions. Each certainly supposes that in the program to prepare the new teacher there must be new learnings.

In thinking about the changes that will be needed in teacher preparation, we could examine in turn the learnings required by each model. But it will be more economical and also safer, insofar as the survival of these particular models may be perceived as uncertain, to try to identify a number of areas in which new learnings would seem to be required by one or more of the models. On this base, we may then wish to project some notions about the impact that the addition of the new learnings will have upon the shape of the formal teacher education program. When we have done this, we may turn our attention to changes in the on-the-job conditions and services that will be needed to support the new teacher more adequately.

Areas of Needed Learning

The areas to follow nominate themselves as those in which the new elementary school teacher will be expected to become more proficient.

Subject specialization. All teachers may be expected to bring to teaching a broader general education than in former years. Such preparation will ensure a better base for developing competency in the range of subject areas now included in the curriculum for children and still thought of by and large as the responsibility of the regular teacher. Many teachers will be encouraged to develop a special competency in one or more of the subject areas. Some teachers will be advised to develop a high level of competency in a single field.

These generalizations would seem to be justified from our review of the new operational dimensions of the elementary school teacher. They concern the relationship of the preprofessional to the professional program. They also suggest the restructuring of the professional program at both the undergraduate and graduate levels.

That the beginning teacher entering the elementary classroom is still generally undereducated as a person in his own right, in the most literal sense, is all too clear. Contact with the academic areas in college has been inadequate to provide the background for teaching today's children. Moreover, one of the major problems in educating the experienced teacher as a specialist is the absence from his earlier education of anything much to build on. He has been shunted into professional education so early in his college career that he comes back unable to reenter the content sequences except at the undergraduate level. The revival of interest in tailoring special courses in the academic areas for experienced teachers, outmoded as it may be historically, arises from this lack as revealed by the needs of the new federally subsidized programs intended to prepare elementary school specialists.

Curriculum and instruction. Teachers may be expected to possess a framework for thinking about curriculum design and development large enough to provide a secure base for exploring new possibilities of improving experiences for children. They need an understanding of instruction that affords a theoretical structure identifying and relating the varied tasks or acts of teaching and that accounts for the function of many kinds of materials and resources in teaching.

We may assume that today's teacher, the experienced teacher, if he has gained such a framework and such a structure, has done so through graduate study. Now the question becomes whether the teacher in preparation, in terms of his probable destiny as executive and professional, needs an earlier start in building a firm foundation in curriculum and instruction. With an affirmative answer, the problem then becomes one of deciding how to include more attention to these areas in his professional undergraduate education.

Staff relationships. Teachers may need to know more than they used to be expected to know about how to work with their immediate colleagues and also how to use effectively an increasing array of persons and services provided for the better education of children.

The theme of the current project of the National Commission on Teacher Education and Professional Standards is "The Teacher and His Staff." The range of staff relationships immediately apparent in the model of the teacher as executive and those that we know exist under the model of the teacher as specialist may be redefined as we alter and improve our model of the new elementary school teacher. However, there has already long existed an agreement that the teacher needs to know his way around better in an institutional setting. The movement in collective negotiation expands the sense of need. What understandings most deserve attention in teacher preparation remain to be determined, but here is a relatively new component for which we must find a place.

Research and experimentation. Teachers who are to occupy a role as relatively independent professional persons may be expected to need the competencies required for using and contributing to new knowledge. As well as those drawn from the broader base in curriculum and instruction already discussed, these competencies include reasonably well-developed skills in testing out, experimenting with, and developing new ideas.

Such competencies can scarcely be expected to have been very well-developed in any undergraduate program of the past; it may be equally unlikely that there will be time available in the future to establish a high level of performance in research and experimentation prior to the graduate years. However, the prospect is that an effort will be made in many programs to set a better preservice foundation in research and experimentation than has existed heretofore and that the graduate education of elementary school teachers will include much more attention to this area than it has in the past.

Professional behavior in general. The new teacher may be expected to need help in many aspects of learning how to behave as a more fully professional person.

What these aspects are, the attributes of behavior that will enable an elementary school teacher to operate more independently in using new knowledge and more successfully in contributing to it, remains to be spelled out in the minds of us all. Yet we can scarcely doubt that as they are spelled out the new concepts of professional selfhood will be incorporated in the program of teacher education.

Here, then, are some of the areas that would seem likely to loom larger in the education of the new teacher. What impact may this expansion of competence be expected to have on our programs of teacher education?

The Education of the New Teacher

Changes in the content of programs for the education of the new elementary school teacher have been identified, however loosely, in the preceding section of this paper. What is of concern here is the reshaping of the program in terms of its segments—the preprofessional, the undergraduate professional, and the graduate. If the changes in content are to be accommodated, changes would seem to be required in the time allocations and proportionate relationships of these segments.

Preprofessional education. At a minimum, it would seem desirable to clear the first two years of college for the full-time general education of prospective elementary school teachers. This minimum provision presupposes, of course, that there will be present in the two-year block a carefully thought out rationale for balance among mathematics and the sciences, the social studies, and the humanities. Such a balanced base is required for the minimal functioning of today's teacher of children.

A strong case can be made for extending this base by a third year of study prior to professional education or the reservation in the upper division of the equivalent of half-time for extension of competency in one or more subject areas. The recent specification of areas of specialization for elementary teachers in California and Texas is indicative of public support in this direction.

Undergraduate professional education. A larger place for preprofessional education would seem to posit a cutback in the amount of time for professional education. Certainly, in these times, if space for undergraduate education cannot be expanded, then the time presently allocated to the professional education in some programs will need to be reduced to allow room for an adequate general education base.

Where this cutback occurs, it may be anticipated that it will be in familiar directions. One is the review of the preparatory courses we have included in the past in order to beef up background in mathematics, the fine arts, the practical arts, and some other neglected areas. A broader general education base should change the picture of need.

Another familiar focus will be the numerous courses in subject methods to determine whether they can be coordinated or combined or perhaps replaced by general courses. This time around, the recent renewal of interest in methodology may provide us with new content to consider. Here also a broader general education base would seem to provide something additional to include in our thinking.

But, of course, if we take seriously the prediction that a broader professional preparation is to be demanded of the new elementary teacher, with more knowledge of curriculum as well as instruction and a sounder beginning in research and experimentation, then we may wonder whether cutting back will answer. Of the fact that we will need to review and revise our present undergraduate professional segment as the general education segment is enlarged, there can be little doubt. Yet bringing the present professional courses up to date and cutting the overlap with general education may not be enough. How do we make room for a broader base for continued professional education?

Graduate education. The reshaping of graduate education for the new elementary school teacher will relate very closely to the expansion of the general education base in the undergraduate years. This much seems clear. The development of more opportunity for subject specialization is at stake. To repeat, the present effort to meet the need for specialist teachers at the graduate level is encountering difficulty because there has been so little to build on in their past education.

We must acknowledge as we try to educate for the new teacher as specialist, the present need for a larger graduate education time block than the customary year in the master's program. Some of the federally subsidized programs to develop specialists are being framed to provide two years of graduate education.

What we may need to do more systematically is to lay out in anticipation a much more comprehensive program of advanced education for the new elementary teacher. The unit of one additional year seems totally inadequate, just as the unit of four years no longer seems to suffice for an adequate undergraduate preparation. In both instances we may need to move toward a large block of time, five years to be provided one way or another for the initial preparation and perhaps three more for advanced education.

Some colleges now offer certificates of proficiency for post-master's programs. This way of recognizing the need for further training will doubtless continue to grow. However, the prospect of designing doctoral programs for elementary school teachers is already upon us. The new models of the teacher as specialist, executive, and professional point the way. School systems are beginning to include truly substantial differentials in their salary schedules for possession of the doctorate. While this response to the changing status of the teacher may seem more immediately related to what is happening at the secondary level, the rewards for advanced education will be quickly appreciated also by elementary teachers.

The dispersal of supervisory functions among elementary school teachers is already bringing teachers into advanced programs of curriculum and instruction to join the number of specialist teachers seeking advanced education in the content areas. The expansion of graduate education in scope as well as time can be taken for granted.

Many colleges of education are studying ways to reshape their undergraduate and graduate programs to meet the need for a new kind of elementary school teacher. At the same time, public schools must review the adequacy of their provision of conditions and services to support the teacher in performing at a new professional level.

SUPPORT OF THE NEW TEACHER AT WORK

That the new elementary school teacher will require certain kinds of different or altered conditions and services to function effectively on the job would seem obvious. Just what these are to look like will depend upon the survival and development of the competing models of the new teacher. However, we may be able to anticipate some of the conditions and services that would seem to be more or less common to the functioning of the new teacher, whether seen as specialist, executive, or professional, and also to define several problems or issues that face us in providing what is needed.

Needed Conditions and Services

The new teacher, like the old, will operate in an institutional setting. The challenge is to strengthen that setting so that it supports the teacher more adequately.

Time for study and planning. Time is needed during the elementary teacher's day, week, and year for personal as well as group study and planning.

We have long since granted the truth of this contention. Sometimes we have tried to provide time "away from children," as we still rather hesitantly refer to the periods set aside for study and planning, by allowing the regular teacher to take a rest break when the teacher of music or physical education turns up. Or we may have dismissed the children at 1:30 on the last Friday afternoon of every month, or even extended the contract to provide a week on duty after school closes or before it opens.

However, these practices do not take care of the teacher's need to have time on the job to prepare for his own teaching, to review new materials and keep track of new curriculum developments, to confer with the speech therapist or counselor or parent on what can be or is being done for Jimmy or Janice, to plan with aides and teacher colleagues for the next day or the next week, and to work with others on the faculty to evaluate and replan the program of the school as a whole.

Doubtless there are new approaches already being developed to provide time for study and planning as a legitimate and, indeed, necessary part of the regular schedule. These will need support and extension as we provide the time basis of more adequate professional functioning in the elementary school.

Specialized local services. A rich local environment of specialized professional services is needed for the support of the new elementary school teacher.

In some situations, such services have been provided more adequately than in others. But if the new teacher everywhere is to be expected to assume new roles and responsibilities, then there must be much more help close at hand, either in the district or perhaps in some new institutional arrangement such as can be found in the multi-district service centers developed under Title III of the Elementary and Secondary Education Act or in the intermediate units that deploy state resources.

These needed services include an adequately staffed professional library, consultants in the subject areas who are truly expert in their fields, general supervisors who know methodology and who can also advise on the development of needed skills of interpersonal and group relations, and specialists in research and experimentation who possess among their competencies the know-how of securing outside subsidy for the strengthening of local innovativeness.

Again, such specialized services are already available to some teachers; the need is to make sure that they are available to all teachers.

Access to broader resources. Relationships need to be established between teachers on the job and the broader resources of professional education available beyond the local district and the adjacent neighborhood.

The new teacher who is to function with an increasing amount of personal authority and self-direction must not be dependent only on what is provided in his own environment. The basis of professionalism is all the knowledge of the field. Access must be open to the best regional and national resources—persons to serve as advisers on the local scene; conferences and workshops to be attended; school systems ahead of the game to be visited; and Research and Development Centers, Regional Educational Laboratories, and Educational Research Information Centers to be related to or consulted.

The financing of wider teacher access to such resources may trouble us at the moment. The financing, however, will follow—indeed it is already following—upon our own resolution to broaden the base of our general professional operation to include the teaching staff as a whole.

This treatment of the conditions and services that will be required to support the new elementary school teacher is fragmentary, and what has been presented has been but partially defined. Yet perhaps enough has been said to indicate the necessity of reviewing how we now support the teacher and the need for beginning to plan how to do so much more effectively.

Problems and Issues

Providing better support for the new elementary school teacher will bring with it several problems and issues that will require a considerable degree of openness to rethink and a good deal of ingenuity to resolve. The brief paragraphs to follow must be regarded merely as notes on the nature of these questions.

New basis for in-service education. Provisions for the continuing professional growth of teachers must be built into the institutional structure in which all teachers function.

Depending on the seeking out of opportunities for their further education by individual teachers and encouraging them to do so by progress barriers or token rewards written into contracts would seem inadequate to the newly recognized need to ensure the high level functioning of all members of the teaching staff.

The problem is how to build provisions for study into the regular work schedule of the staff.

Deployment of authority. The development of greater expertness and self-direction among teachers requires the reconceptualization of relationships in the school setting.

Some functions and responsibilities of official leadership have been and more will be dispersed among teachers as they become newly professional. The negotiation movement is also working toward an increasingly independent status for the precollegiate teacher, one that will be defined rather precisely in legal terms.

How to help shape this deployment of authority is something we need to ponder in the broadest possible terms.

Emergence of new leadership patterns. The deployment of professional authority across a broader base in the school calls for the development of new leadership patterns.

Leadership as a function of office may need to be reassessed in terms of the changing perspective. The redefinition of the role of supervisors as consultants, long since accomplished, may point the way. What the dimensions of leadership in the teaching force are to be is perplexing to many of us. The nature of the principalship in a school with fully functioning professional teachers has also yet to be thought through.

The redefinition of leadership in terms of functions other than office may be a first step to providing ourselves with order in the puzzling problem of reconciling professional and institutional imperatives.

Changes are needed in the conditions and services provided to support adequately the new elementary school teacher on the job. Making these changes will require us to revise some of our old views and invent some fresh ways of working together as a total school staff.

In summary, out of the educational reconstruction of the 'sixties is coming the conception of a new elementary school teacher. This new teacher will need to know more than did the old and thus will require a different kind of education. He will also need different conditions and services on the job in order to function effectively.

Several models of the new teacher are currently under conceptualization. The teacher as a specialist is one model, with a variety of possibilities in the picture—the regular teacher as a specialist for some functions, the team member, the special teacher as such, the auxiliary teacher, and the resource teacher. Another model is the teacher as executive—a manager of resources, a team leader, a coordinator of aides and auxiliaries. A third model is the new teacher as a fully functioning professional, who is thought of as curriculum maker, innovator, or perhaps a specialist in methodology.

Whatever the ultimate model for the new teacher, more opportunities must be available in undergraduate and graduate education to develop specialization, to gain a better grounding in curriculum and instruction, to consider problems of and develop skills in staff relationships, to become more competent in research and experimentation, and in general to learn how to behave as an increasingly independent professional person. Consequently we may anticipate that teacher education programs will attempt to provide for these needed learnings by broadening the general education base, strengthening the professional segment at the undergraduate level, and expanding and extending the program of advanced education for teachers.

Similarly, school systems must review the adequacy of their provisions for supporting the new teacher. We may anticipate that more time will be provided on the job for study and planning, that new kinds of specialized services will be available, and that access to broader resources for professional growth will be ensured. We know that to offer such conditions and services, a new look will need to be taken at the present shape of in-service education and efforts made to restructure present patterns of authority and leadership.

The new elementary school teacher will be harder to prepare and possibly harder to live with. He will demand more of us before he gets on the job and after. Yet we cannot deny the teacher in prospect the opportunities for experiences he needs to become as professional as possible or try to fit him into job conditions unworthy of him or serve him in ways inappropriate to a new level of competency.

Those of us charged with responsibilities in teacher education and those with responsibilities in local school leadership have much to do if we are to make it possible, in turn, for the new elementary teacher to do much more. Yet the promised outcome of our joint efforts is a superior education for tomorrow's children. This promise should be enough to inspire us to do what must be done.